CHRISTIAN ANTISEMITISM

CHRISTIAN ANTISEMITISM

A History of Hate

William Nicholls

JASON ARONSON INC.
Northvale, New Jersey
London

The author gratefully acknowledges permission to quote from the following sources:

From *Karl Marx: Early Writings,* edited and translated by T. B. Bottomore. Copyright © 1963 by T. B. Bottomore. Reprinted by permission of McGraw-Hill, Inc.

From *The Jew in the Medieval World: A Source Book* by Jacob R. Marcus. Copyright © 1975 by Hebrew Union College Press. Reprinted by permission of Hebrew Union College Press.

From Peter Abelard, *A Dialogue of a Philosopher with a Jew and a Christian,* pp. 32–33, by permission of the publisher. © 1979 by the Pontifical Institute of Mediaeval Studies, Toronto.

From *The Siege* by Conor Cruise O'Brien. Copyright © 1986 by Conor Cruise O'Brien. Reprinted by permission of Simon & Schuster, Inc.

From *The Roots of Christian Anti-Semitism* by Malcolm Hay. Copyright © 1981 by the Anti-Defamation League of B'nai B'rith and Alice Ivy Hay. Used by permission of the Anti-Defamation League of B'nai B'rith.

From *The Destruction of the European Jews* by Raul Hilberg. Table on pp. 5ff. Copyright © 1985 by Raul Hilberg. Used by permission of the author and his agents, Raines and Raines.

This book was set in 10 pt. Schneidler by Lind Graphics of Upper Saddle River, New Jersey, and printed by Haddon Craftsmen in Scranton, Pennsylvania.

10 9 8 7 6 5 4 3 2 1

Library of Congress Cataloging-in-Publication Data

Nicholls, William.
Christian antisemitism: a history of hate /
by William Nicholls.
p. cm.
Includes bibliographical references and index.
ISBN 0-87668-398-7
1. Antisemitism–History. 2. Christianity and antisemitism.
3. Judaism (Christian theology). 4. Jesus Christ–Jewishness.
5. Jesus Christ–Person and offices. 6. Christianity–Early church,
ca. 30-600. I. Title.
DS145.N53 1993
261.2'6'09–dc20 92-35713

Manufactured in the United States of America. Jason Aronson Inc. offers books and cassettes. For information and catalog write to Jason Aronson Inc., 230 Livingston Street, Northvale, New Jersey 07647.

To the survivors of the Holocaust,
and in particular to those who have undertaken the task of bearing witness to a new generation

Contents

PART II THE GROWTH OF THE MYTH

PART III THE MYTH SECULARIZED

Preface

A writer who tries to cover as much ground as I have in this book depends to an unusual extent upon the work of others. Without the advantage of the more specialized scholarship of many previous writers, no such book as this could have been attempted. I have tried to record these debts and dependencies in detail in the notes and bibliography. Where there is little disagreement about the history, I have followed standard works, or scholars whose work is widely accepted. Where the specialists are not in agreement, which is often the case, especially in the field of Christian origins, I have followed those that seemed most persuasive, and must hope that my judgment has been correct. In a very few such cases, I have taken an independent line of my own; if I turn out to have been mistaken, I do not believe the general argument of the book will be seriously affected.

However, some debts are broader, and must be acknowledged in gratitude here.

Geza Vermes, in *Jesus the Jew* and later in *Jesus and the World of Judaism*, first taught me to understand imaginatively the fact that Jesus was a Jew (as many others had previously said, without making the same impression). Vermes demonstrated that the memories of Jesus preserved in the Gospels could be filled out in detail by a scholar sufficiently competent in the Judaism of the Second Temple period, so that Jesus' authentic Jewishness could become clear to the reader, and a real separation be made in the mind between the historical man and the myth that grew up so soon after his death, without resort to historical agnosticism. I have learned about Jesus and Judaism from others too, but from no one so much.

In writing about the history of Christian anti-Judaism, I likewise stand on the shoulders of distinguished predecessors, notably Jules Isaac, Edward Flannery, Franklin Littell, the Eckardts, Alan T. Davies, and Rosemary Ruether. While I disagree profoundly with the later, anti-Zionist turn of Ruether's thought, she was the one who first taught us to ask the most disturbing questions about the anti-Judaism inherent in early Christology. It was also Ruether especially who taught us to speak of the "theology of supersession" that has characterized Christianity from early times until our own day. If (as I believe) it is now possible to see further than they could, we owe it to their labors.

My own education at Cambridge (though in many respects among the best then available) gave me little help in understanding Jews and Judaism. I had to find out for myself with the help I could get from friends and books what I now think I should have been taught many years ago. Without the living example of the friends, I am sure I would not have understood what the books meant. Among these friends, Ian Kent, M.D., F.R.C.P. (C), must be mentioned before anyone else. To me and many others he has been a compelling example of what it means to live as a dedicated Jew, with compassion and understanding for all but without compromise of his own commitment. More than twenty years ago, I shared with him in the writing of a book, *I AMness: the discovery of the Self beyond the ego*, the last chapter of which, thought by some to be an anomaly in a book apparently about other things, was the fruit of a coming together of souls as well as minds, and a landmark in the stages of my own development toward the convictions now expressed in this book.

The dedication alludes to a common enterprise that has also meant very much to me. Since 1975, I have been taking part in annual Holocaust Symposiums in Vancouver to communicate to senior high school students the story of a cataclysmic event in world history that their schools were ill equipped to deal with. The most important feature of the symposiums has always been the firsthand testimony of survivors. I have witnessed their pain as they agonized to recover suppressed memories of horror in order to fulfill the almost impossible task of conveying to a new generation what it was really like to live through the Holocaust and survive as a human being, without hate.Through this, and later other shared enterprises with members of the Vancouver Jewish community, I have come to know many Jews as comrades and dear friends, and so to dissipate the vestiges of the stereotype left in the mind by early conditioning. I have tried to emphasize in writing about anti-Judaism that ideas do not explain everything. What has been tragically true in the history of hate is also true in the more hopeful history of reconciliation that has begun. Can there be truth without love? I think not. But a little love may open the heart and mind to truth formerly hidden.

Several people have read parts or all of the manuscript of the book during the years in which it was being written. First among these is Hilary Nicholls, who has read the whole book several times in innumerable drafts of chapters and sections of chapters as they came off the printer. Among other debts that cannot be repaid, I thank her for being adamant in insisting that I make my meaning fully clear to her as well as to myself, in the hope that it would also be clear to eventual readers. Elizabeth Nicholls also read some of the earlier chapters and made valuable editorial suggestions, most of which I adopted. Eugene Kaellis read almost all of the book, until increasing pressure of administrative duties forced him to stop, and as well as providing helpful encouragement also made editorial suggestions, most of which I also adopted. Lloyd Gaston read the first half-dozen chapters in an early draft and saved me from some errors in dealing with the New Testament. Ian Kent checked my use of psychoanalytical literature in Chapter 7 for errors of interpretation. I thank all of them for every kind of help.

None of these is responsible for the use I have made of their help, and needless to say, remaining errors of fact or interpretation are entirely my own.

Introduction

The Holocaust of six million Jews in Nazi-ruled Europe was the greatest outpouring of evil in the history of the planet. No matter how much we learn about the Holocaust, there is always more to defeat the mind's capacity for comprehension and shock the soul. Taking its full measure may be impossible. Its near absolute evil calls in question all hopes for human civilization and threatens faith in divine rule over history. To retain hope in humanity, let alone in God, we must somehow come to terms with it and learn its lesson so that any repetition may be made impossible.

A number of writers have said outright that we cannot comprehend the Holocaust. The very attempt trivializes it, they insist, and removes its uniqueness, assimilating it to other catastrophes, other massacres, atrocious in themselves, but lacking what renders the Holocaust itself without parallel. Many historians, on the other hand, do attempt to account for the Holocaust within categories of explanation they have learned to use in investigating other historical events. They warn us that mystifying the Holocaust by removing it from the historical process may blind us to the early warning signs of a possible repetition.

What defies explanation in the Holocaust is the magnitude of hatred that overflowed upon the Jews. At this point in world history, evil jumped off any scale of computation. Such annihilating hatred cannot be understood as the effect of causes historians normally analyze. When every social, economic, and political factor has been taken into account, the question still remains: why?

Writing about the Holocaust requires us to deal with passions that have nothing to do with reason and calculation. There is no science of the radically irrational. Nevertheless, it makes sense to look at factors often underrated by modern historians just because they are irrational.

The history of the twentieth century ought to have shown us that religion remains a powerful motor of human action. The Holocaust cannot be comprehended without taking into account the way the people of Europe had been taught about the Jews from their childhood up by their own religious traditions.

To say that the Holocaust was the ultimate outcome of antisemitism[1] is illuminating, but only to a point. Many volumes have been written on antisemitism, without satisfactorily accounting for the degree of hatred Jews attracted from their neighbors. Antisemites account for their hatred by accusing Jews of unpleasant racial characteristics and undesirable activities; however, it does not take much investigation to convince anyone of normal goodwill that Jews as a group do not possess these characteristics or take part in these activities. Without exception, the charges that have been leveled at Jews by antisemites are baseless. The origins of antisemitism are not to be sought in Jews but in antisemites.

Antisemitism is causeless hatred. The reasons given for it are always rationalizations of a hate already present in the mind of the antisemite. The antisemite needs such rationalizations to tolerate the inner pressure of a passion that might threaten his or her mental stability if recognized as causeless. We should never be trapped into taking these justifications seriously, trying to see if there was anything in Jewish behavior that might have provided a basis for them.

When Jews do so, they internalize antisemitism and indulge in self-hatred. When non-Jews do so, they collude with antisemitism. There can be no way to understanding along this route. When we attempt to describe the historical development of antisemitism, we do not explain or justify it. We can only show how it grew up and how it was explained by the antisemites themselves.

Nevertheless, although we cannot explain the intensity of antisemitic hate, we do know how to explain the choice of the Jews as its victims. The explanation is not new, but it has understandably been resisted. Many Jewish writers have said, quite simply, that the Nazis chose the Jews as the target of their hate because two thousand years of Christian teaching had accustomed the world to do so. Few Christian historians and theologians have been sufficiently open to a painful truth to accept this explanation without considerable qualification. Nevertheless, it is correct, though perhaps needing fuller substantiation.

Modern antisemitism, though not identical with the historic Christian hostility toward Jews, clearly sprang from it. The links are there to be traced. Secular antisemites had learned from the Christian past that Jews were bad. When they abandoned the religion of their upbringing, they retained its prejudices.

Jews had experienced hostility from their neighbors well before Christianity came upon the scene. Pagan hostility toward the Jewish people was aroused, above all, by the refusal of the Jews to join the ecumenical consensus of paganism, whereby the gods of one people could be satisfactorily equated with those of another. Olympian Zeus was the same as Jupiter Capitolinus, and so on. Jews obstinately refused to admit that the One they worshiped, YHWH,[2] could be identified with these or any other god known to man. Eventually, the Romans at least gave in, and recognized Judaism as a lawful national religion; from 212 C.E. the Jews were Roman citizens.

Pagan calumnies against the Jews seem to be outgrowths of this central rejection. If the Jews would not worship the gods, their religious customs must have been inhuman and barbaric. They were strange and incomprehensible and anything could be believed of them. Thus, pagan anti-Jewishness can be regarded as a specific form of xenophobia, the fear and dislike of the stranger simply because he or she is seen as strange.

Nevertheless, pagan hostility lacked the peculiar intensity of hatred that came to mark Christian anti-Judaism and its secularized child, antisemitism. Sometimes it could even turn into admiration for the purity of Jewish monotheism and Jewish ethics. Not all pagans were antisemites, and some became Jews by conversion. Many more would have done so if it had not been for the barrier of circumcision.

Christian hostility toward Jews possessed a uniquely powerful feature. Christians believed that the Jews had killed Christ, their divine Savior. The myth of the Jews as the Christ-killers has powered anti-Judaism and antisemitism all through the Christian centuries. It is present even in the New Testament, and it has not yet died under the impact of modern critical history.

Like all religions, Christianity is powered by a myth, its charter story that tells believers who they are and where they fit into the divine plan. It is important to this particular myth that it be based in real history. In it, the Jews are cast as the enemies of Christ and God: the Jews that are meant are actual historical people, not just mythic abstractions.

We know from modern scholarship that many features of the myth are historically untrue and are therefore myths in the popular sense as well. Nevertheless, until modern times the myth that tells the Christian story has been firmly believed, and most Christians still do believe it to be literally and historically true.

According to this story, because the Jews rejected and killed Christ, they in turn have been rejected as God's chosen people. The Jews have broken their ancient covenant with God, and he has made a new covenant, sealed in the blood of Christ, gathering to himself a new people, drawn from the Gentiles. This new people has now superseded the old Israel.

The Jews have lost their status as the covenant people, and the new Israel is now the true Israel. As a punishment for this cosmic crime, the Jews have lost their Temple and been exiled from their land. Until the return of Christ they will remain homeless wanderers upon the earth. What theologians are beginning to call the theology of supersession joins hands with the myth of the deicide,[3] Christ-killing people to make the Jews a permanent target for Christian hostility and contempt.

In the Christian state of the Constantinian era theological hostility led to social and legal measures, discriminating against Jews and relegating them to a subordinate status in a Christian world. Raul Hilberg has shown in a famous comparative table[4] how many of the Nazi measures against the Jews, short of the Final Solution itself, were not novelties, but reenactments of older measures of the Christian world, laws of state and church that kept the Jews in their place.

Nevertheless, the Christian world did stop short of a final solution. Christian legislation was governed by a principle apparently first formulated by Augustine in the fifth century: The Jews should be preserved, but in misery. They are to remain in the world as a permanent witness to their own crimes, bearing the mark of Cain, but like Cain, not to be killed by others.

Misery is not extermination. There could be no Holocaust while Christian restriction on genocide remained binding. There could be calumnies of all sorts, even massacres and expulsions of whole communities from countries where they had lived for centuries, but no one could claim Christian sanction for total extermination of the Jews. Loss of Christian authority in a secularized world removed that ultimate restraint, setting Hitler free to act out the last consequences of the ancient hatred.

In the Middle Ages, the myth had already begun to generate popular paranoia. The Christian people had been taught for centuries about the misdeeds of the Jews, how they had rejected and killed their own clearly prophesied Messiah, and how even this was but the culmination of a "trail of crimes"[5] extending from the beginning of Jewish history. About such a people, much could be believed.

The popular Christian mind now began to spin novel and destructive fantasies about the Jews. These are the famous calumnies, from financial greed to ritual murder, the armory of later antisemitism. Unfortunately, they did not die with the Middle Ages. They are still alive in the imagination of large numbers of antisemites, and they are being revived in full strength by the enemies of Israel. It is possible to show that every one of these fantasies can be accounted for by the pathological mechanism of paranoia, and I shall attempt to do so in a later chapter.

If Christian anti-Judaism was now assuming a paranoid form in the mass mind, we are out of the realm of rational justification. Paranoia is transmissible from mind to mind, but it does not go by the route of reason. It can therefore change its rationalization while remaining essentially the same.

This may be the often missing explanation of how the secularized children of Christian parents in the modern world retained their anti-Jewish prejudices even after abandoning the Christian dogma that alone gave them a semblance of plausibility. Detached from its theological justification, hate could live on, unrestrained by Christian limits.

The phenomena discussed so far could best be called anti-Jewish hostility, or anti-Judaism. The modern term, *antisemitism*, often loosely applied to these older manifestations of Christian hate, has different implications and connotations. However much medieval Christians hated Jews, and however much some of them were prepared to do to express their hate, their hate did not take a *racist* form, for the concept of race had hardly been born. Any stigma that might attach to Jewishness was not a permanent characteristic of those born Jewish. It could be washed off in the waters of baptism. A Jewish convert to Christianity was a Christian in the fullest sense, no longer a Jew.

Only in the Spain of the Inquisition did this principle begin to be breached. The forced mass conversions of previous centuries and the sometimes justified supposition that these unwilling converts would do what they could to hold onto their former faith, led to widespread suspicion of the new Christians, or *conversos*, opprobriously called *Marranos*.

Now a new concept, at first resisted by the highest authorities in the Church, grew up in Spain. Those who wished to hold public office had to present a certificate of *limpiezza de sangre*, of purity of blood, showing that they were free of the by then widespread taint of *mala sangre*, bad blood (i.e., Jewish descent). Now Jewishness is being understood in a new way, as a permanent, inborn characteristic that even baptism does not remove. The links between this idea and modern racist antisemitism have not been traced, but ideas once generated have a habit of reappearing elsewhere without apparent connection. At much the same time, Luther was already beginning to believe in inborn Jewish characteristics that rendered Jews impervious to attempts at conversion.

Modern antisemitism is a phenomenon of the new world born in the French Revolution. The secularizing spirit of the Enlightenment, hostile toward all forms of institutional religion, was open to remedying the injustice done to Jews in the old Christian world by their anomalous social position; they were second-class citizens, or more exactly not citizens at all, without legal rights. But the Enlightenment philosophers assumed, along with their Christian predecessors, that there was something wrong with Jews as they were: they ought to be admitted to membership of European society, but only if reformed; they must abandon their exclusiveness and their strange customs. Only then could their inherent potential be realized. Then they could make a contribution to European society, from which both sides would benefit.

This concept of emancipation through reform was embodied in the bargain Napoleon made with the Jews of France, which proved fateful for all subsequent Jewish life in the modern world. The Jews were to become "Frenchmen of the Mosaic persuasion." In becoming French citizens, with the rights of other Frenchmen, they had to give up their own internal jurisdiction under the rabbinic courts, their historic claim to be a distinct people, and their hope of return to their own land. Thus, Jews had to make a severe sacrifice of identity, and take on a concept of religion and its place in society that was novel for them, and inherently Christian, not Jewish.

They were no longer to regard themselves as a people governed by the Torah, a code that covered not only what Christians think of as religion but matters of business and public morality also. They had now to think of religion as a purely private matter, while everything corporate and public was to be governed by the laws of the state. Almost all modern Jews outside Israel have made this sacrifice of national identity in order to live as citizens of the countries of their residence.

The sacrifice did not bring the expected benefits. Jews flocked into the modern nation states, making an astonishing and disproportionate contribution to intellectual, cultural and business life, but they were never fully accepted. Nationalism in its various forms now provided people with new reasons for being suspicious of an old enemy. Instead of the old theological put-downs, people began to speak of the "Jewish problem." The more successful Jews were at adapting themselves to their new environment, the more they were viewed with distrust and even with fear. Even baptism, a route many adopted as "the ticket of entrance to European culture,"[6] did them no good. They were still regarded as Jews in the eyes of their neighbors. The old suspicions still clung to them.

The word *Jew* acquired a new meaning. The secularized culture of the nineteenth century did not regard religious identities as fundamental, but it did see something indelible in the Jewish character. The new concept of race provided a way of identifying what others thought of as inherently Jewish traits.

The nineteenth-century concept of race was a spurious one, part of the century's fascination with biological explanations. It was far more ideological than scientific, though scientists and anthropologists embraced it, as did many others, including some, like Disraeli, who were not antisemites at all. So far as it had a basis in fact, it was an incautious deduction from the findings of philology. The discovery of the relatedness to one another of the various Indo-European and likewise of the Semitic languages led to the fallacious conclusion that there were Indo-European, or Aryan, and Semitic races that spoke these languages. Then the anthropologists "discovered" the superiority of the Aryan race to the Semitic one.

The idea was a gift to those who hated Jews. Now they did not have to apologize for or conceal their dislike. They could give it a scientific dress and call themselves not Jew-haters, which they were, but antisemites, those opposed to "semitism," the influence on society of the Semites (i.e., the Jews).

Antisemites did not then feel compelled to apologize for being such, or to conceal their views behind other more acceptable notions. For a while, there were even antisemitic political parties in Germany and Austria, proudly bearing the title, as well as others that used some form of the title Christian to convey the same meaning. Meanwhile, there were very few Jews to be opposed to. Even in pre-Hitler Germany, where Jewish thinkers and artists were of great importance, less than one percent of the Germans were Jewish.

Hitler claimed great originality for his radically antisemitic views, but for the most part they were inherited from the Catholic antisemitism of the Austrian politics of his youth. Only the will to exterminate was new. When at his Nuremberg trial Julius Streicher, the editor of the scurrilous Nazi newspaper *Der Stürmer,* claimed that if he must stand arraigned for his views on the Jews, so should Martin Luther, he had more than a semblance of justification for his contention.

Nazi antisemitism was anti-Christian as well, and it passed beyond all Christian or even human limits, but it could never have arisen without the Christian past, of which it was the secularized offspring. Without the inheritance of "knowledge" that Jews were bad, there could have been no Holocaust.

The Nazis themselves were able to conceive the radical idea of a final solution of the Jewish problem. They could never have won the cooperation of the Germans and the Eastern Europeans in what had to be done to accomplish it, if they had not been able to rely on the universal heritage of antisemitism in Christian European culture. And perhaps they would also not have been able to accomplish it if the expected trumpet call of protest had ever come from the Christian world outside. That call did not come.

The lesson of the Holocaust has not been learned. Since 1945, antisemitism has, to a degree, become unrespectable in the West, so that even conscious antisemites must now preface their apologias by some such declaration as, "I have nothing against Jews as such, and some of my best friends are Jews, but . . ." Nevertheless, in the world today there are forms of antisemitism hardly less alarming than their predecessors. The old forms are in any case by no means dead, showing clear signs of reappearing not only in Western societies but also in Russia and Eastern Europe, where it now appears that communism did to some extent restrict the expression of antisemitism but did nothing to uproot it.

There are also the new forms of antisemitism, characteristic of the post-Holocaust period, the growing phenomenon of Holocaust denial, attempting to cast doubt on the historical reality of the event itself, and anti-Zionism, which intends to rob the Jewish state of its legitimacy and political respectability in the community of nations by vilifying its actions and policies. These new forms of antisemitism share a common method: the falsification of history. No honest person can doubt that they are expressions of the same ancient hate.

Marxism has produced its own form of antisemitism, which linked up with the old Christian hostility toward Jews in countries like Russia and Poland. It is characteristic of the Marxist Left to deny any authentic national identity to the Jewish people, and today it is difficult for a Marxist, whether Jewish or not, to avoid being an anti-Zionist, denying the legitimacy of a Jewish state.[7]

Have the churches learned the lesson? Some individuals have, and this book owes much to their writings. Corporately, much less has been achieved. Probably the most significant event remains the declaration of the Second Vatican Council, *Nostra aetate.* Without actually proscribing or even mentioning the key word, deicide, and without any expression of repentance for Catholic anti-Judaic ideas and actions, the declaration did nevertheless make it clear that the Jewish people could not be held corporately responsible for the death of Christ. The Catholic church's teaching guidelines that have been issued since the Council interpret the document in a very positive way, and if followed, as they seldom are at the local level, would do much to dissipate the heritage of antisemitism in the Church.

Protestantism has done nothing comparable at the official level, though there have been some remarkable declarations of local church bodies, especially in Europe. The non-Catholic churches nowadays mostly express their views on such matters through the World Council of Churches. In the last few decades, the World Council has been strongly oriented toward the Third World and correspondingly influenced by Liberation Theology. Liberation Theology fuses Marxism with liberal Christianity. Many of its most influential writers are Latin American Catholics, but the same theology in a less precise form now dominates the thinking of the liberal mainstream Protestant churches.

Unfortunately, Liberation Theology is not good news for those who hope to right the millennial wrongs done by Christianity to the Jewish people. It sees Jesus as a revolutionary opposed to the leadership of his own people and to the Torah itself. And its exponents generally have no love for Israel, which they see in Marxist terms as an agent of Western imperialism oppressing the Third World Palestinians.

Theologians open to the Jewish people have so far found it impossible to gain support for a declaration by the major bodies of the World Council repudiating anti-Jewish theology and expressing solidarity with Israel. Instead, the same bodies have issued a stream of pronouncements expressing solidarity and sympathy with the Palestinian cause and reproving Israel for its actions.

In both Christian and secular versions, liberalism has its own form of antisemitism, mild rather than violent, a form of moral superiority based on ignorance of Jewish thought and life, and the uncriticized retention of ancient stereotypes. Liberal antisemitism is not intense enough to launch an attack on Jews, but it is quite strong enough to encourage liberals to see more justice in the cause of Israel's opponents than in Israel's own, and it could lead, as it did during the Holocaust, to Gentile indifference to a Jewish disaster. This form of antisemitism is usually unconscious, if only because incompatible with the liberal self-image of moral superiority, but all the more pervasive and difficult to uproot.

Whether religious or secular, conservative, Marxist, or liberal, all forms of modern antisemitism are branches of the same tree. All of them have inherited from the Christian past the conviction that Jews are bad. For religious antisemites, the Jews are the recalcitrant enemies of God and Christ. For conservatives, they are an unassimilable racial community. For liberals, they are narrow-minded and aggressive, ready to deny to others the political rights they claim for themselves. For Marxists, they are the instruments of American imperialism. New reasons may be given nowadays, but the assumption is old. At the roots of the tree we will find the ancient Christian myth depicting the Jews as the Christ-killers.

In the last few pages, we have briefly traced the development of antisemitism from its mythic roots to its modern secular forms, culminating in the Holocaust, but not ending there. If the Holocaust has not produced a profound moral revulsion from all these and any other forms of antisemitism, nothing will. There are, however, people of good will who do not like their antisemitic heritage but who do not know how to combat it in themselves and others. Jews also need to understand antisemitism better and to become more fully and confidently aware that it has nothing to do with them or their actions. For these readers, a book is still worth writing.

It remains important to trace the links between all modern forms of antisemitism and the Christian past, and I do not believe that it has yet been done clearly or conclusively enough. It is also important to examine the historical foundations of the myth itself by the methods of critical scholarship. Does history bear out the story the myth tells? We can now use the latest developments in scholarship to see the story of Jesus more clearly than ever before against the background of the Jewish faith and life in which he lived. The story emerging from recent scholarship conclusively refutes the anti-Jewish myth. Theologians, however, have yet to come to terms with these historical discoveries.

Scholars may wish to know what methodology I propose to use in approaching this history of hate. I try to make use of some of the newer methods by which religion is being studied in the many university departments of Religious Studies that have sprung up in the last thirty years. The discipline is so new that even its name is not agreed on: some speak of history of religions, others of the academic or scientific study of religion, or of the religious sciences. There is somewhat more agreement on what its proper job is and how it is to be done.

While the academic study of religion differs from theology, there is nothing startlingly new about its approach to history; many scholars who now work in seminaries would be no less at home in religious studies departments. Nevertheless, the academic or scientific study of religion ought to lead to greater sensitivity to the distortions in our perception of religions and their history arising from our own standpoint as modern people, heirs of or participants in particular religious traditions. We will never be able to eliminate our own standpoint, but fortunately self-awareness on this point can lead to new insights into the past. Without the appalling disaster of the Holocaust, I am afraid many of the questions this book attempts to answer would never have been asked, at least by those whose background is Christian.

It should be fully clear to everyone that when we study any religion, we ought not to take the views of some other religion as normative. It is not legitimate to study Judaism from the standpoint of Christian theology, as even critical New Testament scholars have been doing until recently. Even if the object of our study is a religion with which we are personally identified, we must still aim at detachment and objectivity, as well as benefitting from the empathy arising from our participation in it.

We attempt to understand each religion in its own terms, while noting patterns common to all religions. Each religion has its characteristic form of answer to the fundamental questions of life. These answers to the ultimate questions give each religion its identity, remaining distinctive through centuries of historical change. In attempting to identify those traditional and largely unchanging patterns, religious studies is, perhaps, also more open than theology to using the methods of allied disciplines such as anthropology, sociology, and psychology.

This much would probably be common ground. I want to add that such critical self-awareness and detachment need not and ought not to entail a reductionist attitude that denies the reality of the spiritual dimension, or simply ignores it. Unfortunately, much of the work now being done in religious studies is openly or hiddenly anti-religious, to the point of denying the reality of the Spirit. Religions do manifest that spiritual dimension, as well as veiling it in much that is all too human. Part of our task is to see through those veils to the reality beyond. That will sometimes bring us into dialogue with the theologians, whose aim is similar, though their methods are often different.

In pursuance of this greater critical objectivity, Christians and the heirs of Christianity in particular have now to learn to see Judaism, and sometimes even Christianity, through Jewish eyes. Doing so exposes in everyone whose upbringing has been Christian a remarkable ignorance of Jewish faith and life. Our former ignorance continues to become more astonishing to us as we go on discovering it. For those who have been educated by Christianity, it is salutary to begin to see it through the eyes of those who have been its victims. The view is different from there. I still remember vividly a friend whose childhood was spent in Poland saying to me years ago that he could not even pass a building with a cross on it without a shudder of fear.

Christian intellectuals have long seen the need for objective and critical investigation of the origins of their faith. The critical inquiry known as the search for the historical Jesus has been going on for more than two hundred years, and it has not been without result. We do know something now about Jesus as a historical person.

At the same time, the relationship between historical discovery and theology has been under constant debate. Clearly, believers in Christianity cannot wholly separate them. While there is more to be said, it is of first importance to see that while history may and must have an influence on the way faith is articulated in theology, theology must not be allowed to influence the findings of history.

Those who study the history of Christian origins must now learn not to be biased by later Christian beliefs. Historians, including Christian historians, must learn to see early as well as modern Judaism in its own integrity, and not in relation to Christianity, as its forerunner or even opposite. We have no right to assume in advance of inquiry a contrast between Jesus himself and the people to whom he belonged.

Only when what can be done to establish the historical facts has been done may those who wish legitimately proceed to draw theological conclusions. People are coming to recognize that the philosophical claims of religion must at least in principle be compatible with established scientific findings about the nature and history of the world. More slowly, perhaps, they are learning that its historical claims cannot legitimately be incompatible with what historians can recognize as the truth about the past, though religious faith will no doubt go beyond what scientific history can establish.

When we do study Christian origins in this more critical way, something still very novel, even startling, emerges. The supposed founder of Christianity, Jesus of Nazareth, turns out to have had very little to do with Christianity as it developed over the centuries. On the contrary, the more Christianity developed into a new and anti-Jewish religion, the more it betrayed Jesus the Jew. By the time the Gospels were written, one or two generations after Jesus' lifetime, the myth had already begun to take possession of the Christian mind, and Jesus the Jew was no longer remembered as such.

Historical scholarship now permits us to affirm with confidence that Jesus of Nazareth was a faithful and observant Jew, who lived by the Torah, and taught nothing against his own people and their faith. He did not claim to be the Messiah and may even have denied outright that he was. The Jews did not conspire to kill him and were not responsible for his death. He met his end on a Roman cross, condemned by a Roman official for a Roman offense. The myth of the Christ-killers lacks a basis in history. The story it tells of Jewish rejection and malice is not true. The Romans, not the Jews, were the Christ-killers.

These are historical discoveries, but they cannot fail to have theological implications. A number of excellent theologians have written books in the last two or three decades on Christian anti-Judaism and ways to overcome it. None of them, I believe, has drawn sufficiently radical conclusions from the latest developments in the study of Jesus and Christian origins. Even the dialogue theologians have tended to stop historical investigation at a point where it is still comfortable.

If Jesus was, in modern terms, perhaps not altogether applicable to his own times, an orthodox Jew, he cannot be taken as an authority for anything Christian at all. If he did not claim to be the Messiah and was not condemned by his people's highest court for such a claim, his death was not messianic or saving. He was not, in his own eyes at least, a Christian savior, but perhaps a Jewish martyr.

The implications of these discoveries for modern Christianity are devastating and cannot be ignored. Jews can no longer be depicted, either by historians or Christian teachers, as responsible for the death of Christ. Christians may no longer depict the Torah as a rigid and legalistic system, lacking in compassion and devoid of efficacious means of assuring forgiveness for the repentant sinner, because simple honesty precludes it, let alone the discovery of scholarship that Jesus himself lived by that same Torah.

It has become much more difficult to understand why Paul should have rejected the religion of Jesus for his Gentile converts. A vast new question arises. Perhaps Paul's decisions were wrong, if not then, at least now. Christians may now have to choose between Jesus and Paul. Perhaps nothing less than the choice of the Jewish Jesus could effectively rule out new forms of religious anti-Judaism, the anti-Judaism that history shows to be the precursor of antisemitism, and in turn of Jewish annihilation. But the consequences for Christianity of the choice for Jesus the Jew are almost incalculable.

For secular people, these theological questions will be irrelevant. Nevertheless, if the links I shall be tracing in this book are real, secular people should be profoundly disturbed to find that their views on Jewish people and the Jewish state are very likely conditioned by a myth in which they no longer believe. If so, the first step is to make the conditioning conscious, so that a choice can be freely made not to continue an ancient hostility into the very different situation of the modern world.

The purpose of this book is primarily to trace the story. It is a story of a slow and incremental development, and the distance between the beginning and the end of the development is great. Was the end latent in the beginning? Did an initial disagreement between two groups of Jews on how the Messiah should be recognized contain within itself the seeds of Holocaust?

It seems hard to imagine. Yet the fact is that this disagreement between two groups of Jews led, by apparently easy transitions, to a number of momentous developments. So easy were the transitions that they can look quasi-inevitable. They led first to the founding of a Gentile movement powered by a myth in which the Jews were cast as God's enemies, then to an all-powerful Christian church whose best word to the Jews was that they should be preserved in misery until the end of the world, in due course to a lethal paranoia that caused the murder of many thousands of Jews in the middle ages, and finally (or perhaps not?) to a secularized antisemitism that provided the ideological foundation for the greatest crime in human history, a crime whose declared aim was the extermination of every Jew on the face of the planet.

The original Christian hostility toward Jews went through a number of transformations down the course of western history, acquiring different rationalizations. But all its forms shared one element, the most important–Jews were bad.

The metaphor I have used of the seed growing into the tree suggests an organic and causal connection between the first and the latest stages of this long and incremental development. Is the suggestion justified? Many people of good will are likely to deny it strenuously. Good Christians prefer to believe that a form of Christianity originally friendly to its Jewish predecessor has been corrupted by the wrong choices of individual Christians. If so, wrong choices can be reversed, and a purified Christianity can emerge, basically unchanged in its beliefs but no longer anti-Jewish, let alone antisemitic. Others point to an official theology that was never as anti-Jewish as popular attitudes. Thus, they hope, the official theology can survive more or less intact, without its old anti-Judaic consequences.

I no longer feel as confident as I once did that such reforms will suffice. It now appears to me that if Christians want to remove not only all taint of antisemitism from their tradition, but all ideas that have a tendency to lead to it, they must do more than this. It is not enough to deal with the official theology, whose exponents sometimes even defended the Jews. Hatred of Jews draws its justification not primarily from official theology but from the religion by which all Christians live, theologians or laity. Religion's source is not theology but myth.

Ideas that did in fact lead to antisemitic consequences perhaps had an innate tendency to do so. In my view, the burden of proof is now upon those who resist this conclusion. In view of the appalling evils that have followed from them, it is imperative to view such ideas critically, rather than defensively. Many falsehoods must now be eradicated from the way Christians tell the story of their origins to a new generation. This cannot be done without criticism of the central Christian myth, as well as its embodiment in the sacred writings that Christians venerate as Scripture. Can a myth be changed and the religion it has powered survive unscathed?

The Holocaust cannot be undone, nor the six million brought back from the ashes of the crematoria. Only the dead have the right to forgive, and no one, least of all Christians, has the right to forgive on their behalf. Nevertheless, some theologians now believe that repentance for the antisemitism that betrayed Jesus and inflicted unimaginable harm on his people is a spiritual necessity for Christians themselves, whether or not it can earn forgiveness from Jews. Such repentance, if real, cannot fail to lead to theological change.

The secular heirs of the Christian tradition have likewise their own accounting to make with their consciences. Both the Enlightenment and the post-Hegelian Left took over far more from older Christian attitudes toward the Jews than it is comfortable for their present-day successors to admit. In spite of the immense shock of the Holocaust, and the valiant strivings of a small elite to respond, the effort to purge Western consciousness of all traces of antisemitic and anti-Judaic hate has hardly yet begun.

I

Before the Myth

1

Jesus the Jew: 1. Founder of Christianity?

From the time when Christianity first had written documents, the Jew has appeared in its central story as the enemy of Christ. The story of the trial and death of Christ is told to every Christian child, to every adult who attends church, and to every convert being instructed in the faith. Even very secularized people are still familiar with the sacred story through a musical like *Jesus Christ Superstar*, or through the music of Bach, whose settings of the Passion according to St. Matthew and to St. John are enjoyed by many who do not share Bach's Lutheran faith. Christian art tells the same story.

When they hear the story, Christians learn that the Jews were responsible for the death of the Redeemer, the divine Son of God. According to the story they are told, Jewish religious hostility brought Christ to an unjust trial, and Jewish political pressure on the Roman authorities brought him to the cross. The story that every Christian knows best of all depicts the Jews as the killers of Christ.

MYTH AND HISTORY

The image of the Jew as Christ-killer is built into the central Christian myth. This statement introduces a familiar word, "myth," in an unfamiliar sense. In ordinary speech, a myth is an untrue story. When we say that such and such is a myth, we mean that it is untrue and baseless. When scholars who study religion use the word, they understand it rather differently: they mean a story or a group of images in which religious energy and emotion are invested. The story tells the members of the community who they are, giving the community its identity and distinguishing it from others. The myth is the charter of a religious community, the energy center by which it lives. Usually the myth explains such ultimate mysteries as the creation of the world, the struggle between good and evil, and the way human beings can be saved in the future.

Without myths, we would not have religions. Myths tap into deep, archetypal layers of the mind, the levels from which profound religious experiences arise. In turn, religions constantly renew the power of the myth in their adherents by reenacting it symbolically in their liturgy, the rite that unites all believers. Much more than theology, myths determine how the adherents of a religion really feel about the world and about other people. There are also secular myths and even secular liturgies. Nations have them, and so do political movements.

This particular myth has features that render it almost without parallel in the history of religions, and in historical fact it proved to be laden with dreadful consequence for Jews.[1] Such myths typically embody the story of a conflict between cosmic powers, in which order and goodness triumph over chaos and evil. The myth has a hero, and the hero has enemies. By his own cosmic triumph over rival forces, he gives future believers confidence that they too can defeat the forces that menace their own spiritual lives.[2]

The story of the Christian myth does not take place in some timeless realm beyond the historic past, *in illo tempore*, as Mircia Eliade often expresses it in his important studies of myth and religion, or in a dream time, like the myths of Australia. It is set in actual history, in a precise period of time and in a real place.

As the Christian creeds put it, the story of Jesus was enacted "under Pontius Pilate,"[3] an administrator of whom we know something from sources outside the myth. And the enemies of the hero of this story, Jesus of Nazareth, are not personified cosmic forces, but the leaders of an actual historical people, the very people the hero himself belonged to.

The forces of evil, the cosmic adversaries of divine power and goodness, in this story are embodied in Jews who really lived in Jesus' time, some of whom did encounter him, perhaps support him or even come into conflict with him. It is part of the very historicity of this myth, so often rightly emphasized by its interpreters, the theologians, that both the hero and his enemies are historical figures, people who really lived in an actual place and time.

It is therefore impossible to tell the story of this myth without casting Jews in the role of the adversaries. The enmity cannot be altogether spiritualized away and rendered abstract, if only because of the compelling power of the story as it stands. When Christians hear or tell the story, they are uplifted spiritually and given faith and hope. But they must also feel anger and very often hate against those who (according to the myth) conspired against and killed their divine Lord.

The vast majority of Christians who have ever lived have naturally identified the Jews of their own day with the Jews of Jesus' time and have seen them as enemies too. Until recent times, only the most enlightened have ever been able to refrain from doing so. As we trace this history of tragic conflict, we shall find again and again that very devout people, regarded as highly spiritual, even as saints, by their contemporaries and by later generations, have been vicious antisemites. How is this possible? Only the double-sidedness of the Christian myth can explain the paradox of antisemitic saints.

This myth is two-edged and inherently so. It fosters spiritual aspirations toward God and other people, in one of its aspects, while in the other it fosters anger and hostility against Jews. The two aspects can hardly be separated, because both arise from its historical character, which is essential to it. If you try to counteract those aspects of the story that foster hatred of others (while leaving the myth essentially intact), you can only do so by removing the concrete historicity vital to the power of the myth.

This is what happens when people, with the best intentions, say that the real enemies of Jesus were our sins, which brought him to the cross. Theologically, this is no doubt correct, but it cuts the story's anchor with history. That is not what the myth has been saying for two thousand years. The myth has been saying that the Jews killed Christ, and the vast majority of Christians still believe that they did, even when they regard the Jews as only representing and typifying human sin. This myth claims to be true, true in the ordinary sense.

Such a claim is not essential to every religious myth. The historical truth or untruth of its story may be irrelevant to the spiritual function of the myth, as is perhaps the case with the story of Krishna in Hinduism, or the story may actually be true. Sometimes, however, such stories are also myths in the more familiar sense. It can happen that a community has taken it for granted that its myth, the story which is its charter, is historically true, and then discovers that it is not. Can a myth that is known to be untrue, in short, "a myth," still function as a potent center of religious energy?

Contemporary Christianity is somewhat in this situation. For the last two hundred years, the modern techniques of historical inquiry have been applied to the origins of Christianity, in an attempt to rediscover the historical Jesus and his role in the origin of the religion that is everywhere associated with his name. The myth has been subjected to historical criticism, and it must inevitably now receive theological criticism as well, in the light of what it has done to Jews.

The results have been disturbing, and the disturbance continues. The Jesus rediscovered by historians has turned out not to be the Christ portrayed in the myth. And in the newly recovered history of his last days, the Jews no longer play the role of Christ-killers.

However, for decades, until very recently, most ministers in the mainstream Protestant churches had been taught in seminary that the results of this long process of historical criticism have turned out to be negative, leading to ignorance rather than knowledge. The New Testament, it is still widely supposed, gives us very little reliable evidence about the life of Jesus. The story that is the basis of the Christian myth cannot be substantiated by critical history, students have been told, but we do not know what to put in its place.

Only in the last few years has that skepticism been succeeded by renewed confidence in the capacity of historians to arrive at the disturbing truth about Jesus, and the changes have come too late to affect the present generation of clergy. Now that critical history has spread to the Catholic church, the Catholic clergy have also been hearing the same thing from their professors. But the clergy do not know what to tell the laity.

The laity have not the time, or often the capacity, to conduct the detailed studies that would allow them to assess the value of different historical theories and their bearing on faith. If they are simply told the results of biblical criticism, they may lose a simple faith without acquiring a more critical one.

The temptation not to tell them anything is very great. Especially Catholic Christians have continued to learn about the origins of Christianity and such central events as the passion and death of Christ, almost exclusively through the traditional liturgy, and have never heard what critical scholars think about these stories, so central to the Christian myth.

Thus the myth continues to tell millions of Christians all over the world deadly things about the Jews. Weekly and daily, it still reinforces the belief that Jews were the Christ-killers, and breeds in the Christian people a natural suspicion of the Jews of today.

Beyond doubt, the Christian myth has caused immense harm to the Jewish people, leading to the deaths of millions, right up to our own time. Today, echoes of the same myth substantially influence the way the Western world, including liberal people who are no longer attached to Christianity, reacts to events in the Middle East. The ancient suspicion of the Jews still distorts the common perception of the realities of the situation of Israel vis-à-vis her Arab neighbors, giving unwarranted credibility to the propaganda of her enemies.

CRITICIZING MYTHS

No one should doubt that the historical criticism of a myth is a delicate matter. The mere fact of criticizing it, whatever the outcome, arouses feelings of profound anxiety and rage. The myths by which religious people live should be beyond criticism, they usually feel. In a pluralistic society, religious people wish others to refrain from criticizing their myths and may sometimes themselves refrain from criticizing the myths of others. In fact, a pluralistic society could hardly exist without such restraint.

During the time that this book was being written, two events happened that brought to the surface the explosive passions aroused when a religious myth is criticized. Martin Scorcese, a Roman Catholic, made a film based on a novel by a Greek Orthodox writer, Nikos Kazantzakis, called *The Last Temptation of Christ*. The film, like the book, portrayed Jesus as struggling with human temptations, and especially the temptation, remaining with him even on the cross, to renounce his mission in favor of a normal family life with the woman he loved.

While theologically there was little in this portrayal of a very human Jesus that was unorthodox, since the New Testament also portrays Jesus as human and subject to temptation, it caused an uproar, much of which was openly or covertly antisemitic.

Jews were blamed for making a film that was insulting to Christian faith, although its makers were Christian and only happened to work for a company that had some Jews in high managerial positions. (A much more relevant criticism of the film would have been that it was anti-Jewish, reinforcing old stereotypes about Jewish hostility toward Jesus, while not depicting Jesus himself as characteristically Jewish at all. What it did represent as Jewish was substantially distorted.)

What was so disturbing to so many? Primarily, it seems, the depiction in the movie of Jesus' fantasy while on the cross of marriage with Mary Magdalene, including a scene showing normal sexual relations between husband and wife. It seemed that the Christian myth had now assumed a shape in which it was unthinkable to imagine Jesus as having a sexual thought, even an innocent one.

The second event concerned Islam. A British writer of Indian origin, Salman Rushdie, wrote a remarkable book called *The Satanic Verses,* which is primarily about problems of identity, and especially those of immigrants to another culture, who have to contend with more than one identity. In the book, one of his characters, apparently intended to be schizophrenic, has drunken dreams in which he imagines a naturalistic origin for Islam.

The Prophet Muhammad, Islam's founder (lightly disguised as a businessman called Mahound), is not depicted in these dreams as a bad man but as a human being, struggling with the problems of getting a new religion going in a hostile environment. Rushdie depicts him also as tempted to compromise his monotheism but overcoming the temptation. In constructing that part of the book, he uses a tradition many scholars studying Islam find credible, that at one time the Quran contained some verses legitimating a modified polytheism, and that later Muhammad saw his error and removed them. These are the "satanic verses" of the title.

Rushdie certainly did not borrow the phrase for his title because of a detached historical interest in the Quran, or even because it was central to his literary purpose to attack the foundations of Islam. The satanic verses symbolically stand for several other things; the same phrase is also used in quite different contexts in the book. Muhammad and the origins of Islam seem to be peripheral to Rushdie's literary intention.

The outcry in the Muslim world dwarfed the Christian furor over *The Last Temptation of Christ.* The Ayatollah Khomeini called for the murder of Rushdie and pronounced his assassination a religious duty incumbent on all Muslims. The sentence has not been withdrawn by his successors, and some say it never can be. Grotesque (and grotesquely untrue) calumnies about the author and his book circulated in the Muslim world and sometimes found their way into the British press.[4] Even more moderate and westernized Muslims, including academics, pronounced the book a blasphemous insult to Islam and to the Prophet. Rushdie was forced into hiding and remained there, in daily fear for his life.

It is a fundamental Muslim doctrine that the Prophet was human and not divine, and, therefore, presumably capable of error and of correcting his errors. In the current form of the Muslim myth, the Prophet has nevertheless assumed an infallible perfection that in all probability he would not have claimed for himself.

As a result, countless Muslims, who had not read the book and perhaps would not have understood it if they had, came to believe that Rushdie, a modernized skeptic who had never been a Muslim at all,[5] was a Muslim apostate who knowingly and deliberately attacked the Prophet with the intention of insulting him and of blaspheming. This belief has little to do with reality and much to do with the anxiety aroused by an apparent threat to a myth.

The historical criticism of the Muslim myth has hardly begun, at any rate among Muslims themselves. However, the criticism of the Christian myth had already begun long ago, and in view of the Holocaust, many responsible theologians are now convinced that it has still not gone far enough. In particular, it must go further in breaking up the foundations of Christian antisemitism. Now, after the Holocaust, it has become morally necessary to go right through Christian history, examining what Christians have said and taught about Jews, from the accounts of Jesus in the New Testament to present-day developments, to discover if the teachings are antisemitic and if the historical claims on which they are based are justified.

BIBLICAL CRITICISM

Criticism has to begin, therefore, with the New Testament account of the origins of Christianity. Though not originally with this purpose in mind, scholars have been engaged in critical study of the New Testament for a long time. It is still not sufficiently known that in the last two hundred years or so a revolution has occurred in the way we think about the past no less significant than the scientific revolution that was going on at the same time. Like the scientific revolution, the historical revolution also involved the criticism of religion. The methods of historical criticism were first evolved for the purpose of studying the Bible and only later transferred to other fields.

The early critics wanted to see if they could discover how things really happened in the time of the Bible, without being influenced by the dogmatic views of Christianity. The method they began to use was source criticism. They took the daring step of applying critical methods to the books of the New Testament, regarding them as sources from which the history behind them could be recovered. They began to read the Bible as if it were any other book. The idea was a revolutionary one then, and for many it still is. But it soon began to yield results.

Historical criticism generally finds that ancient documents are much better evidence for the time they were written in than for the period they write about. So it proved to be with the New Testament. The New Testament turned out to be excellent evidence for the state of the Church in the last part of the first century, but not such good evidence for the life and times of Jesus himself. However, the early historical critics hoped that by rigorous analysis they could filter out the contribution of the Church and recover a reliable picture of the Jesus of history from their sources.

They greatly underrated the difficulty of the task. Again and again, in the nineteenth and twentieth centuries, scholars have found it necessary to scrap their results and start over again, because they discovered that they were being unduly influenced by the ideas of their own time.

Having, as they supposed, thrown off the influence of traditional dogmas, the nineteenth-century critics now found themselves unconsciously subject to the influence of the liberal progressive ideas of their time. Instead of seeing Jesus as a first-century Jew, they had begun to imagine him as a modern liberal like themselves, teaching abstract and generalized ideas about the fatherhood of God and the brotherhood of man. While they wore those spectacles, they could not see the past as it was.

This tells us something very important about the aims of historical criticism. One of the essential tasks of the critic is to detach him or herself from the assumptions of the present, in order to let the past appear in its objective reality. In antiquity as well, there were historians. They were quite well aware of the need to be critical, according to their own understanding of what that meant. They knew that not everything they had been told was true, and they had a good idea of how to distinguish true from false reports. But they had not yet learned to take off the spectacles of the present when envisaging the past.

The same is true of uncritical readers of the Christian Bible today. They assume that the New Testament Church was like the Church around the corner. This is exactly what fundamentalists do. They think of Jesus and his disciples just like a group of modern Protestant evangelicals, except that Jesus himself is now imagined as so divine that he can hardly be thought of as human any more.

Discovering the truth about the past is not just a matter of hard thinking, like scientific research. It also calls for considerable efforts of detachment from present concerns, as well as the capacity to imagine cultural and historical situations sometimes remote from those of the investigator. The reasoning involved in historical criticism is often very exact and the knowledge required extensive. It is very much like detective work and has the same appeal to the mind. From tiny clues, a fascinating and unexpected picture may be built up. But that is not enough.

In the field of religion, it is especially necessary to become detached from hopes and fears about the effect of one's discoveries. Inevitably, it is important to religious people that what they find will still support the religious identity they cherish and the values they live by. But there is no intrinsic reason why historical discovery should be expected to do this.

Scholars studying religion often try to avoid the difficulty by a scientific objectivity that can amount to detachment bordering on indifference. Impressed by the achievements of the hard sciences, they suppose that a similar kind of disinterestedness will be appropriate in their own enterprise. But this is not the case.

The detachment required in the study of religion is of a more dynamic and empathetic kind. It involves taking seriously the spiritual aims and achievements of our predecessors, while becoming detached from our own contemporary concerns. Without this dynamic detachment, scholars can get out of touch with the very people they are studying, who were themselves neither detached nor indifferent, but passionately committed. In studying Christian origins, Christians need to make their historical imaginations Jewish: for most, that is not easy.

JESUS AND HIS OWN PEOPLE

It is no news that one of the most important questions in the study of the New Testament is the relationship between Jesus and the Jewish people. The New Testament itself thrusts the issue in our face by telling of bitter conflict between Jesus and other Jews, usually identified as Pharisees. The New Testament has given Pharisees a thoroughly bad name among readers of the Christian Bible, and now they have become synonymous in common speech with hypocrisy and meticulousness about the details of religion while missing the spiritual point.

Is this a fair picture of the historical Pharisees? Were they actually like that? Is the picture of conflict between Jesus and the Pharisees, which according to at least some of the gospel writers actually led to his trial and condemnation and subsequent execution, well-founded in historical fact? Did Jesus really bring a new spiritual message, superior to that to which his own people adhered, and thus incur their jealousy and rejection? Did they condemn him for blasphemy because he claimed to be the Messiah, the Son of God? In short, did the Jews kill Christ?

These are the questions that will occupy us in this and the next two chapters. The answer to all of them is no. But we have to see why that answer is correct by looking at the details more closely. The main reason why we are today able to give this clear negative answer to our traditional questions is the progress recently made in understanding what Judaism was like in Jesus' time and applying the knowledge to the study of Christian origins.

Until very recently, Christian historians have not known as much about Judaism as they needed to for their professional purposes. Sometimes, they may not have wanted to find out; they thought they already knew all they needed to know. It is possible to show in detail that the most celebrated New Testament critics of even the recent past had to rely on extremely biased Christian sources for their picture of the Judaism of Jesus' time.[6]

It is no longer regarded as legitimate to get a picture of first-century Jews from hostile references in the Gospels, or from assuming that the Judaism of the day was whatever Paul was against. Yet, this is what Christian scholars were actually doing until quite recently. This means that on the very central issue of the relationship between Jesus and Judaism, all but the most recent New Testament scholarship is out of date and can only be used by experts who know how to correct for its errors.

Fortunately, there are historians today who can teach us about the Judaism in which Jesus lived without misleading us. Some of them are Jews, some of them Christians. They agree on the duty of obtaining as accurate a picture as possible of the religious culture of first-century Judaism as a prerequisite to drawing any picture of Jesus himself. A consensus is developing as to what that religious culture was like. For example, we are beginning to have a clearer picture of who the Pharisees were and what they stood for. They no longer appear as natural enemies of Jesus, and we can now see that he and they stood for many, even most, of the same things. Perhaps Jesus was actually a Pharisee himself.

Once that picture of first-century Judaism begins to crystalize, and we attempt to insert the gospel picture of Jesus into it, something very new and surprising happens. First of all, the picture fits. There are pieces of it that do not, but much more now appears to have been authentically remembered and transmitted than scholars had supposed. The memories of Jesus appear in the Gospels in a misleading context, permeated by the ideas of later Christianity. However, they are still there and can often be disentangled from that context and restored to their original one. Then the stories come to life in a new and far more convincing way. Difficult historical questions remain, but if they are ever to be solved, it will be along these lines.

Second, when thus recovered, Jesus no longer stands out from his background, in sharp contrast, like white on black. That is how he used to appear to readers of the Gospels. It used to seem to Christian historians that he was bringing a new and lofty spiritual message to decadent Judaism. Accordingly, he stood out from his contemporaries as someone different and superior, so superior that he could be regarded as divine where they were human, and the founder of a new religion justifiably destined to supersede Judaism.

Now he seems to be at home in his own world. He is still an individual, with distinctive things to say and a distinctive way of saying them. But his teaching, like his life, does not transcend the Judaism in which it is set (except in so far as genuinely spiritual teaching always transcends institutional religion).

It is part of Jewish faith and life. It does not negate it, it does not replace it with something superior. In the tradition of the biblical prophets, Jesus' teaching was intended to deepen the response to the divine rule of members of his own generation, of his fellow Jews. There is no sign here of a new religion, or even of any interest in anything outside the Jewish people and its destiny.

JESUS THE JEW

Apart from a few radical antisemites, everybody had always acknowledged that Jesus was born a Jew. Throughout Christian history, readers of the Gospels had known that Jesus was born into the Jewish people, of a Jewish mother, circumcised on the eighth day, and brought up to fulfill the commandments of the Torah. But somehow no one, at least among Christian readers of the New Testament, had taken his Jewishness seriously until fairly recently. Everyone had always assumed that no sooner did he reach adult life than he started to utter fundamental criticisms of the religion of his own people, bringing a new message that would soon make it obsolete. And everyone likewise assumed that it was Jewish rejection of this new message that brought him to the cross.

For some time, modern scholars had begun to see more and more clearly that real progress in the understanding of Jesus' life and teaching would only come about when his relationship to Judaism was better understood. As was commonly said, scholars needed to understand "the Jewish background" better than was yet possible. But Jesus, as the founder of Christianity, was the foreground. They took it for granted that the relationship between foreground and background would be contrast. It could only be expected that the contrast would become more vivid as the background was better known and understood.

As early as a hundred years ago, a few Jewish scholars who had interested themselves in Jesus had already given their fellow scholars a warning of what might be found if they went along these lines, but their voices do not seem to have been listened to when they said that they themselves could see no gap between Jesus and Judaism. Christian historians assumed, perhaps, that this was Jewish prejudice.

For Christian writers, especially in the predominant German tradition, it was axiomatic that Jesus was a divinely disruptive force in "late Judaism." The very phrase, so commonly used by these scholars to refer to the religion of the period, was an uncriticized legacy from the old theology of supersession, as we now call it, according to which Christianity had displaced and superseded Judaism in the plan of God. In a truer perspective, the Judaism of Jesus' time was early, not late. It was not destined to be superseded, and it had an important future ahead of it.

Now, such historians as David Flusser, Hyam Maccoby, Geza Vermes, James H. Charlesworth, and E. P. Sanders, among a number of others, both Jewish and Christian,[7] are teaching us to start with early Judaism and then to study Jesus in its light. As Charlesworth a leading Christian scholar on the so-called "Inter-Testamental period" put it, "During the past two centuries, hundreds of attempts have been made by brilliant scholars to place Jesus within the thoughts of the Church. Others, more historically inclined, have endeavored to discuss Jesus and Judaism. Now, I am convinced that the new discoveries, sensitivities and methods compel us to see Jesus *within* his contemporary Jewish environment . . . Jesus of Nazareth as a historical man must be seen *within* Judaism."[8]

E. P. Sanders, writing a little earlier, summarized the findings of the newer research on Jesus: "The dominant view today seems to be that we can know pretty well what Jesus was out to accomplish, that we can know a lot about what he said, and that these two things make sense within the world of first-century Judaism."[9]

Geza Vermes, in an article with the same significant title as his book, *Jesus the Jew*, puts the same thought in this way: " 'Jesus the Jew' . . . is an emotionally charged synonym for the Jesus of history as opposed to the divine Christ of Christian faith that simply re-states the obvious fact, still hard for many Christians and even some Jews to accept, that Jesus was a Jew and not a Christian."[10]

When we do study the history of Jesus within its proper Jewish context, we thus discover a Jew. At every point, what the Gospels tell us about Jesus, where we have reason to believe that their information is authentic, fits in to Judaism. It does not fit nearly as well into Christianity. In fact, if we start from Christianity, as depicted in the New Testament, and try to work back to discover how it began in Jesus, we find very few links from the early Christian church to Jesus – so few, indeed, that only with some ingenuity can any connection be traced between them.

That is, I believe, the main reason why until recently New Testament critics had become so skeptical about the possibility of recovering a satisfactory picture of the life and teaching of Jesus. They had been starting in the wrong place, with an already anti-Jewish church, instead of analyzing this anti-Judaic bias in their sources and filtering it out, so as to reach back to something closer to the original memories of Jesus.

This skepticism is also the outcome of the scholarly tradition, mentioned earlier, in which the majority of present-day clergy have been educated, except in the more conservative churches. The gospel writers and their original readers, it was supposed, did not want to know about the Jesus who had lived in Galilee a few years before. Instead, they wanted to know about the Christ who was now sitting at the right hand of God and would soon return to judge the world and bring in the promised age of universal peace and righteousness. Students of the New Testament have learned from their teachers that the oral tradition of the early Church so molded the stories of the life and teaching of Jesus that the original can very seldom be recovered at all.

They failed to emphasize that somewhere along the line of transmission this tradition had turned profoundly anti-Jewish. But it still preserved accounts that can be re-read today by those who do not share the hostility toward Jews and Judaism of those who transmitted it. They can be restored to something like their original context in Jewish life, and then they come to life in a new way.

It is startling for people brought up in that tradition to discover that the familiar Gospels, which are in the hands of millions, can after all give us all kinds of valuable information about Jesus, once they are read in the right way, that is to say, a Jewish way.

THE REAL JESUS

Let us put the matter in more pictorial terms. In the Western world, Christians generally imagine Jesus as tall, probably with blond hair and beard, blue eyes, and wearing a white robe and an other-worldly expression. Almost certainly, he was short by modern standards and dark-skinned. His black beard was long and untrimmed. He undoubtedly wore earlocks, the *peyot* that are displayed today only by the ultraOrthodox but were once worn by all Jews as a matter of course.[11] We know from the Gospels that he wore fringes on his garments like other Jews. Like other Jews, he wore *tefillin* (called "phylacteries" in the Gospels) when he prayed formally, and perhaps at other times, and took it for granted that others would do the same; he objected only when they were ostentatious in wearing them in public, as some did in his day. He observed the feasts and fasts, and he must have gone to the ritual bath on appropriate occasions to purify himself, as they did, for we know from archaeological findings that the ritual bath was in common use in Jesus' time. He said the customary blessings when he drank wine and when he ate bread. He washed his hands whenever he sat down to eat, though apparently his disciples sometimes neglected to do so, without being reproved by him.

He personally obeyed all the commandments, ethical and ritual, and took part in the sacrificial worship of the Temple when he was in Jerusalem. Like the prophets in whose tradition he stood, he objected to these things only when they were done mechanically, without the intention toward God that made them valid, and without the social morality that God demanded above all.

Jesus was a faithful and observant Jew, according to the *halachah*, the interpretation of the Torah, accepted in his day. He did not regard the Jewish Law itself as mechanical and ritualistic, or those who kept it carefully as spiritually decadent. He loved the Torah and observed it with the deepest faithfulness and spiritual dedication. He lived by it until his last breath.

Jesus was in no way like the gentle Jesus, meek and mild, of much Christian tradition. While he counseled the transcendence of anger to the point of loving enemies, he evidently did not always avoid it himself. His criticism of all religious phoniness is as direct and even brutal as anything to be found in religious history. In this regard, he was the toughest of teachers. Yet his compassion for sinners is rightly regarded as remarkable, and it is this that marked him out as the bearer of a distinctive message concerning divine compassion.

If this message aroused opposition, and it seems that it did, it was not because it was un-Jewish. It was not. Rather, Jesus' convictions concerning the compassion of God for sinners and the way human beings should imitate it went even beyond what some of the devout of his day had been able to imagine of God. And if Jesus was scathing in his criticism of religious phoniness, it was not because he was opposed to Judaism, or regarded it as intrinsically defective, but because he wanted the Torah to be fulfilled by everyone as completely and perfectly as possible, from the heart.

His personal name was Yeshua, in the Aramaic he spoke, or Yehoshua in Hebrew, a very common name usually translated as Joshua. We get the form Jesus from the Greek rendering of his Aramaic name Yeshua, which comes out as Iesous, which is Jesus in Latin and also in English. His parents were Yossef and Mariam, or Miriam. He had brothers called Yaakov (James), Yoset, Shimon (Simon), and Yehudah (Judah). He also had sisters, but their names were not remembered.

In Jewish tradition preserved in the Talmud, which (in spite of medieval Christian attempts at censorship) does contain a few indirect references to him, Jesus is not referred to as the son of Joseph. Of course Jews did not believe in the Christian legend of the virgin birth of Jesus, but in that case we should have expected that he would be referred to as the son of his supposed father, Joseph. He is actually called in these references Yeshua ben Pantera, Jesus son of Pantera. In these earliest sources there is no explanation for the name, but later Jewish tradition took it to mean that Jews remembered that he had not been the son of Joseph but the offspring of a rape or seduction of Mary by a Roman soldier named Pantera.

Christian writers formerly believed that Pantera was not a Roman name but a corruption of *parthenos*, the Greek word for "virgin." They explained the references to ben Pantera as Jewish attempts to discredit the Christian doctrine of the virgin birth of Jesus. A Roman inscription bearing a memorial to a soldier of the same name has actually been discovered in Europe. This explanation will therefore no longer hold up. The tradition that preserved the name Pantera for Jesus' father in all probability has nothing to do with the stories of the virgin birth, and may even be older than them.

A recent writer has suggested that the gospel writers also knew of this persistent tradition, and that the birth stories in Matthew and Luke are intended to show that whatever his human origins, Jesus was born by the will of God in order to fulfill the purpose of God in bringing salvation to the world.[12] The language of the Gospels when they tell the story of Jesus' birth is usually interpreted through the spectacles of later Greek theology. If instead we read them in a Jewish way, we can discover that they do not say that Mary was a virgin when Jesus was born, or that his conception was supernatural, in the sense that later Christians understood it. Even if Jesus was actually conceived as the son of a Roman soldier, especially as a result of rape or seduction, that would not make him illegitimate by Jewish law, since he was born of a Jewish mother and not as the offspring of adultery or of a prohibited marriage.

Jesus was probably born a few years before the date usually reckoned as the beginning of the Common or Christian era, during the reign of Herod the Great. Unfortunately, we have no reliable means of ascertaining the exact date. The methods usually employed depend on the birth stories in Matthew and Luke, which have many obviously legendary elements, and in any case do not agree with each other. He died during the rule of the Roman governor, or Prefect, Pontius Pilatus, which lasted from 26 to 36 C.E.[13] It seems certain that the Romans executed him because they regarded him as an insurgent, on account of his reputation as a claimant to the title of Messiah, whether or not he actually made the claim.

We cannot reconstruct the order of events in his life from the Gospels, because the writers of the Gospels did not know what it was themselves, as was already recognized in the second century. Nevertheless, it is possible to discover the kind of person Jesus was and what he stood for, by a careful comparison of the gospel stories about him with what we now know of the religious environment in which he lived.

To imagine Jesus in a thoroughly Jewish way is very difficult even for Jews, most of whom have also been conditioned to think of him as some kind of Christian. For Christians, it takes real effort. The degree of effort required reveals the anti-Jewish prejudice with which all Christians have been infected, including those who do not think they have any such prejudices. This is the kind of effort the writer and many readers of this book will need throughout, as we move from Jesus, through the origins and early development of Christianity, to its medieval glory and triumph, which was also a time of terror and death for Jews, and on into modern times.

A well-known and authoritative manual of Christian doctrine, used as a textbook in many colleges, has no section at all devoted to the Jews, or to what Christian theologians have said about them.[14] There has been a kind of conspiracy, conscious or unconscious, to render the Jews invisible. Yet, they have been there all along, living their life in obedience to the commandments they have received from God, and their presence, acknowledged or ignored, has been a challenge to Christianity and its claim to be the true people of God. Is it surprising that they have also been hated?

DID JESUS FOUND CHRISTIANITY?

Even as recently as the late 1970s, a justly celebrated New Testament scholar entitled one of his books *The Founder of Christianity.*[15] Like almost everyone else at the time, he assumed that Jesus had been its founder. But can we really imagine the Jewish Jesus founding Christianity? Is not this the very first assumption we have to call in question? How could this authentic and faithful Jew, living according to the *halachah,* have thought of founding a new religion in opposition to the one he loved and lived by?

The Prophets of the Bible were very critical of the Jews of their day, much more critical in fact than the Gospels represent Jesus as being, but they never dreamed of founding a new religion. They envisaged a national repentance from all the sins they excoriated, followed by divine forgiveness and the full restoration of Israel to its status as God's beloved people. Could it have been otherwise with Jesus?

Nevertheless, no new religion was founded in the name of any of the biblical prophets, and it is a fact that a new religion did grow out of Judaism in the first century. It was called Christianity. The name of Christianity, of course, comes from the title Christ (*Christos,* the Greek form of the Hebrew word *meshiach,* our word Messiah), but not from Jesus' personal name; by the time the movement received the name by which it has ever since been known he was already most often referred to simply as Christ, Messiah. But there was no doubt which Messiah was meant.

There were also other first-century messianic claimants. No large-scale religious movement emanated from their careers, however. We shall have to consider why the history of Christianity turned out so differently from theirs. In the case of Christianity, its early leaders acted "in the name of Jesus of Nazareth," whom they proclaimed as Messiah, or Christ. Were they justified in invoking his name to legitimate their actions in spreading a new religion?

This must be our first question, and it will occupy us in the remainder of the present chapter, along with a quick look at the methods of historical criticism of the New Testament, which we shall have to employ in this and the next chapters.

The very name of Christianity shows that in its earliest days it was understood by everyone to be inseparable from the belief that Jesus was the Messiah. A further question to be examined, therefore, in the third chapter, will be the grounds for the belief that Jesus was the Messiah expected by the Jews. We shall find that they are flimsy: in all probability, Jesus himself did not think he was the Messiah, and he may even have emphatically rejected the title when used of him by others.

Before this, however, in the second chapter, we shall have to examine critically the stories in the Gospels that do suggest that Jesus was so condemnatory of the religion of his day that he actually rejected it and was understood by his fellow Jews to have done so. The Gospels do tell a story of growing conflict between Jesus and his fellow Jews, ending in a religious trial before the highest and most solemn court of his people, which condemns him for blasphemy on account of a claim to be the Messiah and hands him over to the Romans for execution. This is the basis of the ancient and long-standing belief that the Jews killed Christ.

Did the Jews kill Christ? We shall discover that the stories in the Gospels that suggest they did are exceedingly improbable. The Jews did not kill Jesus because they had no reason to do so. He was not guilty of any religious offense. It is in the highest degree improbable that such a trial before the Sanhedrin as we read of in the Gospels of Mark and Matthew ever took place. What we read in the Gospels about the trial of Jesus is the product of later Christian imagination, and it reflects Christian, not Jewish, views of the nature of the Messiah.

It was not the Jews but the Romans who killed Christ. They did it for their own political reasons; evidently, the Romans did believe him to be a claimant to the title of Messiah, although he himself made no such claim. No doubt, they correctly understood that from their own point of view a Messiah must be a rebel and an insurgent, since he is expected to deliver the Jewish people from pagan domination. In any case, enough people thought Jesus was the Messiah to constitute a political danger to Roman rule. No one should any longer imagine that it was the Jews who were the Christ-killers.

If Jesus did not claim to be the Messiah and was not rejected, still less killed, by his own people, there is little reason left for believing he could have founded Christianity. Christianity has always been based on the belief that Jesus was the Messiah of the Jews, rejected by his own people. If that central belief is without foundation and must now be abandoned, it becomes much harder to discover anything Jesus said or did that could have led to the development of Christianity from his own work.

In view of these findings, to be justified more fully in later chapters, we should now make it our working assumption that Jesus did not found Christianity, unless and until we find overwhelming evidence that he did. In fact, there is no such evidence.

THE METHODS OF BIBLICAL CRITICISM

How do we know these things about Jesus? We would not have known them by simply reading the New Testament. Even the older methods of biblical criticism failed to bring them to light. (However, many of the nineteenth-century biblical critics came fairly close to our present understanding, though they tended to romanticize or "liberalize" Jesus. When twentieth-century Christian scholarship rejected their theology it also abandoned many of their valid historical findings.)

Perhaps the most momentous development in the whole history of the critical study of the New Testament has been the most recent one, the systematic utilization of Jewish sources to build up a picture of the world in which Jesus lived. These discoveries have suddenly transformed our picture of Jesus himself, making it clear beyond reasonable doubt that he was a faithful Jew, in harmony, not contradiction, with the world of his people.

Nevertheless, the whole previous history of New Testament criticism has not suddenly become obsolete or valueless. Methods of study developed over close to two hundred years are not likely to be jettisoned, and some of these critical techniques, as well as findings, remain indispensable to our inquiry. In fact, the intellectual achievement of the New Testament scholars over this lengthy period is an extraordinary one, perhaps comparable to the skill and innovativeness that went into the discovery of nuclear fission and fusion. It is not so widely known to the general public but is hardly less remarkable.

We shall need to be aware of some of the discoveries of earlier scholarship as we move on to a closer study of what is now known about Jesus. For our purposes, perhaps the first of these discoveries to take into account is the clear finding that the four gospels of the New Testament are by no means contemporary accounts of Jesus by eyewitnesses of the events.

What we have in the Gospels is not a life, or several variant lives, of Jesus, written by eyewitnesses. Instead, we have various disconnected stories of his doings and fragments of his teaching, woven together much later, in a sequence dictated by theology rather than by the memory of the actual course of his life. The whole as we have it has already gone through several stages of transformation from its original Jewish character and is now firmly embedded in a context of a new Christian myth, the charter story of the Gentile church of the latter part of the first century, or even perhaps the early second century. The Gospels already reflect the developing Christian myth, at least as much as they do genuine memories of the real Jesus. To understand Jesus as he was, if that is possible at all, we must remove the stories from their new mythic or theological context and reinsert them into the Jewish milieu of Jesus' own lifetime.

While some healthy disagreement among scholars on the exact dating of the New Testament documents is always to be expected, there is a very solid consensus among the experts that the Gospels are the product of the last third of the first century, whereas Jesus' life belongs to the first third. Thus, there was a considerable gap between the events of Jesus' life and the reporting of them in the Gospels, a gap of one, or in the case of the later Gospels, two generations.

While some critics would assign a date as early as the sixties for the first Gospel to be written, opinion seems to be settling down in favor of a date in the seventies for even the earliest Gospel. The other three can hardly be earlier than the nineties, and one or more of them may even have been composed as late as the beginning of the second century.[16]

What had happened in the meantime? The stories about Jesus, which eventually found their way into the Gospels, had been circulating by word of mouth. They were associated with the preaching of the Christian church, at first to fellow Jews, and soon to Gentiles also, about the redemption that they believed God was bringing about and would soon complete, through his adopted son, Jesus the Messiah. The Church did not tell the stories for their own sake, or for historical or personal reminiscence, but to support that preaching. The beliefs of the missionary church may easily have colored the stories in the course of their telling. Over a generation or two they could have undergone considerable reshaping. They would not have survived at all without that strenuous missionary effort.

Many scholars believe that before the four Gospels of the New Testament were written, some of the stories now contained in them had already begun to be written down. It seems more than likely that the story of the last week of Jesus' life, culminating in his death by crucifixion, had already been written down, perhaps in more than one version, some time before the earliest of the Gospels was composed. To the developing theology of the Church, it was already the most important story it wished to tell about him, exceeding in importance even his spiritual teaching.

It is also possible that, at a similarly early date, a collection was made of certain sayings of Jesus, in which he speaks in the name of the Wisdom of God. This latter collection is now represented in the Gospels of Matthew and Luke, in passages in which the same sayings are reproduced in very similar words; these stories, however, are not found in Mark or John. Many of the same sayings, along with some much less familiar ones, which set the familiar ones in a startling new light, are also recorded in similar words in an early book known as the Gospel of Thomas. It was found in our own century in the Egyptian desert, having been preserved along with other such books by Gnostic Christians, not by the mainstream Church, which apparently wanted to destroy them. The writer of the Gospel of Thomas must have known the same collection of sayings as Matthew and Luke.

The Gospel of Thomas is not the only other Gospel we know of besides the four in the New Testament. In fact, the four are a selection made by the Church, primarily on theological rather than historical grounds, from a larger number already circulating in various sectors of the Church. Each of them presented somewhat different pictures of Jesus, reflecting the views of the communities that composed and circulated them. Many different views of Jesus and his life existed in the early churches, and some of these rejected Gospels may have preserved memories as authentic as those with which we are familiar.

THE SYNOPTIC PROBLEM

We have now reached a point at which we need to discuss a basic question in the systematic study of the New Testament: the relationship between its four Gospels. Readers of the Gospels had noted from early times that the Gospel of John, on the one hand, and the remaining three, on the other, differ greatly in the way they approach the story of Jesus. In spite of differences that are now being much more carefully noted and recognized, the first three Gospels obviously share a common general viewpoint. For this reason, they are called by New Testament scholars the "synoptic" Gospels, from a Greek word referring to this shared viewpoint. (Although the two words are connected by a common derivation, *synoptic* in this sense has nothing to do with our other word, *synopsis*.)

The Fourth Gospel, "according to John," presents Jesus in a very different way from the other three. The writer sees Jesus through the prism of a lengthy period of theological reflection. He is hardly a human character at all; in fact, in this Gospel, he is far more like a walking and talking icon. He utters lengthy and esoteric discourses, works miracles even more remarkable than those recounted in the other Gospels, and is recognized by his disciples as the Messiah from the outset of his ministry. He speaks of his own person without the reticence that characterizes the synoptic Jesus, identifying himself with the divine being in a way hardly thinkable for a Jew.

This Gospel provided the basis for the later development of Christian theology about the divine Christ. Later theologians rethought ideas originally found in the Fourth Gospel in the terms of Greek philosophy and metaphysics. In its prologue we find Jesus presented as the divine Word incarnate. Here this Gospel is already close to the developed Christology[17] of the later church.

These characteristics, obvious to any reader, have led the critics to set this Gospel aside in their historical inquiries and to concentrate on the first three, which do show signs of being more interested in history as we understand it. In fact, however, the first three Gospels are in their own way almost as theological as the fourth, and there may well be places in which the fourth Gospel makes use of authentic historical sources from which the accounts in the synoptic Gospels can be corrected. However, its overall picture of Jesus is clearly much more theological than historical.

Thus, the historical study of the Gospels has for a considerable period been focused on the three synoptic Gospels. They remain central to any reconstruction of the Jesus of history, though we are nowadays gradually learning to take into account evidence not only from the Fourth Gospel but also from Gnostic and other Gospels not canonized as Scripture by the Catholic church.

When we start to read these three synoptic Gospels carefully and critically, we are bound to be struck by both similarities and differences. Although they do in a sense share a common viewpoint, they are by no means identical in either theology or content. Perhaps the first thing to be noticed is that almost everything in the Gospel of Mark is also found in the other two synoptic Gospels and almost always in the same order.

This important observation can be explained in several different ways. The explanation that has been most widely accepted, and which we shall assume to be the correct one, is that Mark was written first, and that the authors of Matthew and Luke made use of Mark as the basis and outline of their own compositions.

However, the material from Mark is by no means all that is to be found in Matthew and Luke; both are considerably longer than Mark. These two Gospels also have a considerable amount of other material in common; the common material consists mostly of those sayings of Jesus, already mentioned, in which typically he speaks in the name of the Wisdom of God. This type of story is not found in Mark.

This fact has led the majority of experts in the field to suppose that the stories in question had been written down earlier in a collection that both Matthew and Luke, as well as the author of the Gospel of Thomas, knew and used. This source is generally referred to by scholars as Q, the initial letter of the German word, *Quelle*, which means source.

This analysis does not exhaust what we find in Matthew and Luke. Each of these Gospels also contains a considerable amount of material unique to itself. In this portion of each Gospel its distinctive character comes out most. Even a casual reader cannot fail to be struck, for example, by the fact that though these two Gospels (unlike Mark or John) tell the story of Jesus' birth, they tell it in very different ways, so differently that it is unlikely that they had a common source.

Their accounts of the "passion," the trial and death of Jesus, also differ at significant points, though here they also depend on Mark. Many of the details of their versions of the passion story must have come from their own special sources of tradition, and not from Mark. It is also not unlikely that the personal contribution of the writer himself appears at such points, reflecting his own theological outlook, and that of the particular church to which he belonged.

Many critics also believe that the source of the special material in Matthew and Luke was likewise some kind of written document. However, it is not necessary to suppose this. All we need to know is that each of them had some distinctive source of information or tradition not known to or not used by the other.

This kind of analysis is not merely academic. First of all, it brings out something of great importance that the ordinary reader is apt to miss. Such readers, especially those educated in traditional Christianity, tend to harmonize the Gospels. They assume that all three, or even all four, are telling substantially the same story, and they feel free to smooth over discrepancies in different accounts of what appears to be the same incident and to supply what is lacking in one source from another.

To careful scholars, this is not a legitimate procedure. We ought to assume that each of the writers told the story as he knew it, and that he did not know, or at any rate did not choose to include, what is not in his own book. If he did know what was in another Gospel but told the story differently, he must have considered that the earlier account was wrong and needed correction. Once we read the Gospels in this careful way, we find that there are quite important divergencies between their ways of telling the story, and even sometimes in the stories that they tell. If we wish to get at the historical truth, we must not harmonize the Gospels but look carefully at their differences, trying to find out why they are there. We may discover that one version appears to be more reliable than another, or even that none of them can be treated as reliable. When there are conflicting accounts of the same incident circulating at more or less the same period, we must conclude that no single authoritative version existed.

THE ORAL TRADITION

The divergencies between the Gospels, once they have been carefully noted, can be helpful to the historian. They are especially useful where we have variant accounts of what appears to be the same incident. As we have seen, these variations can be accounted for in more than one way.

They may well be due to the author in question. He may have had theological or literary reasons for telling the story in this way rather than another. However, he may also have received the story from his church in a different form. Before they were written down, every one of the stories was first told by word of mouth, and this process of oral transmission must have continued for most of the period before the Gospels began to be written. Even if a Gospel writer's account was dependent on an existing written document, this document in turn depended on stories that had been transmitted by word of mouth. How reliable was this earlier oral transmission?

There are many reasons to think that oral tradition in the ancient world was much more accurate than we are apt to assume on the basis of modern experience. It may even have been more accurate than manuscript copying would have been. Nevertheless, the alternative possibility cannot be discounted that while they were being passed down by word of mouth, stories were unconsciously, or even consciously, being reshaped to suit the needs of the communities that told them. Almost certainly, this did happen during the oral transmission of the stories about Jesus. Gradually, perhaps, but strongly, they were colored by the developing myth.

An important school of criticism, usually referred to in English as "form criticism" (the German *Formgeschichte,* or history of forms, is a more accurate description), has grown up around the study of the oral traditions. As its name indicates, this school of criticism began by classifying the various *forms* in which the stories about Jesus were told. As any reader can tell, some of them are about healings, others about teaching, and so on. They also sought to compare the forms they found in the Gospels with forms in other literature outside the New Testament. They thought it possible to establish cross-cultural laws governing the form and development of oral traditions.

If the forms of orally told stories had a general tendency to evolve in the same direction, criteria could be found for assessing the relative age of different forms of the same story. For example, if it were the case (apparently it is not) that stories always grow in the telling, the simplest form of a series of version of a story would be the oldest.

When the form critics began to study the New Testament Gospels in this way, they made one important discovery that is likely to stand. They found that the Gospels are made up of short units of tradition, often corresponding to paragraphs in our English versions. The scholars call them *pericopes*. Each pericope probably constitutes a unit of oral tradition and is likely to have been transmitted separately. These blocks, or units, are linked together by fairly short phrases. Often the links are very small, phrases such as, "immediately," or "after that."[18]

If these linking phrases are removed, it turns out that all the indications of the order of events in Jesus' life have also gone. In a famous phrase, removing the linking phrases is like cutting a string of beads. Once the beads are rolling around separately, we can no longer decide in what order they should be put back together. This is strikingly true of Mark's Gospel. In this respect, however, Matthew and Luke seem to be totally dependent on Mark.

The conclusion is inescapable that the order of the events in Jesus' life, as reported not only in Mark's Gospel but also in those of Matthew and Luke, which follow his order, did not come from tradition; it was Mark's own contribution. As early as the second century, the writer Papias, the first to tell the story of how the Gospels were written, said that Mark did not write the story in order, because he did not know in what order the events had happened. The Gospel of John has a very different order but not necessarily a more (or less) reliable one. *It follows that we have no way whatever of knowing about the order of events in Jesus' life.*

Again, the synoptic Gospels have one chronology, according to which the events of Jesus' public life were contained in approximately a single year, while the Gospel of John has another, allotting about three years to them. Even in the stories of the passion, where the unit of tradition is much larger, the synoptic Gospels and the Fourth Gospel have different chronologies, including a different day for the crucifixion. In this case, John's chronology, placing the crucifixion on the eve of Passover instead of on the day of the feast, has seemed to many historians to be more likely to be correct. It also corresponds to the only Jewish traditions on the point.

The "form critics" did not find they could give us as scientific a basis as they had hoped for distinguishing between earlier and later forms of a story, and thus for establishing which may have been the more authentic. What they did conclude was that however far back they could trace the development of a story, the Church's influence on its shape was always discernable.

The story always demonstrably fitted into its function in the life of the Church. It did not so convincingly fit into any probable situation in Jesus' own life. The critics concluded that they could never find any form that could be identified as pure original tradition from eyewitnesses, uncolored by the needs of the Church for preaching and teaching. The result of form criticism, for the New Testament scholarship of much of the mid-twentieth century, was greatly to increase skepticism about the possibility of genuine historical knowledge about Jesus.

This apparent finding did not disturb the critics as much as one might suppose, since their leaders belonged to a school of thought in (mainly) German theology that distinguished sharply between the historical Jesus and the Christ of faith, regarding the latter, not the former, as decisive for religion. In our terms, this meant that faith was to be directed to the myth, not to the history as critical historians recover it. They did not think that faith should have to wait for the findings of historians, even for their own. Of course it is true that all down the ages, Christians, even theologians, have lived by the myth, with all its emotional power, rather than by the intellectual constructions of theology.

The essence of Christian faith, to these German theologians, lay in the proclamation by the Church of the forgiveness of sins, on the basis of the death and resurrection of Jesus. They heard that proclamation in the preaching of their own churches, and they were confident that the same proclamation had been made by the earliest Christians, immediately after the resurrection.

They did not think it essential to know anything historically about Jesus beyond the fact that he had lived, died, and risen again. Some of them distinguished between the *Dass* and the *Was*, between the "That," which was essential, and the "What," which was not. Christian faith, they thought, needed to know *that* Jesus had been, but not *what* he had been. For a considerable period, theologians lost interest in the historical Jesus, denying his relevance to theology, while concentrating instead on the primitive "proclamation," often referred to as the *kerygma* (from the Greek word for a proclamation made by a herald on behalf of his ruler, sometimes used in the New Testament itself for the preaching of Jesus' followers to their fellow Jews). The preaching of the early Church, not the life and teaching of Jesus, was to be the basis of Christian faith.

Not all scholars, and not all theologians, subscribed to this radical view, nor were all of them as skeptical about the possibility of historical knowledge of Jesus as those that did. Other scholars, especially in the English-speaking world, continued to hope that by patient historical inquiry important knowledge of Jesus could be gained, and they thought such knowledge a necessary foundation for Christianity as they understood it.

Nevertheless, it is fair to say that until about a decade or so ago the dominant school in New Testament scholarship viewed the sources with great skepticism, and treated the Gospels primarily as evidence for the Church of the late first century, rather than for the period of Jesus' own lifetime. Many continue to do so.

ALBERT SCHWEITZER'S CHALLENGE

Another reason for skepticism had surfaced somewhat earlier. I have already remarked that the enterprise of searching for the historical Jesus has had to go back to the drawing board several times already. Sometimes, the reason was the discovery of new methods, such as those of form criticism. At other times, a crisis was provoked by the internal self-criticism of historical scholarship. A very important turning point came about near the beginning of the present century, when Albert Schweitzer published his epochmaking book, known by its English title as *The Quest of the Historical Jesus.*[19]

In this book, Schweitzer subjected all existing research into the life of Jesus to a devastating criticism. Essentially, he showed that it had succumbed to what another wise scholar called "the peril of modernizing Jesus."[20] The early critics had aimed to detach the historical Jesus from the later Christ of dogma. No doubt they had succeeded in this, but they had fallen victim to another and subtler peril. Their Jesus was no longer the Church's Christ, but he was still the reflection of Victorian liberal humanist professors, teaching a religion devoid of the supernatural, and centering on the brotherhood of man and a pacifist ethic. They had devised a picture of someone who had probably never existed.

Schweitzer dealt with the problem in his own radical way. Perhaps more clearly than any of his contemporaries, he saw the crucial importance for our understanding of Jesus of some very unmodern ideas permeating the culture in which Jesus himself lived and thought. The scholars called these ideas "eschatology," or "apocalyptic." There are shades of difference in the meaning of the two words, but they need not concern us. Eschatology is literally the doctrine of the last things, from *eschata*, the Greek word for last. It is the teaching about the end of history, the messianic age.

Today, we have learned to use the term *messianism* in a very broad sense for ideas of this kind.

There can be no doubt that Jesus taught about the "kingdom of God." He was presumably employing eschatological or messianic ideas shared with his contemporaries. Schweitzer believed that these ideas were absolutely central and crucial to Jesus' understanding of his own mission, and that without giving them equivalent importance in our interpretation, Jesus could not be understood at all.

These contentions came as no small shock to a scholarly community that had settled down to believing that Jesus was a liberal reformer who taught about the fatherhood of God and the brotherhood of man. Schweitzer formulated his challenge in a striking way: he called for consistent eschatology or consistent skepticism.[21] Either Jesus must be understood consistently as thinking in messianic terms about the immediate coming of a new age, or we will have to acknowledge that we cannot know what he stood for–the latter alternative Schweitzer called skepticism.

Schweitzer's own consistently eschatological reconstruction of Jesus was brilliant and fascinating, but it did not stand up to subsequent investigation. He believed that Jesus did suppose he was the Messiah in a special sense. According to Schweitzer, Jesus thought he could personally undergo the birth pangs of the messianic age by dying on the cross; in this way he would bring the new age to birth. He imagined that by undergoing a voluntary martyrdom he could put his shoulder to the wheel of history and give it a decisive turn. Already in his dying moments he realized that he had failed and had been mistaken. His words on the cross, as recorded in two of the Gospels, "My God, my God, why have you deserted me?" revealed the agony of disappointment and failure, so Schweitzer thought.

Thus, Schweitzer believed that Jesus was a failed messiah, one who had mistakenly believed himself to be the Messiah, and had not accomplished the coming of the kingdom, which he had believed to be his destiny. This mistake did not detract from the validity of his spiritual teaching for Schweitzer himself. In order to follow it, he gave up his two brilliant careers as a musician and as a theologian, trained as a doctor, and went off as a medical missionary to Lambarene in West Africa.

For a number of reasons, Schweitzer's detailed reconstruction failed to win lasting scholarly acceptance, though a few still uphold it. It now seems that Jesus would not have known of a concept of the birth pangs of the messianic age, since no such a concept has been found in Jewish sources before the tribulations of the second century and the brutal suppression by the Romans of the rebellion led by Bar Kochva, whom many had thought to be the Messiah.[22]

For these and many other reasons, the consistently eschatological interpretation of Jesus came to be replaced by something much more like Schweitzer's alternative of consistent skepticism. Not only the discoveries of form criticism but also those of subsequent developments tended to increase the caution of scholars over saying much about Jesus beyond the bare facts that are beyond dispute.

For a while, a new attempt to give an account of the historical Jesus was debated by the scholars, although the Germans felt considerable theological trepidation, in case the principle should be breached that faith must not depend on historical research but on the proclamation of the Church. The main results of form criticism were accepted: a life of Jesus cannot be written, in view of the nature of the sources. Perhaps, however, scholars could give an account of what Jesus had stood for and show the continuity between that and the preaching of the early Church.

However, the work that was done under the name of this "new quest of the historical Jesus" is not standing up to subsequent criticism. Its Jesus too has turned out to be a reflection of modern needs. It has turned out that the gaps in historical knowledge revealed by previous work have been illegitimately filled by Christian theology.[23] This is especially true of the picture these scholars usually drew of a Jesus in fundamental opposition to the leadership and to the religious ideas of his own people.

REDACTION CRITICISM

I have several times mentioned the likelihood that the gospel writers themselves made an important contribution of their own to the way in which they each tell the story of Jesus. One of the most recently developed methods in the historical criticism of the New Testament studies this element in the making of the Gospels. It is usually called redaction criticism, again from the German term for it. In German, "redaction" means editing. In English, it would be more intelligible to speak of editorial criticism, since the gospel writers can be thought of as editors of the material they had received from their sources, oral and written.

Earlier critics had not taken their contribution as editors seriously. Somehow they come to take it for granted that the gospel writers merely wrote down what they had received, without altering it in any significant way. Not only is this inherently improbable, it also becomes demonstrably false when we start to compare the ways different gospel writers present the same material. It becomes plain that the gospel writers were not passive message carriers but theologians. They were also literary artists of no little skill, using their talents to persuade, as even more recent analysis has shown.

Partly because redaction criticism is a new discovery, its results now seem especially striking. As we shall see in a later chapter, the editorial or creative work of the gospel writers is particularly important for our own inquiry. The later gospel writers in particular introduced important new ways of telling the story of Jesus that made it significantly more anti-Jewish. What has been called the "redactional layer" in the development of the gospel tradition (the work of the gospel writers as editors and reshapers of the material), has been discovered to be notably more anti-Jewish than the sources behind it, written or oral.

We can thus determine that Christianity became rapidly more anti-Jewish during the course of the most creative period of its development. Redaction criticism not only reveals the authors of the Gospels as independent writers, each with a distinctive theological and literary personality, it also reveals them as either reflecting or even perhaps as especially responsible for the anti-Jewish form that the Christian myth came so rapidly to assume.

It had long been recognized that the Fourth Gospel is theology even more than it is history. We must now recognize that the authors of the first three Gospels were also theologians, or mythmakers, with a point of view to put across, though they remained perhaps more interested in factual history than the writer of the Fourth Gospel. We can now see that their anti-Jewish point of view has so strongly colored the telling of the story that substantial doubt is cast on the reliability of all the anti-Jewish elements in their narratives.

It is not easy to separate the literary criticism of the Gospels from redaction criticism. Literary criticism is perhaps the most recent of all developments in New Testament scholarship.[24] A number of literary critics have turned their attention to the Bible, and a number of theologians have adopted the methods of literary criticism in their critical study of the Gospels. The result of this new development has already been to display the gospel writers as conscious literary artists, employing considerable and sophisticated skill to tell a story in the way they want the reader to receive it. The extraordinary and lasting power of the Christian myth on the imagination, including its power to inculcate hostility toward Jews, is due in no small degree to the literary art with which it is presented in the Gospels. Had the story been told by duller writers, such as some of those whose work was not incorporated in the New Testament, it might not have influenced so many so deeply. The vivid accounts of the dramatic trial of Jesus before the Sanhedrin and the less formal hearing before Pilate, as well as many details of the story of his crucifixion, apparently owe much of their form, and in some cases their very existence, to the creative talents of these writers. These are the stories that have done most to make their readers identify with Jesus as the victim, and dislike Jews.

We can now see that the writers of the Gospels used considerable art to give credibility to an anti-Jewish message. Literary skill reinforced a theological lesson: at that stage in the split between Christianity, now fast becoming a new Gentile religion, and Judaism, its parent body, it was important for the writers to teach that the Jews had rejected Christ before they rejected the Church. As Christianity began to make its way in the Roman world, it was apparently also important that the Romans should not appear in the story in an unfavorable light. For both reasons, it was convenient to make the Jews the scapegoat for Jesus' death.

The Jews had forfeited their status as God's beloved people by their rejection of Christ, and the divine favor had passed to the Gentile church that had accepted him. This is how the earliest readers of the Gospels would have understood what they read, even though the message is not spelled out in so many words. Thus, because of their artistic power, the Gospels were extremely effective in stamping anti-Jewish beliefs into the Christian tradition, quite apart from their abiding authority as Scripture for the Church.

CHECKS ON AUTHENTICITY

Literary criticism, like redaction criticism, has tended to increase skepticism about the historicity of what we read in the Gospels. When we see how much theological reflection and literary art intervenes between us as readers and the original story of the Galilean preacher, we can easily begin to wonder if we are simply reading historical fiction, with a very small core of solid truth behind it.[25] This blunt way of putting it does not differ much from the conclusions of the theologians and historians up until the most recent period.

This is not to say, however, that historical scholarship had failed to devise any useful checks on the historical reliability of the materials in the Gospels. A number of these have been widely discussed, and because they will be useful in our own inquiry, we cannot ignore them.

The very diversity of the gospel tradition, brought to light by historical criticism, provides some of the materials for checking its reliability. When we discover that a story is told in more than one strand of the tradition, for example in the Fourth Gospel as well as in the synoptics, or in the material known as Q as well as in Mark, we may feel increased confidence in its historical reliability. This criterion is known as multiple attestation. In the third chapter, we shall examine in detail a story in which Jesus predicted his own death, according to all three of the synoptic Gospels and perhaps the fourth as well. This multiple attestation does not make it certain that Jesus predicted his death, but it leads us to give real weight to the possibility. The criterion is not infallible – nothing in historical scholarship is – since the anti-Jewish elements in the gospel story are also unquestionably attested in multiple strands of tradition. However, in this case we have good reason to believe that they are later additions, as redaction criticism allows us to determine.

More controversial, but also often useful, is the criterion of dissimilarity, as it is called. According to this criterion, we may have greater confidence in the authenticity of elements in the Gospels when they are dissimilar to later Christianity or to the Judaism of the period. Those who use this criterion assume that the transmitters of the tradition are likely to have been influenced either by the original Jewish background of the stories or by the new Christian situation in which they were told. If Jesus is depicted as saying and doing things in accordance with neither the Judaism of his own world, nor the theology of the Church that told the story, we have to take such an account with particular seriousness. This is called double dissimilarity.

An example is the story in which Jesus tells a young man to follow him instead of remaining behind to bury his father. Both ancient Judaism and the Gentile world regarded the duty of burying the dead as especially sacred. Because it was contrary to both Jewish and pagan sentiments, such a story is unlikely to have been invented, and it presents a challenge to the interpreter.[26]

In positive form, the criterion seems unassailably valid, and I shall be using it later in this inquiry. But the criterion does not work so well if (as some do) we try to reverse it, using it negatively, to deny authenticity to all stories that *do* fit either the theology of the Church, or the Judaism of Jesus' own time. It is certainly not impossible that Jesus said and did some things that corresponded to what the Church later came to think, presumably in part at least as a result of what he said and did. Nevertheless, there is good reason for suspicion of stories that represent him as a proto-Christian. On the other hand, it is inherently likely, as I have argued throughout, that Jesus said and did things that corresponded perfectly to the Judaism of his own world.

If the criterion of dissimilarity is applied consistently in a negative way, so as to exclude from our collection of authentic sayings and doings anything that can be parallelled in either Christianity or Judaism, the result is a Jesus totally divorced from history.[27] Why should anyone suppose that he lived outside history, with no connection to his cultural environment? If we attempt to apply the criterion of dissimilarity in such a rigid manner, we shall once again create a Jesus who never existed except in our own twentieth-century imagination, as our predecessors in the nineteenth century had also been doing before their errors were exposed by Albert Schweitzer.

The issue has a special edge for our present inquiry. The gospel writers were Christians and most or even all of them Gentiles; their works were composed late in the first century, after the Church had been going for as much as two generations and had developed its theology to a considerable extent. The breach between the Church and its Jewish parent was already gaping open, and the theology of the Gentile church was becoming steadily more anti-Jewish. There is every reason to think that the gospel writers would have imagined Jesus as more Christian than he actually was. There is no probable reason to suppose that any of them would have imagined him as more Jewish than he was. As representatives of a Gentile church, already opposed to and by mainstream Judaism, they would have had no incentive to do so. What we have discovered already about the influence of theology and literary art on the composition of the Gospels convinces us to the contrary. The Church by this time wanted to play down Jesus' Jewishness and undoubtedly minimized it in the way it told the stories about him. If accounts of his Jewishness have been preserved in a recognizable form, they may well be nuggets of authentic history, very precious in a search for the truth about Jesus.

CONSISTENT JUDAISM OR CONSISTENT SKEPTICISM

Earlier in the twentieth century, Albert Schweitzer had revolutionized New Testament studies with his challenging alternatives, "consistent eschatology or consistent scepticism." As we have seen, the critics have tended toward the pole that he himself hoped they would reject, that of consistent skepticism, and the skepticism has grown with each new critical method as it has been discovered. The result has been a divorce between theology and history, or between faith and intellectual inquiry. It has threatened the integrity of Christianity, fostering the growth of fundamentalism on the one hand, and a somewhat irresponsible use by mainstream theologians of ideas external to the biblical tradition, on the other.

I do not myself believe that Christianity or indeed any religion can in the modern world indefinitely survive a divorce between faith and critical history, any more than it can ignore the findings of science. History does not deliver faith, but it must provide convincing materials on which faith can be based. Without its control, faith becomes arbitrary and irrational, a screen for the projection of all kinds of fantasies, not all of which are authentically spiritual. On the other hand, the inherent difficulty of faith is greatly increased if people are required to believe what their whole education must teach them to regard as incredible.

Fortunately, the latest development in New Testament studies has provided a way out of this impasse by bringing scholarship back into contact with history, while at the same time radically threatening the anti-Judaism that has been both endemic and traditional in Christianity. The rediscovery now going on apace of the Judaism of the first century of the common era has begun to revolutionize the study of Christian origins, while providing us for the first time with the outlines of a truly convincing picture of Jesus the man, as he may have actually existed in historical reality. It is the picture of a faithful Jew.

The time has come, therefore, to reformulate Schweitzer's challenging criterion for valid inquiry into the historical Jesus. He spoke of consistent eschatology or consistent skepticism. Intervening developments since his time have made it abundantly clear that our new criterion for historical inquiry should be both broader and deeper cutting. Now it should be *consistent Judaism* or *consistent skepticism*.

That means we will consistently interpret the Gospel accounts of Jesus in a Jewish way. We will think of Jesus consistently as a faithful Jew, and we will interpret the stories told of him by their original Jewish context, not by what later Christianity made of them. If we do not do this, we shall be doomed to return to the almost complete historical skepticism of the last generation of New Testament scholarship.

I am convinced that the main source of the skepticism into which New Testament studies had increasingly fallen is the attempt to infer what Jesus the Jew was like by starting from the anti-Jewish Christianity of the later first century. Inevitably, such an attempt must fail. The Jesus of history had been lost because scholars had attempted in vain to reconstruct his figure from the starting point of sources already deeply corrupted by a Gentile myth. Only when the influence of the anti-Judaic myth has been isolated and excluded can the sources give us reliable information about Jesus as he was.

The links between the Christianity of the gospel writers and the Jewish spirituality of Jesus himself have become increasingly tenuous with each new insight into the scope of the intervening development between Jesus himself and the final form of the gospel tradition. Scholars have traditionally assumed that the only way to account for Christianity is to suppose that Jesus was somehow its originator. Yet critical inquiry has made this hypothesis increasingly untenable. Since the scholars are honest people, they have been more and more driven back to the admission that they do not know enough about Jesus to confirm their hypothesis.

It happens not infrequently in a scientific inquiry that things reach an impasse where no further progress is being made. This usually happens when the wrong questions are being asked, and asking new questions often breaks up the logjam. Looking at New Testament studies somewhat from the outside, my own impression is that they had reached this point of impasse where an admission of ignorance was the only honest outcome. But the critics are now finding a way out of the impasse through this new development of understanding how Jesus fits into his own background, Judaism, not Christianity.

If we start from the new hypothesis that Jesus was a Jew, and that the record left of him can be explained and understood in Jewish terms, we can finally begin to discern a historical figure that is credible to us. In the last few years, the historical Jesus has reemerged on the scene of scholarship and theology in the form of Jesus the Jew. Both must now take full account of him.

Now, however, we find the origins of Christianity itself harder to explain, deprived of the traditional hypothesis that it was originated by Jesus. But we may not be driven to complete skepticism on that score. The origins of Christianity can also be better understood against a Jewish background, and all the better when we abandon the misleading assumption that it must be directly connected with Jesus. As we have already concluded, if Jesus was indeed fully Jewish, as recent scholarship shows that he was, it is highly unlikely that he could have been the founder of Christianity, and we must learn to account for its origins in other and more satisfactory ways.

THE DIVERSITY OF EARLY CHRISTIANITY

We now turn to another kind of reason for doubting if Jesus could have founded Christianity. This is also a discovery of historical criticism. The new religion that emerged from the events of the life and death of Jesus contained too many divergent movements to have been the product of a single creative mind. At any rate, if Jesus had intended to found a new religion, he did not succeed in doing so in any coherent form. Much more probably, he had no intention of doing so. The Jesus newly revealed by the study of his Jewish environment is not likely to have founded the movements that collectively constituted early Christianity.

Historians used to suppose that early Christianity was united in the legacy left by Jesus; only later did disunity arise, as new and unorthodox interpretations of the tradition developed. We now think it was far otherwise. Early Christianity moved in several divergent directions, and it was not possible to unify them by appealing to the authoritative teaching of a founder.

Only in the second century did it begin to be unified around a form of Gentile Christianity, as a result of strenuous efforts by some of its leaders, most of them associated with the Church of Rome. The effort was never completely successful, and in later centuries new forms of disunity set in. But Christianity never again became as diverse as it had originally been.

If we look back to the state of the Christian movement at the end of the first century and the beginning of the second, we find amazing variety and diversity. However, scholars usually group the many versions of Christianity flourishing then into three main tendencies, only one of which is at all familiar today.

This is Gentile Christianity, sometimes called by the historians Early Catholicism, since it represents the earliest form of the Catholic church of history. It is the ancestor of all modern forms. But alongside it were two other movements, equally popular at the time, and in some places certainly more so, but not destined to survive. It would not have been obvious to an observer in the year 100 that early Catholicism, at that time largely a religion of urban slaves and the underprivileged, was the movement of the future.

One of these competing movements was Gnosticism, which has come into public attention recently as a result of new discoveries. Another, now lesser-known movement was composed of Christian Jews, remaining faithful to their Jewish heritage, while adding to it belief in Jesus as the Messiah. Scholars refer to the various movements that attempted to remain faithful to Christianity's original basis in Judaism as Jewish Christianity.

Obviously, there were sharp disagreements between these movements. Gentile and Jewish Christianity soon parted company. In the second century, the Gentile or early Catholic church fought a sharp, and in the end, largely successful battle to rid itself of Gnosticism and to put down the independent Gnostic communities. At the same time, it stigmatized as heretical all those groups that still held on to Jewish observance.

Gentile Christianity[28]

Christianity began with the preaching of the earliest Apostles of Christ, all of whom were Jewish. It made its appeal to Jews, and as a movement it differed from other forms of Judaism only in its belief that Jesus was the Messiah. Soon its members began to preach to Gentiles and met with success, creating a distinct branch of their movement. Before long, its leadership was assumed by Paul, the great Apostle to the Gentiles. As the name the historians give it indicates, its members were Gentiles, and following the teaching of Paul, they did not consider conversion to Judaism a possible option.

They interpreted Paul's writings as meaning that Judaism was seriously defective, considering that the new faith had superseded Judaism in the plan of God. They soon came to think that the Jews had been rejected by God and lost their place as his chosen people, because of their rejection of their Messiah. They regarded those Christians who attempted to continue their membership of the Jewish people as neither Jews nor Christians, and they fought those who wanted to retain within the Catholic church customs such as keeping Easter at the same time as Passover.

Gentile Christianity differed from the earliest form of the new faith in more than one important way. From the beginning it had rejected the Torah, together with its commandments constituting the human side of the covenant with God. At the same time, it had radically reinterpreted the Jewish Bible, reading it as a complex web of prophecy of Christ and a systematic denigration of Jews and Judaism.

Gentile Christianity soon developed beliefs concerning the role of Jesus that differed greatly from those of the earliest Christians. Gentile Christians believed that Jesus had brought forgiveness to individual sinners through his death, and they came to see him also as a cosmic redeemer. These beliefs were largely based on the teachings of Paul, who had begun the systematic adaptation of an originally Jewish message to a Gentile audience. He, like them, must have been influenced by ideas drawn from the surrounding culture and environment.

The earliest Christians, themselves Jews, had not thought of Jesus' death in this way. It was something that required explanation in the light of their overriding belief that he was the Messiah; on the face of things it was incompatible with it, since it was no part of the destiny of the expected Messiah to be put to death. They believed, however, that with the resurrection of Jesus[29] the general resurrection of all the dead had begun. Perhaps they also saw his death as a martyrdom that could help to atone for the sins of the Jewish people. They could not have regarded Jesus' suffering on the cross as a unique way of obtaining forgiveness for their sins, since (like Jesus himself) they knew that forgiveness was already freely available within the covenant to repentant sinners. The changes introduced by Gentile Christianity were therefore of major consequence, a fact masked from modern people by the greater familiarity of the newer ideas.

Gentile Christianity gained further impetus at a period near the end of the first century, when the original expectation of the Jewish originators of the new movement, that Christ would very shortly return and do all that had been traditionally expected of the Messiah, had died down.

Jesus had preached the imminence of the kingdom, or kingship, of God. After his death, his followers preached the arrival of the messianic age under his auspices. All the earliest Christians, whatever their other differences, were united in the ardent belief that the end of history had come, that it had only a few months or years to run before being utterly transformed into a new age.

They did not think of themselves as originators and shapers of a new religion but as those upon whom the duty had fallen of announcing this new age to their fellow Jews, in the name of Jesus. But Jesus did not return, and as the years passed, it became impossible to sustain the original tension of anticipation of his coming. Gradually, the new movement settled down into history.

The expectation of a new age was too fundamental an element in the original Jewish heritage of the Church to be simply discarded by Gentile Christianity. It had to be retained in some form. In its original form, it meant very little to Gentiles, who had not learned to share the Jewish expectation that God would assert his sovereignty over a rebellious world and deliver his own people. And it did not seem that the expectation would now be fulfilled very soon, in any case.

The expectation of a new age, called eschatology by scholars, was reinterpreted by the Gentile church, now assuming the shape of a new religion. The original contrast between the present age and the new age to come, already dawning in the life of the Christian movement, became transformed into a contrast between the natural and the supernatural. Such a contrast was much easier to understand for pagans, especially the philosophically educated. The terms I have used are actually of later origin, but they provide our best way of understanding how the early Gentile Christians thought.

Now the Church thought of itself as privileged to be the bearer of a new supernatural life of grace, stemming from the incarnation of God in Christ, a divine-human life to which the sacraments of the church gave entrance. The Church could then contrast itself with Judaism, which lacked this supernatural element of grace, stemming from God incarnate. Thus, a Jewish contrast between two historical ages in time became transformed into a Greek contrast between two metaphysical levels, this material world and an invisible, spiritual one.

The new Gentile Christianity became greatly assimilated to the Graeco-Roman culture in which it lived, as it rethought the whole Jewish heritage of Christianity, stemming from the Bible, in the terms of Greek philosophy. Soon the theology of the early Catholic Church would be expressed exclusively in Greek philosophical language, even when it was translated into Latin, and the simpler and more concrete language of the Jewish Bible reserved for popular preaching and devotion.

Greek philosophy was often monotheistic in its theology and ethical in its teaching about personal conduct, but it was pagan in origin and had no natural affinity with Jewish ways of thinking and acting. Gentile Christians felt much more at home with this kind of pagan philosophy than with the Jewish heritage mediated to them through the original Christian preachers, and through the Jewish Bible that had been bequeathed to them as the foundation of their faith. The Jewish Bible in Greek translation was for a long time their only Scripture, but they read it in ways Jews would not have done.[30]

This reinterpretation of eschatology (and soon of all theology) into Greek metaphysical terms led to extremely important changes in the pattern of religion by which the church lived. So effective and sweeping were these changes that it is now hard to imagine Christianity without them. Gentile Christianity, now developing into Early Catholicism, changed the whole pattern of religious life by its introduction of the sacramental system, to become the core of later Catholic Christianity. The sacraments are rituals (significantly called "mysteries" by Greek Christianity) believed to have a supernatural effect on the believing participant.

Like Jews themselves, which indeed they were, the earliest Christians knew nothing of sacraments. They did, of course, possess rites, especially baptism and the breaking of bread, soon to be understood in a sacramental sense. Ideas that may have been the precursors of sacramental theology can be found as early as the writings of Paul. However, the rites which would become sacraments for the Gentile church were originally understood in a Jewish way. Indeed, Paul may have been the one responsible for transforming them into something Gentiles could understand and respond to, in the light of their experience of the mystery religions of their own culture.

The most plausible way to account for the development is to assume, as most historians of doctrine do, that Greek ways of thinking in a Gentile church led to radical reinterpretation of rites originally understood within a Jewish frame of thought. It is most likely true that, as many historians have supposed, the model for the transformation was the Hellenistic mystery religions. These promised the initiate a new life through mysterious rituals of death and rebirth.

The Jewish rites of incorporation into the community, circumcision and immersion, are not comparable in meaning to Christian baptism as it came to be understood by the Catholic church. They more closely resemble naturalization to citizenship of a new country. The earliest Christians must certainly have interpreted the "breaking of bread" as analogous to Jewish common meals of religious significance, such as the meals taken together on the Sabbath, or the Passover seder.

Gentile Christians soon came to think of these rites as having a supernatural effect. They were supposed to transform the believer invisibly, bringing about spiritual effects humanly impossible to accomplish through the identification of the believer with Christ. Membership in a sacramental church meant participation in a supernatural or divine-human life of grace, sharing in fact in the divine-human life of Christ.

The center of this transformation of Jewish into Greek, or in fact pagan, ways of thinking was the new Greek doctrine of Christ, now thought of as fully divine. From the second century on, theologians became centrally interested in the relationship of Christ to God and preoccupied with questions about the divine nature. This too is not a typically Jewish concern, since Jews regard the divine nature as beyond human comprehension, and suspect attempts to explain it as idolatrous.

Now the developing Christian myth presented a problem for monotheists. How could two persons be divine? Yet Christians were convinced that their redemption had been the work of no one less than God. It was now axiomatic to them that Christ was nothing less than divine. Indeed, it was his human nature, originally taken for granted, that now became problematic.

The model on which the theological solution was arrived at was Platonic and Stoic. The Greek philosophers of these schools had already thought of a Logos, or creative Word, the pattern on which the whole universe had been created, its immanent rationality or logic. Since the New Testament had described Christ as the Word of God, it was not difficult to identify this Word with the Word or Logos already spoken of in Greek philosophy. Probably the author of the Fourth Gospel had already done so in his prologue. Thus the theologians came to teach that God had created the world through his Logos, Christ, and had then redeemed it through him also. The Word or Logos was divine, but in a derivative sense.

In the second century, we find the theologians of the Gentile church thinking of Christ primarily as the Word, or Logos, of God, and even as a "second God." The latter term was too risky and threatening to the monotheism to which the church intended to adhere, and it was soon abandoned. Eventually, though not until the fourth century, the complex theology of the Trinity, which also incorporated the Holy Spirit on the same level of divinity, was worked out.

Eventually this transformed Gentile church became the state religion of the

Roman Empire, dominating the world in which Jews had to live. Now there arose a remarkable synthesis between the Graeco-Roman culture of classical antiquity and the beliefs of the Christian movement, already transformed by the impact upon them of Greek and pagan ways of thinking. The Catholic church of history, including its Eastern wing that later became the Orthodox church, was the bearer of this synthesis into the Middle Ages. This classical Christian civilization is in turn the basis of modern culture, itself inexplicable without an understanding of its foundation in the Christian past, though it has broken with its heritage in important ways.

From the pagan world from which they had come, Gentile Christians had inherited many prejudices against the Jews, and these prejudices played in to the anti-Jewish reading of Paul to create a very anti-Jewish outlook in the Gentile church from early times. Christian antisemitism is not at all the same thing as pagan antisemitism, though they are often thought to be continuous with one another. The destructive energy of Christian antisemitism is inconceivable without the myth that the Jews killed Christ, a myth absent from pagan anti-Jewish calumnies, many of which were also leveled against the early Christians. Nevertheless, there was little or nothing in the form of Christianity these Gentiles were receiving to rid them of their preconceived attitudes of hostility and contempt toward Jews, or to cause them to read Paul's writings otherwise than as confirmation and intensification of these existing attitudes.

Gentile Christianity saw itself as a new and superior religion, intended for Gentiles, and adapted to their situation. It is not surprising that very soon theologians were arguing that the Jewish Bible should be discarded, and no longer incorporated in the Christian Scriptures. Looking back, it is in fact astonishing that it was not discarded in the second century.

The reasons it was not discarded will occupy us at greater length in the fifth chapter. They are complex and sometimes surprising. Only its grounding in Judaism could give Christianity the pedigree deriving from an ancient past that people of the day thought a religion ought to have. Novelty, and Gentile Christianity was in fact a novelty, was then considered a very serious drawback in a religion. And of course it was already basic to Christian faith that Jesus had been the Jewish Messiah and that he had died on the cross and thus become the Savior of the world as a result of the rejection and hostility of the Jewish people. Such ideas, un-Jewish as they are, would have been unintelligible without the Bible as their background.

Because Gentile, or Early Catholic, Christianity has had this immense influence on the culture in which we all live today, Jews, Christians, and secularists alike, it is hard to imagine other forms of early Christianity except in this image. Yet, other forms did exist, and at the turn of the first and second centuries they were formidable rivals to Gentile Christianity.

Jewish Christianity

The first Christians were all Jews, like Jesus himself. There is no doubt at all that Christianity originated as a Jewish movement, and in its earliest stages it did not look beyond Judaism. Its members thought and lived in wholly Jewish ways, and they explained even the novel aspects of the new movement by reference to the most authoritative of Jewish sources, the Bible itself.

When historians speak of Jewish Christianity, they do not usually refer to the very earliest form of the Church, Jewish though it undoubtedly was.[31] They mean a group that developed a separate identity later, partly in reaction against the abandonment of the Torah by Gentile Christianity. It is natural to suppose that from the first there must have been some among them who, perhaps like Paul in the period that he remained outside the movement, had doubts about the propriety of bringing converts into the people of God without the proper rites of conversion.

Later, after Paul himself joined the movement, taking the leadership of its mission to the Gentiles, a substantial Gentile wing grew up, composed of persons who had not been formally converted to Judaism and who did not observe the Torah. The group opposed to this development now began to constitute a party or faction within the church. They strenuously opposed what Paul was doing, on grounds that must seem perfectly reasonable from a Jewish point of view. If the messianic age was already unrolling, and the Gentiles were being brought into the covenant in accordance with prophecy, why should they not join the covenant people and enter the messianic time along with it? Paul's actions must have seemed to them reckless and without any basis in Jewish faith or in the authority of the Torah.

On the other hand, another group of no less observant Jews, led by James, the brother of Jesus, were apparently willing to go along with Paul's activities in bringing a Torah-free message to the Gentiles, so long as there was a clear distinction between a Gentile mission on Paul's lines and the original mission to the Jewish people. Gentiles, then, were not to be expected to follow the Torah, but Jews were to be encouraged to continue to do so. Those we now think of as distinctively Jewish Christians were therefore only one wing of a larger group of Christian Jews, all of whom continued to observe the Torah while believing in Jesus as the Messiah.

After twenty centuries of Gentile Christianity, it is natural for us to identify Christianity with non-Judaism and invariably with some degree of anti-Judaism. The existence of an early Christian group that continued to observe the Torah, even though it eventually became unimportant and died out, is an important fact. At least for a time it was possible to believe in the messiahship of Jesus and continue to be an observant Jew.

On the other hand, we must recognize that it was only possible to maintain even this minimal belief in the messiahship of Jesus by supposing that the Jewish community as a whole was in very serious error in its interpretation of the Bible, since it was unwilling to recognize that a crucified insurgent could be regarded as the King Messiah, whose destiny according to everyone else's expectation was to redeem the people from foreign domination and bring in universal peace and righteousness. Jesus had done nothing of this.

From the second generation on, it seems more correct to think of Jewish Christianity simply as the community of those believers in Christ who observed the

Torah and fully accepted the authority of the Jewish Scriptures, whether or not they had been born Jews. This group was distinguished in particular by its practice of making proper proselytes to Judaism of its Gentile converts.

The beliefs of these Jewish Christians are not easy to determine with clarity and precision. They produced Gospels of their own, some of which have survived in fragments quoted by ancient Christian writers. It was believed in the ancient church that they used an original Aramaic version of the Gospel of Matthew. However, the extant fragments of Jewish-Christian gospels do not support this view, and it is not certain if there ever was such a version of Matthew.

In fact, one of the Jewish-Christian gospels (known as the Gospel of the Nazarenes) seems to have been an Aramaic translation back from the Greek Gospel of Matthew, with annotations, additions, and expansions. It seems to have contained the whole of the Matthew we have, including the birth stories. This particular group of Jewish Christians apparently did not differ from the theology of Gentile Christianity on belief in the virgin birth, if that is indeed what they took the story to mean.

Another Jewish-Christian gospel, that of the group known as the Ebionites, was written in Greek. The Ebionites gave their name to Jewish Christianity at large for many writers in the early Church. It was supposed that they had been founded by someone called Ebion. In fact, the word is Hebrew for "poor," and Paul refers to the Jerusalem church by this name. Perhaps they wished to designate themselves as the poor whom Jesus had called blessed. Their beliefs apparently did differ from those of the Gentile church.

Their gospel appears to have been drawn from Matthew and Luke, and it may also have used Mark as a source. It omitted the birth stories. In this gospel the Spirit enters Jesus at his baptism. Like some other Jewish Christians, the authors of this gospel rejected the sacrificial worship of the Temple, attributing the rejection to Jesus himself. A third such gospel, called the Gospel of the Hebrews, of Egyptian provenance, was apparently somewhat more Gnostic or esoteric in character, a fact that may account for its preservation in Egypt, where esoteric Christianity especially flourished.[32]

Something can also be inferred of the beliefs of Jewish Christians from symbols and other artifacts that archaeologists have found. It is clear that they all continued to observe the Torah. Beyond that, it is not easy to generalize. Some groups may have believed in the virgin birth and even the divinity of Jesus. Others certainly did not believe in either.

The later Jewish Christian groups regarded Paul very unfavorably, as a traitor to Judaism (if indeed he had been a born Jew at all) and a perverter of the original message of Jesus. Sometimes their opposition was expressed in disguised ways, in view of the power of the Pauline church. They seem to have been doubtful of Paul's own claim to be a highly educated Jew, trained in the schools of the Pharisees. For them, unlike the Gentile churches, Paul was a disaster for the movement springing from Jesus and his preaching to his fellow Jews. Nevertheless, in due course they too found themselves separated from the main body of the Jewish people by their loyal retention of the belief in Jesus' messianic destiny, now apparently conclusively refuted (in Jewish eyes) by his failure to return to earth and act as the expected Messiah.

Some of the Jewish Christians were certainly involved in esoteric beliefs and ascetical practices, which in themselves tended to separate them from the main body of Judaism. It seems possible that some of them identified Jesus with beings believed in by esoteric groups, such as a great archangel, or even a primordial semi-divine Man, the Adam Kadmon.

If so, the dangers to monotheism the Rabbis saw in esoteric Judaism may have contributed to their rejection of Jewish Christianity. Judaism was tolerant of differences in theology, but much less so of differences in observance. We do not know of ways in which Jewish Christians diverged from their fellow Jews in observance, and there was nothing to warrant excommunication and ostracism in a belief in an unorthodox Messiah, so long as no one thought of him as divine.

There does seem reason to believe that the later movements scholars call Gnosticism[33] originated within esoteric Judaism, and that some forms of Jewish Christianity had very close links with it. The ascetic and esoteric wings of Jewish Christianity must have found a ready association with Jewish esoteric beliefs and practices, or even have originated within such groups. The earlier view of scholars that Gnosticism originated in an extreme Hellenization of Christianity now seems untenable. The traces of Judaism in the Gnostic documents now accessible to us are too many and too pervasive.

Jewish Christianity, at first vigorous, gradually died out, probably because of isolation both from the dynamic development of Gentile Christianity, and from the nourishment of association with the main body of the Jewish people. It was strongly contested from the second century on by developing Catholic Christianity, eager to close the ranks against all forms of heresy. It survived longer outside the Empire than within it, and its eastern forms remained actively missionary.

By the time of the Constantinian revolution, Jewish Christianity was largely a spent force. Nevertheless, it seems to have survived long enough in outlying areas to have influenced the perception of Christianity in the Quran. Muslim Christology is identical with that of some esoteric Jewish Christian groups, and it differs from that of the Catholic church. Muhammad must have known Jewish Christians and their traditions in his earlier years.

As the expectation of Jesus' imminent return died down, since it failed to take place, it would have been natural for Jewish Christianity to go the way of other failed messianic movements, and to be reabsorbed into the main body of Judaism. There have been such movements, both before and after Jesus. Once everyone could see that the supposed Messiah was not going to deliver the people and bring in a new era, belief in him was abandoned with greater or less reluctance, and his followers returned to the main body of the Jewish people. Sooner or later, the new movements fizzled out. However, it is not altogether clear why this did not happen in the case of Christianity.

The main reason seems to have been a feature unique to this particular messianic movement: its appeal to Gentiles and its success among them. Were the links with other forms of Christianity now stronger than the links to the Jewish people, in spite of the failure of the distinctive messianic expectations of the group? Was the belief in a suffering Messiah, not shared by other messianic groups, powerful enough as an interpretation of the tragedies of history to survive refutation of the positive aspects of his messianic vocation? Or was the way barred from the Jewish side? Had the measures taken by the Rabbis against unorthodox forms of Judaism, of which Jewish Christianity was one, been so successful that there was now no way back for disillusioned believers in the messiahship of the crucified?

Whatever the reason, by this time Christianity had ceased to be a movement within Judaism and was regarded by its adherents and detractors alike as a new religion. The new religion continued to have an observant Jewish wing, but its members were no longer regarded as Jews by other Jews. Their association with Gentile Christians who were clearly anti-Jewish may have been sufficient to cancel their Jewish credentials in the eyes of the Jewish authorities.

In fact, both Catholic Christianity and Judaism thought of them as neither Christians nor Jews. Although it may now seem to us that it might have been otherwise, the movement had no historical future, and in all probability it cannot now be revived. Certainly the present-day Hebrew Christians, or "Jews for Jesus," are not Jewish Christians in the ancient sense. Their beliefs are those of evangelical fundamentalism, even if they continue to observe Jewish customs: they hold firmly to beliefs that all Jews must regard as dangerously close to idolatry.

Gnosticism

The third of these movements in early Christianity is generally known to scholars as Gnosticism.[34] Gnosticism was in essence an esoteric spiritual movement, in some respects rather like Buddhism. The term *esoteric* originally referred to something private or secret, being derived from the Greek word *eso*, meaning inside. Its counterpart and opposite, *exoteric*, comes from another Greek word, *exo*, meaning outside. In a religious context, scholars refer to esoteric forms of spirituality or religion, to distinguish them from the conventional or public forms of religion with which we are more familiar, termed exoteric.

Those who practice esoteric spirituality are usually mystically inclined, and like many mystics in all cultures, frequently believe that human beings have within them a divine spark of which one may become aware by various disciplines of concentration and nonattachment. Since such beliefs, if entertained by the spiritually immature, can lead to ego inflation and the development of pantheistic doctrines, they have often been kept secret, revealed only to the initiated, when they are considered sufficiently mature to be out of danger. From this practice of secrecy comes the familiar sense of the word esoteric as something hidden and out of the way.

A number of scholars in the field of comparative religion hold that esoteric spirituality is to be found in all religions and at all historical periods.[35] It differs in its symbolism and practices in accordance with the culture in which it functions, but according to these writers it is always essentially the same everywhere.

If this interpretation is correct, esoteric spirituality cannot be understood by theological or philosophical investigation, but only by inward experience. The secret it protects may seem to some, perhaps, either meaningless or philosophically indefensible, when expressed in intellectual terms, but this does not mean it can be dismissed. As known in intuitive experience it appears to be self-authenticating and not open to the objections of the philosophers and theologians.

One of the classic expressions of esoteric spirituality is to be found in the Upanishads, summed up in the famous phrase *tat tvam asi*, thou art That. But esoteric spirituality is not confined to Asia; it is also to be found in the West, in the Sufis of Islam, the Christian mystics, and the Jewish kabbalists, in distinctive forms and expressions appropriate to each religion.

Esoteric spirituality was also prevalent in the ancient world. Many, including Plato, believed that it had originated in the secret teachings of the ancient Egyptians.[36] That may be so, but we shall probably never know. In antiquity, such teaching was normally never committed to writing. It was believed that spiritual knowledge could only be transmitted from teacher to student, within the spiritual relationship of master to disciple. What could be written down was not the same thing, even if the words were the same. Thus, even if we happen to possess some of the literature of esoteric movements, it is unlikely that we shall understand it as its exponents did, unless we are ourselves practitioners of another authentic esoteric discipline.

In any case, because of this esoteric reticence, much that we might wish to know is simply not available to us. Generally speaking, our knowledge of all such movements is radically incomplete. What we know from the polemical arguments of opponents is probably a misunderstanding, and even when we do possess authentic texts, we cannot be sure that we can understand them correctly. Perhaps our best chance of interpreting them is to read them in the light of the esoteric literature of other cultures, as interpreted by those who do claim to understand them, such as the scholars I have referred to.

This may be our best way of understanding the surviving literature of Gnosticism, which does seem to have been such an esoteric movement, with striking peculiarities of its own, at least in some of its forms. This at least is the impression given by the corpus of Gnostic literature discovered in the late 1940s at Nag Hammadi in Egypt, and now available in English translation.[37] The name, Gnosticism, which has long been given to this particular movement, comes from the Greek word *gnosis*, meaning knowledge. But as we are now in a position to understand, the knowledge referred to is not intellectual or inferential, but arises from direct experience.

As the specialists examine this material with the resources available to them, there is growing agreement among them that Gnosticism must have originated somewhere on the fringes of Judaism. Although much of this literature does not look at all Jewish, especially on a superficial reading, it is becoming increasingly clear that it is permeated with Jewish terms and symbols, and that even in its apparently most anti-Jewish form, it presupposes the structure of Judaism. Probably the earliest form of Gnosticism was fully Jewish, and it was either the ancestor of, or closely related to, the Jewish mysticism of which we first hear in the Talmud, though it doubtlessly originated in an earlier period.

The books discovered at Nag Hammadi appear to have been the spiritual reading of a Coptic monastery, preserved by the monks from destruction in an orthodox crackdown. The Copts are Eastern Christians speaking a form of the ancient Egyptian language, called Coptic. They are descendants of the original Egyptian church but during the Christological controversies of the fifth century remained faithful to their interpretation of the views of their earlier leader, Cyril of Alexandria, now stigmatized by orthodox Christianity as Monophysite.[38]

The rediscovered books include a wide variety of literature commonly called gnostic, some of it barely gnostic at all. Among them are the beautiful mystical work called The Gospel of Truth, often attributed to the Roman teacher Valentinus, as well as the Gospel of Thomas, already mentioned for its affinity with the Q tradition represented in Matthew and Luke in the Christian canon. The works are of varying merit. Only a few of them bear out the picture of Gnosticism obtained from its opponents, the church fathers, who did their best to ridicule it. It is among this small group that we can find evidence of anti-Jewish Gnosticism.

This later anti-Jewish Gnosticism seems to have expressed its alienation from regular, exoteric Judaism by reversing its signs, as it were: what is good in the eyes of mainstream Judaism, such as the creation, becomes bad for this form of Gnosticism; what is bad for Judaism, such as the serpent in Eden, becomes good. The God of the Bible becomes a lesser being, belonging to a metaphysical level far below that of ultimate reality, where the true God exists. But the creator God does not even know that he is not the real deity. Only because he is so deluded can he make the tragic mistake of creating the material world, and thus imprisoning innumerable sparks of the divine in a material envelope.

Thus, neither the Bible nor the teachings of conventional religion, Jewish or Christian, can convey the truth to the seeker. A higher revelation is needed to make known to the imprisoned sparks their true origin and destiny: who they are, where they have come from, where they are going. An emissary from the world of light, far above the level of the deluded creator and lawgiver, must come down and teach them these saving truths.

The Christian forms of Gnosticism believed that this had been the role of Jesus. His esoteric teaching, given to favored disciples, especially Thomas the Twin and Mary Magdalene, in private during his lifetime and after his resurrection but withheld from the future leaders of ecclesiastical Christianity, was supposed to have dealt with these mysteries.

We are far from having adequate critical resources to discover if any authentic ideas, let alone actual words, of Jesus are contained in such works. It has been plausibly argued, however, that the Fourth Gospel in the New Testament is also largely based on an esoteric source, though later edited in the interests of a very different theology. Even the first three Gospels tell us that Jesus did teach in private. Some of his teaching as recorded there suggests that his own fundamental outlook may have been esoteric. The possibility that Jesus was also an esoteric teacher has in my view been dismissed too easily by New Testament scholarship.

DID JESUS FOUND ANY OF THEM?

One person could hardly have founded all three of these movements. They are much too different from one another. They are different enough to be regarded as three different religions, with widely divergent views on the nature of salvation. By the same token, it is far from likely that they stem from a common source earlier than any of them, which could itself be attributed to a single founder. Is it then possible that one of the three could have been founded by Jesus, while the other two arose independently?

We can hardly suppose that Jesus the Jew would have founded Gentile Christianity, though this is in effect the view of earlier historians, before the rediscovery of Jesus' full Jewishness. Nor could the Jesus depicted in the synoptic Gospels, still our most reliable source, have founded the anti-Jewish Gnosticism of the second century. Jesus might perhaps have founded Jewish Christianity and even given it something of the esoteric form it eventually took. But he could only have done so if he had firmly claimed to be the Messiah, and as we shall see in the third chapter, he certainly did not do that.

If we mean by Christianity anything like the movement that developed into the Catholic church of history, we can be sure that Jesus did not found it, since it contains too many anti-Jewish ideas that are almost inseparable from it. That movement in any case is largely the creation of second-century leaders. It has little in common theologically or organizationally even with the work of Paul, the real founder of Gentile Christianity, whose actual theology had little influence on the second century. It was largely an attempt to unify around a common ideology, that of the church of Rome, the very diverse movements that had survived from previous decades. It attempted to suppress its rivals by use of its own prestige as the church of the capital city of the empire and by means of the claim that it represented the most authentic tradition of the Apostles of Christ.

Whether the claim was true or not, it came to be very widely accepted. Behind the second-century unifying tendencies lay, as we have noted, extraordinary variety. It had not proved possible before the second century to unite the diverse forms of Christianity on the basis of commonly acknowledged instructions of a founder. In fact, no such organizational instructions survived, if they had ever existed.

The diversity in early Christianity was altogether too great to make the assumption that it could have had a single founder plausible. When we put that together with the new discovery of Jesus' full Jewishness, we are faced with massive obstacles to acceptance of the traditional assumption that Jesus was the founder of

Christianity. In fact, it has long been abandoned by many New Testament scholars in the dominant tradition.

Instead, we hear of the "Easter faith" of the disciples as the origin of Christianity, and this is much nearer the truth, though what these theologians mean by the Easter faith is something too like the developed Christian myth to have entered the minds of Jesus' Jewish followers at that stage. Christianity does not rest on what Jesus taught himself, still less on what he taught about himself. It rests on what his followers began to teach about him after his death.

However, our question today must be, was that teaching faithful to his own intentions, especially in the anti-Jewish turn it so quickly took? In the past, scholars felt they could cautiously conclude that it was. The more we come to understand Jesus' own Jewishness, the less likely it now seems that that was the case. So far as Christianity is and has been anti-Jewish, it seems to depend on a massive misunderstanding of Jesus himself, of the roots of his spiritual life and of his conception of his own mission.

We must now turn to a more detailed examination of that mission, in order to understand its Jewishness more fully and vividly. We have already learned that the search for the roots of Christian anti-Judaism takes us far back into the origins of Christianity. The same search shows us that anti-Judaism cannot be traced all the way back to Jesus the Jew.

2

Jesus the Jew: 2. Rejected by His People?

The New Testament embodies a Christian myth of salvation. It deeply colors all we read about Jesus in the gospel story. But the Gospels could not altogether escape from history into myth, for the subject of their myth was a historical person. This fact makes it possible for critical history to recover at least the outlines of the real Jesus and to compare him with the way the myth depicted him. When we do so, we can see that even at the comparatively early stage in its development reflected in the Gospels, the myth was already strongly anti-Jewish.

By the time the Gospels were being written, near the end of the first century, the stories about Jesus had taken on a transcendent and cosmic dimension. No longer a Jewish healer and teacher, but a triumphant hero and a savior figure, Jesus defeats his enemies on the supernatural plane, though defeated by them on the plane of history. Having conquered sin and death, he reigns as King on the right hand of God, while his followers await his triumphant return to history, still imminently expected.

As this myth took form, under various historical pressures, it came to level a deadly case against the Jews. The case turned on two charges. It was the Jews (not the Romans, as in historical reality) who were Jesus' earthly enemies, agents in fact of his supernatural foes, the forces of evil. They rejected the more spiritual teaching he brought them because they were attached to their old Law and could not see that Jesus' message of love and forgiveness had made it obsolete. Moreover, though their own Bible had clearly foretold his birth, death, resurrection, and all his doings, they rejected him as their Messiah because they found his claim to divinity blasphemous, condemning him to death and persuading the Romans to carry out the sentence, since they could not. And so they became the Christ-killers. We shall look critically at the first of these charges in the present chapter, and the second in the next.

The myth sets Jesus and his own people at odds with each other, as bitter and irreconcilable opponents. As the developing myth came to exalt Jesus to divine status, his alleged quarrel with Judaism became a divine judgment on a faithless people. Critical history does not find such a quarrel; instead it finds Jesus the Jew, a prophetic teacher who loved the Torah, who wished that everyone would follow it from the heart. And it does not find Christ-killers, but at most, disagreement between Jesus and some other Jews on how best to reclaim sinners.

These are not just academic questions. Because Christians read the New Testament uncritically, through the myth, they came to distrust and often to hate Jews. Seeing the Jews as the Christ-killers, they saw them as belonging to the forces of evil, capable of all kinds of crimes. Viewing them as evil licensed them to inflict evil upon them in their turn. The modern secularized world abandoned the myth, but retained the "knowledge" that the Jews were bad. This "knowledge" made the Holocaust possible.

The rediscovery of the historical Jesus in modern times strikes a blow at the roots of the anti-Jewish myth. That is why it is important for both Christians and Jews, and even for secularized people, to know something of the findings of critical history about the real story of Jesus.

The best historical scholarship now available shows beyond reasonable doubt that both the charges the myth brings against the Jews are false. The real Jesus did not teach anything against the provisions of the Torah his people lived by–he lived by them himself–and therefore could not have been opposed by his fellow Jews for what he taught. He was not convicted of blasphemy in their highest court for any messianic claims, and his people did not encompass his death on that account, or any other.

In the New Testament, however, the myth has been read back into the story of his life: many of the details of the story have been altered in the retelling to fit the new demands of the myth, thus producing a false picture of radical opposition between Jesus and other Jews, especially the Pharisees. Later beliefs about Jesus' messianic status were read back anachronistically, so that Jesus is depicted as claiming in his own lifetime to be what Christian theology would make him after his death. The Gospels speak for the Church, already a predominantly Gentile body, fast becoming in its own eyes the true Israel, the inheritor of all the promises, now lost by the Jews because of their unbelief in their Messiah.

All four of the Gospels in the New Testament were written, it now seems likely, by Gentile writers for Gentile audiences belonging to a movement that from its inception had abandoned the Jewish way of life and was unfamiliar with it. They take the stories about Jesus their predecessors had remembered out of their original Jewish context, putting them into a new one, the context of the rapidly developing salvation myth.

Even the original oral traditions, their sources, had no doubt often taken for granted the Jewish context of the stories, and therefore did not need to record it. This context would naturally have been familiar to those who originated the traditions, and to their first hearers, themselves Jewish. Later, Gentile readers of the gospel stories knew little of it. In reporting events in Jesus' life, the gospel writers sometimes display their own ignorance of Jewish beliefs and customs. At other times, they pass over or misunderstand them. They view the traditions they have received about Jesus through the situation of their own church in their own time, a Gentile movement now facing a radical breach with its Jewish parent.

Until modern times, Christians had always read the story of Jesus through this myth. They had learned the myth from parents and teachers before they began to read the New Testament; when they began to do so, their reading strongly reinforced the myth through which they read it. Most Christians still do read the Gospels in this way. Only those belonging to an instructed minority, conversant with the results of critical scholarship, have begun to question the old reading.

For the most part, profoundly ignorant of Judaism, Christians fail to understand the allusions to Jewish faith and life remaining in the Gospels and do not know how to supply them where they are missing. Thus the mythological aspects of the story seem plausible to them. Jewish readers are able to make these corrections, but until modern times they were discouraged from opening the New Testament at all. Even today they are liable to take the New Testament view of Jesus' relationship to his own people as correct, though they will evaluate the apparent conflict in a different way from Christian readers of the Gospels.

To read the stories correctly, we need knowledge and an imagination open to a Jewish world. We must now learn to extract the accounts of Jesus' sayings and doings from the later context of the myth and restore them to their original Jewish context. We will then find that authentic memories of the real Jesus have frequently survived. The outlines of a credible picture begin to emerge. It is not the picture of any kind of Christian but of a great Jew.

My intention in this chapter, after briefly sketching the pattern of Jewish life as Jesus knew it, is to consider some of the most important of his recorded sayings and doings. I shall concentrate on a few that have been taken to mean that he intended to supersede standard Jewish teaching with a new message and that he was bitterly opposed for it. We shall discover that those aspects of the Christian myth that present the Jewish people in a hostile light are devoid of historical foundation.

JUDAISM IN THE FIRST CENTURY

What was the Jewish world like in Jesus' day? Christian readers especially need to know some basic facts about Judaism then and now, without which they will fail to understand Jesus himself correctly. In Jesus' time, which historians commonly call the Second Temple period of Jewish history, Jewish faith and life had not yet fully assumed the form in which history would know them for the next two thousand years. The fundamentals of Jewish faith were then, of course, the same as they had always been and remain today. In contrast to the pagan world around them, Jews believed in one invisible but active God, who could not be represented by any image and whose requirements from his people were primarily ethical.

The people lived within a covenant with God, which he had established with them on his own initiative after liberating them from Egypt. At Mount Sinai, God had given to the people his own teaching, the Torah, containing his guidance for the way they were to live. The Torah, given through Moses, is both instruction (the root meaning of the word) in the way leading to life, and a legal code governing all aspects of the national life, including those that in a modern state are the province of civil law, not commonly regarded as religious at all.

At Sinai, the people had accepted the Torah from God, promising to obey faithfully all its provisions. What made this people into God's people, after his own choice of them, and their own decision to accept his offer of the Torah, was learning to live by it as fully and obediently as possible. Whenever they did not do so, or abandoned the attempt, God sent prophets to denounce them for straying from the true path, and to promise forgiveness and restoration if they would return to it.

The regulations for the national life given at Sinai included a system of worship, including a variety of animal and vegetable sacrifices for different occasions and purposes. The laws also included regulations for the construction of the sanctuary, originally a portable structure. The sanctuary was believed to house the divine presence, while the people were required to live in holiness in order to be fit for the Presence in their midst.

In due course, the portable sanctuary of the desert wanderings was succeeded by the first Temple, built in Jerusalem by King Solomon and later destroyed in a Babylonian invasion. Reconstruction began when the exiles returned from Babylon under Ezra and Nehemiah, in the fourth century B.C.E. Later, around the close of the millennium, King Herod rebuilt the Second Temple with great splendor, making it one of the wonders of the ancient world.

Jews are not interested in individual salvation. Corporately, the people were saved at the Exodus. The emphasis in the Torah is emphatically upon the creation and building up of a holy people, fit to be the place of the divine indwelling in the sanctuary. The national life is to be governed by ethical principles of fairness and compassion largely absent in the surrounding nations. Even the harsh punishments (later effectively mitigated by the Talmudic rabbis) that the Torah prescribes for those who break its most important regulations, serve the function of maintaining the holiness of the people.

The responsibility of the individual is to remain in the covenant by following its provisions, while cooperating with God in the completion and perfection of his creation. Only in the messianic age will that task be complete. Until then, the world remains unredeemed. It is the task of the Jewish people corporately to reflect the light of God's Torah to the surrounding nations, to speed that day of ultimate redemption.

Not infrequently, both the nation and its individual members failed to live up to their high calling. The Bible is extremely realistic in recording deflections from the ideal, even by personalities of great importance in the history of the people. No one, not Abraham, not Moses, and certainly not the later rulers, is depicted as perfect. The sacrificial system, and especially the observances of Yom Kippur, the Day of Atonement, provided means for dealing with all kinds of sin, intentional and inadvertent, but none of these could be efficacious without repentance.

Even after the loss of the Temple, the Rabbis taught that prayer and deeds of loving-kindness still brought atonement for sins just as efficaciously as had the former Temple sacrifices. The insight could hardly have been completely novel, though the new circumstances made it necessary to emphasize it. It was buttressed by quotations from the prophets, and it must have grown out of the experience of those who already had lived far from the Temple before it was destroyed, but still needed repentance and atonement for straying from the way of the Torah.

Once restored, by appropriate means, the sinner is again a full member of the covenant people, sharing all the benefits God had conferred upon them by liberating them, choosing them as his own people, and giving them the way leading to life. Unlike Christians, Jews do not believe in original sin. The sin of Adam and Eve, whatever it was, affected them alone, and subsequent generations start with a clean slate. However, every human being has to constantly choose between the good and the evil impulse, both present in everyone, and each is personally responsible for their own choices.

In Jewish understanding, God's forgiveness had always been readily accessible; however, there could be no meaning in separating it from *return* to the way of life marked out by the commandments of the Torah. Remaining in a way leading to death, even though forgiven, would not be restoration to life.

Among the provisions for the Temple are appropriate sacrifices to be offered by those who have become aware that they have fallen into sin and seek pardon and return. Such sacrifices, sin offerings and guilt offerings, make atonement for sins committed. Sins against fellow human beings, however, must be put right by appropriate human means before the repentant sinner approaches the sanctuary to seek atonement. Some very serious sins, even though forgiven, may still have to be atoned for by suffering during one's lifetime and ultimately through one's death.

The Hebrew words for repentance are all variations of a common root meaning return. In classical Jewish thought, repentance does not mean indulging in guilt or remorse,[1] but a form of action, a 180-degree turn, to walk once more in the way in which one had already begun, within the covenant with God, a return to the Torah and its commandments.

In Jesus' day, Herod's huge and magnificent Temple still towered over Jerusalem, and the animal and vegetable sacrifices were still offered daily. Its guardians, the priests, were still the authorized interpreters of the Torah; there was as yet no class of ordained rabbis. (Because he was a respected teacher, Jesus could himself be addressed as Rabbi–literally, "my great one"–as could other teachers, but that did not mean that he was an ordained professional interpreter of the Law.)

While the Temple was the center of Jewish worship, as it was of the national life, the great majority of the people, not resident in Jerusalem, saw it at most three times a year, on the occasions when they went up to Jerusalem for the three pilgrimage festivals of *Pesach* (Passover), *Shavuot* (the feast of Weeks), and *Sukkot* (Tabernacles). The weekly *Shabbat*, the Sabbath, a day of complete rest and worship, was in practice much more important to their spiritual life than visits to the Temple in the course of the annual cycle of festivals, though in predominantly agricultural communities these had a significance they cannot have for the present-day urban Jew. Something of the ancient significance of these agricultural festivals is being recaptured today in the kibbutzim of Israel, secular as these traditionally are.

For the rest of the year, the religious life of Jesus' day was centerd on the synagogue, the *Beit ha-Knesset*, or house of assembly. As its Hebrew name indicates, the synagogue is a place where people come together to study the Torah. (Its Yiddish name, *shul*, emphasizes its educational role.) In the time known as the Second Temple period, when Jesus lived, the synagogue had become an institution of vital importance. It had grown up during the Babylonian captivity and was retained after the return, having proved its usefulness when there was no access at all to the Temple.

Every town and village had its synagogue, where the Torah was read and studied, especially on Shabbat. To that extent, first-century Jewish life, at least outside Jerusalem, already resembled the form it would have in later centuries, after the destruction of the Temple.

The teachings of the Torah, originally given orally at Mount Sinai, and in their essentials inscribed on the two tablets of stone, were in due course incorporated in a book, or more precisely in the five books of Moses, the Pentateuch of the Bible. But the book required interpretation. Its origins were old, by the time of Jesus more than a millennium old. Some circumstances had changed considerably since its laws were first promulgated. Moreover, the Torah did not always tell people exactly how to carry out the instructions it contained. There had to be an authorized method of doing so. So the Torah had to be applied, modified in the light of changing circumstances, and generally interpreted to fit specific cases. Originally, this was the duty of the priests. But the priests could not be everywhere, since their functions were performed in the Temple, and there was only one Temple, in Jerusalem.

A class of lay (nonpriestly) interpreters of the Torah therefore also grew up. From the time of Ezra, after the return from the Babylonian captivity, these were called *soferim*, scribes. The translation suggests that they were writers of some kind; probably their original function was to write Torah scrolls, but soon their role in the community became much broader. Their function could perhaps be better rendered by translating the Hebrew literally as "men of the book." The "scribes" were the experts on the Book, that is the book of the Torah, copies of which were to be found in each synagogue.

During this period, near the close of which Jesus lived, the oral tradition of legal interpretation assumed increasing importance. Such a tradition had existed for a long time: according to later belief its essentials came from Sinai itself, having been given to Moses along with the written Torah.[2]

Those who interpreted it were scholars learned in both the written and the oral tradition. They seem to have been called by various names, which overlap to some degree. The greatest of them were known as *hachamim*, wise men or sages. While the sages exercised an important function of spiritual leadership, they could not be equated with any particular class or party. They came from all sections of the community, rich or poor, and included converts among their number. Most were layman, but priests could also be sages. Tradition told that the earliest sages were called scribes.

The sages were also the leaders of the Pharisees, the most popular and influential group among the people at large. Thus, the terms sage (not found in the Gospels), scribe, and Pharisee overlapped and cannot always be clearly distinguished. Since the term sage was reserved for the greatest of these interpreters of Torah, both Pharisees and scribes were a larger group than the sages themselves. The sages were regarded as the successors of the prophets, taking over some of their functions when prophecy was believed to have died out.

The oral tradition provided an authorized interpretation of the application of the provisions of the written Torah to developing circumstances. It remained oral for many centuries, because the text of the book itself was sacred and could not be altered, even when the circumstances for which it was written were no longer in force or had greatly changed. This paradoxically increased the flexibility of the traditional interpretation in adapting to new historical situations. While it remained oral, the tradition was not fully fixed, and there could be debate and even change, so long as the new interpretation could still be made consistent with the old written text. The Soferim, the "scribes," led by the sages, preserved and transmitted the oral tradition, taught it in the synagogues, and often ruled on its application to cases presented to them.

For ordinary Jews in Jesus' time, the synagogue was the main religious center, and they met with the Torah as the scribes interpreted it. By this time there was at least a weekly public reading of the Torah on Shabbat, divided into portions for each week and festival, though these were probably not at this stage exactly the same as the ones that later became traditional.[3] Perhaps a scribe, or someone else, would give an address on the Torah portion. This is how the popular commentaries on the Torah, called Midrash, in due course came to be composed.

The Temple with its priesthood was far away in Jerusalem, relatively inaccessible, especially for Galileans like Jesus, living in an area cut off from Jerusalem and its environs by Samaria, the home of a hostile group. The Temple, in spite of its religious importance, had little influence on their daily life.

The scribal interpretation of the Torah probably represented the mainstream tradition. It was not as radical as some others, especially those of groups like the Essenes, though it would not have been as conservative as the one many of the priests at the Temple followed. The latter belonged to a group called Sadducees, who rejected the oral tradition altogether, adhering to a literalistic interpretation of the written Torah. None the less, since there is no such thing as a completely literal interpretation of any text, the Sadducean literalism was also an interpretation, rivaling others that were current.

The people at large seem to have stuck fairly closely to the provisions of the Bible, though the interpretations of the Pharisees clearly commanded great respect. We also know from archaeological evidence that the use of the ritual bath, or Mikvah, was already quite widespread in Jesus' time.[4] While the Bible does not specifically mention it, the bath is a convenience in carrying out many of the purity regulations it does mention. The well-off also used stone vessels for purification, since it was held that they did not take up impurity, as the more common earthenware vessels would have.

In Jesus' time, there was a good deal of tolerance of diversity of religious opinion among Jews. In consequence, many historians have presented Second Temple Judaism as essentially diverse, lacking an orthodoxy from which other groups could be regarded as diverging. However, it is clear that tolerance was more of theology than of practice. Obedience to the Torah itself was of first importance, and everyone regarded it as such. Given broad agreement in observance, there was wide acceptance of divisions of theological opinion. Certainly, the people had not yet felt the need to close ranks around a particular interpretation of the Torah, as they would after the loss of the Temple.

We also know of several other groups: there were the Essenes, the group thought to have been responsible for composing and preserving the Dead Sea Scrolls, and there were various apocalyptic groups, expecting the imminent arrival of messianic times, including the Zealots, the resistance movement that hoped to throw off Roman rule, and thereby perhaps to bring the Messiah. There were also unorganized spiritual movements, often called Hasidim, especially in the Galilee, where the Zealots were also strong.

Most important of all, there were the Pharisees, who had been a power in the land for perhaps a couple of centuries. They seem to have originated among the Hasidim of the Maccabean period two centuries earlier, devout and faithful Jews preferring martyrdom to deviation from the Torah under Hellenistic influence. From Josephus, the Jewish historian who wrote in Greek in the latter part of the first century, we learn that the Pharisees were extremely zealous for the correct observance of the Torah, and that they were in his own day well respected and very popular among the people. Many of them were scribes and some were priests. They were influential in all areas of Jewish life. Paul says that he was himself a Pharisee, in fact an extremist among them. Josephus also claims to have been a Pharisee, though doubt has been cast on both claims.

The Pharisees were particularly associated with certain oral traditions (perhaps the same as those referred to in the Gospels as the "traditions of the elders") and anxious for their observance in detail, though others regarded them as optional. These traditions, along with the whole oral tradition of legal interpretation, were later collected and to some degree codified in the Mishnah and other portions of the Talmud.

The views of the Pharisees on the interpretation of the Law were generally more humane and liberal than those of the Sadducees. They were also believers in a future bodily resurrection, which the Sadducees rejected, in a considerable element of free will under the divine control of human events and in the efficacy of martyrdom in obtaining forgiveness for the sins of others.

More specific views of what the Pharisees stood for are the subject of continued controversy among the specialists. So far, there is no general agreement about the precise origins of the Pharisees: it is possible that (as some influential scholars believe) they should be identified with groups particularly interested in the voluntary observance of certain purity regulations in the Torah, there imposed only on priests. They may also have been especially interested in tithing. In any case, their central aim, shared by all Jews, was the sanctification of all aspects of life by the commandments of the Torah. Characteristically, they recognized a hierarchy of importance among the commandments, placing those dealing with love on the highest level.

The Gospels tend (though not consistently) to represent the Pharisees, and particularly the scribes among them, as vehement and determined opponents of Jesus, in fact as his typical opponents. Few scholars now believe that this was the historical fact. Jesus may in fact have had little contact with Pharisees, except perhaps on his occasional visits to Jerusalem. In all likelihood, there were very few Pharisees in Galilee by Jesus' time, though that situation greatly changed after the fall of Jerusalem and the failure of the later Bar Kochva rebellion against Rome around 135 C.E. At this date, however, the Pharisees and their influence were largely confined to Jerusalem and the area surrounding it, which Jesus visited relatively seldom and not for extended periods. He may have had little occasion to enter into controversy with them, even if he disagreed with them. Even more importantly, however, Jesus' surviving teaching is very close to what we know of the views of the Pharisees.

The Judaism of Jesus' time was diverse, but its diversity should not be exaggerated. Nor should differences with later forms of Judaism be emphasized, as if the codification of the oral tradition in the second century produced a revolution in belief and practice. That there were varieties and sects within the people is a fact, and clearly there was room for greater tolerance of diversity then than later. Nevertheless, we should not think of the Jewish world of the time of Jesus as essentially fragmented. There was very general agreement on what was meant by observance of the Torah. However, interesting to the modern scholar, especially to Christian scholars, the sects were minorities, and many, perhaps most, Jews of the time would have had little interest in their particular views.

The Pharisees, and especially their sages, had more influence than any other group on the people at large, though they were not themselves numerous. The Essenes seem to have been an esoteric minority living more or less apart from their neighbors. The Sadducees were a priestly and aristocratic group, by definition, not extending into the broad mass of the people. The Church later preserved the writings of various apocalyptic and messianic sects, because they seemed to favor ideas developing in the new Christian movement, but that does not mean that in their own time the sects in question had an extensive influence on other Jews.

Though scholarship still needs to discover more about its precise form at that time, there was surely a mainstream, nonsectarian Judaism that must have been close to the Judaism of later as well as of earlier times. When we compare and contrast Judaism with other religions, and in particular with Christianity, we can see that it did not change substantially from epoch to epoch in its spiritual orientation, in spite of the catastrophes of the loss of the Temple and to a large extent of the Land. With appropriate caution, we can use what we know of the Judaism of periods that are better documented to help us understand the religious environment in which Jesus lived.

ROMAN RULE

Overshadowing all the differences we know of in Jesus' time was the massive fact of Roman occupation. The Jewish people was not at that time a free self-governing people, though the Roman authorities liked to rule indirectly and did not often interfere in the details of daily life, especially in the sphere of religion. As a Roman province, Judaea was then under the administration of a Prefect (referred to in the Gospels as a Procurator), Pontius Pilatus, the "Pilate" of the English versions.[5] Though he sometimes intervened, in brutal ways that more prudent and humane administrators avoided, he normally ruled Judaea indirectly through the existing Jewish administration. Galilee and the trans-Jordanian parts of Herod's former kingdom were ruled, under Roman authority, by his sons Herod Antipas the Tetrarch, and Philip.

In ruling indirectly, Pilate made full use of the priestly aristocracy. Some did not mind this situation very much. The priestly group were not wholly dissatisfied with an arrangement that if anything increased their own power and importance. Others, like the tax collectors, made money out of the situation. Many were hardly affected at all.

But there were those who saw pagan rule over the holy land and the holy people as an abomination and hoped to find ways of putting it to an end. Ultimately, this would be the role of the Messiah himself, who would end pagan rule and restore the kingship of God himself, exercised through the Torah. But human action might have a part in bringing the Messiah. Those who thought in this way are the party described as Zealots. They believed that even a militarily hopeless revolt might bring a catastrophe in which the Messiah would be bound to intervene. Such people were responsible for the revolt of 66–73, which ended in the destruction of the Temple, mass suicide at Masada, and no Messiah.

JESUS AND THE JUDAISM OF HIS TIME

Jesus lived not in Judaea but in Galilee, a rich agricultural land, with hundreds of villages and a few major cities, notably Sepphoris, which is not mentioned in the Gospels, and Tiberias, which is mentioned, though only by John. In Galilee, the Zealots were particularly strong. Some of Jesus' own followers appear to have had Zealot contacts, and one of them actually received the nickname of Simon the Zealot. A few scholars, both Christian and Jewish, have made a case for Jesus himself having been such a Zealot revolutionary. If so, the Gospels must have done their utmost to cover the fact up, but as we shall see, that is not all they covered up. The fact that they do not represent him as a Zealot does not prove he was not.

The strongest argument for believing Jesus was such an opponent of Roman rule is that he was evidently crucified by them as such. Moreover, if it was necessary for the gospel writers to cover up the fact that Jesus was a revolutionary against Roman rule, that would help to explain the fact, which will concern us at length later on, that they attempt to shift the blame for Jesus' death away from the Romans onto the shoulders of the Jewish authorities.

Whether or not we decide that Jesus was a Zealot will probably turn on whether we think such views consistent with authentic records of his teaching on other matters. I do not think the case for regarding Jesus as a Zealot is fully persuasive; while some of his more pacifist-sounding utterances may well have been merely intended to protect himself from Roman attention, I cannot be convinced that he stood for violent resistance to pagan rule. However, Hyam Maccoby, one of the scholars who argues that Jesus was a Zealot, considers that he was not himself a violent revolutionary but one who hoped for a divine miracle to bring in the messianic age.[6] So the question remains open.

The case for thinking of Jesus as a Pharisee, surprising as the idea will be to most readers of the New Testament, is much stronger. It now seems fairly certain that in his own actions Jesus did not contravene the Torah as the Pharisees understood it (let alone as it was generally understood), and that in the most important respects, he and they stood for the same things.[7] He agreed with them on the resurrection, and both he and they taught that the commandments dealing with love were by far of the greatest importance. He taught in parables, as they did, and like them laid great emphasis on the value of repentance.

In any case, it is far from clear that Jesus put forward any systematic religious program of his own that could have come into conflict with that of the Pharisees or any other sect. It is essential to remember that by the time the Gospels were being written, late in the first century, the Church found itself in conflict with the leaders of early rabbinic Judaism, the successors of the Pharisees of Jesus' own time. The writers read the later conflict back into Jesus' lifetime, incorporating a negative picture of the Pharisees into the myth. History does not support this picture. The bad reputation of the Pharisees in the Christian world comes from the Christian myth, overlaying and distorting the historical record.

Some well-qualified scholars, including David Flusser and Hyam Maccoby, even believe that Jesus was or could have been regarded as a Pharisee himself, so great is the similarity between their views and his. However, if the Gospels represent him correctly, Jesus had little interest in either legal scholarship, or in purity regulations, which, according to some prominent scholars, were a major concern of the Pharisees. Even if he was not actually a Pharisee, Jesus probably belonged to the large majority of nonsectarian Jews who sympathized with and respected the Pharisees.

Geza Vermes has suggested that the Hasidim were particularly active in Galilee.[8] He describes them as devout, spiritually inclined people, close to the Pharisees in some respects, perhaps even a branch of the Pharisaic movement, but less concerned with Torah scholarship and more interested in their direct spiritual relationship to God. According to the Talmud, which has a number of references to them, such people were active in Galilee both before and after the time of Jesus.

These were remarkable men, who exercised what the sociologists call a charismatic role in the community. That is to say, they performed important spiritual functions, while occupying no official position. They were not priests or rabbis, or scribes of the Pharisaic or other parties. They enjoyed a direct and unmediated relationship with God, out of which they gave spiritual help and guidance to their fellow Jews.

Some of them, like Jesus, were exorcists and healers. When the Gospels record that Jesus taught "as one having authority, and not as the scribes,"[9] they probably mean that he was recognized as such a charismatic, teaching out of his personal relationship to God, rather than as a learned scholar of the tradition.

In his important and pioneering book, *Jesus the Jew,* Geza Vermes strongly emphasized Jesus' Galilean background, noting that he was a true countryman, constantly thinking and teaching in agricultural images. Vermes also built up a persuasive case for regarding Jesus as a charismatic Hasidic leader, in the Galilean tradition.

Looking at the rival views, I doubt if the evidence of the gospels is good enough to locate Jesus with precision in any of the movements of his day, given the present extent of our knowledge of them. However, from the point of view of this inquiry, that does not matter. What is important is to grasp that the gospel picture of sharp opposition between Jesus and the Pharisees in particular falsifies the real history.

We should probably think of Jesus as a mainstream Jew of his age, with links to the Pharisees, perhaps through the Galilean Hasidim to whom he was close, and perhaps with some affinity also with the esoterics and mystics whose ideas were not yet being committed to writing in his day. He was not a sectarian nor an extremist, at odds with large sections of his fellow Jews. He fits naturally into the Jewish tradition of his day.

JESUS' MISSION AND MESSAGE

Jesus did not appear before his Galilean contemporaries and neighbors in any novel role. He did not present himself to them as a later rabbi would do, giving rulings on difficult questions of Torah law, still less as the preacher of a new religion, expounding new beliefs, nor (as he appears in the Christian myth) as a savior preparing to die for the sins of the world.

He came before his fellow Jews as a teacher, perhaps even as a prophet, telling them that their God was very near to them and that people must respond to him with all their hearts, so that his kingship could be realized in all the details of life. The message was a Jewish one, and by no means unique, since much of what he wished to say was drawn from his great predecessors, the prophets of the Bible, as well as closely resembling the teaching of other Jews both before and after him. What he learned seems to have been intensified by a personal awareness of God's nearness. However, this vision was not a private one; Jesus clearly thought it could be shared by anyone who would turn to God in trust.

If we are to look for anything that distinguished Jesus' message from that of other important Jewish teachers, we shall probably seize on the perfectionism of his ethical teaching, which seems to go beyond even the requirements of the biblical prophets. Some have thought that this perfectionism was so extreme as to set him outside the limits of the Jewish vision of God and man. I shall argue that this is not the case. I think his perfectionism is to be explained by his sense of the nearness of God and his kingdom.

His personal vision of divine nearness seems to have led him to believe that no response could be adequate except one reflecting at the human level God's own perfection. In his teaching, he set standards few have ever been able to rise to. But the requirements, as he saw them, of entry into the sphere of divine sovereignty were not novel, or unique, still less characteristic of some new religion hitherto unknown to his contemporaries. They were nothing more nor less than a radical and uncompromising interpretation of the Torah itself.

It seems clear that this perfectionism was in itself only an intensification of the standard Jewish principle of the imitation of God. In its Jewish context, balanced and supported by the whole structure of the Torah, his perfectionism need not have imposed impossible spiritual burdens on his hearers. Divorced from that background, and inserted into an alien, Christian, tradition of asceticism, such sayings have often been interpreted as making demands even saints could not live up to.

Such impossible demands have often been found spiritually devastating by the devout; others have simply given up the attempt to live by them. The result has often been a double standard absent in Judaism. In a later chapter, we shall see that there is reason to believe that the spiritual stresses introduced by such perfectionism has something to do with the growth of an even more intense hostility toward Jews. If such later interpretations of Jesus' teaching were correct, the more recent opinion that he was fully and authentically Jewish would confront a major problem.

In all probability, however, in its original context such teaching was intended to prepare his hearers for the messianic age, whose imminence he seems to have taught. If so, Jesus was certainly not alone in believing that the Messiah could be brought if Israel would keep the Torah perfectly. However, there is no good evidence that he claimed to be the Messiah himself, or even Elijah, his forerunner.

Jesus seems to have been reluctant to categorize himself and his personal role. Prophet was the only term he seems to have been comfortable with, and he did occasionally apply it to himself. He may have understood his own experience at the time of his baptism by John the Baptist as a calling to some kind of prophetic mission, though the Gospels represent the calling as messianic. If so, he must have been puzzled and in doubt, since prophecy was supposed to have come to an end in his time, except for the future return of Elijah as the forerunner of the Messiah. In the Gospels, Jesus never claims to be Elijah himself.

Though Jesus made no claims for his own person, he seems to have impressed his contemporaries as someone unusual, with a personal authority manifested in his ability to draw others to follow him in a homeless, wandering existence, in the mastery of words displayed in his teaching, especially the parables he told to illuminate his message, and in his remarkable (though not unprecedented) capacity to free people from conditions then believed to be due to demonic possession.

Teachers were normally sought out by their prospective students. Jesus called his own, sometimes brusquely, requiring them to join him in his own wandering life. There was a strong tradition in the developing Christian movement that he had chosen twelve of them for a position of special significance.

The evidence is conflicting on this point. Some traditions do not say anything about the Twelve, mentioning only an inner circle composed of Peter, James, and John. On the other hand, in the early Church, where in due course the Twelve came to be known as the apostles of Christ, more than these twelve seem at first to have been called apostles.

We may no longer be able to determine whether twelve of Jesus' followers already occupied a special position in his lifetime. If they did, their position was clearly symbolic. They must have represented the nucleus of the twelve tribes of a renewed Israel in the kingdom of God. Where Jesus himself would have fitted into such a symbolic picture is even more obscure.

According to the records surviving in the Gospels, Jesus spoke most of all about the nearness of God to his people, Israel. His call to ethical perfection was balanced by teaching about God's special compassion for sinners, those who had strayed from the way of life marked out in the Torah. He told the sinners that God, willing to forgive them and bring them back to the way of life, was actively seeking them out. He himself pronounced the divine forgiveness upon the repentant, and healed the sick in God's name.

His mission, as he himself saw it, was primarily to the sick and the sinners among the people. The two groups largely overlapped, since in the understanding of the time, which Jesus shared, sickness was the outcome of sin, and even of demonic possession. It could not be removed without repentance and forgiveness, and in many cases required the exorcism of the demon by someone with enough spiritual authority to throw it out.

Jesus was apparently such a person. Speaking with authority of divine compassion and readiness to forgive, he was able to remove demons and bring sinners to repentance and forgiveness. The heart of Jesus' message was divine compassion for "the lost sheep of the house of Israel."[10] He believed he had himself been sent to these, rather than to the "righteous persons who need no repentance."[11]

He seems, then, to have regarded it as his own special mission to go to the sinners, those who had abandoned the attempt to live by the Torah. Those of his sayings that the tradition recorded may therefore lay a disproportionate emphasis on a single aspect of Jewish teaching. That does not mean that he necessarily rejected the remainder, but there are vast areas on which the Gospels record nothing of any teaching. In any event, he had no interest whatsoever in the Gentile world, to which the movement that claimed his authority would subsequently turn. His personal horizon was limited to his fellow Jews.

GOD'S KINGSHIP

The gospel writers tell us that Jesus' central role in his lifetime was to proclaim "the kingdom of God." If so, what would that have meant to him or his contemporaries?

Was this a claim that the messianic age had actually come, and therefore that Jesus its proclaimer was himself the King Messiah? We must defer until the next chapter fuller examination of the supposed messianic claims of Jesus, concentrating for now on what he meant by the kingdom of God and its nearness. However, that will already throw important light on whatever may have been Jesus' own relationship to the divine kingdom he proclaimed.

The term usually translated as kingdom originally stood for something much more dynamic than our word *kingdom*. Primarily, Jews view it as a vector of divine energy, an attribute and activity of God himself, reigning as king over the world he had made.[12] We should translate it as kingship, sovereignty, or rule, rather than kingdom, though none of these abstract terms quite catches the dynamism of the original.

The Jewish people had long thought of God as the king both of Israel and of the whole world. For Jewish faith, God is not only the king of his own people Israel, he is the sovereign of the world. All history is under his sovereign rule, yet he restrains its exercise in order to allow the world great freedom. Jews regard freedom as a condition of our humanity; they see human beings as responsible agents in history, but they also recognize that people continually misuse their freedom.

For long historical periods, therefore, the forces of evil, the adversaries of God and his rule, seem to control the world. Yet, since God is the true king, Jewish faith remains certain that one day he will establish his own sovereignty. Peace and justice will reign, and God will be seen by all to be king.

The kingdom of God can also mean God's future disclosure of the truth of his sovereignty, something Jews have usually identified with the age of the Messiah. Even then, however, the "kingdom of God" is not a territory or domain over which God rules or will rule, as the English translation suggests. Instead, it is still God's own kingship, finally asserted and made manifest. Thinking of God in this way goes far back into biblical Judaism, for God was acknowledged as the king of his own people, Israel, before there was an earthly king.[13]

The kingship of God is particularly expressed in his Torah. Acknowledging or accepting the kingship of God concretely means obliging oneself to keep his commandments. Somewhat after Jesus' time, the Rabbis were thinking of the recitation of the *Shema*, "Hear, Israel, the Lord our God, the Lord, is One," as the expression par excellence of acceptance of the yoke of the kingship of God. When they compiled the traditional Jewish prayer book, they associated with the Shema itself passages from the Bible that speak of the need of Israel constantly to be reminded of the Torah, to rehearse its provisions at all times and to teach them to subsequent generations for ever.

This rabbinic interpretation of the kingship of God is of course somewhat different from the messianic one Christian scholars have usually attributed to Jesus.[14] Nevertheless, the association of the kingship of God with the yoke of the Torah may very well have been present to Jesus' mind, perhaps even what he would have thought of first.[15]

In any case, he would not have divorced the triumph of God's sovereignty in a future messianic age, however near, from the fullest observance of the Torah. No Jew thought of the messianic age as a time when Torah would become obsolete. When Jeremiah wrote of a new covenant, he did not imagine new terms but thought of the existing Torah written on the hearts of the people, so that they would now observe it spontaneously. We shall shortly see what Jesus himself thought about the role of the Torah in Jewish life.

GOD'S NEARNESS

I have represented Jesus as characterized by an exceptional sense of God's nearness to human beings and especially to the sinners. According to the Gospels, Jesus made it his central aim to announce that God's kingship had come *near* to his hearers. In the latest translation of the New Testament, the Revised English Bible, quoted above, the translators have attempted to convey the meaning of a difficult Greek verb by having Jesus say: The kingdom of God is *upon you*. More literally, the Greek says: The kingship of God has *neared*, or even arrived. The Greek must reflect a Hebrew or Aramaic word with the same meaning.

The nearness of God has always been an important theme for Jews, from the Bible onward.[16] They have usually thought of his nearness together with its opposite, his farness, or distance. God is both near and far, and we cannot understand the one without the other. These concrete terms are the way in which Jews characteristically think and speak of what others refer to in the more abstract philosophical expressions, immanence and transcendence: God's nearness is his presence or immanence in the world, his farness is his transcendence over it. As it is said, "The world is not his place, he is the place of the world."[17]

"Am I a God near at hand only, not a God when far away?"[18] God's nearness, represented primarily in his choice of and care for Israel, and his fatherly and motherly compassion for human beings, is balanced by his farness, his awesome sublimity, his uniqueness and incomprehensibility to the human mind. Without farness, God would not be God; without nearness, he would not be the God who has sought out and made himself known to Israel.

DIMENSIONS OF NEARNESS

We are getting a little closer to identifying Jesus' distinctive themes. Jesus himself, it seems, had been so profoundly struck by God's nearness that he emphasized it almost to the exclusion of any reference to his farness.

For him, God's kingship was no longer a distant hope, but a present reality. The apocalyptic visionaries to whose ideas Christian scholars have so often linked Jesus' own teaching on the kingdom of God were preoccupied with guessing the time of its coming. Like the first of them, the biblical writer Daniel, they believed in a time scheme for the end of days now being realized, whose signs could be read off by the visionary. But their interest in the future could distract them from the present.

Jesus showed not the slightest interest in any such apocalyptic scenarios. If he talked about signs at all, and he seemed to dislike doing so, it was to refer to signs of the *presence* of the kingship of God, not its future manifestation in a messianic age, whether remote or soon to be experienced. The kingship of God, he said, does not come with signs or wonders. It is in your midst, or among you, or even (according to an older translation, especially favored by the esoterics and mystics) *within* you.[19]

In Jesus' teaching about the kingship of God, the emphasis was all upon the need to respond to the present challenge of its nearness. He collapsed the apocalyptic time scheme into immediacy, bringing his hearers' attention back to the existential reality that they were here and now in God's presence and must respond to it, without waiting for the messianic future.

Did this mean that the messianic age had come? Probably not, for that could not happen until human beings did respond to the nearness of God. The response Jesus called for was the perfect righteousness about which he taught, extending to the imitation of God's own perfection. Jesus' teaching about righteousness is the direct consequence of his vision of the nearness of God.

Jesus also taught that God manifests his nearness in his loving care for his children. This dimension was especially present when he taught about trust in God as Father. When Jesus spoke in Aramaic, which was his everyday language, though he surely knew Hebrew as well, he called God Abba.

Abba means "the father" or simply "father." It was the term used in the family to address the father, as it still is in modern Israeli Hebrew. This is one of the few words of Jesus to be preserved by the New Testament in the original Aramaic, transliterated into Greek letters. Paul refers to it too when he says that God has sent the Spirit of adoption into our hearts, so that we cry, Abba, Father.[20] The writers must have found it unusually important.

Did Jesus go beyond the limits of Judaism when he so emphasized divine fatherhood, speaking to God as Abba, and teaching others to do the same? Hardly. In Jewish understanding, God had always been the Father, as well as the King, of his own people. Jesus must have known liturgical prayers like the *Avinu, Malkenu*, "Our Father, Our King," apparently already in use in his day.

However, Jesus did not balance these two divine attributes as the traditional prayer does. Though he could not help referring to God as the King when he taught about the coming of his kingdom, or kingship, and its character, he does not use this royal language about God in his own recorded prayers or when he teaches others how to pray.

The Aramaic *Abba* seems to differ from the more common and formal Hebrew *Avinu* (alluded to in Jesus' own model prayer, "Our Father") only by invoking the relationship of the individual to God, instead of (as liturgical prayer does) the community's. When God is thought of as the Father of the people of Israel, it was appropriate to address him as *Our* Father, as in liturgical prayer. When it was a matter of the relationship of God to the individual, the domestic and vernacular term Abba could replace Avinu.

Jesus was not the first or the only Jew of the time to call God Abba and to be well known for doing so. Some of the Hasidim of Galilee, with whom Geza Vermes links Jesus, also did so and were called Abba themselves, as a title of respect. Like them, Jesus thought of himself as a son in the Father's house who could confidently make requests to God in prayer.[21] More than likely, Jesus' use of Abba in addressing God was something quite well understood in his own spiritual milieu.

Many critics have supposed that when Jesus spoke of God as his Father, he was laying claim to a unique relationship with the Father as the Son *par excellence*. Apart from the fact that (as Vermes demonstrates in his *Jesus the Jew*) Jesus was not the originator of such language, he can hardly have been claiming a relationship others could not share, since he taught others to address God as Father too. All Jews think of themselves as children of God. The most famous of Christian prayers, the Our Father or "Lord's prayer," is so Jewish in its thought that many Jews have found no theological difficulties with it. What difficulties there are seem to arise from Christian interpretations and associations.

Jesus seems also to have taught that in his extreme compassion God is somehow nearest of all to those who in themselves are farthest from him, the sinners. In this third dimension of Jesus' teaching about divine nearness we may have come upon something sufficiently distinctive to account for the controversies in which he was involved with other Jews. The paradox is striking, even if not altogether without precedent. Isaiah, addressing the whole people, says something very similar. "I was ready to respond, but no one asked, ready to be found, but no one sought me. I said, 'Here am I! Here am I!' to a nation that did not invoke me by name."[22]

In a number of parables, Jesus told stories teaching about the compassion of God for the sinners in particular, the lost sheep of the house of Israel to whom Jesus believed that he himself had been sent. Jesus said that he had been sent to the sinners who needed repentance, not to the "righteous persons who need no repentance."[23] The last phrase has often been regarded as ironic; perhaps it was, but it need not necessarily have been. Those who already observed the Torah from the heart were not among those who most needed Jesus' message of divine nearness and readiness to forgive. The sinners were those who had given up on living by the Torah, and were perhaps in consequence overwhelmed with self-hate and despair.

Only rank Christian prejudice leads people to suppose that Jesus regarded all observant Jews as hypocrites and worse than open sinners. He was an observant Jew himself. He does not seem to have made the modern distinction between ethical and ritual commandments. He kept the Sabbath and the festivals, wore fringes on his garments,[24] and took it for granted that people would put on tefillin (phylacteries) and fast on appropriate occasions.[25]

Jesus did have an acute eye for all forms of phony religiousness. He did not except the outwardly religious but inwardly egotistical from his call to repentance. Nevertheless, he clearly believed that those who observed the Torah were already in the father's household and not among the lost. However, he depicted God himself as in his compassion more concerned for the lost than for those safely in the shepherd's fold. And in defending this mission to the sinners, he seems to have been ready to point out to his critics that it would be unwise to exclude themselves from the category of sinners, since they may well have been guilty of spiritual sins not necessarily less grave in God's eyes than the outward sins of the conventionally sinful.

Jesus' mission to sinners and the way he carried it out in his own conduct seems to have aroused sharp controversy. The controversies Jesus was involved in arose primarily from this mission to the sinners and not from any claim to be above the Law by which his fellow Jews lived. In order to carry out his mission in the way that he himself understood it, Jesus did things that scandalized the devout, raising questions in their minds about his own observance of the Torah.

JESUS AND THE TORAH

Jesus believed that the nearness of God required radical response, a teaching I have characterized as perfectionism. Did the perfect response he thought necessary differ from or even contradict the Torah given through Moses at Sinai?

The common view among Christians that Jesus was rejected by his own people arises from their belief that he held a low opinion of the Torah by which his fellow Jews lived, teaching some superior basis for a relationship with God and a higher and more spiritual way of life than the one laid down there. This idea often leads to a cruder popular contrast between the supposedly cruel and vengeful God of the Old Testament and the compassionate and forgiving God of the New Testament. If he had held such an opinion, it would have been natural for his fellow Jews to reject his teaching. These ideas are so deeply rooted in the Christian mind that people are very resistant to any challenge to them on the basis of the facts. Nevertheless, the facts do not support this ancient prejudice.

The contrast of the God of the Old Testament with the God of the New Testament would have been meaningless to Jesus himself. It was from the Torah and the prophets, as well as from his own spiritual experience, that Jesus learned that God is compassionate and forgiving. Judaism from the time of the Bible on has thought of God's attributes of justice and mercy as in balance, laying almost equal stress on each, while often tipping the balance in favor of mercy.

However, many of the words in the Sermon on the Mount seem to support the notion that Jesus rivals and challenges Moses, by teaching a more perfect way. According to Matthew's report, Jesus seems to put his own teaching above that of the Torah, setting out a series of antitheses contrasting what was said to "the men of old"[26] with his own teaching. If Jesus actually used that expression to mean the teaching of the Torah itself, and intended to supersede it with a superior teaching, the popular opinion would be right. In that case, Jesus would have been claiming superiority to Moses. Such a claim would normally have altogether cut him off from the community of Judaism. If such a claim had been justified, on the other hand, Jesus would presumably have been someone transcending in authority the whole Jewish tradition, at least the Messiah in person. Accordingly, the issue is crucial to the topics we have set ourselves to consider in this and the next chapter.

THE SERMON ON THE MOUNT

A careful reading of the Sermon on the Mount does not support the notion that Jesus claimed superiority to Moses. The critics seem generally to agree that the words of the sermon were not all spoken on the same occasion. Matthew seems to have gathered up various sayings uttered on different occasions to make a set piece version of Jesus' personal torah, or teaching.[27]

Matthew places the sermon in a formal or heightened setting. He may himself have intended to exhibit Jesus as the "prophet like Moses" apparently predicted in Deuteronomy.[28] Others have seen in the arrangement of the five major discourses of Jesus in this gospel an allusion by Matthew to the pattern of the five books of Moses in the Bible. Even the setting of the sermon on a mountain could be an echo of the giving of the Torah on Mount Sinai. These considerations would lend support to the traditional Christian interpretation.

On the other hand, Matthew himself introduces the antitheses between what was said to the men of old and Jesus' own teaching with words that seem expressly designed to rule out such an interpretation. This portion of the sermon begins, "Do not think that I have come to abolish the Torah and the Prophets: I did not come to abolish but to fulfill. Truly, I tell you, until heaven and earth pass away, not a yod nor a crown will pass from the Torah until it is all fulfilled."[29]

(In the English versions, there are various translations of the words I have rendered by "yod" and "crown." The familiar Authorized, or King James, version has "jot" and "tittle." Yod is the smallest and most insignificant letter of the Hebrew alphabet, corresponding to the Greek "iota," which is what the Greek text says here. The Greek word I have rendered by crown was used by grammarians to refer to accents and diacritical marks. At that period, the Hebrew Bible was written without such aids to pronunciation. A crown is a tiny ornament of certain Hebrew letters, already used in writing Torah scrolls. The Jewish mystics have sometimes attached esoteric meanings to these traditional manuscript ornaments; a midrash says that the famous Rabbi Akiva derived heaps of new laws from them. Perhaps Jesus also found mystical meanings in them.)

Luke has an even stronger form of the same saying: "It is easier for heaven and earth to pass away than for one crown of the Torah to fall."[30] It is not likely that Luke would have reproduced a saying so contrary to the views of his readers unless it had been firmly rooted in the tradition and could not be ignored. By the criterion of dissimilarity,[31] therefore, it is extremely probable that Jesus did say something like that. His statement could hardly be more emphatic in its adherence to the Torah as a divine revelation of the right way of life.

There seems to be an echo of controversy in the words, as if they respond to a charge. Perhaps, if the words are indeed Jesus' own, they were spoken as an answer to the charges we shall consider later in this chapter. When Matthew himself placed them immediately before the antitheses, he no doubt intended his readers to understand what followed in their light. However, if the antitheses actually did contradict the Torah, his precaution would have been ineffectual. Do these antitheses contradict the Torah? They do not, and it is hard to understand how Christians, who could read the Torah for themselves in the Bible, could ever have supposed that they did.

THE SERMON AS AN INTERPRETATION OF THE TORAH

The closing words of this section of the sermon are the clue to the way we are meant to understand the antitheses: "There must be no limits to your goodness, as your heavenly Father's goodness knows no bounds." (Matthew 5:48, Revised English Bible. In a more traditional translation: "You must be perfect, as your heavenly Father is perfect.") This is not a criticism of the Torah; it is an interpretation of the Torah in the light of the requirements of the full realization of God's kingship. It is not a revolutionary interpretation, however, but one well-grounded in Jewish tradition. Even the formula, "you have heard it said . . . but I say" appears to have been a standard way of introducing a new interpretation.[32]

Jesus' conception of the goodness required by the kingdom took nothing less than God himself as its standard. Like other Jewish ethical teachers, he understood ethics as the imitation of God, following the passage in Leviticus: "You shall be holy, as I the Lord your God am holy."[33] Accordingly, some of these injunctions are stricter than other interpretations of the Torah, but none of them is opposed to the Torah itself, in detail or in spirit.

Much of the language of the discourse is hyperbolic or exaggerated; some of the sayings can be recognized as parable, not intended to be taken literally. This does not detract from the spiritual ideal set forth, but it should warn us against excessively literalistic and legalistic interpretations, often found in Christian writers.

Like the prophets before him, and the Pharisaic sages who were his near contemporaries, Jesus took the profoundest demands of the Torah, the call for love of God and the neighbor, as the norm for the interpretation of the whole. He saw existing interpretations, involving rights as well as obligations, not as wrong or mistaken, but as making concessions to human imperfection. Religious regulations meant for a whole community normally must make such concessions. Jesus seems to have been addressing a devout minority, especially committed to realizing the kingship of God here and now, by anticipating the perfection of the age to come.

The Torah itself is not in question in these antitheses. Even Matthew appears to wish the reader to contrast them only with a contemporary interpretation that would have been familiar to his readers. In this connection, the scribes and Pharisees (the meaning may be "the scribes of the Pharisaic party") are mentioned.

They were widely known and well respected for their zealousness in fulfilling the Torah in great detail and with considerable strictness, regularly going beyond the letter of the Law in order to be certain of fulfilling it. Matthew may therefore have meant his readers to understand the righteousness of the kingship of heaven as exceeding not the Torah itself, but the most rigorous interpretation of it current in his day. In fact, however, Jesus' teaching, here as elsewhere, does not differ significantly from that of the Pharisaic sages, as the many Talmudic parallels that have been adduced for his sayings clearly show.

The scribes in Jesus' day were developing a systematic interpretation of the Torah whose aim was the sanctification of everyday life. The system they developed was a practical, workable one, though demanding a high standard of personal discipline. The Torah's precepts, so interpreted, can be kept by ordinary people, not just saints or religious virtuosos. But when kept, they bring about a distinctive moral elevation, which has characterized Jewish life down the centuries.

If Matthew (or perhaps Jesus) thought this insufficient for the realization of God's kingship, he was not attacking a straw man. But upholders of the standard Jewish teaching could reply that the teaching of the sermon could only be lived by saints. Ordinary people need to have recognized rights and are permitted to stand up for them.

In several of the antitheses of the sermon, Jesus teaches that avoidance of a specific action forbidden in a negative commandment is not sufficient for the righteousness of the kingship of heaven. There must also be purification of inner motive. As the prophets before him did, Jesus regarded the inner spiritual condition as the root of the outward action.

This is the way he interprets two of the commandments from the Decalogue, specifically referred to in these sayings. (There may also be allusions in other sayings to "You shall not covet," which already extends to inner motivation.) He extends the commandment, "You shall not murder" to include the prohibition of anger and insult, much as the later Rabbis did. Murder is the ultimate outcome of an inner state of hating and rejection of others. For Jesus, the fulfillment of the commandment began in dealing with the inner state leading to the outward action. The requirement of reconciliation between adversaries as a prerequisite for acceptable worship is vividly stated, but it was not a novelty. That is and was standard Jewish teaching.

Jesus interprets "You shall not commit adultery" in the same way. He seems to equate the lustful fantasy in the mind with the outward action that is forbidden, though it may or may not actually follow from it. In view of the impossibility of avoiding sexual thoughts, many of which are lustful in everyone, this saying has caused perhaps more difficulties for Christians than anything else Jesus said. If Jesus really meant to say that the sin of thought is identical with the sin of action, he would have been outside the normal boundaries of Jewish tradition. But this seems to be a Christian interpretation, not required by the original context of the saying, which seems rather to emphasize the fact that lust plans acting out.

The saying on divorce, which belongs in the context of the avoidance of adultery, is best understood in the light of contemporary controversies within the Pharisaic movement.[34] In Jesus' time, the two leading schools, those of Hillel and Shammai, were in disagreement on the conditions for divorce. In this passage, Jesus does not endorse the later Catholic prohibition of divorce on any grounds, which was not advocated by any Jews. Neither of the two schools had that in mind.

Jesus sided with the school of Shammai in its stricter view, against the more liberal followers of Hillel, who were prepared to allow divorce for what may now seem quite trivial reasons. The Torah allows divorce, but traditional practice requires the husband to give his wife a certificate (now called a *get*) representing his formal renunciation of all marital claims and setting her free to marry someone else.

The requirement of a certificate of dismissal is not an idle one, as those unfamiliar with the practice may suppose. To withhold it, as estranged husbands sometimes do, can inflict great hardship on a woman. Siding with the stricter view, Jesus considers the subsequent union of the wife with another man adulterous on both sides. The implication is that making her an adulteress inflicts greater spiritual harm on her even than the withholding of a *get.* Nothing is said about the status of a remarried husband after divorce.

Mark has another version of the same saying, which has had more influence on Christianity, until modern times.[35] In that passage, forbidding divorce altogether, the writer assumes that Jesus is dealing with a situation in which the woman has the right to divorce her husband. Since in Judaism, then and later, only the husband could divorce his spouse, Mark's version cannot be the original form of the saying.[36] Instead, he sets Jesus' words against the background of the Roman legal system, where both spouses had the right of divorce.

Jesus would have had no reason to address this situation when speaking to Jewish listeners. Thus, there is no good evidence that Jesus forbade divorce in all circumstances. The exception for immorality or adultery makes perfect sense in the context, since divorce cannot make a woman an adulteress if she is one already.

The discussion of oaths, which also does not explicitly quote the Torah, seems to refer to the commandment in the Decalogue not to take the name of the Lord in vain. The commandment was strictly interpreted in Jesus' day. Not only was the actual four letter name YHWH never pronounced by anyone except by the High Priest once a year on the Day of Atonement, devout people tried to avoid making use of any name of God. Substitutes were used instead. Hence we often find Jesus in the Gospels speaking of the kingdom of "heaven," for example, instead of the kingdom of God. The commandment was extended in practice to refer not only to oaths, which were permitted but not encouraged, but (as by Orthodox Jews today) to any casual use of a divine name.

Jesus seems to have this practice in mind when urging people not to swear by heaven or earth or by Jerusalem, since all these are intimately associated with God himself. There is not even a suggestion in the text that Jesus intended to criticize the Torah of Moses. In the latter part of the saying, his point seems to be that anyone who needs to reinforce his word with an oath is already considering the possibility of breaking it.

We come now to the famous "eye for eye and tooth for tooth." Here Christian interpreters have traditionally had a field day, contrasting the supposed barbaric requirements of Jewish law with Jesus' more spiritual advice to forgive injuries. Such a contrast between Christianity and Judaism depends upon a literal interpretation of the Torah text unknown to traditional Judaism, and apparently peculiar to Christianity.

In Jesus' day, the accepted interpretation took the text to refer to equivalent monetary compensation. Jesus would never have encountered a literal interpretation and could hardly have been arguing against it. Modern biblical scholarship supports the traditional interpretation Jesus himself would have known. Comparison of the Torah with other Ancient Near Eastern texts makes it highly probable that even the Torah itself originally meant the words to refer to monetary compensation, except in the case of murder, where no amount of money can equal a life.[37]

The remaining words in this paragraph are less controversial. The injunction to give money to those who want to borrow is standard Jewish teaching, as is the duty of giving to beggars and the poor. The famous injunction to go the second mile is another vividly expressed piece of spiritual advice to go beyond the limits normally set by rights.

Finally, nowhere does the Torah say, "You shall love your neighbor and hate your enemy."[38] In the whole Torah there is no command to hate personal enemies. Many Christians (astonishingly) even suppose that Jews did not know of the command to love the neighbor. In fact, so far from being Jesus' invention, it comes from the book of Leviticus, the most priestly and "ritualistic" book of the Torah.

It is extremely difficult to imagine where Matthew could have found this part of the saying. Probably, it is not an authentic saying of Jesus himself.[39] If, as seems likely, the final editor of the Gospel was not Jewish, and perhaps not completely familiar with the Torah, he might have inserted the clause in order to establish a more striking contrast with Jesus' authentic injunction to love enemies. (Even this explanation has to contend with Matthew's familiarity with the Bible, unmatched by his predecessor Mark.)

However that may be, this is one of the most anti-Jewish sentences in a Gospel that, taken as a whole, is among the most anti-Jewish writings in the New Testament. Given that context, we can be all the more sure of the authenticity of other words of Jesus the author cites, bearing witness to his complete devotion to the Torah and its teaching.

The explicit injunction to love *enemies* has been generally recognized as new to Jewish tradition, without going much beyond what can be found elsewhere. Again, Jesus could hardly have intended it as a legal ruling, even if he meant it literally, because only a tiny minority of the most spiritually evolved people could successfully carry it out. (In practice, Christians have not proved better than Jews at doing so, and it could be argued that they have been a good deal worse.[40]) Perhaps the injunction was not intended to be taken literally. It may have been one of Jesus' characteristic hyperboles to drive home a point; no one is to be excluded from the category of neighbor.

Obviously, the last few pages are not intended to be a complete commentary on the teaching of the Sermon on the Mount, generally acknowledged to be one of the most important spiritual documents in religious history. I have addressed myself only to the question of its Jewish character. If the sermon faithfully represents Jesus' personal ethical teaching, the conclusion must be that his teaching remained within the parameters of Judaism, even though it may not have been typical of Jewish ethics, usually more concerned with the ordinary person. If the sermon was meant for saints, they must have been Jewish saints!

Jesus attempted to live by what he taught. He was not the kind of person to break the laws of the Torah casually. If he had in fact done so, it would have been deliberately and consciously, for what he believed to be a spiritual purpose consonant with the central aims of the Torah itself. Once we remove the misunderstandings and distortions of the later Gentile church from the record, there is no good evidence that he did so either deliberately or casually, whether in his actions or in his teaching.

But he did meet with opposition. We must now attempt to understand how this came about, and what there might have been in his words and actions to offend other faithful Jews, without entailing any breach with the Torah itself.

JESUS AND THE SINNERS

The Gospels tell us nothing at all of any opposition to Jesus arising from his teaching about a perfect human response to the divine perfection. If anyone found this un-Jewish at the time, their objections were not important enough to have been recorded. Although we have found this to be the most plausible reason for doubting Jesus' authentic Jewishness today, no such doubt seems to have arisen among his contemporaries. On the contrary, the Jewish criticisms that have survived seem to be based on the opposite charge: Jesus was accused of laxity in his dealings with sinners.

Jesus associated with sinners the devout would themselves have shunned and avoided. He was often in the company of such people and went to their parties. It was natural that he would be suspected of laxity in his own observance, since he associated so freely with people who were perhaps no longer observant at all. This, not imagined claims for messianic authority, or actual perfectionism in ethical teaching, is what disturbed some of his fellow Jews and brought Jesus into sharp controversy with them.

These controversies are very prominent in the Gospels, especially Mark and Matthew, and the reader is led to think that they were the principal cause of Jesus being brought to trial and condemned to death. At the same time, Jesus' opponents are identified as Pharisees.

This must have been a projection back into Jesus' lifetime of the situation of the later Church. By the time that the Gospels were written, the breach between the new Christian movement and its Jewish parent was gaping wide. The new movement was becoming increasingly a movement of Gentiles, and those Gentiles were not being taught to observe the Torah.

Within the Church, Jews were associating freely with nonobservant Gentiles. The two groups shared the same sacred meal, and their religious status was considered to be equal. These developments brought the Christian movement under increasingly severe criticism from Jews who had not accepted the messiahship of Jesus. By this time the leaders of the Jewish community were the successors of the Pharisees of Jesus' time, while other movements in the community had fallen into the background as a result of the loss of the Temple in the revolt against the Romans.

It would not be surprising if analogies were being drawn between the situation of Jesus, associating with the nonobservant sinners and criticized for it by the devout and the scholars, and that of the Church in the closing decades of the century, under sharp criticism from the Jewish leadership of the day in part because some of its Jewish members associated religiously with Gentiles who did not keep the Torah at all. On the other hand, the analogies must have been mostly false ones.

What were the real issues? Jesus taught that God is particularly near to the sinners, and he acted on his own teaching by attempting to imitate God, by being near to the sinners himself. He assumed that the sinners he addressed were already children of God by virtue of their membership in God's covenant people. But they were children who had gone astray, like the prodigal son and the lost sheep in the parables. If the sinner *returns* (as we have already seen, the word is a more exact translation of the usual Jewish words for repentance), it is to his father's house and to privileges that are part of his birthright.

Since Jesus never questions the standard teaching in his recorded sayings, we can assume that he took for granted the need for restitution and reconciliation in the case of sins against other people one had offended.[41] In fact, he expresses the same teaching in emphatic words of his own in Matthew 5:23f. He would likewise have known from childhood that sins against God were dealt with by repentance and by the rites of the Day of Atonement, Yom Kippur. Such offenses (so far as they could be distinguished from sins against the neighbor, which were also sins against God) were primarily, to use a modern distinction that might not have been familiar to Jesus, ritual rather than ethical in character.

There are no sayings in which Jesus calls it in question that God's forgiveness falls instantly upon the sinner's repentance, though other actions may be necessary before full reconciliation and restoration is effected. In his unquestionably authentic sayings, no sacrificial death of his own is in view, and it would be altogether inconsistent with his utterances on the subject to suppose that he thought for one moment that the forgiveness of sins had to wait upon his own death.

THE PRODIGAL SON

The important parables of the prodigal son and the Pharisee and the publican have been held by Christian interpreters to teach something previously unknown to Judaism. These, and other parables in the same group,[42] may well have had a controversial or polemical purpose. They tell stories whose central features may be "likened," as the Rabbis put it in their own parables, to those of the problem in contention. These parables must have been addressed to those who found Jesus' attitudes to sinners open to criticism and were intended decisively to rebut such criticism.

This group of parables teaches that God goes out to the sinners to bring them back, as the shepherd does with the sheep lost in the mountains. (Of course, for Jesus God is the good shepherd, as in Psalm 23, not himself. Jesus sees it as his own duty to imitate God.) The lost state of the sinners attracts the divine compassion in an especial degree, and there is corresponding rejoicing when they do return.

In the story somewhat misleadingly called the parable of the prodigal son, we hear of a father and his two sons, an elder one who is in every respect a good son to his father, and a younger one who has gone radically astray.[43] Christian interpretations have usually focused on the younger son, whose humility and repentance are thought to be the central theme of the story. The elder brother was cast as the representative of Jewish legalism. Later writers also focused on biblical contrasts between older and younger brothers, such as Esau and Jacob, seeing the church as typified by the younger brother and the Jewish people as the rejected elder brother.

However, the real "hero" of the story is not the younger son but the father. When the prodigal comes to his senses and returns to his father's household, the father is so delighted that he comes out to meet him, embraces him, cuts short his prepared speech of repentance, and makes an expensive feast for him. The elder brother is jealous of all this fuss over someone who has actually behaved very badly, pointing to his own record of continuous filial behavior, which has never met with a similar reward.

The father's answer to the elder brother's complaint is the pivot of a correct understanding of the parable. He draws attention to the most important fact in the situation for himself. The son who had been as good as dead is now alive, the one who had been lost is now found. The emotional logic of the father's reply is compelling, without in any way minimizing the former lost state of the repentant younger brother, or the previous good behavior of the elder brother.

In fact, his response to the complaint of the elder brother is as compassionate and tactful as his welcome to the younger. The elder son is always with him, and everything the father has is his also. A special celebration would add nothing. But it is right to rejoice when someone comes back from the dead.

The father's attitude makes perfect emotional sense. It also fits the Jewish attitude to sin and observance of the Torah, corresponding respectively to death and life. To be in the house of the father is to live by the life-giving commands of the Torah.

We should certainly not suppose that the parable teaches anything foreign to Judaism. There is a rabbinic parable on repentance that not only teaches the same lesson, but does so very similar terms, though with less literary elaboration.

> "God says to Israel, open to me a gate of repentance no bigger than the point of a needle, and I will open to you a gate of forgiveness wide enough to drive wagons and carts through." A king's son had traveled a hundred days' journey from his father. His friends advised him to return home, but he said, "I cannot, the trip is too long." Then his father sent him word, "Come back as far as your strength permits, and I will go to

meet you the rest of the way." Thus God says to Israel, "Return to Me, and I will return to you" (Mal. 3:7)[44]

In Christian tradition, the parable has often been interpreted as a radical criticism of Judaism: the younger brother is seen as a symbol of Christianity, relying in faith on divine forgiveness, the elder brother of Judaism, relying on legalistic righteousness. Once we dismiss subsequent interpretations, ancient and modern, one fact comes clearly into view. The attitude of the father to his sons, a humanly possible if perhaps not common one, is meant to constitute the central analogy of the parable. Jesus' hearers are meant to learn from him, not from the younger son. They are not meant to condemn the elder son, who is humanly jealous of all the fuss being made of his brother, who does not deserve it, as he sees it. The elder brother has good reason for thinking he is the more deserving of the two.

If we do not share his view, we fail to see the force of the parable, and the paradox it is meant to bring home to us. The answer of the father to the elder brother asserts the paradox, while making clear that it is a paradox and not a simple idea, except emotionally. This is not legal reasoning or theology but emotional logic, unassailable on its own level. The elder brother is not diminished for his record of obedience and service to the father; he is given full credit for it. He is simply gently rebuked for failing to share in the father's generous-hearted rejoicing.

The parable fits very well as an answer to the charge of welcoming sinners and eating with them, since this is what the father in the parable does. The defense is a powerful one: the clear implication is that Jesus is imitating God when he welcomes sinners. Jesus wants his hearers to see that his own attitude to sinners resembles that of the father in the story, while the father in turn clearly stands for God.

In that case, the elder brother must represent Jesus' opponents, as most interpreters agree. But the critics are also not assailed, as later Christian interpreters supposed, for Jewish legalism and self-righteousness, but simply for failure to rise to the level of God's own compassion for sinners. They are not told that they have misunderstood God's commandments when they themselves observed the Torah, or that they are not members of God's household in good standing.

THE PHARISEE AND THE PUBLICAN

The story of the Pharisee and the tax collector, or publican, illustrates the same paradox, though in this story God does not have a human counterpart.[45] Two men go up to the Temple to pray. One is a very observant Pharisee, the other a tax collector for the Roman occupiers of the land. In this case too, the parable loses its force if we do not take the initial contrast between the two men seriously. Once again, the contrast has often been taken by Christian interpreters to represent a contrast between Jewish and Christian life principles. On the other hand, precisely because it does seem to lend itself rather readily to this kind of interpretation, its authenticity has been suspected by a number of critics. However, such an interpretation is not demanded by the text, and it is likely to be wrong.

The Pharisees, as we have seen, were held in great respect by the community. The tax collector, on the other hand, belonged to a group deservedly disliked and despised. The tax collectors not only collaborated with the pagan occupiers but they made a profit out of doing so as well. No wonder they were classed with the sinners, those who no longer attempted to live by the Torah.

The Pharisee, seeing the tax collector, starts to compare himself with him. In his prayer he thanks God that he observes the sanctifying commandments of the Torah, not even taking the credit for himself. He also mentions some of his extra, voluntary observances, peculiar to his own group. The tax collector does not even dare to lift up his eyes to heaven. He can only say, "God be merciful to me a sinner." Yet, says Jesus, it was the tax collector rather than the Pharisee who returned home justified.

Is there anything un-Jewish in the teaching of this parable, or even an attack on Pharisees as such? Did Jesus perhaps regard the inner repentance of the tax collector and his total trust in the divine mercy, apparently unaccompanied by the outward actions required by the Torah, as superior to the combination of inner repentance and outward acts always upheld by traditional Judaism? Examining Jesus' attitude toward the Torah in the Sermon on the Mount has already led us to be skeptical of such wellworn explanations.

The great value of repentance in the eyes of God was a favorite theme of the Rabbis, and it continues to be central for their successors up to the present. The Talmud tractate Berakoth has a famous saying, quoted (for example) by the great Chief Rabbi of mandatory Palestine, Abraham Isaac Kook, in his own remarkable treatise on repentance, that closely parallels Jesus' teaching in the parable: "In the place where the penitents stand, even the fully righteous are unworthy to stand."[46] A much later saying from a Hasidic master comes even closer to the parable: "Better a sinner who knows he is a sinner than a righteous man who knows he is righteous."[47] There is no reason to suppose that these examples from post-biblical Judaism do not reflect the outlook of Jesus' time, since the later teachers, like Jesus, derived their insights from the Bible.

The most natural interpretation of the parable would therefore be to assume that Jesus meant to teach essentially the same lesson as the later saying in Berakoth. He expressed in a parable the same teaching as the later Rabbi expressed in a brief but rich saying. We can therefore assume that the Pharisees would have agreed with him heartily. God's nearness to the sinner reaches its natural fulfillment when the sinner repents from the heart. The righteous man who has not struggled to repent does not know the same intimate experience of divine compassion. We should not read more into the parable than it says.

JESUS AND THE PHARISEES

The Gospels almost certainly do reproduce authentic memories of serious disputes between Jesus and other Jews. However, to understand them correctly, we must learn to see these disputes as Jewish ones, internal to Jewish faith. Jesus and his opponents, whoever they were, disagreed on what God, the giver of the Torah, meant about the way sinners were to be approached and encouraged to repent.

In fact, once we dismiss the later mythology, we can easily see that the stories of conflict between Jesus and his contemporaries have all the marks of a typical Jewish dispute, including the tough language used on both sides. Debate, even dispute, is normal in Judaism. The Talmud is largely a record of legal debate and interpretation of laws whose authority all sides accept. It seldom records conclusions. Jews will even debate with God. Thus, disagreement with other Jews in itself is far from representing rejection of Judaism as such, on the one side, or exclusion of the opponent from the community, on the other.

Was the dispute one between Jesus and the Pharisees as such? We have seen no reason to think so. Mark, and especially Matthew, represent opposition from the Pharisees as leading to a religious trial before the Sanhedrin, resulting in Jesus' condemnation for blasphemy. The religious leaders are then depicted as manipulating the Romans to get him executed. Conflict on these issues was ultimately responsible, according to these writers, for Jesus' death.

We have here the germ of the myth that the Jews killed Christ. So crucial is the issue for the subsequent development of Christian anti-Judaism and antisemitism that we must take time to look at it with extreme care.

In fact, it is not easy to find anywhere in the gospel stories of conflict between Jesus and other Jews convincing evidence that the issues actually turned on views distinctive to the Pharisees. Vermes, Sanders, and others have shown that it is improbable that Jesus actually differed from the Pharisees, still less Jews in general, on issues such as Sabbath observance and the dietary laws.[48]

While Jesus did heal on the Sabbath, and he may have been criticized for doing so, on those occasions he is shown as healing by word alone, or at most by laying on of hands, neither of which constituted work. The plucking of corn on Shabbat was actually allowed by the school of Hillel, and their view became the halachah. Jesus' own defense of the action, as recorded in the Gospels, is based on the principle laid down by the Pharisees themselves, that a Sabbath law may and must be breached, if there is danger to life, even somewhat remote.

Mark (almost certainly incorrectly) actually represents Jesus as purporting to abrogate the dietary laws.[49] The issue of nonkosher food could hardly have been a live one in an exclusively Jewish culture, in which it was not normally available. It was very much a live one for later Christianity, where the Gentile church had abandoned the dietary laws along with the rest of the Torah, but may well have been under severe criticism for doing so, both from Jewish Christians and continuing Jews.

EATING WITH SINNERS

The gospels do tell us that Jesus ran into severe opposition because of his practice of eating with sinners, and we have just seen that parables such as the prodigal son may have been a defense of this practice. Christian theologians often say that Jesus specifically and deliberately broke the rules of the Torah when he ate with the sinners. In doing so, he is supposed to have acted on a higher spiritual principle than Jewish "legalism," deliberately incurring impurity by associating with them in "table fellowship," and becoming a sinner himself. According to these theologians, Jesus' identification with the sinners to the point of becoming technically a sinner himself, overturned the legal regulations of the Torah, replacing them with the new principle of grace.

We have seen that there was no such conflict of principle between Jesus and Judaism. Once the mythical conflict over Jewish legalism has been ruled out, we are left with a technical question about purity rules. Was a Jew in fact forbidden to eat with sinners on pain of contracting impurity and even sin? To infringe a purity rule does not make one a sinner (except in certain cases, such as the laws of family purity). It leads to impurity, a condition lasting a specified length of time, and removable by specified measures. Impurity simply means unfitness to take part in the Temple liturgy. It is not synonymous with sin. Sometimes the Torah actually requires one to acquire impurity, as in the case of the burial of a relative, since contact with a corpse renders one impure. Even if Jesus had contracted impurity by eating with sinners, that would not in itself have made him a sinner.

Would he actually have contracted impurity from eating with them? Even this seems unlikely. Certain groups, known as *haverim,* bound themselves voluntarily to observe certain additional purity regulations normally binding only upon the priests. Some leading scholars believe that these haverim were identical with the Pharisees. Such voluntary restrictions may (though this is not certain) have included a prohibition on eating with members of certain other groups, those regarded as sinners because of the laxity of their observance, or more broadly with anyone not observing the same purity restrictions as the haverim themselves.

Since such restrictions went beyond the actual requirements of the Torah, they could not oblige anyone who had not taken on the same rules. Jesus did not belong to such a group, and he was not bound by their restrictions. Competent scholars such as Sanders have been unable to find any universally obligatory purity rules forbidding the practice of eating with sinners.

Jesus could not have committed any offense against the Torah by eating with sinners. He could not even have incurred impurity by doing so unless he had been (as he was not in fact) a member of a group that obliged itself to extra purity regulations.

Eating with sinners, therefore, in itself could not possibly have led to a conflict between Jesus and other Jews so severe as to be the basis for the eventual split between Christianity and Judaism. Was there anything at all in Jesus' actions or teaching on which the subsequent split could have been based? Beyond doubt, if so, the gospel writers would have preserved memories of conflict between Jesus and all other Jews–not just Pharisees–on fundamental issues, touching the Torah itself. For that, we will look in vain, even in the Gospels.

In that case, it will be impossible to ground the later split between two religions in the actions and intentions of Jesus. Not only is it no longer acceptable to base

Christian anti-Judaism on the supposed teaching of Jesus, the whole connection between Jesus and later Gentile Christianity, which abandoned the Torah, now turns out to be exceedingly tenuous.

JESUS' CRITICISMS OF OTHER JEWS

While Jesus himself was under criticism in these disputes, he also had strong criticisms of his own to make against certain other Jews. There is good reason to distrust reports of Jesus accusing Pharisees as such of hypocrisy, but we cannot necessarily write off as inauthentic all those passages in which Jesus is represented as denouncing others for hypocrisy or other forms of spiritual error. Many of these sayings are too characteristic of Jesus' own attitudes, as we know them from generally accepted texts, to be easily abandoned. If we retain them as authentic, we must find a convincing target for Jesus' vehement criticisms.

The question of authenticity must also turn on a literary judgment. Do these passages cohere with a general picture of Jesus and the kind of things he said? I must say that reluctantly or otherwise I do recognize in these intensely angry sayings (cf. Grant[50]) a strongly personal voice, which I can regard as the same as we hear in the generally accepted sayings of Jesus.

I also consider that in these sayings, angry and conceivably unfair as they are, there is nothing more than one Jew might say of another. Even if these sayings were uttered as they stand, they could not legitimately be used as the basis of a Christian critique of Judaism. They must have been one Jew's criticisms of other Jews, who, it seems, were equally critical of him. Historians need not share the theological interpretation of these passages as a divine condemnation of God's apostate people.

Jesus certainly could not have been criticizing other Jews for observing the Torah, since he observed it himself. Nevertheless, something important was at stake in an argument with actual opponents. What was it? If the opponents were not Pharisees as such, who were they, and what did they stand for?

JESUS' OPPONENTS

While it is not possible to discover in the reports of these disputes evidence of conflict between Jesus and Pharisees on issues connected with the distinctive tenets of the Pharisaic party, we cannot conclude that none of Jesus' opponents were Pharisees. Jesus was not the only Jewish teacher to lay his finger on the spiritual perils of piety. The Pharisees themselves were remarkably perceptive at doing so, and their own self-criticism provides an illuminating parallel to the sayings in the Gospels.

As Emil Fackenheim has pointed out, Pharisaic self-criticism surpasses in thoroughness and comprehensiveness the criticism embodied in the New Testament. He quotes from Herbert Loewe (coauthor with C. G. Montefiore of *A Rabbinic*

Anthology) a collection of such criticisms Loewe assembled, in the form of a classification of Pharisees by members of their own movement:[51]

> (1) The shoulder Pharisee (who carries his good deeds on his shoulder ostentatiously; or, according to another interpretation, tries to rid himself of the commandments); (2) the sit-a-while Pharisee (who says, "wait until I have done this good deed"); (3) the bruised Pharisee (who breaks his head against a wall to avoid looking at a woman); (4) the pestle Pharisee (whose head is bent in mock humility, like a pestle in a mortar); (5) the book-keeping Pharisee (who calculates virtue against vice, or who sins deliberately, and then attempts to compensate for his sin by some good deed); (6) the God-fearing Pharisee, who is like Job; (7) the God-loving Pharisee who is like Abraham. (The last two categories of course represent those approved of.)

If this is how the most perceptive Pharisees thought of spiritual aberrations within their own ranks, clearly these aberrations cannot have been characteristic of their movement as such. Jesus' rather similar criticisms of the pious, even if directed at individual Pharisees, could no more have been aimed at the whole movement than the internal criticisms assembled by Loewe.

Such distortions of piety are not likely to have been the monopoly of Pharisees, though it is possible that their well-known zeal for observance attracted people of a compulsive and obsessive temperament, who would be inclined to concentrate all their energies on correct observance instead of looking to the spiritual goals that observance was intended to promote.

In fact, if we must suppose that Jesus was addressing his vivid criticisms to any identifiable group at all, it would hardly be the Pharisees but the excessively zealous in any of the movements of the time. For that matter, it would be exceptionally prejudiced to assume that pious aberrations like these are more characteristic of Judaism than of Christianity.

Whoever they were individually, Pharisees or otherwise, Jesus' opponents seem to have had something in common with some of the ultra-Orthodox, or *Haredim* (literally, fearers of God) in Israel today. These are zealots for the strictest interpretation of the Torah, many of whom are eager to encourage or even compel others to live by their own standard of observance, in order to ward off divine wrath from the community at large. They are the people who stone cars driven by secular Israelis on the Sabbath. Paul informs us that he was himself such a zealot before his conversion to the new Christian movement.

Zealous individuals such as these seem always to have been present, in larger or smaller numbers, in the Jewish people. They themselves usually take their stand on the story of Phinehas in Numbers 25. If not every Pharisee was a sage, neither was every Pharisee a zealot of the type that fell foul of Jesus.

What then could Jesus have had against such zealots, if these were the target of his criticism? Essentially Jesus seems to charge his opponents with lack of correspondence between inner attitudes and outward behavior, neglect of the interior dimension of the Torah. The charge lends its sting to the accusation of hypocrisy, even if the actual language may have been conventional.

According to Jesus, outward correctness of behavior in relation to women does not guarantee freedom from mental lust.[52] One can be expert in avoiding impurity from corpses while being just like a whitewashed tomb, impressively pure on the outside but on the inside full of impurity and dead men's bones.[53] Keeping the dietary laws with meticulous care does not guarantee freedom from the much more dangerous defilement of the polluted mind.[54]

In these sayings, Jesus does not suggest that the outward commandment is not necessary or should not be kept. The prophets used similar language about the Temple sacrifices and other observances. Only the Gentile church, which had abandoned the Torah, needed to see them as condemning the observances as such. But his words were offensive to such zealous individuals, whatever their party, and they were presumably intended to be.

JESUS AND THE ZEALOUS

Jesus put love before fear. He saw repentance and trust in God as Father as the heart of all religious acts, regarding the mitzvot as the necessary outward expression of this inner turning toward God. Thus, like some of the Pharisaic sages, he was able to see a hierarchy of importance in the commandments. He refers to the weightier matters of the Law, implying that there are others that may be regarded by contrast as less weighty.[55]

When Hillel was asked to state the essence of the Torah while standing on one leg, he replied, "Do not do to your neighbor what is hateful to you. The rest is commentary. Go and learn."[56] When Jesus was asked a similar question, he gave a similar reply, citing the Shema, the prayer that every observant Jew says twice a day, "Hear, O Israel, the Lord our God, the Lord is one, and you shall love the Lord your God with all your heart and all your soul and all your strength." Alongside the Shema he placed the commandment from Leviticus, "You shall love your neighbor as yourself." His learned questioner, perhaps a Pharisee himself, reckoned it a good answer, not surprisingly, since Jesus' summary also closely parallels several others recorded in the Talmud from Pharisaic teachers.[57]

Again like some of the sages, Jesus interpreted the Sabbath humanistically, when he said that the Sabbath was made for man, not man for the Sabbath.[58] Other controversies on Sabbath observance and fasting refer to the behavior of the disciples, not Jesus' own. There are complaints that the disciples did not fast, or wash their hands before meals. It is extremely unlikely that either Jesus or the disciples omitted the fast on Yom Kippur. What is referred to is more probably voluntary fasts, not yet universally required, but favored perhaps by the Pharisees. The implication in the Gospels is that Jesus himself did observe them, as in the case of the custom, promoted by the Pharisees, but apparently not yet generally recognized as a commandment, of washing the hands before eating.

It may occur to anyone that Jesus might have been involved in breaking the dietary laws, if the sinners he ate with did not observe them themselves. However, this issue is not mentioned in the Gospels, and presumably it did not arise. It was at the level of fundamental attitudes that Jesus and his opponents were far apart; this difference made some form of clash inevitable. Jesus probably understood the issue better than his opponents did, and it is entirely possible that they tried to find fault with him at the wrong level, his observance, without success.

JESUS' REAL OFFENSE

The echoes in the Gospels of disputes about Sabbath observance, hand washing, fasting, and so forth, likewise do not display much understanding of the real issues. The major cause of Jesus' offense in the eyes of his opponents lay elsewhere. As we have already seen, he was undoubtedly charged with associating with sinners. It is not at all difficult to suppose that the zealous people just described would have been deeply scandalized by Jesus' habit of going to parties with tax collectors and other sinners, and above all by such incidents as one in which he permitted a repentant prostitute to kiss his feet, anoint him with costly ointment, doubtless paid for by her immoral earnings, and wipe his feet with her hair.[59] If we assume that the rabbinic etiquette about association with women, even women of good reputation, in any way reflects the attitude of the zealous in Jesus' time, we will have no difficulty in picturing their extreme outrage.[60]

In any period and in any religion, this sort of behavior would have been considered scandalous by the devout, who often consider that the best way to bring sinners to repentance is to ostracize them and certainly not to join in their parties. If these are thought inadequate grounds of offense, because they do not involve an actual breach of Torah, is not this because scholars are looking for an offense great enough to have led to a condemnation of Jesus by the Sanhedrin, which in all probability never took place, while underestimating the shock caused by his unconventional behavior?[61]

JESUS IMITATED GOD

Jesus defended his own actions on a fully accepted principle, the imitation of God, generally regarded as the foundation of ethics by Jewish teachers. He gave additional point to his claim by means of parables that drove home the paradox with which we began this part of the chapter, that God is so compassionate that he is nearest of all to those who are farthest from him. This prophetic but paradoxical insight was of central importance to Jesus and his own understanding of his mission.

Jesus' endeavor to imitate God in his approach to sinners has been twisted into divine condemnation of Judaism, instead of being seen, correctly, as the actions of one faithful Jew, giving scandal to other faithful Jews by the way in which he attempted to emulate the paradoxical compassion of God. The controversy between Jesus and his opponents has nothing to do with those matters that have genuinely divided Christians and Jews. Nor is there good evidence for the belief, common in older scholarship, that eating with sinners evoked such a degree of religious hostility to Jesus that it led to his death.

If Jesus' opponents had had good reason to believe that in such actions he had wished to overthrow the very basis of the Torah, they would have been justified in proceeding against him in a religious court and seeking the death penalty. But we have found no grounds for supposing that they would have had any justification for such a charge. It is noteworthy that the gospel accounts of Jesus' trial do not mention this issue, though there are, as we shall see, other reasons for regarding the trial stories as a whole as unhistorical.

"LET THE DEAD BURY THEIR DEAD"

The Gospels record one occasion when Jesus appears to advise a potential follower to disregard a provision of the Torah. One of those he called to follow him in proclaiming the kingdom is said to have replied: "Let me first go and bury my father." Jesus replied, "You follow me and let the dead bury their dead."[62]

The saying must be genuine, since it is as shocking to Gentile as to Jewish sensibilities. The duty of burying the dead was universally accepted in the ancient world as among the most sacred of all. Sanders argues that at least on this occasion Jesus was prepared to override a provision of the Torah, showing that he did not regard the Torah as absolutely binding or final.[63] Vermes, on the other hand, merely sees in the saying one of Jesus' characteristic rhetorical exaggerations. In the kingdom the dead will be looked after by the dead.[64]

Neither of these interpretations seems so compelling that we need not consider alternatives. The text does not say that there was no other member of the family available to carry out the duty of burial. On the contrary, it implies that there were others, but they were unlikely to respond to Jesus' call. Such people could therefore be described as spiritually dead. The obligation to bury the physically dead fell on the spiritually dead, while the living must hear the call of the kingdom.

What is emphasized in the incident is the critical urgency of responding to the opportunity of proclaiming God's kingship. Jews are required to bury the dead as soon as possible after death, normally on the same day. The delay requested by the mourner was most likely one of a few hours. Even this short delay was intolerable to Jesus. He may (as is often supposed) have perceived the request as an excuse for refusal of the call.

Either way, Jesus' words are shocking, and certainly not typical of Jewish attitudes toward the dead. He must at least have considered that this was an instance where one obligation overrode another that would normally have been binding. Possibly, however, leaving the burial of one's father to someone else, even failing to take part in the customary period of family mourning, did not amount to a clear breach of the Torah if (as appears to be the case) other family members were available to carry out the primary duty of burial.

If so, Jesus' words would not bear on the issue of prompt and careful burial.

Rather, they would bear on family obligations. To leave the burial of a father to others would most certainly be a serious breach of what was universally expected of a son. It indicates, to put it mildly, that Jesus had an unusual attitude toward family obligations and ties.

There is plenty of other evidence in the Gospels, often unnoticed, that this attitude was in fact Jesus' own. It is an attitude with few parallels in the history of religions, except where monasticism is involved, as was never the case in Judaism. Generally speaking, religions lay a strong emphasis upon family obligations and the integrity and continuity of the family. Certainly, both Judaism and Christianity (apart from the latter's advocacy of monasticism for a minority) do. Jesus may have regarded family loyalty as a potential barrier to full response to God.

"HATING" ONE'S FAMILY

In another certainly authentic saying, Jesus said, "If anyone comes to me and does not hate his father and his mother and his wife and children and even his own life, he cannot be my disciple."[65] The words were obviously not intended to be taken literally, nor could they be, for a person who literally hated his own life would be a depressive or a suicide. Such a person could not share the Jewish regard for life as the highest value. Nor was Jesus an ascetic, like so many Christians who have attempted to imitate what they suppose to have been his way of life.

Rather, we seem to be meeting with an idiomatic expression. Jesus may have been speaking about priorities, not emotional attitudes. "Loving" God seems to mean putting him first, choosing him as the first priority. "Hating" members of one's family need not mean having an aversion to them, but putting loyalty to them second to the call of the kingdom. Such words were addressed specifically to those capable of hearing the call to the righteousness of the kingdom and the special way of life that went with proclaiming it to the people.

Elsewhere, we find Jesus commending to the young man in search of perfection the commandment to honor one's father and mother. Whatever he meant by "hating" must presumably have been compatible with obeying the commandment to honor the parents.[66] Moreover, his teaching on marriage and divorce does not imply that he thought these bonds of no importance. Nevertheless, this is a revolutionary saying for Judaism or any other religion.

For a Jew of the first century, the only model for such an attitude to the family would have been the prophet. Prophets were then believed to have undertaken celibacy as the outcome of their unique prophetic calling.[67] We do not know whether Jesus was himself a celibate, or (as we should expect) had a wife, unmentioned in the gospel tradition, whom he too had left at home. In any case, the prophets themselves did not suggest that others should hold family ties lightly.

Jesus seems to have believed that attachments to family would hold a person back from the inner freedom essential for total surrender to God's kingly rule. Some of Jesus' disciples actually did renounce family ties, without however breaking off all relationships, so far as we can judge from the cases of Peter, James, and John, the only ones of whom we know anything relevant. We also read of followers of Jesus who had renounced family ties being told that they would be rewarded a hundred times over in the kingdom of God.[68]

Jesus' attitude toward the family, which as the same saying shows is intended to apply to all natural communities, is another indication that he had no intention of founding a new religion. He was evidently not interested in making new rules for the maintenance of an ordered society, as religious legislators must be.

What is unusual in his teaching, in the general context of Judaism, seems to be accounted for by his sense of the crisis provoked by the nearness of God and the possible imminence of the messianic age if Israel would respond appropriately to that nearness. The man who invoked the duty of burying his father in order to refuse Jesus' call had allowed a religious duty, in itself fully valid but still relative, to stand in the way of an absolute, the spiritual demand of the kingdom of God, here embodied in Jesus' own call to discipleship. Even so, it is surprising that the Gospels record no criticism of this remarkable claim.

DID JESUS "DIE FOR THE GOSPEL"?

In view of what we have so far discovered, there is no need to invoke the explanation of modern German theologians that Jesus "died for the gospel." According to them, his teaching on divine forgiveness was so novel and unwelcome to the Jewish religious authorities that they could not tolerate it, and they were forced to engineer his death. His teaching about divine grace is supposed to have been fundamentally opposed to Jewish legalism. The idea that there must have been any such radical opposition now seems to be demanded by theological prejudice, not sound scholarship. It should be abandoned completely, for good and all. Jesus may not have been a typical Jew, but beyond reasonable doubt he was a faithful and observant one.

Jesus did not die for the Christian gospel, or for any new religious principle, nor was his death the result of Jewish opposition to his teaching. Giving scandal to the pious is one thing, and committing a capital offense against the Torah itself is quite another. It is not realistically possible to find good evidence of such a religious offense in anything Jesus is reported to have taught or done. We must now consider whether Jesus claimed to be the Messiah and whether such a claim could have led to his death.

3

Jesus the Jew: 3. Crucified Messiah?

We are already close to being able to answer the question we set out to answer in these opening chapters: is the myth of the Christ-killing Jews true? We can say with assurance that Jesus did not found the Christian church, and that (as Wellhausen said long ago) he was "no Christian but a Jew."[1] He had no intention of starting even a sect, still less a new world religion. His teaching was not a new and "Christian" teaching, but a personal interpretation of the common Jewish faith, intended as preparation for the coming of the kingdom of God. As we are about to see, he did not claim to be the Jewish Messiah, either in the normal sense or in some new sense later to be enshrined in Christian theology, and he was not rejected by the Jewish people for making such a claim. His vision of the nearness of God illuminated all he said and did, and he believed anyone else could share it, if they would turn to God in total trust, as he had. He would have been astonished and horrified by his own later divinization by the Church.[2]

Jesus belongs essentially to Judaism and only accidentally to Christianity. There is real continuity between all he stood for and the Jewish faith. Between Jesus and Christianity there is discontinuity. The Jesus Christ of historic Christianity is not the Jesus of history. He is a product of the mythmaking mind, basing itself upon historical mistakes and misunderstandings, and even upon some falsifications of history, ultimately shaped by a revolutionary and untraditional reading of the Jewish Scriptures. Christianity did not start with Jesus, but with his followers after his death.

The historical person will emerge from our brief inquiry with his spiritual stature undiminished, perhaps even enhanced. To see Jesus as a human being, wrestling with realistic inner and outer problems, can only lead us to admire the way in which he overcame them. However, one problem he could not overcome: the misplaced enthusiasm of his own followers. This, not Jewish rejection, led to his death. Was his death then a tragedy, without redemptive meaning? From a Jewish point of view, it could be seen as the martyrdom of a righteous man, and therefore, according to the Pharisaic doctrine shared by his followers, of atoning efficacy for the sins of others.

The religious value of the myth is not our present concern. In a subsequent chapter, I will consider its future in the light of these findings. What matters at this point is to show that there can be no basis in the historical Jesus, so far as critical scholarship is able to recover his picture from the sources, for the traditional assertions that he came to pronounce a divine judgment on faithless Jewry, bringing to an end the role of the Jewish people as God's covenant partner and condemning them to the status of homeless wanderers until the end of the world.

Such ideas have nothing to do with the real Jesus. In him we find only affirmation of the Jewish people and the Jewish faith, never condemnation or replacement by another people and another faith. Whatever may be the basis for traditional Christian faith and Christian theology, it cannot be found in the historical Jesus. If Jesus is nevertheless an authority for Christians, that authority can never be rightly invoked to justify Christian anti-Judaism, let alone antisemitism. The only form of religious life for which Jesus' authority could rightly be invoked is observant Judaism. So much is already clear.

The myth tells a very different story, and it is the myth that has governed the thoughts and actions of Christians down the centuries. According to the myth, the Jews killed Christ when he came to them. Although he was the divine Messiah so clearly predicted in their own Scriptures, they would not accept the new, more spiritual teaching he brought from God, clinging to their old materialistic expectations and to the letter of their now obsolete Law. So they conspired to kill him, and because they were not able to do so themselves persuaded the Romans, against their will, to crucify him. They broke their covenant with God, compelling him to make a new one, sealed in the blood of Christ, and uniting all believers in him, while excluding the apostate Jews. In the myth, the Jews are Christ-killers.[3]

The evidence considered in the previous chapter shows that Jesus brought no revolutionary new teaching, contrary to or superseding the Torah. His people did not reject him because he healed the sick or pronounced God's forgiveness to sinners, though some of his fellow Jews were unquestionably scandalized by the freedom with which he associated with the sinners in his endeavor to imitate God by being near to them.

We have still to examine the charge that they, or their leaders, rejected him because he was, and proclaimed himself to be, the Messiah of the Jews, and that he was crucified as such. If this charge also turns out to lack historical basis, there will be no alternative to dismissing altogether the myth of the Christ-killers.

What did Jews mean by the Messiah in Jesus' time? Did Jesus fit their expectation of the predicted redeemer? Could a Jew have believed himself to be the Messiah if he thought of his own mission in the way Jesus did? How could anyone have come to believe that Jesus was the Messiah if he made at most only the ambiguous claims the Gospels record?

We must also examine the claim of the myth that Jesus, though not the expected Messiah, was nevertheless the Messiah in fact, because the Messiah the Jews expected had never been the one God intended to send them. All Jews, including the earliest leaders of the Christian movement, themselves Jews, knew that the Messiah was not expected to suffer. Only by making this revolutionary claim could they maintain that Jesus, who did suffer and die, was nevertheless the expected Messiah of the Jewish people.

Some scholars are beginning to argue that the belief that Jesus was the Messiah played less part in early Christianity than is commonly supposed. Perhaps Paul had really already abandoned the idea, when he began to use the title Christ (the Greek translation of Messiah) freely as a proper name, a kind of surname for Jesus. There are some grounds for thinking that the earliest of the gospel writers, Mark, already regarded Jesus as Son of God and Son of Man, rather than the Messiah. These suggestions come especially from scholars of good will toward Judaism and the Jewish people; they are perhaps intended in part to reduce the opposition between Jewish and Christian ideas of the Messiah.

However, the fact is that nothing was so firmly rooted in early Christianity, and in almost every movement or sect within it, as the belief that Jesus was the Messiah. Although the idea did not initially mean much to Gentiles, who did not expect any Messiah, it was retained by Gentile Christianity and carefully taught to those under instruction. The necessity of retaining it played a major part in the decision of the Church to keep the Jewish Bible in its Scriptures as the Old Testament, under challenge from those who emphasized the utter novelty of Christianity.[4] In the Bible the Church found the proof-texts from which it argued that the suffering Messiah had actually been predicted in advance and that the Jews had rejected Jesus because they failed to understand the plain teaching of their own Scriptures.

Above all, Jesus was known everywhere as Christ, and Christ meant Messiah, although the title soon attracted to itself fresh theological content, as belief in his divinity began to grow and spread. The complete and unchallengeable fixity of the title Christ in all forms of Christianity is sufficient evidence that it was rooted in the earliest and most universal Christian tradition. Without the belief that Jesus was the Messiah, there would have been no Christianity at all.

Among all the images of Jesus, that of the suffering Messiah, the son of God who atoned for the sins of the world on the cross, is perhaps the most dear to the greatest number of Christians. Yet this image still causes the greatest difficulties between Jews and Christians, and it has led to deep-seated Christian hostility toward Jews. Some other ideas about Jesus' identity and mission do not necessarily set Christians and Jews against each other. This does, though, because the claim that he was the suffering Messiah has been rejected by Jews for their own good reasons.

Jews believed then, as those who have retained the ancient expectation still do, in a real, historical figure who will bring about a historical deliverance. He was expected to free the land from pagan occupation, restoring the full observance of the Torah, and bringing in a new era of universal peace and righteousness. Jews have never expected the Messiah to suffer and die in order to bring about a spiritual and other-worldly redemption, while leaving the course of actual history unchanged until his return to earth in glory. Christianity has claimed that its Christ is more spiritual than the Jewish Messiah, stigmatizing the hope of historical redemption as materialistic by contrast.

JEWISH MESSIANIC EXPECTATION

Since the main body of the Jewish people has always rejected the new reading of the Hebrew Scriptures, it is natural to ask what texts the standard messianic interpretation was itself based on. The question turns out to be unexpectedly difficult to answer. There is no doubt, however, about the principal sources of messianic thinking.

Its ultimate origin is the central Jewish concept of the covenant. God will always be faithful to His covenant promises, and He will in the end redeem Israel, even in spite of human unfaithfulness. The concept of redemption, that is, historical, not other-worldly, redemption, underlies and is prior to the concept of the Messiah. The concept of historical redemption is wholly biblical. The Messiah is not spoken of unequivocally in the Bible. Redemption is.

The second source of messianic thinking seems to be reflection on the divine promises to the dynasty of David. The central and prevalent concept of the Messiah in Judaism regards him as a scion of the house of David, in whom these promises will be fulfilled. The Messiah is a righteous and victorious king descended from David. The word *Messiah* itself is simply a transliteration of the Hebrew word meaning anointed. The king was inaugurated in his office by being anointed with oil.

First and foremost, then, the Messiah is a king in the tradition of David. Other concepts of the Messiah, such as a priestly or a prophetic Messiah, found in sectarian literature, are clearly later developments from this central notion. Even those variants still link the Messiah firmly to the covenant promise of redemption.[5]

Messianic expectation in early Judaism seems to have grown up in the period after the last books of the Hebrew canon were composed, but before the canon had been closed. The first sign of the new concept is generally thought to have appeared in the late book of Daniel, probably one of the last biblical books to be written. Our main evidence for the early stages of the development of the concept comes from literature on the fringe of the Bible that did not become accepted into the final version of the canon, the so-called Apocrypha and Pseudepigrapha.

The authors of these books did not always feel the necessity to cite biblical texts in support of their ideas, although in fact they were developments and expansions of hints in the Bible itself. The concept of the Messiah continued to develop in Judaism after the Christian movement began. Some aspects of messianic teaching in the Talmudic texts may even reflect later Christian developments.

Central texts for the expectation of the Messiah seem to have been Isaiah 11 and Psalm 18, apparently inspired by that chapter, which explicitly mentions God's anointed (*meshiach* in Hebrew) in the title and in verses 6 and 8. Psalm 17 also refers to the coming of the son of David. Other texts sometimes employed are Genesis

49:10 and Numbers 24:7 and 17, and from the Prophets, in addition to Isaiah 11, Zechariah 3:8.

In the oldest and most central synagogue prayer, the Eighteen Blessings, sometimes called *the* Prayer, *ha-tefillah*, the Messiah is regarded as a King and the son of David. This is the only concept of the Messiah sufficiently universally accepted to have found its way into the common liturgy. The prayer is thought to have been already in use in the first century, and may therefore have been known to and used by Jesus himself and his followers.

HOW CHRISTOLOGY WAS ANTI-JEWISH

The early Christians maintained that Christ had suffered and died to bring about a spiritual transformation of the world. This transformation, real but hidden, would become manifest in history only upon the return of Christ. If they wished to maintain at the same time that Jesus was the Messiah, as they did, they must also claim that this novel messianic role had been predicted in Scripture, the ultimate source of the regular expectation. The Scriptures had "really" pointed to a suffering Messiah all along. If so, the Jewish people had always been wrong in expecting a conquering king. Such an error must have serious implications.

Years before any of the Gospels were written, Paul was already arguing that when the Jews read the Scriptures there was a veil over their faces, preventing them from seeing the true meaning of what they read.[6] At the root of the split between Christianity and Judaism is a struggle for possession of the Jewish Scriptures, centering on the role of the Messiah. If Jesus was the Jewish Messiah, his life and death, and subsequent resurrection, had to have been predicted in the Scriptures. If they were, Jews do not know how to read their own Bible. If they were not, Christianity as history has known it is either an illusion, or something altogether novel, unprepared in the Bible, as the heretic Marcion argued in the second century. These implications cannot be escaped.

Historical claims can be examined by critical methods. Present-day critical students of the Hebrew Bible, including large numbers of Christian scholars, do not consider the particular texts on which the church has relied to be messianic in their original meaning and context. But this need not necessarily prevent theologians from arguing that in addition to their literal meaning, which critical scholarship can perhaps determine, the texts have a prophetic significance theology alone can assess.

I have defined my critical task in this inquiry as belonging to religious studies, or the history of religions, not to theology. Perhaps not all our questions can be solved outside the sphere of theology, but many can. In the end, however, we shall have to come to theology and evaluate theological claims on their own ground.

LANGUAGE AND SOCIETY

Without entering at this stage into a theological debate, we can say something about the proper use of language in such a discussion. Human language has no absolute meaning. We cannot say what words "really" mean, especially in a religious context. Language derives its meaning from its historical and social matrix. Words only mean what they mean for a society using them to communicate shared understandings and intentions.

The word *Messiah* belongs to a Jewish historical and social context. It does not refer to a presently accessible object in the external world, against which words can be checked. We cannot define it by pointing and saying, "There, that's what I mean when I say Messiah." If a person should appear in history fitting the socially constituted meaning of the word, Jews will say, the Messiah has come. But the word does not have any definable meaning outside this Jewish context. It means what it means for those who originated it and for those who continue to use it in the discourse of their own society.

The earliest Christians could intelligibly dispute with other Jews about the meaning of a word in a shared religious vocabulary, because they were Jews themselves, and they did. But they lost the argument, and the Jewish community went on using the word in the same sense as it had always done. The word *Messiah* was then translated into Greek as Christ, and in its new meaning it became part of the usage of another society, the Greek-speaking Gentile church.

In this new context, the new word *Christ* came to mean what it meant for Christians, but the old word *Messiah* continued to be a Jewish word, bearing its Jewish meaning. *Christ* and *Messiah* are different words, with a different social context and a different meaning. Because the first is a translation of the second, their histories cannot be altogether separated. But objective historians have a duty not to confuse them.

For critical scholarship, the proper meaning of the word *Messiah* will still be the righteous warrior king whose destiny it is to liberate the land from pagan occupation and inaugurate the era of universal peace and righteousness. The Christian concept of the Christ is far outside the semantic range of the word *Messiah*. Unbiassed historians are not permitted to assert (as theologians traditionally have) that, as the Christian Christ, Jesus was *really* the Jewish Messiah.

THE DEVELOPMENT OF EARLY IDEAS ABOUT CHRIST

The earliest Christians were all Jews themselves. Their beliefs about Jesus were cast in a thoroughly Jewish mold, even when they were unorthodox. They differed from their fellow Jews only in believing in a Messiah who did not fit the expectations held by the people at large. They neither abandoned Jewish observance nor departed from the original Jewish concept of historical redemption, though they modified the latter substantially in their new theory.

Other messianic movements in early Judaism centered around claimants whose credentials were more orthodox but who failed to deliver what they had promised. In this case, even the promise was different. However, in its earliest years Christianity did retain some contact with the traditional hope in ways that succeeding generations did not. It looked for Christ to return to earth in a few months or years to fulfill the traditional expectations in a supernatural manner. This hope was not fulfilled and had to be modified to fit the facts. The revised messianic doctrine took the concept still further from Jewish expectation in the direction of an other-worldly salvation.

These beliefs were transmitted to early Gentile Christianity, which quickly transformed a sectarian Jewish belief about a novel Messiah into its own myth of the Christ, a supernatural and cosmic redeemer. From this Christian transformation of an originally Jewish concept, there soon grew on the fertile soil of Greek-speaking Christianity the doctrine of the divinity of Christ. Here, we are even further away from any view of the Messiah that is recognizably Jewish. Perhaps more than anything else in Christianity, its doctrine of the divine Christ separates it from Judaism by an unbridgeable gap.

Between a Jesus we can conceive of as Jewish and the later Christological dogma of Catholic Christianity intervene two immense steps. First, the concept of the Messiah had to be radically transformed, and then this transformed figure was divinized. This double transformation created a new religion with a different concept of salvation centering on a divine redeemer figure altogether unknown to Jewish expectation. The new religion used Jewish themes and symbols to set forth a myth with a totally different structure from anything known to Judaism.

JEWISH OBJECTIONS TO THE CHRISTIAN DOCTRINE

The major objection to maintaining that Jesus was the Jewish Messiah is still the original one brought by Jews from the first. Manifestly, the world has not yet been redeemed. The nineteenth century had been inclined to a different view, in its optimism about human progress expecting the progressive realization of the kingdom of God on earth. The century of Auschwitz and of Hiroshima, of Stalinist mass murders and continuing wars, has disillusioned us. Nor did Jesus, in the manner of the King Messiah, lead a conquering army to free his land and people from pagan occupation and inaugurate an age of universal righteousness and peace. Nor did he lead an uprising that even in failure provoked a divine miracle of deliverance. He could not have been the Messiah the Jews expected and expect.

The disappointment and gradual erosion of the original expectation of Jesus' return led the early Christians to spiritualize the concept of the Messiah. The transformation has already been accomplished in the late gospel of John, where Jesus is represented as telling Pilate that he is indeed a king, but his kingdom is not of this world. Here nascent Christian theology has already parted from its Jewish roots. In Jewish expectation, the messianic age involves a material and political, as well as spiritual, transformation of the world.

Christianity would shortly claim to have supplanted Judaism in God's favor. This claim is the consequence of its new view of the divine and suffering Messiah.

No amount of tolerance and goodwill can obscure the fundamental threat to the Jewish people contained in the heart of traditional Christian belief.

At the same time, the very presence of the Jewish people in the world, continuing to believe in the faithfulness of God to the original covenant, and in our own time restored to their ancient promised land, puts a great question mark against Christian belief in a new covenant made through Christ. The presence of this question, often buried deep in the Christian mind, could not fail to cause profound and gnawing anxiety. Anxiety usually leads to hostility. Only truth, and the acceptance of truth when found, can resolve these deep fears and hatreds.

JESUS AND JEWISH EXPECTATION

We come now to a crucial question. Could Jesus, as a faithful and well-educated Jew, have thought of himself as the expected Messiah, or even as a Messiah of a novel kind such as the church later believed him to have been? Familiar as he was with the prophetic writings, he certainly knew very well what the existing expectation of the Messiah involved. He could only have thought of himself as the Messiah if he believed himself called to fulfill this expectation. If he ever did, he clearly abandoned the idea. The Gospels never suggest that he presented himself as the traditionally expected Messiah. However, the new idea of a suffering Messiah who would leave the historical world unchanged could hardly have meant anything to him as a Jew. The idea could only have grown up later, in the attempt to explain his death consistently with the belief that he was the Messiah.

It is even less easy to imagine that the Jesus who is increasingly being rediscovered by critical scholarship could have supposed himself to be the divine redeemer of Catholic and Protestant credal orthodoxy. Between the Galilean countryman who taught and lived the nearness of God, seeing his own person as without importance in that brilliant light, and the majestic divine being of christological orthodoxy, controlling the universe from his cradle, stands an unbridgeable abyss. If the Jesus now being recovered by critical study of the New Testament in its Jewish environment was also the person depicted in the christological dogma of the church, he himself could not have had the slightest idea of his real identity.

WHAT DID JESUS HIMSELF SAY ABOUT HIS MISSION?

Given the universal Christian conviction that Jesus was the Messiah, it is startling to discover that he may never have claimed he was. The synoptic Gospels nowhere report Jesus as claiming spontaneously to be the Messiah. (The Fourth Gospel, which theologizes history more radically, has Jesus claim to be the Messiah in the novel Christian sense from the beginning of his public career.) Only on one occasion, most clearly in Matthew's version of the incident, does Jesus even appear to assent to the acclamation of his own disciples. Otherwise, the only evidence of a claim is Jesus' somewhat ambiguous assent to the high priest's questioning in the trial scene. There are very strong reasons for regarding the whole scene as unhistorical. It appears to be the free composition of the gospel writers who record it.

At first sight, Jesus' recorded reticence appears strange. It can be explained in two ways. Either Jesus simply knew he was not the Messiah, and therefore he made no such claim, or he realized that his own understanding of his messianic mission differed so much from the general expectation that it would be virtually impossible to explain it to the public until it had been acted out in his death and resurrection. The latter seems to be the view of the gospel writers, especially Mark. Can we now determine which interpretation is correct?

The facts recorded in the Gospels should lead us to reject the interpretation they themselves put forward. Jesus may have wondered at an early stage in his public life whether he was called to the tasks of the Messiah. He might even have experienced the thought as a temptation.[7] If so, he must have abandoned the idea early on, upon deciding that his personal calling was to bring the compassion and forgiveness of God to the sinners, the lost sheep of Israel. Such a mission must have seemed to him incompatible with the expected role of the Messiah. When he became convinced that his mission was going to end in death, that clinched the matter. His role in the coming of the kingdom he announced could not be that of the Messiah. Jesus must have known that he was not the Messiah tradition expected.

If he had thought of himself as the Messiah, he would probably have had no hesitation in assuming the role publicly. Others among his near contemporaries did so. Although mistakenly, as it turned out, they understood their historical role in traditional messianic terms and attempted to mobilize support for their mission. This was the case, for example, with Bar Kochva, a century after Jesus' time. Only if Jesus had quite a different conception of his role would there have been any reason for reticence.

It may not have been a high priority for Jesus to explain his personal role to his contemporaries. If he had wished to do so, however, it would not have suited his purpose to use terms so misleading that no sooner used than they would have to be qualified out of existence. Jesus does not appear to have let himself be misunderstood unnecessarily. There would be little communicative value in announcing that he was the Messiah and immediately going on to explain that he did not mean what everyone else meant, because he was going to die and redeem the world spiritually by his sufferings. This is pretty much what Matthew asks us to believe, as we shall see in a moment.

If Jesus had simply claimed to be the Messiah but meant that he was what Christians would later understand by the term *Christ*, he would not have been understood by his hearers. If he really meant to say that he would redeem the world spiritually by his sufferings, the conclusion of anyone who believed him would have been that he was some kind of martyr. There are probably links between the Jewish idea of martyrdom as an atonement for the sins of others and the later Christian view of Jesus' role.

No Jew ever thought of a martyr redeeming *the world* by his death. Only after Jesus' death and the Christian belief in his resurrection had grown up would such a concept have meant anything to anyone. We cannot plausibly attribute it to Jesus in his lifetime. Even after his death and supposed resurrection, when it had begun to take mythical form and had been allotted scriptural proof texts, it impressed only a minority of Jews as consistent with the hopes they had learned to cherish.

It is difficult to reconstruct Jesus' actual conception of the relationship between his own mission and the kingdom whose nearness he announced. His message was undoubtedly linked to Jewish messianic expectations, but he does not seem to have understood them in the conventional way. He seemed to show little interest in the Messiah, and he did not openly identify himself with that figure. The Messiah, it seems, belonged to the future, Jesus' mission to the present.

WAS JESUS MISTAKEN?

Ever since Albert Schweitzer first suggested it, scholars have occasionally argued that Jesus did suppose that he was the Messiah, but that he was mistaken. Few writers have been as honest as Schweitzer in facing the implications of this position. If Jesus supposed he was the Messiah, he was quite certainly mistaken, if the term is to bear its Jewish meaning. Schweitzer and others credit Jesus with the expectation that the messianic age would come very shortly as a result of his own work, in a matter of months or years. He was no less certainly mistaken if this estimate of the time of the kingdom was off by a couple of thousand years or more. Such a delay does not modify the expectation, it nullifies it.

Though this is seldom clearly recognized, any contention that Jesus thought himself to be the Jewish Messiah, even in novel senses not central in the Judaism of his time, entails the same admission that he was mistaken. In Judaism, the Messiah is always expected to bring in the messianic age. Even if Jesus thought that he could do so, he did not.

The difficulty arises even with E. P. Sanders' carefully qualified contention that Jesus' actions and words were messianic in character and that it was therefore a fair inference that he regarded himself as the Messiah. If he regarded himself as the Messiah in any sense that would have been intelligible to a Jew, he was mistaken.

There is no reason why the conclusion that Jesus was mistaken should trouble the historian on theological grounds. The problem arises at a different level. Among other recent interpreters, Vermes recognizes that Jesus was a person of great spiritual stature as well as of good education in the Jewish tradition. If so, it will seem inconsistent to attribute to him an unintelligible, megalomaniac, or seriously mistaken view of his own role in history. The efforts of the gospel writers to attribute to him a messianic claim are fraught with difficulties and inconsistencies, but these are not likely to be his own.

Jesus seems to have understood God's kingly rule as a present reality, calling for immediate decision but in no way precluding a future consummation affecting the whole world. It would be fully consistent with such a belief to teach that the kingdom can be entered here and now, by repentance and faith and a commitment to the righteousness "exceeding the righteousness of the scribes and Pharisees." Like other Jews before and after him, he probably believed that if people would fully respond to God's present kingship, the messianic age would come .

Vermes was able to give a full account of Jesus' teaching on the kingdom of God without attributing any role to Jesus himself beyond that of prophet, the only title he seems readily to have accepted for himself. It would be simpler, as well as more in accordance with Jesus' own authentic words, to assume that for him the kingdom was the kingdom of *God*, not his own kingdom.

As the German theologians put it, in a famous phrase, at a certain point the "proclaimer became the proclaimed." Jesus' own role in his lifetime was to proclaim the kingship of God. Others then began to proclaim him as the king. While this reversal may even have begun to happen in Jesus' lifetime, there is no good evidence of self-proclamation by Jesus. We find instead reticence, avoidance of the question, perhaps equivocation or secrecy, and even outright denial of any personal messianic role. For Jesus, the kingdom is present because God himself is present in his kingly rule, not because it is present in his own ministry.

WHAT DID OTHERS BELIEVE OF HIM?

Those around Jesus, including his own followers, did understand messianic expectations in more traditional ways. If (as Jesus seemed to be announcing) the kingdom was coming, they assumed that the Messiah would be there to bring it, and if Jesus was connected with its coming, he must be the King Messiah. This was probably what the crowds supposed, and so did Jesus' close followers, especially Peter. Jesus' opponents, whoever they were, including the Romans when eventually Jesus came to their notice, would have assumed that this was also how Jesus thought of himself. The Romans would have regarded him as a subversive, and that is certainly why they eventually crucified him.

This is the difficulty that Mark, and subsequently Matthew and Luke, faced in writing their gospels when they came to deal with the problem of how Jesus had seen his own mission. Long before they came to write, the Church had settled down to the conviction that Jesus was the Messiah, while radically redefining the concept to fit the actual history of Jesus. Thus, in the eyes of the early Christian community, their own conviction that Jesus was the Messiah now took precedence over the accepted definition of the Messiah.

The death and resurrection of Jesus became central to the new concept, together with his expected return. In its new Greek dress, as "Christ," this novel messianic theory proved quite acceptable to Gentiles, who had no previous assumptions about what the term Messiah ought to mean. By the time the Gospels were being written, the new Christian doctrine had quite lost its novelty for the Church. The gospel writers themselves were thoroughly accustomed to the transformed concept, and no doubt they firmly believed that it went back to Jesus himself.

READING BACK THE NEW CONCEPT INTO THE STORY

Mark and his successors therefore needed to represent Jesus as having taught in his lifetime that he was the Messiah in the new Christian sense. As I have argued, it would have been highly confusing and misleading to Jesus' Jewish hearers if he had actually claimed to be the Messiah, while intending the novel Christian meaning of the term. In any case, the traditions the gospel writers had received almost certainly did not say he had. These writers therefore had to represent Jesus as equivocating, affirming and denying simultaneously, or affirming in private while denying in public. The result is highly confusing, presenting major difficulties to the present-day historian.

I think it highly probable that the gospel writers not did not receive any traditions in which Jesus had claimed to be the Messiah but actually were confronted with at least one in which he denied it outright. In view of their beliefs, it was impossible for them simply to accept this tradition and reproduce it unaltered, but neither could they simply ignore it or gloss over it.

PETER'S ACCLAMATION OF JESUS AS MESSIAH

All three of the synoptic Gospels tell a story of a particular occasion on which Peter acclaims Jesus as the Messiah. In the fullest version of the three, Matthew, Jesus himself appears to provoke discussion of his mission in order to elicit from the disciples a profession that they believe he is the Messiah, praising Peter's acclamation in the strongest terms when he receives it. Such an explicit claim is without parallel in the three synoptic Gospels, apart from Mark's version of the trial scene, not followed by the other two.

Most scholars treat the incident as of central importance for understanding Jesus' work. The account in the Gospels also proved significant for the later history of the church, because the Catholic church regarded Matthew's version as the biblical basis for the papal claims to primacy and supremacy.

Since (as the gospel writers, especially Matthew, tell the story) Jesus appears to accept Peter's acclamation, the interchange between them used to be taken as proving that Jesus did regard himself as the Messiah. Does critical history still support this view? The passage is a test case for any non-Messianic interpretation of Jesus' mission, and we will therefore examine it in more detail.

The story is found in three places, in each of the three synoptic Gospels (Mark 8:27–33, Matthew 16:13–23, and Luke 9:18–22; it may also be alluded to in the Gospel of John; cf. John 1:40–42; 6:67–69).[8] There must have been a strong tradition that such an incident had taken place. However, the writers disagree on several important features of the story.

Older interpreters used to harmonize passages like these, ignoring the discrepancies and building up a composite picture based on all the accounts. In this case, the effect would be to treat Matthew's version, the fullest and most elaborate of the three, as the normative one, as the older theological tradition did. On that procedure, we will conclude that Jesus definitely claimed to be the Messiah.

Critical scholars regard this procedure as illegitimate. They consider it more honest to examine the differences between the accounts, looking for reasons why they differ. When we come to do that here, the results can be illuminating. The differences are substantial. As the literary critics point out, where such differences in the versions exist, each implicitly declares the others to be fictions.[9] Closer examination strongly suggests that Matthew and Luke were aware of a problem, and that they considered that Mark had failed to solve it. Each of them presents a new and different version, handling the problem in his own characteristic way.

THE THREE ACCOUNTS COMPARED

The three writers agree that Jesus himself brings about the discussion. He takes the initiative in asking the disciples about the speculations going on in the crowds, and after receiving an account from them he challenges them directly on their own view of him. Peter makes himself the spokesman, declaring that Jesus is no less than the Messiah.

Only in Matthew does Jesus directly assent to Peter's acclamation. However, in all three versions, Jesus immediately forbids the disciples to say anything to anyone about it. Apparently in explanation of the prohibition, he goes on to tell them that he will be tried and put to death; then after three days he will rise from the dead. In Matthew alone, Jesus' predicted sufferings are directly attributed to the Jewish authorities. Mark and Matthew say that Peter then expostulates with Jesus, and he receives a shattering rebuke. On this vitally important point Luke is silent.

All three writers append a short address by Jesus to both disciples and people, in which he speaks of self-renunciation.[10] Its central sentences might be a commentary on a decision of Jesus to renounce messianic pretensions. "What does anyone gain by winning the whole world at the cost of his life? What can he give to buy his life back?"[11]

Should we believe that Jesus predicted his death and resurrection? The more radical critics have usually taken it for granted that the whole story is a prophecy after the event and without historical value. This certainly seems to be true of the prophecy of the resurrection. Jesus certainly would not have predicted his resurrection in a messianic context, since no one expected the Messiah to rise from the dead–it was no part of his destiny to be killed, in the first place. If the Gospels correctly report the disciples' astonishment and disbelief at the first reports of a resurrection, we have to conclude that Jesus had not prepared them for anything of the sort. Nor could he have predicted a trial of the sort the writers will shortly describe, since in all probability there was no such trial.

On the other hand, there should be no difficulty in taking seriously a report that Jesus predicted his death. It required no supernatural prescience to guess that the messianic excitement springing up around him would attract the attention of the

Romans if it went on. More than likely they would move against the supposed ringleader of the agitation. Precisely this agitation is the context of the conversation with Peter, even though we may think that it happened somewhat later than Mark tells us, nearer to the last weeks in Jerusalem. (The gospel writers did not know the order of events in Jesus' life.)

I regard Jesus' unequivocal prediction of his own death as the core of this tradition. In its original Jewish context, his answer would have been very awkward for Peter's expectations. Jesus' emphatic words must likewise have presented a major difficulty to the gospel writers when they came to write their accounts.

What would Jesus' prediction of his death and injunction to be silent about messianic hopes have meant in a Jewish context? Jesus' reply would have been decisive. When he said that he expected to be put to death, this was the same thing as saying, "I am not the Messiah – forget it." If so, Jesus' imposition of silence on his followers becomes hardly mysterious. As Vermes points out, Peter himself could only have understood Jesus' reply as an outright denial.[12] Both Jesus and Peter knew that the role of the Messiah was to be a victorious deliverer.

In Jewish expectation, as we have seen, the Messiah does not get killed, either by his countrymen or by an occupying power. He delivers the people from foreign occupation and rule. When Peter acclaimed Jesus as the Messiah, this is what he hoped for, not some spiritual transformation devoid of this worldly political content. And this is what Jesus denied unequivocally.

We should not assume, therefore, that even the earliest account, Mark's, is simple and unvarnished tradition. Mark's account is no less theological than those of his later successors; indeed, from a literary-theological point of view it is much more sophisticated than Luke's. Luke deals with the embarrassing features of the story by brevity. He plays the whole incident down, omitting as much as he can.

Mark presents the encounter in the light of the new doctrine of the suffering Messiah, devised by the Church after Jesus' death: he adds to it some features of his own, both literary and theological, making the incident pivotal to the structure of his composition and perhaps introducing a theory of a "messianic secret," a concealed and private teaching of the new doctrine. If so, Mark presents Jesus' words as the first and enigmatic disclosure to the inner circle of a new secret doctrine, not to be made known to others until the resurrection has come.

Mark seems to have retained the outline and content of the original tradition of the discussion, while transforming its meaning by the literary context into which he puts it. Matthew used a different method. He did not employ Mark's literary devices but directly inserted new material into the dialogue, the effect of which is to reverse its meaning.

In Matthew alone, Jesus responds positively to Peter's acclamation, praising him for it and telling him that it has come to him by divine revelation. He goes on to appoint Peter to a position of authority in the Church, giving him the new name of Rock, the rock on which the Church will be built.[13]

However, Jesus continues, as in the other versions, by strictly ordering the disciples to tell no one he is the Messiah, an injunction now much harder to account for. Peter's expostulation and Jesus' answering rebuke are subtly reworded to make it appear that Peter is sorry for Jesus' predicted sufferings rather than indignant at his denial that he is the Messiah.[14]

Otherwise, what stands out in the inserted material is its ecclesiastical character, which may lead us to suppose that it originated well after Jesus' lifetime. The word *church* occurs here, almost uniquely in the Gospels; the only other time it appears is in another passage in Matthew, close to this one. Matthew was writing at a fairly late date, almost certainly not earlier than the last decade or two of the century, when the organization of the church was rapidly assuming its historic form.[15]

If Peter understood Jesus' injunction to silence and its explanation as any Jew would, that would explain his vehement expostulation with Jesus, reported by Mark and Matthew (though not by Luke). Probably, therefore, both his acclamation of Jesus and his subsequent expostulation are historical. He may have been grieved at the prospect of his master's imminent death, but he was still more disappointed at the immediate frustration of his messianic hopes, and he was not inclined to take No for an answer.

Jesus' even more vehement rebuke to Peter, in response, has to be a still more emphatic denial that he is the Messiah. At the same time, he introduces a further reason for refraining from such speculations – since Jesus is not the Messiah, they are spiritually dangerous to him, for they could only deflect him from the path actually marked out for him by God.[16]

Perhaps the order of Jesus' words has been slightly altered in the tradition. Perhaps Jesus did not predict his death as a certainty already accepted as the will of God but as the likely outcome of the messianic excitement now growing up around him. He may have vainly attempted to put a stop to it by the injunction to say nothing more about such fantasies.

If so, he would have meant to point out to Peter that if he continued to spread such rumors there would have to be a Roman reaction, and Jesus would then lose his life. The injunction to silence would be a means of self-protection for Jesus. In that case, of course, Jesus' words would still have been a denial. If he was not the Messiah, he was as vulnerable to death as any other man.

Thus, in a Jewish context, the core of the story, especially the features common to two or more of the accounts, becomes both intelligible and plausible. However, it does not appear in the Gospels in its original Jewish context.

It has undergone development and transformation, and it has been fitted by the writers into the Christian myth of the dying and rising Messiah. In its original form, the tradition must have been a decided embarrassment to the theory embodied in the myth, recording as it did Jesus' own unequivocal and extremely emphatic denial that he was the Messiah.

The gospel writers had to do something about the difficulty, and we can get at what they were each doing by careful comparison of the three different versions. As can now be seen, each in his own way transforms Jesus' denial into a new form of messianic claim. The writers would by now have been reading back into the tradition the well-established theory of the double coming of the Messiah, first in earthly suffering and then on the clouds of heaven in glory. For the Church, it is no longer a shocking novelty but a commonplace, long meditated upon and elaborately furnished with scriptural justification.

"Of course" that is what Jesus had really meant. He could not possibly have intended to deny that he was the Messiah. Surely, he really intended to convey to his disciples the new doctrine of the suffering Messiah. Peter could not have been rebuked for calling Jesus the Messiah, he must have been rebuked for failing to accept the necessity for Jesus to suffer on the way to his eventual messianic glory.

THE ORIGINS OF CHRISTIAN MESSIANIC BELIEF

Given that these were the convictions of the gospel writers, it is noteworthy how restrained they are in presenting Jesus as a messianic claimant. Nowhere else do the synoptic Gospels represent Jesus as spontaneously claiming to be the Messiah. In the trial scene he seems to give ambiguous assent to the High Priest's direct question, but apart from the ambiguity and the differing versions, it is just at this point that we can be most certain that the trial is not historical, for there was nothing blasphemous in a messianic claim, nor would the High Priest have used the language of later Christianity.[17]

This reticence on the part of the gospel writers indicates a powerful constraint in the earliest tradition. There must have been a firmly rooted memory that Jesus had never claimed to be the Messiah, or had even denied it. The writers display their respect for the tradition in the small extent to which they tamper with it to conform it to the myth. This same respect for tradition today makes it possible to rediscover the Jewish Jesus.

If Jesus denied that he was the Messiah, how are we to account for the evident conviction of Peter, and perhaps others among his close followers in Jesus' lifetime, that he was the Messiah? Perhaps there is no great mystery. The crowds, impressed by Jesus' healing miracles, regarded him as a major prophetic figure from the past, resurrected or reincarnated. It would not be a big step beyond that for intimates of Jesus, who were no doubt in a better position than the crowds to gauge his full stature, to accord him the highest position available.

His proclamation of the nearness of the Kingdom of God would have lent color to their hopes. Perhaps their Jewish education was not as good as Jesus', and they did not at first note the discrepancies between his developing mission and the accepted role of the Messiah. The similarities were obvious enough, since Jesus spoke with authority of the nearness of the kingdom of God. Or perhaps, like the disciples described at the end of Luke's Gospel, they kept hoping that he would eventually do what the Messiah was supposed to do. But it was just these hopes that were an embarrassment and a mortal danger to Jesus.

They were an embarrassment, since they would deflect him, if he went along with them, from his real task of recalling the lost sheep of the house of Israel and introducing them through repentance and faith to the kingdom of God. And they may actually have led to his death. If the disciples violated Jesus' prohibition on telling anyone that he was the Messiah, the rumor may have spread more widely, giving Jesus the reputation that in fact did lead to his accusation before the Romans and eventual execution as a subversive.

The leaders of the early Church seem to have been fully aware of the conflict between Jesus' own teaching and current messianic expectations. They dealt with the conflict by remodeling the expectation to fit what had actually happened to Jesus. Mark's gospel incorporates a particularly striking presentation of the remodeled concept of the Messiah projected back into Jesus' lifetime. He represents Jesus as teaching the new concept to the inner circle of his disciples, while enjoining silence on them in public. They, however, cling obstinately to the conventional expectations, and are they therefore astonished when everything happens as Jesus had predicted. The "messianic secret" cannot be understood even by those closest to Jesus, until events make its true significance clear.

In fact, however, the new concept could hardly have arisen without the combination of two essential factors: the disciples' conviction in his lifetime that Jesus was the Messiah, in spite of his own denials, and the later resurrection visions reviving their expectation in new forms after it had been demolished by his death.

At the end of his Gospel, Luke represents Jesus as opening the meaning of the Scriptures to conventionally minded disciples in a mysterious resurrection appearance, teaching them the new interpretation of the infant church. No doubt, the infant church did believe that it was guided by the spirit of Jesus in drastically reinterpreting the Jewish Scriptures to fit what had happened to him, creating an altogether novel concept of the role and destiny of the Messiah. Attributing such a concept to Jesus in his own lifetime presents obvious difficulties for the historian.

The Gospel of John solves the problem in a different way. For this Gospel, Jesus was the Messiah from the very beginning (though in the new Christian sense). He could have been recognized as such by those with sufficient faith, even at the outset of his ministry, perhaps three years before his death. But though he was the messianic king, his kingdom was not of this world. It was and always had been a purely spiritual kingdom. In John's version, the kingdom was present already in Jesus' ministry, and it was fully realized in his spiritual victory on the cross.

This gospel still strongly affirms the traditional idea that Jesus had been the Messiah, although on its writer's own showing, he had little in common with the figure of traditional expectation.[18] The Fourth Gospel deals with the tension between biblical expectation and the history of Jesus by abandoning the historical role of the Messiah and the attendant hope for a transformation of the world.

THE SON OF MAN

Many critics who believe Jesus *did* regard himself as the Messiah in a novel sense think he may have been influenced by certain sectarian concepts of the Messiah, including some found in the Dead Sea Scrolls. Vermes argues persuasively that such scholars have exaggerated the importance of these minority concepts of the Messiah, which had little influence on the mass of the people. In any case, they do not differ radically in their conception of the historical role of the Messiah from the standard expectation, diverging from the mainstream concepts not so much on the Messiah's role as on his background and origins. Even in these variations, he remains a deliverer, not a suffering martyr.

However, one such supposed concept has assumed central importance in many modern reconstructions of Jesus' understanding of his own mission, and we should therefore discuss it briefly. This is the mysterious "Son of Man." In the synoptic Gospels the expression is found only in Jesus' own mouth, and in many cases, though apparently not in all, it obviously refers to himself.

By the time the Gospels were written, the church had come to use it as a new title for Jesus, filled with the significance of its own revolutionary messianic doctrine. The Son of Man must suffer, but he would come again on the clouds in glory to judge the world. Did Jesus think of himself as the Son of Man in this messianic sense?

A number of theologians and well-respected critics continue to maintain that Jesus had already begun to call himself the Son of Man, in preference to Messiah, because he was able to fill the less familiar term with the new content, implying his future death and resurrection, and subsequent coming as judge. They share the widespread assumption that the Son of Man was an existing Jewish messianic title, based on the figure "like a son of man," in Daniel 7:13, who is to come on the clouds of heaven to the Ancient of Days and sit on a throne. The later apocryphal book of Enoch also speaks of a being like a son of man. The important doctrine of Jesus' second coming appears to have been largely drawn from such texts.

On the basis of the same passages, Vermes and others have convincingly argued that there was no Jewish messianic concept of the Son of Man.[19] As Vermes points out, from Daniel in the Bible to the late apocalyptic book of Enoch, wherever the expression Son of Man is used, it does not function as a title of the Messiah; it always simply means a human being, which is the original meaning of the expression. If there had been such a title as Son of Man, it would simply have meant "the human being," a concept so vague as to be meaningless, unless contrasted with something else, as in Daniel. There, the contrast is with symbolic animal figures. In Daniel, it is plain that the author means the human figure in his apocalyptic vision to stand not for any individual but for the people of Israel.

When, apparently after Jesus' time, some Jews did begin to think of the figure in the texts as messianic, the phrase, "one like a son of man," still did not become a title, but continued simply to mean a human being. The later interpreters of the texts are much more interested in the thrones that are to be set, and the function of the human figure who will sit on one of them. In all these cases, the human figure comes on the clouds of heaven *to* the divine being, not *from* him, as in the Christian myth.

It is clear from the synoptic Gospels that the Church remembered that Jesus did speak of himself as the son of man. But what did he actually mean? The expression in the Greek of the Gospels, more literally, "the son of the man," is a strange one, making no more sense in Greek than in English; it is obviously a Semitism.[20] For grammatical reasons, it has to have come from Aramaic rather than Hebrew, and the scholar must look to Aramaic sources, rather than the Bible, for parallels that can explain the idiom. Vermes has been able to find examples in Galilean Aramaic of an idiom that appears to be the one Jesus employs in the Gospels.

In these Aramaic texts, a speaker refers to himself as "the son of man" in two contexts in particular, where modesty is appropriate and where coming disaster is to be alluded to. For many British readers, it would be appropriate to translate such cases with the pronoun "one," used by upper-class speakers of British English to avoid saying "I," where this is felt to be drawing too much attention to oneself. Jesus refers to himself as "the son of man" in somewhat similar contexts.

Evidently, the gospel writers (or, perhaps more probably, the traditions they are reproducing) still sometimes understand the usage correctly, since they occasionally substitute "the son of man" where "I" appears in an earlier version and vice versa. The current English versions of the New Testament are therefore misleading the reader when they capitalize the expression, as if it were a recognized title; it is to be hoped that future versions will refrain from doing so.

In view of Vermes' research, increasingly accepted by other scholars competent in the field of Aramaic, we must now be more than doubtful that Jesus could have identified himself with an existing messianic figure called the Son of Man. For the same reasons, he could not have spoken of the future coming of the Son of Man. On certain occasions, he did refer to himself as "the son of man," or "this son of man," as other Aramaic speakers did in similar contexts. In all probability, these are the only authentic instances of the use of the expression by Jesus.

Only later, when the tradition had been translated into Greek, and the original meaning of the idiom lost sight of, was it possible to blend Jesus' own usage with references in Daniel and perhaps elsewhere to the figure like a son of man, thus creating a new messianic title unknown to Judaism. The Gospels seem to reflect a "secondary, midrashic development, more understandable in Greek than in Aramaic,"[21] in which Jesus is represented as speaking of the future coming to earth of the son of man. The new messianic concept was then read back into Jesus' lifetime, and "Son of Man" placed in his mouth by the Gospels in meanings he had not intended and in contexts where he himself had not used the expression.

Some scholars, such as Rudolf Bultmann, who believe in the authenticity of such passages suppose that Jesus sometimes meant to refer to someone other than himself. These passages are thought to come from the Synoptics Sayings Source, or Q. However, if we accept the above explanation, these passages cannot represent actual words of Jesus. Jesus would not have spoken of the future coming of a Son of Man, in any event.

It turns out that the "son of man" is indeed an important expression, but for reasons very different from the traditional ones. It brings to us a vivid recollection of how the real Jesus thought and spoke of the possibility of his own death.

JESUS' ENTRY INTO JERUSALEM

Was there any reason for Jesus to expect his own death as a result of *Jewish* rather than Roman opposition? He had aroused intense opposition by scandalizing the zealots with his unconventional behavior. Nevertheless, giving scandal to the pious is one thing and committing a capital offense against the Torah itself quite another. It is not realistically possible to find good evidence of an offense of this order in anything Jesus is reported to have done up to this point. By the time he began to predict his death, we can safely assume that he had not done anything of the sort.

Could he then have had it in mind to do something of major significance later that might have put his life at risk from the Jewish authorities? Two possibilities need to be examined, since Sanders in particular regards them as important clues to Jesus' messianic intentions, and a source of official opposition. Jesus' entry into Jerusalem on a donkey, to the applause of a small crowd waving palm branches and shouting,[22] has been thought to be an acted claim to be the Messiah, recognized as such and welcomed by the crowds. All four gospels record the incident, with many differences of detail. The account in the Fourth Gospel is the simplest, stating, probably correctly, that the incident was not thought significant at the time but only in retrospect.

The synoptics add the mysterious story of the prearranged acquisition of the donkey colt, which Jesus rides from Bethany to Jerusalem. Matthew and John give a reference to Zechariah 9:9 (the primary text underlying all versions) to suggest that Jesus fulfilled this messianic prophecy when he rode a donkey into Jerusalem.

So remote is the final editor of Matthew from the scene that he misunderstands the conventions of Hebrew poetry, and he mistakes the parallelism of "an ass, and a colt the foal of an ass," as referring to two different animals, and therefore has Jesus arrive on or with two donkeys. (This would lend support to the views of those who believe the final editor of Matthew's Gospel to have been a Gentile. Other versions rather improbably represent Jesus as riding an unbroken colt.)

Sanders takes the story to be basically authentic, reflecting Jesus' messianic aims. Others have thought the whole story a creation of the gospel writers, attempting to provide a suitable fulfillment for messianic texts they or others had found. The case for this is strong, as a detailed examination of the way the writers handled the texts shows.[23]

Vermes thinks there was a small demonstration by Jesus' followers, shouting and waving branches, but believes that the use of a donkey was simply due to the fact that it was a convenient means of transport, only later given messianic significance by the Church. It was as a prophet, Vermes tells us, not as the Messiah, that Jesus was welcomed by the crowds when he came into Jerusalem.

The passage from Zechariah underlying the story implicitly presupposes the normal view of the Messiah as a victorious king: the Messiah rides a donkey out of humility, instead of the war-horse a warrior king would normally ride. The prophet emphasizes the Messiah's humility, of which riding the donkey is a symbol.

In itself, there could be nothing significant in seeing Jesus himself riding a donkey. It would have been his normal way of getting about, when he did not walk. If it was hot that Pesach, the donkey would have made the long climb up the hill less fatiguing. No one would have attached any significance to his riding on a donkey, except by contrast with something else, as in the prophecy itself.

If therefore, the incident had been intended as a messianic claim addressed to those who did not yet recognize him, not only Jesus but his intended audience would have had to be aware of the detailed meaning of the prophecy, by which the Messiah contradicts instead of fulfilling what would naturally be expected of him. Moreover, for the symbolism of arriving on a donkey instead of a war-horse to be understood, the crowds would have had to know already that he was the Messiah.

The argument is really circular, defying common sense. It is hard to see Jesus making any messianic claim in this incident, though the demonstration may have reflected the beliefs of some of the onlookers that he was indeed the Messiah. By the time the gospel writers were looking for scriptural references, they were using them out of context as proof texts, and they probably did not stop to think out the reasoning.

JESUS AND THE TEMPLE

One more event remains to be examined before we come to the trial. Sanders also thinks that the incident generally known as the "cleansing of the Temple" was a conscious assertion by Jesus of messianic authority, provoking the opposition of the authorities. He attaches great importance to the story, regarding the cleansing of the Temple as one of the few solidly attested historical facts in Jesus' life on which a reliable interpretation of his intentions can be based.

He further believes that Jesus' action was misunderstood as an attack on the Temple and that this led the priests, perhaps in alliance with the Pharisees, to have him arraigned before the Sanhedrin. In my own view, the nature of the evidence does not permit such confident conclusions, and I do not believe the incident can bear the weight Sanders wishes to place upon it.

Jesus' action in the Temple took place in the last few days of his life, when he went up to Jerusalem to keep the Passover festival. He is reported to have overthrown the tables of the money changers in the outer courts, expelling them from the Temple precincts.[24] His action has usually been regarded as a protest against commercialism in the sacred precincts and as a purification or cleansing of the holy place.

This interpretation is the one favored by the gospel writers themselves, as is shown by their choice of biblical quotations to support their account. Since, on their interpretation, Jesus would have upheld rather than attacked the sanctity of the Temple, he could hardly have aroused opposition intense enough to lead to a capital charge.

Sanders agrees that Jesus was upholding the sanctity of the Temple, but he does not accept the explanation of the gospel writers. His own explanation is a little difficult to grasp at first reading. He considers that Jesus' action in overthrowing the tables was intended as prophetic symbolism, like the actions of some of the biblical prophets. Jesus prophetically foresaw a disaster for the Temple at some time before the messianic age arrived, and he enacted this symbolically by overturning the tables. His main aim, however, was to proclaim the final *restoration* of the Temple in the messianic time. When he overthrew the tables, he may have spoken (in the name of God) some such words as, "Destroy this Temple and in three days I will raise it up," words that were in fact attributed to him by others. His violent action was then taken (mistakenly) to be a threat to the Temple.

Sanders thinks the trial before the Sanhedrin was provoked by this incident and the hostile reaction to it. Sanders does believe in the broad historicity of the trial, though not in the details, since the disciples could not have known what actually took place behind closed doors. He postulates an alliance of the priests with the Pharisaic leadership to deal with Jesus, prompted by his threats to the Temple, as they supposed them to be.

Accordingly, Sanders believes that the usual explanation of the incident, which sees Jesus as protesting against commercialism in the sacred place, is incorrect. The exchange of currency in the Temple environs, against which Jesus is supposed to have been protesting, was actually unavoidable, Sanders thinks, given the necessities of the sacrificial system. Pagan coinage, which bore an image regarded as idolatrous, would not have been acceptable currency for the purchase of sacrificial birds and animals by those who had not brought their own. The money changers would have exchanged Roman coinage for Jewish, which could then be used without sacrilege for the purchase of the birds or animals required for their sacrifices by all those who lived more than a short distance from Jerusalem.

Jesus appears to have taken the sacrificial system of the Temple for granted. According to Sanders, he could not have opposed particular features of it without calling the whole system in question. In that case, there must have been some other reason for his actions. This is why Sanders offers his own novel explanation.

Now, the synoptic writers do mention the Temple in their accounts of the trial, attributing the allegations that Jesus threatened its destruction to false witnesses. In the end, they relegate these charges to the background, making Jesus' condemnation turn on a charge of blasphemy, based on his failure to deny that he was the Messiah, when the question was put to him explicitly.

The writer of the Fourth Gospel retains the charges in his own very different and much more convincing account of Jesus' interrogation by the priestly leadership. However, the author of this Gospel antedates the Temple incident itself to the beginning of Jesus' ministry, on a previous visit to Jerusalem on a pilgrimage festival, which he alone records. He offers an allegorical interpretation of the saying, "he spoke of the Temple of his body."[25] It is interesting, however, and perhaps insufficiently noticed, that this writer does assume that Jesus spoke some such words as, "Destroy this Temple and in three days I will raise it up."[26]

Unlike Sanders, Vermes lays little stress on the incident, assuming in his brief reference to it that Jesus was concerned to keep business dealings out of the actual precincts of the Temple. Sanders can hardly be correct in assuming that commercial transactions of this kind, though certainly necessary to the sacrificial system, necessarily had to take place in the actual Temple area. Why could they not have been undertaken in the immediate neighborhood, but outside the sacred area? This seems inherently more appropriate to the holiness of the sanctuary. Perhaps therefore, actual abuses of the sanctity of the Temple had grown up over time.

If Jesus really did wish to keep commercial transactions out of the sacred precincts, this would show his reverence for the Temple. On the other hand, it has sometimes been suggested that he was opposed in principle to the Temple cultus, that is, the sacrificial system as such. The whole matter is unquestionably puzzling, and there may be something behind the accounts now difficult to recover.

THE "TRIAL" OF JESUS

We have now arrived at a central point in considering the historicity of the myth of the Christ-killers. We are confronted in the Gospels with several different accounts of Jesus' condemnation and death, differing in many important respects but essentially in agreement in laying the blame for his death on the Jewish religious authorities.

In the earliest gospel, Mark, followed by Matthew, we find what purports to be an account of a full-scale religious trial of Jesus before the highest Jewish court, the Sanhedrin, leading to his condemnation for blasphemy, an offense carrying the death penalty. The blasphemy is supposed to consist in claiming to be the Messiah, the Son of God. The Jewish court could not carry out the capital sentence under the Roman occupation. The authorities therefore hand Jesus over to the Romans, not for the religious offense of blasphemy but on the political charge of being a messianic claimant, and he is executed (unwillingly) by Pilate, the Prefect.[27]

In Luke's Gospel, there is an account superficially resembling Mark's and Matthew's and often confused with theirs, but in fact it is substantially different.[28] Jesus is brought before the "council," but there is no formal trial or condemnation. Even Pilate does not try him but acts as his defender; the reader naturally receives the impression that Jesus is crucified by the Jewish crowd. What Luke describes is in effect a lynching of Jesus by the Jews.

The Fourth Gospel has a much more plausible story of a hearing in private before the high priest, leading to a decision to hand Jesus over to the Romans to stave off heavy reprisals against the population at large over the messianic agitation centering around Jesus. Even this Gospel, however, retains the highly improbable account of Pilate attempting to avoid the outcome but yielding to Jewish agitation.[29]

In all four Gospels, the whole tendency of the accounts is to exculpate the Romans, who beyond question actually tried and executed Jesus for sedition, and transfer the blame to the Jewish people. Through the centuries, these accounts have been the principal basis for the notorious charges against the Jews as Christ-killers and deicides. The question of their historicity is of central importance.

We can say straightaway that the accounts of a religious trial before the Sanhedrin cannot be grounded in historical truth.[30] The reasons are numerous and overwhelming. To begin with, the writers represent the judges as condemning Jesus for blasphemy. The basis of the offense is said to be his claim to be the Messiah or failure to deny it when the question was put to him by the high priest.

It is not a religious offense at all in Jewish law to claim to be the Messiah. Even if Jesus had made the claim, which so far he had not, he could not have been charged or condemned by the Sanhedrin for it. Moreover, there is nothing blasphemous in a Jew claiming, even falsely, to be the Messiah. So far, all the claimants have proved to be mistaken, but they have not been accused of blasphemy.

In Jewish law, blasphemy involves an improper use of the great name of God, YHWH. There is no suggestion in these sources that Jesus was ever accused of such an offense, and in fact he is often represented, as he actually is in this context,[31] as avoiding even innocent use of the word *God*, as pious Jews still do.

An unfounded claim to be the Messiah could only be blasphemous for those who regard the Messiah as the divine Son of God. Since Jews did not and never have believed that the Messiah will be the Son of God in this sense–which Jews find idolatrous and offensive–it would have been impossible for his judges to have regarded a claim by Jesus to be the Messiah as constituting blasphemy.

Only in Christian eyes would an unfounded claim to be the Messiah be blasphemous, since only Christians regard the Messiah as divine. The accounts of the trial in Mark and Matthew therefore presuppose, and require for their intelligibility, a substantial development in Christian theology. Such a development could only have occurred outside the original Jewish environment of Christianity and would have been inconceivable at the time and in the circumstances of Jesus' trial. These writers have already lost touch with essential features of the Jewish religious outlook, and they are addressing themselves to a purely Gentile audience.

No Jewish court could have condemned Jesus for blasphemy. It is quite clear, therefore, that in this central respect the accounts in Mark and Matthew of a religious trial before the Sanhedrin are devoid of historical basis; it follows that no theological conclusions can legitimately be drawn from the words here attributed to Jesus.

There are also major problems with the procedures attributed to the court. We have no evidence coming from Jesus' time of the rules of judicial procedure governing the conduct of hearings before the Sanhedrin on a capital charge. We do have precise evidence dating from somewhat later, in the Talmudic period. Vermes, like several other scholars, thinks it reasonable to suppose that at least the majority of these regulations would have already been in force in Jesus' time. Following the Jewish scholar Paul Winter in his influential book *The Trial of Jesus,* Vermes concluded that if indeed such a trial as the Gospels describe took place, the Sanhedrin achieved the considerable feat of breaking just about every rule in the book on a single occasion.[32]

One of the most relevant of these rules prohibits holding a capital trial by night or on a festival. We are asked by the synoptic writers to believe that Jesus was arraigned before the full Sanhedrin on the evening of the Passover celebration. Given the especial sacredness for Jews of the first night of Passover, such a claim alone will strain the credulity of anyone who has ever thought about its implications. Once again, only a Gentile audience, ignorant of Jewish laws and Jewish feelings, could have found it credible. There are many other instances of improper procedure in the hearing as recorded. They alone would have been sufficient to invalidate the trial and make a death penalty grossly illegal.

The gospel writers do strongly suggest that there were serious improprieties in the handling of evidence, and that there was a miscarriage of justice. If procedural irregularities had been all that was wrong with their accounts, it might have been possible to conclude that a trial actually took place, but was conducted in an irregular manner. But the procedural questions are of relatively minor importance in the accounts compared with the major issues just discussed.

The writers themselves in the end dismiss them as irrelevant, since they believe that Jesus was convicted of blasphemy out of his own mouth by his acknowledgment of the messianic claim. Jesus' condemnation is in their eyes providential and divinely willed, though the Jewish people are none the less to blame. His death on the cross "must" come to pass and be the means of the world's salvation.

The historicity of the whole affair is more than suspect. Paul knows nothing of it,[33] and the accounts in the first two Gospels are both conflicting and highly tendentious. As for Luke's even more tendentious account of what amounts to a Jewish lynching of Jesus, while Pilate uselessly attempts to declare him innocent, it is even less worthy of credence.[34]

From anything we know from other sources of the character and conduct of Pilate, the accounts in all four Gospels of his inadequate attempts to defend Jesus against a Jewish mob howling for blood are so improbable as to border on the ludicrous. Pilate was eventually relieved of his post for brutality in his administration excessive even in Roman eyes.[35] It is not easily conceivable that this administrator, who did not shrink from massacres, would have gone through scruples of conscience on whether it was legitimate, in view of the nobility of Jesus' character, to yield to Jewish demands for the crucifixion of one individual.

Matthew adds an even more devastating but no less improbable touch when he has the crowd shout, "His blood be on us and our children,"[36] words that have been used down through the centuries to justify many a pogrom and persecution. The myth has already taken over from history.

WHY DO THE GOSPELS FALSIFY HISTORY?

The conclusion cannot be escaped that the accounts of the trial in the synoptic Gospels are false to history. As well as the demands of the structure of a rapidly developing myth, they undoubtedly reflect the need of the Church to be in good standing in the Roman world at the time they were written. The Romans come out reasonably well from these gospel accounts, collectively and individually, while the

Jewish authorities are represented as unscrupulous and unjust and the crowds as bloodthirsty. We do not know if the device worked to save Christian lives in the dangerous times of the first century. We do know that it cost countless Jewish lives in the subsequent centuries.

Was this falsification of history deliberately and knowingly undertaken by the gospel writers? It seems impossible to say. If these writers were Gentiles, remote in culture and religious background from the Jewish events they chronicle, and powerfully influenced by the demands of the myth, perhaps they might have supposed that they were recording events truthfully. If so, however, they are not likely to be reliable witnesses in their picture of the Jewish world in which Jesus lived, or of the events of his life, even though (as we have argued) some historical truth can be extracted from their narrative by critical methods.

THE ROMANS WERE THE CHRIST-KILLERS

The upshot of the gospel accounts is to divert attention from a solid historical fact, nevertheless unmistakably present even in their own accounts, that Jesus was condemned by a Roman court on a Roman charge, and put to death by a method of execution then used only by the Romans. So successful is this diversion of attention that to this day countless Christians believe that the Jews killed Christ.

No one today blames the Italian people, the putative descendants of the Romans, for what their ancestors did in crucifying Jesus. The supposed guilt of the Jews has echoed down history, justifying innumerable massacres. Even today, innocent Jewish schoolchildren are being called Christ-killers by their schoolmates. All this is based on these stories. To demonstrate their falsehood is not just a scholarly obligation but a human duty.

What part, if any, did the Jewish authorities play in the events leading up to the death of Jesus? Vermes, like a number of other scholars, is prepared to accept the broad historicity of the substantially different account in the Fourth Gospel.[37] There is no mention of a blasphemy charge, or indeed of any other. The chronology is different, since the interrogation before Annas is supposed to have taken place on the night before the beginning of Pesach, instead of during the festival itself, and the nature of the hearing is altogether different. Instead of a full-dress religious trial before the Sanhedrin, we have an informal hearing before Annas, the father-in-law of the high priest Caiaphas, continued in the latter's house, resulting not in a religious condemnation but a political decision to hand Jesus over to the Romans to save life.

The decision appears to have been justified by an argument of Caiaphas that it was expedient for one man to die for the people, rather than for the whole nation to be destroyed.[38] As a political leader, the high priest seems to have judged that the messianic enthusiasm gathering around Jesus would inevitably be interpreted by the Romans as a sign of incipient revolt. The Romans evidently knew enough about the Messiah to know that he was supposed to be the King of Israel. Any messianic claimant necessarily challenged the authority of Rome. Messianic agitation could lead to very severe reprisals, in which many would lose their lives. It was therefore arguably necessary and legitimate to sacrifice one man for the common good. From this point of view, it is irrelevant whether or not the priestly authorities thought that Jesus actually was a messianic claimant. The fact that he was widely thought to be one, and that the crowds were in consequence becoming excited about him, was judged sufficient.

Josephus records a parallel case, in which a similar decision was taken for similar reasons.[39] Here we seem to be on much more solid historical ground. The Jewish leadership, though not the people as a whole, did play a part in the execution of Jesus, but the motivation was not religious but political. The action of the priestly authorities, who had to operate under a ruthless occupation, could be ethically defended, as could analogous actions during the Holocaust. Under that kind of pressure, ideal justice has sometimes to give way to iron necessity.

WHY DID JESUS DIE?

Jesus did not die for the gospel or for any idea associated with Christianity. He did not die because his teaching about divine love and forgiveness to sinners offended Jewish legalism. He did not die because he claimed to be the Messiah, the son of God. He did not die because the Jewish people rejected their Messiah when he came to them. He was not killed by the Jews.

He died, so far as we can now determine, because of the enthusiasm of his own followers and of the crowd, who insisted on treating him as the Messiah in spite of his own precautions. The resulting popular enthusiasm grew into a danger for the people at large, recognized as such by the political leadership. If the Romans got wind of the messianic agitation around Jesus, they would have correctly regarded it as subversive. Their punitive measures would have been indiscriminate, involving the loss of more lives than those of the messianic claimant and his immediate followers. The risk was genuine that many innocent and uninvolved people would lose their lives.

In these circumstances, according to the account in the Fourth Gospel, which looks rather credible up to the point of the interrogation by Pilate, the authorities decided that it was necessary for one man to be sacrificed to avert much more extensive losses of life. In the event, only one man did die. The Romans were satisfied with the elimination of the supposed leader, and they made no attempt to eliminate Jesus' following along with him. The hard decision of the authorities must have seemed justified by its outcome. Twentieth-century experience renders it at least intelligible.[40]

Jesus was a victim not of Jewish hostility toward his teaching, which was Jewish in any case, nor of injustice in a religious trial improperly conducted, but of the ruthless practices of an occupying power. The decision of the Jewish political authorities to hand him over to Pilate as a subversive did lead fairly directly to his death. However, they may have regarded it as unavoidable, by this stage in the development of events. Jesus in no way deserved his fate, especially as he had personally done all he could to discourage the messianic agitation that constituted a public danger.

In any case, moral responsibility for Jesus' death rests squarely on Roman, not Jewish, shoulders. He was condemned to death by a Roman court with little interest in justice and none of the careful procedural safeguards of Jewish religious trials. He was put to death by perhaps the most barbarous method of execution that has ever been employed by a state. If he may be said to have died for any religious reason at all, it was for Judaism, not Christianity. He may legitimately be regarded as one of many Jewish martyrs to Roman rule.

The time has come, and came long ago, for Christians to drop all accusations against the Jewish people in the death of Christ. The facts set out in this account of his death are no longer in dispute among serious and impartial scholars. There can be no doubt that the Romans bear the responsibility for Jesus' death, which they and not the Jews actually brought about. If any person is to blame for Jesus' death, it is Pontius Pilate, so implausibly represented in the Gospels as his defender. In any scholarly inquiry, many conclusions remain uncertain. This is not one of them. The Jews are innocent of Jesus' death.

II

The Growth of the Myth

4

Paul and the Beginning of Christianity

How could Christianity have grown out of the life and work of Jesus the Jew? The question now stares us in the face. It will not be easy to answer, and perhaps it never will be answered with certainty. The right way to answer the question will be the way we have already used in attempting to imagine what Jesus himself was like: this time, stripping off later developments, we must try to imagine the earliest form of Christianity for what it was, a Jewish messianic movement. Then we can start to see how the original beliefs of this movement were transformed into the Christian myth, in which the Jews appear as the enemies of Jesus – the Christ-killers.

Modern critical methods have made it possible to trace the outlines of a history of Jesus surprisingly different from the story that has been familiar to the Western world for two thousand years. We have learned of the life and death of a Jewish teacher who taught from his own direct experience of the nearness of God and his compassion for sinners. He aroused opposition from the pious and the zealous because he attempted to enact in his own doings the divine nearness and compassion for the "lost sheep of the house of Israel,"[1] but did not himself stray from the Torah God had given to his people.

But he also gained a reputation among his followers and the crowds for being something he did not claim to be, the Messiah who was to deliver his people. He saw it for an illusion and did what he could to dispel it, but in vain. And because of that illusion he lost his life while still a young man. He was crucified by the Romans as an insurgent, a pretender to the throne of his people, but his death seems to have averted a greater loss of Jewish life, which would have followed a Roman crack-down on the movement associated with him.

Several forces were at work in the process that transformed this human story into one of the great salvation myths of history, the foundation of the most influential religion in the world. The belief of some of Jesus' followers that he was to be the Messiah had been shattered by his death; now it received renewed energy from the visions of his resurrection. In trying to understand how he could have been the Messiah, they did what other Jews would have done: they looked in the

Scriptures for predictions of historical events in their own time, seeing in them redemptive significance.

They found what they were looking for, but in this case the search quickly led to an anti-Jewish outcome. So differently did the leaders of the new movement now read the Bible of their people that they soon created a virtually new book, the Christian Old Testament. The Old Testament is not the Jewish Bible. It is an extremely novel reading of the Septuagint Greek translation of the Hebrew Scriptures.[2] So reread, the Bible is no longer the history of covenant and Torah but a complex web of predictions of the life, death and resurrection of Jesus the Messiah.

Another important element in the transformation was the mythmaking propensity of the human imagination, working on the material of Jesus' story to give it universal significance and conform it to archetypal patterns found in other such myths. I do not mean to say dogmatically that Jesus' story lacked inherent significance for others. I am trying to understand the way in which the early Christians articulated the significance they saw in his story; they made use of mythical thinking.

This chapter opens a new section of the book, which I have called "The Growth of the Myth." So far, with the assistance of critical scholarship, we have been trying to pierce through the myth to discover what the real Jesus might have been like. Now it is time to reverse the process and consider how the myth grew up around memories of his life and death.

While the myth did not attain its full anti-Jewish proportions until the Middle Ages, its development was most rapid in the first years of the new movement. It must have been largely completed by the time of the composition of the earliest Christian documents to have survived, the letters of Paul to the various churches he was associated with. It is likely that Paul himself played the major role in the development and articulation of the myth. Little needed to be added after the Gospels appeared, near the end of the first Christian century. Even the second century theology that saw the Church as the true Israel, superseding the old in God's favor, is already implicit in the New Testament.

At this stage, we can hardly speak of theology. Even Paul and John, the "theologians" among the New Testament writers, are not theologians in the later sense, articulating dogma through philosophical analysis. The myth had already been influencing large numbers of people before anyone with a Greek university education began to work on systematically analyzing it and reconciling it with existing thought.

Throughout Christian history, the myth has directed emotions and actions more than theology did. The myth was usually more anti-Jewish than the official theology, though there were times when theology caught up. Perhaps that is one reason why the standard histories of doctrine have said so little about the palpable reality of Christian hostility toward Jews. It has taken a new critical principle to bring the extent of the hostility to awareness. Anti-Jewishness was the creation less of the theologians than of the popular mind.

In Paul, the developing myth is certainly *non*-Jewish in structure, in spite of his abundant use of Jewish themes and ideas, but it is perhaps not intrinsically *anti*-Jewish. By the time the New Testament was complete, however, the myth had already become the charter story of a new, predominantly Gentile, and by now strongly anti-Jewish religion.

The New Testament tells Christians whatever they would need to make them hostile toward Jews. Already the Jews are the Christ-killers. Hostility toward Jews is not a late corruption, absent from the foundation documents of the church. It is there already.

THE FIRST DAYS OF CHRISTIANITY

If the story of Jesus had ended with his death, nothing would have been heard of Christianity. However, it did not end there but was followed by a strange epilogue. Shortly after Jesus' death and burial, those who had known him in his lifetime began to experience visions convincing them he was still alive. The visions were contagious; more and more of his original followers experienced them, including a group of five hundred at once, according to Paul. Paul too finally received a vision, considerably after the original series had come to an end.

Christianity did not begin with Jesus and his teachings; it began in consequence of these visions, when his former disciples came to believe that he had risen from the dead and was therefore the Messiah after all. More precisely, it began when they started to bring the story of their new convictions to their fellow Jews.

We may be inclined to imagine that what they brought to the Jewish people was the Christian gospel of salvation through the death of Christ, as we know it from later history. Countless readers have gained that impression from the late book of the Acts of the Apostles, which features major utterances to Jewish audiences by Peter and by Stephen, the first Christian "martyr." Modern theologians have taught that the earliest preaching of the disciples of Jesus to their fellow Jews was the Christian gospel of the forgiveness of sins. This is hardly conceivable. Only the Gentile world would have needed a gospel of forgiveness. Jews already knew about divine readiness to forgive the repentant.

The speeches in Acts do retain some early traits, which have led some scholars to believe that Luke preserved characteristics of the first preaching of the apostles.[3] Nevertheless, in all probability, Luke had no way of knowing what was said on such occasions. In the manner of ancient historians like Thucydides, he wrote the speeches himself, putting down what he thought it appropriate for Peter and his associates to have said. Accordingly, the speeches largely reflect the beliefs of the church of his own day, very late in the first century, or perhaps into the beginning of the second. We can only suppose that the earliest preachers taught the later Christian gospel if we do what the New Testament itself does, and retroject later beliefs to a stage in Christian history when they had not yet developed.

We have to reconstruct the earliest form of the Christian message from clues in the New Testament, since we no longer have it anywhere in its original form.

Whatever Peter and others actually said on such occasions, they said on the basis of Jewish ideas common to themselves and their audiences. We can safely assume that the first Christian message proclaimed Jesus as the Jewish Messiah, albeit a novel one, and not as the Divine Savior of later Christianity. It was a message addressed to Jews and not to the world at large, having nothing to do with the religious destiny of the Gentiles.

Possibly, the new message also spoke of Jesus' death as a martyrdom atoning for the sins of the people. The Pharisees would have had no difficulty with this claim, if so, for they also taught that the martyrdom of a righteous man could have atoning efficacy. Paul tells us that he received from tradition that Jesus "died for our sins according to the Scriptures."[4]

It is not likely, however, that the earliest preaching claimed that Jesus had also died for Gentiles, as Paul does. Nor it is likely that the earliest preachers thought that the atoning value of Jesus' martyrdom was connected with his messianic role. Probably, they saw his resurrection as designating him as the future Messiah on his return to earth. His death was in itself an obstacle to thinking of him as the Messiah, an obstacle now cancelled for believers in his resurrection. At most, Jesus's death was regarded as the martyrdom of a righteous man.

It may not have been long before the new movement did address itself to Gentiles. In a few years, Paul had already assumed the leadership of the Gentile mission, and he was dominating it with his new gospel for the Gentiles, expressed through his own theological and literary gifts. Even he was probably not the first to bring the new message to a Gentile audience. Not many years after that, the movement had become a Gentile religion, already opposed to, and therefore by, its Jewish parent.

RESURRECTION VISIONS

The earliest surviving account of Jesus' resurrection is in Paul's first letter to the Corinthians, and he speaks only of visions.[5] The dramatic stories of an empty tomb and of physical manifestations of Jesus' risen body belong only to the much later accounts in the Gospels. As Pinchas Lapide has pointed out, if the New Testament accounts of the resurrection of Jesus are arranged in what scholars generally believe to be their chronological order, each successive account is longer and more detailed than its predecessor.[6] Paul has four sentences. Of the gospel writers, Mark has eight sentences, Matthew twenty, Luke fifty-three, and John fifty-six, taking up two chapters. Here truly is a story that grew in the telling.

The reports in the synoptic Gospels are inconsistent with one another, as well as with Paul's earlier account and with the presumably later one in John. Paul's early account does not agree with those in the Gospels at any point.

It is an obvious if surprising conclusion that there was no universally acknowledged tradition in the Christian movement of how the resurrection had happened. Like the stories of Jesus' death, all the accounts of the resurrection in the Gospels are strongly influenced by the belief that Scripture is being fulfilled in the events they describe. Unlike Paul's version, the Gospels tell of an empty tomb, together with some kind of supernatural announcement of the resurrection, though the identity and number of the messengers varies, from one young man in Mark to two men in Luke to one angel in Matthew. With the important exception of Mark, the earliest, the Gospels also describe resurrection appearances of Jesus himself, though their accounts differ greatly from one another.[7] Geza Vermes believes that the story of the empty tomb is too firmly embedded in the tradition to be disregarded, and that it must be the one solid fact underlying all these stories, but he thinks we shall never know how the tomb came to be empty.[8]

Clearly, whatever it was, the "resurrection" of Jesus was no ordinary historical event. However, the historian need have no difficulty in principle with the earliest accounts, which refer to visions, not physical events. There is no doubt that these visions transformed the outlook of the disciples, impelling them toward beliefs and actions that would later prove to be the basis of a new religion, opposed to Judaism, the religion of Jesus himself and the one in which they themselves had been born and brought up.

THE BIBLE REREAD

The death of Jesus had put and end to hopes among his disciples that he was to be the Messiah. Apart from personal grief, the disciples were profoundly dispirited at the evident loss of their hope of the redemption of Israel through Jesus. This fact, clear from the sources, shows that the disciples had not at that stage begun to imagine the novel concept of a suffering Messiah.[9] It was not something Jesus had already taught them, so that they would be prepared to see his death as part of a divine plan of redemption. His execution by the Romans came to them as a devastating shock and the clear refutation of all their messianic hopes. If he had predicted his death, they do not seem to have taken him seriously. Their hopes for messianic redemption were too strong.

The visions of Jesus as alive, once accepted as authentic, put matters in a different light. If God had now vindicated Jesus by raising him from the dead, the shame and ignominy of his death as a criminal had been cancelled. Even his failure to accomplish the victories predicted of the Messiah might be explained. The way was open to interpreting his death in a positive way, as part of God's plan of redemption. They could once more believe that Jesus had been the Messiah, though a thoroughly unexpected one. His death could be seen as a martyrdom atoning for the sins of others, and perhaps as more.

If God had raised one person from the dead, this must be the beginning of a general resurrection of all the dead. Many Jews, especially Pharisees, expected that all the dead would rise again at the end of history to take part in the messianic age. If Jesus had actually risen from the dead, the final transformation of the world must have begun to unroll.

The resurrection of someone from the dead would not prove that he was the Messiah. Nobody expected the Messiah to rise from the dead–he was not expected to die. Rather, when others rose from the dead, they would owe their resurrection to the work of the Messiah.

Nevertheless, Jesus had been crucified as a supposed Messiah. The scholars appear to be in agreement that it is a solid historical fact, indeed one of the few absolutely reliable facts at our disposal, that the Romans crucified him under the title of "The King of the Jews." If God had vindicated Jesus by raising him from the dead, then the ironically bestowed royal title had after all been literally true. The executed rebel must have been the King Messiah.[10]

Peter may have taken the lead at this point, as the much later stories in the Gospels and Acts suggest. Always in the forefront of those who had believed Jesus to be the Messiah in his lifetime, he now seems to have returned to the task, emboldened by the resurrection visions and convinced that he had been right all along. But it was not a simple matter to reestablish a crucified insurgent as the Messiah. For anyone who had not themselves experienced resurrection visions, the notion must have seemed altogether absurd.

To convince anyone else that Jesus was the Messiah and perhaps to clarify the new idea in their own minds, Peter and his friends needed something more than stories of a resurrection that even those who now told them had themselves apparently regarded as incredible when they first heard them. The belief that Jesus was after all the Messiah required a foundation in biblical prophecy, the ultimate source of the regular expectation of the King Messiah.

The New Testament books would not be written for decades to come or canonized as Scripture for generations more. Jesus' followers were Jews. They went to the Jewish Bible for confirmation of their new convictions. Like all other Jews at that time, they believed implicitly that the whole text of the Bible had been divinely given and that every word and phrase of it was full of meaning, even previously unsuspected meanings.

Through the Torah and the Prophets, God had made his will known, including the pattern of future history. Especially for people who looked forward eagerly to the coming of the messianic age, the Bible was an inexhaustible store of necessary information about the character of the new age and the way it would come about. All that was needed was to search the Scriptures expectantly.

Peter and his associates, joined perhaps now by Yaakov (James), the brother of Jesus, who seems to have assumed the leadership of the Jerusalem community at an early stage, set about looking for the necessary proof texts. In all probability they did not search at random. They knew what they were looking for and more or less where to find it. They used the existing messianic texts, already interpreted as such by the tradition, and they looked, following existing Jewish methods of scriptural interpretation, for other apparently related passages that might fit the extraordinary history of Jesus himself, paying particular attention to texts about a righteous sufferer vindicated by God.

How long the process of finding the texts took we cannot say at all precisely. But it must have been substantially accomplished by the time Paul joined the new community, probably some two to five years after the death of Jesus, since allusions and citations in his letters make it clear that he already knew many of the texts that would later become traditional in all parts of the Church.

We have no contemporary documentation for this period, but it must have been the most creative in the whole history of Christianity. During that short time, the foundations of the whole edifice were laid and decisions taken by the new movement that would shape for many centuries the future relationships between Christians and Jews.

Two were critical. First, deciding to adopt a radically novel interpretation of Scripture to justify claims on behalf of a crucified and resurrected Messiah set the new movement immediately at odds with fellow Jews who could not accept the new interpretation. No other messianic movement of the period would have required so radical an adjustment from its supporters. The future of the movement within Judaism was already in question. The second decision set the new movement even further apart from its Jewish origins: Gentiles were soon joined to the movement without conversion to Judaism, yet regarded as full members of the people of God, perhaps even with a status superior to that of continuing Jews.

In time, and no long time, the new reading of the Hebrew Scriptures led to their simultaneous transformation into and displacement by the Christian Old Testament–virtually a new book with the same text, so differently did the Christians read it. First of all, the leaders of the new movement had found texts appearing to justify their belief that Jesus was the Messiah. In due course, as more and more such texts were found, it began to seem as if virtually the whole Bible was nothing else than a set of complex predictions of every detail of Jesus' life and even of the life of the Church. By the time the Gospels were written, the idea had become so fixed that the Old Testament could be used as a source of information about events in Jesus' life where existing traditions provided conflicting information or none.

Finally, the Church had to lay claim to the Bible as its own. The new meaning had so completely taken over from the old that the only remaining function of the book was Christian. The next century would see a bitter struggle for the retention of this transformed book in the new Christian Bible. Winning the struggle meant co-opting the book from the Jews, denying them the right to it. It must become the book of the Church.

The second decision was perhaps even more fateful. From very early on, the members of the new movement began to address Gentiles as well as Jews and to experience greater success among them. They may have been led in this missionary enterprise by Greek-speaking Jews from the Diaspora who had been present at the inception of the new movement. Already precariously rooted in Judaism because of its innovations, the new movement was soon much more attractive to Gentiles; before long, it was first predominantly and before very long almost exclusively composed of Gentiles.

Did the earliest Christians make full proselytes to Judaism of the Gentiles who believed in their preaching? It seems more than possible that they, or at least some of them, omitted to circumcise and immerse their converts, while nevertheless treating them as if they were fellow members of the Jewish people. When Paul tells us that he persecuted the members of the new movement, it seems most likely that their offense in his eyes was not just preaching to Gentiles but joining them to a Jewish movement without going through the proper procedures for converting them.[11]

There would have been nothing contrary to Jewish law in attempting to convince fellow Jews that Jesus was the Messiah, provided this activity was not accompanied by innovations in action breaching the existing *halachah* (the accepted manner of observing the Torah). There was nothing in the teaching of Jesus that would have led his disciples after his death to break with Jewish observance in their own behavior, and there is no evidence that they did so at this stage.

However zealous Paul was at that time, on his own testimony, zeal alone does not account for activities that he himself would later call "persecuting" the new movement. He must have had some objective reason for his extreme displeasure with the movement, and it is hard to imagine what else it could have been. Simply announcing that Jesus was the Messiah could not have aroused that kind of reaction, for there is nothing contrary to Judaism in a messianic claim.

The very implausibility of this particular claim, from a Jewish point of view, rendered it negligible. The joining of Gentiles to the Holy People without circumcision and commitment to the Torah was an innovation that cut at the very roots of Jewish identity as hitherto understood.

If this is the case, the development of Christianity into a new religion was already implicit in some of the earliest activities of the leadership of the new movement. The seeds of future opposition between the new religion and the old were likewise present in these earliest developments. The new movement could not make the claims it wished for Jesus without at the same time accusing the main body of the Jewish people of rejecting their Messiah and misreading their Scriptures.

If the members of the Christian movement were the only Jews to understand the true meaning of the Scriptures, God must have revealed his purposes only to them; alternatively, they were the only Jews faithful enough to understand what God had all along meant to convey through the Scriptures about the way he intended to redeem Israel. Either way, the Christian movement in its own eyes now constituted the faithful remnant of the people of Israel. The small group of Christians were the true Jewish people. Before long, the claim would be made explicitly.

Joining Gentiles to the covenant people without making them converts to Judaism could not fail to arouse the strongest Jewish opposition. As we shall see later in this chapter, conversion was, and is, closely analogous to naturalization into another people. Because this people was collectively a party to a covenant with God, whose terms included living by the Torah, it must be assured that the convert joining the people intended personally to observe the Torah in full along with people to whom he would now belong.

No such demand was made on converts to the new faith, at least in the areas where Paul's own influence was dominant. On the contrary, Paul forbade his converts to observe the Torah. As the Christian movement became more Gentile, its criticism of mainstream Judaism turned increasingly hostile, and it was soon transformed into global rejection. Before long, the new religion would claim to have superseded the old in God's plan and in his favor.

The original leaders of the movement probably could not have foreseen the effects of their actions. Jesus himself had shown no interest whatever in a mission to Gentiles, on the contrary, and he had therefore left them no guidance on the matter of proselytism. Passages in the Gospels in which Jesus speaks of a universal mission are by common consent of the critics late additions. The new leaders had to improvise decisions to meet unforeseen developments.

Whatever differences of opinion there may have been between the leading personalities in the movement, then and later, on other matters, they were united in the conviction that the risen Christ would shortly return to earth to carry out all the traditional functions of the Messiah. They did not look forward to twenty centuries of history or more. They expected history to come to a glorious end in a few months or years at the most. No doubt, the urgency they took for granted justified in their eyes innovations that in other circumstances would have been long pondered and discussed, and their effects on Jewish unity carefully assessed.

THE TEXTS

When the new movement went to the Bible to find support for its messianic beliefs, it found numerous texts that appeared to provide it. By modern critical standards, they do not. Either they refer in their original context to events in the prophet's own time, or to the victory of the messianic King of normal Jewish expectation, or they are Greek mistranslations of the Hebrew original, or their resemblance to the events of Jesus' story is random and accidental.

A famous text that actually depends on such a Greek mistranslation of the Hebrew original is the proof text for the virgin birth of Jesus. "A virgin shall conceive and bear a son, and his name shall be called Immanuel."[12] Here the Hebrew simply says a young woman, without any reference to a virgin, and the context makes it clear that the reference is to the prophet's own time. Such texts could only be supposed to refer to Jesus by wrenching them out of context or reading them against the intention of the original writer.

However, this way of reading the Scriptures as prophecies of later times was not altogether peculiar to the Church. Other Jewish groups, such as the Essenes, were reading the Scriptures in much the same way but for different purposes. There were no modern biblical critics in first-century Palestine. However, Christian use of mistranslations was soon apparent to Jewish opponents, and the novelty of reading the Torah and the Prophets as predictions of an unorthodox Messiah made their acceptance of the new reading unlikely.

The concept of a suffering Messiah who would shortly return from the dead to inaugurate the full messianic age was more startlingly novel than any of its contemporary counterparts, such as the Essene reading of the Bible. The concept of a suffering Messiah is apparently unknown in Jewish sources before the tribulations of Roman persecution in the suppression of the revolt of Bar Kochva in the following century, and only hinted at then.[13] The various sectarian concepts of which we know still seem to assume that the Messiah will personally inaugurate the new age by a victory of some sort.

The texts that the leadership of the new movement found in the Torah, the Prophets and the Psalms, came to be known as the Testimonies. They are the real foundation of Christian theology. The texts are referred to many times in the New Testament, they are quoted and paraphrased in the Christian liturgy, and they formed the basis of Christian instruction from the first. In the following centuries they would be collected together in books called Testimonies.

Most of the same texts are still familiar to present-day Christians. In fact, many of the most important are also familiar to countless people who have not maintained a connection with the Christian church. Handel set many of them to immortal music in his oratorio, the *Messiah*, reinforcing by the beauty and emotional power of his work the conviction that the texts were messianic.

Space precludes reproducing here the new texts discovered and used by the earliest Christians, but it will be helpful to the reader who wishes to examine them to give some references. Hosea 6:2 was taken as a prophecy of the resurrection. The Psalm texts that many scholars believe refer to the enthronement of YHWH as King were also pressed into service, along with many other texts from Psalms, including Psalms 8, 16, 18, 22, 69, 89, 110, 118:22 (cf. Isaiah 8:14, 28:16).

Many of these psalms refer to the sufferings and subsequent vindication of a righteous person, and thus they could be taken to apply to the history of Jesus. Psalm 22, taken in Jewish interpretation to refer to Esther, not the Messiah, seems to have been chosen because of the reference to the dividing of the garments of the sufferer. It therefore no longer seems as certain as it formerly did that Jesus actually recited it on the cross, or that if he did he had in mind his own subsequent vindication.[14] Among other prophetic texts made use of were Daniel 7 and Daniel 2:34f, as well as Zechariah 12:10.

The Daniel texts with a little improvisation around them gave the concept of the Son of Man, discussed in the previous chapter, though the direction of his journey on the clouds was reversed to fit the expectation of Jesus' return. Out of this web of texts the searchers constructed a whole new midrash, weaving together the passion, resurrection, and heavenly enthronement of Jesus as Messiah.

The cycle of songs in Isaiah 42 and 52–53, about a suffering servant of the Lord, must have become important at a fairly early stage. Like most of the other texts the early leaders found, the songs had not previously been regarded in Jewish interpretation as referring to the Messiah.[15] Indeed, it seems likely that early interpreters of the Bible did not think of them (as modern scholars do) as a cycle at all, but as isolated texts.

There is no reliable evidence that early Judaism derived a particular figure of a Suffering Servant of the Lord from these texts, especially under that name. It would therefore not be correct to assume that the early Christians identified Jesus with a previously recognized Suffering Servant, as scholars have often believed.[16] The idea of the suffering servant developed gradually, within Christian rather than Jewish reflection on the texts.

In Jewish interpretation, when the figure of the servant of the Lord is discussed at all, he is generally taken to symbolize the people of Israel and his sufferings those which have been its historical destiny. The Christian movement began to read these texts as pointing to Jesus and his ignominious death. Read in this way, the texts allowed them to interpret his death as meritorious and bringing forgiveness for the sins of the people. The Pharisees believed that the death of a righteous person could atone for the sins of others. Perhaps, then, faith in the death of Jesus as an atonement originated with the belief that he had died as an innocent martyr. If so, this is yet another link between the early Christian movement and the Pharisees, later to become enemies. James, soon to be the leader of the Jerusalem church, was close to the Pharisees.

The scriptural case for the belief that Jesus was the Messiah is based, and has from the beginning been based, on these texts. If they had not been important to the Church, theologically as well as apologetically in the defense of Christianity against its critics, it is unlikely that the Jewish Bible would have retained its status as scripture for the Christian church, as it did, since it no longer had the traditional function of embodying a Torah to be learned and observed.

In the second and succeeding centuries, the concept of Christ had moved far away from its roots. Now that he had become a divine Savior, having little in common with the Jewish Messiah, there were great pressures to discard the Old Testament, but the needs of theology and apologetic proved paramount. For a considerable period, the reread Septuagint translation was the Church's only Bible. Only gradually did the New Testament writings come to be regarded as Scripture too.

The Christian leadership had to show that Jesus' messiahship had been revealed in advance by God to the Jewish people and that his suffering and resurrection and eventual return were predicted in advance in Scripture, for otherwise no Jew could possibly have believed in the messiahship of the crucified. This original need, dating from the earliest days, became so fixed in the Church's tradition that the argument, and the Scriptures on which it was based, had to be retained later on, even in a wholly Gentile world.

There, the Jewish Scriptures meant little, and they were largely misunderstood. Some who did to some extent understand them could reproach the Church for retaining the Jewish Scriptures without obeying the commandments contained in them.[17] The very name of Christianity linked it inseparably with the claim that Jesus had been the Messiah. Although the word Christ was eventually filled with new content by the Gentile church and came to refer to the divine Son of God, no one could entirely forget that it had originally meant the same as the Jewish word, Messiah. But if Jesus was the Messiah, his role must have been prophesied in the Jewish Scriptures.

In the second century, it would have been much less embarrassing for the Gentile church to follow the example of Marcion, the heretic who believed that the revelation of God in Jesus was wholly new and without previous preparation, and jettison the Jewish Scriptures altogether.[18] The Church had the difficult task of attempting to explain why it retained the Jewish Bible while ignoring the specific commandments contained in it. But to abandon its basis in the Bible would have been fatal to the Church's own theology. It would also have removed an important defense against the charge that Christianity was a novelty, always considered a reproach in the ancient world.

However, the Church's interpretation of the Jewish Bible was in fact a wholly novel one. New meanings had been given to familiar texts, and new texts, hitherto not thought messianic at all, had been found and mobilized for the task. What began as total and outrageous novelty soon became normal, even obvious, for the new movement.

It became more and more clear to the members of the new movement that this was what God had "really" meant to say in the Bible about the Messiah. Indeed, they soon came to feel that this was the true meaning of the whole Bible; in their eyes, its main purpose was no longer to set out the story of God's choice of a people and his gift to them of a way of life, but to point forward to Jesus, the crucified and risen Messiah.

Around the key texts, everything fell into place. Jewish history was reread as pointing to and culminating in Jesus. Before him, everything had been provisional and prophetic. Now had come the age of fulfillment. The history recorded in the Bible, and the whole complex of personal and social ethics found in the Torah, ceased to have inherent significance. The Church saw them as the shadows of night when the day has come.

SECTARIAN THEOLOGY

There was one not inconsiderable difficulty in the way of this revolutionary reinterpretation of the scriptures. It did not commend itself to most Jews as plausible or faithful to the revelation God had given them. In their initial enthusiasm for their discovery, the leaders of the new movement doubtless felt that the new interpretation had only to be pointed out to be accepted by all their fellow Jews. Everything was now so clear to them that it must soon be clear to everybody else.

Their own conviction that Jesus had risen from the dead and the consequent exhilaration, which they interpreted as the gift of the divine Spirit, also expected in the last days, gave them utter confidence that they were right. The messianic age had dawned and would soon be full day. They were privileged to know in advance what everyone else would very soon know too.

In the meantime, their task was to proclaim the good news to their fellow Jews and to anyone who would listen. Some of them believed what they heard, but (as we know from the New Testament itself) most did not. The new interpretation of

Scripture was too much at odds with everything they had learned and there were none of the expected signs that the messianic age had arrived.

Jesus had been no conquering king, though no doubt a righteous sufferer, and the people continued to be under pagan rule. The only evidence for the claim was (from their point of view) a few preposterous accounts of a dead man, not inherently qualified for the messianic role, coming back to life, together with the claim of the members of the movement to possession of the Spirit, a claim not necessarily self-authenticating.

The rejection of the new concept of a suffering Messiah by the vast majority of the Jewish audience to which it was first addressed and its rapid acceptance by Gentiles provoked a crisis in the community, reflected, rather than described, in the New Testament. The crisis must have begun at an early stage, but it took decades to be absorbed and resolved. In relation to the Jewish people, the new community became more sectarian and inward looking; simultaneously it became more oriented to the Gentile world, where its ideas were finding greater response.

It began to regard itself in truly sectarian style as not merely the new but in due course also as the true Israel.[19] The claim that God had revealed his redemptive purposes to them alone eventually led the new group to the further claim that they alone constituted the covenant people.

We find similar ideas among the Qumran community, but there the hope remains that the rest of Israel will come to share their views and that finally the whole community will again be one. As the Christian movement became more Gentile in composition and the distinction between it and its Jewish parent more evident to both parties, the hope of convincing the majority began to vanish. The conviction hardened that it, and *not* the Jewish people, was God's true Israel, the people of the covenant promises.

The new sect began to see providential significance in the obstinate failure of other Jews to perceive the true sense of scripture. Paul, writing to the Corinthians at an earlier stage in these developments, speaks of a veil that covers the eyes of the Jewish people whenever they read their Scriptures.[20] The new sectarian community, considering its own to be the only correct interpretation of the Bible, regarded the standard and accepted interpretation among the Jewish people as the result of blindness, perhaps divinely caused, like the hardening of Pharaoh's heart at the time of the Exodus from Egypt. This concept is plainly visible in the speech of Stephen in Acts 7, composed by Luke in the nineties or later, but perhaps correctly reflecting the outlook of some members of the new movement in its earliest days.

The New Testament itself does not tell us much about the stages in these crucial developments. To some extent we have to infer them from what we know of the history of the developing church. It seems likely that no one ever sat down and thought through the implications of what was happening at such a speed. We do not find until much later a full theological justification of the split with Judaism. We will not find it in Paul's letters, nor in the Gospels. Where the thoughts of the early Christians are not clear, and perhaps were not clear even to themselves, we must look at their actions and determine the significance that they must have had for them as Jews and how they would have been regarded by other Jews.

The fundamental attitude of the emerging Church to Judaism stands out from the fact that while Jews were baptized by the Church, Gentiles were not circumcised (except by the minority of Jewish Christians, whose importance quickly dwindled). As Geza Vermes (among others) has shown, the Christian understanding of baptism owed much to the existing Jewish understanding of the meaning of circumcision, and thus, it must in some sense have replaced it.[21] We cannot avoid the inference that belief in Jesus as the Messiah soon came to be determinative for membership of the new community, replacing the normal and recognized means of entry into the Jewish people.

THE CRUCIAL BREAK

Now, for the first time, we can observe the beginnings of the Christian anti-Judaism that would in due course develop into full-blown antisemitism. The new movement was compelled by the logic of its own beliefs to deny legitimacy to the main body of the Jewish people. A theological disagreement was already turning into a rejection of another group, a rejection heavy with consequences for the Jewish people in the centuries to come. The infant Church alone understands Scripture, and the Jews no longer understand its meaning. God's covenant people no longer understand God's purposes for them, and they have turned away from their historical fulfillment. All this is the consequence of the Church's claim that Jesus was the Messiah, although he had not fulfilled any of the prophecies.

This is no minor difference but a total change not only in the way the biblical texts concerning the Messiah were read but also of the very meaning and function of the Torah and the Prophets. The fundamental and original claim of Christianity, that Jesus is the Messiah, or Christ, entailed repudiating the right of the Jewish people to determine the meaning and function of the Scriptures that had been given to them. After this redefinition of the meaning of the Torah, it was no great further step to break away from its commandments, as Paul and Gentile Christianity did. Soon the Jews would be accused of legalism, and even of outright disobedience to God, for continuing to observe them.

Moreover, once Gentile Christianity added the repudiation of the Torah to the claim that Jesus was the Messiah, it had to take over the Jewish Scriptures as its own; giving them a wholly new sense, it attributed to them a novel function. It had to deny them to the Jewish people, or else renounce any claim to be in continuity with God's dealings with the human race in past centuries.

The Christian movement attributed the failure of the majority of the people to accept its own new reading of the Scriptures to blindness to their true meaning. But failure to interpret the Scriptures correctly, on this scale, could only be a symptom of something deeper. A people that failed to recognize its Messiah because it failed to read its Scriptures correctly could only be regarded as an apostate people: Israel must, temporarily at least, have departed from the covenant.

The newly formed church was therefore the only group in Israel remaining faithful to the covenant. And when this sectarian community actually aligned itself with the Gentile world, where it found a readier response to these ideas, a second fateful step had been taken in the alienation of the Church from its Jewish origins and in the growth of its historic claim to have superseded Israel as God's people.

Ideas that in their original Jewish context were merely sectarian acquired a new and dynamic significance when taken over by a predominantly Gentile church. They now became anti-Judaic. What has been called "the theology of supersession" was not full-blown until the following century, but its seed is present here. By early in the second century, the Church was already beginning to regard itself as not only the new but also the *true* Israel.

What is most astonishing about these developments is the dynamism and speed with which they were carried out. Scholars have sometimes supposed that the speed of the development cannot be explained on the hypothesis we have so far found most fruitful: Jesus himself did not believe he was the Messiah. So rapid a development presupposes, in their opinion, preparation for it in the lifetime of Jesus, by teaching about his messianic role, and the novel form it would take. But they have then to account for the failure of the disciples to foresee either Jesus' death or his resurrection. I have already argued that Jesus himself had explicitly contradicted the idea that he was the Messiah. No doubt, the visions of the resurrection, once accepted as genuine, seemed to confer certainty that the final age had dawned and that everything had changed and was now new. That would be enough to produce the dynamic changes we know occurred.[22]

MYTHMAKING

The earliest Christian concept, that Jesus was the fulfillment of the Messianic hopes of his people, was itself mythical, in the technical and neutral sense in which I have been employing the word. It inserted a historical figure into a preexisting myth of redemption. But it remained within the limits of Jewish faith, and it postulated only so much cosmic significance for Jesus as the Messiah inherently possesses.

It seems reasonable to suppose that the growth of a new salvation myth was in some way connected with the movement of Christianity into the Gentile world. The prologue to the Gospel of John, identifying Jesus with the divine Word, already fuses Jewish and Gentile thinking into a synthesis on which later incarnational theology could be grounded. Its terms are for the most part Jewish, but they appear in a framework that is strikingly non-Jewish.

Some of the early critics used the concept of myth to deny Jesus' real existence, making many of the more cautious among their successors suspicious of any mention of myth. The latter react especially strongly against suggestions that the story of Jesus was made up to fit the shape of some preexisting myth, such as the widespread Near Eastern myths of a dying and rising fertility god, or some Egyptian myths. I am not suggesting anything like this. I am convinced of Jesus' real existence and of the historicity of his life and death as a Jew. The elements of the earliest Christian faith are likewise Jewish.

However, the mythmaking imagination soon began to play upon the story of Jesus, investing it with meanings it did not originally possess. When the Messiah became the Christ, a new myth was born. A Jewish redeemer (as he had originally been thought to be) became the Savior of the world. The title Savior, applied to anyone but God, does not correspond to an existing Jewish concept, nor is Judaism a religion of salvation in this sense.

Christians began to see the death of Christ as a cosmic struggle with the forces of evil. On the cross, Christ defeated the devil and overcame sin and death. Now something new and different is to be required of members of God's people. No longer are they to observe the Torah given by God, now they are to believe in the power of the Savior's victory. Through belief and participation in the sacraments, they are enabled to participate in the victory of the Savior. To a very great extent, this later Gentile-Christian view of Christ is already present in the letters of Paul. The myth has already burgeoned out. Paul was a Jew, but these are not Jewish ideas.

Mythical thinking does exhibit common patterns. Not every myth is a fertility story, explaining the seasons of the year and how to make the crops grow. Many scholars believe that there are traces in Genesis of ancient Near Eastern creation myths, depicting God's victory over the monsters of chaos.

In the Bible, such scholars believe the ancient stories have been transformed by monotheistic faith, but creation is still depicted as a victory. God's enemies are no longer the monsters of the deep. Now he conquers the *tohu vavohu*[23] of chaos, ordering it by imposing distinctions on it. Whether or not these scholars are right in seeing traces of long superseded and half-forgotten myths in the Genesis story of creation, such ideas remind us of another mythical pattern closer to the one to which the story of Jesus appears to have been conformed.

The Jewish concept of Messiah was not rich enough in associations for non-Jews to power a Gentile religion. The word was retained in translation, but it needed and received a new mythical content. Jesus gained universal significance as the hero of a salvation myth at the expense of losing his Jewishness. But the cosmic struggle envisaged by the myth needed to be embodied in the details of the story.

If the divine Christ defeated cosmic enemies, the human Jesus must have had to face human enemies. Of course, he did, in the shape of the Romans. Why did the mythicized version of his story not cast the Romans as his primary enemies? A precritical or fundamentalist Christian might reply that historically it was in fact the Jews who encompassed his death because his religious claims challenged theirs. We have seen good reason to disbelieve this explanation.

The New Testament naturally does not draw aside the veil behind which the transformation of history was effected, and we have to speculate on the motives of those who managed it. As we have seen, the most likely explanation is connected with the movement of Christianity out of Judaism into the Roman world. On the one hand, the new movement was rejected by Jews, so that it must have seemed natural to think that the Jews had rejected Jesus beforehand. On the other, the Church needed to make its way in a Roman world where the Jews were less popular than they had been in the past and would later be again. Deliberately or not, they began to tell the story in such a way that the Romans would look better and the Jews look worse.

Now the human embodiment of the cosmic struggle between Christ and the forces of evil becomes Jesus on trial before the Sanhedrin, driven to his death by Jewish blood-lust and fanaticism against the ineffectual resistance of half admiring Rome. Now the Jews have become the enemies of Christ and finally the Christ-killers. In late strata of the New Testament, the charge became explicit.

In what is probably a late interpolation into the earliest surviving Christian writing, the first letter of Paul to the Thessalonians, we read that the Jews "killed the Lord Jesus," a patent falsification of the history recorded elsewhere in the New Testament.[24] In the Fourth Gospel, Jesus is represented as telling the unbelieving Jews that they are the children of their father the Devil, not the children of Abraham, still less of God, as they believe they are.[25] The new myth is now inseparable from profound hostility toward Jews.

PAUL, THE FIRST MAJOR THINKER OF CHRISTIANITY

Can we be more specific about the origins of the new myth? Hyam Maccoby, in a controversial book that came to my knowledge only late in the writing of my own,[26] argues cogently that Paul was personally the creator of the Christian myth. In the letters of Paul, the earliest surviving Christian writings, the story of Jesus the Jew has already been transformed into a cosmic myth of salvation. Now helpless humanity can only receive in faith the salvation brought from heaven by a quasi-divine Redeemer. The Torah Jesus lived by now appears as a temporary measure, no longer as God's chosen way with humanity and with the Jewish people as its nucleus and representative. Paul's Gentile converts need not–and must not–live by the commandments of the Torah.

Paul shows no interest whatever in the historical Jesus, whom he never met. The details of his life, his teaching, even the circumstances of his death, play no part in his scheme of salvation. Thus, Jesus' own adherence to the Jewish way seems to have been irrelevant to Paul's scheme of salvation. All depends on the descent to earth of the Savior, his death and resurrection, and his return to heaven.

This scheme, as Maccoby points out, has much more in common with Gnosticism than with Judaism. Man's part is no longer, as in Judaism, to cooperate with God in bringing his creation to perfection but to receive the gift of grace and live in the power of the Spirit now poured out on the Church. Through faith and baptism, the believer becomes identified with Christ's death and resurrection, dying to sin and rising to new life.

Nevertheless, Paul puts forward this essentially non-Jewish, perhaps latently anti-Jewish, scheme of salvation as the destined fulfillment of God's former dealings with the Jewish people. He represents himself as fully qualified to put forward this revolutionary interpretation of Judaism by virtue of his own Jewish birth and education as a Pharisee. Although his letters are addressed to Gentiles, they are full of complex arguments about the meaning of the Jewish Scriptures, transformed in his radical new interpretation into a prediction of Paul's own gospel for the nations.

These facts have led many of those who reject the old opinion that Jesus was the founder of Christianity to regard Paul as its real founder. Whether or not he was technically its founder, no one can deny that Paul played the major part in the transformation of a Jewish messianic sect into the nucleus of the most influential of all the world religions. If Paul did not personally create the Christian myth, he was certainly the one to give it its earliest and perhaps most powerful literary expression.

Nevertheless, the interpretation of Paul's ideas has been endlessly difficult, and continues to be unresolved among those most qualified to have an opinion. At present, much of the debate centers on the question of whether Paul, like later writers, was himself anti-Jewish, as the traditional interpretation of his ideas unequivocally requires.

THE TRADITIONAL INTERPRETATION

Was Paul anti-Jewish as well as Jewish, if indeed his own origins were Jewish, as he emphatically claims? In present-day terms, was he a Jewish antisemite? Did he insist that his Gentile converts should not observe the Torah because he believed it had lost whatever spiritual value it once possessed? If so, he would not have been the last Jewish convert to Christianity to turn against his own people and their faith, misrepresenting both to his new coreligionists. From the formative period of Christian theology in the first five centuries, down to our own day, most of those who have studied his writings have taken it for granted that he was indeed an alienated Jew who turned to an altogether new faith, rejecting the old as he did so.

Even today, Protestant theologians usually interpret his thought in the light of Martin Luther's distinction between the Law and the Gospel. According to Luther, Paul taught that the Law cannot save but only condemn, for it imposes standards unaided humanity cannot reach. Only the Gospel of the forgiveness of sins, based on the death and resurrection of Christ, can reconcile men and women to God and permit them to live according to his will in the power of the Holy Spirit.

In that case, the work of Christ has superseded the Jewish way of covenant and Torah. Christ has brought a new covenant, abolishing the old, and bringing its historical mission to an end. Not only is the Torah obsolete, but it also is and always was a way of slavery to commandments. In contrast, the gospel is the way of liberty in the Spirit. Worse still, the Jews, who had never obeyed the Law in any case, have killed Christ and persecuted his apostles. They can be saved only when they turn to Christ. In the end, however, they will all be converted to him, at his return.

Those who believe Paul taught such ideas are able to cite many passages from his own writings in support of their interpretation. If they are right, he must be held responsible for the theological anti-Judaism that soon grew up in the Church and proved to be the ancestor of later antisemitism. In any case, since his writings so eloquently set forth the Christian myth, inherently anti-Jewish as it turned out to be, he can hardly escape all responsibility for the implications later generations found in it.

WHAT IS WRONG WITH THE TRADITIONAL VIEW?

The principal difficulty with this traditional interpretation, as some Jewish scholars were the first to point out, is that it involves the assumption that Paul, the highly educated Pharisee, as he tells us he was, misunderstood the most elementary points of his own Jewish faith. He should have known that a person is not saved by keeping the commandments of the Torah. The word *saved* does not belong to the Jewish vocabulary. If, however, we are to look for an equivalent, we would have to say that all Jews are corporately saved by the divine act of delivering the people from Egypt and giving them the Torah to live by. Thus Jews do not concern themselves with the question of individual salvation as Paul does.

He must also have known quite well that "all Israel has a share in the life of the world to come."[27] In Christian terms, salvation for the Jew is by grace, not works. The commandments are a gift, not an obstacle course.

If, as he says, Paul really had an impeccable Jewish background, he must have known these basic facts about Judaism from his childhood: it is almost inconceivable that he could have regarded the Torah as a means of self-justification and therefore as an impossible burden. In themselves, the commandments of the Torah are by no means out of reach. Countless Jews have successfully kept them down the centuries. Indeed, Paul says he was himself blameless in this respect.

The contradiction can be resolved in one of two ways. Either Paul was not really a Pharisee of advanced scholarly accomplishment, as he himself claims, or the traditional interpretation that involves making him ignorant of basic Jewish beliefs is wrong. Most Jewish scholars, who know their own tradition best, have tended to discredit Paul's claim to be an advanced student of Pharisaic learning. Maccoby, for example, analyzes passages that have been taken to be particularly characteristic of Paul's Pharisaic background, arguing that Paul does not display the scholarly or logical expertise of a trained scholar in the Pharisaic tradition.[28] On this showing, he simply would not have measured up to the standards of the schools he is supposed to have attended. Christian writers, especially recently, have been more inclined to question the older interpretation of Paul, explaining his ideas as far more Jewish than had traditionally been supposed.

Maccoby concludes that the autobiographical passages in Paul's letters are to be viewed with skepticism. His own very different interpretation of Paul's personal history and religious ideas is part of a total reconstruction of Christian origins that has been severely criticized by some Jewish as well as Christian scholars for lack of attention to the details of the historical evidence. I have not adopted it here, for somewhat similar reasons, though I am impressed with Maccoby's ability to build up an alternative historical picture to the traditional one, explaining much that the latter cannot.

He believes, as we have seen, that Jesus was associated with the Zealots, that he did regard himself as the Messiah in something like the traditional sense, and that he hoped for a divine miracle that would deliver the people from Roman rule. Along with some ancient Jewish-Christian sources, Maccoby rejects Paul's claim to have been "a Hebrew of Hebrew-speaking parents" and to have been a Pharisee. He believes Paul was a convert from Gentile origins who failed to master either the Jewish way of life or Jewish scholarship. Embittered by his failure, he turned to the new messianic movement and created a world religion out of it on the basis of his own ideas.

Maccoby finds three sources on which Paul drew in the creation of the Christian myth. These are the following: (1) The Gnostic dualistic view of the world, in which humanity lives in a realm of darkness and despair, from which it can be rescued only by the descent of a savior from the world of light; (2) the pagan myths of dying and rising gods, current in the environment in which Paul grew up, together with the mystery rituals whereby the initiate could become identified with the god; and (3) Judaism itself, with its vast historical perspective from the creation to the end of the world, into which he could insert the new myth, giving Christianity the ancient pedigree that won it credibility in the Gentile world.

Maccoby does not believe Paul ever consciously thought out the new myth or adopted it as part of a deliberate strategy. He sees Paul as a compound of sincerity and charlatanry, like many contemporary evangelists. He believes in fact that the myth was created by Paul's unconscious mind, and rose to his consciousness more or less fully formed at the time of his crisis, when he had his vision of the risen Jesus.

Maccoby's case is not done justice to by a brief summary. His thesis has great explanatory power, and it can be supported by evidence Maccoby himself does not mention, such as the favor Paul enjoyed among the second-century Gnostics, who recognized in him a kindred spirit[29]; this awkward fact is often ignored by Christian scholars.

However, Maccoby's reconstruction involves treating much of Paul's autobiographical writing as self-serving and even mendacious, while building a considerable structure on the foundation of the later Book of Acts, generally treated by recent scholarship as less reliable than Paul's own writings. His methods lead to speculations about the real story that are not necessary to the present book, whether or not they are correct. Along with nineteenth-century scholarship, Maccoby also postulates a much sharper opposition between James and the Jerusalem church, on the one hand, and Paul and his colleagues in the Gentile mission on the other, than can be directly demonstrated from the sources. Later in the present chapter, I offer a more cautious account of their relations.

As we have already seen, the myth had anti-Jewish aspects that in due course would become the seed of full-blown antisemitism. Did these already include the casting of the Jews in the mythic role of "sacred executioner," as Maccoby puts it? This was the part they played in the developed myth, as we find it sketched in the Gospels and fully attested in later sources. The Christ-killers have a necessary function in the myth.

The question that now concerns us is whether this was already so for Paul. If so, we cannot avoid attributing to Paul the anti-Jewish views characteristic of second-century and later Christianity. Other recent scholarship casts doubt on this, seeing Paul as divided, with intense loyalties to Judaism conflicting with thoughts and actions quite unacceptable to other Jews. Unlike Maccoby and a number of other Jewish writers, some Christian scholars, of whom E. P. Sanders and Lloyd Gaston are perhaps at present the most influential, consider that we must now presume Paul did know the elementary facts of Judaism, and much more besides.

According to his own statement, if we choose to believe it, his own Jewish background was extremely solid. "Circumcised on the eighth day, of the people of Israel, of the tribe of Benjamin, Hebrew-speaking of Hebrew-speaking parents, in regard to [observance of] the Law a Pharisee, in regard to zeal a persecutor of the church, in regard to the righteousness which is within the Torah blameless."[30]

Although he mentions these things in a context implying that this is not something he ought to boast about (and indeed the implication is that there may be another, higher kind of righteousness), he does not decry his qualifications. In a similar context in another letter, he contrasts the new covenant with the old, the covenant of Sinai, praising the overwhelming splendor of the new. But he does not in fact say anything against the old covenant, except that it is not the new.[31]

Perhaps the word *splendor* may give us the clue we need. Paul tells us he had a vision of a new stage in the plan of God that impressed him as being of such overwhelming splendor that everything he had ever known paled by comparison. Yet he loved the people of his birth and upbringing. It was not any defect in the Torah, these interpreters argue, that caused him to praise the new way as far surpassing the old. It was because of what he believed he had understood in the moment when the risen Christ appeared to him and called him to be an Apostle to the Gentiles.

Paul believed that when God raised Christ from the dead, he had inaugurated a new and final stage in his dealings with human beings. What was now coming about was new, but it had been promised long before to Abraham, when God told him he would become the father of many nations. Paul understood the word *nations*, as other Jews did, as synonymous with Gentiles. Now, in the last days, the promise was to be fulfilled, and the Gentiles, hitherto excluded by their own choice and its consequences, would be brought in to share in the divine mercy.

From the time of Moses, God's dealings with humanity had been effectively confined to the Jewish people, for they alone had accepted a covenant relationship with him. Now, with the coming of Christ, all the prophecies were being fulfilled, and God's compassion and his saving action were broadening into an immense sweep to include the whole human race.

Paul believed he had been singled out by God for a glorious destiny of his own.

He was to bring to all who would listen the good news of the opening up of the covenant to the Gentiles. His task was to bring the Gentiles in before the final act of world history, the return of Christ.

Paul seems to have believed that Christ would not come back before his own mission had been completed. Clearly, then, he did not have to convert every human being in the world. His preaching to the Gentiles was a kind of symbolic proclamation. From his letter to the Romans, we can gather that he thought his task would be complete when he had preached the good news in Spain, which he, like his contemporaries, thought of as the limit of the world.

Gaston and scholars who think along similar lines argue that interpreters of Paul must take much more seriously than they have Paul's own statements that his calling was exclusively to the Gentiles and that he had no mission to the Jews. He therefore suggests that all Paul's negative statements about the Torah really refer to Torah as experienced by the Gentiles, who had rejected it. Gaston cites evidence from the Midrash to suggest that Paul may have believed that for Gentiles the Torah now works only condemnation and death, whereas for Jews, who had accepted it, it is a way of life. God has therefore provided a different means of salvation for the Gentiles through the death and resurrection of Jesus Christ. On these and related principles of interpretation, Gaston offers a remarkable rereading and even retranslation of Paul, which presents a very unfamiliar picture of him.

However, it is not clear on this view why Gentiles should not have a part in the life of the world to come, as Jews thought the nations could, either by keeping the Noachide laws or by conversion to Judaism. In Paul's day, Jews were energetically seeking proselytes. Gaston believes that Paul thought Gentiles, having once rejected the Torah, had no second chance of accepting it, and that God must provide them with a different path. If that was indeed Paul's view, he did not get it from the Pharisees.

It would not follow from such ideas, if Paul held them, that the Jewish people had been rejected. To them, as he says, the promises had been given, and they had enjoyed the blessings of the covenant all along. But now the time had come to move on with God to the fulfillment of his ancient promises, and to a new and even more glorious stage in his dealings with the human race. Nor need it mean that Paul regarded the Jews as Christ-killers. If we regard the later book of Acts as an unreliable source for Paul's life and ideas, as these scholars do, we shall find little to suggest that Paul blamed the Jews for Christ's death. The most famous passage that does so, the text in 1 Thessalonians that says the Jews "killed the Lord Jesus" is probably an interpolation by a later writer. In Paul's authentic writings,[32] Jesus' death is clearly voluntary, and he has no apparent interest in the agency, Jewish or Roman, by which it came about.

For Paul, it seems, the resurrection of Jesus had opened the new age of which the prophets had spoken. But God's work was still hidden and secret. The messianic age had not yet come in fullness. To share in its benefits along with the Gentiles to whom Paul preached, Jews also had to believe in the risen Christ and in God's new act in raising him from the dead and inaugurating the new age. God was creating a new people for himself, growing out of the old, and composed of those Jews and Gentiles who believed in the preaching by Paul and his colleagues of Christ crucified and risen.

According to writers like Sanders and Gaston, Paul believed that God had not deserted his own people and never would. The covenant remained in force. As he says in Romans 11, Israel is the stock into which the new branches of the Gentiles have been grafted. But the stock supports the branches, not the branches the stock. By God's mercy the privileges of the covenant had now been extended to the Gentiles, on special terms appropriate to their different historical destiny. This, if these writers are correct, is the gospel that had been entrusted to Paul, as the Apostle to the Gentiles.

THE VISION FADES

Paul lived and, according to tradition, died a martyr in the energy of this glorious vision of God's final work in the history of the world. In its light, all he had known before became dim. But after his own death, it was not long before the vision faded into the common light of day.

Christ did not return. The new age did not come. History was not transformed but went on as before. The vision became harder and harder to reconcile with everyday reality, and it had to be drastically reinterpreted by the leaders of the Church. From a messianic movement, living in the presence of the final future, Christianity became a religion in ordinary history. Now, the radically new event of the Christian gospel, which Paul believed had already transformed all history, bringing about nothing less than a new creation, became the mere novelty of a new religion in rivalry with an old one.

In future, Paul would be read by the Church as the first theologian of a gentile religion in rivalry with Judaism. His own contrasts between the messianic time and the history of preparation for it became transformed into an apologetic defense of one historical religion against the claims of another. In an unforeseen historical situation, Paul's writings came to mean something very different from what he had perhaps intended. They became what he himself may not have been, anti-Jewish, and so they have remained until this day. And they have been authoritative, as part of the Scriptures of the New Testament, in fixing that anti-Jewish theology in the dogma of the Church.

His actions in making converts to his own movement without making them Jewish proselytes now became all important, and nothing in his theology could be read as mitigating the rejection of Judaism they implied. Only in the last few years have scholars begun to read him in the context of his own vision and to imagine the conflict that may have existed in his mind between an old and a new love.

Nevertheless, it is important to remember that such a modern recovery of Paul's theology, even if valid, was in no way shared in the ancient world. The Paul the second century thought it knew, author of Hebrews, Colossians, and Ephesians, and the letters to Timothy and Titus, as well as the letters now regarded by scholars as authentic, was the foremost critic of Judaism, providing the ammunition for most of the later theological onslaughts on his own people. Above all, the myth stood in his writings and in the belief of early Christianity as its charter story.

The debate goes on, and it has not yet led to a new consensus. If anything, views are becoming more divergent. Unfortunately, a fully worked out and widely agreed interpretation of Paul's life and thought is not yet available. In spite of the very great importance such an interpretation would have for this inquiry, we shall have to be content for the present with much less than that.

Attempting to resolve current controversies in Pauline scholarship would certainly be beyond the scope of this book. Nor, perhaps, is it necessary to my argument to do so. What Paul actually thought is one thing, what he was taken to mean is another. His role in the development of Christianity into a new and anti-Jewish religion was on any showing pivotal.

If it is too soon to attempt a sketch of Paul's religious ideas that might command common assent among those most qualified to judge, there is something else we can do that may throw important light on the question that does concern us. We can concentrate on his actions in making converts to the people of God without requiring conversion to Judaism, and we can consider what these actions must have meant. Noting how he justified and explained them (to the extent that he did so at all in his letters) will take us some way into his theological ideas, but only as far as is necessary for our purpose. This is what the Jews of his own day would have done. Like other Jews, they could tolerate wide divergence of belief but insisted on unity in observance of the Torah.

More than anyone else, Paul was responsible for the spread of Christianity among the Gentiles, where its historical future lay. If he was not the first to take the decision to admit Gentiles into the people of God without conversion as Jews understood it, and without requiring of them the observance of the Torah, he put all his own authority and energy behind that decision.

Paul thus opened the way for a vast influx of Gentiles into the Church. Jewish proselytism could never have achieved comparable success, because the requirement of circumcision stood as a formidable barrier in the path of the convert. Many educated people in Graeco-Roman society, who shared Jewish belief in one God and who were impressed by Jewish ethics, became semi-proselytes, observing almost everything Jews did, except that they held back from circumcision. Circumcision is painful, even under modern conditions, and it was then often interpreted as equivalent to castration. Moreover, after the Jewish revolt in the reign of Hadrian, it was forbidden by Roman law, and the prohibition was not formally revoked when other restrictions on Jewish life were loosened.

Paul's decision to abandon the normal requirements for conversion made it possible for them, as for other Gentiles, to enter the community without this barrier. More than any other factor, these decisions were responsible for the rapid development of Christianity into a new religion, soon strongly opposed to, and in due course by, the Jewish people from which it had sprung.

A JEWISH APOSTATE?

Paul was a Jew who did some very un-Jewish things. He converted Gentiles to the people of God without imposing on them the normal requirements of the *halachah* for conversion.[33] More, he actually strongly discouraged his converts from undergoing circumcision or observing the Torah, substituting faith in Christ for adherence to the existing covenant and its requirements. It is also fairly clear that when among these Gentile converts, he himself lived as they did, without observing the specific requirements of the Torah falling only on Jews. (However, he apparently expected his converts to keep the ethical commandments, though on his principles the theoretical justification for this is not obvious, and was questioned at the time.)[34]

Where Jewish and Gentile Christians lived together, he seems, though not perhaps consistently, to have expected the Jews to give way to the Gentiles on points of observance that might have created difficulties for the unity of the new community.[35] From a Jewish point of view, all that adds up to apostasy. These actions were undoubtedly largely responsible for the growing alienation between Gentile Christianity and the Jewish community.

PAUL'S ACTIONS

When Paul admitted Gentiles in considerable numbers to the people of God, without requiring them either to be converted according to the accepted Jewish standards, or to observe the Torah when they had become converts, these actions were altogether unacceptable for other Jews, including some other Christian Jews. They regarded them as destructive of the very basis of Judaism. They involved nothing less than a complete change in the prevailing understanding of Jewish identity and of the covenant with God on which it was based.

Existing Jews could not regard these converts as Jewish, although they appear to have supposed that Paul did. In fact, he did not encourage them to regard themselves as Jews either. But he did teach them that they belonged to the people of God, as much as or perhaps more than Jews themselves.

The importance of Paul's action in making irregular converts of Gentiles, while acquiescing in, or actually supporting, the baptism of Jews by his colleagues in the Church, has perhaps been underestimated by more recent scholars, especially those who have concentrated on his theology, attempting to interpret it in more Jewish ways. The importance of what he *did*, whatever he thought, was certainly not underestimated at the time, either by Christians of Jewish origin who wished to remain Jews, or by the main body of the Jewish community.

We have no direct evidence of the latter's opinion of Paul. He does not seem to be mentioned in Jewish writings of the period. The low opinion of Paul held by Christian Jews can be gathered from their own literature, where he sometimes appears in disguised form.[36] In the New Testament, a letter attributed, probably wrongly, to James, the leader of the Jerusalem community, attacks a divorce between faith and action that could have been deduced from Paul's teaching on justification through faith.

While Paul does not seem to have intended such a divorce as the writer of the letter attacks, we can see how Christian Jews, with a traditional Jewish understanding of the inseparability of faith and obedience to the commandments, might have interpreted Paul. Whoever he was, the writer of the letter certainly knew that Paul, while stressing faith, did not encourage his converts to observe the Torah.

WHO WAS A JEW?

To understand properly what Paul's actions would have meant, we need to know how Jews think of their own identity, and therefore how converts, or proselytes, come to share that identity. In an expression famous in discussions among Jews today, we need to discover *who is a Jew,* and who was regarded as a Jew in Paul's day.

A recent book by Lawrence Schiffman, *Who Was a Jew?,*[37] appears to have answered these questions, setting the split between the Church and its Jewish parent in a clearer light than before. The split actually occurred, Schiffman believes, on the issue of Jewish identity, not on the beliefs of the Christian movement, unorthodox as these were. Jews could tolerate wide divergences of belief, so long as there was unity in observance of the obligations of the covenant. The Christian movement, by its abandonment of the Torah, threatened that unity at its roots.

Schiffman made a careful analysis of the texts in which the rulings of the tannaim on Jewish identity and conversion are to be found. The tannaim are the Jewish scholars of the period between the destruction of the Temple in 70 C.E. and the codification of the Mishnah at about 200 C.E. Until then, the tradition had been handed down by word of mouth, possibly over many centuries.[38]

Schiffman found that at least from approximately the time of the return of the Jews from exile in Babylon in the fifth century B.C.E., it had been universally understood that Jewish identity was primarily hereditary. Being a Jew was the same as belonging to the people of Israel. Already at that time, the main requirement was to be born of a Jewish mother. Although status within the Jewish people, as priest, Levite or Israelite, was inherited from the father, Jewish identity itself was derived from the mother. If a male, the child of a Jewish mother was circumcised on the eighth day, sealing his existing share in the covenant of Abraham.

From that time on, he was obligated, along with the whole community, to observe the commandments of the Torah. The people had assumed these obligations when they entered into the covenant with God at Mount Sinai. The duty of observing the commandments fell on the people corporately and also on every individual according to his status and position. Women had different obligations from men, and priests from Levites and Israelites, or laity.

Jewish identity, once gained in this way, could not be lost. Neither heresy nor apostasy could cut the tie with Judaism, once established by birth and circumcision. Heresy was understood to mean beliefs not in accord with the prevailing understanding, while apostasy referred to a non-Jewish way of life, deliberate actions not in accord with the Torah. Actions, however, were much more important than beliefs in determining a person's status in the community.[39]

BECOMING A JEW

How then did one become a Jew, if not born of a Jewish mother? Jews in this period were not only willing to make converts but actively sought to do so. A reference to proselytism in the Gospels, whether or not it is an authentic saying of Jesus, clearly establishes the prevalence of Jewish missionary activity at this period, confirming what is known from elsewhere.[40]

To become a Jew meant nothing less than changing one's heredity and acquiring a new hereditary identity that would be passed on to one's children. At the same time, it involved sharing in both the benefits and the obligations of the covenant that God had established with the Jewish people at Mount Sinai. Further, it involved sharing in the historical destiny of the Jewish people. As a result of Roman persecution, beginning not long after Paul's time, the decision to do so became a burden for the convert, as well as for the born Jew, not to be lightly undertaken.

To acquire this new heredity, therefore, a prospective convert, if a male, had to meet four requirements: (1) to accept the obligations of the Torah in full, (2) to be circumcised, (3) to be immersed in the ritual bath, the mikvah, and (4) to bring a sacrifice to the Temple. (In the case of a female, circumcision was naturally omitted, and immersion became of central importance.) After the destruction of the Temple, the requirement of sacrifice was discontinued, since it could no longer be fulfilled. However, in Paul's time it was still in force. No doubt converts from the Diaspora would eventually journey to Jerusalem to fulfill their obligation.[41]

PAUL'S CONVERSIONS

Paul imposed none of these four requirements on his converts, unless we count baptism as fulfilling the requirement of immersion. In fact, it seems to have had a different meaning from Jewish immersion, though the rite itself was similar. He did not require acceptance of the Torah, he did not require circumcision, and he said nothing about sacrifice. Not only did he not require these steps, he forbade them, as the discussion of the matter in his letter to the Galatians shows.[42]

What did he do? He had his converts immersed, or baptized, in the name of Jesus Christ, simply on profession of faith.[43] Instead of accepting the obligations of the Torah, the Gentile convert had to believe on the name of Jesus. He did not and must not take on the obligation of fulfilling the commandments of the Torah in detail. For Paul, "love is the fulfilling of the law."[44]

Paul's detailed ethical teaching does turn out to be closer to traditional Judaism than this theory might suggest. However, it would certainly not have been regarded by Jewish teachers as remotely fulfilling the requirement on a convert to accept the Torah as a whole and to share with the Jewish people in its obligations and benefits.

WHAT DID PAUL INTEND?

Did Paul himself think he was converting his Gentile followers to what today we call Judaism? In our modern sense of the word, the term is out of place in Paul's period. Where we do find it, in Paul himself and other ancient writers, it does not mean the Jewish faith; it means Jewish practices. He clearly did not intend to convert Gentiles to Judaism, in that sense of the word. He discouraged them strongly from adopting Jewish practices.

On the other hand, it does seem clear that he intended to bring them into the people of God, the people which had so far been defined by its acceptance of the Torah as its own side of a covenant with God. He must therefore have believed that the requirements for entry into the people of God had changed in some radical way as a result of what God had done in Jesus the Messiah.

Paul may have believed that through Jesus' resurrection God had opened the covenant to the Gentiles on new and special terms. Now, for them at least, faith in the risen Christ had become decisive for admission into the people of God, replacing adherence to the community and acceptance of the Torah.

Paul himself could not have supposed that he was making converts to Judaism when he baptized the Gentiles who came to faith in Jesus Christ. He undoubtedly knew quite well what the *halachah* for conversion was. If he did not follow it, it was not by accident or by mistake, but because he meant to do something else. Nevertheless, Jewish authorities at the time seem to have assumed that it was his intention to make conversions to the Jewish people.

For them, this would have been the natural interpretation of his actions. Christianity was not yet regarded as a new religion, with different membership rules from Judaism. Later, they would have accepted that Christian baptism had nothing to do with conversion to Judaism. At the time, they correctly saw that Paul meant to incorporate his converts into the people of God and drew the conclusion that he had done so improperly. They naturally did not share Paul's messianic faith in the arrival of the new age, and the new form of the people of God.

They could only suppose that Paul was purporting to bring his converts into the existing covenant people. If so, his converts were irregular and had not become Jews, and Paul was seriously at fault in what he was doing. He was deceiving himself and his converts alike, and in fact creating a schismatic community. In the latter respect at least, they were correct in their judgment. After the excitement of messianic expectation died down and Jesus did not return, Gentile Christianity did rapidly become a new religion, quite distinct from its Jewish origins.

Paul seems to have thought he was making converts to a new form of the same people of God, growing out of the old in fulfillment of prophecy. Membership in this renewed people was open to Jews and Gentiles on the same terms, faith and baptism. Paul himself did not intend or expect to found a new religion. He never expected history to last long enough for that to happen. In his own mind, he was doubtless initiating his converts into the people of the age to come, beyond history, but now, as it were, overlapping with history.

As a result of these actions, as Paul himself tells us, he was five times compelled to submit to the punishment of the *makkot*, the thirty-nine lashes.[45] He himself calls what happened to him persecution, not punishment, and associates it with Jewish rejection of his activity as a missionary to the Gentiles. In fact, the Jewish community must have punished him for making converts without imposing the proper requirements on them. Since in their view Paul's Gentile converts were converts improperly made, they had not been converted at all and remained Gentiles. The Jewish authorities would have had no objection at all to conversions performed according to the *halachah,* even if such converts were taught to believe that Jesus was the Messiah.

Paul could have avoided the punishment by totally separating himself from the Jewish community. His acceptance of the sentence of the courts shows that he must have maintained his membership in the synagogue. He must have accepted the authority of Jewish judges, even though he strongly disagreed with them, and was not prepared to obey their rulings. The fact that he referred to these floggings as "persecution" is not likely to have increased regard for the Jewish leaders among his Gentile readers.

Beyond question, however unorthodox his actions, Paul continued to think of himself as a Jew. He may have become an apostate for the sake of his mission to the Gentiles, but an apostate was still a Jew.[46] Paul thus invoked in a new context the analogy of Christ's shameful death, by actions of his own that were shameful in the eyes of other Jews.

PAUL'S SELF-REVERSAL

It seems quite possible that Paul was now being "persecuted" for the very same practice for which he had himself earlier persecuted the Church, before he joined himself to the new movement. Perhaps, as Lloyd Gaston suggests, this is what he meant when he said in the letter to the Galatians[47] that he was now building up what formerly he pulled down. This makes his actions more, not less, remarkable. It shows that he fully understood the implications of what he was doing.

If so, why this 180 degree self-reversal? It certainly arose from the event in which he believed himself called to be the Apostle to the Gentiles. Since he is reticent about its nature, we cannot tell if the event was a vision, a mystical experience, or something that happened while he was studying the Scriptures, as Gaston thinks possible. (The famous account in Acts in which Paul "sees the light" is much later and conflicts in several respects with the little Paul says himself.) Paul ranks it with the resurrection appearances received by the other apostles before he himself joined the Church. It seems to have convinced him that Jesus was indeed the Messiah, presumably because he did experience him as risen from the dead.[48]

The same experience of the risen Christ had convinced him that it was his own calling to preach the Messiah Jesus among the Gentiles. In the final days of history, the Gentiles, according to prophecy, were to be brought in and would worship the one God in Jerusalem, along with the people of Israel. As we saw earlier, it would be Paul's personal task to bring them in, and so prepare the way for the return of Jesus.

But why should this entail the abandonment of the normal requirements of conversion? As we saw, Maccoby argues that it was at this point that the Christian myth sprang more or less fully formed into Paul's conscious mind. The myth does view salvation differently from the way Jews had always done. If so, conversion to the Jewish people and joining in its covenant with God might not, in Paul's eyes, have been the way for the Gentiles to find salvation. He no doubt saw their lot, and if more traditional interpreters are correct, the lot of the whole human race, Jewish as well as Gentile, as hopeless apart from faith in the work of Christ.

Nevertheless, abandoning the requirements of conversion was (I believe) the very practice that had previously aroused his passionate indignation, because it was so destructive of Jewish identity. Even if Paul supposed that he was introducing the Gentiles into a new stage in the history of the people of God, why not do as the Jewish Christians did, and make proper proselytes of the Gentiles, so that they could enter the new age along with the covenant people?

RECEIVING THE HOLY SPIRIT

In his letter to the Galatians, dissuading his earlier converts from undergoing circumcision, Paul clearly supposes that his most powerful argument is his appeal to the agreed fact that the Galatian Christians had received the Holy Spirit by hearing the preaching of Paul's gospel and not by the mysterious "works of law" (whatever they are).[49] He says elsewhere that the Spirit is the Spirit of liberty. Here he is at pains to point out that the Spirit, without working through specific commandments, leads the believers into actual fulfillment of the Torah, especially the key commandment, You shall love your neighbor as yourself.

Evidently, whatever was meant by receiving the Holy Spirit, it was something he did not expect any of the Galatians to dispute. They knew what he meant, and it was common ground between them that it had taken place. Though he does not say so in so many words, we can infer that Paul does not think the Holy Spirit available within the covenant of Sinai to Jews who had not yet believed in Jesus as the Messiah. What could he have had in mind?

Today, educated Christians are accustomed to the idea that receiving the Holy Spirit is not subject to empirical testing. Only among charismatic groups who associate the possession of the Holy Spirit with ecstatic phenomena such as speaking with tongues would it be natural to treat reception of the Spirit as an empirical fact from which conclusions could be drawn in this confident way. Should we therefore assume that Paul too equated the event of receiving the Spirit with verifiable ecstatic phenomena?

It looks as if he did, at least when he wrote Galatians, though he is much more cautious in 1 Corinthians 12–13. Even there, however, he does not go so far as to deny outright that there is a one-to-one correspondence between ecstatic phenomena and the gifts of the Spirit, as a mainstream, noncharismatic theologian would today.

It seems to follow that the principal advantage that Paul saw in his way of faith over the way his Galatian converts proposed to adopt was that it led to the reception of the Spirit. Evidently, living by the Torah had not produced similar ecstatic phenomena that could be interpreted as manifestations of the Spirit. If indeed Paul thought that Jews did not possess the Spirit unless they too had believed in Jesus, we may have an answer to the question that has been puzzling us.

The outpouring of the Spirit on all flesh was to be a sign of the messianic age, a radically new epoch. It is Paul's eschatological scenario, derived from the prophets, and now (as he believes) being fulfilled as a result of the resurrection of Christ, that permits him to assert the superiority of the new way over the old.

He is not asserting the superiority of a new religion over an old one but the superiority of eschatological fulfillment over ordinary history. Later, when the expectation of the return of Jesus and the imminence of the new age had died down, his ideas would be misunderstood. Christians would soon use them to claim superiority of Christianity as one *religion* over Judaism as another, a concept remote from Paul's own mind.

The earliest Christians did not think of themselves as belonging to a new religion but as a community living in the end-time. The powers of the age to come had been poured out upon them, and they lived in history as though beyond and outside history. There was no difference in this respect between Paul and the Jerusalem church.

This was not a time for making regulations that would govern an institution for centuries to come. Matters were decided ad hoc and in the light of the overwhelming conviction of the imminent return of Jesus to inaugurate the new age in its fullness. Whether or not the Gentiles were to be converted to Judaism, it would not be long before all such matters, important as they now were, would become irrelevant. Paul and his converts were living in the last days, and the time remaining was very short. There was certainly no time for nonessentials.

The coming of Christ and his death and resurrection had inaugurated a new age, which would last forever. The Jews and Gentiles who believed in Christ were the new people of God who belonged to the age now dawning. The proof of this was to be found in the ecstatic phenomena, such as speaking with tongues, that accompanied acceptance of the new gospel, as well as the spiritual changes in the converts that followed. Paul and the other Christians interpreted these happenings as the prophesied outpouring of the Holy Spirit in the last days.[50]

He therefore believed he was bringing his Gentile converts into the people of the new age. By the same token, this new people, the body of Christ, was not identical with the people as it then existed, the Jewish people from which Paul himself claimed to have come. It was a new creation, a new humanity; Christ himself was the second Adam, the root of the new humanity as Adam had been the root of the first. Nevertheless, the new people was not wholly new; it was the old people renewed. The new people was still "the Israel of God."[51]

THE GOSPEL FOR THE JEWS

What would Paul have said to a Jew who came to believe in Jesus as the Messiah? Would he have wanted to "convert him to Christianity"? We do not know. Paul is emphatic in his own writings that he himself had no mission to Jews. Only the later Book of Acts promotes the view that he went first to the synagogues and only turned to the Gentiles when rejected there. He did, however, approve of a parallel mission to Jews, conducted by others. He must have agreed with its leaders that there was a message to be preached to Jews also and that acceptance of it would make an important difference to the spiritual destiny of those who believed in the new message.

What could have been its content?[52] No documents have survived that would give us this information directly. We have no theological treatises from James or Peter, the leaders of the mission to the Jews. We have to infer what the message to Jews was from Paul's writings, from later works such as Acts, and from the probabilities of the matter.

Undoubtedly, the gospel for the Jews concerned the novel sense in which Jesus was now to be regarded as the Messiah and the expectation that he would shortly return to earth to bring in the messianic age as it had traditionally been understood. The missionaries probably concluded with a call to repentance and baptism, and a promise that the gift of the Holy Spirit would follow, in order that the new believers could enter into the benefits of the messianic age, already present in advance of its full coming.

Paul himself does not tell us in so many words, as Acts does, that Jews who accepted the message were also baptized, or immersed, in the name of Jesus Christ, as Gentiles were. What little he does say on the subject makes it extremely likely that they were.[53] Acts tells us that they were baptized from the very first, and that Christian baptism was believed to be something different from the baptism of John the Baptist, since it conveyed the gift of the Holy Spirit, as the latter did not.[54]

Paul's own doctrine of baptism is an extremely high one. It meant dying with Christ to the old life, rising again with him, and rebirth into the new creation.[55] No less than conversion to Judaism by circumcision and immersion, baptism involved a radical change of identity and a new relationship to God. If Jews were also baptized, in the eyes of the Christian movement as a whole the way of covenant and Torah could not in itself have been adequate for entry into the benefits of the new age.

Acts also tells us that Paul was accused by the Jews of going about in the Diaspora and teaching Jews to forsake observance of the Torah.[56] However, we cannot directly confirm that from anything he says himself. If he is telling the truth, it may simply have been an inference from what he had been reported as saying about the Torah when addressing Gentiles, or possibly from the fact that he had himself become an apostate in order to be a missionary to Gentiles, sharing their status and embracing the same way of salvation as he preached to them. However, as we shall see later in the chapter, he did also encourage other Jewish missionaries to the Gentiles to omit observances that in particular circumstances caused difficulties for the unity of the new community, and perhaps this was the real basis of the charge.

To suppose that he systematically dissuaded fellow Jews from observance would be a further substantial step beyond the point to which the evidence has so far taken us, and it would contradict what Paul says himself. He had himself no mission to Jews, whether in the Land or in the Diaspora.

A DOUBLE COVENANT?

Some modern scholars believe that Paul held something like the double covenant theory associated with the modern Jewish theologian Franz Rosenzweig.[57] According to this theory, simply put, Christians come to the Father by faith in Jesus Christ through the new covenant, but Jews are already with the Father through the existing covenant of Sinai. If Paul did believe that, he would have thought that the Gentile converts he made acquired the same status before God that all Jews already possessed by birth.

Paul's own writings do not confirm that this was what he thought. He seems to have believed that his Gentile converts had a new status, not yet possessed by Jews who had not accepted the gospel, but open to them also on the same terms, faith in Jesus Christ. The new status of believing and baptized Jews must have been different from the one they already possessed under the covenant of Sinai, and superior to it.

Again, we are obliged to infer this from the fact that he approved of the mission to the Jews, though he did not himself take part in it. He further seems to have believed, according to Galatians, that Gentile Christians could lose their own status as a result of adopting Jewish practices, and perhaps even as a result of conversion to the Jewish people.

If Paul had believed in some kind of double covenant, as some present day theologians do, he would have been opposed to any mission to the Jews, as these contemporary theologians are. He certainly would also have been opposed to immersing Jews, unless it meant in these cases something very different from what in his own writings he tells us baptism means. If Paul had thought that baptizing Jews cast doubt on their existing status before God, and that such a doubt was not justified, we can be sure that he would have vehemently opposed it.

Since he supported, or at the very least did not oppose, the mission to the Jews, which involved baptizing them in the name of Jesus Christ, it follows that, in his view, faith in Christ did add something of great importance to the existing status of

Jews, as well as Gentiles. Nor would he have so strongly opposed anyone requiring his Gentile converts to be circumcised and to observe the Torah, if he had not believed that through faith in Christ they had already gained this new status before God. Clearly, he believed that the new status could not be added to by adopting Jewish practices and might actually be lost.

However, Jews as well as Gentiles could and should belong to the renewed people of the end-time. The new people was the faithful remnant of the old, according to Paul. Paul certainly did not hold the views of second century and later theologians that the Gentile church had simply superseded the Jewish people as God's people. The new creation was the old re-created. The new people was still Israel and the inheritor of all the promises to the old people of Israel.

Jewish birth, however, did not automatically confer membership in the people of the new age. It ought naturally to lead to it, since the new age and the new people were the fulfillment of Jewish expectation. But birth into the community and abiding by the laws of the Torah were no longer enough. In order to belong to the people of the new age, the Jew, like the Gentile, had to believe in Jesus the Messiah. The Jew, like the Gentile, also had to be baptized into the name of Jesus. Jewish converts would thus also acquire the same new status before God, that Paul feared the Galatian Judaizers might lose by conversion to Judaism.

PAUL AND JAMES

Paul's views on conversion to Judaism were not the only ones in the early church. In Chapter 2 of the letter to the Galatians we have his own version of a discussion in Jerusalem leading to agreement on the demarcation of missionary activity between himself, as the one responsible for the mission to the Gentiles, and the Jerusalem leadership, with overall responsibility for the mission to Jews. The same conference is apparently described in Acts 15. Galatians 2 also contains Paul's account of a serious disagreement he himself had with Peter on related matters. The altercation with Peter had taken place at Antioch before the events dealt with in Galatians. We can therefore use this chapter to discover or infer the views of other early Christians on the matters that were of such importance to Paul.

It seems to emerge from these passages that there were at least three views on the matter in the early church. Paul's views have now been discussed. It seems clear that there were Jewish Christians who were altogether opposed to him and his actions, though according to some recent scholarship they are by no means so frequently mentioned in Paul's own writings as used to be supposed. What is now becoming clearer is that James and his friends in the leadership of the Jerusalem church did not themselves belong to this group, but were supportive, for reasons we must attempt to understand, of Paul's Torah-free gospel for the Gentiles.

Acts 15 provides a somewhat different account than Galatians of the meeting leading up to the Jerusalem agreement, sometimes known as the Apostolic Council. According to Acts, the meeting was called to deal with the most serious issue facing the young Christian movement, the terms on which Gentiles should be admitted to it. It has thus often been thought of as the first ecumenical council of the Church.

Paul in Galatians says the meeting took place because he himself, as a result of a revelation, had gone up to Jerusalem, along with his close colleague Barnabas, to confer with the leadership there. He had gone up fourteen years after his only previous visit, during which he had spent a couple of weeks with Peter, but otherwise had not met the remaining leaders, except James. The first visit had occurred three years after he had joined the Christian movement and begun to preach to the Gentiles. On this second visit he laid before the notables the gospel he had been preaching to the Gentiles, in order, as he says, that he "might not be running, or have run, in vain."[58]

The issue was precisely the question of whether or not the Gentile converts should be circumcised. If the leadership had insisted that they should, Paul would have been running in vain, presumably because the new movement would have been split on a fundamental issue, not because Paul would ever have admitted that he had been wrong. However, the Jerusalem church did not insist on circumcising the convert Titus, a Greek, whom Paul and Barnabas had taken along with them as a test case. This was in spite of the demands of certain people, whom Paul characterizes as "false brethren" who had insinuated themselves "to spy out the freedom they had in Christ Jesus."

The leadership had nothing against what he was doing. Paul is careful to say that he does not care who they were, and that he did not accept their authority as binding on himself; this suggests that his readers may have thought it more natural to suppose that they actually had the right to exercise authority over Paul's actions.

When they saw that he had been entrusted with "the gospel of the uncircumcision," just as Peter had been entrusted with the gospel of the circumcision, and that the same [God] who was working in Peter in his mission to the circumcision was likewise working in Paul in his mission to the Gentiles, James and Kephas [Peter] and John, "the ones who were supposed to be somebody," gave him and Barnabas the right hand of fellowship for their mission to the Gentiles, corresponding to their own mission to the Jewish communities.[59]

While there are significant differences between this account and the one in Acts, especially on the conditions attached by the Jerusalem community to the agreement, they seem to be describing the same occasion. According to Paul but not Acts, the Jerusalem leadership made no conditions, only requesting that Paul should remember the poor, which he says he was glad to do anyway. Evidently, the Palestinian communities were suffering economic hardship. The term *the poor* may also have become technical: a group among the Jewish Christians was later known as the Ebionites. The later Christian writers would suppose that it was founded by somebody called Ebion, but in fact the name comes from a Hebrew word meaning poor. In any case, Paul was responding to an appeal to the basic Jewish virtue of charity to the poor. Whatever his views on the Torah for Gentiles, he acknowledged this value for himself.

According to Acts 15, James behaved like a bishop of a somewhat later period, chairing the meeting and formulating the consensus. He requested Paul to impose on his converts a few rules that are very close to what later became known in Judaism as the Noachide covenant. Although the details were fully formulated only much later, it is known that ideas of this kind were already in existence, and the account in Acts confirms it.

These few moral and ritual rules were believed to be binding on the whole human race, as a result of God's earlier covenant with Noah after the flood. It is important to notice that the Pharisees, like later Jews, believed that righteous Gentiles who observed these precepts as the commandments of God had as much chance of entering the world to come as Jews who observe the Torah. The specific commandments of the Torah associated with the unique priestly status of the Jewish people are not binding on Gentiles, in the view of most Jews.

If this is what James had in mind (supposing Acts to be correct in this instance), he must have considered that the Gentiles need not be converted because it was not necessary for them to be Jewish in order to participate in messianic redemption. What was necessary was the basic righteousness symbolized by the Noachide covenant. Thus, although going along with Paul's Torah-free mission to the Gentiles, he would still have been in accordance with the *halachah*. He would not have considered them converted at all, regularly or irregularly, and would have had no need to consider their Jewish status.

James must have shared with Paul the expectation that in accordance with prophecy the Gentiles would be brought in at the end of days to worship the God who had revealed himself to Israel. Both no doubt believed that this was now happening. James also shared with Paul the expectation that the final end, the return of Jesus to earth, was very near.

Whether or not he accepted that Paul had been called to a special eschatological role of Apostle to the Gentiles, in view of the imminence of the end there was simply no need to go into the question of conversion. At the end, when it came, God would bring them in anyway. James need not have agreed with Paul on the necessity of doing so before the end. In fact, James was a much more central Jew than Paul, as the favor he enjoyed with the Pharisees confirms.

Quite possibly, both accounts of the meeting are broadly correct, and not in conflict with one another, though on this view Paul is being slightly tendentious in his own version. He insists that James and the others did nothing to infringe on his own independence and freedom, and were quite happy with his own Torah-free mission to the Gentiles. It does not follow that James also accepted Paul's theoretical justification for his actions, which we have attempted to understand above. Paul would certainly have understood James' own reasoning, but he did not choose to discuss it with the Galatians, if so.

PETER AND THE EMISSARIES FROM JAMES

Paul goes on in the same chapter to discuss a conflict of his own with Peter. Since it dealt with questions of Jewish observance, Paul's account of the argument should help us to understand the nature of the differences between Paul and other members of the Christian movement on that vital issue and the views of the various parties to the dispute. However, as reported in Galatians, the argument and the issues it actually turned on are not easy to understand, and we shall have to follow a rather complex discussion of its details in order to arrive at any sort of clarity about the conclusion.

Antioch, an important city in what is now Turkey, seems to have been the headquarters for both diaspora missions, that of Peter to the Jews, and that of Paul to the Gentiles. The demarcation between them was social or ethnic rather than territorial. Antioch had a large Jewish community, apparently bilingual in Aramaic and Greek. We have seen that the Gospel of Matthew was probably written there, and some scholars believe that of Mark was as well. According to Acts, Antioch was also the place where the Christians were first recognized as a separate religion and given the name by which they have since been known, though this must have happened later than Acts suggests. Even at this point, however, the problems were surfacing that eventually did lead to the emergence of a new religion.

As a result of the missionary work emanating from Antioch as a base, the Christian community there was a mixed one, containing members of both Jewish and Gentile origin. This presented basic problems, which had to be solved. The principal Christian rite, known as the breaking of the bread, was a common meal. Could Jews take part in this with Gentiles, and if so on what terms? The unity of the community required all to share in this meal, which was interpreted as a communion with Christ and with one another.

It has usually been supposed by Christian scholars that the Jewish members of the community would not have been permitted to eat with the Gentiles at all, and that in order to do so they would have had to break with the Torah altogether. More careful investigation has failed to substantiate the prevalent view that there were Jewish rules of purity that forbade eating with Gentiles.[60] At most, a minority of Jews, bound by special voluntary rules of purity, might have had such a difficulty, and even this is not certain.

There is another obvious difficulty, however, which would have affected everybody. According to the dietary laws binding on all Jews, they must not eat food that is not kosher, conforming to the regulations laid down in the Torah and codified by the sages, or which has been offered to idols. The problem, then, was not eating with the Gentiles as persons but eating their food, and doubtless also sharing their plates and other nonkosher utensils. This was no minor problem, in view of the centrality of dietary laws for all Jews.

Paul solved the problem radically, in his usual way. The Jews in the community should eat with the Gentiles and not bother about the dietary laws. This was his own practice. Among Gentiles, he seems to have lived like them. He became in fact an apostate "for the sake of the gospel."[61] His colleague Barnabas, and perhaps others in his group, had been doing the same. It appears that Peter had been willing for a time to follow their example when in Antioch.

According to Acts, Peter had had a vision that removed his scruples about the dietary laws, freeing him for missionary work among the Gentiles. Since this account is tied up with the theory of Acts that both Peter and Paul went to both Jews and Gentiles, directly contradicted by the firsthand testimony of Paul, we should probably view it with skepticism.[62] However, vision or not, Peter was now sufficiently impressed with the need for unity to go along with Paul and Barnabas in eating Gentile food. Whether he saw clearly that this meant joining them in apostasy, we do not know.

Then, Paul tells us, some people came from James and objected to what Peter was doing. Following a hint in Acts 15, these unnamed persons are often identified with a group who wanted the Galatians to be circumcised. Paul charges that the latter did not keep the Law themselves. Some recent scholars accordingly believe they were Judaizers, imitators of certain Jewish practices, not actual Jews. Or, as Segal suggests, they may have been content with a standard of observance less rigorous than Paul's own in his days as a Pharisee, a standard he accordingly treats with contempt.

If so, the people mentioned in Galatians cannot have been the same as the emissaries from James. James and his friends were fully observant Jews who believed in the messiahship of Jesus. It would hardly have been a fair characterization of James and his associates to suggest that they themselves did not keep the Law. There is no evidence in Paul's writings of such hostility toward James. He would hardly have slandered him in that way. James was also greatly admired by the Pharisees, as we know from Josephus; they are unlikely to have admired him as they did unless his observance met their standards.

Older interpreters of Paul set the incident in the context of an ongoing struggle between Paul on one side and Jewish Christianity, led by James, on the other, over the issue of the conversion of the Gentiles to the Jewish people. Since evidence is lacking in Paul's actual words for any such struggle between Paul and James, we should probably suppose that if there were Christian Jews who objected to Paul's actions, James was not among them. In any case, it is Peter, not Paul, that his emissaries have come to rebuke.

The arguments of the emissaries from Jerusalem were sufficiently persuasive that Peter and even Barnabas, Paul's closest colleague, gave up eating with the Gentiles, as did the other Jews. Paul does not tell us what the arguments were. He accuses Peter and by implication Barnabas of cowardice, of acting not out of conviction but out of fear of the Jews. He says he stood right up to Peter and told him he was wrong: he was not (literally) "walking straight according to the truth of the gospel."[63]

We do not hear that the emissaries criticized Paul himself. Their concern was with Peter and his actions. This may help us to guess what their arguments actually were. It seems most likely that they wanted the Jerusalem agreement kept on both sides. Paul was to conduct a Torah-free mission to the Gentiles, while Peter, as an observant Jew, was to lead the mission to the Jewish diaspora. It would have been fatal to this mission if it could be said that its leader was not himself observant, and had in fact become an apostate. The anxiety of the emissaries was justified.

They did not necessarily object to what Paul himself was doing, which was covered by the agreement and was his own responsibility. Paul was not expecting his converts to become Jews, and they understood this. Although Paul does not say so, they must have been very unhappy at his influence on Peter, however. They also seem to have awakened a Jewish conscience in Barnabas. He was not so eager as Paul to be an apostate for the sake of the gospel.

At some point, Peter seems to have proposed a different solution to the problem. (This is not described by Paul in so many words, but it seems to be the implication of what he does say.) Instead of the Jewish contingent conceding to the Gentiles, why should not the Gentiles be the ones to concede and eat kosher food along with the Jews in the community? Then the problem would disappear.

This is what really aroused Paul's indignation with Peter. He accuses Peter of traducing the gospel. How can Peter, who is himself (though a Jew) now living like a Gentile, expect the Gentiles to "Judaize"? (To *Judaize* meant to adopt Jewish practices, not to be converted to Judaism–that was not the issue.)[64] Are we to conclude that Peter had until then altogether abandoned observance and in effect ceased to be Jewish? Peter may well have been confused and inconsistent, but it is in the highest degree unlikely that he would have abandoned observance altogether if he was conducting a mission to the Jews. He may have temporarily yielded to Paul's pressing arguments, but in the long run Peter was a Jew and he knew it. He saw the full force of the complaints of the emissaries, and he returned to observing the dietary laws.[65]

For Paul, on the other hand, it was a matter of principle that in any such clash, Jewish Christians should concede to the Gentiles, and not the other way around.[66] This tells us something of great importance about Paul's opinion of the relationship between the Torah and the new way of faith in Christ. If there is a conflict between them, the latter, not the former, must be decisive. As for the mission to the Jews, that was not Paul's priority.

DIFFERENT VIEWS IN THE EARLY CHURCH

The incident allows us to understand better the position of several different parties in the early church on the question of the membership of the Gentiles in the covenant people. The group Paul disparagingly calls the "false brethren"[67] were not a party to the dispute in Antioch. Paul insinuates that they are not really Christians but Jewish spies in the Church. Incidentally, that is a hostile enough remark to cast doubt on Paul's remaining sympathy with his original faith.

It is rather more likely that they were Christian Jews of the Pharisaic party, close to James in their standard of Jewish observance, but differing from him on the correct solution of the Gentile problem. In their opinion, the Gentiles should be properly converted and enter the messianic age along with the rest of the Jewish people. As E. P. Sanders reminds us, this was a perfectly reasonable position from a Jewish point of view.[68] However, Paul's partisanship on the issue has made it appear otherwise to generations of Christian readers.

James's solution was equally in accordance with the *halachah*, but carried with it the implications that his emissaries drew out in the discussion at Antioch. The two groups in the Church would have to live separately to the extent that living together made it difficult for Jews to remain observant. For James, the Jewish people and their covenant obligations remained fundamental. The Gentile converts to the new movement were in a sense secondary, perhaps even anomalous.

Paul found this intolerable. The unity of the new people, the Christian community, must take priority over the requirements of Jewish observance, and if this meant apostasy for the Christian Jews, so be it. This is surely as significant as any of Paul's theoretical statements for our understanding of what he thought about the status of Jews and Gentiles in the people of God.

However we understand the letter to the Galatians, Paul most emphatically believed that his Gentile converts ought not to undergo a Jewish conversion. However, there seems to have been unanimity in the early Christian movement that Jews who came to believe in Christ needed to be baptized, with the implication that this did bring about an alteration in their status before God no less radical than circumcision itself. Presumably, Paul's arguments were successful. In any case, on the larger scene, he prevailed.

The future of the Church would not lie with Jewish Christianity but with the way taught by Paul. In Paul's time, Jewish Christians were still active missionaries. Soon the path of Jewish Christianity would be followed only by those who had been born Jewish, or who were the children of Jewish Christians. As time went on, there would be fewer Jewish Christians. If they had little future among the Gentile churches, they had even less among the Jewish people. Meanwhile, the Gentile churches became increasingly anti-Jewish, and soon they came to believe that they had supplanted the Jewish people as the true Israel.

The Rabbis of the period after the destruction of the Temple felt a need to unify the Jewish people around their own teachings and to exclude rival interpretations. They took action against various heretics, among them the Jewish Christians. Soon the latter became, as Jerome called them, neither Jews nor Christians. Gentile Christianity made its way rapidly in the Roman world, and in four centuries it became the official religion.

5

The True Israel: Battle for the Bible

By the time we reach the second century, there can be no question that the myth has become anti-Jewish as well as non-Jewish. During the last years of the first century and throughout the second, the Gentile church was engaged in establishing itself as a separate movement from its Jewish parent, laying claim to the whole inheritance of Israel. Like the Essenes of Qumran, the original Christian movement within the Jewish people had claimed to be the new Israel. No doubt, the new movement at that stage saw itself as the nucleus of a renewed people to embrace all Israel, as the Essenes did. The Gentile church believed it was the *true* Israel; the claim was exclusive and excluding. The sacred texts of Israel belonged to the Church, and all the promises contained in them applied to the Gentile church. The Jewish people was no longer the Israel of God, and they had no right to the Bible.

Even in its earliest days, the movement had needed to assert that it alone understood the Scriptures correctly. Now the Gentile church went further. The Scriptures belonged to it, and it alone. They always had. The Bible had predicted the life, death, resurrection, and return to earth of Jesus the Messiah. It had also predicted that the Jewish people would be superseded as the people of God by the church of the Gentiles. The Church was the Bible's true subject and theme, and in the Church alone it would find its proper place as Old Testament beside the New.

The Jewish people had no claim to be the covenant people spoken of in the Bible. Always disobedient and unfaithful, they had now finally forfeited their position as God's people, continuing to exist only as a witness to their own crimes. The church's claim invalidated the Jewish people completely. The claim took shape in the years when the Church was separating from the Jewish people, but was not abandoned when the separation was fully accomplished. It still remains standard Christian teaching, in spite of the efforts of a few.

There was in reality no sharp historical dividing line between a period in which Christianity was a Jewish messianic movement and one in which it had become a Gentile church living by an anti-Jewish myth. Symbolically, however, the writing and canonization of the books of the New Testament can be taken as the division.

But the New Testament was not written all at once, and some more extreme anti-Jewish ideas generally associated with a somewhat later period may have made their appearance before the last books of the New Testament were written. Dogmatically, most Christians regard the New Testament as the foundation document of the Church. Everything after that has less authority. Everything before is only an element in the authoritative synthesis of the new faith. Historically, it was not as clear-cut as that.

Once the New Testament had been completely written and assembled into a new scriptural canon, the Church was clearly distinct from its Jewish forebear, a new religion with its own Scriptures. Earlier, the Church had already adopted the Greek version of the Jewish Bible as its own. The addition of the New Testament changed the existing Bible into the Christian Old Testament. The Greek Bible had already been so transformed by the way Christians were now reading it that it had become virtually a different book with the same text, as we have several times noted. While the Church's decision (against powerful and persuasive opposition) to incorporate the Jewish Scriptures in the Christian Bible affirmed Christianity's roots in Judaism, it no less strongly affirmed its own counterclaim to be the true Israel, the heir to all the promises.

The period in which the later books of the New Testament were being written was also the time during which the central anti-Jewish myth was growing into its historic form. The oral and written stories already circulating about Jesus' doings, and especially the story of his death, were now being written up with conscious art into gospels. Mark and his successors created a new literary genre whose aim was to persuade their readers that the hero of this story was indeed the divine Son of God, the Messiah who had suffered and risen again, the present and future King of the world, the hero of the great new myth of salvation.

At the same time, the Church and its Jewish progenitor parted and went their separate ways, not without mutual hostility, considerably more intense on the Christian side. Here too we cannot point to any exact date for the division. The commonly accepted date of 85 C.E. may be too early. In any case, it did not mark a definitive cutoff of relations between Jews and Jewish Christians. The break was gradual. It had started much earlier, when Gentiles were first baptized but not circumcised, and it was not complete until late in the second century.

PAUL IN THE EARLY CHURCH

We cannot justifiably align Paul himself with the anti-Jewish attitudes of the later books of the New Testament and other Christian literature of approximately the same period. But when we thus speak of Paul, we mean the Paul who is being painstakingly recovered by modern scholarship, not the Paul the ancient world, Jewish or Gentile-Christian, thought it knew, the author of all the books traditionally attributed to him.

Paul's complex and difficult theology was neither widely understood nor influential in the next decades. Some of Paul's own circle, like the author of the letter to the Ephesians (if, as most New Testament scholars believe, he was not in fact Paul himself), understood him, but few others did, even Luke, the author of Acts. A later New Testament author, writing under the name of Peter, says that there is much in Paul's writings that is hard to understand and can be distorted by ignorant readers.[1] We can agree about the difficulty and acknowledge that his views were in fact considerably distorted by later readers.

However, his actions were more influential than his thoughts. When he abolished Jewish requirements for conversion in the areas of his mission, Paul effectively created the worldwide Christian church. Whether, if Paul had not come on the scene and made Gentile Christianity possible, a vibrant Jewish Christianity would have made its way among the Jewish people and survived down the centuries as a Jewish sect, it is impossible to say. It seems unlikely.

Esoteric and ascetic tendencies among many Jewish-Christian groups would have attracted the suspicion of the Rabbis, already concerned at what they regarded as a threat to monotheism among Jewish esoteric groups.[2] They would probably have been forced to take measures against the spread of Christian ideas in any case.

Judaism was missionary and successful in the earlier part of the first century. If a wise and informed observer had then been asked which, if either, of Christianity and Judaism was likely to become the religion of the Empire, he would have said Judaism. But after the first disaster of the Jewish revolt and the destruction of the Temple in 68–70 C.E., the second disaster in the 130s of the Bar Kochva rebellion, leading to the loss of the city of Jerusalem and the right to live in Judaea, put an end to any such hopes. Had it been otherwise, Jewish Christianity might have shared the successes of a missionary Judaism. Even so, the demand for circumcision would have remained a major obstacle.

Christianity could offer the monotheism and at least the personal ethics, but after Paul, it did not need to require circumcision as the price of entry. Moreover, it offered a powerful myth of salvation the pagan mind could understand. In the Roman world, the future lay with Christianity, and in all probability Judaism, or Jewish Christianity, could never have played the same role. Probably, the successful transformation of Christianity into Greek terms paved the way for a success that no form of Judaism could have enjoyed in the Roman world.

If Paul's theology had been better understood, perhaps the new movement would not have become as anti-Jewish as it did. The traditional anti-Jewish reading of Paul began quite early. One passage in Paul's writings lent support not merely to anti-Judaic ideas but also to the real hostility toward the Jewish people that borders on later antisemitism. A text in the first letter to the Thessalonians accuses the Jews of "killing the Lord Jesus and the prophets," and "driving us out."[3]

The tone as well as the content of the passage is so unlike what we find in writings of Paul agreed to be authentic that a number of scholars have concluded that it must be an interpolation by a later writer. It concludes with the statement that retribution has now at last overtaken the Jews. The only event of which we know that could be interpreted in this way is the destruction of the Temple in 70, unless the passage was interpolated as late as the second century and refers to the second disaster following upon the Bar Kochva revolt. Either way, Paul could not have written the passage in question, since both events occurred after his death.

At least one writer sensitive to the anti-Judaism in early Christianity has argued that the passage in 1 Thessalonians represents an early and therefore immature stage in Pauline thinking,[4] like the letter as a whole. In fact, it seems more probable that if Paul ever did think anything like that, it would have been late in his life. In any case, the discrepancy in tone, as well as the apparent reference to the disaster of the loss of the Temple and the destruction of Jerusalem, seems too striking to be ignored. The passage is most probably an interpolation.

On the assumption that someone interpolated the passage referring to the Jews as Christ-killers at some time in the first century, it must have circulated more or less as soon as the letter itself did in its original form. Believed by its readers to be by Paul himself, the passage would then have influenced the views of the literate leadership of the Church, as well as of the lay Christians who regularly heard the letter read in church. From very early times it would have been taken for granted that the concept of the Christ-killers had his own very high authority.

The passion narratives in the Gospels were giving dramatic color and detail to the same version of events. The passage in Thessalonians should probably be ranked with other late strata of the New Testament, including the Gospels in their final form. On the common assumption of the critics that the second letter to the Thessalonians is not by Paul, we might guess that whoever did write it was responsible for the interpolation in the first.

This final layer of the New Testament is unmistakably anti-Jewish. Even in its most Jewish portions, its tone reflects the bitter family quarrel that had led to the banning of the Jewish Christian leadership, somewhere around the final decade of the first century C.E. The Christian movement, especially that part of it which remained observant, did not generally think of itself as a new religion but as the true Jewish faith. It had not wished for the breach and resented it when it came.

No doubt the Gentile church viewed the break somewhat differently. It had no interest in remaining Jewish. Nevertheless, the breach must have resulted in part from increasing Jewish hostility toward the memory of Paul and his work, upon which Gentile Christianity now largely depended for its theological and structural basis. We can see the traces of these controversies in Acts, which seems to defend Paul against Jewish charges while making the Pharisees, the forerunners of the Jewish leadership in Luke's own time, friendly to Paul.

THE BREAK WITH JUDAISM

In *Who Was a Jew?* Lawrence Schiffman clarified the actions of the Jewish leadership, making them more intelligible than New Testament scholars had previously found them. The latter had generally assumed that the decisive break between Christianity and its Jewish parent occurred with the introduction of a nineteenth "blessing," the *birkat ha-minim*, the curse against heretics, into the Eighteen Blessings, the great synagogue prayer said three times every day.[5] Schiffman shows that the break was more gradual, perhaps beginning somewhat later than the date usually assigned for the introduction of the new "blessing." It was not complete until Christianity became recognized as a Gentile movement and no longer as a Jewish heresy.[6]

After the fall of Jerusalem to the Romans in the year 70, a group of Rabbis under the leadership of Yochanan ben Zakkai formed an academy at Yavne on the coast, with Roman permission. This is the group to which Judaism owes its survival through two thousand years of exile into the present. They were faced with an appalling catastrophe, the loss of the Temple, and the consequent departure of the divine Presence from the midst of the people. With the Temple they had also lost the sacrificial system of worship and the means of atonement for sin. How could Judaism continue?

In answering this question, the Rabbis had a major advantage over rival groups within the Jewish people. They themselves came from the Pharisaic tradition, a primarily lay movement, centered on the synagogue, not the Temple. Their interest was in the study of Torah rather than in the Temple and its sacrifices. There are hints that some of them already preferred the study of Torah to animal sacrifices. They were able to absorb the catastrophe and chart the course that Judaism was to follow for the next two millennia.

It was through them that the Jews became the people of the Book, as they are often called. They were able to create a "portable fatherland,"[7] with a religion independent of sacred places. The tie to the land of Israel remained, but for many centuries it would be a constant hope rather than a daily reality for all but the few Jews who continued to live there.

For the Rabbis, the loss of the Temple was a catastrophe, but not a fatal one. Although the sacrificial system was no longer available, prayer was still acceptable to God. Perhaps the divine Presence was even sharing their exile. Atonement could come about through repentance and deeds of loving-kindness. Around this time, a new word, *teshuvah,* began to be used for repentance, marking the high valuation already placed on it, noted in a previous chapter. God would respond with compassion to the repentance of his children, and his forgiveness would be instant. A number of the Rabbis spoke habitually of God as the Father who is in heaven, just as Jesus had done.

The Rabbis also undertook the task of collecting and codifying the various traditions about how the Torah should be observed. Their testimony and their debates were recorded in the Mishnah, which began to be written down, under the leadership of Yehudah ha-Nasi, or Judah the Prince, also known simply as Rabbi, at the close of the second century. The Mishnah formed the core of the later Talmud, most of which is commentary on and interpretation of the Mishnah.

MEASURES AGAINST THE HERETICS

In view of the catastrophe they had to confront, and the imminent danger to the survival of the Jewish faith, the Rabbis felt it necessary to close ranks around their own interpretation of the Torah. The purpose of the new "blessing," or rather curse, against heretics was to make it impossible for their leaders to lead the prayers in the synagogue, since they would not be able to say it.

Its introduction is generally dated about 85. However, since we read that Rabban Gamliel II was responsible for having it composed, and he was not formally installed as Nasi, or Patriarch, until 96, after the death of the Roman Emperor Domitian, it may in fact have been somewhat later. The curse did not imply denial of Jewish status to the heretic. As we have seen, Jewish status could not be lost. It is therefore not entirely correct to say, as Christian scholars commonly do, that Christians were now expelled from the synagogue.

Who were the heretics? They are described by the term *minim*, which literally means "kinds" or "sorts," or perhaps "divisions." Among those whom the Rabbis regarded as heretics were Sadducees, the priestly party, who denied the resurrection and did not recognize the traditions that came to be known as the oral Torah. However, the Sadducees were soon of little significance; with the loss of the Temple, they no longer had a power base. The Rabbis were also opposed to the Zealots, whose messianic enthusiasm had led to the revolt and so could be blamed for the loss of Jerusalem and the Temple, as well as of many Jewish lives.

It is likely that they viewed the messianism of the Christians with equal suspicion. Neither the Zealots nor the Christians had delivered the promised messianic age. By this time, after the destruction of the Temple and the bloodshed of the Hadrianic persecutions, it was only too painfully obvious that the new age had not arrived. The Rabbis may also have found certain esoteric tendencies among the Jewish Christians threatening to monotheism, as Alan Segal suggests.[8] However, their most important and fundamental objection to Jewish Christianity must have been the practice of the rest of the movement of accepting Gentiles into the community without proper conversion.

Whatever the reasons for their objection to Jewish Christians, they still regarded them as Jews, though Jews who had gone astray, and therefore as *minim*. At some point, they began to call Christians *nozerim*, probably meaning Nazarenes, followers of Jesus of Nazareth. Jesus is regarded as a Jew who had been a miracle worker or magician and had been hanged (i.e., crucified) on the eve of Passover.[9]

The Christians the Rabbis met with in the Galilee were Jews, having every intention of remaining so. The Rabbis did not at this stage have to take account of Gentile Christianity, since they did not yet meet with it as a significant force that affected them. What the rabbis hoped to achieve by the curse on the *minim* was to make it impossible for heretics, Christian and otherwise, to feel comfortable in the synagogue. They would either have to abandon their heresy or worship in their own congregations.

In due course, as the threat from the heretics began to seem more serious, the Rabbis introduced further measures intended to isolate them from the main community. These measures restricted not only religious but social contact. It was forbidden to derive any benefit from the heretics. One could not even be healed by them. It appears that, in the tradition of Jesus himself, some of these Galilean Christians specialized in healing. Some Rabbis thought it better to die than accept healing from a heretic.[10]

The Rabbis also had to consider the status of the sacred books of the heretics, "the books of the *minim.*" Part of their own internal activity at this time was the determination of the canon of Scripture, which had not yet been fully fixed. Several books that were already part of the Greek Bible and relied on by the Church for some of its proof-texts were now excluded. The Church, in response, relegated them to a secondary status, and they became known as the Apocrypha.

In the technical terminology of the Rabbis, sacred books were referred to as those that "defiled the hands." Their holiness communicated itself to those who handled them. After handling them, the hands could not be employed for other purposes without first washing. Such books must not be destroyed or discarded, since they contained divine names and must be saved from a fire, even on the Sabbath. Rabbinic literature records debates about whether Christian books had such a status, and it was determined that they did not.

The question was raised by the fact that not only did the Christians possess their own Torah scrolls and books of the prophets, but they also had begun to write their own sacred books, which contained quotations from the Jewish Bible and also included divine names. Many of the Rabbis thought that these books ought to be destroyed on account of their heretical teachings. On the other hand, the Tetragrammaton, the name YHWH, appeared in Christian books, and was arguably entitled to the same reverence there. In fact, it is now known that the Tetragrammaton was written in Hebrew letters even in many Greek Bibles of the period, such as the Gentile Christians used.[11]

Some Rabbis contended that unlike Jewish books, Christian books should not even be saved from a fire on the Sabbath, in spite of the Tetragrammata they contained. On a weekday, the Tetragrammata could be cut out and the remainder of the book destroyed. Others found even this too liberal, and they prefered to destroy the books, divine names and all. No doubt the differences of opinion reflect differing judgments on the severity of the threat posed by Christianity, as well as differences in personal temperament.[12]

Again, it must be emphasized that these stringent measures did not imply that Christians of Jewish origin had lost their status as Jews. In spite of all such restrictions, this status could not be lost. However, this did not apply to their converts, unless they had been properly converted according to the *halachah.* Although no discussions on the matter have been found, there is no question that Paul's converts and their successors would not have been regarded as Jewish at all. Paradoxically, there would have been fewer restrictions on Jewish contact with them: the Jewish heretic was less forgivable than the Gentile. The Jewish heretic knew the Lord, and he knew his Torah, but he had turned away of his own accord. The Gentile was in ignorance, and he was less to blame.

THE RABBIS AND GENTILE CHRISTIANITY

Between 150 C.E. and the time of Constantine, the Rabbis began to realize that the real threat came from Gentile Christianity, by now explicitly anti-Jewish. Sometime after the period of the important early Christian writers Justin and Origen, in the late second century or early in the third, they seem to have added to the curse a mention of Christians, *nozerim*, as well as *minim*, heretics.

From the third century on, the church fathers polemically interested in Judaism speak of a Jewish practice of cursing Christ three times a day in the synagogue. Since the Eighteen Blessings is the only prayer actually said three times a day, the reference must be to a later text of the *birkat ha-minim*, mentioning Christians explicitly. Such a text has been found in the Cairo Geniza, a repository for Jewish sacred books. Like other material found there, it represents Palestinian Judaism in the period after the compilation of the Mishnah. Whether it also represents an earlier or even the original text of the blessing is less certain but possible.[13]

By this time, the Rabbis were aware that Christianity was no longer a Jewish movement. They were not interested in the Jewish status of heretics and apostates, which was never in question, but in the status of Gentiles who were known to be anti-Jewish and eventually in alliance with an increasingly anti-Jewish Roman state. The question now became whether the Christians should be grouped with idolaters, because of their doctrines that seemed to infringe on monotheism, or recognized as irregular worshipers of the one God who had revealed himself first to the Jewish people. Either way, they were a threat against which stronger measures had to be taken.

The measures taken by the Rabbis, with the aim of avoiding all possible confusion between Christianity and Judaism, may seem extreme, especially to Christians. They effectively separated Jewish Christians, not to mention Gentiles, from the body of the Jewish people. As Schiffman points out, if they had not held fast to the *halachah* on conversion, Gentile semi-proselytes in large numbers would probably have taken advantage of Paul's practice, without necessarily agreeing with his theology, to claim full membership of the Jewish community.

The result, as Schiffman suggests, might well have been a new religion, nominally Jewish but in reality no longer so.[14] A new religion did in fact grow up, but it could not be confused with Judaism. Dilution of the Jewish people would in all likelihood have weakened it, making it unable to stand up successfully to Roman persecution, as in the event it proved capable of doing.

EDITORIAL BIAS IN THE GOSPELS

All four Gospels reflect the growing breach with Judaism, displaying anti-Jewish attitudes that had been absent in their source material, as redaction criticism reveals. We have already considered some of the effects of this editorial bias when attempting to recover the historical reality behind the gospel accounts of Jesus.

There we were concerned with eliminating its influence on our understanding of history. Our interest now shifts to the role of the gospel writers in creating the anti-Jewish beliefs of historic Christianity. Before we were concerned with the original history, now with literature and its effects on later history.

The literary creations we call Gospels are remarkable works of art, but it would not be out of place to call them propaganda literature, in the original sense of the word, *propagating* the faith of Christians. They embody authentic historical memories of the actual Jesus, but they use them in the service of the new salvation myth. The Gospels were the principal agency implanting the anti-Jewish myth in the minds of generations of later Christians up until the present day.

One of the most important literary methods used by the writers of the Gospels related the traditions they had received to texts found in the Greek Bible. In fact, they frequently structured their narrative around such texts. Randel Helms goes so far as to suggest, on the basis of his own careful literary analysis, that these writers were so convinced that the events of Jesus' life and death had been predicted in advance by God in the Bible that they felt at liberty to use the texts as a source of historical information, even "correcting" existing traditions by this means.[15] Accordingly, we cannot separate the role of the gospel writers in creating the anti-Jewish myth from the Christian takeover of the Jewish Bible. The two are inseparable, as they are part of the same process.

We have already noted in Chapter 2 that the gospel accounts of the opposition of other Jews, especially the Pharisees, to Jesus reflect the situation of the Church at the time the Gospels were composed, not the situation of Jesus' own lifetime. No doubt, Jesus did become involved in controversies with his fellow Jews, but his opponents could hardly have been the same groups whose reasoned rejection of the new movement now confronted the Church. The reputation of the Pharisees among Christians all down the centuries as hypocrites, petty legalists, and dishonest opponents originated in these accounts; it has nothing to do with the historical Pharisees. However, the Church identified the Pharisees of Jesus' time with their own opponents, the Rabbis who were now proscribing Jewish Christianity. Of course, such traits are no more characteristic of the Rabbis than of their predecessors, the Pharisees.

THE TRIAL OF JESUS IN THE GOSPELS

The vividly told stories in the Gospels of the trial and death of Jesus led to even greater hostility toward Jews. As literature, their drama and poignancy make these some of the greatest stories ever told. In our earlier examination in Chapter 3 of the historical worth of the accounts, we concluded that they are largely untrue. We must now examine the same stories from a different point of view, to show how they reflect and mark the rapid development of the anti-Judaic attitudes already at work in the Church.

The gospel version of the trial and death of Jesus unequivocally presents the Jews as responsible for his death, even though they did not themselves carry it out–because they could not, not because they did not wish to–and therefore as Christ-killers. In reality, as we have seen, Jesus was put to death by the Romans, for their own reasons. The gospel writers plainly tampered with history considerably in composing the picture they left for future generations to meditate upon.

Recent New Testament scholarship has paid a great deal of attention to the role of the gospel writers as editors of materials they had received from the oral and written tradition. In this editorial or redactional layer of the gospels, once analyzed out, we can best trace the rapid growth of the myth of the Jews as the Christ-killers. They could have played no such role in the original traditions of the Christian movement, closer to the actual events.

Each of the gospel writers in his own way distorts earlier traditions about the way Jesus met his death in order to place the Jews in a more unfavorable light and make the Romans by contrast look better. The tendency increases as time goes on. It is already present in Mark, but Matthew, Luke, and (in his own very different way) John each considerably accentuate it.

One clear finding of criticism has been the discovery that at the time the gospels were being written there was no authoritative account of the trial of Jesus available, nor even any agreement that there had been a trial at all.[16] The differences between the accounts clearly show that no gospel author attributed binding authority to the accounts of the other writers.

Our earliest written sources, the letters of Paul, display no knowledge of any trial of Jesus, nor of the specific charges placed by Mark in the mouths of Jesus' accusers.[17] It is hard to imagine that such dramatic events would have been passed over in silence by Paul, if he had known of them. Since Paul was only too ready to interpret Jewish legal measures against infant Christianity as persecution, he would surely have spoken of Jewish persecution of Jesus himself if he had believed there had been anything of the sort.

Since Mark was the earliest of the Gospels, the later accounts might be expected to conform closely with his. In fact, they do not. Among the three later Gospels, only Matthew directly depends on Mark's version of the trial. Luke (in part) and John use other sources, having more in common with one another than either do with the version in Mark and Matthew.

Neither Luke nor John explicitly speaks of a trial at all. Mark's trial scene was either not known to or (more probably) had no authority for these authors, writing perhaps a quarter of a century after Mark. Each "corrects" it in the light of his own theological understanding of the significance of the events. John may even have had a more reliable source of historical information at his disposal than the other writers, but the theological character of his reading of what happened is still more striking.

MARK'S CREATION OF THE TRIAL

We must conclude that Mark or his immediate sources created the vivid scene of the trial of Jesus before the religious Sanhedrin. The historical finding that there was no authoritative tradition of a trial means that even Mark, the first to depict one, had no reliable accounts to go on, perhaps none at all.

Mark was the literary originator of the calumny that the Jews were really guilty of Jesus' death, and that a religious court tried him, basically for his messianic claim, condemning him to death for blasphemy and persuading the Romans to execute him, by representing this claim as a threat to Roman power. While this literary creation did not impose a detailed stamp upon all the succeeding Gospels, their authors share with Mark the intention of removing the responsibility for Jesus' death from the Romans and placing it on the shoulders of the Jews.

Each does it in his own way. An action in fact undertaken by the Romans for their own political reasons, in which the Jewish role at most consisted in identifying and handing over the leader of a supposed resistance movement in order to save the lives of his followers and of other Jews, is progressively transformed into a Jewish plot to get rid of Jesus for religious, not political reasons.

MATTHEW'S VERSION

Matthew follows Mark, presenting an account of a religious trial ending in the condemnation of Jesus for blasphemy. However, he makes many detailed changes in the story showing that he intended to present the Jews in a more unfavorable light than even Mark had done. Mark may simply have wished to shift the blame off the Romans. Matthew clearly intends to fasten the guilt of Christ-killing upon the Jews.

He presents the Jewish leadership in a more aggressive role than Mark had, while treating the leadership as fully representative of the people at large.[18] Matthew plays down the role of the scribes, apparently because some scribes had supported the Christian movement, while greatly enhancing the role of the elders of the people as its representatives. The various groups involved are unanimous in the wish to condemn Jesus.[19]

By comparison with Mark, Matthew depicts the High Priest as much more pushing when he questions Jesus: he clearly aims for an outright confession of guilt. Matthew also significantly changes the wording of the High Priest's questions: he no longer asks Jesus if he is "the Messiah, the son of *the Blessed One*," but "the Messiah, the son of *God*." On Jewish lips, these words would have violated the custom of refraining from naming God directly. In fact, the High Priest is made to be the blasphemer instead of Jesus.[20] Mark's account, though already fictional, respects Jewish sensibilities in its language. Matthew's does not. Yet there is good evidence that Matthew, or his sources, knew much more than Mark knew about Judaism.

In Matthew, the leadership is determined to get a condemnation, and stops at nothing to do so. In Mark, witnesses disagree in their testimony, which is accordingly thrown out. Here the leaders deliberately attempt to secure false witnesses.[21] The express intention is to have Jesus put to death.[22] When Judas repents, confessing that he has spilt innocent blood, the leadership shows no sympathy but treats him with brutality, perhaps contributing to his subsequent suicide.[23]

Most critics regard the Barabbas story as historically improbable; if he existed, however, Barabbas was probably a Zealot freedom fighter. Whether or not that is the case, Matthew, in contrast to Mark, paints the crowds as clearly *choosing* Barabbas for release in preference to Jesus, while Barabbas is represented as a criminal, to make the maximum possible contrast with Jesus. Moreover, the choice is repeated for emphasis.[24]

The crowd actually demands Jesus' crucifixion, literally howling for his blood. Finally, in the passage that above all others has justified the charge of Christ-killing in Christian eyes, the crowd consciously takes on itself the guilt for Jesus' death, in effect pronouncing a curse on this and future Jewish generations, in the notorious words, "His blood be on our heads and our children's."[25] Meanwhile Pilate, in a gesture characteristically Jewish and not Roman, washes his hands to show his own innocence in the death of Jesus.[26] On the cross, Jesus is reviled by the Jews, not just by Roman soldiers, as in Mark.[27]

These many and sometimes subtle changes transformed Matthew's version into a much more anti-Jewish document than its predecessor. The object of his hostility is not just the leadership but the people as a whole, corporately blamed for the death of Jesus.[28] As in the other Gospels, Jesus is depicted by contrast as a noble and dignified victim of injustice, suffering in resignation to the will of God. As the contrast is sharpened between innocent victim and bloodthirsty accusers, the Jews look worse and worse. Matthew's Gospel could be called the charter of antisemitism, although its author also preserves from his sources evidence of Jesus' own adherence to Judaism.

Matthew's version of the trial shows the issues that by his time have come to separate Jews from Christians. He presents Jesus as convicted by the Jews on two separate counts, his claim to be the Messiah, and his claim to be the Son of God. These are the claims that the Jewish people of his day reject and that the Christian movement must uphold against them.[29] Exactly the same two claims are prominently featured in Matthew's account of Peter's confession of faith, examined in Chapter 3. Peter tells Jesus that he is the Messiah, the Son of God, while Jesus praises him for his insight.[30]

We have to conclude that Matthew's anti-Judaism is not primarily motivated by the need to present a favorable image in the Roman world, as Mark's is. Matthew is directly concerned with Jewish rejection of the claims of the Christian movement concerning Jesus as Messiah and Son of God. The Gospel comes out of the split between the Church and the main body of the Jewish people, which began somewhere around 85–100 C.E., though it was not complete until many decades later.

LUKE'S NON-TRIAL

Luke's account of the passion also surpasses Mark's in its hostility toward the Jews. While the intention of the writer is certainly to transfer the guilt for the death of

Jesus from the Romans to the Jews, an aim accomplished with singular thoroughness, it is not clear which is his primary object, to exculpate the Romans or to incriminate the Jews. Probably, as in Matthew's case, it is the latter.

Like Matthew, Luke involves the whole people in the guilt for Jesus' death. The Pharisees are not held especially responsible; in a number of passages, especially those coming from Luke's special source, they are represented as friendly to Jesus, as they are friendly to the Church in Luke's second volume, the Acts of the Apostles. Both Luke and Acts seem to be hostile toward the Temple and the Temple establishment, the High Priest, and the Sadducees, who appear in a prominent role in the accounts of Jesus' condemnation and death. But their role is not contrasted with that of the people: the priestly establishment appear precisely as the leaders of the whole Jewish people, who are thus the real culprits.

Luke does not follow Mark throughout–he apparently depended on a different source for much of his account of the condemnation and death of Jesus. Where he does, his editing shows that he sharply increased the Jewish role in the events leading up to Jesus' death and even the death itself. Unlike Mark, Luke does not attempt to portray a formal trial with religious charges and a verdict of guilty. The hearing before the Council in the house of the High Priest is in no sense a trial: there are no witnesses, there is no confession by Jesus that he is the Messiah,[31] there is no charge of blasphemy, and no verdict is passed.[32]

The reader receives the impression that "Jesus was not tried and condemned but lynched."[33] Luke so plays down the role of the Romans that the natural way to read the narrative is to think that the Jews were the ones who actually carried out the crucifixion of Jesus.[34]

The role of Pilate, already subjected by Mark to considerable imaginative restructuring, is further developed by Luke in the same direction, to such an extreme that, as Gaston puts it, "this is [now] the chief function of Pilate. He does not interrogate, he does not condemn, he does not execute, he only declares Jesus innocent."[35] Or as the same critic puts it elsewhere in his article, "Pilate (and to a lesser extent Herod) appears in the gospel in the role of a defence attorney, desperately trying to dissuade the people from their undertakings."[36]

Luke has thus managed to achieve a 180-degree reversal of history, presenting the official who in fact sentenced Jesus to death as his defender against the blood lust of his own people. Here the foundation is laid for the role of Pilate in the apocryphal "Acts of Pilate," a legendary version of the events that in turn provided the basis for the view of Pilate as a saint, traditional in some of the Eastern Churches. But if Pilate is a saint, what by contrast are the Jews?

As Gaston points out, in Luke, Jesus' real trial is before his own people. The people "demand" that he be crucified (Luke 23:22f) and their voices "prevail." After ineffectual protests, Pilate finally delivers up Jesus to *their* will (v. 24). By contrast with theirs, and with history, Pilate's role is to show that Jesus was innocent of all charges, including religious ones.

Gaston sums up by saying, "What earlier in the gospel was a warning coupled with a call to repentance has in the passion narrative become a prediction and no repentance is possible. Although it is expressed very subtly in the gospel, the Jews as such have been irrevocably rejected."[37]

In his Gospel, Luke joins Matthew in the task of depicting the Jews as the Christ-killers, adding a distinctive contribution of his own. In Acts he continues the enterprise. The speeches to the Jewish people of the Christian leaders, in the first five chapters, all accuse the Jews of direct responsibility for the death of Christ, even implying that they were guilty of *crucifying* Jesus, a punishment the Jewish courts had no power to inflict.[38]

True, in these speeches Luke represents the early Christian leadership as offering some mitigation of the charges: the people and their leaders acted in ignorance and in accordance with a plan of God, and repentance is possible. In this respect, Luke is not at one with later Christian anti-Judaism, but he nevertheless provides it with some of its material.

In Acts, the main purpose appears to be to defend Paul against charges of apostasy beginning to be made against him by Jewish teachers. Luke wishes to show that Jewish guilt justifies the Church in distancing itself from the people. At the same time, he attempts to drive a wedge between the past leadership of the people, the Sadducees, and the current leaders, the Pharisees and their descendants. The Pharisees appear in Acts as the friends of the Church, including Paul, and a link is established between Paul and the grandfather of Gamliel II, the leader or *nasi* of the Yavne community at the time Luke was probably writing.[39]

Presumably Luke's motives in his restructuring of past history were not the same as either Matthew's or Mark's, but his distortions of past reality are no less drastic and perhaps more. The tendentiousness of the editorial material in all these Gospels is so striking, once properly analyzed, that it induces intense skepticism in the informed reader about the historicity of any of these accounts. We are entitled to conclude unequivocally that the anti-Jewish passages in these writings, and above all the attempt to depict the Jews as the Christ-killers instead of the Romans, represent the propagandist needs of the Church at the time the accounts were written. What the real history was we have already seen.

JOHN'S ANTI-JUDAISM

In the Gospel of John, probably written about the turn of the century, the Jews do not appear so clearly as the Christ-killers, but the Gospel as a whole has long been recognized as perhaps the most hostile toward the Jews of the four. John's account of the events leading up to Jesus' death seems at many points to have been dependant on a source not known to or used by the other three gospel writers, more closely related to historical reality. Nevertheless, even he depicts Pilate, contrary to all historical probability, as unwilling to condemn Jesus and only giving in reluctantly to Jewish demands.

By this point in his narrative, the writer's understanding of the Jewish role in the events leading up to Jesus' death has changed completely. (Is he now using a different source?) Inconsistently with the account of the hearing in the house of the High Priests he has just given, and inconsistently with Jewish law (since the Messiah is not regarded as divine, even if called the son of God), the leadership now say to Pilate, "We have a Law, and by this Law he ought to die, because he made himself the Son of God."[40] Though this account of events had so far presented the motivations and actions of the Jewish leadership in a generally more plausible light than the other Gospels, the total effect is still to make them largely responsible for Jesus' death.

The Gospel of John has a distinctive way of speaking of Jesus' opponents. Seventy-nine times the expression "the Jews" appears in this Gospel, compared with five times each in Matthew and Luke, and six times in Mark. Its author feels no identification with the Jewish people and views them from a distance from which their internal distinctions and differences are no longer significant. He sees them in a uniformly hostile light.

Jesus is hardly thought of as a Jew himself. The Jews are now distinct from Jesus and by implication from the Church, and they are opposed to him. Yet, this is not perhaps the consistent view of this Gospel. Granskou observes that the Gospel of John hovers between two views, one in which Jesus brings a spiritual form of Judaism, opposed to the Temple and formal worship, and another in which he brings a new religion, altogether distinct from Judaism.[41]

In the Gospel as a whole, the passion story dominates the structure of the book. Mark's theory of a messianic secret plays no part at all. Jesus is openly recognized as the Messiah from the beginning, explicitly proclaiming himself as such. John the Baptist in acclaiming him as the Lamb of God already refers to the crucifixion as a sacrifice for the sins of the world. Jesus' opponents are seeking to kill him long before the final climax.

Their motivation is satanic. The Jews are the children of the devil (8:31.) At the same time, there are hints that Jesus died for the people, such as the remark of the High Priest, understood by the author of the Gospel in an ironic sense, and the depiction of some prominent Jews as believers in Jesus.[42]

As in Luke, Pilate appears as the defender of Jesus against his own people. The figure of Pilate is being reconceived by all these writers to make points in a polemical struggle between the Church and the Jewish people. This ruthless official, fired for brutality excessive even by Roman standards, can hardly have been the uxorious and indecisive character, troubled by ethical scruples about putting Jesus out of the way, depicted by this and the other Gospels. This is not the Pilate of history. Like the Jewish leadership in the Gospels, he is the creation of Christian anti-Judaism.

It has been said that the Fourth Gospel is the most Jewish and the most anti-Jewish of the four. Perhaps this is true. In some respects it shows more knowledge of Jewish matters than the others, and in its account of the hearing before the High Priests it is probably closer to history than its synoptic counterparts. But like Matthew, this writer is embittered by the breach with the synagogue. If he stood for an esoteric Judaism centered on Jesus' private teaching, he and his friends have been sharply informed by the Rabbis that there is no future in Judaism for such views.

If these are the opinions of a final editor, he has no continuing loyalty to Judaism, if indeed he had personally ever been Jewish, which many scholars consider improbable. Whoever he was, his part in laying the foundations of later Christian antisemitism at least equals that of the other gospel writers. The solemn reading of the Johannine account of the Passion of Jesus in the traditional Good Friday liturgy has fixed the anti-Jewish picture of Jesus' death in the imagination of millions of Christians down the centuries. Now it will be very difficult to efface.

Perhaps even more familiar to Catholic Christians is the prologue to the Gospel, read at every mass in the Tridentine rite. In these majestic and quasi-credal lines we hear that the incarnate Word of God came to his own, and his own received him not, while those who did receive him became the sons of God. In its own way, the prologue states the new doctrine that the covenant has passed from the unbelieving and rejecting Jews to the Gentile church. This passage is also remarkable for the way in which it alludes to central Jewish themes while inserting them into the context of a mythical structure altogether non-Jewish.

THE NEW TESTAMENT AND ANTI-JUDAISM

The final stages of the composition of the Gospels, sometimes called by the critics the redactional stage, may not be the latest stratum of the New Testament. Some of the letters may be even later. But the Gospels in their finished form set the tone for future Christian attitudes toward Jews. They have imprinted on Christian history the stereotype of the Jews as determined but hypocritical opponents of Jesus and in the last analysis Christ-killers. No uncritical reader of the New Testament could easily come away with any but the most negative opinion of Jews. While the New Testament does not encourage racist views, for these were the invention of later periods, it sees little hope for Jews except in conversion to Christ. Israel has no continuing validity as the covenant people.

Whatever Paul's own views may have been, and we have discovered that he is very difficult to understand, even with the help of the tools of modern scholarship, he has been read and interpreted in the context of the rest of the New Testament, and in particular of the Gospels. The New Testament in turn has been read in the light of Christian teaching as it later developed, a teaching in which the election of the Jewish people is regarded as canceled on account of their rejection of the Messiah and their crime of killing him.

It is possible to read the New Testament in this way, because the seeds of the later theology of supersession are in fact already present in it. *Christian anti-Judaism is not a later distortion of an originally pure religion. It is embedded in the foundation documents of the faith.* By the completion of the New Testament, the basis for later anti-Judaism and antisemitism had already been firmly established.

Against such influences, traditional Christianity, which accepts the binding authority of the New Testament Scriptures, has no theological defense. Only critical scholarship, driven by a passion for truth and for justice for the Jewish people, can disentangle Christianity from its legacy of anti-Judaism. In a later chapter we shall see how difficult even that enterprise is.

THE LETTER TO THE HEBREWS

Since the breach between the new religion and its parent body took place at different times in different places, we cannot precisely date the beginnings of the new theology of supersession, corresponding roughly to the emergence of Gentile Christianity as a distinct entity, altogether separate from its Jewish origins. Even within the New Testament, most of which belongs to the first century, there is at least one book having more in common with later theology than with its companions in the New Testament. This is the mysterious Letter to the Hebrews.

The letter continues to baffle New Testament scholars. Its authorship, destination and purpose remain unknown, in spite of many attempts to solve the mystery. The title, *To the Hebrews*, is not part of its text and it was added later. Traditionally, Hebrews was supposed to be by Paul and must have circulated from an early date along with the collection of his letters. However, neither its theology nor its elegant literary style are those of Paul, and only very conservative readers still claim it as his.

The critics are unanimous in rejecting Pauline authorship, though at least one has suggested that it comes from the Pauline circle.[43] If this is correct, Hebrews reflects in its own idiom a theology generally shared by Paul and his team of bright young men. On the other hand, if Paul's views were anything like the interpretations of recent scholars such as Sanders and Gaston, the author of Hebrews can have had little in common with Paul beyond their common Christianity.

While Paul remained a Jew, in spite of his conviction that the resurrection of Jesus was a cosmic event ushering in a totally new epoch, the author of Hebrews is so convinced of the superiority of Jesus to Moses, and of the new covenant to the old, that he can no longer be called a Jew, even if he had once been one. No one can speak of the covenant of Sinai as abolished and replaced by something better and still be a Jew. The claim for the superiority of Jesus to Moses is an absolute breach with Judaism and the manifesto of a new religion.

Paul never went as far as that, even when he spoke of a new covenant. Jeremiah had predicted a new covenant,[44] but it differed from the old only in that God would put his Torah in the hearts of the people, so that they could keep it better. None of the prophecies in the Bible of the renewal of the covenant ever suggest that the existing one will be abolished. If the Letter to the Hebrews was actually addressed to Jews, or to Christian Jews, its purpose must have been to dissuade them from fidelity to Judaism, or from returning to Judaism from Christianity.

The old covenant is not simply inferior to the new: it is no longer in force and has been canceled and abrogated by God himself (7:18; 10:9). Jesus is the bringer of a new covenant in every way superior to the one given through Moses (7:22). In the view of the author, the old covenant is not merely surpassed by the new because of the latter's excellence: the old was already defective and incapable of fulfilling its function (7:18; 8:7).

It is from this letter that we get the familiar name, New Testament, for the Scriptures of the "new covenant," since its author plays upon the double meaning of the Greek word he uses to render the word "covenant," *diatheke*, which also means testament, or will. The covenant of Sinai, the foundation of Judaism then and now, is not merely old in relation to new (8:8,13; 9:18; 12:24). Compared with the new covenant, it is both inferior (7:22), and obsolete (10:9). Such a theology need not involve hostility toward Jewish people as such, but it is profoundly anti-Jewish in the sense that it degrades and invalidates Judaism in relation to Christianity, the religion of the "new covenant."

THE LETTER OF BARNABAS

A further stage in the growth of the myth and its attendant theology of supersession is documented in another writing, outside the New Testament canon, but roughly contemporaneous with its later portions. This document, known as the Letter of Barnabas, is strongly anti-Jewish in tone, in this respect probably surpassing anything in the New Testament. But as in the case of the most anti-Jewish books in the New Testament, Matthew and John, its author knows a good deal about Judaism and argues in very Jewish terms for a case intended to invalidate Judaism. It is also clear that his arguments are not original: he is the heir to a tradition that has already been using scriptural proof-texts to establish the superiority of Christianity over Judaism. The texts are often quoted in translations found only in Christian authors. Such ideas go well back into the first century, even if they lack contemporary documentation.

The origin of the letter of Barnabas has long been debated among scholars. A recent essay by Martin B. Shukster and Peter Richardson[45] argues for a location in Syria-Palestine and a date in the reign of the Roman Emperor Nerva (c.98 C.E.). During the reign of this Emperor, anti-Jewish attitudes in the Empire, which had been strong in the reign of his predecessor Domitian, relaxed, and there was even a project for rebuilding the Temple in Jerusalem.

The authors argue that the letter of Barnabas was written in view of this project, which seemed to threaten the already prevalent Christian belief that the destruction of the Temple had been a punishment inflicted by God on the Jewish people for their killing of the Messiah Jesus. "Within a Christian context, this apparent rehabilitation of Jewish status raises afresh the question of who possesses the covenant."[46]

Some members of the community are already arguing that "the covenant is both theirs and ours" (4:6),[47] a position that would recognize the legitimacy of both religions. For the author of the letter, this position is absolutely untenable. The

Jewish people has been altogether superseded as the covenant people by the Church. The Christians are the "new" people (3:6, 5:7, 7:5, 13:1–6), and the "true heirs of the promise" (5:7, 6:17, 15:7, 16:9) and of "the covenant" (4:6–8 [cf. 14:1–5:19], 13:1–6). God had already rejected the Jewish people when Moses broke the tablets (4:8).

The polemic of the letter is directed against two central Jewish institutions, the Temple and the house of study. The repeated direct and indirect references to the Temple seem to suggest an anxiety that its rebuilding would seriously compromise the Christian claim, leading to defections to Judaism from among the faithful. The polemic against the house of study is more concerned with the interpretation of Scripture and the Christian claim to know the meaning of Scripture better than Jews do.

Like the writer to the Hebrews, Barnabas argues that the Jewish priesthood and sacrificial system have been abolished by being fulfilled in Christ, the true sacrifice. The sacrificial system of the Temple is no longer in force and cannot bring about the remission of sins, which the blood of the cross, mediated to Christians through the preaching of the good news and baptism, is alone able to effect. Any rebuilt Temple would now be illegitimate. There is a genuine and legitimate Temple, but it is spiritual, found in the Christian believer.

Barnabas was faced with real expertise in scriptural interpretation from his rivals, the pharisaic and rabbinic scholars in their house of study. They knew the Scriptures backward and forward. They stood in a tradition of interpretation that had centuries behind it but could be developed in a highly creative manner, as it was at the time. Moreover, the interpreters belonged to the same tradition and community as the authors of the biblical books themselves (though the ancient world did not see it in that way, since it believed in the divine authorship of the Scriptures).

In contrast, the church and its teachers had no choice but to put forward novel interpretations, remote from existing tradition. Barnabas argues that these novel interpretations, which he calls "knowledge" (actually *gnosis* in the Greek), are the fruit of divine inspiration through the Spirit. Nevertheless, anyone aware of both interpretations might easily consider that the Rabbis were on much surer ground than the teachers of the Church.

In the context of Barnabas' polemic, themes appear that will become familiar in later Christian literature. Christians possess a superior righteousness. Jews are given to works of evil. The spiritual worship of the Church is superior to the sacrificial cult of the Temple, which the prophets had already denounced, showing that God does not require sacrifices and burnt offerings but a spiritual service.

The dietary laws have been carnally misunderstood by the Jews, since they really have a spiritual meaning in the overcoming of the flesh, a meaning Christians understand but Jews do not. It is the divine intention that Christians should rightly understand these things from their reading of the Scriptures, under the guidance of sound Christian teachers. Christians have the true circumcision of the heart, which is exactly what enables them to understand the Scriptures correctly.

For Barnabas, the Christian believer is the Temple of God, and at the same time the divine presence dwelling within him is the source of right interpretation of Scripture, novel and astonishing as it may turn out to be. The superior Christian status can only be retained if the Christian remains faithful to teachers such as Barnabas and does not "become like them" (i.e., the Jews). Hence, it may be correct to interpret his strong anti-Jewish language as a dissuasive. Christians are being tempted back to Judaism by the quality of rabbinic scholarship and the relative openness of some Jewish teachers. If this goes on, the Church will collapse. Strong rhetoric is called for. We shall see that this situation will be repeated many times in the centuries to follow.

THE THEOLOGY OF SUPERSESSION

The Christian literature of the second century and onward has taken on a new tone, already foreshadowed in the later strata of the New Testament. The new tone is one of rejection of the Jewish people, based on the claim that God had himself rejected them because of their rejection and killing of their Messiah, Jesus. Christian writers now claim that the Church has altogether taken over the position of the elect people of God from the Jewish people. We are learning to call this development *the theology of supersession.*

Israel has been rejected and displaced, superseded by the Church as the new Israel, which is also now the true Israel. Already in the writers of the New Testament we have met (at least by implication) the claim that the Church is the new Israel, the renewed Israel of the end time. The Essenes also claimed to be the new Israel, but they saw themselves as the nucleus of a reformed people. The Church claims something more far-reaching: it is the *true Israel*, and it can trace its own pedigree back to the beginning. The exact words may not be found until the writings of Justin, but the idea is certainly present in Barnabas, written probably in the closing years of the first century, and we have found similar thoughts in Hebrews, within the New Testament canon.

The new teaching would be a standard feature of Christian theology from then until the late twentieth century. It is still the standard view, though the theologians of dialogue with the Jewish people have at last begun to question it. The growth of the theology of supersession is the major second phase in the incremental development of anti-Jewish attitudes in the Christian church, completing the shape of the myth.

In the first phase, the Christian movement, still a sect in Judaism, sought to prove that Jesus was the Messiah and that his unique history had been predicted in Scripture. The first century struggles between the Church and its Jewish parent had centered on Christology, the novel Christian claim that Jesus, though crucified and an apparent failure, was nevertheless the Messiah on the ground of his resurrection. While the church remained Jewish, the claim for Jesus' messiahship had been paramount in the dispute with the main body of the Jewish people. Meanwhile, the

Gentile church began to develop its revolutionary new salvation myth, already largely worked out in the letters of Paul.

In the second century, the ground of the conflict shifted and broadened. The issues between the Church and the Jewish people were no longer simply christological, though the newer view that Jesus as Son of God was actually divine made the christological issue even more serious and divisive than before. The conflict was now no longer so much between two views of the nature and destiny of the Messiah as between two claimants to be God's people, or even two different views of God's dealing with human beings in history. The claims had become irreconcilable.

The writers of the period continue to claim that the Jews have been rejected by God because of their own rejection of his Messiah, a claim that will be made by Christians down to the present day. But the claim is now surrounded and supported by a greatly enlarged list of alleged Jewish crimes.

Jewish rejection of Jesus is now held to be the outcome of a basic flaw in the people manifest since its beginnings, only coming to a head in their killing of the Christ when he came. It is not only their view of the Messiah that is mistaken: they had been wrong about God, about worship and about ethics, and they never lived up even to their own mistaken standards. The Jewish people had been rejected by God because they deserved to be.

However, God had always foreseen, even intended, this development, and he has now provided himself with a people drawn from the Gentiles who would be worthier of their election. Such a position, with only minor variations, appears to have been common ground among second-century Gentile Christians and their successors in the following centuries, taken for granted in controversy among themselves, as well as in their apologetic writings addressed to the pagan world.

ISSUES BETWEEN JEWS AND CHRISTIANS

In view of the thesis of this book, it is important to evaluate this early religious opposition correctly and without exaggeration. If Christians were religiously opposed to Jews at this period, so of course were Jews to Christians. There were serious theological differences between Jews and Christians at this period, and neither side can be blamed for standing up for its own position. In the ancient world, it was customary to do so with vigor and with strong language.

However, the opposition between Christians and Jews was not a symmetrical one. Jewish opposition to Christianity may have had several causes, as we saw earlier in this chapter. In addition to those already discussed, Jews were now confronted by the belief of the Gentile church that Jesus was divine, a belief probably not found among Jewish Christians, at least in any explicit form.

The Rabbis had already become uncomfortable about the threat to monotheism of various Jewish Gnostic doctrines, which they regarded as acknowledging "two powers in heaven."[48] In the second century, the Church's theology, which referred to Jesus as the divine Word of God, or Logos, and as a "second god," must have seemed altogether beyond the pale of monotheism to the Jewish scholars, although the theologians of the Church did not intend it as such. On this central issue there could be no compromise for mainstream Jews.

However, Jewish theological objection to Christian beliefs did not entail a need to convert Christians to save them from damnation. Beliefs totally unacceptable for Jews themselves might not be an obstacle to the salvation of non-Jews, who had not experienced the divine choice nor entered into a covenant that required very specific forms of obedience.

Those who observed the precepts of the Noachide covenant,[49] without embracing Judaism, had every chance of salvation in the world to come. At this time, the members of the Church did observe these precepts.[50] Jews could thus hope for the salvation of their Christian neighbors in spite of their heretical doctrines, as well as of righteous pagans who abjured idolatry and observed the ethics of the philosophers.

The curses on the *minim* primarily concerned the dissemination of their doctrines within the Jewish people, though in later times the strong and persistent opposition of the Church to the Jews eventually engendered a counter-opposition to Christians as such. In contrast, Christians believed that nobody could be saved except through the death and resurrection of Christ.

Jews do not have to define themselves in relation to Christianity, whereas Christianity cannot escape defining itself by reference to Judaism. The asymmetry begins at that point. It is impossible to state the beliefs of Christians without mentioning the Jews. Judaism can ignore Christianity, as the Talmud does, almost completely. Since the Jews reject all the Christian claims, what Christianity has to say about them is bound to be negative. Simply in order to affirm its own faith in Jesus, Christianity had to provide a rival interpretation of the Jewish Scriptures, an interpretation rejecting the Jewish reading as a whole.

Rejection of particular interpretations might merely constitute an internal disagreement between different Jewish groups. A total difference in the way Scripture is read and understood is a far more serious matter, involving rejection of the basis of Jewish faith in the covenant of Sinai and of Jewish commitment to the commandments of the Torah as the divinely required human response to God's deliverance. Christians seldom realize how great the difference is, since they do not regularly encounter Jewish interpretations. Even Christian Old Testament scholarship, supposedly scientific and impartial, largely ignores Jewish writers and Jewish biblical interpretation.

What for Jews is the constitution of a commonwealth now becomes for Christians a cryptogram for Christ. Jews read the Bible as an account of God's choice of the Jewish people to be his people and of the terms of the covenant that he made with them when he did so. These terms oblige the Jewish people to a unique way of life, higher than that required of the surrounding nations. The commandments imposed by God as part of the covenant not only require a high ethical standard from individuals, they also include all kinds of laws for the community, dealing with matters that today belong to civil law. The Torah is not just about religion, it is also about the state and about business relationships. In fact, it governs all aspects of life.

The first five books of the Bible hold a special place and are called the Torah *par excellence*, since they contain the various commandments, laws, and regulations by which the Jewish commonwealth was and ideally still is governed. The remaining sections of the Bible, the Prophets, including the historical books, and the Writings, occupy a slightly lower place, since they are not Torah in the most direct and immediate sense. They are commentary on Torah, to be read, but they are not in the same sense the commanding word of God.

In the synagogue service on Saturday morning and in the private study of traditional Jews, the whole Torah is read each year; it is accompanied by the Haftarah, selected passages from the Prophets (which in the Hebrew canon include the historical books of Joshua, Samuel, and Kings), but much of the prophetic literature remains unread, except by students of the Bible. The Writings are read on festival days, but otherwise, except for the psalms, are less studied by the people at large.

Since the Gentile church had abandoned the covenant with all its corporate and personal legislation, it was not obvious that the Jewish Scriptures should be retained at all. Yet for a considerable period they constituted, in the Septuagint translation, the only Bible of the Church. Later, various "apostolic writings"[51] were added to the canon and entitled the Scriptures of the New Covenant, or New Testament.

In the absence of an ethical and legal system arising from the covenant, the Hebrew Scriptures no longer bore their original meaning. They were read as prophecy, not as Torah. In their transformed meaning, they were now understood as pointing forward to Christ and his Church. Those provisions of the Torah that could not be given a prophetic or symbolic meaning, pointing to Christ, were simply ignored and treated as obsolete.

The Jewish Bible was given a new name: it became the Old Testament (i.e., the Scriptures of the Old Covenant). Since the Old Covenant had been abolished, according to the Church, its only remaining meaning was prophetic or typological. Thus, when the Bible of the Jewish people was taken over by the Church as its Old Testament and set alongside the New Testament, in the light of which it would now be read, its meaning was transformed. It became a new and different book.

The struggle of the Church with Judaism inevitably centered on a struggle for possession of the Jewish Bible. The Church could not maintain its claim that Jesus was the Messiah, along with the conviction that in consequence the Torah was not binding upon Gentile Christians, without carrying out this annexation and transformation of the Jewish Scriptures.

OTHER SECOND-CENTURY WRITERS

As we move further into the second century, the same themes reappear in Christian literature, sometimes in milder, sometimes in more hostile language. The former

Platonist Justin, writing somewhere around the middle of the second century (he is said to have suffered martyrdom from the Romans in 165) dealt with the relation of Christianity to Judaism in a set-piece dialogue, the protagonists of which are himself and a Jew, Trypho.

We do not know whether Trypho was a real person or whether the dialogue is one that had actually taken place and been recorded by Justin. In any case, the views that Justin attributes to his Jew, Trypho, are plausible ones, that a Jew of the period might have advanced in dialogue with Christians, and the tone of the exchange is not hating, though hard-hitting on the Christian side.

The views advanced by Justin himself in the controversy are based on the testimonies already used by Barnabas. Justin spells them out in detail, with a wealth of accurate quotation, even recognizing differences between the Septuagint translation and the Hebrew.

Justin's own position precludes absolute hostility toward Judaism. As a Christian Platonist, he wishes to claim what he sees as the best in Judaism, along with the best in paganism, for the activity of the Word or Logos who became incarnate in Christ. Like other writers of the period, he must also emphasize the links between Christianity and Judaism in order to establish the antiquity of Christianity to rebut pagan objections.

On the other hand, Justin has no doubt whatsoever that Christianity has completely superseded Judaism. God's "true Israelite people" are those that confess Jesus as the one who fulfilled the Scriptures, as the new Law and the new Lawgiver. There is a place in this people for those who retain Jewish observances while believing in Jesus (i.e., for Christian Jews, provided they do not compel other Christians to be observant). Those who do insist on these observances, however, are wicked and uncomprehending, and will not be saved. Those who in their synagogues anathematize believers in Jesus as the Messiah must repent in order to be saved.[52]

Justin was apparently the first to claim in so many words that the Church is the true Israel (*Dialogue* 11, 123, 124). However, if the words cannot be found before Justin, the idea is certainly present earlier, clearly implied, for example, in the words of the Letter to the Hebrews on the superiority of the new covenant.

Justin believes that the Jews killed Christ, but he does not regard their suffering in the persecution under Hadrian, including the destruction of Jerusalem, as punishment for this crime. Nevertheless, for him as for later writers, circumcision functions as a kind of negative identity designator and no longer as the sign of the covenant between God and his people.

However, Justin is no antisemite. He even says that Christians should pray for the repentance of the Jews, in order that they may participate in the future salvation of God's people. Jews may continue to exist alongside Christians, but their hope lies in conversion to Christianity, not in Judaism itself.[53]

Another approximately contemporary second-century Christian, Melito of Sardis, uses much stronger language. His work was much less influential than Justin's, and to this extent less important for our inquiry. Nevertheless, it is illuminating to see how intense theological anti-Judaism could be, even in one who knew a great deal about Judaism and had a large and powerful Jewish community among his neighbors.[54]

Melito was a leader, perhaps the bishop, of the Christian community in the Asia Minor city of Sardis. He wrote a number of works, only a few fragments of which have survived, apart from the one we are here concerned with, the *Peri Pascha*, "Concerning the Passover, or Easter."

The Greek word *pascha*, originally rendering the Hebrew *Pesach*, came to mean either Passover or Easter. The ambiguity, surviving in the Romance languages such as French, Italian, and Spanish, though not in English, is relevant to Melito's argument: he was what was then called a Quartodeciman, that is, he belonged to a community that celebrated both Good Friday and Easter on the same day as Passover, the fourteenth (*quartodecima* in Latin) of the Jewish month Nisan. Their festival could most correctly be described as the Christian Passover. The Roman usage, which eventually prevailed, was to celebrate Easter on the Sunday following the Passover, so that the celebration of the Resurrection would always occur on a Sunday.

Melito's long and highly rhetorical poem contrasts the two Passovers, Jewish and Christian, showing the complete superiority of the latter. The Christian Passover, like everything else that is Christian, is superior to the Jewish in the same way that a finished work is superior to a model or plan. Judaism is God's preliminary sketch for Christianity. But once the final construction is in place, the plan is useless and obsolete. Whatever value it formerly had is now completely lost.

In his account of the Passover, Melito depicts the Jews in relation to Jesus in a role analogous to that of the Egyptians in relation to the Jews at the Exodus.[55] He blames them for rejoicing in their own Passover at the very time that they were crucifying Jesus, thus becoming responsible for the death of the true paschal lamb.

The responsibility of the Jews for the death of Jesus assumes in Melito's poem a peculiar vividness and awfulness we have not hitherto met with. Melito's Christology and Trinitarian theology is much more advanced than that of Justin, going beyond later Christian orthodoxy, though not beyond popular devotion and preaching, in its unqualified identification of Christ and God.

Melito was what was called a modalist monarchian, in the technical language of the theology of the time. That is to say, he was a strict monotheist, then called monarchians, and he believed that the one God, as it were, alternated roles in his dealing with men, appearing in three modes successively, first as Creator, then as Redeemer, and finally as the Spirit in the Church. Thus, Melito sees Christ as directly involved in the history of Israel before the incarnation.

He also sees God as crucified:

> He who hung the earth is hanging;
> he who fixed the heavens has been fixed;
> he who fastened the universe has been fastened to a tree;
> the Sovereign has been insulted;

the God has been murdered;
the King of Israel has been put to death by an Israelite right hand.[56]

Deicide appears in these verses, for the first time, apparently, as the prime accusation against the Jewish people. The charge has not yet been formally withdrawn by the Roman Catholic church.[57] Since Melito's writings had little currency after his lifetime, his charge of deicide was probably not immediately influential. Chrysostom and others revived it in the fourth century, probably independently, and it became a standard part of the controversial armoury of Christendom.

In spite of the reluctance of the Church to deprive itself finally of so formidable a weapon against the Jews, the charge has more rhetorical than theological force. On any theistic assumption, God cannot be killed. However, the doctrine can hardly be called unorthodox, since the Christology involved is the same as that implied in the hallowed tradition of calling Mary the Mother of God. According to this widespread and popular theology, the Incarnation of God in Christ permits the virtual identification of his divinity and humanity, so that what happens to the one happens also to the other.

Many widely accepted forms of Christian theology and devotional writing have blurred the distinction between divinity and humanity in the same way. The more fervent Christians, especially the monks, have tended to identify Christ with God without qualification; often the same elements in the Church have been the most anti-Jewish. It is therefore interesting to notice that Melito is referred to in other Christian writings as "the eunuch," which at that period probably means a celibate ascetic, following the ancient interpretation of Jesus's words about those who have made themselves eunuchs for the sake of the kingdom of heaven.

The intense and dramatic tone of the poem, of which the example quoted is typical, and the rhetorical use of antithesis pervading it naturally tend to heighten the anti-Jewish atmosphere and charge theological opposition with hatred. Contemplation of the awesome event of the death of God is inseparable from recollection of the ultimate crime, committed by none other than the Jews.

MARCIONISM, A REJECTED POSSIBILITY

Justin and Melito may also have been concerned with a challenge to Christian theology from another quarter than the Jews, that of the heretic Marcion. Marcion had much in common with the Gnostics of the time, who denied that the God of the Bible, the creator of the world, is the true God. While his thought may have originated not in Gnosticism, but in a radical interpretation of Paul's theology,[58] Marcion seems to have come under greater Gnostic influence later.

He shared with the Gnostics the separation of the one God of Christian orthodoxy into two, and their denial of the full humanity of Christ. The God and Father of Jesus Christ was not the same as the God spoken of in the Old Testament as the creator and the giver of the Law to Israel. Jesus came from a wholly other God, far above the god of creation and law. Marcion therefore created a new version of the Christian Bible, abandoning the Old Testament altogether, as the product of an inferior God, and reducing the New to the letters of Paul and a single gospel, an expurgated version of Luke.

By this time, the inferiority of Judaism was a given, shared by orthodox and heretic alike. Marcion accounted for this inferiority by his theory of antithesis. Judaism and Christianity were opposites. Christianity was something utterly novel, the revelation of the unknown God.[59]

Judaism, together with its Bible and all its religious practices, was not a human invention, however, but a revelation, though a revelation of an inferior god. This god was real for Marcion, and Judaism correspondingly had for him a certain validity denied it by the orthodox. Since Jesus was the emissary of the unknown God, it was understandable that the Jews could not recognize him, and in fact he did not fulfill their messianic prophecies.

Marcion's views were extremely popular, gaining the allegiance of a substantial proportion of Christians. Meeting his challenge contributed to the development of second-century Christian theology and to the formation of the canon of the New Testament. The challenge could be met only by conceding to him (since it was in any case common ground) the inferiority and obsoleteness of Judaism, even while the Church's theologians argued for the retention of the Jewish Bible as the Old Testament of the Church.

If, like Marcion, the Church had felt able to dispense with the Jewish Scriptures, it would not have been necessary in refuting him to adopt a position so opposed to the Jewish people. Marcion was convinced of Jewish inferiority, to the extent of characterizing the God of the Bible as a lesser and inferior god to the one revealed in Christ. However, he was for this reason able to be more tolerant of Jews and Judaism than could the orthodox Church.

To say that the Jews worshiped a different God was the contemporary equivalent of saying that Judaism was a completely different religion, not a false version of the true religion. Marcion also saw that since Jesus was not the Messiah predicted in the Jewish Scriptures, the Jews were not to blame for not accepting him as such. The Church, in contrast, retained the unity of God and the grounding of its new covenant in the old at the cost of denigrating and invalidating the Jews.

Looking back on the controversy from a modern perspective, it may not seem altogether clear why the Gentile church did not in fact simply cut its links with Judaism and approach the Gentile world as an entirely new religion. Modern liberal Christians are so convinced of the ethical inferiority of Judaism that it is hard to see what meaning the "Old Testament" continues to have for them. Voices are occasionally heard suggesting that it should now be dropped altogether.

Why did the Church of the second century, which held equally or more negative views of ancient Judaism, not follow Marcion's example and jettison the Jewish Bible? In that way the Church could have avoided the necessity of a hostile and polemical relationship toward Judaism. While doubtless continuing to maintain the inferiority of Judaism as a rival religion, it could have exercised a certain tolerance toward it, as Marcion did in his own terms.

There appear to have been several reasons for the course actually adopted by the Church, perhaps none of them individually compelling, but in sum decisive. The controversy with Judaism on the messiahship of Jesus was too deeply embedded in the tradition, including the New Testament books, to be abandoned, even though its relevance to contemporary Gentile Christianity was now much less than it had originally been for the infant Church.

Openly abandoning the claim that Jesus had been the Jewish Messiah and rethinking Christology in entirely Gentile terms would have seemed too revolutionary a step, although that was what the theologians were implicitly doing with their new doctrines of Christ as the divine Word incarnate. To go all the way might have meant abandoning the New Testament along with the Old, since the New depends so much upon the latter.

Among pagan critics, a common charge against Christianity was its admitted novelty, regarded as a serious reproach by the ancient world. Paganism recognized national religions, especially when their antiquity could be demonstrated. Christian apologists could partially rebut the charge of novelty by stressing Christianity's origins in Judaism, since the genuine antiquity of the latter was well recognized in the pagan world, while at the same time disengaging it from various aspects of Judaism that pagan critics found objectionable, such as its exclusiveness and distinctive way of life.

As the anti-Jewish polemic developed, theologians began to claim that in a sense Christianity was even older than Judaism. Since Christ was the Logos, the creative word of God, he had been active in the world from its beginnings, long before Judaism came on the scene. The patriarchs of Judaism before Moses could be claimed as Christians before their time, as could the pagan philosophers like Socrates.

The status of the humanity of Jesus was a third issue raised by Marcion, though somewhat less sharply than by later Gnostics, who denied the need for undergoing martyrdom under persecution, consistently with their denial that the flesh did or could play any part in the redemption of the spirit. (The Marcionites, however, like the Catholics, did submit to martyrdom.) Unlike moderns, Gnostics had no difficulty with Jesus' divine or quasi-divine status in theology but could not see how he could also have taken on human flesh, the polluting envelope of the spirit and the product of the deluded creator god of Gnostic theory, who was not the true God whom Jesus represented. They therefore regarded the humanity of Jesus as a kind of illusion or phantom, barely concealing his divine nature.

The Church wished to reclaim the real humanity of Jesus from the spiritualizing Gnostic onslaught; its challenge was serious and widespread, having gained the allegiance of considerable sections of the Church. The reclamation of Christ's humanity could only be accomplished by reclaiming the Creator, the same God to whom the Jewish Bible bore witness. The challenge of Marcion and the Gnostics had to be met by an assertion of the unity of God and the goodness, within limits, of the created world and of human flesh. Only the retention of the Jewish Bible as Scripture for the Church could make this stand possible. But this carried with it the necessity of denying the Bible to the Jews.

TERTULLIAN ON THE INFERIORITY OF THE JEWS

As recent studies of Marcion and the theologians who responded to him have shown, the necessities of the controversy drove theologians like Tertullian and Irenaeus to an even more intense anti-Judaism.[60] How far is Tertullian, whose anti-Judaism seems exceptionally intense, representative of Christian theology during the period in which he lived?

Tertullian was a North African, a resident of Carthage, probably of Berber descent, but thoroughly Romanized by his education as a professional rhetorician, a speechmaker for his clients. He was an important theologian and no marginal figure, in spite of his eventual defection from the Catholic community to the Montanists, a more rigorist group. His treatment of the problems of the Trinity effectively defined the terminology for succeeding Western theology up to the present.

A Catholic writer, David Efroymson, did important work on Tertullian in his Temple University Ph.D thesis, which has attracted attention from writers on Jewish-Christian relations; it has not so far been published commercially. He sharply brings out the implacable hostility toward Judaism Tertullian found it necessary to employ in his defense of the Church's co-option of the Jewish Scriptures. His and other studies have established that the same anti-Judaic themes are common to Justin and Irenaeus before him (though Tertullian, with his rhetorical skills, presents them more vividly), and likewise to the major church fathers Ambrose, Augustine, Cyril, and Chrysostom after him.[61]

Perhaps Tertullian, for temperamental or other reasons, had an unusual personal dislike of Jews, but he did not invent the ideas through which he expressed it. The most significant thing for our own inquiry is that when the controversy between the Church and Marcionism broke out, the inferiority of Judaism from every point of view was already common ground between Marcion and his opponents. It was by now so firmly established in Gentile Christianity that it could not be questioned either by revolutionary thinkers or the defenders of orthodoxy.

Efroymson showed that Tertullian, who wrote against the Jews in more contexts than any other theologian of the period, actually has more anti-Jewish material in his controversial book against Marcion than in those in which he attacks Judaism specifically.[62] What should we conclude from this?

Ruether's earlier studies of the Christian literature *adversus Judaeos*,[63] the polemical literature specifically directed against the Jews, had demonstrated the existence of a whole series of common anti-Jewish themes in writers from the second century onward. Tertullian made his own contribution to the stock of polemical anti-Jewish topics, but Efroymson's findings show that anti-Judaism was even more important to the Church when it attempted to state its own central theological themes. The opposition between the old Israel and the new provided the very structure on which theological thought was now based. This has continued to be the case, even when the need for anti-Jewish polemic was no longer urgently felt.

Tertullian was able to save the unity of God and the antiquity of Christianity against Marcion only by adopting Marcion's own principle of antithesis.[64] Marcion had claimed that the inferiority of Judaism was the result of its being the revelation of an inferior god. Tertullian and his contemporaries and successors replied that the admitted inferiority was due not to God but to the people to whom he had given Judaism. The principle of antithesis was not Marcion's invention, however. It was already a commonplace of theology: that was the way the Church was reading the Sermon on the Mount.

Tertullian argues that all the commandments of the Torah, which pagans and Christians alike regarded as degrading and unworthy of enlightened people, were given to the Jews to curb their tendency to idolatry, sensuality, and greed–a tendency unique to them and not shared with the rest of the human race. Their "trail of crimes"[65] had culminated in the killing of Christ. The Jews had always been unworthy of their election, and now they had finally lost it. God's choice had been transferred to a people, the Gentiles, capable of living by higher standards than those that had been imposed on the Jews.

In his careful investigation of Tertullian's writings against the Jews in various contexts, Efroymson found no less than twenty-three counts on which the Jews are accused of iniquity. They rejected or killed both Jesus and the prophets. They persecuted Jesus' disciples and later Christians. They spread calumnies against Christians. They displayed envy or jealousy against Christians or Gentiles. They were guilty of pride (national or ethnic). They were contentious about the meaning of the words of the Bible. They committed idolatry. They forgot or were ignorant of God. They lacked faith or hope, and they were blind. They manifested *duritia*, hardness or stiff-neckedness. They were impatient and mocked God's own patience. They were ungrateful and senseless. They were generally disobedient and sinful. They were and are worldly, earthy and sensual, and gluttonous. They indulged in empty ritual. Their religion was obsolete and sterile. They were unready for and unworthy of the gifts of God. They were hypocritical and petty. They even aided and abetted the Marcionites.[66]

Although this catalog of iniquity is largely drawn from a one-sided reading of prophetic denunciations of the people in the Bible itself, omitting the promises of forgiveness and redemption upon repentance, Tertullian does not hesitate to refer it to contemporary Jews. After all, they are the heirs of those who killed Christ, their ultimate crime.

The picture of the Jewish people is set in vivid contrast to the people who have superseded them, the Gentile Christian church. Christianity is in every way the antithesis of Judaism. Efroymson presents Tertullian's "constructive anti-Judaism" (i.e., the points at which it follows from what he wishes to assert positively about Christianity) as circling around the ideas of God, Christ, the Church, and the law.

Tertullian's view of *God* is not peripherally but essentially anti-Jewish. Marcion had complained, like modern liberals, that the Jewish God was too occupied with justice to the exclusion of mercy (an idea that would come as a considerable surprise to Jews who read the Bible through Talmud and midrash). Tertullian's explanation is not that God is harsh, but that he had to deal with an impossible people, with whom only hard measures would work. What God does with Christians is different from, superior to, what he was able to do with Jews, because he has much more responsive material to work on.[67]

The Jews are blamed for their absolute monotheism, their refusal "to count in with [the one God] the Son, and after him the Spirit. . . . It was God's will to make a new covenant, for the very purpose that in a new way his unity might be believed in through the Son and the Spirit, so that God who had previously been preached through the Son and the Spirit, might now be known in his own proper names and persons."[68]

The Jews had never properly understood that God is Father, because they had not known him. They failed to understand that he is God of all, supposing, incredibly, that he was primarily concerned with the Jews.[69] These are familiar modern accusations too, and it is interesting to see how far back they go. As the quotation above suggests, the theologians believed that God had actually revealed his character as the Trinity in an obscure way even in the Old Testament, speaking through his Son and Spirit. Many of the divine appearances described in the Bible, and often regarded by Jews as mediated by an angel, were understood by the Church as manifestations of the Son or Word of God.

Jews are blamed for failing to recognize this and for clinging obstinately to their excessive monotheism. Moreover, God had made known his own intentions, finally to be realized in the Church, clearly enough, but the Jews had refused to see it. The father of Christ "has hidden things by first setting them forth in a document of prophetic obscurity, such as faith might earn the right to understand. . . ."[70]

Efroymson comments, "So the God of Tertullian speaks, clearly enough so that Jews should have understood, but not so clearly that they did understand. Understanding is a Christian prerogative, and misunderstanding is Jewish. And God speaks in ways that insure that the distinction is preserved."[71]

God is wise, not foolish as Marcion had suggested, in giving the Jews laws that brought him into contempt with the enlightened. The laws were needed because of the deep-seated sinfulness of the Jews. The law of retribution was needed because of the hard-heartedness of the Jews. The food laws were needed because of their gluttony. The sacrificial laws were aimed at their tendency to idolatry: God did not really need the sacrifices, but they were what Jews were used to and could serve to detach Jews from idolatry and attach them to himself. The laws governing domestic and public life were likewise aimed at Jewish hardness of heart. In any event, all the laws had also a prophetic meaning, only to be understood in the Christian dispensation.[72]

God is in fact merciful, inasmuch as he keeps on forgiving the ungrateful Jews, even though his mercy was wasted on them. However, he also punishes when it is appropriate. Efroymson comments, "Tertullian seems to enjoy talking about God's severity and justice more than about his mercy; he certainly engages in it more frequently."[73] All God's punitive actions were thoroughly justified by the iniquitous behavior of the Jews on whom they were inflicted.

Above all, their loss of the Temple and the Land is just punishment for killing Christ and called down on themselves when they cried, "His blood be on our own heads and on our children's." Finally, in a vivid fantasy of the Last Judgment, Tertullian gloats over the spectacle of the anticipated punishment of the Jews, on which he will turn "an insatiable gaze," and taunt them with their rejection of Christ.[74]

When Tertullian treats the now classic motif of the replacement and supersession of Israel by the Church as the chosen people of God, he represents it as the deliberate plan of God, rather than a divine improvisation to deal with the failure of an earlier project. All had happened by God's will and had been prophesied in advance. The only reason given is the iniquity and the obsoleteness of Jews and Judaism. ". . . [O]ne meets here a God who is as antagonistic towards Jews and Judaism as Tertullian is. Never is he described as 'loving' Israel, or 'regretting' her loss. . . . Anti-Judaism is in this God's blood; he is infected with it, and it is contagious."[75]

The second theme of Tertullian's constructive anti-Judaism deals with the relationship of *Christ* to Judaism. The divinity of Christ is crucial to Tertullian's polemic. It is the essential difference between Christianity and Judaism. The Jews however constantly reject that which is more than human, or divine. Since in Tertullian's Trinitarian theology, which laid down the future terminology for Western Christendom, the Father and the Son are of the same substance, those who had not recognized the Father were not able to recognize the Son when he appeared.

Jesus is like the Father in his dislike of and opposition to Jews. He resembles the Father in "coming down hard" on the Jews.[76] They in turn are the instigators of hatred against Christ. Hatred against Christ is a focal point of Jewish hatred: before Christ it had been directed against God, and now it is directed against the Church. Above all, their hatred is shown in the suffering and death of Christ. "The Jewish crucifixion of Jesus is . . . an essential element in his explanation of the replacement of Judaism by Christianity."[77] Theology fully reflects the drama of the myth.

In Tertullian's account of the teaching of Jesus, it is superior to Judaism, whatever the point at issue. The results of Jesus' work are always the demise of Judaism or the superiority of Christianity. In a work of Tertullian's directed specifically against the Jews, there is an eloquent climax. Jesus is ". . . the giver of a new law, the heir of a new testament, the priest of new sacrifices, the purifier of a new circumcision, and the observer of a new sabbath–one, that is, who would suppress the old law, establish the new covenant, offer the new sacrifices, repress the antiquated ceremonies, and suppress the old circumcision with its sabbath."[78]

Not unexpectedly, when Tertullian turns to the direct consideration of the *law*, new and old, the theme is treated in the same way, representing Christianity as antagonistic to and greatly superior to Judaism. Law is an important category of Tertullian's thought, so much so that some historians think he was a lawyer himself, and even the terminology he utilized in his influential theology of the Trinity has been explained as legal metaphor. Whether he was a lawyer or simply a professional rhetorician, he certainly thought in legal terms and used them with variety and richness. Unlike Marcion, he does not construct an antithesis between law and gospel, but between old law and new law. For him, as for much later Catholic thought, Christianity is the new and better law.

To make way for this new law, he conceives of the old law as abolished or abrogated. In some particular cases, however, such as the decalogue, it continues to bind Christians or is even rendered more severe by the teaching of Jesus about sins of the will or heart. Alternatively, the law has been transformed and renewed, given a spiritual import that was always inherent in it. Always, however, the law is given an anti-Jewish meaning.

The law is transformed by Jesus: Christian forgiveness replaces Jewish vengeance, Jewish bondage is replaced by Christian dignity. On the other hand, more is expected of Christians, who need no Jewish laxity. As Efroymson remarks, Tertullian manages to say almost simultaneously that Christian law is at once *less* binding, since the burdens have gone, *more* binding, since the precepts of the higher righteousness have been extended beyond Jewish limitations, and *better* than that of the scribes and Pharisees.[79]

The law is spiritually fulfilled in the spiritual circumcision, the circumcision of the heart, which Christians have received. They celebrate divine and eternal sabbaths, offering spiritual sacrifices. Everywhere, the law is shown to have had a secret meaning, ignored by Jews but brought to light in its fulfillment in the Christian church.

The controversy with Marcion involved Tertullian in one centrally important but tricky debate, the justification for retaining the Bible without keeping the laws contained in it. Marcion raised the problem sharply, but he was not the only one to do so. The pagan critic Celsus is scathing on the subject, and Origen, the Christian writer who replied to him, is in some difficulties with his reply. How can Christians allege that the Jewish Bible is authoritative for them, if on principle they do not do what it explicitly says?

Marcion agreed with the Church on the abolition of the law, but was ready to attribute its original promulgation, along with the Bible that contained it, to the inferior god of the Jews. Consistently, if the Church wanted to attribute the Jewish Bible to the father of Jesus Christ, the only God, they should have accepted its authority in its plain sense. According to Efroymson, Tertullian has no one standard answer to the charge, but uses all his armory of arguments, each in appropriate contexts.

"The one constant factor is that nothing Jewish can ever be Christian." What God demands of Christians is always not what the Jews did: it is either less, or more, or better, as we saw above. Christians are called to transcend Judaism in every imaginable way.[80]

Finally, Tertullian represents the Gentile *church* as a new and superior people, supplanting the old in accordance with God's design. As a Gentile people, drawn from all nations, it is superior to the ethnocentric Jews. Gentile means non-Jewish and in Tertullian's anti-Jewish scheme it becomes a code signifying whatever is more than, other than, and better than Jewish.

The original distinction between Jews and Gentiles, made by the Bible and adhered to by Jews, is retained, but Tertullian has reversed its meaning. The Gentiles, originally considered worse off, are now held to be superior to the Jews, precisely on the ground of lacking what for the Bible had been the great advantage of the people of Israel over the nations, the sanctifying and life-giving commandments of the Torah. The Gentiles have replaced Israel because they are a worthier and more honorable people.

Christian *worship* is superior, for Christians can call on God the Father in prayer, which Jews could not because the hands they would raise in prayer are red with the blood of the prophets and of the Lord. The spiritual sacrifices offered by the Christians are better than the carnal ones formerly offered by the Jews. The theme of spirituality versus carnality will become a commonplace of Christian polemic against the Jews, even when all vestige of factual pretext has disappeared, as Christian liturgical worship grows in complexity and magnificence to surpass the ceremonies of the synagogue.

Efroymson ends his study of Tertullian with memorable words, the last of which have already been quoted by others. His conclusion comes with all the greater force when one has worked one's way through the details of his study of the ancient writer's anti-Judaism. He first reminds us that Tertullian was by no means the last to use these themes, to exploit this "caricature" of Judaism for polemical purposes:

> Eusebius will use it as a launching pad for his history of the Church, contrasting the triumph of the Church with the calamities that befell the Jews in "punishment" for their treatment of Jesus. Athanasius will use it to show that the Arians[81] are "no better" than the Jews. For Augustine, one of the "real" errors of the Pelagian[82] vision will consist in the "Jewishness" of Pelagianism, and the Pelagianism of the Jews. The synod of Elvira will legislate against the Jews as non-Christians. And Ambrose will prohibit the rebuilding of a burned synagogue, because the Jews have no rights; they will have become not only non-Christians, but almost non-persons. *The road from here to Auschwitz is long, and may not be direct, but one can get there from here.*[83]

Tertullian was not unique. In the writers whose anti-Judaism has been studied by historians, he holds a special place. But he was not an innovator, and the themes he explored were not dropped after his time. Chrysostom seems to have hated Jews even more than he did, and he used themes, including that of deicide, that Tertullian did not.

The shocking thing about Tertullian is not that he accused the Jews of things no one else thought of but that so much he said so long ago is still familiar to someone with a Christian education. How many modern Christians have not heard that Judaism is a religion of vengeance and Christianity one of compassion? How many have not heard that Christian worship is more spiritual than the sacrifices of the

Temple? How many have not heard that Jesus brought a new teaching, superior to Judaism, and that the Jews hated him and conspired to kill him because of it? Above all, how many millions up to our own time continue to hear that the Jews killed Christ? To this day, and in peaceful North America, innocent Jewish children are being confronted by their Christian classmates with the same accusation.

In Tertullian, theology has caught right up with myth. All the skills of a sophisticated rhetorician and philosopher are here bent to the denigration of the Jews. Though he ended in schism, his views continued to influence orthodoxy until today. Tertullian's ideas are not dead, even though few if any responsible Christian writers would after Auschwitz marshal them in the same organized and deliberate campaign of polemic.

6

Jews in a Christian World

Christianity began as a tiny minority movement, often persecuted by the Roman authorities. In the fourth century it acquired power, becoming the state religion of the Roman Empire. How would the installation of the Christian myth in the apparatus of state affect the Jews? The new Christian empire found the Jews in a fairly secure position, enjoying full rights as citizens, and even a few privileges. As the myth began to influence legislation, the state withdrew first privileges, and eventually rights as well.

From 212 C.E. the Jews had been Roman citizens, with clearly defined rights under the law. With the triumph of the Church in the reign of Constantine, Jews found themselves in a Christian world for the first time. For a while, their situation did not deteriorate significantly. It was not long before it did. Christian rulers whose outlook had been formed by the Christian myth were not likely to regard Jews as eligible for the same status as Christians, and they did not, though the tradition of Jewish citizenship in the Empire would last for hundreds of years more, in East and West alike.

From the fourth century until the Islamic conquests, most Jews had to live in the new Christian world. Thereafter, more Jews lived under Islam than under Christianity; their fate under Islam was usually more like that of the Jews who lived in Christendom than is generally acknowledged, but their story is not our primary concern in this book. In Christendom, the social and legal situation of Jewish people was increasingly determined by the myth of the Christ-killing Jew, now incorporated in the more comprehensive imperial myth of Roman and Byzantine Christendom.

THE CHRISTIAN STATE AND THE JEWS

Constantine was the first emperor to embrace Christianity publicly. Perhaps at first he was not able to distinguish the God of the Christians from a supreme deity pagans could recognize, such as the Unconquered Sun. Probably, however, in due course he became a sincere and reasonably well-educated Christian, thinking it his duty as a ruler to make laws that would be pleasing to the God he worshiped.

He soon allied himself with the Church, making it a cornerstone of imperial policy, though he personally did not receive baptism until his deathbed, in conformity with prevailing ideas about the dangers of sinning after baptism. Nevertheless, like his successors he was accounted a very exceptional Christian by the leaders of the Church, a kind of universal bishop outside the Church. He was even spoken of as a "thirteenth apostle," or as "equal to the apostles."[1]

As a Christian, he could not allow himself to be worshiped by the citizens of the empire as his predecessors had been. Emperor worship was not a profound religious act, but it had great political significance: it has been described as the ideological glue that held the varied elements of the empire together. Constantine needed a new adhesive, and he found it in Christianity, his own new faith. The empire should be Christian, and this common religion would bind it together even more effectively than the outmoded worship of the emperor.

In the Edict of Milan of 313, soon after attaining power, Constantine removed existing legal disabilities upon Christians, including those remaining from the recent persecution under Diocletian. Christian property confiscated or otherwise lost during the persecution was also restored. Freedom of religion for others was simultaneously left open.[2] It is sometimes said, for example in J. Stevenson's valuable collection of documents of the period, *A New Eusebius*, that Constantine did not go back on this principle, though his successors did. This may be true so far as paganism was concerned, but it is not true for the Jews. Erosion of Jewish rights and privileges already began under Constantine, the very first Christian emperor.

In the following decade, the emperor summoned the first ecumenical council of the Church to decide a theological dispute over the Arian heresy that threatened to spread everywhere from its origins in the church of Alexandria. When the council of bishops met at Nicaea in 325, he sat in on and perhaps presided over the proceedings, and he personally testified to the orthodoxy of the creed which it adopted. His political purpose was certainly to maintain the unity of the empire by preserving the unity of the Church.

If heresy and schism threatened political unity, did Judaism too as a rival religion? Judaism had long been recognized as a legitimate national religion, whose legality was beyond question. Pagan culture had not found Jewish religion threatening. There was no reason it should now be thought to menace the new imperial state church, so long as it kept to itself, remaining solely a national religion for those born Jews.

The strength of the Jewish diaspora had led, however, to renewal of universalist and therefore missionary ideals. Judaism was again a rival to Christianity, and a serious one, attractive not only to enlightened pagans but to many Christians as well. The Church exercised continuous pressure to keep this rival under control. The state did not always respond to this pressure with the alacrity the Church would have wished.

There was probably no consistent imperial policy of discrimination against the Jews. Emperors, standing upon established legality, often sought to maintain the rights of Jews against the wishes of the bishops to restrict them. Gradually, however, they yielded to these pressures; by the time of Justinian in the sixth century, Jews were no longer first-class citizens and no longer safe from even religious interference by the Christian state. Even though the empire did not have an explicit anti-Jewish policy, Jews gradually came to be considerably worse off than they had been under pagan emperors. They were described in insulting language in imperial legislation, and they were seen as a threat to Christians, from which the latter needed legal protection.

The laws of Constantine did not make serious inroads into the position of the Jews, but they foreshadowed legislation introduced by his successors that would in due course take away many of their privileges and some of their rights. In the development of this legislation we can trace the gradual erosion of the Jewish position under continuous ecclesiastical pressure.

Imperial legislation was generally issued in response to particular situations, often embodied in letters to officials who had sought for a ruling on a problem confronting them. An emperor's reply had the force of law. The laws of successive emperors were eventually collected together in codes.

The codes did not reduce the laws to a system, simply collecting together existing legislation still in force, and not explicitly withdrawn, while incorporating additional rulings by the emperor responsible for the new code. Such additions were known as novellas (Latin, *novellae leges*). Generally speaking, the laws found in the later codes refer to the date and place of their original promulgation, permitting us to trace in detail the growth of anti-Jewish legislation under successive emperors.

The first such code was that of Theodosius II, compiled in the middle of the fifth century, and the most important and complete Justinian's, from the sixth century. It added material for the guidance of lawyers, which later became the foundation of the study of Roman law.

"The path from Constantine to Justinian is a continuous one, and one marked by ever-increasing severity," said James Parkes in his early but still unsuperseded study of Jewish-Christian relations in the period.[3] Constantine's successors gradually moved to restrict first the privileges and then the rights of the Jews as members of a legally recognized religion.

As Parkes put it on a later page:

> The period is marked throughout by one consistent characteristic. In so far as popular feelings were concerned there might be ups and downs. In so far as legislation was concerned, a right once lost was never permanently regained. The restrictions were continually reinforced. The path towards their mediaeval position and the mediaeval ghetto was followed relentlessly and without deviation. The Theodosian code (the earliest) embodied the maximum of their rights. Lawlessness and ecclesiastical enthusiasm from time to time encroached thereon, but it never cancelled any provision in a manner favourable to them. In the end, all the different systems under which they lived "finished under the influence of the Church by considering the Jews

ethnically as strangers, and religiously as unbelievers, and in this capacity as persons deprived of civil rights, and subject to special restrictions."[4]

LAWS AGAINST JEWS

When Constantine did make the first move against the Jews, he aimed it directly against the missionary enterprise of the Jewish diaspora. In a law of October 18, 315, he forbade Jewish measures against converts to Christianity from Judaism and discouraged conversions to Judaism. Physical attacks against those who had forsaken Judaism for Christianity were to be punished with death; anyone who should join "their nefarious sect" and attend their meetings was to suffer the "deserved" penalties along with the Jews (possibly even death, from the context).[5]

The law aimed at the prevention of Jewish proselytism, and it restrained Jewish actions intended to avoid the erosion of their own religion through conversions to Christianity. If these policy aims could be achieved, the interests of the Roman state did not necessitate further measures against the Jews. However, this was just the beginning.

A further measure of Constantine, not aimed directly at the Jews, nevertheless affected them adversely. On March 7, 321, the emperor ruled that Sunday was to be a day of rest for all except farm workers in the fields. This was the first of a host of subsequent laws regulating Sunday observance, many of which still exist in modern societies.

The idea of a day of rest, of course Jewish in origin, had been unknown to the Roman world before it came into contact with the Jewish people. Christians adopted some of the observances of the Jewish Sabbath, transferring them to Sunday, originally a working day. While the Church remained a persecuted minority, Christians had gotten up early on Sundays to worship and then gone to work. Now legislation was introduced to make Sunday a day of rest for all as well as worship for Christians.

Such measures always discriminate against Jews. Owners of Jewish businesses lose a day of business since they cannot work on Saturdays but are then not able to make up for it by working on Sundays. The impact is not so strongly felt in the modern world, where so many Jews are assimilated or no longer observant, but it must have been serious in the fourth century.

Another law affected Jewish slave owners. It also appears to have originated in Constantine's time, though only recorded later, in the Theodosian code, and not precisely datable. According to this law, a Jew who circumcises a slave forfeits his ownership, while the slave gains his freedom.[6] Subsequent rulings would modify this law, usually by making it more severe.

At the time, neither Jews nor Christians had yet called the institution of slavery into question: the economy depended on it. However, the Torah, both written and oral, contains many rulings designed to humanize the institution as much as possible. Since the slave of a Jewish household lived close to the family, it made life much easier for both sides if he or she were also Jewish and could take part in the family observances.

To circumcise such slaves was by no means Jewish aggression; it was a friendly act, intended to make the slave more of a participant in the close-knit family life of the Jews. It also entailed obligations on the owner to treat him even better than before. The *halachah* called upon Jewish slave owners to circumcise their slaves, or else sell them.

Christians, however, began to regard it as intolerable that a Christian should be a slave to a Jew, since servitude should be the lot of the Jewish people. It was equally or more intolerable that a Christian should be degraded to the lower status of a Jew by conversion and circumcision. The new law made it practically impossible for observant Jews to own slaves, unless the slaves were already Jewish, since they were in conflict with the laws of their own religion if they retained them without circumcising them and subject to severe legal penalties from the state if they did make proselytes of them. In the circumstances of the time, the economic penalty was heavy.

Constantine also made a law requiring the Jews to participate in the public office known as the decurionate, inflicting a serious new burden on them. The *curiales*, as the members of this group were called, had to collect imperial taxation, and if there was any deficit from the required amount, they had to make it up from their own resources. The wealthy, then as now, practiced tax evasion, and poverty was common. The position of the curiales was a most difficult one. Moreover, it was a hereditary class, and the only way to escape from it and its obligations was to become a serf or a monk, as many did.

In pagan days, Jews had been immune from the office, because it involved sacrificing to the pagan gods. Under the Christian empire, the reason for immunity presumably no longer applied. It was, however, customary to exempt those who had religious obligations from these duties. The clergy of the Catholic church were exempt; the same privilege was accorded to "two or three" in each Jewish community, and eventually to all who were occupied with religious functions. Thus, while the new law did not directly discriminate against Jews, the loss of their former immunity involved economic hardship except for the few who were exempt.[7]

Constantine was succeeded by his son, Constantius. In his ecclesiastical policy he favored dogmatic formulations to which Arians as well as (he seems to have hoped) followers of the theology of the Council of Nicaea could assent. However, this reconciling policy failed in its hope of unifying the church around vaguer doctrinal statements. Unlike the Arians themselves, he extended no comparable toleration to the Jews.

A law of August 3, 339, considerably strengthened the existing measures against Jewish slave owning. If a Jew bought a pagan slave, the slave must be immediately and automatically confiscated to the imperial treasury. If a Jew bought a Christian slave, the purchaser also forfeited all the rest of his property. In either case, the penalty for circumcising the slave was no longer forfeiture of the slave but death.[8]

Constantius made two other laws worsening the position of the Jews. Any

Christian who married a Jew forfeited the whole of his property to the treasury, and any Jew who married a Christian woman working in the imperial factories (*gynaecaea*) was to be put to death, and the woman returned to the factory.[9]

Constantius' successor, Julian, called the Apostate by the Church, was friendly to the Jews, more so than any previous foreign ruler.[10] He formed the intention of restoring the sacrificial worship of the Temple, of which he approved. Letters and other documents that have survived show his sympathy and compassion for the Jewish people, and a proclamation given at Antioch in 362 expresses his intention to rebuild Jerusalem and restore the Temple of God.[11]

It seems that his motives were not only sympathy toward Jews. Julian had left Christianity in favor of Hellenic culture, and he was no friend of the Church. He was fully aware that his actions would damage Christianity by historically refuting its claim that Jewish exile was a divine punishment for the killing of Christ. Some Jewish resettlement of Jerusalem actually began, but the whole project fell to the ground when Julian was killed the following year while on a campaign.[12]

None of Julian's laws has survived, but his letters imply that he did take measures to improve the legal position of the Jews. Certain laws of one of his successors, Gratian, reimposing the curial burdens of the Jews, presuppose that they previously had been removed.[13] Gratian's restored law now included the Jewish clergy, who had to postpone their religious duties until their public functions had been discharged or pay for substitutes. Parkes considers this the "first real infringement of the rights of Judaism as a lawful religion."[14] By modern standards, however, the prohibition of proselytism was already a substantial infringement of religious liberty.

Gratian also reenacted the prohibition of conversion, increasing the penalties. The convert and the Jewish missionary responsible must both be punished.[15] The same emperor also added to the legislation on Jewish slave ownership by providing for the compulsory sale to Christian masters at a fixed price of the Christian slave of a Jew, or one he had converted to Judaism.[16]

The impact of Julian's tolerance otherwise survived his reign for a while, up to the accession of Theodosius I, the Great, in 379. No wholly new anti-Jewish legislation was promulgated during that time, and one or two edicts marginally improved the situation of the Jews for a time.

The legal status of the patriarchate was consolidated. The patriarch or *nasi*, originally styled Ethnarch by the Romans, ruled over the Jewish people in the empire as a semi-autonomous community governed by the laws of the Torah. The patriarchal family were supposed to be descendants of King David and at many periods kept up at Tiberias a court of almost royal dignity and splendor. The Romans permitted the patriarch to collect taxes from the Jewish community throughout the empire, on the model of the old temple tax.

The reigning patriarch was also accorded a title of nobility by the Roman state, that of Praetorian Prefect. An edict of Valens exempted officers of communities "subject to the Illustrious Patriarch" from service on municipal councils. Another, of 368, forbade the billeting of troops in synagogues.[17] Valens, himself an Arian, showed complete tolerance to the Jews.[18]

Under Theodosius I, an orthodox emperor, and his sons, Arcadius and Honorius, the position of the Jews worsened sharply. Even though the edicts themselves were not so severe as they would later be, the language in which they were expressed was particularly insulting to Jews.

Even an edict nominally intended to protect Jews began with a preamble stating that the intention is to "suppress the power and insolence of the contemptible Hellenes, Jews and heretics. Therefore, all we permit is that they shall no longer be persecuted and in future their synagogues shall not be seized and burned down."[19]

Various laws describe the Jews as a *feralis secta,* a savage or animalistic sect, speaking of their *turpitudo,* wickedness, and *flagitia,* outrageous crimes, while their meetings are termed *sacrilegi coetus,* sacrilegious gatherings. To be converted to Judaism is described as *Judaicis semet polluere contagiis,* to pollute oneself with Judaic contagion. To serve the Jews is *indigna servitudo,* unworthy servitude.[20]

Theodosius I brought in the first law terming marriage between a Christian and a Jew adultery; anyone could inform on the couple.[21] Even when marrying among themselves, Jews must observe Christian regulations on affinity by marriage, more restrictive than the biblical ones still observed by Jews. The practice of polygamy, still permitted to Jews as in biblical times, was also now prohibited by the state.[22] Possibly, as Parkes argues, the prohibition against building new synagogues or beautifying existing ones dates from this time.[23]

However, Theodosius, a strong emperor, sometimes stood up for the rights of the Jews. Some of his laws even protect the Jews against the officiousness of imperial officials.[24] In a letter addressed to the governor of the Eastern provinces, he refers to what appears to be becoming a more general situation.

> It is sufficiently evident that the Jewish religion is prohibited by no law. We are therefore seriously disquieted to learn that in certain places Jewish meetings have been prohibited. Your Excellency will, on receipt of this order, restrain with suitable severity the excesses of those who under the name of the Christian religion are committing illegal actions, or attempting to destroy or ruin synagogues.[25]

In a similar context, as we shall see shortly in more detail, he attempted to stand up to the formidable bishop Ambrose of Milan, who had blamed him for applying the law, by requiring a Christian bishop whose flock had burned down a synagogue to compensate the Jewish community by restoring it. Admittedly, the attempt failed under the stress of ecclesiastical blackmail, but the incident shows that the attitudes of church and state still differed.

Theodosius I was succeeded by his two sons, Honorius in the West and Arcadius in the East, theoretically as joint rulers, in practice dividing the empire between them. Honorius ruled from various places in Northern Italy, while Arcadius continued to administer the Eastern Empire from Constantinople.

Where economic matters were concerned, Honorius, who was clearly short of money, was severe on the Jews. He was faced with invasion of Italy by various barbarian tribes, including the Goths; Alaric sacked Rome in 410, during his reign.

In 399, Honorius appropriated the tax money normally sent by the Jews to the patriarch in Jerusalem, describing him as "the ravager of the Jews," a role Honorius clearly preferred to exercise himself.

The action is also significant, as Parkes points out, in that it marks a clear sense that the empire is now divided. Honorius regarded the tax as the export of funds to a foreign province, expecting the Jews to feel the same, since he stated that he is preserving them "from this exaction."[26]

In the same year a new prohibition appears, which remained in force until the nineteenth century and was revived by Nazi Germany. Jews were now forbidden to hold public office. During the fourth century, the abolition of pagan sacrifices on state occasions had made possible the entry of the Jews into many public functions, some honorific, some burdensome, like the decurionate. Fifth century Christians no longer felt that this was appropriate to the status of the Jews as they conceived it.

Honorius at first promulgated blanket legislation prohibiting the Jews from exercising any public function whatsoever. "Jews and Samaritans who are deluding themselves with the privileges of imperial executive officers are to be deprived of all military and court rank."[27] Since this provision proved unworkable, a new measure made more specific rulings: those already in official functions were to remain until retirement and would then receive the customary pension, as a once for all concession. Any Jew serving in the army was to be immediately reduced to the ranks.

On the other hand, Jews could continue to serve as lawyers and could enjoy the two-edged privilege of the decurionate. Honorius added, "These things ought to be enough for them, and they ought not to take their omission from government service as a slur,"[28] "words [as Parkes remarks] reminiscent of the utterances of modern antisemitic polemists."[29]

On the other hand, much of his other legislation was more tolerant of the Jews than might have been expected, or than that of his brother in the East. In both portions of the empire, laws were promulgated during the fifth century on the question of sanctuary. Under the economic pressures of the time, people were falling into debt and taking sanctuary with the Church to avoid their creditors. Violation of sanctuary was normally regarded as a crime, and is so described in the code of Justinian. Jews who took sanctuary had to convert to Christianity. Honorius, recognizing the economic distress that caused some Jews to flee to sanctuary and to baptism, permitted them to return to Judaism without penalty, a remarkably liberal attitude for the period.[30]

Honorius also revoked the imperial legislation on Jewish slave-owning, permitting Jews to own Christian slaves so long as they were not made proselytes to Judaism. The master was simply forbidden to interfere with the slave's religion, without any penalty being laid down; on the other hand, anyone who interfered with their possession of Christian slaves was to be severely punished.[31]

Arcadius, the brother of Honorius, had acceded to the imperial throne of the Eastern Empire at the age of seventeen. He lived in a period when anti-Jewish rhetoric in the Church was reaching new heights, or depths; the sermons of his contemporary, John Chrysostom, are a conspicuous example.[32] In the reign of

Arcadius, things began to deteriorate for the Jews, doubtless under similar ecclesiastical pressures to those exercised on his father, Theodosius.

A law of 396 imposed a petty vexation by interfering with the operation of the Jewish slave markets, which were in themselves legal and under imperial protection. Later in the same law we find attacks upon the patriarch, despite his high rank in the Roman nobility. The patriarch himself was insulted, his rights questioned, and his officials challenged. Still, this remained on the level of words.[33]

Arcadius also permitted the violation of sanctuary, ordering Jews to be expelled until their debts were paid.[34] After giving Jews a broad immunity from curial responsibilities, he withdrew the measure and fell into line with his brother's legislation.[35] He reduced their judicial autonomy and may have taken away their right of giving evidence in a Christian court. Either he or his brother Theodosius II, who succeeded him, seems to have prohibited the building of further synagogues, since such a law was already in force in 415, when it is referred to in connection with the degradation of the patriarch from his rank.[36]

Valentinian III, a later Western successor of Honorius, repeated the law prohibiting Jews from holding office, adding that he did not wish Christians to serve such persons, "lest by their office they find occasion to corrupt the venerable Christian faith."[37] Valentinian also enacted a law forbidding Jewish or Samaritan parents to disinherit their children or grandchildren if the latter should convert to Christianity; if they attempted to do so, the will should be regarded as null and void, and the case treated as one of intestacy. The only exception was to be if there was clear documentary evidence that the children or grandchildren in question had committed serious offenses against their parents or grandparents, in which case they should only inherit a standard amount, though they must also be punished for the offense. This is a clear case of the state interfering in family matters for purely religious motives.[38]

THEODOSIUS AND HIS CODE

The legislation of Theodosius II was much more anti-Jewish than anything seen previously, in language as well as provisions. Insulting language now becomes a regular feature of laws referring to the Jews. The first matter to be dealt with by Theodosius II was the Jewish manner of celebrating Purim. Purim, a comparatively new feast, not referred to in the Torah, had been introduced during the Second Temple period. It celebrates the deliverance of the Jews from a Persian pogrom, described in the Scroll of Esther, which is read in the synagogue on that day.

The celebration takes a high-spirited form: Jews are traditionally commanded on this day to get so drunk that they can no longer distinguish between "Blessed be Mordechai," and "Cursed be Haman." This is pretty drunk and only ultra-Orthodox Jews observe the commandment literally nowadays. Jews were now forbidden by Theodosius to burn the effigy of Haman the oppressor or to use the feast to mock the cross, on pain of the loss of their existing lawful privileges.[39]

Since Jews were now experiencing their Christian rulers as oppressors, it was inevitable that the identification with Haman would be made, and no one should be surprised if something of their resentment at their treatment crept into the celebration of Purim. About ten years after the law was promulgated, a case occurred at Inmestar, which was alleged by a later Christian historian to have led to the death of a Christian boy. He was submitted, it was said, to a mock crucifixion, and so ill-used that he died. A Jewish historian remarks that the Jews must have been drunk at the time.

However, the authenticity of the account has been questioned by other historians, in view of the falsity of later legends of Jewish atrocities against Christian children. Parkes, on the other hand, sees no reason to question the veracity of the story. We have no contemporary or firsthand accounts of the event, described only by a later Christian writer. In view of the long and painful history we are examining, unconfirmed Christian sources must be regarded as potentially prejudiced on all matters connected with Jews. The question cannot be decisively settled either way.[40]

There seems greater reason for confidence in accounts of riots between Jews and Christians in Alexandria, which led to considerable loss of life on both sides. Parkes thinks the events at Inmestar and Alexandria were probably responsible for the degradation of the patriarch Gamliel in 415 from his Roman status of Prefect. The patriarch had been accused of contravening the anti-Jewish laws by building synagogues, circumcising slaves, and judging cases between Christians. He was demoted and warned against committing similar offenses.[41]

The Church leadership appears to have lobbied for the abolition of the office itself, since the quasi-royal status and associated ceremonial of the descendant of the house of David seemed to contradict Christian claims for Jesus as the Messiah, son of David. A law of 429 contained in the Theodosian Code refers to the abolition of the "Patriarchal exemption," directing the Sanhedrins of the two provinces of Palestine to hand over to the imperial treasury the taxation money collected with imperial permission for the patriarchate.

We learn from this edict that the patriarchate had already been abolished and the former single Sanhedrin split into two. The government seems to have taken advantage of the death of Gamliel to decline to recognize a successor. This was the end of an institution that had endured for three and a half centuries, uniting the Jewish nation, both in Palestine and in the diaspora, around a leader recognized as the legitimate successor of the kings of the house of David.[42]

If there was hostility toward the Jews at the official level, there was more at the grass roots. Even Theodosius II, hostile toward Jews as he was, found it necessary to issue edicts forbidding mob violence against them, reminding the populace that there were law courts in which Jews who committed crimes could be tried. The edict refers to the widespread burning of synagogues and houses, and assaults on individuals. However, the edict continues, "Just as we wish to make provisions for the benefit of the Jews, so we consider also that a warning should be addressed to them that they must not presume upon their security to commit outrages against the Christian faith."[43]

In the same context, we learn of the extraordinary phenomenon of an emperor being restrained by the intervention of a famous ascetic, Simeon Stylites, from restoring to the Jewish community of Antioch synagogues stolen from them by Christians. Simeon lived for thirty-seven years at the top of a pillar fifty feet high. He was held in great veneration on account of his austerities, as a man of singular holiness.

Today, we have to ask what kind of holiness is displayed in the use of spiritual power to perpetuate injustice. Unfortunately, the case is not unique. Again and again we shall find in the annals of Christian history that a person celebrated for holiness displays anti-Judaism fully proportional to his fervor for Christianity. The emperor was induced to apologize humbly to the Church for his just action and to leave the stolen property in its hands.[44]

The third novella of Theodosius introduces more systematic legislation against the Jews. Newly constructed synagogues are to be forfeited to the Catholic Church. Jewish office holders are to be degraded, even if they have been decorated by the state. The repair of a synagogue incurs a substantial fine. Imperial permission is conceded for the repair of a synagogue actually in danger of collapse, although it is not to be beautified by decoration. Jewish courts are still permitted to deal with private cases between Jews. Jews are to be eligible for all the burdensome public offices. The death penalty is introduced for "corrupting the faith of a Christian." As Parkes remarks, there is no further pretense that these regulations are justified by any Jewish lawlessness. This is straight religious discrimination.[45]

THE CODE OF JUSTINIAN

Justinian reigned over the remaining Byzantine Empire from 527–565. The eighth- and ninth-century Byzantine codes were based on his work, and it continued to influence medieval legislation in the East up to the end of the Byzantine state at the fall of Constantinople to the Turks in the fifteenth century.

Thus, the status of the Jews in the Byzantine world remained essentially as laid down in the code of Justinian. Moreover, other areas of Eastern Europe not actually under Byzantine rule were also under its cultural influence. Imperial Russia and the other Slavonic countries, with some exceptions, received Christianity from the East, Russia not until the tenth century. Their attitudes toward Jews reflected not merely the now well entrenched myth, but the legal position of the code of Justinian.

Justinian found in the Theodosian code over fifty laws relating to the Jews. He abolished more than half of these as superfluous or out of date. What is interesting to us is not only his new laws but also those he omitted. Most importantly of all, perhaps, Theodosius' formal statement of the legality of the Jewish religion was left out.[46] The status of the Jewish religion before the law was therefore no longer defined at all from this point, and could be altered by the decision of an administrator.

The fifth-century laws protecting the position of the Jews were also left out. All immunities for synagogue officials were simply dropped, especially the law of Arcadius that put them in the same position in this respect as the Christian clergy. The Patriarchate and the tax on the Jews for its support, known as the *aurum coronarium*, were not revived. Laws allowing Jews the right of excommunication of members of their own people, and of trying with their own judges cases affecting Jewish law, were likewise omitted. A law of 537 interpreted existing legislation in such a way as to require the Jews to bear the full burdens of municipal government without any of the honors normally attaching to the office.

The new legislation definitely worsened the position of the Jews. Novella 131 put canon law, the law of the Church, on the same level as state law. This could not fail to hurt the Jews, since canon law was generally much less restrained in its attitude toward the Jews than imperial legislation.

The implementation of regulations directed against the Jews (and other religions) was now no longer the responsibility of provincial governors alone, but it was to be shared between them and the bishops. This guaranteed that the Jews would be worse off than before, since the state had usually, though not always effectively, tended to protect the Jews from the Church in the name of legality. The law actually required the bishops to let the emperor know if they found the civil authorities lacking in zeal in their implementation of anti-Jewish legislation.[47]

Justinian fancied himself as something of a theologian, and his interventions in religious affairs were more specific and detailed than those of most of his predecessors. Justinian went further than any of his predecessors by actually intervening in a direct way in Jewish religious affairs, paralleling his theological interventions in the affairs of the Church.[48] A dispute had occurred in one Jewish community between those who wanted the Torah reading to be in Hebrew only and another party who wished for a Greek translation to accompany it. Those who supported Hebrew alone seem to have feared that the reading of the Greek translation would replace the customary sermons on observance and other aspects of the tradition that followed the reading of the Torah. The dispute was brought before the emperor.

Justinian actually took it upon himself to regulate the conduct of the synagogue service in his Novella 146, explicitly stating that his aim was to persuade the Jews to draw closer to Christianity and to the Christian interpretation of the Torah. He supported the party favoring the use of a Greek translation, advocating the use of the Septuagint, though the version of Aquila[49] was also permitted. Christians favored the Septuagint because some of its incorrect translations of the Hebrew Bible had been incorporated in the christological proof-texts on which the theologians relied.

The law went on to state, "But what ye are wont to call *Deuterosis* [i.e., the Mishnah] is entirely forbidden, and the Heads [sc., of the synagogues] shall see to it that the law is not interfered with and is carried out properly." Here again we meet with what might almost be called the touching illusion of Christian theologians and rulers that in the absence of the "veil," that is, if Jews were not indoctrinated by their traditional way of interpreting the Bible, they would at once see that the christological reading was the natural meaning of the text. The expectation always proved mistaken.[50]

Parkes rejects the obvious suggestion that Justinian was motivated by anti-Jewish prejudice, suggesting that his motives were "grandmotherly." He thinks Justinian felt exaggerated responsibility for the religious well-being of his Jewish subjects, and he wished to protect them from false doctrine.[51] There was certainly a parallel between his theological interventions in church affairs and this incident. No such explanation can be accepted today as an excuse for illegitimate interference by the state in the practice of a legally tolerated religion, explicable only on Christian theological grounds. While the action did remain unusual, it evinced a hostility toward, as well as misunderstanding of, post-biblical Judaism still normal in Christian thought in our own time.

Justinian's changes in the legal status of the Jews in fact as well as theory had an adverse affect on them. Deprived of the protection of their status formerly contained in the Theodosian code, they had no legal recourse in 535 when in Borion in the province of North Africa Judaism was outlawed, the synagogues were closed, and the Jews were subjected to forced baptism.[52] The case was exceptional, but it shows what was now possible. Nor did Justinian's measures bring about greater religious peace, as he may have hoped. The Jews smarted under the new restrictions, and they did what they could to protest against them.

THE END OF THE WESTERN EMPIRE

The situation was somewhat different in the West, its effective separation from the Byzantine Empire having already occurred before Justinian's time. Not his code but the earlier code of Theodosius was inherited both by the papacy and by the barbarian kingdoms that superseded the Empire in the West. In the West, the institutional legacy of the empire was divided between the papacy and the new kingdoms.

The imperial office came to an end in the West in the fifth century, when the last, by this time insignificant, Roman emperor, Romulus Augustulus, was deposed by the Goth Odoacer. From then on, the Ostrogothic monarchs ruled in Italy, while the papacy inherited much of the glory and responsibilities of the defunct imperial throne. In the East, the empire survived until the Turkish conquest in the fifteenth century, retaining the particularly close relationships between church and state that had always characterized it, sometimes referred to as Caesaropapism.

The barbarians wished to Romanize themselves, not to barbarize the empire; they showed great respect for Roman law, as defined in the code of Theodosius, the one they knew. The papacy retained the tradition of Roman legality, too, Roman law providing the basis for much ecclesiastical legislation. The legal status of the Jews in the West, even in the barbarian kingdoms, long reflected the somewhat milder position of the Theodosian code.

AMBROSE THE BISHOP AND THEODOSIUS I

The encounter between Ambrose and Theodosius I over the burning of a synagogue is a remarkable example of the way the Christian myth and the growing power of the Church could influence state policy. It is therefore worth looking at in detail.

In the year 388, at the city of Callinicum on the Euphrates, Christian rioters, encouraged by the local bishop, had burned down a synagogue. The governor of the area, the military Count of the East, was reluctant to enforce on his own authority the law that required restitution by the Christians for the damage done, and he wrote to the emperor, who ordered him to carry out the law by punishing the rioters and requiring the bishop to rebuild the synagogue at his own expense.

The matter came to the attention of the bishop of Milan, Ambrose, a theologian and a strong-willed character, who had himself been a Roman governor at the time he was elected bishop. Ambrose wrote to the emperor requesting him to rescind the order, in terms reminiscent of those later to be used by popes to the civil rulers, assuming a degree of social equality that perhaps his past position as a governor made natural, even adopting in his tone a certain superiority, as a priest of the church addressing a layman.

Ambrose argues that the emperor is putting the bishop in an impossible dilemma. If he obeys the imperial order he will be an apostate, if he disobeys it he will risk becoming a martyr, and in either case the Jews will triumph over the Church. Even if the order is rescinded, in accordance with Ambrose's request, others may now offer to have the synagogue restored out of their own funds, or the count, following precedent, may order this to be done. Then the Jews would be able to put up an inscription outside the synagogue: "The Temple of Impiety, built from the spoils of the Christians." If the Emperor is moved by the need for discipline, he should reflect that the cause of religion is of greater importance.

In any case, there is no need to make such a fuss about the burning of a synagogue, "a home of unbelief, a house of impiety, a receptacle of folly, which God himself has condemned." In fact, Ambrose states outright that it was not a crime at all to burn a synagogue. The emperor should punish him, Ambrose, instead, for though he had not actually himself burned down the synagogue in Milan, which had lately been destroyed by fire, it was only due to his own tardiness in getting round to it, and the fact that God had already destroyed it in the meantime.

Ambrose alleges (although we possess no independent evidence for his statements) that the Jews had destroyed a number of important churches during the reign of Julian, and that no one had required them to pay compensation. So why should Christians have to do so now? There is no need to fear their revenge: "Who will avenge them, God whom they have insulted, or Christ whom they have crucified?" Finally, he tells the emperor he has no need to fear breaking his oath to administer the laws. Ambrose will take care of that. How can God be displeased at an action undertaken for his honor?

The following Sunday the emperor was present at the liturgy in Ambrose's own cathedral in Milan, and Ambrose preached a sermon on the Church and the synagogue, depicting the richness of the former and the poverty of the latter. When he came down from the pulpit, the emperor said to him, "You were talking about me." Ambrose replied, "I dealt with matters intended for your benefit." Then the emperor said, "I had decided too harshly about the repairing of the synagogue by the bishop, but that has been put right. The monks do commit many crimes."

After an altercation with one of the generals present, whom Ambrose addressed in much less courteous tones than those he employed with the emperor, he made it clear that he did not intend to proceed with the liturgy, the mass itself, until the emperor unequivocally promised to rescind his order. Not to proceed would have been tantamount to excommunicating the emperor. After some hesitation and delay, Theodosius gave way and delivered the explicit promise that Ambrose required.

In a letter he wrote to his sister, a nun, with an account of the incident, Ambrose tells her that he would not have proceeded with the liturgy without a clear undertaking from the emperor. He goes on to say that he felt the action was very acceptable to God and that the divine presence was manifest in the service as it went on.[53]

Theodosius felt obliged to retreat before this display of the power of the Church, but evidently he was not convinced, for we find him a few years later again making a law forbidding the burning of synagogues. It is already clear that the emperors, in spite of their anti-Jewish legislation, were the only protection the Jews now had from the enmity of the Church, and that in the absence of such protection they would have been a good deal worse off than they were.

From the time of Constantine, the canon law of the Church begins to deal with the relations between Christians and Jews. We can easily see from these acts that the Church had taken the lead in bringing about the deterioration of the position of the Jews in the empire and that Justinian's enshrining of canon law in state law would prove a serious blow.

THE CANON LAW OF THE CHURCH

Our earliest information about the attitude of the Church comes from the canons of the Council of Elvira in Spain, presided over by Ossius, the bishop of Cordova, who was Constantine's ecclesiastical adviser. The council is generally dated in the year 306, in the reign of Diocletian, but Robin Lane Fox, in his book *Pagans and Christians*, argues convincingly that the issues dealt with by the council fit better with the situation early in the reign of Constantine himself, around 312.[54] If so, we can discern parallels between the ecclesiastical policy in regard to the Jews of Ossius himself, and Constantine's state policy in the same area, which Ossius, as his adviser, must have had a considerable part in making.

The council found it necessary to make regulations affecting the relations between Christians and their neighbors, including both pagans and Jews. Canon LXI forbids Christian parents to give their daughters in marriage to heretics or to Jews, on the ground that there can be no communion between believers and infidels. The penalty for parents who transgress the rule is excommunication for a period of five years. Canon L forbids Christian people to eat with Jews; the offender is to abstain from the communion of the Church, that he may learn to amend. Canon LXXVIII deals with adultery between a Christian man and a Jewish or pagan woman. The adulterer is to be cut off from the Christian communion.

Canon XLIX contains a surprising and revealing provision. It forbids the Christian people to seek the blessings of Jews for the fruits of their crops, lest the Christian benediction be rendered invalid and unprofitable. Such practices are not forbidden unless they are prevalent. This canon tells us therefore that at this time and place Christians were on friendly terms with their Jewish neighbors and that the latter were still engaging in agriculture and had not yet been confined to mercantile and banking roles in a Christian society.

We can also learn that the Christian laity held a superstitious belief in the magical efficacy of the blessings of the rabbis, presumably thought to be more powerful than those of the Christian clergy. Christians seem at many periods to have held Jews in a kind of superstitious awe and to have attributed to them magical powers for good or ill. In the Middle Ages, Christian magic seems to have appropriated from the Jewish practical Kabbalah the use of permutated divine names for theurgic purposes. These beliefs died hard, and there are traces of their survival even among the Nazis during the Holocaust.[55]

Space does not permit the examination of the whole history of the canons passed by various Catholic synods, dealing with the relations between the faithful and the Jews. In his important and widely respected book, *The Destruction of the European Jews*, Raul Hilberg prints a remarkable table of comparisons between the canonical laws of the Church in the medieval period and the later measures of the Nazis, showing beyond doubt that the latter were not original but followed a known precedent.[56] The table has been quoted several times before by other writers, but it is sufficiently striking to reproduce once again; I give it in Hilberg's original form, though (e.g.) the date given for the Council of Elvira may be too early.

CANONICAL LAW	NAZI MEASURE
Prohibition of intermarriage and of sexual intercourse between Christians and Jews, Synod of Elvira, 306.	Law for the Protection of German Blood and Honor, September 15, 1935 (RGB1 I, 1146).
Jews and Christians not permitted to eat together, Synod of Elvira, 306.	Jews barred from dining cars (Transport Minister to Interior Minister, December 30, 1939, Document NG-3995).
Jews not allowed to hold public office, Synod of Clermont, 535.	Law for the Re-establishment of the Professional Civil Service, April 7, 1933 (RGB1 I, 175).
Jews not allowed to employ Christian servants or possess Christian slaves, 3d Synod of Orleans, 538.	Law for the Protection of German Blood and Honor, September 15, 1935 (RGB1 I, 1146).

CANONICAL LAW	NAZI MEASURE
Jews not permitted to show themselves in the streets during Passion Week, 3d Synod of Orleans, 538.	Decree authorizing local authorities to bar Jews from the streets on certain days (i.e., Nazi holidays), December 3, 1938 (RGB1 I, 1676).
Burning of the Talmud and other books, 12th Synod of Toledo, 681.	Book burnings in Nazi Germany.
Christians not permitted to patronize Jewish doctors, Trulanic Synod, 692.	Decree of July 25, 1938 (RGB1 I, 969).
Christians not permitted to live in Jewish homes, Synod of Narbonne, 1050.	Directive by Göring providing for concentration of Jews in houses, December 28, 1938 (Bormann to Rosenberg, January 17, 1939, PS-69).
Jews obliged to pay taxes for support of church to the same extent as Christians, Synod of Gerona, 1078.	The "Sozialausgleichsabgabe" which provided that Jews pay a special income tax in lieu of donations for Party purposes imposed on Nazis, December 24, 1940 (RGB1 I, 1666).
Prohibition of Sunday work, Synod of Szabolcs, 1092.	
Jews not permitted to be plaintiffs, or witnesses against Christians in the courts, 3d Lateran Council, 1179, Canon 26.	Proposal by the Party Chancellery that Jews not be permitted to institute civil suits, September 9, 1942 (Bormann to Justice Ministry, September 9, 1942, NG-151).
Jews not permitted to withhold inheritance from descendants who accepted Christianity, 3d Lateran Council, 1179, Canon 26.	Decree empowering the Justice Ministry to void wills offending the "sound judgment of the people," July 31, 1938 (RGB1 I, 937).
The marking of Jewish clothes with a badge, 4th Lateran Council, 1215, Canon 68. (Copied from the legislation by Caliph Omar II [634–44], who had decreed that Christians wear blue belts and Jews, yellow belts.)	Decree of September 1, 1941 (RGB1 I, 547).
Construction of new synagogues prohibited, Council of Oxford, 1222.	Destruction of synagogues in entire Reich, November 10, 1938 (Heydrich to Göring, November 11, 1938, PS-3058).
Christians not permitted to attend Jewish ceremonies, Synod of Vienna, 1267.	Friendly relations with Jews prohibited, October 24, 1941 (Gestapo directive, L-15).

CANONICAL LAW	NAZI MEASURE
Jews not permitted to dispute with simple Christian people about the tenets of the Catholic religion, Synod of Vienna, 1267.	
Compulsory ghettoes, Synod of Breslau, 1267.	Order by Heydrich, September 21, 1939 (PS-3363).
Christians not permitted to sell or rent real estate to Jews, Synod of Ofen, 1279.	Decree providing for compulsory sale of Jewish real estate, December 3, 1938 (RGB1 I, 1709).
Adoption by a Christian of the Jewish religion or return by a baptized Jew to the Jewish religion defined as a heresy, Synod of Mainz, 1310.	Adoption by a Christian of the Jewish religion places him in jeopardy of being treated as a Jew. Decision by Oberlandesgericht Königsberg, 4th Zivilsenat, June 26, 1942 (*Die Judenfrage [Vertrauliche Beilage]*, November 1, 1942, pp. 82–83).
Sale or transfer of church articles to Jews prohibited, Synod of Lavour, 1368.	
Jews not permitted to act as agents in the conclusion of contracts between Christians, especially marriage contracts, Council of Basel, 1434, Sessio XIX.	Decree of July 6, 1938, providing for liquidation of Jewish real estate agencies, brokerage agencies, and marriage agencies catering to non-Jews (RGB1 I, 823).
Jews not permitted to obtain academic degrees, Council of Basel, 1434, Sessio XIX.	Law against Overcrowding of German Schools and Universities, April 25, 1933 (RGB1 I, 225).

A number of these provisions will be recognized as not new but simply reenactments by a synod or council of laws already found in the Theodosian Code, or subsequent legislation by the Empire in the West, or of earlier Church rulings. In some other cases, when the Church synods had preceded the state, the canons in Hilberg's list are reenactments of earlier measures. Yet other provisions, such as the badge, go beyond anything found in Roman law and testify to the capability of the medieval Church to legislate for Jews as well as for its own members.

We do not know whether the Nazis researched the Church canons or the Roman law books looking for measures that could be reenacted. What is clear is that their anti-Jewish legislation was not original but inherited an attitude as well as specific provisions stemming from the Christian Roman Empire and the medieval Catholic world.

Over this history as a whole, we can discern the gradual and incremental development of antisemitism out of the original anti-Judaism of Christian theology. Hilberg's table shows that this development was substantially complete by the end of the Middle Ages. Only nineteenth-century racial theories needed to be added, and the restraining hand of traditional Christianity rejected, for the stage to be set for Holocaust.

THEOLOGICAL ANTI-JUDAISM IN THE CHURCH FATHERS

In the previous chapter, we examined the anti-Jewish theology of the second-century Church through one very influential writer, Tertullian. We must now broaden the canvas considerably and look at the views on the Jewish people of a number of other leading theologians of the ancient Church, the Church fathers, as they are called.[57]

Their ideas on the subject are principally to be found in writings specifically directed against the Jews, the so-called *adversus Judaeos* literature. Efroymson showed that anti-Judaic themes are by no means confined to this category of writings and can even be more prominent in works where the controversy is with others than Jews. Ruether in *Faith and Fratricide* demonstrated that over several centuries the themes remained essentially the same, varying only in tone from writer to writer. Her work and Efroymson's complement and reinforce each other, leaving no doubt as to the views of the Church on the Jews in the formative period of its theology.

The *adversus Judaeos* tradition contains almost no themes we have not already encountered in Tertullian. One of the most striking aspects of this literature is the continuity of the tradition of anti-Jewish testimonies, from the period before any of the New Testament was written, right on into medieval times.

Christian theology originally took shape at a time when the Septuagint was the only Bible of the Church. The very early origin of the continuing anti-Jewish tradition of the Testimonies is shown by the fact that even into medieval times, it continued to rely primarily on the Greek Old Testament as its source of texts, making little use of the New Testament.[58] New Testament references were of course eventually added, but they did not become central to the tradition.

The biblical texts on which this controversial literature relied were collected together in the later Books of Testimonies. There were many such compilations, and they continued to be produced into medieval times. The material contained in them provides the basis of all kinds of anti-Jewish literature, sermons, treatises, dialogues, stories, and dramas.[59]

With the exception of scholars such as Origen and Jerome, the writers of the Church were unable to read the Hebrew text of the Bible: the prophecies were always quoted in Greek. This caused difficulties for Christian apologetics, since Jews could justifiably point out that in a number of cases important to the Christian argument, the Greek translation did not faithfully represent the Hebrew.

A famous case, which turns up in controversy even today,[60] is the text in Isaiah, usually translated, "A *virgin* shall conceive, and bear a child, and they shall call his name Immanuel" (7:14). The Greek version used by the Church has the word *parthenos* here, which the older English translations render as virgin.

Parthenos usually, though not always, does mean that. The Hebrew, however, is *almah*, which simply means any young woman, not necessarily a virgin, since an *almah* can also be a married woman. In its context, the text refers to a person contemporary with the prophet, perhaps his own wife, and it has nothing to do with the supposed virgin birth of Jesus, centuries later.[61] The whole point of the prophecy is that it will be fulfilled in a very few years.

When the Jews pointed out mistranslations of this kind, they were accused by Christians of falsifying the Bible, of "altering the Scriptures." Partly as a result of such controversies, the Jewish community soon began to produce new Greek versions of their Scriptures, such as that of Aquila, early in the second century. Aquila was a Roman aristocrat who converted first to Christianity and then to Judaism and became a protégé of Rabban Gamliel. His work was intended to supersede the Septuagint, eliminating the mistranslations used by Christians as proof-texts.

Two major themes run through this controversial literature. The first is the rejection of the Jews by God and the election of the Gentiles as the true Israel in their place. The second is the inferiority of Jewish law, worship and scriptural interpretation and their spiritual fulfillment in Christianity. We have already met these themes in Tertullian and other writers, but they can be documented in a wide range of authors from different localities and of different dates, up to the sixth century, where Ruether ended her study.

Central to both themes is the idea that the Jews rejected and killed Jesus, the Messiah sent to them by God. This is why they have lost their status as the chosen people. However, the writers attempt to show that this cosmic crime was no isolated incident. It arose out of the very nature of the Jewish people; it was the culmination of a "trail of crimes" committed by the Jews all down their history.

The Jews failed to recognize their Messiah because they were carnal, sensual, instead of spiritual like the Church. Their expectation that the kingdom of the Messiah would be an earthly one contradicted God's true intentions: he sent a Messiah with a spiritual mission, whose kingdom was not of this world. In contrast, the Church was in every respect spiritual: its doctrines, its law, its worship were all spiritual, altogether superior to those of the Jews.

This thinking was based on a double standard and considerable self-deception. It considered the nonsacrificial eucharistic worship of the Church as the fulfillment of the universal spiritual worship predicted by Malachi (1:1–11). The equally nonsacrificial worship of the synagogue it stigmatized as illegitimate. The Church looked on the fall of the Temple as a divine cancellation of *all* legitimate Jewish worship.

Christian writers tenaciously maintained these contrasts even when the Church developed into a large scale organization with considerable property holdings and a magnificent ritual of worship, as well as a set of rules of behavior different from but no less concrete than those by which Jews were bound. The contrast between the two religions was in fact a purely theoretical one, which could hardly have withstood the test of empirical comparison. The theologians could only render the contrast plausible by attributing to the Jews all sorts of wickedness of which they were not in fact guilty.

They achieved this aim by means of a remarkable and unique method of scriptural interpretation. The method is already present in Barnabas, before the end of the first century, and even he was clearly not its originator. Christian writers treated all the criticism of Jewish behavior found in the prophets, which from a modern point of view can be called Jewish self-criticism,[62] as a straight description of "the Jews" as they are. The other side of the prophetic message, the promise of forgiveness and future restoration for Israel upon her repentance, they denied to Israel and applied to the Church.

> By this method, one gains an unrelieved tale of evildoing and apostasy, said to be characteristic of "the Jews," divorced from the message of future hope, which is applied to the Church. This turns the Jewish Scriptures, which actually contain the record of Jewish self-criticism, into a remorseless denunciation of the Jews, while the Church, in turn, is presented as totally perfect, and loses the prophetic tradition of self-criticism! This also means that the heroes of the Old Testament become the heritage of the Church, while the Jews are read as a people who never accepted or responded to their prophetic leaders and teachers.[63]

The central crime of killing Christ is taken as paradigmatic, and it is projected back to the very origins of Jewish history: the Jews are seen as apostate from the start. The Jews are not only killers of the prophets (cf. 1 Kings 19:10) but also idolaters, law breakers, and sinners of every description.[64]

Apparently, their tendency to idolatry and vice was something they had picked up during their stay in Egypt. It would not have done to trace it too far back, to the patriarchs; they had to be claimed for the Church as forerunners of spiritual Christianity. Eusebius alleges that "everything that Moses forbade they had previously done without restraint (sc., in Egypt)."[65] The fourth-century preacher of Antioch, John Chrysostom, in characteristically unrestrained language tells his audience that "they built a brothel in Egypt, made love madly with the barbarians, and worshipped foreign gods."[66]

The episode of the golden calf is constantly brought up as evidence of the supposed Jewish mania for idols. Barnabas thinks God rejected the Jews right from the start because of this incident. Moses broke the tablets to show that God had withdrawn his election from the Jews and reserved it for the future Church.[67] John Chrysostom and others say the Jews constantly tried to kill Moses. Such writers did not press the point too hard, however, because this would tend to put Moses in too favorable a light, whereas they needed to show that his legislation was inferior to their own.

The idolatry manifested in the incident of the calf continues once the promised land is reached, characterizing the whole history of Israel. In contrast, the faithful Gentiles have turned away from idols to the worship of the living God.[68]

A set of texts is collected to prove the depravity of the Jews: they were blasphemers against the name of God (Isaiah 52:6), they were rebellious and resisted the spirit (Isaiah 64:2), they were gluttonous (Exodus 32:6), they were sensualists (Deuteronomy 32:15), and they were adulterers (Jeremiah 5:8).

Here we see the technique of interpretation in action. Christian writers read these prophetic warnings to Israel, intended to lead to repentance and restoration, as unqualified condemnations of permanent Jewish characteristics.

The theme of sensuality, in particular, is a favorite one of the former monk, John Chrysostom. Contrasts such as these may rest to some extent upon the increasing tendency of the Church to define monastic asceticism as the norm of Christian life. Judaism does not encourage asceticism; in fact, Jewish teachers have tended to be suspicious of it when it made its appearance among pious Jews. They usually regard it as ingratitude for God's gifts in the creation, for which Jews themselves regularly bless and thank God. They see in the ascetic life a risk to the love of the neighbor and participation in the common life of the community.

Many of the most violent of the Christian controversialists were monks, who looked down on the Jews as carnal and sensual because of their affirmation of marriage, of normal bodily life, and of the created world in general. John Chrysostom, a presbyter in Antioch at the time he preached his vitriolic sermons against the Jews, had so injured his health by his austerities when he was a monk that he was obliged to return to ordinary life.

Such contrasts between Jews and Christians, however misleading and unjust in their language, may have had a certain basis in the fact that the two religions did and largely still do have somewhat different attitudes toward the creation and toward the life of the body. But such theological differences provide no foundation for a Christian claim to superior spirituality, especially when the contrast is generalized to apply to all aspects of religion, including scriptural interpretation.

The Jews are regularly characterized as people of the letter, in contrast to the Church, as the people of the spirit. Christian writers contrast their own preference for allegorical or "spiritual" interpretations, necessary to them if they wanted to make the Jewish Bible mean what their theology required, with a Jewish preference for historical or literal ones. When it suits them, however, these writers can take biblical metaphor literally: the Jewish people is called a harlot, cast off for being "wanton between the legs,"[69] and their synagogues whorehouses.

John Damascene, a later writer, says God gave the Jews the Sabbath because of "grossness and sensuality" and an "absolute propensity for material things." Aphraat equates the synagogue with Sodom and Gomorrah, and he alleges that like these cities, Jerusalem will never be rebuilt.[70] The Jews are regularly accused of infanticide, of sacrificing their own children to idols, or even of cannibalism, of eating their own children.[71] Chrysostom calls them "godless, idolaters, pedicides, stoning the prophets and committing ten thousand horrors."[72]

This escalation of polemical rhetoric beyond all plausibility, let alone evidence, is perhaps in part to be accounted for in the particular context of Chrysostom's sermons by their function as a dissuasive. They were addressed to members of his congregation who did not see Jewish religion in this light at all but as spiritually attractive in ways the Church was not. In the city of Antioch, many Christians were attending Jewish services and following Jewish customs and might well, in due course, be led to convert.

The almost hysterical character of Chrysostom's sermons may be a testimony to the seriousness of the threat to his hold over his flock presented by a flourishing and attractive Judaism. We could even conclude that the more extreme his rhetoric, the better testimony it becomes to the high level of Jewish religious life in his immediate environment. If so, the sermons really prove the opposite of his own case. Much of the anti-Jewish polemic in the fathers may have been intended as a dissuasive to Judaizing Christians.

As before, the central charge is the killing of Christ, and in a sense, all else follows from this. The Jews, having rejected and killed their Messiah, have been rejected irrevocably for another people, the Gentile church, who will respond to God.[73] Augustine in the same period regards the killing of Christ as an inherited characteristic of Jews, persisting into later generations, like original sin. "This is said about Christ, whom you, in your parents, led to death . . . "[74] The Jews are always the Christ-killers.

Early in the fourth century, at the first ecumenical council at Nicaea, the Church for the first time had formally defined the divinity of Christ, in the phrase (as rendered in the commonly used English translation of the Nicene Creed) "God of God, Light of Light, Very God of Very God, being of one substance with the Father." This new dogma encouraged escalation of the language concerning the killing of Christ.

After Nicaea, Christian writers can describe the Jews as enemies of *God*, guilty of cosmic treason and *lèse majesté*. Chrysostom, writing some decades after Nicaea, is fond of this theme, actually using the notorious term *deicide*, later to be a standard Christian charge against the Jews, not formally abandoned even at Vatican II.

Ruether describes a passage in which Chrysostom uses a rhetorical device, in which the terms of the argument are related in the form ABBA. The device allows him to draw bizarre conclusions. As he supposedly has demonstrated, the Jews were in former times prone to every vice, idolatry, and lawlessness, but God did not cast them off. Finally, they committed the ultimate sin of killing Christ, which is beyond forgiveness. Now, too late, they start to observe the Mosaic law. They no longer worship idols, stone the prophets, or eat their children.

But they are much more hated by God now than they were before. When God wanted them to keep the law, they broke every commandment. Now that Christ has come and God wants to abrogate the law, they perversely insist on keeping every detail. Their present virtues are much worse in God's eyes than their previous vices, because of their guilt for the murder of Christ; in fact, their present faithfulness to the law is only one more expression of their rejection of Christ.

This ingenious argument allows Chrysostom to continue to refer the Old Testament language about idolatry, harlotry, and demon worship to the synagogue of his day, although he has just admitted that contemporary Jews do not do anything of the sort. So he can go to describe the present synagogue as a brothel and a house of demon worship.[75]

The sermons of Chrysostom have been admired down the centuries for their "spiritual beauty." It was for his eloquence as a preacher that John gained his added name of Chrysostom, which means "golden mouth." He is one of the most honored of the early theologians or fathers. His writings are regarded in the Eastern Orthodox Church as part of the Holy Tradition, second only in authority to Scripture itself. His name was later given to the liturgy of the Byzantine Church, to become the most widely celebrated of all Eastern Orthodox rites.

Chrysostom's writings were studied down the centuries by clergy and monks, especially in the Eastern Orthodox Church, helping to form their attitudes toward the Jews. His reputation for holiness also earned Chrysostom the title of Saint, by which he continues to be known in both the Orthodox and Catholic churches. Those who claim, as some conservative Catholics do to this day, that this kind of anti-Jewish attitude is an authentic part of the tradition, have Christian history on their side.[76] It is not tradition but the modern conscience that renders such language unacceptable, no matter where it is found.

What, then, are we to make of this "golden mouthed" preacher, whose "spiritually beautiful" sermons include such obscene and mendacious rhetoric against the Jews? Does the beauty of the other sermons cancel out the hatefulness of these, or ought we to conclude that the presence of unmistakable hate here casts doubt on the authenticity of the saintliness apparently manifested elsewhere?

The phenomenon is not unique to Chrysostom; one almost begins to conclude that the more fervent the Christian, the more likely he is to be violently anti-Jewish. But is fervor the same as authentic holiness? The fervor of these writers' devotion to their image of Christ is not in doubt. Unfortunately, at the center of that image is the crucifixion, and without exception they believed it to be, if not the actual work of the Jews, beyond doubt their fault. Could one love the crucified without hating those who crucified him?

CONTRASTED PAIRS: THE CHURCH SUPERSEDES ISRAEL

From the Letter of Barnabas on, Christian writers make use of various contrasts in the Bible between pairs, such as Jacob and Esau, Sarah and Hagar, and Rachel and Leah, to provide the raw material for figurative contrasts destined to live long in Christian history. For the Rabbis of the Talmud, Edom and Esau stood symbolically for Rome and in due course for the imperial state church. The Church now claims to be Jacob and in turn casts the Jews as Esau. The text about the two nations struggling in the womb of Rebecca–"one shall be stronger than the other, and the older shall serve the younger"–is taken to refer to the Church and the Jews.[77]

Several writers see the Jews as Cain, the murderer of his brother Abel. Thus, the Jews become the murderous older brother compelled to wander the earth as a reprobate among the nations, the Gentile church. This notion already foreshadows the medieval myth of the wandering Jew, destined to move about the world until the end of time, never finding rest. The mark of Cain is identified with circumcision and in turn connected with Hadrian's law barring the Jews from entering Jerusalem.

Circumcision functions in the imagination of such writers as a kind of negative ID. Indeed, circumcision is no longer a mark of divine favor but of reprobation.[78] The murderous Jews are being punished by God with exile and exclusion from their city and their land, in accordance with the mistranslated text of Psalm 69:24, "Their back bow thou down always."[79]

The relationship between Isaac, the child of Sarah, the freewoman, and Ishmael, the child of Hagar, the slave girl, becomes a stock image in the Middle Ages for the servitude of the Jews to the Church. Already in Cyprian we find the figure of the weak-eyed Leah as a "type" of the synagogue, contrasted with the beautiful Rachel, a "type" of the church, who after remaining long barren brought forth Joseph, a type of Christ.[80] Later, Leah's weak sight is connected with the Pauline veil over the eyes of the Jews when they read the Scriptures, and in medieval carvings of church and synagogue, the synagogue is depicted as blindfolded.

The rejection of the Jews has its counterpart in the choice of the Gentile church to succeed them as God's chosen people. "The heart of the *adversus Judaeos* tradition is the proof of the election of the Gentile church and its inheritance of the election of the rejected Jews."[81]

The contrast between the Jews and the nations, a basic theme of the Bible itself, is turned backward and given the opposite of its original meaning: now the Gentiles instead of the Jews are the people of God. After the end of the first century, few writers attempt to maintain the Pauline idea that Israel is the stock on to which the Gentile church is grafted. The election of the Gentiles and the rejection of the Jews have to go inextricably together.

Since the Gentile church is already prefigured in the Old Testament, it turns out that the Church is the real meaning even of Israel itself. "Essentially, there is one covenant, *promised* to Abraham, *foretold* by the prophets, and *fulfilled* in the Gentile church, who accepted the Messiah promised to Israel."[82] The message of election refers to a *believing* people: the Jews are not such a people, but the Gentiles are. Since the Jews never accepted God, the covenant with them was abortive, and it was replaced by one with a people who did accept God, the prophets and the Messiah. In short, the Church is, and always has been, the true Israel.[83]

How do these writers substantiate their thesis? Ruether found that the basic method of proving the election of the Gentiles was to read all texts about Israel as the light of the nations, about the rule of the future Davidic king over the nations, and all praise for non-Hebrew peoples, as prophecies of the Gentile church, while these texts were read in antithesis to those condemning Israel, taken literally and regarded as irrevocable.[84] Thus, Christ was seen in the Davidic king in the Psalms, and in the suffering servant of the Lord in Isaiah, and the enemies of these persons taken to be the Jews.

Christian biblical interpretation understands the gathering of a faithful people from among the Gentiles as the fulfillment of the messianic expectation of the ingathering of exiles to Mount Zion at the time of final redemption, and denies that gentile converts to Judaism are such a fulfillment. Ruether comments:

> Needless to say, this exegesis calls for extraordinary distortion of the actual meaning of the biblical texts. There, the Israel which is chastised and the Israel whose messianic fulfilment is predicted are the same.
>
> The messianic fulfilment of Israel includes the ingathering of believers from among the nations. In the Church's reading of these texts, however, the messianic Israel is identified with the believing Gentiles, in antithetical relationship to the chastised Israel, the reprobate Jews.[85]

After Constantine and his successors established the new Christian empire, the theme took a novel political twist. Now the theologians of the triumphant Church identify the Christian empire with the predicted reign of Christ on earth for one thousand years, and they regard it as a fulfillment of the scriptural promise to the Davidic king that he would rule, as Christ does in Christendom, "from sea to sea and from the river to the ends of the earth" (Psalm 72:8). The overthrow of paganism by the Church becomes the prophesied vanquishing of idolatry and overthrow of the demons.

Writers such as Eusebius, a contemporary of Constantine who as a kind of court bishop did much in his own writings to shape and spread the ideology of the new empire, fuse that ideology with the existing messianic universalism of the Church. The imperial Christian ideology speaks of the empire as if it covered the whole world and of the rule of the Christian emperor as if it were identical with the rule of Christ.[86]

In contrast, the Jews foolishly continue to look for a Messiah who has already come but whom they have rejected when he came. They have already been restored from two captivities, but this third one is final, and it is useless to look for the Messiah to bring this captivity to an end. In our time, the traditional theory has broken down against the empirical test of history, since the Jewish captivity or exile is in fact being brought to an end by the events of the twentieth century.

For these writers, it is vain for the Jews to continue to look for a Messiah, and even perverse, since they are supposed to know from Scripture that the Messiah has already come. Indeed, the Messiah they still look for is not the real Messiah but the anti-Christ. This notion would become prevalent enough over the course of time to be incorporated in the medieval ritual for the baptism of converts from Judaism.[87]

The Church was presented with an acute apologetic problem when it retained the Jewish Bible as its own Old Testament while declining to keep the Law contained in it. The usual way of dealing with the problem was to attempt to show that the Jews misunderstand the original meaning of the Law when they take it in its literal sense. The Jewish understanding of the Law is carnal, of the flesh, while the Christian, allegorizing interpretation is spiritual. A second argument is that the Law is intrinsically unworthy; God's intention in promulgating it was punitive, not redemptive, and in consequence it is now both historically and morally out of date.[88]

Both these arguments depend on a claim that goes back to the Church's original controversy with fellow Jews concerning the messiahship of Jesus. The Jews cannot read the Scriptures correctly. They read the letter, and only the Christians can see beneath the letter to the spiritual meaning, which is precisely the Christological interpretation of the texts employed by the Church.[89]

Many of these writers criticize the Jewish Law from the same point of view as an enlightened pagan: the Law is irrational, or degrading, or promotes idleness. They do not adopt the standpoint of the Bible itself, for if they did, it would be much more difficult to evade its contention that the Torah embodies man's obligations under the terms of the covenant. This is one point at which Christian anti-Judaism does seem to have continued the arguments of its pagan counterpart.

Eusebius and others offer another way of overcoming the difficulty, which also shares the pagan standpoint in many respects. Here we find the notion of a pre-Mosaic religion as the true forerunner of Christianity. By means of this idea, Judaism can be relegated to an intermediate period and seen as a purely temporary provision by God for specifically Jewish needs. It is hard to find a New Testament foundation for the idea, though it is possible to read Paul as implying something not altogether unlike it. Ruether thinks that the foundations of the idea are to be found in a combination of Jewish haggadah on the virtues of the patriarchs with the Greek notion of a golden age of all the virtues in pre-historical times.[90]

According to Eusebius, the patriarchs, Abraham, Isaac, and Jacob, were not Jews but belonged like Christians to a universal race, neither Jew nor Greek. There was neither idolatry nor crime when they lived. Men were virtuous without prescriptive law because they followed the universal law of conscience written on their hearts, which is the same as the natural law of Greek philosophy. Abraham's intention was to spread a universal "natural religion," suitable for everyone, not Judaism, suitable only for Jews. Christianity restores this universal natural religion, in its final and fulfilled form.

Thus Christ not only brings a new covenant but also restores the original covenant, the universal spiritual religion of patriarchal man before the Mosaic dispensation. This universal spiritual religion is often identified with the Ten Commandments, the basic law that preceded the fuller Law of Moses, intended for Jews only. Eusebius and his colleagues appear to have forgotten that the Ten Commandments were also given through Moses at Sinai, but they probably have in mind the notion that the ritual law belongs to the second set of tablets, given by God after Moses had broken the first, as a "second Law." The whole idea seems to owe something to the Jewish theory of the Noachide covenant, but with the values reversed.[91]

The Mosaic dispensation, Eusebius argues, was never intended to be other than temporary, until the coming of Christ. It was on a lower moral level than the spiritual patriarchal religion that was restored by Christ. It was limited in time, to the period from Moses to Christ, in place, since it applied only to Palestine, and in use, since it was to be observed only by Jews.

It did not have the purpose, as the Bible had stated, of raising the Jews above the spiritual level of the surrounding nations, but rather of raising them up to the general level, below which they had fallen during their stay in Egypt. The Mosaic Law was intended as a preparatory training for the Jews, who as a people are morally worse than others, to ready them for the restoration of the natural law when Christ should come.[92]

Similar reasoning dealt with the subjects of the Sabbath and of circumcision. The text of Isaiah 1:13 was used to prove that God dislikes Sabbaths in principle, no matter how they are observed, and it was characterized as a merely natural rest, devoid of spiritual benefit. It was given only to restrain the Jews from their pursuit of material gain for one day a week.

Circumcision, the theologians argued, was a purely national distinguishing mark, intended to separate the Jews from the surrounding idolaters, and it was no longer needed when the whole world had become Christian and abandoned idolatry. Circumcision was indecent, in contrast to the modest Christian sealing on the forehead in the rite of chrismation, and its sole purpose said to be the restraint of the sexual proclivities. It was also regarded as inferior to baptism on the ground that women could be baptized but not circumcised.

All these laws were given only to restrain people who possessed an inordinate tendency to vice, a characteristic, as we have already seen, thought to be distinctive of the Jews. Neither the patriarchs before them nor the Christians after them needed such provisions. On the basis of Ezekiel 20:25, "I gave them statutes that were not good, and ordinances by which they could not have life," such writers attempted to prove that the Mosaic Law was intrinsically evil, given only as a punishment, and not expressing the true and final will of God.[93]

The law that was thus abrogated for the Jews had found a spiritual fulfillment in the Christian Church, among men and women who do not only observe outward forms but observe the inner, spiritual meaning of the commandments. God has removed their hearts of stone in his new covenant, giving them hearts of flesh. Christ, the new lawgiver, has given a universal spiritual law, written on the hearts, a law that in accordance with prophecy has gone forth from Zion, not Sinai like its predecessor. Christians have been redeemed from the curse of the law, a law that no one could keep properly and which did not save those who attempted to observe it.

The spiritualizing explanation covers the same ground that we have just surveyed from another point of view, showing how, in the view of the Christian apologist, all the Jewish observances have a counterpart in the life of the Church, which in every case is at once more spiritual than and also supersedes its Jewish forerunner. "Circumcise your hearts and not your flesh" is taken to signify (contrary to Hebrew idiom) that the *real* meaning of circumcision is repentance.

Thus it can be made to appear that the Christians, not the Jews, are the truly circumcised, as if they had a monopoly of repentance. John Damascene, the great systematic theologian of the Eastern Church, teaches that the real meaning of circumcision is "the cutting away of fleshly desires." The implication, of course, is that Christians do this, while Jews do not. Such theologians argued that the patriarchs before Moses had been righteous without circumcision, and therefore it was not needed now. They appear to have forgotten that circumcision was first given as a sign to Abraham himself.

On the same reasoning, the dietary laws do not prohibit unclean animals but animalistic forms of behavior. The Sabbath is proved not to be binding by biblical arguments: the patriarchs did not observe it, for it had not yet been given. Joshua had circled Jericho with his trumpets on the Sabbath as well as the other days of the week. The Maccabees actually fought on the Sabbath–a particularly heartless argument, since it ignores the loss of life and painful spiritual struggle the Maccabees had actually undergone before determining that they were indeed permitted and obligated to fight on the Sabbath when attacked, since God had said of his commandments that "a man shall *live* by them."[94]

The Sabbath was said to be an insult to creation, since the seventh day was as much a part of the world as any other day: the Sabbath really refers to the eschatological eighth day of creation, the day of final rest, which is celebrated in advance on the Christian Sunday. Ascetics like John Damascene can turn the argument around, and say in effect: why only *one* day for God, when *we* give all of every day to him?[95]

As Ruether points out, all these arguments show how little detailed knowledge of Judaism the writers had. They are certainly altogether out of touch with the development of halachah in the postbiblical period of Judaism, by means of which the Torah is applied to contemporary situations through careful and earnestly debated jurisprudence. They argue with stereotypes of Judaism, assuming, and probably possessing, only as much knowledge as any Gentile who had heard of Jews might have of them.[96]

By similar reasoning the Christian writers attempt to show that the sacrificial cult of the Jerusalem Temple has been spiritually fulfilled in Christianity. Here, however, their arguments have an extra edge, derived from their knowledge of the destruction of the Temple, which is regularly interpreted as the divine punishment for the crucifixion of Christ. The various prophetic denunciations of the Temple and its sacrifices, such as Amos 5:21, Isaiah 1:11–13, and Jeremiah 7:21ff., are collected together to show that God had always rejected the sacrificial system.

The prophets themselves had intended their denunciations to apply only to sacrifice separated from social morality. The theologians argue that the sacrificial system was only a temporary expedient against idolatry, obsolete once the habit had been finally broken, as it were. It had never reflected God's true will. God had intended it only for local application, for the Jews only, and not for any other peoples.

The eucharistic liturgy now becomes a new Temple cult with its priesthood. The Christian rules concerning fasting and abstinence become a new set of dietary laws. Sunday becomes the new Sabbath. Easter becomes the new Passover. All these are interpreted as if they were purely spiritual and could legitimately be contrasted with Jewish "outwardness." Thus, as Ruether puts it, the Christian theology of spiritualization of the Jewish past in the life of the Church becomes false consciousness: the theologians represented these institutions as being what they were not, and at some level they must have known they were not.[97]

From the fourth century on, Christian eucharistic worship acquired a public and liturgical character. It ceased to be a domestic, or semi-domestic rite, like the Jewish observances from which in all probability it had originally been derived. Splendid churches were built and the liturgy took on appropriate ritual magnificence. The officiants at the liturgy correspondingly came to be regarded as priests in a special sense.

A mistranslation of Psalm 40:6 is taken, following the version in Hebrews 10:5, "Sacrifice and offering thou didst not desire, but thou hast prepared a body for me,"[98] to prove that God has abandoned the Temple sacrifices in favor of the worship of the Body of Christ, offered through the priestly ministry of the eucharistic celebrants. Thus, the eucharist itself comes more and more to be interpreted in sacrificial terms, and to the extent that it is, contrasted favorably with the sacrifices formerly offered in the Temple.

This development marks a further stage in the departure of the Church from the biblical interpretation of law and rite within the covenant with the people of Israel. Philo and Hellenistic Judaism had understood the allegorical interpretations they offered as the inner meaning of the outward commandment, which still remained obligatory. "When Christianity fused the Philonic dualism of letter and spirit with the messianic dualism of the historical age and the messianic age, this made the relationship of letter and spirit antithetical and supersessionary. This was originally done in a mood of expectation of imminent eschatological crisis."[99]

Later, however, the eschatological tension died down; the Church no longer lived in daily expectation of the return of Christ and the fulfillment of all the messianic prophecies. In fact, it settled down into history again, and it became a religion like any other. Expectation of the second coming of Christ was postponed indefinitely, though apocalyptic ideas could be revived from time to time under pressure of unusually threatening historical circumstances.

The original contrast present to some extent in Jesus' own teaching between the fulfilled kingdom of God and Judaism as a religion became transformed into a contrast between two historical religions. Nevertheless, the original eschatological language continued to be used. Christian writers apply the language of messianic fulfillment, now in a Graeco-Roman cultural environment translated into a claim for superior spirituality, to rites and observances that are in reality no less historical and material than those of the Jewish people. In spite of that, the theologians argue that the Christian rites are intrinsically superior on account of their supposed spirituality.

THE CHRISTOLOGICAL INTERPRETATION OF THE OLD TESTAMENT

All these ideas are collected up in one theological principle, which is also historically the root of the whole scheme. In a systematic way, the Scriptures of the Jewish people are interpreted christologically. The idea of the christological fulfillment of the Jewish Scriptures is the foundation of all traditional Christian theology, making frequent and specific appearance in the *adversus Judaeos* literature. It is the earliest and most consistently employed Christian theological method. It is the basis of the collections of "testimonies" that originally formed the basis of theology in general and specifically of the controversial literature.

Liturgy went in the same direction. As the monks began to base their life of corporate prayer on the daily recitation of the psalms, they learned to interpret the speaker in the psalms, originally David or his descendant, as Christ in his body the Church. As we saw, this method frequently permitted the theologians to interpret the enemies of the Davidic king as the enemies of Christ, and both as the Jews. The annual retelling of the Passion story at Easter, later embellished with liturgical dramas and passion plays, used the same methods, even more vividly depicting the Jews as the killers of Christ.

Sacred art also depicted the objects of Christian faith in images drawn from the Old Testament. In the traditional icons of the Orthodox church, the Holy Trinity is depicted in the form of a painting of Abraham entertaining angels unawares before the destruction of Sodom and Gomorrah. In the icons, the Persons of the Trinity are shown as three identical young men, one of which has a cross in his halo to show that he is Christ.[100]

The icon reflects the theological tradition that understands the Old Testament appearances of God, often reinterpreted by later Jewish tradition, even within the Bible itself, as mediated by angels, as theophanies of God the Word. As even the earliest Christians seem to have believed, every detail of the life of Christ, as well as his death, resurrection, heavenly Lordship, and eventual return, had been prophesied in advance for those who could understand.

The Jews did not "understand." They interpreted the Bible very differently, through the oral Torah, now being codified in the Talmud, a process that went on concurrently with the developments in Christian theology we have been describing. The rabbis believed that the oral Torah was as old as the written one, indeed that it had also been given at Sinai, but not written down until Yehudah ha-Nasi began the process at the end of the second century C.E. with the codification of the Mishnah. When the written Torah and the oral Torah were read as mutually complementary, such Christian interpretations could not arise, and were not felt to possess the least plausibility.

Accordingly, the Church had to undertake a polemic against the way the Jews interpreted their own Scriptures. This polemic would in later centuries be concentrated on the Talmud. The Talmud became identified with the Pauline veil over the eyes of the Jews when they read the Scriptures. Medieval Christians would burn it, not only because it was thought to contain anti-Christian sentiments, but above all because it contained the Jewish interpretation of the Scriptures.

The theologians of the early Church continued and developed the hints of criticism of Jewish biblical interpretation found in the New Testament. They accused Jewish interpreters of blindness, of literalism, of carnality. The polemic combined the Pauline doctrine of Jewish blindness with the Johannine doctrine of Jewish carnality and demonic influence and the Matthaean doctrine of Jewish hypocrisy.[101] All three criticisms could be conflated in a single anti-Jewish charge, more formidable than anything found in earlier years.

Developing Christian theology gave extra force to the polemic as it increasingly thought of Christ, following the prologue to the Gospel of John, as the incarnation of the Word of God. The Word incarnate in Christ was also the Word by which God had created the world, and the Scriptural Word of revelation, as well as the Word by which history was providentially directed.

Along the lines of the Johannine prologue, it could therefore be argued that the Jews by their rejection of Christ the Word had proved that they had never at any time received God's Word, and accordingly had never known God through their Scriptures. The prophetic gifts were now all transferred to the Church, together with the Holy Spirit, and lost to the Jewish people.

Ruether sums up in some powerful sentences: "Everything in Judaism becomes 'Old Testament' in relation to the Christian "New Testament." The relationship between the two testaments becomes a triple supersession: a supersession ontologically, morally and historically. Everything Jewish is, at best, an outward 'shadow,' which symbolizes on a bodily level the spiritual meaning realized in the Christian dispensation."[102]

We have already traveled a considerable distance along the road from the Jewish Jesus to full-blown Christian antisemitism. Jesus' original prophetic criticism of some of his Jewish contemporaries in the light of his vision of the kingdom of God has been transformed into the polemic of one historical religion against another. The claim of the earliest Church, that Jesus had been constituted Messiah by his resurrection, in spite of the incompatibility of his earthly life and death with the messianic prophecies, has been transformed into a systematic denial to the Jews of the right to their own Scriptures and their own interpretation of their Scriptures.

The claim of Jesus and his disciples that the kingdom of God was in the midst of their contemporaries has been transformed into the claim of the Catholic church to supersede the Jewish people as the elect people of God. And Jewish reluctance to accept a novel interpretation of the Scriptures has become the culpable blindness of a people that had always been the enemies of God.

All this centers on the calumny that the Jews killed Christ: in the theology of the Church, the calumny becomes dogmatized into an unassailable fact, and the cornerstone of Christian polemic against the Jews. It is projected back even to Sinai, and the divine rejection of the Jews dated to that point. It is projected forward on to the contemporaries of the Church, still the Christ-killing Jews.

It governs the whole relationship between Jews and Christians, and it has continued to do so to this day. Only in the last years, when horror at the Holocaust has joined with critical scholarship to light the fuse to explode the myth of the Christ-killing Jew, has it become possible to conceive of that relationship in other terms. What these might be is still far from clear.

Ruether and others are rightly opposed on ethical grounds to the continuation after the Holocaust of a theology that justifies the claim that Jesus is the Messiah by means of an anti-Jewish use of the Jewish Scriptures. I am less optimistic than Ruether that these christological affirmations can now be disentangled from their original anti-Jewish scriptural justification while remaining recognizably in continuity with Christian tradition. A Christology that abandoned the anti-Jewish "left hand" would be left without a basis for the claim that Jesus was in any sense the Jewish Messiah. Critical history leads honest Christians to the conclusion that Jesus himself never made the claim.

Would not this renunciation also involve the return of the "Old Testament" to the Jews? This ecumenical gesture could entail exceedingly awkward consequences for contemporary Christianity, for (as Chrysostom observed long ago), "Don't you realize, if the Jewish rites are holy and venerable, our way of life must be false?"[103]

GREGORY THE GREAT AND THE JEWS

The policy of the medieval popes toward the Jews was governed in large degree by the inheritance of Roman law, embodied for the West in the Theodosian Code, still containing provisions upholding the legality of the Jewish religion and protecting Jews from oppression and violence from Christians.

Because of the particular responsibility they felt for upholding Roman legality, the popes were in general more respectful of Jewish rights than were other elements in the Church, such as the monks and friars, or the inferior clergy, sometimes protecting Jews from onslaughts from these quarters. Nevertheless, it would hardly be correct to describe any of them as friends of the Jews.[104]

They fully believed the Christian myth of the Christ-killing Jews, and the theology of supersession, based on it. The Jewish law had been abolished and replaced by the new, spiritual law of the Church, which they administered. In particular, the popes inherited the theology of Augustine, according to which the Jews were destined to survive until the second coming of Christ as a witness to their crimes. They were to be *preserved, but in misery*.

Popes attempted to reconcile these two elements in the traditional position; some leaned toward the tolerance implicit in the concept of preservation, others emphasizing rather the misery that ought to be the lot of the Jews, in view of their crimes. Preservation should not be so emphasized that the Jews acquired any sort of equality with Christians, but misery should not be so emphasized that their lives were endangered. This position is not friendly to the Jews, but neither is it genocidal.

The principal author of the papal position on the Jews was Pope Gregory I, known as Gregory the Great, who ruled from 590 to 604. Gregory was a Roman aristocrat, and he had been a Benedictine monk before his reluctant election to the papacy. The office of the pope at that time involved secular rule over the extensive papal territories, known as the Patrimony of Peter, as well as vast influence over the whole of the Western church, which regarded the Pope as the successor of Peter, the Prince of the Apostles, and as the first bishop of the whole Church. Gregory's rulings had the force of law in his own territories, and he carried great authority everywhere else. As an administrator, he sought to apply the principles of the Roman legal heritage, modified by the theological legacy of the church fathers.

Gregory's views on the Jews are to be found in his sermons and in letters containing rulings on specific cases brought to his notice. While he issues his rulings on cases in specific terms, not precisely applicable to other cases, he also sets forth the principles guiding him in reaching his decisions. His rulings accordingly proved useful to future generations of popes for the guidance of their own actions. They would quote him again and again in their rulings.

Gregory came into contact with the Jews as pastor and as administrator. In his sermons and in many of his letters, we meet with the familiar themes of the anti-Jewish theology of the church fathers, already sketched out earlier in the chapter. Little is distinctive, beyond his conviction that there is nothing to be gained by coercing the Jews into conversion to Christianity, for a faith brought about by coercion is likely to be insincere.

On the other hand, Gregory had no objection to using economic and social inducements to conversion, so that the status of the new convert could be seen to contrast clearly with the "misery" of his former coreligionists. There was hope that the children of such "rice Christians" might in due course find a sincere and genuine Christian faith.

His administrative dealings with questions about the Jews displayed the distinctive balance of antithetical considerations through which the pope applied the Augustinian theology in the practical sphere. The balance between "preservation" and "misery" in Gregory's practical decisions can also be accounted for by the double legacy of Theodosian law and patristic theology. The law made it clear that the Jews had rights as citizens and as adherents of a legal religion. The theology of the fathers made it no less clear that these rights ought never to go so far as equality with Christians.

Gregory's phrase, *sicut Judaeis non,* the first words of a letter, taken according to ancient practice as its title, and frequently quoted in the titles of subsequent papal rulings, stands for this balance of antitheses. The principle was formulated in the context of an incident in which a local bishop had expropriated a synagogue and turned it into a Christian church. The Jews of Palermo had complained, through the good offices of the Jewish community in Rome, that a synagogue and its guesthouse had been taken over by the bishop and consecrated as a Christian church. In Gregory's view, this action was clearly illegal: "*Just as* licence ought *not* to be presumed *for the Jews* to do anything in their synagogues beyond what is permitted by law, so in those points conceded to them, they ought to suffer nothing prejudicial."[105] The italicized words are translations of the Latin, *sicut Judaeis non.*

The action of the bishop was condemned–"our brother has acted rashly"–and Gregory would have preferred that no action be taken to consecrate the church until the matter had been sorted out. However, now that the synagogue had been consecrated as a church, it could not be returned to Jewish use. Even according to the civil law, buildings could not be used for another purpose once consecrated to Christian use.

Victor, the bishop, had evidently hastened to consecrate the synagogue as a church before Gregory could require him to return it. He must now pay for the buildings, making them the legitimate property of the Church, and ensuring that the Jews "should in no way appear to be oppressed, or suffer an injustice." The books and ornaments that had been seized at the same time were to be returned to the Jews without question.

Edward Synan, in his useful book on papal attitudes toward the Jews in the Middle Ages, offers an astonishing explanation of the principles underlying the pope's ruling. "Here we encounter," Father Synan informs us, ". . . a Christian conviction fully grounded in the spirit as well as in the letter of the Pentateuch–namely, *What has been given to sacred uses cannot be withdrawn without sacrilege.*"[106]

Apparently, it does not occur to even this relatively enlightened Catholic writer, whose book appeared in a series intended to "foster brotherhood" between Christians and Jews, that the synagogue had already been given to sacred uses. The Jews might have considered that taking it from these uses and employing it for Christian worship, which at this period they doubtless regarded as idolatrous, would be at least equally sacrilegious. Certainly such reflections do not seem to have occurred for a moment to Gregory himself.

Gregory's other rulings on matters involving the Jews seem to have stemmed from the existing legal position embodied in the Theodosian Code. He followed its precedent when forbidding the employment of Christians as Jewish slaves. Here too Synan offers a surprising defense of the pope's actions, implying that they were guided by a theologically grounded view of the human person that made slavery in any form inappropriate. He thus contrasts Gregory's outlook favorably with that of some of his modern critics, who believe he acted unjustly in taking away Christian slaves from their Jewish owners.

However, Synan does not bring any examples of the pope's condemnation of enslavement of Christians by Christians, and we must conclude that Gregory's real objection, like those of other Christians of the period, was to the indignity of the superior Christians being enslaved by the inferior Jews, whereas their own status should be one of slavery.[107]

Gregory deals with the building and location of synagogues in a similar style. The Jews are not to build new synagogues, but old ones must not be taken away from them. If the Jews worshiping in a synagogue near a church disturb Christians at their worship by their chanting of their own prayers, they can be made to move their synagogue to another location. Again, it would not have occurred to the pope to suggest the possibility of a church being moved to avoid disturbance to Jewish worshipers.

The *sicut Judaeis non* dictum was constantly referred to by subsequent popes confronted with the question of what to do about the Jews and ultimately incorporated in a constitution of that name, originally, it seems, composed by Pope Alexander III and revised by Innocent III (1198–1217), who added an introduction.

The constitution in question protected the Jews from forced baptism, from violence or injury to their persons or property, from disturbance at their own festivities, or from violation of the sanctity of their burial places. The penalty for infractions is to be excommunication. Innocent added the proviso that these provisions are not to protect the Jews in any plotting against Christians.[108]

Of course, all these things did happen to the Jews in the Middle Ages, but in an otherwise black history, it is important to note that they did not happen by the will or permission of the central authority of the Western church, the papacy. When they did, the Jews could sometimes appeal to the papacy for protection and vindication.

The papacy's regard for the inheritance of Roman law, and its own position as the upholder of legality, made for a milder policy toward the Jews than the Church as a whole would have liked. Their theological position on the subject the popes shared with their Catholic coreligionists.[109] We shall see in the next chapter what sort of popular attitudes the more enlightened administrators had to contend with.

7

Popular Paranoia

In the high Middle Ages, the myth became the vehicle of intense popular hatred. Now, anti-Jewish passion in Christian civilization reached its climax. Christian culture came to fullest expression in philosophy, mysticism, art, and architecture. Simultaneously, hatred, fueled by and expressed through the ancient myth of the Christ-killers, broke out in unbridled violence – sometimes under the leadership of venerated saints. Jews were massacred and tortured, and soon whole Jewish populations were expelled from countries where they had long resided. The imagination of the Christian people began to devise far more deadly calumnies against the Jews than the theological offenses with which they had so far been charged. Most of them have survived in the popular mind to the present day.

In this period, we first hear of the blood libel, the baseless accusation that Jews practiced ritual murder in order to consume the blood of their victims. Christians charged their Jewish neighbors with desecration of the consecrated host from the mass, and with poisoning the wells of Christians and causing the plague, the Black Death that ravaged Europe in the fourteenth century. Christian society denied the Jews all occupations except banking, and as a result they became the creditors of Europe. Soon, we begin to hear of Jewish love of money and Jewish skill at acquiring it. (As Israelis joke, Jews have not yet lost this reputation, in spite of the state of the economy of Israel.) This is the period from which classical antisemitism later drew its store of images of the Jew as evil, powerful in uncanny and magical ways: in the Christian imagination the Jew finally became the agent of the devil himself, the ultimate supernatural origin of all evil.

Even at this point in the long development, it is probably not yet true to speak of antisemitism in the modern racist sense. Christians still identified Jews as members of a religious community, not yet as a race. But the racist antisemite of modern times can hardly think of anything bad to say against Jews that had not already been said by the medieval Christian.

By the end of the Middle Ages, however, Christians were already beginning to think of Jewishness as a permanent characteristic, now incapable of being removed by baptism. No longer only a religious status, it was connected with blood, or descent. When coupled with the already demonized image of the Jew, this can properly be called antisemitism.

Though it originated in the social consequences of the forced conversions of the fourteenth and fifteen centuries, this early antisemitism can only be explained by the distorted picture of the Jew already flourishing in the popular imagination in the late Middle Ages. Although many Jewish converts to Christianity perished through the Inquisition, the Church was still able to guard against the last consequence of antisemitic hatred, genocide itself. The traditional doctrine that the Jews must be preserved until the Second Coming of Christ still saved the Jews from corporate extinction. Nevertheless, the new concept of the permanence of Jewish blood, and therefore of Jewish behavior, even in the baptized convert, was a further fateful step toward Auschwitz.

"The year 1000," writes Edward Flannery, "found Jews in conditions reasonably stable for the time. Two centuries later they were almost pariahs. In three, they were terrorized."[1] If our findings so far are correct, the word *stable* must be something of a euphemism. But there can be no disagreement with Flannery's characterization of the development that followed.

The medieval image of the Jew was not merely distorted but completely false. That should be altogether clear to us today. How could the Christian people have been willing to believe their Jewish neighbors capable on religious grounds of such inhuman atrocities, when the educated among them had access to the Scriptures by whose laws the Jews of their day continued to live? We can only conclude that the myth and the doctrinal teaching embodying it had far more influence on the Christian mind than the Scriptures themselves. Doubtless this was in part due to the general illiteracy of the population, which met with the Scriptures only in selective quotation in the liturgy, and then the Old Testament was placed in the context of a Christian interpretation.

No one who knew anything about actual Jews could have given credence for a moment to the allegation that Jews are compelled by their law to use the blood of a Christian child in the baking of the unleavened bread of the Passover season. What the Torah in fact requires is a respect for life so strict that it forbids the consumption of even animal blood. Yet medieval Christians did implicitly believe the libel, and many have continued to do so, right up to the twentieth century. The same libel was the basis of the most recent, post-Holocaust pogrom against Jews in Poland on July 4, 1946, in which forty-three Jews lost their lives.[2] The notions on which the blood libel was based were officially contradicted by the highest authorities in the Church. At the same time, they were encouraged by the cult of fictitious child martyrs, enjoying the approval of the same authorities in the Church.

False beliefs so extreme cannot be accounted for by the characteristics or behavior of their objects. They are devoid of rational basis and can only be explained by the state of mind of those who harbor them. It is useless to ask what Jews did that could rationally account for these beliefs, even by way of misunderstanding. The historic Christian prejudice against Jews never had anything to do with the characteristics of actual Jews or with their conduct. The proper question is, what was going on in the Christian mind that could cause Christians to imagine and believe in such atrocious falsehoods?

In attempting to answer the question, we are almost inevitably led to the notion of paranoia. Paranoia is a pathological condition, in extreme cases a form of insanity. The evidence compels us to the conclusion that medieval Christianity was indeed insane on the subject of the Jews, and it possessed the power to act on its insanity.

Whether in this case insanity should mean diminished responsibility is another matter. If we had to be the judges of medieval Christianity, we might conclude today that such a plea in mitigation was unacceptable. This particular form of insanity is also chosen. It can be cured, if the will to health is present, by getting to know actual Jews. The opportunity to do so had not completely and everywhere disappeared by the end of the Middle Ages. Those who hated Jews were still morally responsible for their actions.

ABELARD'S PICTURE OF THE JEWS

Not many possessed the will to mental health on the subject of the Jews, even among popes and saints, the highest spiritual and administrative leaders of the Church. One who did, and showed it by understanding how Jews felt about their lot, was Peter Abelard. Strenuously opposed by Bernard of Clairvaux, he became a virtual outcast from the theological and ecclesiastical community, partly because he was willing to employ regard for empirical facts as well as theological theories in his philosophical inquiries.

Abelard believed a person was morally bound to follow his own conscience. Accordingly, citing the prayer of Christ, "Father, forgive them, for they know not what they do," he argued that the Jews were not morally responsible for the death of Christ. Indeed, if their leaders had believed him guilty under the law they were administering, they would have sinned if they had failed to condemn him.

Abelard wrote a dialogue between a philosopher, a Jew, and a Christian, in which he put these moving words into the mouth of his Jewish protagonist:

> I, along with you, have a common faith in the truth of the one God; I, perhaps, love him as much as you, and besides, I exhibit this love through works which you do not have. If these works are not useful, what harm do they me even if they were not commanded, since they were not forbidden? And who could censure me if I work more generously for the Lord, even if I am not bound by any precept? Who would censure this faith which . . . greatly commends the divine goodness and enkindles in us a great charity towards him who is so solicitous for our salvation that he deigns to instruct us by a written Law? . . .
>
> Whoever thinks that our persevering zeal, which puts up with so much, is without reward, affirms that God is most cruel. Surely, no people is known or even believed to have endured so much for God as we constantly put up with for him; and no one ought to claim that there can be any dross of sin which the furnace of this affliction has not

> burned away. Dispersed among all nations, alone, without an earthly king or prince, are we not burdened with such great demands that almost every day of our miserable lives we pay the debt of an intolerable ransom? In fact, we are judged deserving of such great contempt and hatred by all that anyone who inflicts some injury on us believes it to be the greatest justice and the highest sacrifice offered to God. For they believe that the misfortune of such a great captivity has only fallen on us because of God's supreme wrath, and they count as just vengeance whatever cruelty they visit on us, whether they be Christians or pagans . . .
>
> Consider the kind of people among whom we wander in exile and in whose patronage we must have confidence! We entrust our lives to our greatest enemies and are compelled to believe in the faith of those without faith. Sleep itself, which brings the greatest rest and renews nature, disquiets us with such great worry that even while sleeping we can think of nothing but the danger that looms over our throats. No pathway except the path to heaven appears safe for those whose very dwelling place is dangerous. When we go to neighbouring places we hire a guard at no small price, in whom we have little confidence. The princes themselves who rule over us and for whose patronage we pay dearly desire our death all the more to such a degree that they then snatch away the more freely what we possess. Confined and constricted in this way as if the whole world had conspired against us alone, it is a wonder that we are allowed to live. We are allowed to possess neither fields nor vineyards nor any landed estates because there is no one to protect them for us from open or occult attack. Consequently, the principal gain that is left us is that we sustain our lives here by lending money at interest to strangers; but just this makes us most hateful to them who think they are being oppressed by it. However, more than any tongue can do, our very situation is enough to speak more eloquently to all of the supreme misery of our lives and of the dangers in which we ceaselessly labour.[3]

Beyond doubt, this contemporary picture faithfully depicts the condition of the Jew in medieval Christendom. I do not know whether Abelard knew real Jews, though we might conclude from this text that he did. Apparently he knew some Hebrew, but not much, though his friend Heloïse is said to have read it as easily as Latin.

The Dialogue does not in all respects accurately represent the religion of the Jewish participant. Like other Christians of his time, Abelard seems to have seen the Jews through the prism of the Old Testament as Christians read it, and known little of post-biblical developments. Undoubtedly, Abelard shared in most respects the theological views of the church concerning the Jews, in spite of his daring recognition that they were not to blame for the death of Christ and his noble attempt to feel with their sufferings.

Peter Abelard was not canonized as a saint, though some have thought he deserved to be. But his imagination and compassion were equal to the task of depicting the state of the Jews in his time as it was and as Jews themselves experienced it. If he had a peer in this respect, his work has not come down to us. Certainly his principal critic, Bernard, saint though he is considered, could not enter such a world of imaginative compassion for other human beings unless they were also his fellow-Christians. The fact that Abelard was capable of it proves that it was possible, and that the outlook of the times did not wholly preclude it.

Not all medieval Christians still had the opportunity of getting to know Jews and dropping the paranoia, since in some countries, including England, there were soon no Jews, because they had all been expelled. But by the same token the paranoia of English Christians could no longer be acted out, though literature shows us it did not disappear along with the Jews who were its object.

In most European countries Jews still lived, and the opportunity existed, as it had in former centuries, to find out what they were actually like. No doubt, some continued to avail themselves of this opportunity, got to know their Jewish neighbors, and discovered in them no counterpart of the paranoid image.

Fewer and fewer did so, it seems, as time went on. The legislation of the Church had begun to take effect. It aimed at separating Christians from their Jewish neighbors. Eventually, the Jews were herded into ghettos where they lived their own lives apart from the Christian people around them. The Jew had now become unknown, alien, misunderstood, and if for no other reason regarded as uncanny, magical, and dangerous, the object of superstitious fear.

THE CRUSADES: BERNARD AND THE JEWS

The new situation of the Jews had first become apparent at the time of the First Crusade in 1096. When the crusaders were setting out on their long and arduous journey to the Holy Land, to free Jerusalem and the places where Christ had walked from infidel rule, it occurred to them that they had not to go all that distance to find infidels who were displeasing to Christ. They could gain as much merit, perhaps, for the salvation of their souls, by killing the infidels in their midst, the Jewish population of their own lands.

As a result, in a number of cities in the Rhineland, the crusaders fell upon the Jewish population, offering them sometimes the alternative of baptism or death, not always even that choice. The Jews offered such armed resistance as they were able, but it was not much, and it did not for long stay the inevitable outcome.

They sought the help of the more decent churchmen, who sometimes aided them for a while but, as the pressure mounted, yielded to crusading fury. The archbishop of Mainz, who attempted to protect the Jews of his city, had to flee for his own life. In that city alone more than one thousand Jews lost their lives, either at the hands of the crusaders or at their own.

In the end, they resorted to an ancient means of preserving their faith at the cost of their lives. They slew first their wives and children and then themselves, in an act of *kiddush ha-Shem*, a hallowing of the divine name in voluntary martyrdom, rather than submitting to baptism or a more atrocious death at the hands of the crusading mob.

The horrors of those days lived on in Jewish literature, as did the glorious memory of the martyrs who chose to die rather than profane the name of God by apostasy to a faith that by now appeared to them idolatrous as well as brutal.[4] About ten thousand Jews in all are said to have lost their lives at this time, either by massacre or voluntary martyrdom.

When the crusaders reached Jerusalem, they took a further opportunity to revenge themselves on the infidels, including those they thought of as the killers of Christ. Under their leader, Godfrey of Bouillon, they spent the first week after the capture of Jerusalem disposing of the inhabitants of the city.

Godfrey wrote to the pope, "If you want to know what has been done with the enemy found in Jerusalem, learn that in the Porch and in the Temple of Solomon, our people had the vile blood of the Saracens up to the knees of their horses."[5] As for the Jews of the city, they were shut up in a synagogue and burned alive. The crusaders then went to worship in the Church of the Holy Sepulchre and give thanks for God's blessing upon their arms. The horrors recurred at the time of the second Crusade, in 1146. This time, it was a monk of Clairvaux, Ralph or Rudolph by name, who first drew the attention of the crusaders to the engaging possibility of killing the infidel at home. He told the soldiers it was their duty first to kill the Jews, before proceeding east against the Saracens. Ralph's preaching was responsible for massacres at Cologne and several other German cities.

Ralph's abbot in his monastery of Clairvaux was no less a person than St. Bernard, one of the most venerated of medieval saints, highly regarded for his devotional writings, expressing his mystical love of Christ. Because he is a saint, held in high honor by Catholics and others, it is important to look especially closely at his attitude toward the Jews, as revealed in these incidents. We can expect that we will learn what Catholics at their best thought of Jews.

Bernard was the official preacher of the Crusade, commissioned to the role by the pope himself. In his capacity as abbot, he was also theoretically responsible for the actions of his own monks, under a vow of obedience to him, as Ralph was. Bernard disavowed personal responsibility for Ralph's actions, claiming that he had been absent from his monastery without leave. However, as Malcolm Hay points out, a monk does not leave his monastery without the permission, or at least the knowledge, of his abbot.[6] Bernard could hardly escape all responsibility by such disclaimers.

Nevertheless, he is to be believed when he denies emphatically that he had given Ralph authority to preach a Crusade against the Jews. He also did not omit to condemn his preaching of murder. However, the reasons he gave for doing so, in a letter to the archbishop of Mainz, seem strangely inadequate today.

The letter contains no outright condemnation of Ralph's actions on ethical grounds. Probably the archbishop of Mainz had complained about Ralph's infringement on his own ecclesiastical jurisdiction, and this was the occasion of Bernard's reply. Nevertheless, that does not wholly account for Bernard's disproportionate emphasis on ecclesiastical over moral offenses.

First and it seems foremost, Bernard censures Ralph for leaving his monastery and preaching, instead of remaining in his monastic calling. Further on in the letter, he lists his faults in chronological order, so that it is difficult to be sure of their relative importance in Bernard's mind. "I find three things most reprehensible in him: unauthorized preaching, contempt for episcopal authority, and incitation to murder."[7]

Even if Bernard did think the last of the three the most serious, the mere fact of juxtaposition in such a list trivializes the real offense. The rest of the letter is scathing enough in what it says about Ralph; but his offense is represented as ambition, the fault of a proud individual with tendencies to heresy, rather than murder by proxy.

Bernard himself, when he preached the Crusade, had already told people it was meritorious to kill the infidel. Ralph seems to have drawn the not unnatural conclusion that it was no less meritorious if the infidel was Jewish instead of Saracen, and rather more easily accessible.

From Bernard's point of view, the conclusion was certainly unwarranted, even perhaps heretical. But what was wrong with it, in his eyes, was not that it was simply ethically impermissible to call for the murder of Jews; the issue for him was that it broke with the Church's traditional view that the Jews (alone among infidels) must be preserved until the return of Christ, as a witness to their own crimes.

Nevertheless, whatever his reasons, there is no doubt that Bernard was strongly opposed to the killing of Jews, and he did what he could to stop it. The letter Bernard wrote to the archbishop of Mainz about the matter initially having had little effect in stopping the slaughter, Bernard determined to visit the Rhineland himself. In spite of hostile demonstrations from the mob, he did succeed in quelling their fury, saving the lives of many Jews. For this the Jewish communities held him in gratitude for a long time afterward. A sixteenth-century Jewish writer said of him, "If the mercy of God had not sent that priest, not a single Jew would have escaped with his life."[8]

The killings continued, though on a smaller scale, not only in Germany but even in France, not far from Bernard's own monastery. Bernard called Ralph to his monastery and reprimanded him, though still without, so far as we know, attempting to punish him for incitement to murder.

Bernard also wrote an encyclical letter to the bishops of the Rhineland and Bavaria, making it clear to them that it was their duty to put an end to such actions. This letter too is curiously restrained in its terms, perhaps because it had to serve more than one purpose. It was also sent to the people of England. The letter does not refer specifically to the killings in the Rhineland. When he writes about the killings of Jews, Bernard again refers primarily to excess of zeal, not to the wickedness of the act itself. Here too, his main concern seems to be to uphold a traditional doctrine: the Jews must be preserved as witnesses to their crimes.

Once again we meet with the spectacle of a highly venerated saint who seems to have been unable to see Jews as fellow human beings. Bernard could see them only as role-players in a Christian theological drama. According to historians of spirituality, Bernard was a mystic of the first rank. His case, like that of others we have met with, and yet others still to be considered, raises questions about what we mean by spirituality and sanctity. Should it not mean something more than extreme devoutness and attachment to orthodox doctrine and include the capacity to value all human beings as created in the image of God, whatever their religious affiliation?

We cannot doubt that Bernard was a good man, according to his lights. But these lights did not shine as brightly on the Jews as we would like to think today. He would protect the Jews from slaughter, but not because he cared for them as human beings; his concern was for Christian orthodoxy. Leaving aside the unique personality of an Abelard, this was the best that medieval Jews could hope for from their Catholic neighbors.

JEWS AS LENDERS

In the period after the First Crusade, the economic and social condition of the Jews in Europe changed. Increasingly, they were denied all occupations but banking, though this condition never seems to have become absolute. The Jews became the agents of the princes. The princes used the freedom of their Jewish subjects under their own law to make interest bearing loans to non-Jews to enrich themselves, at the expense both of their own subjects and of the Jews.

The Jews made the loans, but the princes took a heavy cut of the proceeds. Thus, the Jews became hated for actions that were really the responsibility of others. The Jews lost their freedom and became serfs of the princes, becoming legally their property, without rights over against their princely owners.

Previously, Jews had made a livelihood in a variety of occupations, both in the West and in the Byzantine Empire, as craftsmen and traders, as well as in international commerce, the role for which they had been best known in the period up to the First Crusade. As Christian commercial activity expanded, with the growth of the guild system, Jews were increasingly excluded from commerce as well as other activities. Commerce, including international trade, became a Christian monopoly. Jews could not join the various guilds that operated the trade because such guilds were united by Christian rites and oaths.

At the same time, the European economy increasingly demanded supplies of capital for its functioning; these were then hard to come by. Much precious metal had been withdrawn from circulation and converted into ecclesiastical and state regalia. The Italian city-states developed a flourishing international trade with the Muslim countries in the period after the First Crusade, eliminating Jewish competition, while at the same time tying up European money supply in financing their ventures. Many Jews retained supplies of capital from their former successes in international trade. In their new and straitened circumstances there was not much they could do with it except lend it to those who needed to use it.

The Catholic church in the Middle Ages read the Old Testament as absolutely forbidding usury. The philosophers and theologians also shared the opinion of the Greek philosophers that the growth of money through interest was unnatural. The Church thus found itself in constant tension with the spontaneous development of the economy from an agricultural to a mercantile and early capitalist stage. Capital was needed, and it was impossible to expect people who had it to regard it otherwise than as a commodity. Those who possessed it could hardly be expected to give it away, except to family or friends; its use had to be charged for like any other commodity.

The Church constantly attempted to forbid the lending of money at interest. Ways around the prohibition were constantly found and the needed financing supplied, to mutual benefit. In the end, the Church gave up the unequal struggle and came to terms with the changing economy. In modern times, of course, the churches have usually been strong supporters of the capitalist system and opposed to the socialist theory, which shares the medieval view that the growth of money through interest is unnatural.

The Jews read their own Scriptures differently, through the tradition of the oral law, now codified in the Talmud and responsa. They understood the Torah to mean that interest must not be charged to fellow Jews, who were to be treated as family.[9] However, there was no objection to charging interest on loans to non-Jews. Gradually, the Jewish view also changed, under the pressure of economic reality, and it became clear to many Jewish ethical theorists by the close of the Middle Ages that consumer loans were a matter of mutual benefit and that fellow Jews should not be excluded from these benefits.

With the takeover of the commercial field by Christian merchants, the Jews could no longer make commercial loans from their capital supply. The remaining field of economic activity open to them was the making of consumer loans, for which there was a considerable demand. By modern standards, interest rates were extremely high. Frequently, creditors could not keep up payments of both principal and interest. The interest defaulted on was added to the principal, so that loans had to be repaid by compound interest.

Few borrowers had good enough credit with the Jewish bankers that their loans could be obtained without security. In most cases, some property had to be offered as collateral and its value negotiated with the lender. As a result of defaults, the Jewish bankers came into possession of a substantial quantity of secondhand goods that they could sell at a profit.

There were good reasons for these developments, other than the supposed usuriousness of the lenders. Capital was in very short supply, driving the price up. The risk was very high, especially for Jewish lenders, who were exceedingly vulnerable to default because of their weak social and legal position. Nevertheless, contemporary authorities were in agreement that when Christian bankers did engage in the business of making loans, they charged higher interest rates and were less humane in enforcement than their Jewish counterparts.

Eventually, Italian and German bankers became strong competitors of the Jews, and without driving them out of business altogether, they brought their monopoly to an end. In due course, the making of loans became far more characteristically an Italian than a Jewish activity. Nevertheless, present-day Italians do not have to contend with a reputation for usuriousness.

It is interesting to discover the kind of purpose for which Jews did make consumer loans. A valuable source of this knowledge is the list of loans and their purposes made by an English Jew known as Aaron of Lincoln, who lived in the second half of the twelfth century. He died in 1185, and at that time the outstanding loans amounted to three-quarters of the annual income of the English exchequer, or £15,000 in the currency of the time. He had made loans to borrowers in twenty-five counties, including two cathedrals and nine monasteries, for building purposes. It is intriguing to reflect, therefore, that some of the most notable church buildings of medieval England may have been financed in part by Jewish capital and not simply by the collective efforts of the English people, as is commonly supposed.[10]

SERFS OF THE ROYAL CHAMBER

During the period that Jewish activity in the making of consumer loans was developing, the social situation of the Jews was changing. For legal purposes, they became essentially the property of the princes they served as financial agents. During the twelfth century, the theological concept of Jewish servitude gained ground, and it was increasingly reflected in secular legislation. The activities of Jews had so far been regulated by charters, which both declared the royal interest in the banking carried on by the Jews and afforded the Jews some measure of protection. Now a new concept arose, whereby the Jews, being condemned for their crimes to perpetual servitude, came under royal and imperial jurisdiction as "serfs of the Royal (or Imperial) chamber."

As in the case of the preceding charters, these measures were not wholly unwelcome to Jews since they gained from them a status that could be legally enforced, thus acquiring some protection where none would otherwise have existed. They were seldom treated literally as slaves or serfs. They remained at liberty, and they were free to carry on their economic activity under royal or imperial protection. However, they were subject to confiscatory taxation, for which there was no redress. When they died, the kings considered themselves free to take possession of Jewish estates, regarding themselves as the heirs, since the Jews were their property. It became a proverbial saying that the Jews were the sponges of Europe, soaking up Christian wealth, only in order themselves to be squeezed dry by the princes.[11]

Documents from the period show rulers referring to "my Jew" and requiring his return from elsewhere. On eighteen occasions between 1198 and 1231 documents show rulers of principalities and duchies promising to return their respective Jews. A royal order, countersigned by "Jew-owning" princes and dukes, put it in the following way: "Nobody whatsoever may keep the Jew of another lord; and wheresoever a man shall find his Jew, he shall be entitled to seize him by right, as being his slave and property."[12]

In Germany, the Emperor Frederick I employed the concept of imperial ownership in laying down the rights of the Jews of Regensburg in a document of 1182. Stating that the Jews belonged to the Imperial Chamber, he announced his concern for their welfare and intention to protect them. Frederick II made use of the expression "serfs of our Chamber"[13] first in Italy and then over the rest of the Holy Roman Empire.

Frederick was engaged in a major power struggle with the Church, and the Jews were a factor in this struggle. Against ecclesiastical claims to jurisdiction over the Jews, formulated by Pope Innocent III, he maintained that "according to the accepted law, the Jews are directly subject to us, both in the Empire and also in our Kingdom." In a charter of the city of Vienna, issued in 1237, he stated that it was on account of the "intolerable sin" of the Jews that he himself as the heir of the Roman Emperors had become their lord, since "Imperial authority imposed everlasting servitude on these Jews from ancient times as punishment for the sin" of Christ-killing.[14]

The image of the Jew as Cain, the murderer of his brother, justified both the claim of the Church to exercise jurisdiction over all Jews throughout Christendom and also the delegation of this authority to the secular rulers.[15] Pope Innocent III declared in 1205, "God is not displeased but rather finds it acceptable that the Jewish Dispersion shall live and serve under Catholic kings and Christian princes." Nevertheless, this jurisdiction could also be employed by the Church to protect Jews from application of one side only of its own two-sided theology, as in the famous Constitution on the Jews, reissued by the same pope in 1199. Although the Constitution contains opprobrious language, it does provide for the protection of Jews in a Christian society, and it could be appealed to when abuses occurred.[16]

Whatever the theory, the Christian princes used the Jews for their own ends. They could allow the Jews to expand their banking businesses when it suited them, and they could take as big a cut of their profits from the enterprise as they chose. If the Jews were to make a living, they had to take account of such confiscatory taxation in setting their own interest rates, which were thus forced up. The result was that the Jews were hated even more than creditors usually are, though they were not responsible for the level of interest they were forced to charge.

CREDITORS MASSACRED

However, all these developments did lead to the medieval image of the Jew as a greedy and oppressive moneylender, an image that survives to this day. Circumstances had compelled the Jews in the medieval world to adopt the profession of banker, as a service to the rest of the world and at that time only Jews could perform. These circumstances are responsible for the unfortunate and undeserved reputation for exceptional financial greed and corresponding expertise that has clung to Jews into modern times.

The hatred of the Jews that arose in this way was sometimes acted out in violence. In the English city of York, on Shabbat Ha-Gadol, just before Passover, in the year 1190, a violent onslaught on the Jews of the city took place. It seems to have been inspired in part by the attacks in France in 1171 on Jews suspected of ritual murder and by riots in other English cities earlier in the same season of Lent. The attack was led by their creditors, as the contemporary chronicler, William of Newburgh, allows us to discover.

The Jewish community in York was a wealthy one, and its creditors included the local nobles. The status of the community as belonging to the King's Jews failed in this case to protect them. In any event, the King, Richard I, was overseas on one of his numerous military adventures when the attack came. The Jews attempted to defend themselves, their wives, and their children by shutting themselves up in the castle of the city. Realizing that defense was proving vain, many committed corporate suicide after the example of the Rhineland martyrs. Some who had sought to save their lives by the promise of conversion were nonetheless murdered.

William of Newburgh recorded the fact that the leaders of the plan to massacre the Jews–he calls it "a daring plan"–were some of the nobles who were heavily in debt to the Jewish bankers. We also learn that after the massacre the documents recording the debts to the Jews who had perished, known as *starrs*, were destroyed. William evinces no sympathy for the Jews, though he is shocked at the bloodshed. The plan, daring or not, certainly had the advantage of simplicity: the most effective way to liquidate a debt is to liquidate the creditor. An inquiry failed to result in the punishment of those who had perpetrated the massacre.[17]

Not only did the Jews suffer physically at the hands of those who disliked them because they themselves owed them money but the Church also increasingly attempted to prevent their carrying on of this business, essentially the only one now left to them. The Church could not directly prevent Jews from lending money to Christians, since they were not under ecclesiastical jurisdiction. The Jews themselves acknowledged no legal or moral validity in the Church's prohibition of usury, since they were guided by their own traditional understanding of the Torah.

Since it had no legal or moral leverage on Jews themselves, the Church could only resort to permitting Christian debtors to default on the interest or the principal of the loan. This action had the effect of transferring large amounts of Jewish capital to Christian hands. Several times the Church declared a moratorium on the repayment of debts to Jewish creditors for those taking part in the Crusades. Bernard was among those who did so, in connection with his preaching of the Second Crusade. This financial inducement considerably assisted his recruiting drive, though it unjustly impoverished the Jews.[18]

Ben Sasson comments, "As long as the political, economic and social organization of Christian society was based exclusively on Christian cohesiveness, there was no hope of abolishing Jewish usury without completely undermining the existence of the Jews." The other side of the situation was that the same Christian cohesiveness had made it virtually impossible for Jews to earn their living other than through banking, though this situation did not prevail absolutely in all areas of Europe. In Castile, usury was not even the main livelihood of the Jews.[19]

THE BLOOD LIBEL

There was at least a semblance of basis for the charge of usuriousness, since Jews actually did engage in the business of making loans at interest. There was not even that much color for the other charges that began to be made in the Middle Ages and led to the death of large numbers of wholly innocent Jews. The blood libel, as Jews call it, first made its appearance in the middle of the twelfth century. This is the accusation that Jews ritually murder a Christian child at the season of Passover and mingle the child's blood with the unleavened bread they eat at that time.

The first recorded case of the accusation occurred in the year 1144 at Norwich in eastern England. The body of a twelve-year old child called William was found, and the Jews were accused of murdering him. He had engaged in business dealings with the Jews as a skinner and was well known to them. No doubt suspicion arose for the simple reason that they treated him in a friendly manner, and it was assumed this must have some hidden purpose.

The Jews were believed by many of the locals to have kidnapped him and kept him for a few days until the actual day of Passover. On that day, according to the accusation, under the supervision of the head of the synagogue, they bound and gagged the child, tortured him, stabbed his head with numerous thorns, fastened him to a cross (without using nails since this would have led to the discovery of the perpetrators of the outrage), and finally killed him with a stab in the side. All this was supposed to be a horrible mimicry of the events of Christ's passion.

The information confirming these fantasies in the mind of the local Christians came from a Jewish convert to Christianity, now a monk, Theobald by name. He told a bizarre story of how the Jews of Europe, being obliged by their law to do so, and with the aim of avenging themselves on Christ, on whose account their exile had arisen, selected a community each year to perform the sacrifice of a Christian child at Passover. The choice of city was supposed to be made at a grand gathering of Jewish leaders at Narbonne in southern France, where there was indeed a flourishing Jewish community.

Theobald claimed to have been present at Cambridge when, the lot having fallen on Norwich, all the synagogues of England by letter or personal representative gave their consent to the deed. He claimed to have been fully aware of what was done. Later, however, he heard of the miracles that had come about through the intercession of the martyred child, became afraid, and forsook Judaism for Christianity.[20]

Not for the last time, a Jewish convert to Christianity was willing to malign and traduce his former coreligionists in order to gain credit with his new associates. The Christian population knew virtually nothing about Jews by this time, and their fantasies were based on Christian models. They were only too ready to believe a lying convert who told them what they wanted and expected to hear.

A popular cult of the child martyr, soon to be known as St. William of Norwich, speedily grew up and miracles began to occur through his intercession as the medieval account mentioned. Pilgrimages to his tomb were frequent and doubtless profitable for the citizens of Norwich.

Another such case was that of Hugh of Lincoln, who was found dead in 1255. The Jews of the city were accused of crucifying him, and after taking him down from the cross, removing his intestines, no doubt for magical purposes. The story turns up in Chaucer's *Canterbury Tales*, completed in 1387, when there had been no Jews in England for almost a century. He gives the story to the Prioress, who is not represented as an attractive character; no doubt, her morbid dwelling on the horror story is not meant to be to her credit. Nevertheless, there is no reason to suppose that Chaucer himself disbelieved it.

Marcus also reproduces a contemporary account, in this case Jewish, of an incident at Blois, in France, in 1171, in which similar accusations were made against the local Jews after a boy's body was found in the river. A Jew selected as the principal accused failed an ordeal by water. A number of the Jews were imprisoned. They attempted to ransom themselves with money and the cancellation of debts owed to them, but in vain. Thirty-one of them were put to death, some by the sword, some by burning. Those who were burned died bravely as martyrs.[21]

Not everyone took much notice of the accusation against the Jews of Norwich, but once the libel had been started it seemed to acquire a life of its own. Toward the end of the century it reappeared in various English cities, though the Jews were not in all cases punished. There are 150 recorded cases of the charge of ritual murder, and many led to massacres of the Jews of the place.

In Germany, the problem created by the persecution of the Jews on this ground became so serious, since so many Jews had lost their lives, that the Emperor Frederick II decided to conduct an inquiry into the truth of the charges. He first asked a number of leading churchmen whether they were well-founded, but he received inconclusive answers. He then convened a conference of converts from Judaism, who showed conclusively that Jews do not harm children and have no use for Christian blood. In any event, Jewish teaching, as they informed him, inculcates abhorrence of the ingestion of blood. The emperor issued a Golden Bull, forbidding the accusation.[22]

Pope Innocent IV also issued several bulls to the same effect. One issued in 1247 stated: "They [the Jews] are falsely accused that in the same solemnity [Passover] they receive communion with the heart of a murdered child. This, it is believed, is required by their Law, although it is clearly contrary to it. No matter where a dead body is discovered, their persecutors wickedly cast it against them."[23]

Other popes, including Gregory X, Martin V, Paul III, and Nicholas V, also vindicated the Jews from the charge of ritual murder, but this did not stop it from being widely believed. The accusation continued to be made into the twentieth century, and it is even showing signs of revival today.

One of the last reported cases occurred in Czarist Russia in the first decade of the present century, when a Jew called Mendel Beilis was accused of the ritual murder of a Christian boy. He would doubtless have been convicted and executed but for an international outcry.

The story, altered in many of its details, was the basis of a remarkable novel by Bernard Malamud called *The Fixer,* and of a film of the same name, starring Alan

Bates. As noted earlier, the calumny could still be used as a pretext for killing Jews in post-Holocaust Poland. The same libel is being revived in our own day by the enemies of Israel.[24] It has also resurfaced very recently in Catholic Italy, in the revival (or hitherto unnoted continuation) of a medieval cult of a child martyr, San Domenichino de Val, supposedly murdered by the Jews for ritual purposes in the year 1250 in Saragossa, Spain.[25]

So many Jews were being accused of ritual murder in eighteenth-century Poland that Cardinal Ganganelli (afterward to be Pope Clement XIV) made a careful investigation of the whole matter. He concluded that with two exceptions, the incidents at Rinn and Trent, the stories were without foundation. More modern and critical scholars have concluded that his cautious approval of even these two cases was largely motivated by the Church's sanction for the cultus of the children in question as martyrs. In the judgment of more recent scholars, there is not a single case of ritual murder that stands up to critical investigation.

The accusations could never have been made by anyone who knew anything actual Jews or about Judaism. As even the more honest medieval authorities were ready to admit, Jews are forbidden by the Torah to consume blood in any form. The laws of ritual slaughtering require that all the blood be drained out of the animal, and that it then be salted and washed to absorb whatever remains. Even the tiny speck of blood in a fertilized egg renders that egg forbidden to the observant Jew. In the Middle Ages, almost all Jews were observant.

Apart from the Torah itself, Jews would have been restrained from harming children by their traditional love of them. Children represent life, the highest value in Judaism. The Jew who might have been guilty of these charges was not the real Jew but a fantasy in the sick imagination of the medieval Christian.

Catholic scholars have more recently attempted to point out that the Church's approval of the cult of such imaginary child martyrs does not guarantee the authenticity of their legends, and that it is the piety of the faithful, not the story, which is being approved. However, there can be no question that the approved cultus, with its apparatus of authenticated miracles and annual pilgrimages, did much to fasten the legends in the popular Christian mind and to contribute to the obloquy in which the Jews were held. Flannery's comment is apt. "The ritual murder calumny stands in the judgment of history as the most monstrous instrument of anti-Jewish persecution in the Middle Ages."[26]

CHARGES OF DESECRATION OF THE HOST

A little later, after the definition of the dogma of transubstantiation by the Fourth Lateran Council in 1215, a new libel surfaced, known as host desecration. According to this calumny, the Jews obtained a consecrated host from the mass, with the assistance of a Christian who retained it from the administration of communion, took it to their synagogue or homes and subjected it to every indignity, including trampling on it and sticking pins into it. Their object was supposed to be revenge on

Christ, symbolically repeating their original crime of crucifying him. In many cases, it was believed, the victim responded in a miraculous way by bleeding, bringing about the conversion to Christ of a number of his tormentors. The accusation was made for the first time at Belitz, near Berlin; all the Jews of the town were burned. One hundred instances of the charge have been recorded, in many cases leading to massacres.

This accusation is particularly bizarre, because it assumes that Jews themselves actually believe not only the doctrine of transubstantiation but also a particularly materialistic, and strictly speaking heretical, popular version of it. Of course, no Jew believes such a doctrine in any form. To a Jew, the host is simply a piece of bread; he could not suppose that doing anything whatever to it could have any effect on Christ, even if he wished to harm him. This is neither the first nor the last instance of the Christian supposition that Jews actually believe Christian doctrines and are therefore not sinning in ignorance.

The classic case is the original myth of Christ-killing, from which these medieval libels appear to be more or less remotely derived. The Church not only believed that the Jews crucified Christ but also that they knew quite well whom they were crucifying, and thus were fully guilty of deicide.

By the high point of the Middle Ages, the Jews were being accused, by a Christian population that believed its own accusations, of indescribable crimes, bloodlust, insatiable hatred of Christ, and infanticidal acts, while at the same time they were supposed to believe in Christian dogmas.

Flannery comments that these charges "indicate[s] the course the Jewish image was taking. Unbeliever and usurer; now ritual murderer. Gradually stripped of his human features, the Jew assumes a satanic guise."[27]

THE JEWS AND THE DEVIL

The term *satanic* is well chosen. Joshua Trachtenberg has shown with precision and copious documentation that this is exactly how the Jews were imagined in the Middle Ages.[28] The identification of the Jew with the devil–and of the devil with the Jew–is abundantly clear, not only from literary sources but also from engravings and the mystery plays and passion plays. Some of the latter have survived in modern times and are still performed. The most famous of them is the Oberammergau play, which retains antisemitic elements that continue to trouble both Jews and Christians of goodwill but apparently not the villagers of Oberammergau.

In the Christian myth, the Jews figure as the enemies of Christ and therefore of God. Given that, it was perhaps a natural step to equate them with the ultimate and cosmic enemy, the one who sought to destroy all God's work in creation and redemption alike.

Today, belief in the devil has faded from the Christian consciousness, except in very conservative groups. It is not easy to imagine how real he was to the medieval mind. He was at least as real as God and perhaps more so. To medieval man, the devil was a very present and terrifying reality, awesome in power and cunning, obscene in appearance and behavior and constantly seeking the damnation of every Christian. In the late-night service of Compline, recited every night by the monks and others who were obliged to say the office, the psalm (91) speaks of the adversary "going about, seeking whom he may devour." The terror was real and very close.

There was no escaping him by good living, for the higher up the ladder you climbed in your austerities and holiness, the more certainly he would be ready to attack and deceive you, bringing about your downfall. If he succeeded, he would be your tormentor for all eternity in the fires of hell.

Nor was the devil a mere theory for medieval man. Man experienced him, knew his cunning temptations, smelled his sulphurous smell, and sometimes even saw him, horns, tail, and all. Everyone knew what he looked like. He appeared in many forms of Christian art, high and low. As Trachtenberg shows us, he regularly appeared with features supposedly Jewish and even wearing the badge of shame, at this stage commonly a yellow circle.

The Jew showed his association with the devil in part by the *foetor judaicus*, the Jewish stink, the sulphurous smell of the devil himself. Since Jews would use any means, including Christian blood, to rid themselves of the stink that revealed their origin as the children of their father the devil, as the Fourth Gospel calls them, if they did not smell of the devil it did not prove they had no such smell. It only proved their cunning. The less they smelled, the more certain it was that they had worked hard to rid themselves of a stink none the less innate.

Modern historians who are shocked, and rightly so, by the blood libel and the charge of desecration of the host sometimes fail to see that the identification of the Jew with the devil is something worse still. Since the devil is not vivid to them, they forget that he was to the medieval mind. Once the Jew has been identified with the devil, nothing is too bad for him. With such an enemy, there can be no compromise. Thus, it is important to remember that this identification, while widespread at the popular level, did not receive official sanction, and the ancient doctrine that the Jews must be preserved as a witness to their crimes held firm. Only when that had gone would the way be clear for genocide. Nevertheless, as the libels gained an increasing grip on the popular mind, the Church's doctrinal defense against the destructive power of the forces of hate became weaker, almost too weak to stem the tide.

THE FOURTH LATERAN COUNCIL

The Council of 1215 was the fourth in a series of church councils organized by the popes and held at the Lateran church in Rome. These were the first exclusively Latin councils, meetings of bishops under the presidency of the pope, to be claimed as ecumenical (i.e., councils representing the whole Church and binding upon it).

Innocent III, a particularly energetic church politician, fought a strenuous and ultimately losing battle with the empire for supremacy. The calling of the Fourth Lateran Council was an instrument in this aggressive papal policy. Part of its purpose was to symbolize the authority of the supreme pontiff in all matters. It was in conformity with this claim to universal authority that the council enacted legislation concerning the Jews.

The canons of the council dealing with the Jews essentially reenacted the old imperial legislation on the status of the Jews, considered in the previous chapter, thus asserting the right of the Church to act in the same capacity as the empire in legislating for its Jewish citizens. By reenacting the old legislation on the Jews, with additions, the council affirmed the Church's own claim to be the legitimate successor of the empire, at a time when a rival claim was being made by the Holy Roman Emperor, Frederick.

The Jews were, in part, symbols in a power struggle between church and state. At the same time, there were actual differences of opinion between the two parties on how the Jews should be treated. As was normally the case, the princes, led by Frederick, were inclined to a more positive view of their social status in a Christian realm because of the services they could render. The Church, on the other hand, wished to reaffirm the social consequences of the old theology of supersession.

We have already discussed the disastrous consequences for the Jews of the definition by the Council of the dogma of transubstantiation. Other canons dealt with them directly, assuming authority over their actions. Innocent had already reenacted the Constitution on the Jews, which afforded some protection, though no inherent rights, in spite of insulting language.

The council enacted five canons dealing with the Jews.[29] The first of these attempted to control Jewish interest rates by threatening a social and economic boycott. Jews were to repay interest considered excessive by the Church, and Christians were compelled to join an eventual boycott under threat of excommunication.

The princes, in fact the moving force behind Jewish banking enterprises, were commanded not to be hostile toward Christians as a result of these measures but to restrain their Jewish subjects "from so great an oppression." Without the cooperation of the princes, which was unlikely to be forthcoming, the Church could do little about Jewish interest rates. Jews were also to be compelled to pay tithes to the Church on any Christian property that came into their possession as a result of Christians defaulting on loans, "so that the church be preserved against loss."

A second canon carried with it far more serious consequences for the Jews. This second canon required Jews (and Saracens), both male and female, to wear a distinctive dress. The purpose of the canon was to prevent sexual relations arising between Christians and Jews.

Its enactment indicates both that Jews and Christians were not distinguished at this time by either speech or dress, and also that such relations did in fact spring up. Clearly, the church teaching that inculcated distrust and even hatred of Jews did not always prevent friendships from occurring; once the barrier of conditioned distrust was broken down, there was naturally no mutual aversion, and normal sexual attraction could arise between Jew and Christian, with consequences the Church found distasteful.

The canon, which borrowed from an earlier Islamic ruling, did not lay down what form the distinctive dress of Jews should take. However, as a consequence of its enactment, local jurisdictions in many places required Jews to wear "the badge of shame." At this period this was not the yellow Star of David the Nazis would require when they reenacted the medieval legislation, but a yellow circle. The yellow was supposed to stand for the Jewish love of gold. In many places Jews were also required to wear a yellow conical hat. This measure was extremely successful in imposing social isolation on the Jews of Europe, contributing markedly to the aversion in which they were generally held. Abba Eban describes the badge as "a personal ghetto in which every Jew had to live."[30]

The canon also forbade Jews to go out in public during the three days before Easter and especially on Good Friday. The canon explains that some of them on those days "do not blush to go forth better dressed and are not afraid to mock the Christians who maintain the memory of the most holy Passion by wearing signs of mourning." All this really indicates is that Jews wore their normal Sabbath finery on the Saturday that fell within these three days, and that Christians chose to interpret this as an insult and a mockery of themselves and their mourning for the death of Christ. It is unlikely that Jews had any such motive in mind.

A third canon reenacted the old legislation, going back as far as the Theodosian Code, and in the West to the Third Council of Toledo of 589, prohibiting Jews from holding any public office that would place them in a position of superiority over Christians. It would eventually be revived by the Nazis.

Another canon, pointing forward to the troubles of the Jews in Spain during the period following the Reconquista, deals with the tendency of Jewish converts to Christianity to retain Jewish rites and customs. Jewish converts usually did attempt to do so, especially if their conversion had occurred under pressure or duress, always arousing the suspicion of the Church. The canon requires "a healthy compulsion" to be exercised against such tendencies, and ironically (or sarcastically) quotes the provision in the Torah against wearing a garment of mixed wool and linen as a justification for prohibiting such religious mixtures.

A further canon required Jewish lenders to remit all interest on loans to those who had joined the Crusades; any such interest already received had to be paid back. Even on the principal itself, the secular power was instructed to declare a moratorium on payments for anyone who alleged difficulty in meeting them. Jewish lenders had to deduct from the principal of the loan the income received from mortgaged property during the absence of the debtor on the Crusade.

Abba Eban sums up the consequences for the Jews of the Fourth Lateran Council:

> To the Lateran Council must be laid the blame for the anti-Semitic epidemics that swept Europe in the thirteenth and fourteenth centuries–outbursts predicated on allegations which the higher clergy knew to be false, but for which they had already paved the way. Once these outbursts had been set in motion, nothing the Pope or the bishops might say could impede their awful consequence. Indeed, the princes of the Church frequently remained silent, and by so doing lent an air of complicity to the

unrestrained fury of the mob. Papal bulls decrying the slaughter of the Jews were of no avail; under torture, Jews would make detailed confessions to crimes they had never committed, and thereby justify the behaviour of their persecutors. Besides, upon the death of the "culprit," all debts and mortgages to him were automatically cancelled; the spoils were divided among his Christian accusers.[31]

THE TRIAL OF THE TALMUD

Christians had long believed that the Talmud was the main obstacle to Jews believing in Christianity. In due course, they also came to imagine that it contained various insults to Christ and his mother, thus constituting an attack on the sanctity of the Christian faith. Presumably (in so far as it had any basis at all) the idea arose from the occasional references in Talmudic literature to Jesus as ben Pantera. The present text does not contain insults to Christianity. However, it was inevitable that in due course, as Christian power increased, the Talmud would become a target.

The trial and burning of the Talmud at this period was instigated by a Jewish convert to Christianity, Nicholas Donin, who informed Pope Gregory IX that it contained blasphemies. In 1239, the latter ordered the bishops and secular rulers of France, England, Spain, and Portugal to seize all Jewish books and examine them. In most cases they dragged their feet, but the pious King Louis IX of France took energetic action.

In 1240, King Louis IX caused a disputation to be held in Paris, in which four prominent French rabbis were compelled to meet with Donin. The disputation actually took the form of a trial of the Talmud. The Jewish representatives were permitted only to defend themselves, not to advance positive arguments for their position.

In the same year, the Pope's order was carried out in Paris, and on March 3, 1240, Jewish books were seized and handed over to the Dominicans and Franciscans to be examined. The Talmud was condemned and twenty-four cartloads, no doubt all accessible copies, were burned. The burnings took place probably in 1242 and perhaps also in 1244, in Paris and elsewhere. The result was the end of rabbinical studies in northern France, the community that had nourished the great biblical commentator Rashi of Troyes.[32]

In 1247, however, the Jews successfully petitioned Pope Innocent IV for relief, on the ground that the Talmud was an absolute necessity for the practice of their religion. They obtained from him a ruling that burnings of the Talmud were to cease and the books returned to their owners if they contained nothing injurious to Christian faith. The pope in this case was influenced by the tradition embodied in the Constitution on the Jews, which affirmed the theological necessity of protecting the Jews from outright persecution, though it did so for Christian reasons and not because any inherent rights were conceded to Jews.[33]

Marcus prints the reluctant letter of Odo, the papal legate, who had to carry out the pope's order to return the Jewish books to their owners. Odo details the events of the previous years, giving the text of papal letters, and he argues that the books should not be returned, since they had been found to be full of errors and to have turned the hearts of the Jews away from "an understanding of the spirit, and even of the letter" of the Scriptures.

He refers to the Talmud as the source of the veil that covers the hearts of the Jewish people. It is "the chief factor which holds the Jews obstinate in their perfidy." (At this stage, perfidy probably still had its original meaning of false belief, but was rapidly acquiring its present sense.) He also denies the claim of the Jews that the Talmud is a necessity for the practice of their religion.[34]

It is not clear whether Odo had any personal acquaintance with the text of the Talmud. More probably he relied on the word of the Dominican examiners and of Donin himself. From these events stems the antisemitic fantasy of the Talmud Jew: the Talmud is an evil book and the cause of Jewish wrongdoing. Such ideas resurfaced at the end of the nineteenth century, and they have not yet wholly disappeared. Without exception, they are based on either ignorance or forgery, and they cannot survive confrontation with the text of the Talmud.[35]

THE BLACK DEATH

Early in 1348, the Black Death struck Europe, spreading with terrifying rapidity. While we know today that it was an outbreak of bubonic plague, spread by rats and fleas, medieval Europe did not possess this knowledge. It saw the plague as a terrible divine intervention, doubtless a punishment for human sin. Nevertheless, people were not content to accept divine action in humble resignation. If the plague had occurred by the will of God, human instruments might nonetheless have been involved, and if God could not be blamed, they could.

As more and more people were struck down, panic grew, and with it the need to find some way of discharging the passions of terror and rage. The explanation most favored was that the wells had been poisoned. This was not a new idea. As recently as 1320–21, when epidemics of disease had occurred, the lepers had been blamed for doing so.

This was an emergency of a greater order, and an even more uncanny instigator had to be sought. It will be no surprise that blame fell on the Jews. That spring, as deaths multiplied, Jews were attacked. At Narbonne and Carcassonne, Jews were dragged from their homes and burned to death. Others were tortured, and under duress they gave their captors what they wanted.[36]

Seeing the danger of a runaway persecution of the Jews that might far exceed the limits of the Christian doctrine of preservation in misery, the pope of the day, Clement VI, issued a bull prohibiting the killing, looting, or forced conversion of Jews without trial. This had some effect, especially in the papal states and in the Avignon area, where the pope then lived, but the panic rage against the Jews was spreading northward like a forest fire.

In September, formal trials were held in Savoy. The charges were based on material derived from forced confessions under torture, which in turn owed their nature to the fantasies of the interrogators. Jews were supposed to have taken part in an international conspiracy with its center at Toledo in Spain, from whence emanated messengers carrying poison in little leather bags. The messengers were said to have been under instructions from their rabbis to drop packets of poison in Christian wells and to coordinate their plans with their coreligionists everywhere. The accused were found guilty, and eleven of them were burned to death. The remainder had to pay a heavy tax in order to remain in Savoy.[37]

The confessions elicited in Savoy were widely distributed by letter, provoking further accusations against the Jews in Alsace, Switzerland, and Germany. A meeting of representatives of the Alsatian towns was held to decide on action. The representatives of Strassburg attempted to refute the charges, but they were heavily outvoted. In September, Clement VI again attempted to stem the tide by issuing a further bull, in which he said that Christians who blamed the Jews for the plague had been "seduced by that liar, the Devil."[38]

He pointed out that everybody, including Jews, was falling victim to the plague. It existed equally where there were no Jews and where Jews did live they were suffering from it like their neighbors. He urged the clergy to take the Jews under their protection, and he offered to do so himself at Avignon. However, this enlightened voice was hardly listened to.

In January 1349, the Jews of Basel, amounting to several hundred in number, were burned to death in a wooden house constructed for just this purpose on an island in the Rhine. The town council of Strassburg, which had attempted to prevent such outrages, was deposed by popular vote, and the new council, without waiting for the plague to reach their city, apprehended two thousand Jews and took them to the burial ground, where all who would not accept conversion were burned at the stake.[39]

Another characteristically medieval reaction to the disaster now made its appearance. If the plague was God's punishment for sin, penance was the appropriate response. There sprang up groups of flagellants, penitents who went from town to town, whipping themselves as they went with leather whips tipped with iron, until the blood flowed, in expiation for their own sins and those of the communities around them.

The flagellants soon became a substantial movement, with their own masters who imposed their own discipline upon them, which was no longer that of the Church. The groups of wandering flagellants were sometimes several hundred in number, and they would perform in the city squares to the awed attention of the population. Groups of such flagellants are vividly depicted in Ingmar Bergman's film *The Seventh Seal*.

After what we have learned about earlier Christian ascetics, it will again be no surprise that they did not confine themselves to penance and self-blame but turned upon the Jews. "In every town they entered, the flagellants rushed to the Jewish quarter, trailed by citizens howling for revenge upon 'the poisoners of the wells.' In Freiburg, Augsburg, Nürnberg, Munich, Königsberg, Regensburg, and other centers, the Jews were slaughtered with a thoroughness that seemed to seek the final solution."[40]

In March 1349, the Jewish community at Worms, four hundred strong, adopted the hallowed solution of *kiddush ha-Shem*, burning themselves to death inside their own houses. The community at Frankfurt-am-Main took the same course in July, setting fire to a large part of the town. In Cologne, the town council attempted to dissuade the mob by using the rational arguments of the Pope, but the flagellants prevailed.

Mainz had the largest Jewish community in Europe. Emboldened perhaps by their numbers, its members actually resisted their persecutors, killing two hundred of the mob. However, the enraged multitude descended upon them in full force, and seeing that resistance was in vain, that community too set fire to their homes. Six thousand are said to have perished in the flames. At Erfurt, there were no survivors of a community of three thousand. The last attacks were at Antwerp and Brussels, where entire Jewish communities perished in December of the same year.[41]

By this time, both church and state had had enough. The flagellants had gone too far and not only against the Jews. The authorities were finally ready to take action against these anarchic elements in the community. City fathers ordered the gates closed against them. Clement VI called for their dispersal and arrest. The great University of Paris denied their claim to divine inspiration. King Philip VI forbade public flagellation on pain of death, and the masters were pursued by the local rulers. The movement subsided as suddenly as it had arisen.[42]

The majority of the surviving Jews had fled to Eastern Europe, where at that time they could expect more rational treatment. Some filtered back westward, and in many places, once the plague was over, Jews were invited back to fulfill their former functions, though on worse terms than before. Even in the aftermath of the plague, Christian Europe found its Jews indispensable. But the Western European communities were never the same again, and the future of European Jewry now lay in the east.

It is sometimes said (e.g., by Abba Eban)[43] that the Jews did indeed to some extent escape the plague, and that this accounted for the suspicion that they did so by such satanic means as they had employed in setting it on the Christians. It may well be that their partial isolation from the surrounding population and their relatively higher standards of hygiene played a part. Such practices as the obligatory washing of hands before eating could not fail to keep down the spread of many infections. Moreover, as city dwellers, the Jews were less liable to rat-borne infection than were the agricultural population surrounding them. However, in the conditions of the time, even Jews could not altogether escape, and we have the contemporary witness of Clement that they suffered as their neighbors did. The suspicion that they had means of escape denied to others was without foundation.

THE FRANCISCAN ASSAULT ON THE JEWS

It is perhaps not surprising, in view of their own dedication to ascetic poverty, that the Franciscans should have paid unfavorable attention to the economic activities of the Jews. It is more surprising that saints among them should have preached against Jews with such vehement hostility and disregard for truth.

Bernardino of Siena, one of these Franciscan saints, is the author of a beautiful hymn to the Holy Spirit, known in English translation by its opening words, "Come down, O love divine." Bernardino, like a number of other Franciscans, was concerned with the economic exploitation of the poor by the moneyed classes. He devoted twenty-three sermons in Latin and some in Italian to economic problems. Although strongly opposed to usury, he did not consider that a man who had been compelled by the state to loan money at interest should be regarded as a usurer, thus supporting financial practices in vogue in many of the Italian city states.

When it came to the Jews, however, he considered that they should be exposed to the full and unconditional prohibition of usury. In their case, he employed no such careful moral reasoning, but gave full vent to religious hostility. The saint's views on love, where Jews were concerned, may be gathered from the following quotation: "In respect of abstract and general love, we are permitted to love them. However, there can be no concrete love towards them."[44]

The Franciscans themselves were to a certain extent in competition with the Jews as granters of credit, though they did not originally charge interest themselves. They promoted the establishment of Christian loan funds to assume debts owed to the Jews, known as the Monte di Pieta fund. In other places they went into direct competition with the Jewish finance houses. Eventually, in the sixteenth century, the pope determined that the Christian establishments could also charge a low rate of interest.

Another Franciscan saint, John of Capistrano, was known as "the scourge of the Jews." He led an orchestrated campaign against the Jews, employing diplomatic activity at the courts of the rulers as well as popular preaching. He also made use of the powers of the Inquisition, vested in him as a legal scholar. His influence led to various libels against the Jews and their expulsion from several communities. He obtained the cancellation of charters previously granted to Jews. Especially in the kingdom of Naples and Sicily, his influence was extremely deleterious to the Jewish communities, continuing after his death.

Eventually, he carried his campaign against the Jews outside Italy to Austria, Germany, and Poland, in conjunction with his efforts against the Hussite movement. In 1453 he took part in a ritual murder trial in Breslau, which led to the deaths by fire of several Jews and the expulsion of their whole community from the city. He claimed to have been told that the Jews were spreading a "dreadful idea" among Christians, that every man can be saved by his own faith.

His admirer and disciple, Bernardino da Feltre, was yet another Franciscan Jew-baiter. He was principally responsible for one of the most famous of the blood libels, the case of Simon of Trent. His anti-Jewish sermons in the city whipped up an already growing anti-Jewish feeling, and when a rumor spread about the disappearance of a two-year-old child named Simon, the population were ready to believe in the guilt of the Jews. The whole Jewish community of the city was arrested and tortured to obtain confessions, some of which, though in conflicting form, were naturally obtained. Some were sentenced and executed; the remainder of the community was expelled.

The pope initially refused to endorse the growing cult of the supposed victim, but in due course he yielded, and Simon was canonized as a saint in 1582. In 1965 the canonization was withdrawn; the Church admitted that a judicial error had occurred. This was the last remaining ritual murder case to be officially repudiated by the Church.[45]

THE ORIGINS OF THE CALUMNIES

Jews do not smell of sulphur. Jews do not desecrate the host. Jews do not consume Christian blood or blood of any kind. Jews as a group are no more attached to money than anyone else, perhaps less so. The accusations were and are false in every particular. Nevertheless, there is no doubt that they were believed, and some people believe them still. Why?

All the libels must be ultimately derived from the original myth that the Jews killed Christ. However, a reasonable person, such as Abelard, would view this fact, if he believed it to be such, in its context. He would understand that the Jews could not be corporately blamed; even their leaders at the time could only have acted in accordance with the laws it was their duty to administer. Nobody could reasonably conclude, from the supposed historical fact that Jewish leadership had once been instrumental in bringing about the death of Jesus, that more than a thousand years later Jews were drinking the blood of Christian children or desecrating the host.

Since the charges are so remote from any rational basis, we must look for irrational causes. Hatred of this nature and fantasies so perversely remote from the truth cannot be adequately explained by the history of ideas. A more powerful instrument is required. We need somehow to get into the mind of the medieval Christian to comprehend the passions at work there and the forces generating them.

Modern depth psychology, which explores the irrational aspects of the mind, can perhaps assist us to do so. For our purposes, its most suggestive contribution is the concept of paranoia. However, before we consider the role of paranoia, it may be important to look at other forces operating on the medieval Christian psyche that may have increased the inner tensions exploding in hatred of the Jews.

Like all other religious and ethical systems, and (as Freud reminds us) civilization itself, Christianity involves a considerable degree of restraint on the instinctual drives. Freud and the psychoanalytic tradition, following him, analyzed the mind into three main energy locations: the superego, the ego, and the id.[46] The superego can be thought of as the internalized commands of the parents. It becomes an inner voice, speaking with great authority to require social and ethical restraints. Freud did not distinguish the superego from the true conscience, but we may feel free to do so, without underrating the power of the superego to enforce from within the restraints that external society requires.

The id is the location of the instinctual drives, primarily sexuality and aggression.

These are biological drives, resembling though not identical with the instincts of animals, and oriented to the biological imperatives of survival and the continuation of the species.

Thus the mind contains both the biological imperatives of survival, shared with the animals, and the distinctively human pressures to restrain these instinctual demands. Society could not exist if the instincts were followed without restraint: Freud supposes that otherwise a man would possess every woman who attracted him and attempt to kill every male rival. The superego, as the internalized voice of society, represented originally by the parents in early childhood and later by teachers and other authority figures in society, is altogether necessary to civilization.

Between the superego and the drives, there is an unavoidable conflict. Each is pulling in opposite directions. The drives require satisfaction so that the species may survive, the superego restraint in the interests of living with others in an orderly society.

Everyone experiences these conflicts to some degree. When the superego is particularly exacting, the instinctual side of human nature reacts with anger, even rage, to the frustrations thus generated. Usually, however, the authority of the superego has been such that the legitimacy of its demands could not be consciously called in question. This is especially the case where a religious authority, standing in for God, or the internalized image of God himself, becomes the superego.

Then the demands of the internalized conscience cannot be questioned without blasphemy. All questioning, and especially all rebellious and angry reactions, will normally have to be suppressed. But since they cannot be simply disposed of by suppression, they have to go somewhere else.

They are accordingly repressed below the level of consciousness, continuing to exist and operate, but now unconsciously. Since they are still present, they can affect both thinking and conduct. The presence of such rebellious reactions may be manifested in thinking by bizarre ideas that do not fit in with consciously held views of reality, since they actually are determined by unconscious forces; and in conduct by behavior that does not correspond to the conscious ideals of the person.

In the opinion of Freud, health is normally achieved when the psyche attains a balance between the socially necessary demands of the superego for instinctual restraint and the biological needs of the instincts for satisfaction. The ego, the third energy location, has the task of achieving this balance between the opposing forces by mediating between the demands of the other two levels of the mind. It accomplishes this in part through its orientation to external reality, instead of inner fantasies, unlike the other two centers of psychic energy.

A strong ego is capable of warding off excessive demands either from the instincts or from the internalized conscience. If it is successful in its task, the inner conflicts common to us all need not surface, and no excessive stress will be consciously experienced. But a strong ego also needs reinforcement from society, and without it, it will certainly be weakened. If either the superego or the instinctual drives become too strong for the ego, stress surfaces in consciousness, and the harmony of the normal healthy personality is broken up. The result is either excessively scrupulous behavior, if the superego is too demanding, or behavior unacceptable to the conscience, if control of the instincts is lost, or even both.

NEW PRESSURES ON THE CHRISTIAN PSYCHE

There is reason to believe that during the period when the calumnies against the Jews were developing, the superego of medieval Christians was becoming more exacting than before. This was particularly true for a very influential group in the Church, the clergy, and the religious orders of monks. These were especially prominent in the development of anti-Jewish ideas, though it was often left to others to act them out.

From the eleventh century onward, a reform movement, emanating from the monasteries of Cluny and led by Pope Gregory VII, brought about a considerable tightening of discipline in the lives of the clergy and monks. This was the period when clerical celibacy was being newly enforced in the Western church. Earlier, celibacy had not been strictly required of the clergy in practice, although it was usually considered to be the ideal. In the Eastern Orthodox church, the parochial clergy have never been expected to be celibate. On the contrary, they have to be married. (However, their bishops are drawn only from the ranks of the celibate monks.) The clergy of the Western church were now expected to conform much more closely than before to the monastic model, including celibacy and a life devoted to prayer.

A second factor, affecting primarily but not exclusively the devout, was the development of devotion to Christ crucified. During the period we are considering, there was a substantial change in the Church's understanding of what Christ had done on the cross to save the world. In the period of the Church fathers, the formative period of Christian theology, the cross had usually been viewed in dramatic or mythological ways; Christ had conquered the devil on the cross, emerging victorious from the struggle with the ultimate forces of evil. This earlier view has been described in a famous and influential book by the Swedish theologian, Gustaf Aulén, called *Christus Victor.* When represented in art, this earlier theology led to the depiction of Christ as calm and victorious, without emphasis on the effects of his sufferings.

In the scholastic period, different views of the atonement arose; theologians now came to see Christ's death on the cross as a sacrifice of his own body offered by him to the Father on behalf of a sinful world. Christ was the sinless victim, suffering on behalf of the sins of humanity. According to Anselm, writing in the eleventh century, the "weight" of sin is such that the smallest sin requires the atoning value of the sacrifice of the sinless humanity of God incarnate. Such a concept necessarily induces guilt and self-hatred as well as repentance. If even a passing sexual fantasy or a hostile thought against another has brought my savior and my God to a terribly painful death, what does this say about me?

The older view was expressed primarily in the liturgy and in Christian art. The new view, besides greatly altering the way in which the crucifixion was represented in art, lent itself also to dramatic and emotional preaching and to devotional meditation. The laity in general were not given to meditation, but preaching was an important element in their lives. They were largely illiterate, they had no radio or TV, and the sermon, especially if preached with eloquence, was the most exciting event of the week and must have had a powerful emotional effect.

The passion plays, actually an offshoot of the liturgical drama itself, were a new medium for the education of the Christian masses that had grown up at this period. They dealt with the death or passion of Christ, which was depicted as vividly as possible.

Those who were supposed to have been responsible for his death were no less vividly portrayed. The Jew, the villain of the piece, was usually depicted in contemporary dress, with moneybags hanging from his belt, wearing the yellow Jewish hat, and sometimes with red hair, not uncommon among Jews in fact, and a symbol of evil to the audience.

The more strongly the emotions of the audience were engaged with the sufferings of Christ, the more they hated those who were supposed to have caused them. In a collective form, the Jewish people appeared in the character of Synagogue, portrayed as blindfolded, with broken banner, and grasping a goat's head, a symbol of Old Testament sacrifices and of Jewish stubbornness and unchastity.

During the same period, the character of Christian art itself, the other most important medium by which the beliefs of the Church were inculcated in the faithful, changed remarkably in the West. No longer was the norm in art the icon, which attempted to convey spiritual concepts through the use of nonrealistic techniques. Now Christian art became realistic and humanized, and the crucifixion was increasingly depicted in vivid detail. The development reached its culmination in the period of the Reformation and Counter-Reformation. Its end point can be seen in the famous triptychs by Matthias Grünewald in the hospital at Isenheim. Here the dying Christ on the cross is portrayed with the luminescence of a decaying corpse.

What Christian art did for the senses, meditation did for the imagination. The devout Christian in prayer and meditation increasingly concentrated on the humanity of Christ and on the details of his suffering on the cross. This was also the period during which devotion to the Precious Blood of Christ became popular in the Church. The earlier, dramatic or mythological view of Christ's victory on the cross did not lend itself to focussing attention on the sacrificial value of his blood. By the end of the Middle Ages, Christ's blood had become a central object of devotion, remaining so in modern piety, both Catholic and Evangelical. Christ's blood saves the sinner, and it even intoxicates the devotee, as in the popular prayer, the *Anima Christi*. In miracle story after miracle story, we hear of statues and crucifixes and consecrated hosts bleeding, sometimes to convince unbelieving Jews of the atoning value of the death of Christ. While we cannot show that the growth of the new devotion to the cross and to the blood of Christ directly caused such phenomena as the blood libel, we can say that they grew up more or less simultaneously. It is likely that the same psychological influences were at work in both. The imagination of the medieval Christian was certainly obsessed with blood as his forefathers' had not been. Who had shed that blood?

From the thirteenth century on, the Franciscans were pioneers of the devotion to the cross. They are usually and rightly associated with dedication to poverty. This was not unique to them, although Francis, their founder, expressed an ideal shared with others in uniquely poetic terms in his hymns to the lady Poverty. The other major order of friars, the Dominicans, also lived in voluntary poverty. The monks, in contrast to the new mendicant orders of friars, often enjoyed a much higher standard of living than the surrounding laity, although the property they possessed was not owned by any individual in particular.

Both the Dominicans and the Franciscans called for "apostolic poverty," living as Christ and his apostles had done, in dependence on the charity of the faithful and the providence of God. The Franciscan order was racked by controversies, which split it more than once, on the degree to which the ideal of poverty was to be taken literally. It may not be accidental that campaigns against the Jews in the later Middle Ages, directed specifically against their practice of usury, were so frequently led by "spiritual" Franciscans of the stricter observance.

No less important than poverty for the Franciscan ideal was the mysticism of the cross, which had also been central in Francis' own spiritual life. His meditation on the cross had been so profound that he was the first to receive the "stigmata," replicas in his own body of the five wounds of Christ, which bled continuously. Christian life was increasingly seen as one of penance for sin. The life of the penitent must aim at ever increasing identification with Christ crucified, "filling up that which is lacking of the sufferings of Christ," a quotation from Paul that became of the greatest importance for devotional theology.

The body and its instinctual needs must be put to death and the ego crucified with Christ. The reward would be resurrection with Christ, symbolically to a new spiritual life past the crucifixion of the ego in this world and in the next to reign with Christ for eternity. What the Franciscan friars practiced, they also preached to the laity. Their principal function in the Church was as itinerant preachers.

The whole devotional life of the medieval Christian was oriented to blood and death. Meditation on the inevitability of death and the vanity of life was recommended to all. Many kept a skull in their rooms to remind them of death. To the extent that a medieval Christian identified with the ascetic ideal, he or she must view life as a continuous martyrdom, a continuous killing of nature, in order that a supernatural life of grace might arise from its dead body.

Only those who have attempted to follow such an ideal can imagine the psychological stresses it induced. Moreover, it did not necessarily produce the imagined effect. All too often, instead of supernatural humility and charity, the result was, at first, the excited illusion of a spurious holiness, and later in life, iron fanaticism. Not infrequently, the resulting fanaticism was directed against the Jews.

UNCONSCIOUS RAGE AND REBELLION

If we accept in general terms the psychoanalytic account of the mind and its levels, it is not difficult to understand how such effects followed from these causes. Christ crucified became the internalized superego, or ego ideal, and the ego weakened in the absence of any social reinforcement for a nonascetic way of holiness. The instincts were allowed no legitimate gratification; even thought or imagination of sexuality or aggression was felt to be sin. Human friendship was viewed with suspicion by the devout, on the assumption–by no means illusory in these circumstances–that it could give rise to sexual attachment.

The instinctual side of human nature must, as it were, have cried out in extreme pain, "What's in all this for me?" And since the answer was nothing, the reaction of nature must have been intolerable rage. The rage must have been unbearable not only in its intensity but because of the impossibility of ever expressing it, or even allowing it into consciousness. Unlike Jews, Christians are not permitted to get angry with God. The utterly forbidden rage had to remain buried below the surface of consciousness. If it ever came close to surfacing, the result could only be insupportable guilt. For the sin against the Holy Ghost there is no forgiveness.

DISPLACING THE OBJECT

Keeping it unconscious did not make the rage go away, however, and the mind had to find some acceptable outlet for it. Rage could, with the implicit sanction of the Church, be deflected outward on to the enemies of Christ, and above all toward the Jews. This displacement outward of the forbidden wishes is paranoia. Jews did not (generally speaking) practice asceticism. They married, owned property, and some even became rich bankers. And, the medieval Christian would reflect, they had rejected Christ crucified. Indeed, did they not kill him themselves? In spite of all this, they continue to claim that they are God's chosen people and that we are not. They are doing what I long to do, but may not. And they are getting away with it.

The devout Christian was living under ascetic demands that denied the legitimacy of an ineradicable part of his own nature. He was therefore driven to self-rejection. Against such denial and rejection, the instinctual drives could only rebel. Finding no inner or outer response, the rebellion had to be directed outward against a surrogate target. The Jews were available. The more intense the guilt and self-rejection, the greater the rejection and hatred against the Jew.

Theodor Reik, in his psychoanalytical study, *Myth and Guilt: the Crime and Punishment of Mankind*, points out that the origin of guilt is not necessarily, as is often supposed, sexual transgression. He cites evidence that sexual misdemeanors in themselves excite only a moderate degree of guilt. In contrast, much more guilt is experienced when the temptation is overcome for a while, and chastity endured.[47]

The fantasy of the forbidden delights is then if anything even more vivid, and since it now cannot be gratified, aggression is aroused against the authority that prohibits enjoyment. The guilt is not due to the sexual fantasies as such but rather to the murderous aggression aroused by the demand of internalized authority for total chastity in thought, word, and deed.

The origin of the feeling of guilt is therefore the fear of withdrawal of love. If the authority that forbids, originally a parent, and now God, should ever discover this inner rebellion and homicidal rage, surely he would no longer love the sinner. The emotional history of Martin Luther, of which we know something, owing to his own frankness, proves that in at least one case, clearly not untypical, this analysis is not mere speculation.[48]

Thus, the Jew could stand for the repressed and therefore unconscious rebellion of the Christian against the ascetic demands of Christ. The Christian imagined the Jew as much more given to acting out the demands of the instincts than was actually the case, since Jews also are required to restrain the instincts through the discipline of the Torah. The Jew was imagined as hating Christ and taking bloody revenge upon him; but in reality it was the Christian who inwardly hated Christ for the demands he was believed to make for instinctual renunciation and the denial of life. The Christian gained a double satisfaction: he could fantasize the acting out of his own hatred of Christ by another, and he could discharge some of the hate and assuage some of his own guilt by the bloody punishment of the offender. Hatred of Christ can never be consciously acknowledged. By projecting the hatred on to the Jew the Christian can gain partial relief from the strain of conflict and its suppression. The Christian relieves the inner tension, but the Jew pays the price, not seldom with life itself.

This explanation does seem to account in general terms for the medieval Christian's hatred of Jews, as well as for the fact that it was not evoked by anything Jews were actually doing. The fantasies of Christians about Jewish actions originated in the dynamics of their own unconscious minds.

However, we need to offer a more concrete explanation for charges of ritual murder and host desecration. These bizarre charges were not only false, they precisely and specifically contradicted the outlook and behavior of real Jews. That seems to point to something more specific in the Christian mind, not so far brought to light.

EATING CHRIST'S BODY

Reik's analysis of myth and guilt may provide an answer, though it will be a profoundly disturbing one. He directs our attention to the presence of cannibalistic fantasies in the Christian unconscious:

> While murder does not figure in the ritual of the great monotheistic religions, cannibalistic rites are daily performed in the Mass of our churches. Not the slowly vanishing customs of Central Australian tribes, but the living liturgy of Christianity bears witness to the strength and ineffaceability of cannibalistic trends in our civiliza-

> tion. The eating of Christ's body and the drinking of His blood are the most important parts of the Eucharist. Religion, the loftiest and most sublime creation of the human mind, has at its center the most savage and bloodthirsty ceremonial in a cannibalistic rite.[49]

Reik does not mean that Christians literally perform cannibalistic acts when they receive communion. Nor does he suppose that eucharistic theology speaks of a literal eating of flesh and blood. He is referring to what goes on in the unconscious mind. The unconscious mind does not operate with subtle intellectual concepts, but is altogether crude and literal. If the Church teaches that the faithful receive the body and blood of Christ in the bread and wine of the sacrament, the unconscious understands exactly that, with no ifs or buts. For the unconscious mind, communion *is* eating Christ's flesh and drinking his blood.

Moreover, even the theology of pagan cannibalism is itself not as crude as we suppose. Pagan cannibals do not eat others out of hunger, nor because they enjoy the taste of human flesh. They do so as a solemn religious act, in order to incorporate into themselves the potency of the one they eat. That is why they eat their enemies and sometimes their kings, and that no doubt is why they sometimes ate Christian missionaries. The aim of eating is identification with the one eaten. In the title of Reik's chapter, "You are whom you eat."

Is it possible that such fantasies lurk beneath the surface of the minds of civilized people? The psychoanalysts, who have the best reason to know what goes on in the unconscious, assure us that it is possible. We know that lovers not infrequently say to each other, "I love you so much I could eat you." Nevertheless, these fantasies of eating are nowadays very deeply repressed as a rule, more so even than fantasies of killing others.

Originally, as Reik believes, killing was only a means to eating. For this reason, he modifies Freud's anthropological myth, which describes the murder of the primitive father by the brothers in order to gain possession of the women of the horde. (Freud developed his own view in *Totem and Taboo*, and other works. The criticisms Freud's speculations have been subjected to may be of somewhat less force against Reik's modification.) Instead, Reik supposes that the purpose of the primal murder was eating, to incorporate the godlike potency of the father.

There are, moreover, uncomfortably close affinities between this cannibal theology and eucharistic theology. Does not the Gospel of John say, "Unless you eat the flesh of the Son of Man and drink his blood, you have no life in you"? The purpose of the sacramental eating of Christ's body and drinking his blood is to unite the believer with Christ, to incorporate him into Christ's body, to fill him with the supernatural life of Christ. For the language of the unconscious, it is difficult to imagine a closer parallel, short of literally eating the dead body of Jesus. At the conscious level, the distinctions are all-important. For the unconscious, which operates at the level of symbols, the differences are without significance.

Again, I do not wish to be misunderstood, or to give needless offense. No one should suppose that there is anything cannibalistic about even the high Catholic doctrine of the eucharistic presence of Christ. Rather, we are attempting to comprehend the way the doctrine may have been understood at the unconscious level. From there, not from the interpretation of doctrine in the conscious mind, came the murderous impulses of medieval Christians. It is the unconscious fantasies we must attempt to explain, if we are to understand why Christians acted in ways their faith should have forbidden.

PARANOID PROJECTION

I can find no adequate explanation without taking into account the mechanism of paranoid projection. Christians were subconsciously aware that they imagined and took satisfaction in literally killing and eating Christ, and drinking his blood. Since they could not allow this awareness to come to full consciousness, it surfaced only when they attributed the same wish to Jews.

No doubt, too, they harbored infanticidal fantasies. As Freud considered, many psychological effects are "overdetermined," that is, have more than one cause. The prevalence of actual infanticide in Christian society in the Middle Ages is well established by contemporary documentation. In an age without birth control, or modern medical care, children were certainly not always welcomed.

Infanticide was not only a fantasy, but an all too frequent fact. It could not fail to be in people's minds, whether or not they were themselves parents. Nevertheless, it was forbidden by the Christian conscience. The more devout, so far from acting it out, would not permit themselves to think of infanticide as something they themselves might wish to do.

Together, cannibalistic and infanticidal fantasies could account for the origin of the blood libel. Such fantasies were, and are, too horrifying, especially for people committed to a religious life, to be admitted into full consciousness without the aid of psychoanalysis. They could come to expression only in a projected form; the hated Jew could bear the burden of the Christian's fantasy, and the guilt could be discharged by killing the Jew in punishment.

The charge of host desecration can likewise be explained as paranoid projection. There is no doubt that Jewish hostility toward Christ was real enough by this stage, in view of what Jews had suffered from his supposed followers. However, they could hardly find satisfaction for their hostility by maltreating a piece of bread that in their eyes had nothing to do with a long dead apostate from Judaism. Who might believe that the host provided a means of harming Christ, should they wish to do so?

If we are correct in supposing that many medieval Christians harbored a huge amount of unconscious hostility toward Christ for his ascetic demands, a hostility which could never in any circumstances be openly expressed, we may also suppose that they would have found unconscious satisfaction in imagining the Jews trampling on and sticking pins in the host. They imagined that the Jews were doing it for them. But since the wish was totally forbidden and overwhelmingly guilt producing, the imagined perpetrator had to be effaced from the earth by death, lest the thought leak into consciousness that Christians themselves would like to do that.

Even the charge of usuriousness is explicable as paranoia, though we do not need psychoanalytic insight to understand that the debtor who goes so far as to wish to liquidate his creditor, and sometimes actually does so, is strongly attached to money. The accusation of greed comes ill from those who murder their creditors, and even if they do not, fail to condemn those who do.

The explanatory power of the concept of paranoia is not exhausted by these specific instances. As the Middle Ages wore on, the accusations seem to have fused and coalesced into the image of the Jew as demon, and the devil as Jew. Psychoanalytically, the devil clearly stands for the rejected instinctual side of the psyche. There may be other associations, too, such as the stern, accusing father, but the medieval picture of the devil, with horns, tail, and cloven hoof, undoubtedly represents the side of bodily nature we share with the animals. Whether or not there is in fact a spiritual force of cosmic evil, as many very spiritual people assure us is the case, the devil of the medieval imagination, who was also the Jew, stood for the rejected sexuality and aggression of the Christian, projected outside himself.

Once this stage is reached, specific accusations are no longer needed, but on the other hand any and all accusations become plausible. Once the Jew is identified with the ultimate enemy of God, he is capable of anything. He is endowed with superhuman cunning and deceitfulness; indeed, he is constantly and secretly conspiring against all the works of God.

Perhaps this is the germ of the more modern notion of a Jewish conspiracy against the Christian world. On the other hand, this too may be a paranoid projection, since the Church most certainly did, especially at this period, attempt to rule the world for Christ, regarding all earthly authority as delegated by itself. Like the devil, the Jew is seen as secretly plotting to take over the realm of God's kingdom, to pervert it for his own evil ends.

THE TRANSMISSION OF PARANOID SYSTEMS

Paranoia can also explain the persistence into modern times of such mythical calumnies against the Jews, even when the former rationalization for them is no longer possible or available. A paranoid system of this kind does not require intellectual justification, and it does not submit to rational criticism. It was not generated by intellectual processes, and it cannot be refuted by them. There is no use arguing with a confirmed antisemite, for rational argument does not touch his fantasies. He is literally insane on the subject of the Jews.

No doubt such medieval Christians would have been paranoid even if there had been no Jews in their environment. As Hitler once said, if there had been no Jews, it would have been necessary to invent them. Beyond doubt, however, it was Christianity that identified the Jew as the one on whom these fantasies could be plausibly projected in that society. The paranoid fantasies of the medieval Christian found a social and consensual support from the ancient myth of the Christ-killers, embodied in the doctrines of the Church.

Once established, however, antisemitic paranoia no longer needs Christian doctrine as a rationalization. It first developed and flourished in the medieval world, where the imagination was peopled with Christian symbols. But the paranoid system was powerful enough to survive the modern questioning, and even repudiation, of traditional Christianity. It continued to exist in the post-Christian world of Nazi Germany and Stalinist Russia, and it continues to exist today, though now taking new forms.

A paranoid system is not transmitted by intellectual discourse. Antisemitism is passed from mind to mind by hints and tones of voice, and perhaps even more directly. Originally acquired in the most sensitive phases of childhood from parents, it is almost ineradicable except by genuine repentance and a firm will to truth. Its presence and origins must be brought to consciousness before it can be let go. With or without the assistance of psychoanalysis in some form or other, this will not easily be achieved.

In the modern Western world at least, there are no longer many conscious and acknowledged antisemites. However, the paranoia persists. The Jew remains an object of suspicion and distrust. More and more people are openly expressing doubt of the reality of the Holocaust, and some are informing us that we have been taken in by a Jewish plot designed to bring about the establishment of the racist state of Israel.

More and more people are questioning the legitimacy of the claim of the Jewish people to their own land; their defensive measures are characterized as a violation of Palestinian rights, or as expansionist aggression. Palestinian propaganda is widely believed, even when based on stories that are objectively false. Zionism, the national liberation movement of the Jewish people, is characterized as racism, and the Jew is called a Nazi. When such irrational charges are made, who can doubt that those who make them have a psychic need to displace their own hate and guilt on to others?

Today, we can see with crystal clarity that the medieval charges against the Jews were altogether without foundation. It may not be so easy today to discern that the contemporary charges are no less false, but honest and unbiased inquiry displays them for what they are. Today, too, paranoia is at work. As in the Middle Ages, the charges made against the Jews in our own time are a much better guide to what is going on in the mind of the accusers than to actual Jewish behavior.

8

Inquisition and Reformation: The Turning of the Tide?

By the end of the fourteenth century, it might have seemed that things could hardly get worse for the Jews. But even worse was yet to come. The fifteenth century saw the Expulsion from Spain and the beginning of the Spanish Inquisition's attack upon the numerous forced converts of the time. As the Middle Ages came to an end, a new concept emerged in Spain, the precursor of modern racism, Jewish blood as a hereditary stigma, persisting for generations even in the descendants of converts to Christianity.

Was that the historical low point, after which only improvement was possible for Jews? While the Reformation somewhat improved their conditions, the improvement was limited. The Reformation, at least in its Lutheran form, was medieval through and through in its thinking, not premodern as liberal historians used to suppose. Only in areas influenced by the Reformed tradition can we discern the beginnings of a genuinely new attitude among Christians toward Jews, foreshadowing the dialogue that has tentatively begun in our own time.[1]

Those accustomed to contrasting the modern and the medieval mind, attributing a more enlightened outlook to the twentieth century, generally expect the end of the Middle Ages to have been a turning point, after which more tolerant attitudes appear. The Holocaust casts serious doubt on this assumption. So-called medieval attitudes have not yet come to an end in the non-Jewish world. In any event, for the Jews, in many places the Middle Ages ended only in the first decades of the twentieth century, if then.

THE FATE OF SPANISH JEWRY IN THE FIFTEENTH CENTURY

During the fourteenth and fifteenth centuries, an extremely large number of Spanish Jews was induced to receive baptism. The pressures exercised on them were economic and social as well as religious. A few also converted spontaneously. The latter were often drawn from the more mystical groups among Spanish Jewry;

among them were antirationalists, like Abner of Burgos, who became Alfonso of Vallodolid. They were disillusioned with the whole religio-legal system embodied in the Talmud, supposing that Jews could only find redemption if they put their faith in a Messiah who had already come, as Christians claimed. Such converts were often especially zealous in the mission to their former coreligionists and willing to employ harsh measures against them.

Another such convert, Rabbi Don Solomon Halevi, became Bishop Pablo de Santa Maria of Burgos. His children joined him in conversion to the Catholic faith, though his wife remained faithful to Judaism. One of his children actually succeeded him in the see of Burgos. Another convert, Joshua Lorki, became Geronimo de Santa Fé, and he took a prominent part on the Catholic side in the famous disputation of Tortosa, held in 1413–14, in which Jewish and Christian theologians debated the truth of their respective faiths, under conditions extremely disadvantageous to the Jewish representatives.

The numerous conversions of Jews created a new problem for Spanish society and for the Church. Suddenly a substantial number of "New Christians" were to be found in society, no longer subject to the social, ecclesiastical, and legal disabilities of Jews but clearly of Jewish descent and often of Jewish upbringing. Their allegiance to Christianity could reasonably be questioned, since in most cases their conversion had been far from spontaneous.[2]

The New Christians themselves showed little desire to be assimilated to the majority. They kept their identity as a distinct group, frequently retaining their ties with other Jews. They were suspected, often rightly, of holding on as best they could to their old faith and practicing it in secret. Sometimes they seem to have kept up Jewish observances without altogether knowing why. Such practices as putting out the best tablecloth and silver for dinner on Friday night may have been retained as family customs, without their religious significance being understood. Others exposed themselves to the malicious curiosity of their neighbors by refraining from lighting fires on Saturdays, purchasing their meat from a butcher who was also a new Christian, or buying large quantities of vegetables before the season of the Jewish Passover.

Still others went much further, doing their best to hold on to their Judaism in secret while outwardly appearing to be Christian. Usually they married only among themselves. They kept up traditional Jewish ceremonies and many continued to eat only kosher food. Until the sixteenth century, they retained some knowledge of Hebrew. They also instructed their children in their beliefs, though babies were not circumcised, since this would have led to death on discovery.

Their creed, imparted to their children at the normal age for becoming Bar Mitzvah, was, "Salvation is possible through the Law of Moses, not through the Law of Christ." The language and concepts of this creed are Catholic, not Jewish: even those most determined to remain Jewish could not fail to be influenced by their surroundings over a period of time. However, they continued to keep the Sabbath and the Day of Atonement.

In worship, their customs were partly Christian and partly Jewish. Usually they knelt, like Christians, for prayer instead of standing or sitting, and the prayers were often said, instead of chanted, as Jewish prayers were. Since fasts could easily be concealed, they were more faithfully observed than the feasts. But the feast of Purim was especially popular among them, in view of their natural identification with Esther, who had kept her descent and religion secret.[3]

Suspicions that the New Christians still wished to be Jews and tried to hold on to their Judaism brought down on them the hostility of the Christian majority. The new Christians gained for themselves an opprobrious name, the *Marranos*. The name has stuck to them, and is widely used in the history books. However, there seems to be some doubt about its meaning; while some explain it as related to a Hebrew word for turning, in Italian the same word means swine. Almost certainly this was the original meaning of the Spanish word. If so, it seems better not to refer to the group as *marranos*, but to use other names employed at the time, such as the New Christians, or the *conversos*.

A new concept now appeared, without precedent in Christian history. From the middle of the century, some Spanish religious orders began to require the qualification of *limpiezza de sangre* (i.e., Christian descent on both sides), and they continued to require it until the nineteenth century. In the ideology of the time, the opposite of *limpiezza de sangre* was *mala sangre*, or "bad blood." During the same period, a statute was passed declaring the *conversos* unfit to hold office in the Spanish state, or to bear witness against Christians. Pope Nicholas V condemned its instigators, but the statute was reenacted in 1467.

These are revolutionary concepts by comparison with all previous Christian tradition. As I have frequently emphasized, Jews had always been defined by the Church as a religious, not a racial, community: whatever supposed stigma attached to being Jewish was effaced by baptism, in the eyes of the Church, and apparently also those of the people at large. The new concepts defining Jews by descent and not by religion were not in conformity with church doctrine, and they were even contested by some of the better instructed converts. They were widely held in Spain and elsewhere, in consequence of the forced conversions and the presence in the Church of large numbers who could be suspected of holding on to their Judaism.

From a Jewish point of view, Jewish status is indeed primarily a matter of descent. Even apostasy to another faith, which will cut all social ties and remove the right to the privileges of being a Jew, can be effaced by repentance. Here too, repentance means return to what one originally was.

However, it was not because they became acquainted with Jewish law on the point that Christians now began to define Jewishness by descent. They had begun to regard Jewishness as an undesirable hereditary trait, incapable of removal by baptism. The only basis for the new view was the suspected or real tenacity of the converts in holding on to their former practices and beliefs. The Christians failed to see that such tenacity was a moral trait, not a hereditary characteristic.

The concept of *mala sangre* could be called antisemitic in an exact sense, no longer just anti-Judaic, like all the former manifestations of hostility toward Jews, however extreme or ill-founded. However, even at this point in the long incremental development, the term antisemitism is still an anachronism. Properly speaking, it should be reserved for the modern period, since it depends on racial theories that did not make their appearance before the nineteenth century. Nevertheless, we can hear at this point a distinct "pre-echo" of the nineteenth and twentieth centuries. Once Christians begin to define Jews by descent, regarding them as such even when they have been baptized, and to view them with suspicion and dislike simply because they are Jews, a Rubicon has been crossed.

Historians have not been able to find any clear connection between these Spanish innovations and the racial theories of the nineteenth and twentieth centuries. Nevertheless, once ideas are in the air they seem to make their appearance independently in different places and spread without apparent links. Not long afterward, we find the old Luther, who had turned against the Jews for their failure to respond to his new gospel, beginning to regard them as intrinsically incapable of improvement. Soon the prevalent Christian view will be, "Once a Jew, always a Jew." Never supported by official theology, over the next few centuries this prejudice became more widespread than the corresponding orthodoxy. It prepared the ground for the secular racism of modern anti-Christian antisemitism.

A second consequence of these developments was the introduction of the Inquisition in Spain, for the express purpose of dealing with the *conversos*. In the Protestant world, the Spanish Inquisition is usually associated with the persecution of Protestants. However, there were few Protestants in Spain at any time, though there were many in its dominions, and its primary role was the rooting out of crypto-Judaism in the Church. Any adherence, however slight, to customs or behavior considered Jewish was sufficient evidence of this heresy.

The strongest opponents of the New Christians argued that the local courts, episcopal and papal, were not dealing drastically enough with the menace of crypto-Judaism and demanded the introduction of a sovereign Spanish Inquisition. The pope of the day held to traditional orthodoxy on the subject of converted Jews, trying to maintain some kind of control over the excesses of the Spaniards.

In 1483, however, the Dominican Tomás de Torquemada was appointed Inquisitor-General of both Aragon and Castile. His name has become legendary for ruthless zeal in the prosecution of heresy. It has been suggested that his zeal against the New Christians can be traced to his own Jewish descent. However, his Jewish origins have not been convincingly demonstrated. Whatever the cause, his enthusiasm for rooting out Judaism in the church is incontestable.

The Inquisition had no jurisdiction whatsoever over Jews as such. Its role, defined in its formal title, the Holy Office for the Faith, is internal to the Church and concerns the preservation of orthodoxy. Its procedures reflect this role, as well as medieval assumptions about the way to get at truth. The court, as Ben Sasson reminds his readers, considered itself to be motivated solely by a loving concern for the spiritual health of the person under investigation, a health that could only be assured by a full adherence to the Catholic faith.[4]

The person investigated needed no defense counsel, since the court was in any case on his or her side. Nor did the accused need to be present when all evidence against them was heard by the court, for the same reason. When the inquisitor found himself compelled to pronounce the person an irrecoverable heretic, the final act of exclusion from the Church was one of pruning the vineyard of the Lord, or of surgery, without which the health of the body could not be assured.

The procedures introduced by Torquemada allowed full scope for the introduction of gossip and slander. Once the court was set up, a period of grace of thirty to forty days was established, during which the inquisitors could receive confessions or any voluntary evidence. During this period, the suspect might confess to minimal transgressions, in the hope of escaping more serious charges. His neighbors and acquaintances would then report to the court any behavior they chose to regard as suspicious.

The accused might call his neighbors as witnesses for the defense, only to find that they were his accusers. While they might testify that he behaved in public as a Christian, they would also often mention their suspicions that in secret he followed Jewish practices.

Once the suspicion was raised, torture would be employed to extract a confession, which would usually be obtained. (The twentieth-century reader can hardly fail to note the parallel with the trials of deviationists in Stalinist Russia, vividly depicted in Arthur Koestler's *Darkness at Noon,* and even with the interrogations of contemporary Soviet Jewish dissidents like Natan Sharansky and Yuli Edelshein.)

The Inquisition itself did not punish, other than by excommunication, unless one considers the tortures inflicted during the investigation to be punishment in advance of conviction. (Marcus reproduces a horrifying and moving account, drawn from the records of the Inquisition itself, of the ordeal of a woman who seems really not to have understood the offense with which she was charged but was nevertheless cruelly tortured until she confessed to whatever her inquisitors wanted.)[5]

Nevertheless, in the organic Christian state, heresy was considered a threat to the body politic as well as to the Church. Therefore, once the Inquisition had convicted a person of heresy, it would hand over the accused to the secular arm. The state would then profess its own Christian and Catholic character by an "act of faith," in Spanish *auto da fé,* an expression that became synonymous with the ceremonial burning of the heretic at the stake. The first such *auto da fé* took place in 1481, before the appointment of Torquemada. The sentence on the accused was always pronounced, and the punishment carried out, on the spot.

Many of the condemned found the courage at the point of death to affirm their Jewish faith, and they died with the Shema on their lips, as Jewish martyrs had since Akiva. Though death by burning at the stake was a common punishment, it was not the only one. Sometimes the victim would be flogged, imprisoned, or banished.

At least two thousand *autos da fé* were carried out in Spain and Portugal and their dependencies, and about 400,000 persons tried by the Inquisition in these countries during the three and a half centuries that it operated. About 30,000 of them were put to death. The Inquisition was abolished only in 1834, though its activities in its final years had considerably slowed down for want of suitable victims.[6]

The Spanish Inquisition was a disaster for the New Christians, but it was the prelude to an even greater disaster for Spanish Jewry as a whole. In 1490, an accusation of ritual murder was brought up against the New Christians, the case known as the Holy Child of La Guardia. All the accused were burned in the following year. The public feeling aroused by the case, exploited by the Inquisition in spite of its lack of basis in fact, increased animosity toward the New Christians as a group and also toward the unconverted Jewish population of the country.

In 1492, all Jews who refused conversion were expelled from Spain. In fact, the majority did accept baptism. According to recent scholarship, those who refused conversion and underwent expulsion and exile amounted to 100–150,00. The last remaining Jews left on August 2, 1492, the ninth of Av in the Jewish calendar, always kept as a day of fasting and mourning for the destruction of the Temple. On the same day, Columbus sailed for the Indies, to find America.

Many Jews fled to Portugal, where they encountered even more determined and successful attempts to turn them into Christians by force or persuasion. At first the Inquisition was not employed against former Jews in Portugal, and those who converted had an opportunity to consolidate a crypto-Jewish existence and to build up the basis of survival. Mass conversion, rather than expulsion, put an end to Portuguese Jewry. No known Jews remained in Portugal by 1497.

Some of those expelled from Spain and Portugal, including especially *conversos*, fled to South America and maintained a precarious existence there. There is evidence that many of Columbus' crew, including perhaps himself, were New Christians hoping to find a freer life. Indeed, the whole expedition seems to have been their enterprise, both in its planning and financing. It was largely funded by Luis de Santangel, a financier of New Christian extraction, and a principal patron was Gabriel Sanchez, High Treasurer of Aragon, himself of full Jewish descent.[7] Nevertheless, the Inquisition pursued the New Christian exiles to the Spanish dominions in the New World and many perished there.[8]

Most of those expelled from the Iberian Peninsula made their way south to North Africa and then eastward. Some turned northward to the Netherlands and even in due course to Britain. Today some of the oldest and best established Jewish families in Britain are Sephardic. (The name *Sephardic* comes from the Hebrew words for Spain and Spanish.) Yet others found their way back to the Turkish domains and then to the Land of Israel, establishing themselves especially in the northern part of the country. They found greater tolerance in the Turkish empire than they had experienced under Christianity. Safed in upper Galilee became an important center of mysticism and kabbalah under the leadership of exiles and their descendants.

The Expulsion is an event of incalculable importance in Jewish history. In the history of antisemitism it is not a novelty, unlike the new emphasis on blood and descent. Other expulsions had preceded it, less remarkable in their extent and consequences. Nevertheless, this was always called *The* Expulsion, and it marks yet another incremental stage in the development of original Christian anti-Judaism into full-blown modern antisemitism.

Medieval paranoia, in Spain and Portugal at least, had now reached its climax: Jews were seen as a deadly menace to Christian society, an alien presence that could not be eliminated by forced conversion and assimilation, but must be physically removed. Christian society could go no further toward genocide without losing its Christian character and abandoning the old Augustinian belief that the Jews, though in misery, must be preserved as a witness to their own crimes.

The final step awaited modernity and its abandonment of remaining Christian restraints, together with the complete overcoming of the old religious definition of the Jew by the new racial one. But the racial definition had already made its appearance in fifteenth-century Spain. From this point on, the Holocaust became a possibility.

THE COUNCIL OF TRENT: A CATHOLIC TURNING POINT?

The sixteenth century saw several movements for reform, not all of which gave rise to Protestant churches. There was also a Catholic Reformation, though it is usually regarded, not altogether correctly, as simply a response to the challenge of Luther, Zwingli, and Calvin, and therefore termed the Counter-Reformation. In fact, there was a strong internal Catholic impetus for reform, already manifested in the Conciliar Movement of the previous century. It aimed at dealing with abuses, curbing the exclusivity of papal power by giving balancing power to assemblies of bishops known as Councils, and purifying existing doctrine. Some of its leaders attempted to enter into dialogue with Luther on the key questions of justification by faith, and gospel and law.

The great Council of Trent, which met during the middle years of the sixteenth century, laid down the guidelines for the reformed Catholicism of the succeeding centuries. Though its work has often been criticized in the light of the much more radical reforms of Vatican II, Trent's achievement ought not to be underestimated. From some points of view, it could be regarded as a more successful reform than those of the Protestant churches, and the fact that its work stood until the twentieth century is not just a testimony to Catholic conservatism, but to the comprehensiveness and solidity of the reforms it introduced.

Trent even dealt with the question of the guilt for Christ's crucifixion, in a paragraph from its Catechism that seems to have gone almost unnoticed until the birth of Jewish-Christian dialogue in our own time. It reads:

> In the guilt of the crucifixion are involved *all* those who frequently fell into sin; for as *our* sins consigned Christ to death on the cross, most certainly those who wallow in sin and iniquity themselves crucify again the Son of God. This guilt seems more enormous in us than in the Jews since, according to the testimony of the apostle, if they had known it they would never have crucified the Lord of glory; while we, on the contrary, professing to know him yet denying him by our actions, seem in some sort to lay violent hands on him.

Elsewhere, the Council affirms that the crucifixion was Christ's free decision, and that theologically all humanity is responsible for the death of Jesus on the cross.

Geoffrey Wigoder comments, "Tragically, these guidelines, laid down four centuries ago and so enlightened for their time, were consigned to oblivion and only recalled in the Vatican's 1985 'Notes.' "[9]

The background to this rethinking of the guilt for the crucifixion lies in medieval spirituality. Meditation on the cross interiorized the myth. Christ's death, no longer a cosmic victory over the powers of evil, becomes part of an inner spiritual transaction between the believer and God. Human sin, not Jewish hostility, now becomes the cause of his death. We find the same idea in modern Evangelical thought. In this way, the myth loses much of its anti-Judaic force. But myths are powerful and not so easily disposed of. The Catholic masses continue to this day to think of the Jews as the Christ-killers, forgetting the godly admonitions of the council. So too do many Evangelicals.

Trent's statements are not modern documents. They assume the "gospel truth" of the New Testament accounts of the death of Jesus, as does Vatican II in the twentieth century. We cannot expect to find in them modern insights drawn from historical criticism, such as those examined in the first three chapters of this book. In their absence, this is probably as far as Christians could go in the criticism of their own myth and its anti-Jewish consequences.

THE REFORMATION AND THE JEWS

Martin Luther was not a modern man. His mind was still haunted by the same demons that peopled the imagination of his medieval predecessors. The devil himself was a palpable reality to him, and as the champion of Christ and his gospel, Luther frequently found himself in single combat with him. On one occasion, he successfully repelled the adversary by throwing an inkstand at him.

In Luther's universe of mortal struggle between good and evil, God and the devil, the Jews too had a role to play, and it was not on the side of God. Along with the Turks and the heretics within the Church, they were instruments in the devil's war against the true gospel of Christ. At least as far as the Jews were concerned, the Lutheran Reformation still belonged almost entirely to the medieval world.

Luther's opposition to the Jews was rooted in the ancient mythical thinking of the Church. His universe was formed by a myth of cosmic conflict, in which the Jews continued to play the part of the antagonist, the enemy of the divine Son of God, and of all God's redemptive purposes. In spite of its humanistic connections, the Reformation did little to dissolve this mythical thinking, or to encourage people to approach Jews as real people, instead of characters in a mythic drama.

Luther's own theology was simply an articulation of this compelling myth. While it cast the Jews in the role of adversary, it had nothing to do with modern racial theories, though modern racists would later use it for their own purposes. But the role of the Jews in his theology tied in directly with themes of central importance to him in his own theological struggle with the papal system. It would be a mistake to think of his attitude toward Jews merely as a peripheral remnant from the past.

In Luther's thought, as for his present-day successors among the theologians, the Jews stood for a legalistic relationship with God, in contrast to the true relationship of grace and faith. What Luther supposed to be the Jewish religious principle was altogether antithetical to the principle of the gospel, for which he was engaged in a life and death struggle. Neither the young Luther, who is sometimes supposed to have been a friend of the Jews, nor the old Luther, who was apparently their enemy, saw any place for the unconverted Jew in the world of grace. On the other hand, since he was not a racist, Luther was more than ready to welcome a Jewish convert into the arms of the gospel.

In that respect, Luther remained consistent. Where he held different views at different times, it was on the susceptibility of the Jews to conversion. In his youth, in the first flush of enthusiasm from the discovery of the new gospel, he was relatively optimistic, thinking that the Jews might share his excitement at the discovery of a more biblical theology and find in the church of the Reformation gospel a more welcoming home. In his deeply pessimistic old age, the Jews had come once more to seem to him obstinate and unconvertible, requiring at best "a severe mercy."[10]

The following quotation will make the contrast between the earlier and the later expectations clear, though without the foregoing explanation of the consistent thread in Luther's understanding of the Jews, this isolated quotation could mislead, and often has. In 1523, Luther wrote in his tract, *That Jesus Christ was a Born Jew*:

> I will . . . show by means of the Bible the causes which induce me to believe that Christ was a Jew born of a virgin. Perhaps I will attract some of the Jews to the Christian faith. For our fools–the popes, bishops, sophists, and monks–the coarse blockheads! have until this time so treated the Jews that to be a good Christian one would have had to become a Jew. And if I had been a Jew and had seen such idiots and blockheads ruling and teaching the Christian religion, I would rather have been a sow than a Christian.
>
> For they have dealt with the Jews as if they were dogs and not human beings. They have done nothing for them except curse them and seize their wealth. Whenever they converted them, they did not teach them either Christian law or life, but only subjected them to papistry and monkery. . . . I have heard myself from pious converted Jews that if they had not heard the gospel in our time [i.e. in its Lutheran form] they would always have remained Jews at heart in spite of their conversion. For they admit that they have never heard anything about Christ from the rulers who converted them.
>
> I hope that if the Jews are treated friendly and are instructed kindly through the Bible, many of them will become real Christians and come back to the ancestral faith of the prophets and patriarchs . . . [In Luther's theology, inherited in this respect from the age of the church fathers, the prophets and patriarchs were proleptic believers in Christ, whereas the Jews of Jesus's time and the later Talmud had corrupted this pure biblical faith] . . .
>
> If we wish to make them better, we must deal with them not according to the law of the pope, but according to the law of Christian charity. We must receive them kindly, and allow them to compete with us in earning a livelihood, so that they may have a good reason to be with us and among us and an opportunity to witness

> Christian life and doctrine; and if some remain obstinate, what of it? Not every one of us is a good Christian.[11]

Even here, in this humane and charitable approach to the Jews, it is clear that the issue is conversion. The Jews are to be "made better," a theme that recurs in the Enlightenment's approach to Jewish emancipation. The Jews are now seen individually as human, but Luther does not attempt to comprehend or evaluate positively the Judaism by which they live.

The tone of Luther's later writings on the Jews is certainly very different from the foregoing. But the underlying theology has not changed.[12] Luther had no doubt changed psychologically. The stresses of a life of conflict and often of disappointment had perhaps worn him down. Or as Erik Erikson suggests, the unresolved conflicts of his childhood surfaced in late middle age and drove him to the brink of psychosis.[13]

Perhaps the gospel of grace had failed in the end to bring to Martin Luther himself the deepest healing, right down to the center of the self, in the unconscious. In the depth of his soul, Luther could not believe in himself as the object of God's unfailing love, and therefore, he could not truly love himself or others.

Whatever the cause, in these late writings the charitable temper of the earlier Luther has been replaced by one of hate and rage where the Jews are concerned. The mythical spectacles distorting his view of the historical role of the Jews had been there even in Luther's earliest writings on the subject. What is new in the last pamphlets is the emphasis on Jewish intransigence and obstinacy, which the younger Luther had hoped could be overcome by Evangelical kindness.[14] The concept of "severe mercy" follows from this disillusionment with the prospects of large-scale Jewish conversion.

> What then shall we do with this damned, rejected race of Jews? Since they live among us and we know about their lying and blasphemy and cursing, we cannot tolerate them if we do not wish to share in their lies, curses, and blasphemy. In this way we cannot quench the inextinguishable fire of divine rage (as the prophets say) nor convert the Jews. We must prayerfully and reverently practice a merciful severity. Perhaps we may save a few from the fire and the flames. They are surely being punished a thousand times more than we might wish them. Let me give you my honest advice.
>
> First, their synagogues or churches should be set on fire, and whatever does not burn up should be covered or spread over with dirt so that no one may ever be able to see a cinder or stone of it. And this ought to be done for the honour of God and of Christianity in order that God may see that we are Christians, and that we have not wittingly tolerated or approved of such public lying, cursing and blaspheming of His Son and His Christians . . .
>
> Secondly, their homes should likewise be broken down and destroyed. For they perpetuate the same things there that they do in their synagogues. For the same reason they ought to be put under one roof or in a stable, like gypsies, in order that they may realize that they are not masters in our land, as they boast, but miserable captives, as they complain of us incessantly before God with bitter wailing.

> Thirdly, they should be deprived of their prayer- books and Talmuds in which such idolatry, lies, cursing, and blasphemy are taught.
>
> Fourthly, their rabbis must be forbidden under threat of death to teach any more. . . .
>
> Fifthly, passport and traveling privileges must be absolutely forbidden to the Jews. For they have no business in the rural districts, since they are not nobles, nor officials, nor merchants, nor the like. . . .
>
> Sixthly, they ought to be stopped from usury. All their cash and valuables of silver and gold ought to be take from them and put aside for safe keeping. For this reason, as said before, everything that they possess they stole and robbed from us through their usury, for they have no other means of support . . . Such evilly acquired money is cursed, unless, with God's blessing, it is put to some good and necessary use . . .
>
> Seventhly, let the young and strong Jews and Jewesses be given the flail, the ax, the hoe, the spade, the distaff, and spindle, and let them earn their bread by the sweat of their noses as is enjoined upon Adam's children. For it is not proper that they should want us cursed *Goyim* to work in the sweat of our brow and that they, pious crew, while away their days at the fireside in idleness, feasting and display. And in addition to this, they boast impiously that they have become masters of the Christians at our expense. We ought to drive the rascally lazy bones out of our system.
>
> If however we are afraid that they might harm us personally . . . . . . then let us apply the same cleverness as the other nations, such as France, Spain, Bohemia, etc., and settle with them for that which they have extorted usuriously from us, and after having divided it up fairly let us drive them out of the country for all time. For, as has been said, God's rage is so great against them that they only become worse and worse through mild mercy, and not much better through severe mercy. Therefore away with them. . .[15]

At his trial in Nuremberg after the Second World War, Julius Streicher, the notorious Nazi propagandist, editor of the scurrilous antisemitic weekly, *Der Stürmer*, argued that if he should be standing there arraigned on such charges, so should Martin Luther. Reading such passages, it is hard not to agree with him. Luther's proposals read like a program for the Nazis, or for a modern Arab state such as Syria. Nothing can be said to condone or palliate such words.

Nevertheless, in one sense Streicher's Lutheran self-defense cannot be sustained. Luther was not a modern racist antisemite, and he would still, even at that stage, have welcomed a Jewish convert as a fellow Christian without reservation. But if anyone still doubts that theological anti-Judaism is the true precursor of modern antisemitism, Luther's words should remove such doubts.

Though Luther was not the out-and-out antisemite some modern writers have depicted, he was also far from being the originator of a more tolerant attitude toward the Jews, such as we generally associate (without convincing evidence) with modernity. Some Lutherans did defend the Jews against the medieval calumnies, as did Andreas Osiander, who also disagreed with Luther himself on his attitude toward the Jews.[16]

In spite of such exceptions, the Reformation as a larger movement, for which Luther was by no means the only person responsible, did not at first make much difference to the status of the Jews in European society. Sometimes it even made it worse. In fact, the main contribution of the Reformation to the well-being of the Jews seems to have been an accidental one.

It gave rise to the beginnings of modern pluralism, though none of its leaders had any thought of doing so, for they stood for the unity of the Christian world as much as did the Catholic church. By breaking up the unity of medieval Christendom and creating a variety of religions and sects, the Reformation made the differences between all forms of Christianity, on the one hand, and Judaism, on the other, seem less stark, less a difference of black and white and more a matter of degree.[17]

Much of the religious hatred formerly directed at the Jew was now directed by Protestants against the Catholic church and specifically against the Pope, and Catholics could now hate the Protestants instead of or as well as the Jews, thus lessening the intensity of the hatred to the extent that it was dissipated over a wider area.

The Reformation was not therefore the precursor of modern liberalism but (in the areas it influenced) the last kick of the medieval world. Nevertheless, it did lead to intellectual and social changes that would in due course prove to be somewhat favorable to the Jewish people, still living in a Christian world. The new possibility of religious pluralism, following on the abandonment of the older hope of a single Christian world, is only beginning to be realized in our own time. It was undoubtedly an outgrowth of the new diversity among Christians themselves. The presence of a variety of sects within the same society made tolerance of some kind a practical necessity for the preservation of social unity. It likewise accelerated processes that would eventually lead to secularization.

For the first time since the last days of the Roman Empire, Christians could regard society as transcending the Church, for it bound people together even when religion divided them. For many centuries, Christians had viewed society as an organic union of church and state.[18] If the new society emerging from the breakup of medieval Christendom, no longer bound up inextricably with a particular orthodoxy, was to have shared values, these must of necessity be derived from a common ground. The realization could not be delayed indefinitely that this common ground of ethical values was in fact shared by Christians with Jews. It would take rather longer for a few to realize that these same values actually owed their origin to the Torah itself. More commonly, they would be explained as derived from natural law, or a common human heritage of ethical and social values, needing no religion for their justification.

These changes occurred more slowly in the areas in which Lutheranism was strong. The religious wars in the Holy Roman Empire ended in a compromise, commonly summed up in the phrase, *cuius regio, eius religio*. Each ruler could determine for himself the religion of his domain, and it would of course be his own. Thus, the small states into which Germany especially was divided were either Catholic or Lutheran, but not both. The principle of the unitary state was preserved at the cost of the breakup of the larger unity, which could no longer be sustained.

In countries where the Reformation did not take a Lutheran form, it was less possible to preserve the remnants of the unitary state. Calvin made an attempt for a while in Geneva, and the established churches of England and Scotland continued the theory. But monarchs and other civic rulers were neither strong enough nor consistent enough to preserve these orthodoxies unchallenged over a lengthy period. Alongside both these churches others grew up, holding more radically to Reformation principles as they interpreted them and unwilling to conform to institutions so closely allied to the state, an alliance they regarded as illegitimate. Even in these countries, Catholicism preserved a tenuous existence.

Calvinists frequently experienced persecution and exile themselves, under the impact of Catholic power. For those who did, like the Huguenots, it was no longer so easy to interpret Jewish misfortunes as an expression of divine wrath, a very old idea still vivid to Luther.[19] Solidarity in misfortune made the first breach in the theology of supersession. Calvinists began to think of a single covenant in which Jews as well as Christians shared, and of a divine sovereignty and compassion directed to both.

More than Lutherans, they began to read the Jewish Bible, the Old Testament, as the word of God. The Latin Bible, surrounded as it was by a liturgical midrash, was poetic and beautiful, but it no longer had much to do with God's covenant with his people the Jews, or the Torah in which he had marked out for them the way of life. The "Old Law" had been so taken up into the New that it had lost its original identity.

Luther did not change that very much. The antithesis of Law and Gospel, fundamental to his own theology, could only imply a corresponding antithesis between Judaism and Christianity. The Old Testament still contained intimations of Christ and of the religion of grace, but in itself it stood for the religion of Law. Luther characterized the most Jewish of the New Testament letters, the Epistle of James, as an *epistola straminea*, "a right strawy epistle."

The Calvinists held a different view of the relationship between Law and Gospel. Calvin knew of a "third use of the Law," as guidance for the conduct of life for the justified Christian, living in the covenant of grace. Without knowing it, he had in fact come closer to the original Jewish understanding of the function of Torah in personal and corporate life. Thus, Calvinists could look to the Old Testament as guidance for the building of new societies that had thrown off the Catholic yoke, or (later) that of the established churches of the Protestant world.

Calvinists began to read the Christian Bible as a single book with a common theme spanning the two Testaments, with less of Luther's sharp antithesis between law and gospel. Once they had learned to value more highly the Scriptures by which Jews themselves were living, they could not fail in due course to approach actual Jews with greater understanding and sympathy.

It is thus not accidental that many of the more enlightened present-day theologians now contributing to the Jewish-Christian dialogue share a Calvinist theological background, though they belong to a variety of denominations. Perhaps the same respect for the Old Testament as the word of God inspired the Huguenots of Le Chambon in France, during the German occupation, when almost every family protected at least one Jew from capture and deportation to the death camps.

THE HUMANISTS

None of the early reformers were liberals in a modern sense. Even humanists such as Erasmus would hardly qualify as liberals by modern standards. Erasmus himself was decidedly anti-Jewish.[20] Nor were the humanists and the Reformers seen by the people of their own time as being on different sides, though ultimately their work did lead in different directions. Both groups made use of humanistic scholarship in their approach to the Bible, preferring to work from accurate texts, and from the original Hebrew and Greek, instead of using the traditional Latin Vulgate.

This brought them under severe criticism from traditionalists, who were right from their own point of view to sense a threat. Every translation is an interpretation and the Vulgate embodied a Christian one. Closer attention to the original text and language of the Bible, and to its plain sense, without allegory or typology, could not fail to lead to a more biblical theology, and to corresponding discontent with traditional ideas. The main theological achievement of the Reformation was the discovery of this renewed and more biblical, dare one say, more Jewish theology.

We could add that it was not in fact post-Enlightenment liberalism that eventually brought about improving relations between Christians and Jews in the period after the Reformation and in the modern world. Liberals have not usually been, and in general still are not, sympathetic to Judaism, or to Israel, the Jewish state, despite standing for a tolerance alien to older views. The Calvinistic Netherlands, well before enlightened France and Germany, first extended (and never withdrew) civil rights to Jews.

Liberal acceptance of Jews, on the other hand, has always depended on Jews conforming themselves to liberal standards, or to their willingness to be assimilated to the majority culture.[21] Real recognition of Jews as Jews has tended rather to come from those who could understand the outlook of the Jewish Bible and how Jews themselves lived by it, even though this was different from the way in which Christians did so. In this company Calvinists hold an honored place.

III

The Myth Secularized

9

The Napoleonic Bargain: "Frenchmen of the Mosaic Persuasion"

For large numbers of Jews, the advent of the modern age opened up a new epoch in their relationships with their Christian neighbors. Suddenly, their situation changed fundamentally. They were beckoned out of the ghetto into participation in the dynamically changing world of modernity. They came out in the expectation that the centuries of horror had at last come to an end. At last they were to be treated as equals and fellow citizens, and their talents would find scope for expression among their peers.

Within a century and a half, two-thirds of European Jewry would be annihilated in the Nazi Holocaust. Jews had entered with high hopes into modernity; in the outcome, it proved far more destructive to them than all the Christian centuries that had preceded it. In the Holocaust, the unbelievable became reality.

Is it possible to account for this unparalleled event, even in part? Many have thought not. The absolute evil of the event itself defies all rational explanation and makes fools of historians who attempt to trace its origins by means of the categories with which they are familiar. But we can explain why the Nazis chose the Jews as their target, and at this point in our inquiry we are close to being in a position to do so.

In the final chapters of the book, we must attempt to understand how the ancient Christian hostility toward Jews was transmitted to the modern world and there raged unchecked by the safeguards of traditional theology. Against uncaused hate, there are no final safeguards. But it is possible to hope that historical truth can dissolve antisemitic mythology. When mythology has been dissolved by history, Jews can appear as they are. Then, perhaps, others can learn to acknowledge a common humanity with them.

Our first task must be to attempt to comprehend the nature of modernity, what made it novel, and how its transformation of European and American society affected the Jewish people. This will occupy our attention in the first part of the present chapter, before we turn to consider the events of the period in greater detail.

From the period of the Enlightenment, the ancient Christian myth became secularized. It mutated in consequence into new forms, descendants of the old, religious myth, and sharing many of its characteristics, but no longer explained in religious terms. Liberals, Marxists, and Nazis, as well as Christians of a conservative stamp, continued to blame Jews for the evils of society, but less was now heard of the old theological calumnies. The calumnies that survived the transformation of the myth into secular terms were mostly those of medieval paranoia, the myths generated by the popular unconscious. These proved more tenacious than the theology that had been their original basis.

Modernity did break in many ways with Christian mythology, but most of the leaders of thought in the new nations it brought into being continued to regard the Jews as aliens and potential enemies, as a problem for which solutions would be sought. Not only did they continue to regard the Jews as an alien people, unassimilable while they remained a people, but they continued to attribute to them much the same characteristics as had medieval paranoia.

At least for the Jews, modernity began with the Enlightenment and the French Revolution. Until this time, Jews had been living for many centuries in a unitary Christian society, without the rights of citizens, because they were not regarded as belonging to Christendom. Jews had no legally recognized place in a Christian society, except as serfs or tolerated residents. They had lost their status as Roman citizens and no equivalent had been allotted them.

Before the modern age, every traditional society, with insignificant exceptions, had been based on a shared religious myth, embodying a sacred teaching and sacred laws. Each such society constituted a unity allowing no room for other peoples, defined by the worship of other gods. If you lived in the territory of a particular god, you must worship him and obey his laws along with the other citizens. Thus, in ancient Judaism, in the First Temple period, there was apparently no provision for rites of conversion.[1] There was to be one law for the citizen and for the stranger. You could become a citizen by adhering in full to the laws of the land and worshiping the God of Israel.

In such societies, sacred law governed even those aspects of social life that modern people no longer associate with religion.

The very concept of religion, which involves a distinction between religion and a different sphere, unconnected with it and free from its control, which we now call the secular area of society, had in fact been unknown in all traditional societies. It is still unknown where such societies survive today, as in much of the Islamic world.[2]

In such societies, everything was subject to the rule of the sacred. Accordingly, neither secularity nor its opposite, religion, existed as concepts. By the same token, a plurality of religions within a single society was unthinkable. Jews and Muslims could live in a Christian world–or Jews and Christians in a Muslim world–only as second-class citizens, though in fact not as citizens at all, at best as a tolerated minority of aliens.

Only in the Christian West had the now widely recognized distinction between the religious and the secular domains been able to develop. This distinction proved to be the foundation of modern religious pluralism. It arose for reasons peculiar to

Western and indeed to Christian history. From its beginnings, Christianity did not fully resemble traditional religions. Beginning as a movement within Judaism, and then moving out into the Gentile world, it left behind the social legislation of the Torah, which for the Jewish people completed the structure of a traditional religious society.

The early Church was a small and private movement without aspirations to rule society, whose end it confidently expected. Lacking a social legislation of its own, it tacitly accepted this essential feature of society from the Roman state in which it lived. Even when Christians began to make the laws themselves, after the Constantinian revolution, they did so at first as rulers of the state, rather than in their capacity as churchmen.

Soon, however, the Christian ruler became a sacred personage. In the course of centuries, medieval Christendom, in both East and West, did come to resemble a more traditional society with a religious basis, on which all aspects of common as well as private life rested. At the same time, especially in the Western church, its philosophers and theologians, remembering and valuing the inheritance of classical antiquity along with that of the Bible, began to make distinctions that would in due course evolve further and lead to the notion of the secular domain.

Medieval Christian philosophers had attempted to mediate between the Bible and classical Greek philosophy. In the course of this enterprise, they had learned to make distinctions between natural law and divinely revealed law, between nature and grace, and between the natural and the supernatural. Thus, the concept of a secular domain had already showed signs of being a possibility for medieval thought. But the possibility was not yet actualized in medieval society.

The European Middle Ages distinguished between the two swords, of the church and of the state. But the Church struggled to assert its authority over kings and emperors, and not always successfully. Kings and emperors were anointed and crowned by the Church to signify that their authority derived from God. Thus they too became religious personages, as popes, bishops, and priests already were. In the Orthodox church, in Eastern Europe and in Russia, Byzantine Caesaropapism lived on with little modification. The Emperor, or the czar, remained a hieratic figure, a kind of bishop outside the formal structure of the Church hierarchy.

Where all was sacred, nothing was secular, even though some areas and things were defined as profane. However, it was precisely by sacred law that the nonsacred had been designated as profane. The very word *secular*, coming from a Latin word meaning a period of time, originally implied no contrast with religion; the contrast was with eternity. The Catholic church still speaks of secular priests as opposed to religious, meaning those who belong to an order. In our sense of the word, both are religious.

The modern secular society incorporating religion, and even a variety of religions, within itself–and therefore transcending religion–was a novelty in world history.[3] Intellectual concepts had to come first, before social novelty could be based on them. From the first beginnings of such ideas in medieval philosophy, through the Renaissance, to the thinkers of the Enlightenment, there was a lengthy and complex intellectual development. It was undoubtedly hastened by the breakup of the unity of Christendom in the period of the Reformation, leading to the long and bloody Thirty Years War between Catholics and Protestants. These events made it possible and even inevitable to contemplate a society embracing more than one religion.

When society caught up with thought, the process was sudden and violent. In a few years of intense upheaval, the French Revolution, following hard on the heels of its American forerunner, changed a traditional society, with a long and magnificent history rooted in the ancient and medieval worlds, from the old basis to the new. Others would soon follow. But for the world in general, the French Revolution marked the symbolic turning point.

THE NEW SOCIETIES OF MODERNITY

Nothing like these developments had ever happened before. The advent of the modern age brought about revolutionary novelty in the social, political, and technological spheres. Everywhere, myth was to be replaced with reason. Society would no longer be based on religion, with its myths and its sacred laws. From now on it would be founded on human reason and shared values, as defined by the leaders of the new thinking, the philosophers of Enlightenment.

Skepticism began to replace religious certainties as the foundation of thought. Science and technology flourished, set free from Aristotelian science. The political and social revolution soon led to the Industrial Revolution. The Industrial Revolution in turn led to the technological revolution and the present revolution in information and communications, creating the so-called global village. In the late twentieth century, the media, which do not identify themselves with any religious community, have become a major cultural force, emphasizing the secularity of the majority culture and increasing the alienation of those who look to other sources of inspiration for their lives.

In the course of a century or so, changes occurred whose counterpart in dynamism and magnitude had not been known for millennia, if ever. If members of the great civilizations of the ancient world could have been transported to early eighteenth-century Europe or America, they would have found much of the culture intelligible or even familiar to them. The agricultural and commercial basis of the economy, the construction of buildings and roads, the means of transportation, and in due course postal communication, had all changed little. Even the institutional structures of society, such as monarchy and aristocracy, would somewhat resemble those they had known. There had been greater changes in religion: the temples and sacrifices of their day would be missing. The invention of printing had transformed the dissemination of ideas, including religious ones. Even so, the place of religion in society remained not unlike the one they had known.

By the end of the nineteenth century, even members of an eighteenth century society would have been bewildered by what was going on in the new world, and they probably would have found great difficulty in adapting themselves to it. Nineteenth- and twentieth-century society had already become far more unlike seventeenth- and eighteenth-century society than the latter had been to the societies of three millennia ago.

A little later, the generation of my own parents lived through the invention of the telephone, electric light, the automobile, the airplane, television, the atomic bomb, the jetliner, the space rocket, and the computer. They lived through two world wars, the advent of the totalitarian state, the Nazi Holocaust, and the break up of the great colonial empires. They saw the rise of communism, though not its fall, the polarization of the world between the two superpowers, and the growing importance and influence of the Third World. In their own countries, they saw the breakup of traditional social structures and growing democratization and homogenization of social groups.

THE JEWS IN THE MODERN WORLD

How did these unprecedented intellectual and social changes affect the Jews? Suddenly, and almost without intellectual preparation, a people who had lived for centuries as a closely knit minority, apart from their neighbors, was introduced to the complex and turbulent life of modern nation states. In these states, nationalism began to replace religion as the social bond. Loyalty was now accorded to the nation. In the societies that were still not based on the concept of a single nationality, such as the Austro-Hungarian Empire, emancipated Jews had no community to identify with, since they did not belong to any of the several nations that now made up the Empire. Without religion as the bond, a new one had to be found, and soon the novel concept of race made its appearance, replacing religion as the foundation of identity and unity for the new nations. Jews had no more place in a society based on race than they had previously enjoyed in a society based on an alien religion.

The revolution in thought and in social structure had abolished the domination of the Church, which had so far been the principal agent of anti-Jewish hostility. There was reason for Jews to hope that they could now find toleration and acceptance within a more pluralistic society. To some extent they were able to do so, especially in America and even in Europe. They could not foresee that these apparently beneficent developments would also lead to antisemitism properly so-called, which in the end proved more destructive to the Jewish people than all the forms of religious hostility they had previously experienced.

Large sections of the Jewish people were precipitated into the maelstrom of modernity. Others were not, at first. In Russia, and the areas under its domination, the Middle Ages lasted almost unaltered until 1917. The Enlightenment and the French Revolution had little lasting influence, and it was left to the Russian Revolution to bring modernity almost overnight, in a particularly intense and ideological form, to places where millions of Jews were still living their traditional way of life.

Nowhere, however, had traditional Christian anti-Judaism been as violent and hateful as in the world of czarist Russia. There, in fact, we must recognize an extraordinary fusion of the old religious anti-Judaism with the new racial antisemitism of the West, a fusion that shows very clearly the continuity between them. Even after the downfall of the czarist regime, antisemitism continued to flourish in Communist Russia, almost (though, as we are now beginning to see, not entirely) unchecked, even though it was supposed to have been abolished by the *fiat* of party and state.

In fact, many Jews did adapt themselves with striking success to these changes. There was a remarkable explosion of Jewish talent in the sciences, medicine, literature, music and the other arts, and the financial and commercial world, as Jews flooded into the emancipated post-Enlightenment world. Beyond question, the contribution of emancipated Jews to the modern nation states has been disproportionate, as the number of Jewish Nobel prizewinners exemplifies. But, perhaps out of envy, these achievements were held against them by large masses of people, instead of being to their credit.

Soon, the presence of emancipated Jews in the new nation states evoked new forms of hostility. True antisemitism now made its appearance. For the first time Jews were explicitly identified as a race, whose characteristics could never be eliminated even by conversion to Christianity, still less by mere assimilation to a secular society. The ancient hate was now to be explained in a new way. Supposed racial characteristics of Jews were identified by the new pseudoscience, and the old calumnies found a new center. Deprived of the old restraints of Christian theology, antisemitism became genocidal in less than a century.

In this and the following chapters we shall try to understand how all this happened. Our own societies have not yet analyzed and dealt with their own heritage of genocidal antisemitism. It is regarded as a temporary aberration, confined to Nazi Germany and to a particular time, and needing no serious attention elsewhere and later. Nazism is seen, perhaps, as simply a throwback to more primitive ways of thinking, without roots in modernity, which can therefore afford to ignore it. The lesson of the Holocaust has not been learned. We do not see that genocidal violence is also a characteristic of modernity. In consequence, antisemitism is breaking out again at the present time, and could once more take an extremely destructive form, even after the Holocaust, whose repetition so many confidently regard as unthinkable.

LIBERAL ANTI-JUDAISM

The modern, liberal ideology had ostensibly abandoned mythical thinking in favor of rationality and empiricism. But myths about Jews had not died. In the Nazi ideology, they were overt and lethal, but the liberal world had not fully exorcised them either. Present for the most part below the level of explicit conscious thought, the old myths weakened the West's defenses against genocide. Christendom had been able to defend itself against the genocidal tendency of its own anti-Judaism by means of the Augustinian doctrine that the Jews must be preserved until the end of the world as a witness to their crimes.

The defense was inherently fragile, and it did not prevent terrible persecutions and atrocities, but it may have saved the Jewish people from extinction. Now the myth could continue to flourish without that safeguard. Nazism repudiated the safeguard along with the rest of Christian theology, while retaining and intensifying the antisemitic myths. Liberalism also abandoned the theology but continued to collude with the myths.

The liberal culture of the West (like the churches) failed to mobilize the world against the Nazi Holocaust while it was in preparation and while it was known to be going on. If anything, liberals at that time preached tolerance and understanding of German grievances against the treaty of Versailles and the Nazis' wish to redress them, while continuing to believe in the possibility of peace with Germany long after it had ceased to be realistic. In America, liberals were so hostile toward the thought of war that they long turned their faces from the necessity of going to war against Hitler. Only Pearl Harbor made war inevitable.

Western liberals unconsciously collaborated with Hitler's genocide even while it was known to be in motion. The events leading up to and during the Gulf War proved to be a rerun, in most respects, of the thirties. Liberals and pacifists preached appeasement, indifferent to the obvious fact that appeasement could only be at the expense of Israel and its people, let alone Kuwait, Saddam Hussein's first victim. They continue to preach understanding for Arab grievances against Israel and condone Arab violence and terrorism, while blaming Israel for its attempts at restraining them.

Forty-five years after the full revelation of the consequences of destructive antisemitism in the Holocaust, liberal thinking at the end of the twentieth century does not seem able to stand alongside Jews to protect them against the renewal of antisemitism. Antisemitism is reappearing in the West in the form of hate literature, vandalism, and desecration of synagogues and cemeteries. In the Soviet Union and in Eastern and Central Europe, where the grip of the totalitarian state has been loosened, the old antisemitism is surfacing in a virulent and widespread form. There is every possibility that once more Jews could be made the scapegoat for economic and political distress. It is not yet clear whether the new and inexperienced democracies of Central Europe know how to protect their Jews against a renewed alliance of nationalism with ancient antisemitic hatreds.

Antisemitism is also mutating into new forms, of which the most conspicuous are denial of the historical reality of the Holocaust and anti-Zionism, hostility toward the Jewish state. Holocaust denial has become a minor industry of pseudo-scholarly falsification of history, while anti-Zionism is constantly expressed in gross distortion by the media of the events and issues of the Middle East conflict, supporting governmental policies that once again place the safety of the Jewish people in doubt. New outbreaks of antisemitism are also taking place in the black communities of North America, partly reviving traditional Christian themes, partly stemming from the no less traditional anti-Judaism of the Left. Liberals continue to place the highest priority on freedom of expression, fearing the dangers of censorship, while less educated and sophisticated minds than theirs, especially among the young, can easily be taken in by the outpouring of hate against the Jews.

In the Arab world, except in Egypt almost completely untouched by modern liberalism, the alleged distinction between anti-Zionism and antisemitism has almost completely disappeared, if it was ever a reality. Anti-Judaic hostility, contrary to what is often said by Arabs and their apologists, has deep roots in Islam, going back to the life of the Prophet himself and to the words of the Quran.[4] Islamic anti-Judaism was, to be sure, not as intense as Christian anti-Judaism, for Muslims did not think of Jews as Christ-killers, but they certainly regarded them as untrustworthy, to be opposed and kept in their place. Like Christianity, Islam entails a theology of supersession, applying both to Judaism and Christianity. However, whereas some Christian theologians have begun to criticize their own theology of supersession, there is no sign of Muslim theologians even beginning to do so.

Arab rage against Israel has revived these darker aspects of Islam and borrowed from Western antisemitism some of its own most disreputable themes. Now even Holocaust denial has made its appearance in an organ sponsored officially by the PLO and evidently with the approval of its leadership.[5] Arab antisemitism, though an important and underestimated reality, is not our concern here. What is important and significant for this inquiry is the degree to which Christians and their secular heirs in the West are willing to excuse antisemitism and give it tacit support.

The task of comprehending the evolution of modern antisemitism, and dealing with its continuing presence below the surface of our liberal culture remains urgent. We began with an attempt to comprehend the reasons why the Jews were singled out for the Holocaust. We now begin to see that that task will not be the conclusion of our inquiry. Since Jews are still hated, even after the revelation in the Holocaust of the genocidal potentiality of antisemitism, the inquiry must continue and go on to examine the events of the present day. The forces that led to the Holocaust are still active. Until they are identified and eliminated from society, there is no enduring safety for Jews.

Does the liberal world of post-Christianity in the late twentieth century share in some measure with the atheistic Marxist world and the anti-Christian Nazi world a deep-seated hostility toward Jews? All three of these modern ideologies, which have (it may seem) little else in common, exhibit distaste, to say the least, for Jews and for Judaism, except in a very untraditional form. When the far Right and the far Left get together in a common hatred of Jews, while liberals stand by doing nothing, Jews are again in mortal danger.

Is there perhaps some undiscovered factor common to all three that accounts for the resemblances (significant even if partial) in their attitudes toward the Jews? Did the various types of secularized society in the modern, post-Christian age, whether totalitarian or liberal democratic, each to some degree inherit the anti-Judaism of the religion they had consciously repudiated? There is good reason to think so.

When these modern societies needed a scapegoat, one had already been identified for them by many centuries of Christianity. Prewar Germany had nothing to fear from a Jewish minority of less than one percent. Marxism had no inherent philosophical reason for antipathy to Jews, and in fact, considerable reason for regarding their faith as a relic of past stages in the development of society. Liberalism should have stood for the acceptance of all on the basis of common humanity.

How could any of these three diverse ideologies have concluded that Jews were bad, on the basis of their own ideas about the world? They could only have all "known" it because they had inherited the idea from a past all three shared in common. In that case, we must be prepared to find that the Holocaust had roots running through the French Revolution, the great harbinger of modern, enlightened society, as well as in the anti-Judaism of the *ancien régime*.

THE ENLIGHTENMENT AND THE JEWS

When, in the period of the French Revolution, Europe abandoned the organic, religiously based society of the Middle Ages, it attempted to build the social order on foundations requiring no mythical or religious sanction. The Jewish people, however, had remained a traditional society, even when they were a minority in a Christian world. As societies, and not just as individuals, the Jewish communities had continued to observe the Torah as the basis of their common life. The Torah was still to a very great extent the constitution of a commonwealth, the code of legislation governing corporate and civil behavior, and not just the basis of personal and private morality. Jews had lost their land and much of the legislation applied only to conditions in the land. However, they remained a community. They had been oppressed, sometimes very severely, but they had succeeded in retaining their identity as a distinct self-governing society under the Torah. Could they still retain that identity in the new, enlightened world?

While some of the thinkers of the Enlightenment had been somewhat sympathetic to Jews, believing that they had an important contribution to make to the new society, others continued to be extremely hostile toward them. Even those who saw a place for Jews in the new society thought that they needed to be made "better." By abandoning their old-fashioned ways, their dress, their ritual rules, their language, their exclusiveness and refusal to intermarry, their dependence on usury, and by taking their place in liberal society, they would in fact be changed for the better.

Many Jews thought so too. Among Jews, there was a corresponding movement of Enlightenment, known as the *Haskalah*, and its leaders also hoped that Jews could move into the mainstream of European culture, abandoning their old-fashioned ways, which kept them apart from their fellow citizens, and make a contribution proportionate to their abilities.

Acceptance was not to be unconditional. It would depend on Jews abandoning the features of their own traditional way of life that conflicted with the new ideology. Opponents of emancipation argued that this was impossible. They reasoned from the correct perception that the Jews constituted a people, with its own identity and its own loyalties. Such a people, they thought, could not be integrated into the nation state, the institutional embodiment of a different people.

Many Jews protested that they could indeed leave their traditional way of life behind and become full and loyal citizens of the new states. Even when they attempted to do so, however, antisemites would argue that they had not done so sincerely and that they still stuck together with their fellow Jews more than with their fellow citizens. Antisemites also claimed that they had other loyalties and other goals, sometimes imagined in sinister terms as a conspiracy to take over and rule the states of which they had become citizens. Ironically, the antisemites, who hated Jews, saw them correctly as a people, not just a religious group, whereas those who stood for toleration could not tolerate the Jews as a community with their own way of life but could accept them only as individuals with a diminished Jewish identity. Thus the Jews were in a no-win situation.

The concept of conditional acceptance was embodied in what I have called in the title of this chapter "the Napoleonic bargain," which proved to be the model on which all modern societies, legally or socially, would deal with what came to be known as "the Jewish problem." Napoleon's actual measures were both preceded and followed by similar ones in other countries, embodying the same concept of conditional emancipation. However, what happened in France can serve as the symbol for what happened in many places.

When Napoleon finally decided to incorporate the Jews into the new French society, he imposed conditions on them whose consequences proved to be far-reaching, and not only in France. Jews were to be accepted as fellow citizens, but on the condition that they stopped being traditional Jews, and became "Frenchmen of the Mosaic persuasion." They were to abandon their status as a distinct people, governed by the laws of the Torah, administered by their own rabbinic courts, and to become Frenchmen, distinguished from other Frenchmen only by their religious or "Mosaic" persuasion. They were to abandon hope for a messianic restoration of the commonwealth of Israel in its historic land. The role of the Torah was now to be restricted to religion as Christians were coming to understand it, to private morality and personal relationships. For Jews, all this meant a substantial loss of identity and it meant taking on (for them) a wholly novel conception of religion and its place in a total society.

Napoleon's concept was new to the Jewish people and alien to the ways by which they had hitherto lived. It offered glittering possibilities, but the price was heavier than has usually been supposed. Even when they paid the price in full, Jews were not permitted to realize all the possibilities the bargain seemed to offer. Europe (and to some extent even America) did not after all accept them as equals and fellow citizens, but continued to regard them as a foreign body in society, alien and threatening.

The Napoleonic bargain was applied in one form or another in all the European nation states (though not in Czarist Russia). In analogous, though less explicit, ways the same bargain was already in force in America, the earliest society to be based on the principles of the Enlightenment. There, Jews were at that time fewer than in

Europe, never coming to constitute a legally distinct community. The American heritage of religious nonconformity, entailing the constitutional separation of church and state, made room for Jews as well as for a variety of Christian groups. But all must salute the flag and give an overriding loyalty to the common life of the new republic. American Jews are perhaps the most assimilated of all.

Wherever the Napoleonic bargain was applied, the traditional unity of the Jewish people was disrupted. Modernity hit the Jewish people much harder than it did Christians, because adjusting to it would require much more profound change for Jews. Inevitably, different groups reacted in different ways to the impact of modernity. The resulting controversy was bound to be intense: so much depended on a correct decision. Any decision was certain to be fraught with consequence for all future Jewish faith and life, as well as for the place of the Jews in the new world coming into being.

Some were all for embracing modernity with both hands and altogether abandoning traditional Jewish ways that were in conflict with it. Others suspected that modernity was likely to lead Jews away from God and his Torah and rallied round a very conservative interpretation of the halachah. Still others sought compromises giving appropriate weight to both modernity and tradition.

Wherever Jews entered the modern state, they found themselves embracing a concept of religion traditionally unknown to them and therefore also alien to their existing way of life. In fact, there is no traditional word for religion in Hebrew, and the modern Hebrew word *dat* had to be adapted from sources outside the existing vocabulary.

By the time of Napoleon, it had already become possible for Christians to think of themselves as Frenchmen of the Christian persuasion rather than as Catholics who happened to live in the territory of a French monarch, himself a Catholic like themselves and like other monarchs. Neither Christians nor their secular heirs could see any reason why Jews should not think of themselves in the same way. Indeed, it was clear that some of their leaders, especially among the Sephardim of South-Western France, had already begun to do so. But thinking of themselves as Frenchmen first meant much bigger changes for Jews than for Christians. It meant a radical transformation of Jewish identity. The consequences are still with us in every modern state where Jews live, including Israel.

FRENCHMEN OF THE MOSAIC PERSUASION

Everywhere in Western Europe and America, Jews were becoming "Frenchmen of the Mosaic persuasion" instead of members of a Jewish commonwealth. A genuinely traditional form of Jewish life in due course ceased to exist and is found virtually nowhere today, its surviving elements having been destroyed in the Holocaust. Even the most Orthodox and traditionalist of Jews in these societies found their experience of Jewish life radically transformed by this new conception of the place of religion in society. Suddenly religion, in the new narrow sense borrowed from Christianity, became central to their understanding of what it meant to be Jewish, in ways in fact not traditional for them at all.

Traditionally, what we are accustomed to call religion had been simply one aspect, though an important and central one, of a complete way of life. The laws regarding religion found their place among others governing business, social life, and the relationship of groups in the community to one another. Moving into an environment with a Christian conception of the place of religion in society, leaving behind the public and social aspects of the Torah, and adopting for themselves this new conception of religion, in subtle ways heavily Christianized even the most Orthodox of Jews.

Indeed, perhaps the effect on the most traditional Jews, the least recognized by themselves or by others, was the most profound, inasmuch as they now focused their intense loyalty to tradition on the details of religious observance that differentiated them from other Jews whose observance was laxer or more adjusted to modern conditions. Thus their dedication to being Jewish became focused on religion to a degree Jews had hardly known before, and indeed was not characteristic of the tradition. Today, even the most conservative of all Jewish groups, the non-Zionist ultra-Orthodox in Israel, who attempt to maintain the life of the East European shtetls in modern secular Israel, have been transformed, without themselves recognizing the fact, by this new Christian form of religiousness into a style of Jewish existence unknown to the original shapers of the tradition they revere.

The options explored by the various groups in modern Jewish life parallel in many ways those adopted by analogous groups in modern Christianity. But in the Christian world, none of them touched the identity of the whole community as Jewish conflicts did. Not surprisingly, the conflicts within the Jewish community, between the Reform and Orthodoxy, and between the assimilated and the still observant, and within each of these groups, were hard fought and often bitter. They continue to this day, both in the Diaspora and in Israel.

Many Jews had their own reasons for wishing to enter modernity. The difficulty of doing so was greatly increased by the fact that modernity was to so great an extent a phenomenon of Christian history, not a spontaneous evolution arising from the dynamics of their own history. Modernity had evolved in the Christian world, and it was already more or less fixed in its outlines when Jews entered it and borrowed its outlook.[6] Most Jews who embraced modernity did so because the consequences of remaining excluded from it seemed intolerable.

Many Jews almost completely lost their Jewish identity in the process. Some even surrendered it intentionally. In the nineteenth century, many accepted baptism as "the ticket of entrance" to the liberal Christian world. Later, many more simply abandoned Judaism and lived as secular people among others. Especially in Eastern Europe, a substantial number of Jewish intellectuals embraced the revolutionary philosophies of the Left, hoping that the "Jewish problem" could be solved by the submergence of Jewish identity in a Marxist utopia.

Another group became Zionists, believing that the way out of antisemitic hatred and discrimination was to be found only in a Jewish state, where Jews need not apologize for their existence and could defend themselves. But the Zionists did not attempt to revive in their national home the traditional Jewish community living under sacred law: they made no attempt to restore a Torah-governed state, in any case. Israel was to be a "normal" modern nation-state, like the others.

Among secularized intellectuals who continue to identify themselves as Jews or Israelis, most are unaware that many of the liberal values they cherish as Jewish have actually been absorbed from the Christian and post-Christian West, in the period after the Enlightenment, and are not necessarily authentically Jewish at all. This is even harder for many of them to see because they participate in the modern rebellion against the religious domination of thought and life, and they therefore view traditional forms of Judaism with a contempt and hostility as much Christian as Jewish.

Even those who did their utmost to forget their Jewish identity were not allowed by others to forget it. In fact, post-Enlightenment society now bestowed upon Jews a new identity, not of their own making, and foreign to their traditional understanding of themselves. Deprived of their identity as a people living under the Torah, and in many cases no longer identifiable even as "Frenchmen of the Mosaic persuasion," Jews were now to be regarded as a race. But in the new nation-states, themselves largely based on racial or quasi-racial concepts, there could be no place for members of an alien race. This was especially true in Germany, where the Romantic movement spoke of the *Volk*, the ancient Aryan race in its pure German form. Jews could now no longer be accepted even as "Frenchmen (or Germans) of the Mosaic persuasion." Once again, they were aliens, unassimilable even when they did their utmost to assimilate.

Ancient fear and distrust still lingered under the surface of liberal culture. Even the paranoia of the Middle Ages had not been dissipated by the Enlightenment. Transmitted at the unconscious level from generation to generation, it continued to influence the actions of the post-Christian world, even when these actions were no longer explained by Christian ideas.

As for the Jews themselves, all of them had made a heavy sacrifice of identity, often far heavier than they themselves realized, in order to enter the new world of modernity, in which at last they might find toleration. For many of them, the sacrifice was in vain. In spite of all their efforts, and in spite of the outstanding contribution that they were making to the societies that they joined, Jews remained objects of suspicion, unwelcome, a "problem" that awaited final solution.

ENLIGHTENMENT VIEWS ON RELIGION

The philosophers of the Enlightenment took a skeptical and critical view of revealed religion. It seems likely that they had been profoundly disillusioned with revealed religion by the religious wars and other conflicts within Christendom let loose by the crisis of the Reformation. Christians had been fighting to the death over what (in the eyes of the philosophers) was most doubtful in their beliefs, instead of agreeing on what was most certain. Instead, the philosophers sought a religion that could be firmly based in reason instead of revelation, and therefore would not lead to irrational conflicts over unprovable assertions.

Christianity was characterized by an emphasis on credal orthodoxy, just as it required faith as the primary religious virtue, on which all others were held to depend. In these respects it differed from Judaism, which has always emphasized action more than theology, so much so that many have argued that the concept of theology is actually foreign to Judaism. The Jewish people has traditionally been held together by a common observance of the Torah, not by a common creed. Whereas Christian controversies have been primarily about what to believe, Jewish ones have usually been about what to do.

Judaism might well have appealed to the philosophers of the age of Enlightenment, and to some it did. It could appear to be more rationally based than Christianity, and less exclusive in its requirements for salvation, since any righteous person, Jewish or not, could be saved. Its ethical principles were rationally acceptable and could be defended without reference to the specific revelation at Sinai, or so it seemed to some. Moreover, they seemed to be essentially the same as those which Christianity advocated, if only because Christianity had drawn much of its ethics from Judaism. What later came to be called, misleadingly, the "Judaeo-Christian ethic," could serve as the basis for a commonly shared system of values that could be rationally supported and did not need revelation to authenticate it.

However, the simple monotheism and rational ethics of Judaism were wrapped up in what was called "positive religion." Positive religion, a favorite term of the day, was contrasted with natural religion. To the thinkers of the time it meant religion that was invented by priests, full of superstitions and rules for the control of society. It depended on the irrational concept of divine revelation, which permitted the guardians of the supposed revelation, the priestly caste, to exercise domination over society.

The monotheism and the ethics of Judaism were not identical with natural religion, though they resembled it. They were bound up with a traditional way of life and ritual rules that seemed as irrational and outmoded as the ethics seemed rational. The potential value of Judaism for an enlightened age could only be achieved if the monotheism and the ethics could be separated from the ritual commandments and the distinctive way of life. Jews had a contribution to make to the new age, but traditional Judaism could not make that contribution. Jews had to be made better before they could be acceptable. Even those who thought that Judaism had an essential contribution to make to an enlightened society were convinced that only a radical reform of Jewish ways could make that contribution possible.

Other Enlightenment thinkers were almost as hostile toward Judaism as their orthodox Christian predecessors had been. Sometimes, their expressed hostility toward Judaism seems to have been a safer way of venting their hostility to their real enemy, the Church. In other cases, it seems that, as would happen so often in the succeeding decades, abandoning the faith of the Church did not entail parting with its anti-Jewish prejudices. The Enlightenment stood in principle for tolerance and freedom of individual opinion, in part because it was skeptical of all religious certainties, but since it had failed to free itself from the anti-Judaic hostility of the Church, it could not extend that tolerance to Jews as members of a community.

Jews could enter the new age as individuals, but not as members of a traditional religious community. As Clermont-Tonnerre put it in 1789, "Everything for the Jews as individuals, nothing for them as a community." Only as individuals could Jews be tolerated, never as full Jews in the traditional sense, since Jews had not hitherto regarded themselves as religious individuals, but as sharers in a communal way of life.

During the seventeenth century, Europe had been swept by a tide of rationalism.[7] In its thinking on religion, this new rationalism was crude and prejudiced, by the critical standards of later experience. Its greatest representative, Spinoza, did grasp the possibility of a genuinely scientific criticism of the Bible, but his insights would not be followed up for many decades. True historical criticism did not begin until late in the eighteenth century, and it only got properly under way in the nineteenth century. Seventeenth-century critics of religion tended to focus on the Old Testament, seeing it as a tissue of myths, full of unbelievable stories of prophecies and miracles. While it was Christianity that was actually under attack, such a critique could hardly fail to perpetuate ancient hostilities toward Judaism.

Eighteenth-century thinkers focused their criticism rather on positive religion in general, contrasting it, as we have seen, with natural religion. Natural religion (a construct of the eighteenth-century imagination, that could hardly have existed in actual history) was exceedingly rational. It consisted of an argument for the existence of a very abstract God and a nonspecific morality that could theoretically be assented to by members of any religion, as well as by the philosophers of antiquity on whose thought it ultimately depended. Such a religion, though the term religion is hardly appropriate, could appeal to philosophers in their studies. Devoid of emotional or spiritual content, it had no chance of becoming the foundation of a society, or a living faith for the broad mass of a people.

Its intellectual basis ultimately went back to the medieval distinction between the natural and the supernatural, between the spheres of nature and of grace. This in turn corresponded approximately to the contributions to Christian civilization of Graeco-Roman antiquity, on the one hand, and of Bible, on the other. But whereas the medievals usually grounded nature in grace, while distinguishing between them, the deists and other enlightened philosophers attempted to cut away the sphere of grace and revelation altogether, leaving only natural religion and natural law. Just as the medievals had asserted that natural reason can tell us *that* God is, even though not *what* he is, the philosophers of this period were inclined to believe in the existence of God, though not in his attributes as Jews and Christians had formerly understood them. Essentially, they were abandoning the biblical contribution to Western civilization in favor of the philosophical contribution of antiquity.

Once rationalism took a turn toward empiricism, the concept of God became even more tenuous. Hume ironically perhaps, and Kant rigorously and intentionally, located God outside the realm of rational demonstration, in that of faith. The traditional arguments for the existence of God, inherited from the medieval philosophers, were now subjected to a devastating criticism, from which they have not yet recovered.

In this development of ideas, it was not to be expected that Jewish faith and life would fare very well. While Judaism could sometimes be used as a stick to beat Christian dogmatism, and Jewish morality was occasionally commended as more rational than Christian, the fact that the Jewish understanding of God and his commands was rooted in the Bible meant that the enlightened philosophers could have little real sympathy with it. From their point of view, it was really no better than Christianity, although since they had not themselves felt Judaism as a restrictive weight, they could sometimes view it more dispassionately.

Thus, the most liberal thinking of the seventeenth and eighteenth century on religion tended to favor toleration of the Jews in so far as they were not Christians, but could only be comfortable with them if they were substantially changed. A very abstract, enlightened, and (from a traditional point of view) greatly attenuated Judaism could be acceptable to the age. The concrete faith and life of a Jewish community, observing the Torah in full, could not.

NATHAN THE WISE

Perhaps the most positive appreciation of Jews that we can find in this period comes from G. E. Lessing, who wrote about the Jews in more than one of his works. Lessing knew and greatly admired the enlightened Berlin Jew Moses Mendelssohn. He used him as the model for the central character in his play, *Nathan the Wise*. One of its central themes is the very modern notion that the three great religions of the West, Judaism, Christianity, and Islam, are children of the same father.[8]

Lessing's central thesis on the three religions is embodied in the allegory of the three rings, told by Nathan himself. According to the story, in the East there once lived a man who owned a wondrous ring, which had the property of rendering its wearer beloved by God and man, so long as he wore it in faith and confidence. He made a will, bequeathing the ring to the dearest of his sons, and enjoined upon him to do the same for the dearest of his own sons. The owner of the ring would always become the head of the family.

Eventually, the ring descended to a father of three sons, each of whom he loved equally. He had weakly promised each one of them that he should inherit the ring. To solve his problem, he had two perfect copies made of the original ring, and before his death, separately and without telling the others, gave each of his three sons one of the rings and his blessing. Each, of course, then claimed to be the head of the household but could not make good his claim because the rings were now indistinguishable from each other—"almost as indistinguishable as the true religion now is."

Nathan tells his interlocutor, Sultan, that he himself has no way of distinguishing in truth between the three great religions. Each depends on history and tradition, which (he implies) is not susceptible of rational proof, but must instead be accepted in faith and trust. Each of us naturally trusts our own flesh and blood, and accepts from them what they tell us, unless there is reason not to. Thus it is natural for Jews, Muslims, and Christians alike to believe in their own religion.

The sons went to court with their claim. Each swore, truthfully, that he had received the ring from the father with his love and blessing. Each insisted that his father could not possibly have deceived him, and that the fraud, if any, must be the work of his brothers.

The judge, told that the ring had the power to make the wearer beloved, inquired which of the three was most loved by the other two, since a false ring could not have this effect. If, as seemed to be the case, each loved himself the best, the natural conclusion would be that all the rings were false.

Finally, however, the judge advises them to leave things as they are. Let each go on believing his ring the true one, and try to live up to the promise that it would make him beloved by practicing the virtues of friendliness and devotion to God. Perhaps in a thousand thousand years a wiser judge may then be able to render judgment between the three sons.

Elsewhere in the play, Nathan defends himself against the accusation that the Jews themselves had introduced the religious division between human beings by thinking of themselves as the chosen people. He replies that he did not choose his people any more than anyone else did. "I am a man first and a Jew second, and you are a man first and a Christian second."

While the parable has won much praise for its message of mutual religious tolerance, it is important to look at it a little more closely, for its message is a very modern and indeed skeptical one. Lessing's Nathan shares with the age the notion that only rational demonstration can give certainty. The claims of positive religion cannot be rationally supported. They depend on the contingent facts of history, which can never be the basis of a rational proof.

In fact, since faith is uncertain, ethics will be the only solid support for religion. The message is borrowed, perhaps, from a saying of Jesus, "By their fruits you shall know them," but put into a modern context. What is left from this enlightened critique of positive religion is not twentieth-century interfaith dialogue, based on mutual respect and appreciation, but the deist remnant of an abstract God and a purely rational ethic.

Lessing puts his enlightened message into the mouth of a Jew, who is thus depicted as less of a dogmatist than his Christian or Muslim counterparts. The Jew is represented as the proponent of natural religion, opposed to the dogmatism of positive, or revealed, religion. But it is abundantly clear that though Lessing is able to respect an enlightened Jew, he has no more use for traditional Judaism than he has for Christianity in its positive form. Even for this most sympathetic of Enlightenment philosophers, Jews must be reformed before they can find a place in tolerant liberal society. The Jew he depicts in Nathan has been thoroughly reformed.

While Nathan's humanist claim that he is a man first and a Jew second can easily be defended on Jewish grounds, in the context it seems to lend support to the very concept we have symbolized by the formula, "Frenchmen of the Mosaic persuasion." It is not a large step from the universal but abstract humanism of Nathan-Lessing to the nationalism of the nineteenth century, and enlightened liberalism was to prove weak before its onslaught.

Not long after Lessing composed *Nathan the Wise*, C. W. Dohm, an official at the Prussian court, wrote at the instigation of Moses Mendelssohn a book called *Civil Reform of the Jews*, in which he proposed that Jews should be granted equal rights and complete freedom in their choice of occupation. He called for freedom of worship, including the opening of synagogues, abolition of ghettos, admission of Jews to schools, and permission for them to take part in science and the arts.

However, he wanted to make bookkeeping in Hebrew illegal in order to prevent deception and increase trust. Jewish schools should be supervised to prevent the influence of antisocial attitudes toward those of other religious views, and the teaching of "the pure and holy truths of rationalism" required, in particular the obligations of citizens toward the state. Moreover, where a Jew and a Christian of equal qualifications were candidates for the same post, the Christian should be preferred.

Clearly, even this benevolent representative of enlightened thought considered the Jews dishonest in tendency and inclined to hate Christians and feel no loyalty to the state. Dohm's views had considerable international influence on proposals for Jewish reform and emancipation.

NONCONFORMITY AND TOLERATION

In the previous century, the case for toleration of Jews had been argued as an incidental conclusion from the requirement of tolerance between the Christian groups. Roger Williams, the Puritan preacher who founded Rhode Island, claimed in 1644 that "true civility and Christianity may flourish . . . notwithstanding the permission of divers and contrary consciences either of Jew or Gentile." He argued that since the coming of Lord Jesus, it is the will of God that "freedom of religion, a permission of the most Paganish, Jewish, Turkish or anti-Christian conscience be granted to all men, in all nations and in all countries."[9] This hardly sounds like a commendation of Jews, but it is a radical demand for freedom of religion, from which American Jews would later profit.

In 1689, the English philosopher John Locke, in political theory an apologist for the Glorious Revolution of 1688, wrote a "Letter concerning Toleration," in which he affirmed that "There is absolutely no such thing under the Gospel as a Christian commonwealth." The early Christian church had had no connection with the state and was in fact a voluntary society. Thus, "[n]either pagan, nor Mahometan, nor Jew ought to be excluded from the civil rights in the commonwealth because of his religion."[10] But Locke did not therefore, like Lessing a century later, argue that there is no real or rationally based distinction between Judaism and Christianity. For him, Christianity itself was essentially reasonable, though he attenuated Christian dogma very considerably in the name of reason. Thus, he proved to be the precursor of the English Deists.

In intellectual circles, Jews did become more acceptable through the spread of humanistic scholarship. Christian Hebraists increased in number, and chairs of Hebrew were founded in a number of universities. Sometimes these could even be filled by Jews. Others studied Hebrew and Judaism with the aim of converting Jews. Even they, however, defended Jews against the traditional calumnies, when they were revived in such a book as the notorious *Das entdeckte Judentum* (Jewry Exposed, 1700) by Johann Eisenmenger. Eisenmenger himself was arrested, but his book (though initially suppressed in response to Jewish indignation) would in due course become a source book for later antisemites.

JEWISH APOLOGETICS

Sensing the changing climate, apologists to the Gentile world began to appear from within the ranks of the Jewish people themselves. Simone Luzzato, a rabbi from Venice, published in 1638 his essay on the Jews of Venice. He argued that the presence of a Jewish community brought advantages to Venice and to all other states. Wherever Jews live, trade and commerce flourish. Jews developed the economy, did not acquire landed property, and did not seek political power.

Similar arguments were put forward by the Sephardic Jew Menasseh ben Israel, in his address to the Lord Protector of England, Oliver Cromwell, petitioning for the return of the Jews to England. However, ben Israel added a messianic turn to the argument. He argued on the basis of biblical prophecy that the end of the age and the coming of the Messiah awaited the presence of the Jews in the farthest parts of the earth first. England, as the most northerly and distant realm, must have its Jewish presence. Cromwell was ready to be convinced, if not by the messianic at least by the commercial argument. He himself stood for religious tolerance, except for the Church of England, and he was ready to have the Jews back. But others opposed the idea strongly, and it did not pass into law. From that time on, however, Jews began again to live in England unmolested, and some of the oldest English Sephardic families owe their origins to this period.

John Toland, a leading Deist, explicitly basing his reasoning on Luzzato, argued in 1714 for the grant of rights of citizenship to Jews, in his *Reasons for Naturalizing the Jews in Great Britain and Ireland*. In France, Montesquieu argued along similar lines. Christians had fostered the role of Jews in European trade when they had prohibited usury in the Middle Ages. Under the threat of expulsion and confiscation of property Jews had invented the letter of exchange, rendering their property safe from seizure. Commerce could become international and secure, and princes were forced to govern more humanely and virtuously, in their own self-interest. Thus, Montesquieu hinted that Jews had actually played a beneficial part in the development of the European economy.

In his *L'esprit des lois* (1748) he argued for universal tolerance, and he pleaded eloquently for Jewish victims of the Inquisition. Nevertheless, even those best disposed to Jews among the Enlightenment thinkers were convinced that Jews needed to be reformed. In particular, they must be weaned away from the Talmud and return to biblical simplicity. None of the philosophers was bold enough to argue for full tolerance for traditional Judaism.

ANTI-JUDAISM AMONG THE PHILOSOPHERS

Other eighteenth-century thinkers were much less well disposed toward Jews. Herder regarded them as "a parasitic plant, clinging to almost all the European nations and sucking their marrow." However, he looked forward to the day when it will no longer be asked who is a Jew and who is a Christian, since Jews will live according to European laws and contribute to the well-being of the state.

Voltaire, the most prominent writer of the day, was generally regarded in his own time as the leading antisemite among the philosophers. His intolerance of Jews extended even to the enlightened among them. He regarded the Jewish character as immutable, persisting from ancient times into his own. Such a view foreshadowed nineteenth-century racism. While Jews are no longer objected to as Christ-killers, many of the old calumnies still stick to them. On this premise, Jews were incapable of the reform that Enlightenment thinkers regarded as a prerequisite to their incorporation in modern society.

Various explanations have been offered for Voltaire's attitudes toward the Jews, apparently inconsistent with his general philosophical position. While he apparently had had unfortunate experiences with two Jewish individuals, he himself considered these of no importance in the formation of his outlook. Arthur Hertzberg argues that in his repudiation of Christianity Voltaire went back to ancient pagan attitudes to Judaism.[11] Certainly he repeated at length the arguments of pagan antiquity against the Jews.

At the intellectual level, it seems to be true that Voltaire did set the Greeks against the Jews. In all probability, however, his opinions, like so much else we have examined in this inquiry, were rationalizations of emotional attitudes acquired very early in life and never adequately criticized. We can safely assume that Voltaire already "knew" that Jews were bad before he went to antiquity to find reasons for his conviction. In this sense, we can agree with those who argue that his attitudes were vestigial relics of Christianity. If so, they were an important channel through which Christian hostility entered the secular, post-Enlightenment world in secularized form.[12]

As Hertzberg himself puts it:

> The idea of freedom for all sorts of intellectual ideas was the major intellectual force for liberating the Jews at the end of the eighteenth century. The idea of re-making men to fit properly into the new society was the seed-bed of totalitarianism. The notion that the new society was to be a reevocation of classical antiquity was the prime source of

> post-Christian antisemitism in the nineteenth century. The vital link, the man who skipped over the Christian centuries and provided a new, international, secular anti-Jewish rhetoric in the name of European culture rather than religion, was Voltaire. The defeat of the emancipation of the Jews existed in embryo even before that process began.[13]

Hertzberg establishes the importance of Voltaire as a link between the old anti-Judaic hostility and the new antisemitism, but in his concentration on the history of ideas he fails to perceive that ideas are often rationalizations, in this case of the old Christian paranoia. The pagan critique of Jews was no more intellectually defensible than its Christian counterpart. For a man of Voltaire's intellectual stature to embrace it argues a powerful emotional pressure distorting rational thought.

Some have argued that the invective of Voltaire and others was really directed against Christianity, with the aim of undermining it by sapping its biblical foundations in Judaism. But they could have achieved the same aim by praising Judaism and emphasizing its differences from Christianity. That it did not occur to them to do so must be significant.

In his *Philosophical Dictionary*, Voltaire described the Jews as "a totally ignorant nation who for many years have combined contemptible miserliness and the most revolting superstition with a violent hatred of all those nations that have tolerated them. Nevertheless they should not be burned at the stake."[14] Given the language in which Jews are described, the rejection (stylistically an afterthought) of burning at the stake did not stand much chance of warding off destructive Jew-hatred. Voltaire's hostility toward Jews recurs again and again in his writings, up to the end of his life.

The materialist d'Holbach wrote of Jews in even more opprobrious terms:

> The revolting policy of the Jewish legislator (sc. Moses) has erected a stone wall between his people and all other nations. Since they are submissive only to their priests, the Jews have become the enemies of the human race . . . The Jews have always displayed contempt for the clearest dictates of morality and the law of nations . . . They were ordered to be cruel, inhuman, intolerant, thieves, traitors and betrayers of trust. All these are regarded as deeds pleasing to God. In short, the Jews have become a nation of robbers . . . They have become notorious for deception and unfairness in trade, and it may be assumed that if they were stronger, they would, in many cases, revive the tragedies that occurred so frequently in their country . . . If there are also honest and just people among them (which cannot be doubted) this means that they have rejected the principles of that law clearly aimed at creating trouble-makers and evil-doers.[15]

As Hertzberg tells us. ". . . [d'Holbach] argued that the Jews were a creation of a climate and an environment that made them totally and hopelessly foreign to Europe. This was, of course, a long step toward the notion about race that was to be held by Gobineau in the next century."[16]

Such language, coming from a supposedly enlightened philosopher, who firmly rejected the Christian myth along with Christian institutions, shows only too clearly the persistence of medieval paranoia in the post-Christian world. The language is strongly reminiscent of the medieval calumnies we have already considered in a previous chapter. The same ideas are familiar even today in the utterances of those who detest Jews, while echoes of them ring in the current denunciations of Israel by liberal Europeans and North Americans.

Fichte, a founder of Germanic romanticism in philosophy, went even further. A protégé of Kant, he wrote in extravagant terms in praise of the German spirit, which he saw as the chief bearer of universal values. He is generally considered the first important theoretician of German nationalism. He believed in a mysterious spiritual connection between the divine life and that of the German people, a connection once enjoyed by other nations, but now lost by them and retained only by the Germans. In effect, the Germans were the chosen people. These were the seeds of ideas that the Nazis turned into an ideology for the masses.

Fichte sought to defend German culture against Napoleonic imperialism, writing as he did while Berlin was under French occupation. But the values associated with Napoleon and the French revolution were those of rationalism, liberalism, and legalism, opposed to the pseudo-mystical thinking of the new Germanism. Soon these revolutionary values would be associated with the Jews, as opponents of a regime from which they had nothing to expect and under which they had suffered profoundly. For such reactionary thinkers as Fichte, Jews became symbols of modernity, to be opposed along with it.

Obviously, there could not be two chosen peoples. If the Germans had been chosen as the bearers of divine life in the world, the Jews could have no such role. Consistently with his rejection of all that he conceived to be Jewish values, Fichte actually denied the Jewishness of Jesus, perhaps the first thinker since Marcion to do so, but by no means the last, especially in Germany. Fichte considered the Gospel of John, which he found more congenial than the others, to be the only one that was trustworthy. Because this gospel does not furnish a Davidic genealogy of Jesus, Fichte felt free to conclude that his descent was uncertain. Since he was such a pure representative of the German spirit, Jesus could not have been Jewish.[17]

In his treatment of the Jewish question, Fichte combined the two arguments we have met with already: the Jews were morally corrupt, and they constituted an alien state within a state. However, he did not share the view that the Jews could be reformed by removing their distinct communal identity and absorbing them as individuals into the nation-state. He was convinced of Jewish hostility toward the rest of the world, and he was certain that they would never become loyal citizens. "Give them civil rights?" he wrote, "I see no other way of doing this except to cut off all their heads one night and substitute other heads without a single Jewish thought in them. . . . I see no alternative but to conquer their promised land for them and to dispatch them all there."[18]

Fichte was perhaps the first antisemite to embrace Zionism (in advance of its invention by Jews) as the solution to the Jewish problem. In 1938, the Nazis were still implementing this solution: Eichmann collaborated with the Irgun Zvai Leumi in organizing the illegal immigration of Jews into Palestine from Nazi-dominated Germany and Austria.[19]

Kant, not widely known as an antisemite, put the Enlightenment position succinctly in his *The War of the Faculties*. "The euthanasia of Judaism can only be achieved by means of a pure moral religion, and the abandonment of all the old legal regulations" (sc., of Judaism). Thus, for the most influential thinkers of the Enlightenment, there were only two possible solutions, each of which involved the "euthanasia" or death of Judaism. Either the Jews were to be reformed out of existence, or they were to be exported or expelled once more. One is reminded of Raul Hilberg's sinister formulation of the progress of antisemitism. If the Middle Ages said to Jews, "You shall not be allowed to live among us," the modern age said, "You shall not be allowed to live as Jews." It would be left to the Nazis to say, "You shall not be allowed to live."

Because we take antisemitism so much for granted, it is important to emphasize yet again that such ideas are not and were not then self-evident. The philosophers of the Enlightenment who argued that Jews must be reformed before they could enter modern society, or who considered them incapable of reformation, did not base their opinion on a careful and unprejudiced study of actual Jewish life. They knew little or nothing of actual Jews. Jewish need for reform, let alone their incapacity for it, was assumed, never demonstrated.

The philosophers' concept of what Jews were like had quite another source. It came from the millennial Christian myths about Jews as Christ-killers, legalists, usurers, and so on. It was by Christian standards that the Jews were supposed to be in need of reform, not by their own, or even by those of unbiased inquiry. The philosophers did not need to conduct a fresh investigation into Jewish life because they already "knew" how bad Jews were, even when they were ready to blame Christian influence for these defects. The source of their knowledge was the New Testament, the Church fathers, and popular Christian tradition, in short, the myth. It would be left to our own times for the non-Jewish world to make the first beginnings of the criticism of that myth, too late to save six million European Jews.

THE FRENCH REVOLUTION

The French Revolution opened up the whole Jewish question in debates in the National Assembly of France and in the corresponding discussions in the Batavian (Dutch) National Assembly. The Revolution stood for the new world of modernity and the rights of man, a world in which old religious intolerances could no longer be justified. Inevitably, therefore, the question of the status of the Jews in the new regime was discussed at length.

Even the most conservative, clerical members of the National Assembly did not argue for continuing to deprive the Jews of human rights. All agreed that they should have freedom of movement and choice of occupation. Disagreement centered on what we have already singled out as the key issue: did the Jews constitute a separate people, or could they be integrated into the new state? Ironically, as we have already seen, it was those who argued against the grant of full citizenship to the Jews who maintained the traditional (Jewish as well as Christian) view that they did, while those who stood for greater tolerance also denied the Jews their full identity as a people under the Torah.

In the discussions of December 1789, the clergy and other conservatives argued that "the word *juif* is not the name of a sect, but of a nation which has laws of its own, according to which it has always acted and wishes to continue to act. If you define the Jews as citizens, it is as if you had said that Englishmen and Danes could be French citizens, without papers and naturalization and without ceasing to be Englishmen and Danes." The radicals, of whom Robespierre was the spokesman, argued that "[t]he evil qualities of the Jews emanate from the degree of humiliation to which you have subjected them. . . . Any citizen who fulfils the conditions of eligibility has the right to public office."[21]

Abbé Henri Grégoire was the most prominent churchman in the movement for emancipation. He had been influenced in his political thinking on the subject by Dohm's writings. Grégoire came from Jansenist circles in the French church that had for some time been friendlier to Jews than traditional Catholics. They believed that the conversion of the Jews must precede the second coming of Christ, and that this end would be accomplished by treating them with kindness and tolerance.[22] Earlier, he had won an important prize from the Society of Sciences and Arts in Metz for an essay on the renaissance of the Jews.

In Grégoire's solution, the Jewish communities as such would be dissolved and replaced by private associations concerned only with religion in the narrow Christian sense. A government representative would chair all Jewish gatherings and everything would be conducted in the language of the country. (Grégoire was personally opposed to all dialects, but he had a particular dislike of Yiddish.) The aim was emancipation by assimilation, as with other liberals.

In the assembly, Grégoire moved a motion in favor of the Jews, but met with much opposition. The assembly and the country were both strongly divided on the issue, and there was much political agitation on both sides. Similar debates took place in the Dutch or Batavian National Assembly in 1796. There, too, conservatives argued that the Jews still hoped to return to the land from which they had been banished and were therefore strangers in all other lands. Liberals and radicals argued that the Jews were not a nation but a people of one faith, having no state of their own.

In spite of the adoption in August 1789 of the Declaration of the Rights of Man, which provided that "[n]o man shall be molested for his beliefs, including religious beliefs," the assembly failed to resolve the question in the debates of December of the same year. The following January, the (mainly) Sephardic Jews of Bordeaux and Bayonne–those "known in France by the name of Portuguese, Spanish and Avignonnais Jews"–were granted the status of "active citizens." Those granted these rights numbered between three and four thousand. It was only at the end of September 1791 that the assembly finally passed a law enfranchising all Jews. The second decree also embraced the Ashkenazic communities of the northeastern border of the country and of Alsace and Lorraine, numbering about thirty thousand, much poorer, with a few exceptions, than the Sephardim of the south, and subject to much more antisemitism.[23]

Wherever the revolutionary armies went, they carried the same principles with them. They expelled the pope from Rome in 1798, revoking the discriminatory laws of Rome on the Jews. Similar measures were taken in other captured Italian territories. In 1898, the kingdom of Westphalia in Western Germany granted equal rights to the Jews, but as elsewhere, with the decline of French influence the state reverted to older attitudes.

Only in Prussia did matters evolve in the same direction for internal reasons. After the defeats by the French in 1806–1807, there was much pressure for liberalization, and in 1812 an edict was issued declaring Jews to be "countrymen and citizens of the state." They were to be subject to the same civil obligations, including military service, as other citizens, while their matrimonial laws were placed under civil jurisdiction, although marriages under Jewish law were recognized as valid civil marriages. Only in the government service was the principle of equality compromised.[24]

THE NAPOLEONIC BARGAIN

It was left to Napoleon in the first decade of the nineteenth century to resolve the question in a more stable way. We have already considered the background to his thinking. It is now time to look somewhat more closely at the details of his treatment of the Jews, if only for its symbolic importance for the whole modern age.

Napoleon had originally followed the conservative line, regarding the Jewish people as a nation rather than as a religion, but he eventually took a more liberal course, wishing for the reformation rather than the expulsion of the Jews. His policy evolved over several years in reaction to changing circumstances before reaching full clarity. After his return from his victory at Austerlitz in 1806, he received a petition from the citizens of Alsace-Lorraine, where the greatest number of Ashkenazi Jews lived.

The citizens in question had acquired during the revolution a considerable amount of property confiscated from the clergy and aristocracy. However, they lacked the funds to work these properties and had in consequence to borrow from Jewish bankers. As a result of inflation, they found themselves unable to pay off their debts. Naturally, they blamed the Jews.

Napoleon took their complaints seriously, and on his return to Paris he determined to impose restrictions on the Jewish usurers. His first intention was to impose an indefinite moratorium on all debts owed to Jewish bankers. At that time he was influenced by an article in a leading newspaper that argued that the emancipation of the Jews had been one of the greatest mistakes of the revolution. The writer contended that the Jews could never become true citizens unless they became Christians. The implication was that once again the Jews should be expelled.

However, Napoleon now began to think, characteristically, in more grandiose terms, which led him in a different direction. "It would be a weakness to chase away the Jews," he declared. "It would be a sign of strength to correct them."[25] The emperor had now borrowed an idea from the liberals, while incorporating it into his own imperial ideology. He persuaded the National Assembly to follow up a more limited, one year moratorium on debts to the Jews with a call for the convening of a Jewish assembly of notables to study the situation.

The assembly met in July 1806 under the chairmanship of Abraham Furtado, a financier who was already disposed to think of himself as a Frenchman first. The assembly was welcomed with ceremony, including a guard of honor. However, its proceedings were opened by a speech from Napoleon's representative for Jewish affairs, Comte Molé. The speech was abusive and uncompromising, containing a denunciation of the practice of usury. The delegates, who had been led to expect considerable forward movement on their question, were stunned and on the defensive.

Molé then presented them with twelve imperial questions, dealing with the relationship of the Jewish community to the French body politic. They were examined on Jewish laws of marriage, including their attitude toward polygamy, the validity of civil divorces, and mixed marriages, on the nomination and jurisdiction of rabbis, on whether Jewish law prohibited them from entering the professions, and whether it encouraged usury. Finally, they were asked whether the Jews considered France their country and whether or not they would defend it. Here they could answer enthusiastically, "*Jusqu'à la mort!*" (until death).

The other questions gave them somewhat more difficulty, but in the end their answers were also affirmative. They concluded by expressing their full readiness to comply with Napoleon's wish, transmitted to them by his delegate: "*Sa majesté veut que vous soyez Français.*" (His Majesty's will is for you to be Frenchmen.)

The assembly had something of the character of a commission of inquiry, and its findings had so far no legal status. Napoleon wished to invest them with the utmost possible solemnity. He determined therefore to revive the ancient Sanhedrin in his own domain of France and to call upon it to pass the new understandings, the answers of the Provisional Assembly, into Jewish law. Every congregation would send representatives, so that its findings would be accepted by the whole community.

Napoleon wrote to them, "I desire to take every means to ensure that the rights which were restored to the Jewish people be not illusory . . . to find for them a Jerusalem in France."[26] Molé required the decisions to be taken by this Sanhedrin to be placed side by side with the Talmud; they should gain the greatest possible authority in the eyes of Jews everywhere. Clearly, this was not a spontaneous evolution of Jewish law, but a development imposed from the outside, which the Jews of France were willing to go along with in order to achieve their aim of emancipation.

The Sanhedrin finally met in Paris in February 1807. Its function, according to Napoleon, was to represent "the organization of the Mosaic religion" in the state of France. In order to meet Napoleon's wish that the revived body should resemble its ancient predecessor as closely as possible, it had the traditional number of seventy-one delegates and was presided over by a *nasi* (president or chairman), an *av bet din* (vice-president), and a *hacham* (second vice-president), as tradition required. The rabbi of Strasbourg, David Sinzheim, was appointed *nasi*.

In its very first session the Sanhedrin ratified the decisions of the assembly and gave them legal sanction. It yielded on every point except mixed marriages, the issue to which Napoleon himself attached the greatest importance. The Sanhedrin managed to find an acceptable compromise on this point also. Mixed marriages, though not sanctioned by Jewish religion, were to be recognized as binding if they took place under civil auspices. The Sanhedrin delicately reminded the Emperor that this was also the position of the Catholic church.[27]

Abba Eban comments:

> With the decisions of the Sanhedrin the Jews of France renounced rabbinical jurisdiction, corporate status, and the hope for a return to the Land of Israel. From now on, their destiny was to be linked inseparably with that of France. As Abraham Furtado declared: "We are no longer a nation within a nation. France is our country, Jews. Your obligations are outlined; your happiness is waiting." The Sanhedrin's renunciation of separate nationhood marked an important turning point in Jewish history, and set the tone of Western Jewish life for the next century and more.[28]

However, the Sanhedrin's renunciations of traditional Jewish self-understanding did not win for the Jews of France the promised full acceptance as Frenchmen. As we shall see, during the course of the nineteenth century, antisemitism grew dramatically in France, taking on a racist character foreign to older Christian tradition and assuming an intensity perhaps even greater than that which characterized its German counterpart in the same period. In fact, it is even possible to wonder why the Holocaust did not take place in France rather than Germany, and it is no surprise at all that Vichy France was so ready to collaborate with the German occupiers in the rounding up of its Jewish population for deportation and extermination.

French antisemitism came to a symbolic climax in the Dreyfus affair of 1894 and the following years. Dreyfus' trial was to be reported by a young Jewish journalist from Austria, up to that point as assimilated as a Jew can be. Theodor Herzl received such a shock at the revelation of the depth of hatred of the French for their Jewish countrymen that he turned in quite another direction, one hitherto embraced, though almost unknown to him, only by some Eastern European visionaries. The new direction, which would in due course become the received view in almost all Jewish communities, was to be called Zionism.

Like Napoleon's bargain, which it renounced as null and void, Zionism embraced aspects of both conservative and radical views. Like the more conservative views, Jewish as well as Christian, Zionism was to reaffirm that the Jews are a people, a nation like other nations, with the right to and need for a state of their own. Jews could never hope successfully to be "Frenchmen of the Mosaic persuasion." In reaffirming their traditional identity as a people, Jews would also lay claim to their traditional country.

In order to do so, however, they had to break with the traditional Jewish belief that only the Messiah could restore the people to their land. Moreover, they made no attempt to restore rabbinical jurisdiction over the whole community under Jewish law. (The distinctive Israeli concept of the status quo retained rabbinical jurisdiction over personal status in matters such as marriage, while preserving the monopoly of Orthodoxy among the Jewish religious groups.) The Jewish national home was to be a nation like the other nations, a "normal" modern state. One could say that, for the Zionists also, observant Jews were to become Israelis of the Mosaic persuasion. The modern age had been internalized even by those Jews who most wished to rebel against the antisemitism of liberal western society, and some of its most basic assumptions were to be carried over into the new thinking of Zionism.

THE INFAMOUS DECREE

Napoleon did not fulfill his own side of the bargain. In spite of his promises to the Sanhedrin that Jews would now be regarded as Frenchmen, he proceeded to make special laws governing Jews only. In March 1808, he promulgated two edicts. The second of these became known to Jews as the "*décret infâme,*" the infamous decree.

The measures were nominally intended as transitional, with the aim of accomplishing the more complete integration of the Jews into the French state. In fact, they were discriminatory and should have been unnecessary on the assumptions on which the discussions with the Provisional Assembly and the Sanhedrin had been carried on. The second decree imposed restrictions on Jewish loans, required Jews to have special permits in order to engage in trade, forbade migration of Jews from other areas to North-East France, and prohibited the practice (allowed to other French citizens) of finding a substitute for military service under conscription.

According to the final paragraph of this second decree, "[t]he instructions in this order will be implemented over a period of ten years in the hope that at the end of this period, under the influence of the various measures undertaken with regard to the Jews, there will no longer be any difference between them and other citizens of Our Empire. But if, despite all this, Our hope should be frustrated, implementation will be extended for whatever length of time seems appropriate."[29]

In the first decree, establishing the arrangements for the structure and organization of the Mosaic religion within the state, the rabbis were enjoined to see to it that the Israelites (as Jews were henceforward to be called by those who wished to avoid the by now inherently insulting name of Jew) should regard military service as a sacred task, exempting them for its duration from any religious obligations incompatible with it. Thus, the interests of the Mosaic religion were clearly to be treated as subordinate to those of the state.

In the measure establishing the organization of the Mosaic religion, provision was made for a hierarchical system: there was to be a consistory in Paris, supposed to help the state authorities in the task of regulating the lives of Jewish individuals, and all individual and communal Jewish affairs were to be overseen by this consistory. Protestant affairs were somewhat similarly regulated. The aim was not the promotion of the internal well-being, religious or social, of the Israelite community; it was to make them easier to govern.

Outside the borders of France, where Napoleon continued to hold sway, the "infamous decree" was also in operation to varying degrees. The Duchy of Warsaw, created out of central Poland, postponed the granting of equal rights to Jews on the basis of the decree. In Westphalia, on the other hand, emancipation was granted.

After the defeat of Napoleon at Waterloo, following close upon the failure of his Russian campaign, there was a considerable reaction back to the former state of affairs, especially in the Italian states. There the Jews were stripped of their newly acquired rights and returned to the ghetto. In Frankfurt, the Jews were also returned to the ghetto. In Lübeck, the whole community was expelled.

THE CONGRESS OF VIENNA

In May 1814, after the defeat of Napoleon that led to his banishment to Elba, the French signed a peace treaty with the victorious allies, which provided for a congress to meet at Vienna the same year to deal with most of the remaining issues left over by the defeat of Napoleon. Among the principal tasks of the congress was the drawing up of a constitution for the new German Federation, consisting of thirty-six states. Most of these had belonged to a union known as the Rheinbund, which Napoleon had created. The constitution would also deal with the Jewish question.

The congress included among its delegates both men of considerable intellectual stature, such as the great scientist and explorer Friedrich von Humboldt of Prussia, who stood for full equality for the Jews, and reactionaries of various types. The Jews sought to lobby for emancipation, both directly and through their friends among the delegates. The two largest and most influential states, Prussia and Austria, were on their side, and they were willing to provide for full emancipation in the proposed constitution. The representatives of the smaller states were mostly eager to undo the emancipatory measures of Napoleon.

Humboldt was personally sympathetic to the Jews, regarding them as constituting "so peculiar a religious and world-historical phenomenon that not the worst minds have raised doubts as to whether its existence can be explained in a human way only. . ."[30] He recommended full equality to the congress as the only just, logical, and politically wise solution to the problem.

However, such principled and forward-looking views were not characteristic of the congress' deliberations, which fell to hard bargaining, in which the formulations of the constitutional position of the Jews became increasingly vague. The delegates were subjected to considerable pressure from home, especially from the burger class, which feared the economic rivalry of the Jews. What was originally a fairly liberal draft was finally passed in an ambiguous form, by no means so favorable to the Jews as its advocates had initially hoped.

The article on the Jewish question was divided into two parts: Part One promised that a future Federal Assembly would in due course deal with the whole Jewish problem with a view to arriving at a common solution that would be applicable to the whole of Germany. However, nothing was done to implement this provision for a considerable period, in view of the reactionary climate that now set in. The Romantic movement had fostered new thoughts of a pan-German Christianity, a neo-medieval notion that had no more place for the Jews than had its model.

The text of Part Two of the article had originally been intended to safeguard the existing, newly acquired rights of the Jews. In its original formulation, it stated that "the rights already conceded the Jews *in* the several federated states will be continued." However, the delegate from Bremen successfully moved an amendment to strike the word "in" and replace it with "by." This slight verbal change had the intended effect of nullifying most of the recent gains of the Jews, since only three of the states had actually granted citizenship to the Jews. Their rights elsewhere had not been enacted by the states themselves but by the French occupying power.

Restrictive measures against the Jews remained in the legislation of many of the German states for many years, but the Jews gradually succeeded none the less in acquiring economic and cultural rights. Jewish poets and literary figures gave their people a more favorable image among the intelligentsia, while bankers boldly used their economic power on behalf of their coreligionists. The Rothschilds, now becoming an international force in the banking world, refused to make loans to governments that oppressed Jews. They also inspired others to stand up for themselves and fight for their rights.[31]

Nevertheless, the early part of the nineteenth century saw the loss of many leading figures to Christianity. The poet Heine was among them, though like Disraeli in England he remained well disposed to the people of his ancestry and wrote of them in favorable terms. Between 1800 and 1810 one tenth of the Jewish population of the German states purchased what Heine called "the ticket of admission to European culture" in the form of baptism. Few of them became enthusiastic Christians, and soon it was enough to renounce Jewish observance and become secular Europeans. Among those who took the route of baptism were four of the children of Moses Mendelssohn, the great Berlin apostle of enlightenment. One of them became the father of the composer Felix Mendelssohn. The path of the enlightened Jew was not to be an easy one to hold to.

PROGRESS TOWARD FULLER EMANCIPATION

The "infamous decree" continued to govern French policy for the stipulated period. However, it also set limits to any reversion to prerevolutionary attitudes. When after the final defeat of Napoleon in 1815 the monarchy was restored in France, and Catholicism again declared to be the religion of the state, no fresh restrictions were imposed on the Jews. When the decree expired in 1818, the government stood firm against popular agitation for the renewal of restrictions, and French Jews continued to enjoy equal rights under the law.

Alsace-Lorraine remained a center of anti-Jewish hostility, which broke out in times of social upheaval, such as the revolutions of 1830 and 1848, even to the extent of rioting and violence against Jews, but the tide of emancipation was not rolled back. After the July 1830 revolution, the government proposed that the Jewish religion be placed on an equal footing with the Christian churches. Their clergy, including those of the French Protestants, received salaries from the government. The proposal was approved by the legislature, and rabbis received their salaries from 1831.

In 1846, the special Jewish oath in the law courts was removed. This was the last law affecting Jews only, and from this point on Jews were no longer treated legally as a separate group. The revolutionary constitution of 1848 contained a general affirmation of the principle of non-discrimination in all public appointments.

Previously, support of Jewish emancipation had been associated with the program of the revolutionaries. Its embrace by more conservative governments, such as the French, now made it much more widely acceptable, even to monarchies elsewhere. Toleration for Jews could now be seen as a normal feature of good government, not threatening even highly conservative rulers.

In England, Jews were already full citizens, subject to no special laws. Nevertheless, they did suffer under some restrictions common to all who were not members of the Established Church and a few peculiar to themselves. All candidates for public office and for university degrees had to take an oath on "the true faith of a Christian." Sometimes the same oath was required even for the purchase of land. Non-conformists and Catholics could take such an oath. Naturally, Jews could not.

In 1828–29 Parliament discussed the Catholic Emancipation Bill; several laws were passed during the discussions, eliminating restrictions on both Protestant non-conformists and Catholics. No steps were taken, however, to alter the oath, and thus permit Jews a fuller entry into public life.

When the Reform Parliament of 1833 met, Robert Grant, an M.P. sitting in the Whig interest, reintroduced a measure abolishing all restrictions on Jews, which he had earlier worked for in 1830. His bill won the eloquent support of the historian Macaulay. It passed in the Commons, but it was thrown out by the Lords, with the support of King William IV. Successive attempts to win passage in the succeeding years all failed similarly.

However, outside Parliament, some progress was made. In 1831, the City of London devised a form of the oath that a Jew could take in good conscience, and thus could be free to engage in commerce and trade. Later, Jews were allowed to be called to the bar, hold municipal office, and serve on juries. When University College, London, was founded in 1837, Jews were permitted to become undergraduates. In Oxford and Cambridge, however, the link with the Church of England remained until 1871, affecting nonconformists as well as Jews. Also in 1837, Moses Montefiore, later to be a prominent figure in the efforts of Jews to return to their own land, was elected to be a sheriff of the City of London and knighted by the Queen. By 1840 there were no more public restrictions on Jews, except the right to sit in Parliament. This now became the key issue, and a group of influential Jews began to work for its removal.

In 1847, the City of London elected Baron Lionel de Rothschild as one of its members of Parliament. There was in fact no formal restriction on Jews being elected as members, but a Jew could not take his seat, because he could not take the oath. The prime minister now took the opportunity to propose the abolition of this form of discrimination, and the Commons supported him by a considerable majority. Among those who spoke in favor were Disraeli, Peel, and Gladstone; the latter had previously been on the side of discrimination against Jewish M.P.s, and now changed his mind. Once again, however, the Lords were strongly opposed and succeeded in defeating the measure.

Rothschild did not press the matter, renouncing his seat so that the city could be properly represented in Parliament, but he was reelected at the next election. Again the Lords defeated the measure that would have allowed him to take his seat. A year later, another Jew, Sir David Salomons, was elected, and he attempted to take his seat by omitting the contentious phrase when he took the oath. He was removed from the chamber and heavily fined.

Finally, in 1858, after thirteen attempts, both houses passed a bill allowing each house to determine its own form of oath. British Jews were now free to enter all forms of public life, though certain honors remained closed to them, as to Catholics. Especially the more prominent among them won considerable social acceptance by the upper classes from that time on. King Edward VII numbered several Jews among his personal friends. Widespread antisemitism only began to reenter the British social climate with the advent of large numbers of immigrants from Eastern Europe, many of whom settled in the East End of London.

In Central Europe, the progress of emancipation was slower. After the defeat of Napoleon, the monarchs of Russia, Prussia, and Austria entered into a "Holy Alliance" that reaffirmed their common Christian heritage. Intellectual opinion swung against liberalism. Now the popular cry was for the "German spirit" over against the "French spirit" associated with the occupation by Napoleon. Enlightenment concepts were now regarded, unhistorically, as foreign to Germany and a manifestation of alien ideas. Instead, romanticism became all the rage.

In spite of its achievements in literature and music, in the social sphere romanticism attempted to hark back to the Middle Ages. The new mood envisaged a Christian state on medieval lines. Once again, Jews were faced with a social climate into which they had no chance of fitting, and the movement of enlightenment among Jews themselves took a heavy blow.

The reaction after the Congress of Vienna hit the German states hardest of all. In most of them, the status of Jews reverted to what it had been before the French conquest. In Frankfurt, the Jews were pushed back into the ghetto, and they were expelled from several of the Free Cities, including Bremen and Lübeck. Bavaria retained the old pre-Napoleonic restrictions. Prussia decided to apply the Emancipation Law of 1812 only in the areas that had formerly belonged to it, while in the substantial areas added to its territory by the Congress former laws would continue to apply.

In the Rhine area the Prussians extended the "infamous decree" indefinitely. During the 1820s, even the 1812 law was gutted by a provision that Jews be barred from government and municipal offices and from holding posts in the public service.

In Austria many restrictions remained or were restored. The number of Jews permitted to reside in the country remained limited and the regulations were strictly enforced. Various special taxes fell on the Jews, and their occupations were restricted by a measure providing that "the customs, way of life and occupations of the Jews be rendered harmless." In Vienna, only two hundred families had the right of settlement, while thousands lived semilegally as servants, subject to police harassment.

During the 1830s, Jews attempted to campaign once more for equal rights in several of the German states. However, they failed to win the necessary support of the liberals, who were either weak politically or hesitant to embrace the Jewish cause. Only in the state of Kurhessen did the Jews achieve the equality they sought. Within the Austro-Hungarian Empire, the Hungarian Diet did decide to grant the Jews rights equal to all other citizens who were not members of the nobility, but the upper house failed to approve the resolution, proposing instead the cancellation of the "toleration fees" current in the Empire and of restrictions on residence, occupation, and ownership of real property. The concessions were further reduced by the central administration of the Empire in Vienna.

During the 1840s the climate swung somewhat in favor of the Jews. In 1843, the Landtag of the province of the Rhine passed a resolution supporting Jewish equality, and agreed to approach the Prussian king for his support. Other legislatures passed similar resolutions. In due course, the Landtag of all Prussia passed a comprehensive law defining Jewish status essentially in terms of the provisions of 1812. In 1847 a Law on the Status of the Jews granted them equal rights with Christians "to the extent that there is no instruction to the contrary in the law."

Jews could now serve in posts in state and municipal government, apart from those connected with judicial, police, or executive authority. They could serve as teachers in several kinds of school, and university professorships of medicine, science, and philology were opened to them, but they remained debarred from teaching religious subjects or the humanities. At the same time restrictions on movement and occupation were removed.

The widespread revolutions of 1848 opened up the Jewish question more widely. Jews were prominent in the revolutionary movements in Berlin and Vienna. They were also distinguished among the casualties of the fighting and were buried along with the other dead. When the Kaiser left Vienna, a Jew, Adolf

Fischhof, was made head of the General Security Committee that governed the city. Several Jewish deputies sat in the all German Parliament of May 1848, and one of them was elected deputy-speaker.

However, the revolutionary assemblies of both Germany and Italy did not take Jewish rights for granted, but instead debated the matter vigorously. The old argument was brought up that Jews did not belong to the body of the nations. Gabriel Riesser, who had been elected deputy-speaker in Germany, succeeded in having a measure passed that would grant legal equality to all, irrespective of their religion.

In the Austrian Diet, Jewish delegates campaigned for the abolition of the remaining restrictions and for full equality, but the matter had not been resolved when the meetings came to an end. In the Hungarian Diet, measures for Jewish equality failed to win the support of even the liberal Kossuth, who regarded them as premature. However, in 1849, a few days before the final collapse of the revolution, the diet did pass a resolution granting equal rights to Jews.

The revolutionary movements of 1848 also engendered serious forms of backlash against the freeing of Jews from old restrictions. Hostility toward Jews was particularly evident in areas where they could be identified in the popular mind with the former oppressive regime. In Bohemia and Moravia, Jews were identified with Germany because they themselves spoke German; in Pressburg (now Bratislava) the inhabitants demanded the expulsion of the Jews. Public opinion forced the Jews out of the Hungarian National Guard.

In France, the traditional antisemitism of Alsace-Lorraine also made itself felt in riots that had to be suppressed by military force. In Rome, the ghetto was opened and the Jews allowed to reside anywhere; when they emerged, however, they were met with violence.

After the suppression of the 1848 revolutions, governments everywhere granted their peoples new constitutions "of their own free will." Some of these included provisions, among others intended to placate liberals, which virtually granted equal rights to Jews. Franz Josef of Austria, in March 1849, granted a constitution that affirmed that civil and political rights "are not dependent on religion." Thus, even right wing circles were once more encouraged to assent to the principle of emancipation. The restored Prussian monarchy published a constitution in 1851 in which Christianity was recognized as the state religion. However, Clause 12 of the 1848 constitution, recognizing the equality of all religions, was also retained, in spite of the inconsistency of having two contradictory provisions in the same text.

The 1850s were a reactionary period, after the 1848 upheavals, but the cause of Jewish emancipation continued to advance slowly. The unification of Germany under Prussia was facilitated by an alliance between Bismarck and the liberals. To gain liberal support Bismarck was willing to offer the liberals concessions on the Jewish question, among others. In November 1867, the united Reichstag, now with a liberal majority, passed a resolution banning all religious discrimination. This was followed in June 1869 by a law affecting the united Germany that allowed Jews to enter government service, including the judiciary and university posts. The 1860s also saw a liberal trend in the Austro-Hungarian Empire. A new Austrian constitution of 1867 granted full equality to the Jews. Hungary passed a similar law, but required some Jewish reforms as a condition.

In Italy, however, things got worse. Jews had enjoyed legal equality in the Sardinian kingdom since 1848, but the papal states imposed new restrictions. European public opinion was aroused against these backward conditions by the Mortara case of 1858, in which police kidnapped a child from a Jewish family on the pretext that he had been secretly baptized by a servant during a severe illness. The child was put in a monastery and never restored to his parents, despite widespread international protest.

However, with the Risorgimento and the spreading rule of the Sardinian royal family, better conditions for Jews were extended over widening areas of Italy. In 1870, the temporal power of the pope was abolished and his rule confined to Vatican City. Rome was declared the capital of a united Italy. Henceforward, there was to be somewhat greater toleration for Jews in Italy than elsewhere in Europe. In spite of Fascist efforts, destructive antisemitism never took root among the Italian populace, and many remained friendly to their Jewish neighbors. However, the role of Italy in the international politics of the late twentieth century does not suggest that antisemitism had by any means been uprooted from the Italian mind.

Switzerland held out against Jewish equality for a long time, Jews even being prohibited from residing in the country, except in the region of the Aargau, but without civil or political rights. Other countries attempted to bring pressure on the Swiss to liberalize their laws, but without success. Only in the 1874 Federal Constitution was Jewish equality finally granted in the whole federation, completing the process of emancipation in central Europe.

The nineteenth century brought legal emancipation and equality to Jews, albeit at considerable sacrifice, and with great loss to the traditional unity and integrity of the Jewish people. But it did not bring real and universal social acceptance to them. Antisemitism in its true modern sense, which we must now consider, was a reaction to Jewish emancipation. Jews were never felt by their fellow citizens to be so alien as when they mixed freely with others and had abandoned most of what had hitherto been distinctive in their way of life. Old hatreds persisted, and new rationalizations were devised for them. Both the Left and the Right continued to be hostile to Jews, and in due course the new racist antisemitism was combined in many Christian circles with the old theological hatreds. The readiness with which the new antisemitism could be integrated into the old theological anti-Judaism is perhaps the strongest evidence that they were not essentially different. The new was the deadly offspring of the old.

10

Secular Antisemitism

Emancipation led to antisemitism. When Jews began to move with relative freedom in European society, sharing citizenship and civil rights with their neighbors, the latter found new justifications for hating them. But they were still hated above all because they were Jews. What did that now mean? Previously, their Christian neighbors had thought of Jews as members of an alien and false religion, adherents to a broken covenant. Now secularized antisemites would hate them as members of an alien and inferior race, unassimilable by those among whom they lived, a dangerous source of pollution for the cultural and racial purity of their neighbors.

Substantial numbers of Christians would also borrow racist ideas from the new secular antisemitism and incorporate them into new forms of their old theological rejection. In the latter part of the nineteenth century, Christian antisemitism also becomes racist, and (with rare exceptions) directed against all who are Jewish by descent, whatever their religious adherence.

Most of the non-Jewish world now took it for granted that all Jews, whether observant, secular, or Christianized, together constituted a unique group in society, whom it might still be appropriate to hate. The new reasons were not after all absolutely new. They owed something to the old ones, and we shall find clear lines connecting the old and the new forms of anti-Judaic hostility to one another.

By far, the most important line of continuity between the old and the new was not intellectual at all. This was the paranoia inherited from the Middle Ages and transmitted from mind to mind at a nonrational level, often below the level of conscious thought. Paranoid hatred for Jews is picked up in early childhood from the attitudes of parents and teachers. No intellectual indoctrination is needed to make an antisemite. Looks and tones of voice are sufficient for the sensitive mind of a child. Loyalty to parents will make the impression permanent. Only a strong and independent conscience can shake off such powerful early conditioning.

Causeless hatred for Jews came first, and conscious reasons for the hatred were always rationalizations. Whatever people thought and said against Jews was only a way to account for a hatred already in their minds and passions; the semiconscious aim of antisemitic ideas was to assist the antisemite to feel comfortable with his or her own hatred, by furnishing it with spurious justification.

Christian parents could therefore transmit their own dislike of Jews to their offspring without its essential character changing even when the latter subsequently became secularized. The definition of a Jew could change, and the reasons for thinking ill of a Jew could be modernized. What did not change was the constant assumption of others that there was something uniquely bad about Jewish character and Jewish behavior that justified hostility and discrimination. The rationalizations would differ. The hate did not.

Throughout the centuries during which the Church had been teaching people what to think, Christians had marked out Jews as their one constant target for hate, even though they sometimes hated others too. Loss of Christian influence on society did not change that. Understanding the spurious reasons by which the new antisemites explained their hatred is much less important. If Jews continued to be hated in the modern secular world, while some now hated them even more than before, it was because the Church had successfully taught the world (even if not in so many words) that the Jews were the right people to hate. The effects of the teaching lasted even after the teacher had lost much of her ancient authority.

The reasons for hating Jews, whether theological or secular, have always been bad reasons, that will not stand up to critical investigation, as we have found throughout the present inquiry. Nevertheless, they still need to be exposed, so that the irrationality and baselessness of all forms of antisemitism can be confronted head-on and dealt with by the conscience at the proper level. There is also an intellectual line of descent from older Christian anti-Judaism to the new secular antisemitism, at least in some of its forms, and it remains important to trace it.

So far, I have attempted to be consistent in reserving the term *antisemitism* for hostility toward the Jews based on supposed racial grounds, while using *anti-Judaism* and its variants for the traditional, religiously based hostility. The dividing line was the possibility of effective conversion: on the older, Christian view, a Jew ceased to be a Jew upon baptism. Now the assimilated Jew was still a Jew, even after baptism or abandonment of any form of religion. From the Enlightenment onward, it is no longer possible to draw clear lines of distinction between religious and racial forms of hostility toward Jews.

Once Jews have been emancipated and secular thinking makes its appearance, without leaving behind the old Christian hostility toward Jews, the new term *antisemitism* becomes almost unavoidable, even before explicitly racist doctrines appear. Emancipated Jews had often abandoned their religion for Christianity, or for no religion at all. They could no longer be identified by their religion. However much they tried to join their neighbors, their neighbors refused to assimilate them. Jews remained aliens. They were still considered a distinct group, whether as individuals they remained Jewish, converted to Christianity, or became altogether secularized. In the eyes of their neighbors, all were still Jews. This is a new way of defining Jews, unknown to traditional Christianity and not easily conceivable before emancipation.

The secular antisemite can no longer object to Jews for religious reasons. He may object to their religion, since he objects to all forms of religion, but he must deny to Jews an authentic religious identity. If he wishes to distinguish Jews from their neighbors at all, which on his own secular assumptions he should not, he must regard them as a social group defined only by their descent. Indeed, once they abandoned the Torah, that is what assimilated Jews had effectively become.

It is only a small step from hostility toward Jews as a social group with a unique descent to full-blown racist antisemitism, and historically also it did not take long for this step to be taken. I shall therefore now begin to use the more familiar term *antisemitism* to denote all the new secular forms of hostility toward Jews, while acknowledging that the full racist doctrine emerged only later in the nineteenth century.

THE LEFT-WING HEGELIANS

Hegel, the great Berlin idealist, was the dominant figure in philosophy in the nineteenth century. In spite of the popularity in the twentieth century, especially in the English-speaking world, of empiricist thinkers, whose ideas are more consonant with the scientific outlook, Hegel's shadow still extends over a vast area of modern thought. His most remarkable disciple and critic, Karl Marx, still dominates the outlook of a considerable portion of the world, but Hegel's influence is by no means confined to the Marxist current of thought. Hegel's indirect legacy is also apparent in the prevalence of social criticism, Marxist and otherwise, in intellectual circles, and indeed wherever the form of critical thinking called dialectical is practiced. By general consent, Hegel is acknowledged to be one of the hardest of philosophers to understand, though some of his interpreters write much more clearly than he usually did.

Hegel is also a principal link between the older theological and the modern, secular thinking. He is one of the few modern philosophers whose work explicitly reflects Christian themes. In fact, he intended his system to be a rational explication of Christian faith in a modern or enlightened form. It was not without substantial justification that his left-wing critics accused him of being theological, instead of basing his philosophy on reason alone.

Fewer have noticed (perhaps because the idea was until recently taken so much for granted) that his system also incorporates the ancient theology of supersession, according to which Christianity has replaced Judaism, while incorporating in itself all that was true in its predecessor.

Hegel's thought traces the movement of the absolute Spirit through history, as it continuously acquires self-knowledge through objectification of modes in its own being. The historical development of the movement of thought, as each new philosophy negates its predecessor and at the same time takes it up into itself in transfigured form, successively presents in time that which is eternally present in the being of the Absolute. What is true of philosophy is also true of religion. Religions also negate and subsume their historical predecessors.

For Hegel, Christianity is the final religion: it embodies the unity of God and man, of which the Incarnation of God in Christ is the historical expression. In negating its immediate predecessor, Judaism, Christianity also takes up into itself in a higher form what was true in Judaism, as well as the truth in all its other predecessors from the beginnings of religion.

Hegel writes of Judaism with respect, a respect rare in Christian thinkers. But this does not mean that for him the Jewish faith has a continuing historical destiny alongside Christianity. For Hegel, no less than for the church fathers, Christianity comes to bring Judaism to an end. From the point of view of Hegel's system, this is not an ultimate loss, since Judaism is not simply negated. Since it is taken up into Christianity in transfigured form, it is therefore in a sense still present in it. Once Christianity appears on the scene, however, Judaism has no further historical role or destiny.

Hegel attempted to rationalize Christianity completely, thus converting theology altogether into philosophy, but there is no doubt that theology is at the root of his system. One might even guess that the very idea of *Aufhebung*, the subsuming of a past phase in the history of thought into its successor, is simply a philosophical version of the old Christian idea of the supersession of Judaism in its fulfilment by Christianity. Even in this enlightened way of thinking, Christianity is still understood as replacing Judaism at the same time as it fulfills it.

A number of Hegel's most important followers, known as the Left Hegelians, among whom Feuerbach and Bruno Bauer were prominent, were critical of elements in Hegel's system that they thought inconsistent or insufficiently critical. They accepted his dialectical method and his historical orientation, but they disagreed with him on the application of the method to the historical material before them.

Just as Hegel believed Christianity to be the final form of religion, he also believed the Prussian constitutional monarchy, somewhat idealized, to be the final form of the state. In various ways, the Left Hegelians criticized both these assumptions. They argued that Christianity might indeed be the final form of religion so far; however, thought could still move on to the negation of Christianity, and if Christianity was the final religion, its negation could only mean the negation of religion as such. Similarly, the Prussian monarchy could also be negated by further historical change, and in particular to democracy, in which every individual would embody the principle of sovereignty, so far confined to the person of the monarch. Thus in various ways they looked forward to a further historical epoch in which religion would no longer be supported by the state: it would become a private matter, or perhaps even cease to exist in any form, while in the state itself, democracy would prevail.

KARL MARX AND ANTISEMITISM

The argument between Karl Marx and Bruno Bauer, on what was coming to be known as the Jewish question, or the Jewish problem, illustrates ways in which the Left Hegelians continued Hegel's scheme of thought and pushed it further, while disagreeing with him and with one another on important matters of content.[1] The same argument also reveals something of great importance for the present inquiry: certain traditional Christian assumptions about Jews and Judaism were being transmitted to the modern secular world through Hegel and his intellectual descendants. While there can perhaps be debate about whether Bauer or Marx were antisemites in the strict sense of the term, they were certainly among those who laid the foundations for the left-wing version of antisemitism, later to become so prominent in the Soviet Union and in much of the rest of the world.

People often wonder how Marxism in its Soviet Communist form could have turned out to be so antisemitic, since they regard Marx himself as a Jew. Moreover, his theory had apparently left no place for racial distinctions. Doubtless the main reason is simply paranoia transmitted from the Christian past, still powerfully influencing the minds of the masses in the Communist states, as well as those of the Marxist intellectuals themselves.

However, we cannot absolve Marx himself of responsibility for providing ideas to justify the inherited paranoia. Marx was not in fact a Jew, except by descent. If anything, he was a Christian. Unless we share nineteenth-century assumptions about the all-importance of race and breeding, we should not think of him as a Jew in any sense that throws intellectual light on what he thought about Jews or anything else.[2]

Karl Marx's father, Herschel Levi, early embraced the diffuse and free-thinking religion of the Enlightenment. After the setbacks to emancipation following on the Congress of Vienna, he found it necessary for career reasons to adopt Lutheranism, a year before the birth of his son Karl. Herschel was hardly more than a conventional Christian, before or after joining the Church, but given his Enlightenment views, "conversion" was not an important issue for him. He changed his last name to Marx, from one of his father's given names, and he took the Christian name of Heinrich. Karl Marx's mother was a Philips, of the same family as the founders of the present Dutch electronics giant.[3]

Karl was the descendant of learned rabbis on both sides of his family, but he received no Jewish education and apparently not much of a Christian one, though some of his high school essays did deal with Christian topics. He was baptized in the Lutheran church at the age of five and brought up in the family as a Christian in the liberal tradition of the Enlightenment. His father would read to him from the works of Voltaire and Racine. As we have seen, Voltaire was no friend of the Jews; his writings are full of unfavorable references to Jews.

When we turn to Marx's own writings, we cannot help being struck by their extremely hostile tone when they do refer to Judaism or to individual Jews. Jewish thinkers sympathetic to his ideas attempt to defend Karl Marx from the charge of being an antisemite, in spite of the evidence to the contrary.[4] For a hundred years Jewish Socialists refrained from translating Marx's writings on the Jewish question into Yiddish or Hebrew.[5]

As Sydney Hook acknowledges, however, Marx certainly used the epithet Jew in a highly opprobrious sense.[6] In the famous theses on Feuerbach, he uses the expression "dirty Jewish" as a characterization of a form of economic activity. In private correspondence, among many other such references, he characterized Lasalle, a prominent socialist who had not converted to Christianity, as a "Jewish nigger," and spoke of detecting a "Jewish whine" in his utterances.

Marx described the Jewish refugees from Poland as "this filthiest of all races, [who] only perhaps by its passion for greedy gain could be related to [the Jewish capitalists of] Frankfort."[7] In the 1850s, he sneered at those who fought for the seating of Lord Rothschild in the House of Commons. "It is doubtful whether the British people will be very much pleased by extending electoral rights to a Jewish usurer."[8]

More important still, in the discussion with Bauer, now to be examined, dealing explicitly with the Jewish question, Marx firmly identifies Jews and their practical religion with "hucksterism," or "haggling," that is, with commerce having a crass profit motive. What else is this but the old medieval identification of the Jews with usury and greed, as in the comment on Lord Rothschild just cited?

He did not derive this identification from any objective study of contemporary Jewish activities, a study that his family connections would doubtless have made possible. He must have learned it from the Christian mythology surviving among those with whom he was brought up and spent his formative years and from the attitude of the Germans of his own intellectual milieu to emancipated Jews.

Marx, who was critical of so much, failed to be critical of anti-Jewish ideas widely held in the circles in which he moved. One might also speculate that the knowledge of his own Jewish descent, which he desired to repudiate, may have made him especially hostile toward others who did not repudiate it as he did. If this is not antisemitism–and I think it is–it certainly served to perpetuate and encourage antisemitic ideas among those who would later treat his writings as holy writ. Marx takes his place among a long line of former Jews who did not scruple to slander their own people in the Gentile world.[9]

Bruno Bauer had written a substantial essay on the Jewish question, *Die Judenfrage*, published in Brunswick in 1843. He also wrote a smaller discussion of the question, entitled *Die Fähigkeit der heutigen Juden und Christen frei zu werden* (The capacity of present day Jews and Christians to become free), in a work called *Einundzwanzig Bogen aus der Schweiz* (Twenty-one Sheets from Switzerland). The following year, Marx replied critically to each of these essays in separate articles of his own.[10]

Together, Marx's two articles constitute his final views on the Jewish question, to which he did not explicitly return. Although they did not circulate widely in his own time, they are the basis of modern Communist theory about the Jews. They also have substantially influenced the thinking of many left-wing, non-Zionist Jews about Jewish identity and destiny, and hence (directly and indirectly) about Israel, though of course Marx did not refer to Israel.

Erich Fromm calls the articles brilliant, and in a special sense perhaps they are, provided the reader is able to ignore the anti-Jewish prejudice and post-Christian triumphalism that lie at the basis of the argument and vitiate it. In contrast, Isaiah Berlin calls the reply to Bauer "a dull and shallow composition."[11]

Marx and Bauer were in very sharp theoretical disagreement, and it is therefore particularly instructive to observe the assumptions they shared. These are presumably at least the legacy of Hegel, and in all probability the common view of the society they both belonged to. Both assume almost without argument that in order for the Jews to be emancipated they must cease to be Jews. Both also believe that Jews, although not yet emancipated, already exercise disproportionate power in society through the control of financial institutions.

These are very familiar ideas in the outlook of the traditional antisemite, and neither of the two has learned to criticize them, empirically or theoretically. For Marx, the Jew is the essential capitalist. His religion is money. The abolition of capitalism and the abolition of Judaism are essentially identical.

The two differ, however, mostly because Marx is the more radical thinker of the two, carrying ideas Bauer begins to formulate to their logical conclusion. Bauer believes that Jews are incapable of emancipation while they remain Jews, and that likewise Christians are incapable of giving emancipation to them while they remain Christians. Jews lag behind the development of history, and in order to be emancipated they must first become Christians, though the Christianity that they should embrace is one already in process of dissolution. Like the new post-Hegelian theologians, of whom Bauer himself was one, they should study historical criticism and take part in the radical criticism of Christianity.

Both Jew and Christian must come to see religion as simply an outmoded stage of development in the human mind, a snakeskin to be sloughed off. Ultimately, the political emancipation of both the Jew and the Christian will come about through the abolition of religion, which will be effectuated when the connection between the state and religion is thoroughly broken and religion becomes a purely private matter.

Marx, however, considers it essential to ask, not only who should emancipate and who should be emancipated, but what is emancipation. His own answer is that political emancipation, as considered by Bauer, is not real emancipation. Real emancipation is human emancipation, the identification of man with himself as a social being, what Marx, following Feuerbach, called *species-being.* "The political emancipation of the Jew or the Christian—of the religious man in general—is the *emancipation* of the state from Judaism, Christianity, and *religion* in general."[12] But from this purely political point of view Christians have no right to ask Jews to renounce their religion, as Bauer claims.

This is still a theological controversy. "The theological doubt about whether the Jew or the Christian has the better chance of attaining salvation is reproduced here in the more enlightened form: which of the two is *more capable of emancipation*? It is indeed no longer asked: which makes free–Judaism or Christianity? On the contrary, it is now asked: which makes free–the negation of Judaism or the negation of Christianity?"[13]

Political emancipation leaves religion still in existence, while withdrawing privileges from a particular religion. "The emancipation of the state from religion is not the emancipation of the real man from religion. We do not say to the Jews, therefore, as does Bauer: you cannot be emancipated politically without emancipating yourselves completely from Judaism. We say rather: it is because you can be emancipated politically, without renouncing Judaism completely and absolutely, that *political* emancipation itself is not *human* emancipation."[14] Marx argues that Jews cannot be emancipated as human beings without cutting themselves off completely from the faith of their people and ceasing to be Jews.

Establishing the rights of man is no solution, since such rights are based on egoism, not on the transcendence of egoism by identification with the social being of man. (Here Marx, remarkably, argues like many a conservative, who considers duties, not rights, to be fundamental to society.) In the French and American movements for human rights, man was not yet liberated *from* religion or property, he was only liberated *for* them.

In the second reply to Bauer, Marx's specific views on the Jews come out much more clearly and polemically. Now Marx disengages himself from Bauer's theological formulation of the question, and he asks, what specific *social* element is it necessary to overcome in order to abolish Judaism?

> Let us consider the real Jew: not the *Sabbath Jew,* whom Bauer considers, but the *everyday Jew.* Let us not seek the secret of the Jew in his religion, but let us seek the secret of the religion in the real Jew.
>
> What is the profane basis of Judaism? *Practical* need, *self-interest.* What is the worldly cult of the Jew? *Huckstering.*[15] What is his worldly god? *Money.*
>
> Very well: then in emancipating itself from *huckstering* and *money,* and thus from real and practical Judaism, our age would emancipate itself.[16]

Marx sees in Judaism a universal antisocial element of the present time, whose "historical development, *zealously aided in its harmful aspects by the Jews,* has now attained its culminating point" (emphasis mine, here only). "In the final analysis, the *emancipation of* the Jews is the emancipation of mankind from *Judaism.*"[17]

Marx considers that Judaism, thus understood, has in fact taken over the Christian world, so that it now shares completely in Jewish egoism and commercialism. "The Jew, who occupies a distinctive place in civil society, only manifests in a distinctive way the Judaism of civil society."[18] Practical need or egoism is the basis of civil society. "The god of *practical need and self-interest* is *money.*"[19]

> Money is the jealous god of Israel, beside which no other god may exist. Money abases all the gods of mankind and changes them into commodities. Money is the universal and self-sufficient *value* of all things.

> It has, therefore, deprived the whole world, both the human world and nature, of their own proper value. Money is the alienated essence of man's work and existence; this essence dominates him and he worships it.
>
> The god of the Jews has been secularized and has become the god of this world. The bill of exchange is the real god of the Jew. His god is only an illusory bill of exchange.[20]

These passages display with extraordinary clarity both the spiritual insight of which Marx was capable and its no less remarkable vitiation by anti-Jewish prejudice. Unfortunately, however, his thinking is so closely integrated that the two are inseparable. In these passages, at least, you cannot have the one without the other. A Marx without antisemitism would no longer be Marx.

He goes on to explain how Judaism as he understands it has taken over Christianity.

> Christianity is the sublime thought of Judaism; Judaism is the vulgar practical application of Christianity. But this practical application could only become universal when Christianity as perfected religion had accomplished, in a *theoretical* fashion, the alienation of man from himself and nature.
>
> It was only then that Judaism could attain universal domination and could turn alienated man and alienated nature into *alienable*, saleable objects, in thrall to egoistic need and huckstering.[21]

Marx concludes:

> As soon as society succeeds in abolishing the *empirical* essence of Judaism–huckstering and its conditions–the Jew becomes *impossible*, because his consciousness no longer has an object . . . The *social* emancipation of the Jew is the *emancipation of society from Judaism*.[22]

Even if we attempt to minimize the antisemitic elements in this thinking, by emphasizing the emancipatory and ethical context in which they appear in Marx's own writings, we cannot fail to see that for his later followers, the actual communists of the twentieth century, including the men in power in the communist states, such ideas would inevitably encourage the perpetuation of ancient hates and foster them where they had been weak or nonexistent.

During the nineteenth century, the antisemitism present in Marxist doctrine seems to have remained largely latent. The German social democratic parties avoided it, and it is unlikely that so many Jews would have seen hope for themselves in the Russian revolution had the party been as antisemitic then as it later became.

However, the peculiar conditions of Russia had a destructive effect upon Soviet Communism, wedding Marx's anti-Jewish ideas to the inherited hostility toward Jews of the East European world. Indirectly, in more recent years, Soviet influence upon the international Left has spread the same hostility toward Jews far and wide in the form of determined hostility toward Israel.

Marx thus succeeded, both directly and indirectly, in impressing upon the far Left two assumptions he took over uncritically from the Christian world of his upbringing: that Judaism will and must be superseded and abolished by a further stage in historical development, and that Jews are inherently characterized by an obsession with money, that they are essentially capitalists. In the Marxist utopia, there will be no Jews.

It is therefore part of Marxist dogma that Jews do not constitute an authentic national group. Whether in the Union of Soviet Socialist Republics or in Israel, they had (unlike others) no essential justification for constituting themselves a distinct nation. Their presence in the Middle East was therefore a colonialist aggression on the rightful owners of the land, the Palestinians. Essentially, such Marxists regard Israel as an arm of imperialism, a tool of America. Israel can be supported tactically, as the Soviet Union did at the time of its achievement of independence, but there is no inherent Marxist reason for doing so.

Similarly, such left-wing Jews in the Diaspora, who are numerous and vocal, though a small minority among all Jews, see no future for their own people as a people. The true destiny of Jews is complete loss of identity in a Marxist utopia. They can have therefore no sympathy whatsoever for the revival of Jewish national identity brought about by Zionism and the founding of the state of Israel.

On the contrary, they are bitterly opposed to Israel, as perpetuating the illusory identity of the Jews and delaying their absorption into humanity in general. Many such Jews identify themselves as Jewish only when they wish to criticize Israel and its doings. Such alienated Jews may be thought of most charitably as among the remoter casualties of antisemitism.

Like Hegel, Marx was a link of the greatest importance between the old Christian anti-Judaism we have been examining in earlier chapters and the new modern antisemitism still so prevalent near the end of the twentieth century.[23] Certainly he had a blind spot about religion: he failed to grasp that it is a powerful motor of historical change, naively sharing the Enlightenment view that it would soon disappear. Perhaps this made him take less critical notice of particular religious ideas, since they would disappear along with the whole of which they were a part.

Be that as it may, his own anti-Jewish attitudes seem to have made it particularly easy for him to be uncritical of inherited prejudices against Jews. Since he could not use an idea without integrating it into his own systematic thinking, antisemitism became embedded in Marxism, and perhaps cannot now be removed without breaking up the system of which it is a part.

It will therefore be interesting to see whether the theoretical critique of the whole Marxist scheme, which the Left must now undertake after the collapse of the Communist system in Eastern Europe, will also lead to a critical reevaluation of the important role antisemitism has played in left-wing thought, including its analysis of the Middle East conflict. One can hope.

Unfortunately, Marx was not the only antisemitic influence on left-wing thinking. Some of the early French socialists, including Leroux, the actual inventor of the word socialism, Fourier, one of its two principal founders, and Proudhon, one of its most important theorists, held very similar views to those of Marx. Fourier called the Jews "parasites, merchants, usurers," and considered their emancipation "the most shameful of all recent vices of society."[24]

Leroux, a Christian, like Marx identified the Jews with capitalism, regarding them as the incarnation of Mammon, living by the exploitation of others. For him, the only solution to "the Jewish problem" was the conversion of all Jews to Christianity.[25]

Proudhon wrote in public in a more moderate manner but in his journals like a Nazi:

> That race poisons everything by meddling everywhere without ever joining itself to another people. Demand their expulsion from France, with the exception of individuals married to Frenchwomen. Abolish the synagogues: don't admit them to any kind of employment, pursue finally the abolition of this cult . . . The Jew is the enemy of the human race. One must send this race back to Asia or exterminate it . . . By fire or fusion or by expulsion, the Jew must disappear . . . What the people of the middle ages hated by instinct I hate upon reflection, and irrevocably.[26]

The French Socialists stood aside in indifference from the Dreyfus affair. In 1898, there was published a manifesto from the Socialists calling for "non-participation in the Dreyfus affair on the grounds that while the reaction wishes to exploit the conviction of one Jew to disqualify all Jews, Jewish capitalists would use the rehabilitation of a single Jew to wash out 'all the sins of Israel.' " The manifesto was signed by many of the leading Socialists of the time. Even when the Socialists did finally take a stand, they expressly declared that the Jewish aspect of the affair was irrelevant.[27]

Thus, the two main streams that came together in European left-wing thinking, the Marxist and the French Socialist, shared a common antipathy to Jews, expressed in remarkably similar terms. Again, one must look for a common source, and it is obvious enough by this time what it was. The words of Leroux, himself a committed Christian, made that clear enough, if any doubt still existed.

THE NEW RACIAL DOCTRINES

The concept of race was a novel one for the Christian world; it had usually accepted the biblical view that all human beings are descendants of an original pair. The idea of race was originated in the eighteenth century by early anthropologists, such as Buffon and Linnaeus. Goethe believed that Adam was the ancestor only of the Jews, while Voltaire thought that blacks were an intermediate species between the whites and the apes.[28] The full flowering of the theory of race came in the nineteenth century, when it captured the outlook of all kinds of people, including many who saw in it no antisemitic implications.

Benjamin Disraeli, a convert to Christianity, puts into the mouth of one of the characters in his novel, *Tancred*, an idea that was doubtless his own. "All is race; there is no other truth." Disraeli was so far from being an antisemite that he took an exaggerated and romantic pride in his own origins, and in his novels he presented Jewish characters such as Sidonia in *Coningsby* in a highly idealized light. Many have supposed that such characters as Sidonia and Alroy were intended as self-portraits.

Disraeli does seem to have believed that Jews shared the same racial origins as the Arabs, and he dreamed of a great political revival in the Middle East, in England's interests, in which Jew and Arab would share. Perhaps Disraeli, who had joined the Church of England more to secure his own future than out of genuine Christian convictions, compensated in his own mind for his religious desertion of his people by allotting them a racial significance that was untraditional. Jewish identity, so defined, could be claimed by converts like himself as well by continuing Jews.

Nevertheless, the new racial theories being espoused by anthropologists and philosophers were a gift to antisemites. Such ideas did not appeal to the Left, which would generally follow Marx in seeing class, not race, as the key to history. The Right, and especially those with a romantic concept of the people, in German the *Volk*, took readily to racist theories.

Conservatives and supporters of the *ancien régime* liked the idea of race because it fitted in so well with their own traditional emphasis on the importance of family and breeding. Originally, the idea of the races of mankind was a broad one: the races were divided by color, into the white, the black, and the yellow. The notion of particular races within these broad divisions came later and owed something to an illicit application of the findings of philology.

Late in the eighteenth century came the important discovery of the relationship between the languages of the group dubbed Indo-European, or by German scholars Indo-Germanic. Around 1780, Sir William Jones, a British administrator in India, set out to learn Sanskrit. He observed to his surprise that many of the most common and therefore most primitive words in Sanskrit were extremely like those in Latin and Greek, which he already knew. There were likewise similarities in grammar. In a paper he read in 1786, he presented for the first time the theory that the Sanskrit language has a strong affinity to Latin and Greek, and also a less strong one to the Celtic and Teutonic language groups, including English.

Later study confirmed his theory and added the discovery that the same affinity exists with the Slavonic group and two of the three Baltic languages, as well as with the Iranian languages of Persia and Afghanistan. Linguists now agree that all these languages must have had a common ancestor, sometimes called the Indo-European language. Of course this language no longer exists, but a fair amount is known about it from the comparative study of its descendants.

Early in the nineteenth century, the German orientalist Lassen drew the conclusion, for which there is in fact no evidence, that the speakers of this family of languages belonged to a single common race, which he called after the language group the Indo-Germanic race. Lassen opposed this Indo-Germanic race to a Semitic race, of which the Jews and the Arabs, who likewise spoke languages with a close family relationship, belonged. He also determined that the Semitic race was inferior. "The Semites," he wrote, "do not possess that harmonious equilibrium between all the powers of the intellect which characterized the Indo-Germans."[29]

The Indo-Germans were frequently called Aryans, after the Sanskrit term, meaning noble, which the Indo-European speakers who had invaded the Indian subcontinent from the north applied to themselves. Those who wanted to identify themselves with this supposed superior race attributed to it all the most desirable creations of the human spirit. Many also believed that the Germans were now the purest representatives on earth of this Aryan race. They had also a duty to preserve its purity by refraining from intermingling with the inferior races.

In this scheme of things, the Jews were not originally regarded as a distinct race. Rather, they had originated by just such intermingling between the Indo-Germanic and other races. Soon, however, the concept of a Semitic race began to be applied exclusively to the Jews. It was convenient to identify the old enemy of Christendom by means of the new, pseudoscientific term, Semite, and thus to find new, likewise "scientific" reasons for holding them in contempt.

The actual term, antisemitism, was coined, according to most scholars, by the German journalist Wilhelm Marr, as late as 1879, to characterize various existing forms of political opposition to Jews. In its original meaning, antisemitism did not denote opposition to some cultural or intellectual movement called Semitism. Antisemitism is simply the attitude of those who were against the influence on society of Semites (i.e., Jews). At the time the word was coined, it was not something for which they felt any necessity to apologize, because *Antisemitismus* was a more respectable, since ostensibly more scientific, term than *Judenhass*, hatred of Jews, which is what it was.

Antisemites were and are not opposed to all so-called Semites but only to Jews, and not always to all of them as individuals but primarily to Jews as a group in society. They have usually gotten on very well with Arabs, from the Grand Mufti on. Thus, the "quibble" (as Abba Eban rightly called it) of Arab antisemites, that they cannot be antisemites because they are themselves Semites, has no basis in the origin of the term. (For that matter, as we have already seen, there are Jewish antisemites too.)

Nevertheless, the attitude for which the term *antisemitism* became convenient certainly did not originate with the term itself. Earlier in the century, there were already plenty of influential antisemites who viewed Jews as members of a race and found racist reasons for disliking them. All the same, Jews were disliked because they always had been, and the new racial reasons were nothing more than excuses.

In the earlier years of the nineteenth century, antisemitic ideas flourished more in Germany than elsewhere. Jews were prominent among the new men who were running industry and commerce, and among these, they were the most easily identified group. They attracted to themselves a resentment aroused by the success of a whole new class.

After the Congress of Vienna, intensely anti-Jewish pamphlets and books began to appear. The most inflammatory of these was *The Mirror of the Jews*, by Hartmann von Hundt-Radowsky. He alleged that all Jews were criminals, and he advocated selling them off to plantations or mines, castrating them, or even killing them. "I myself," he wrote, "do not regard the killing of a Jew as a sin or crime, but as a mere police offence."[30]

His and dozens of other such pamphlets played a part in the incitement of the anti-Jewish passions that found expression in the famous "Hep! Hep!" riots of 1819. The riots were so called after the battle cry of the rioters, which has been explained as the initial letters of *Hierosolyma est perdita,* Jerusalem has been lost.

After Marx, the most influential German antisemite was probably the composer Richard Wagner. In this, as in so many other respects, Wagner is an enigma and a contradiction. He owed a considerable debt to Jewish musicians, which he often went so far as to acknowledge. Meyerbeer among others had assisted his career, by doing much to get his early operas performed and accepted in Paris. But in 1850 an anonymous pamphlet appeared, written by Wagner under the thin veil of a pseudonym, and later to be revised and issued under his own name. Its title was *Das Judentum in der Musik.*

He wrote of Jews as a people of mongrel origin who had debased humanity. The Jews had contributed nothing to European culture, belonging as they did to no European community and speaking no European language properly. Jews were inherently incapable of music, since its foundation was in song, "speech aroused to the highest passion." Mendelssohn was a mere copyist without originality, appealing only to people's wish to be amused.[31] Judaic works of music, he alleged, produce in us the feeling of hearing a "poem of Goethe's being rendered into Yiddish."

Some Jewish musicians and critics could not help admiring Wagner's musical genius, and some Jews have been consummate performers of his works. Nevertheless, what Wagner wrote in his pamphlet cannot (as some would like to argue) be wholly separated from his music, which would so captivate the Nazis in the next century. In any event, his musical aesthetic rejects the Jewish component in European culture, even when it does not ostensibly, as in the Ring cycle, hark back to a Teutonic paganism untouched by Christianity or its Jewish and biblical roots.[32] In Israel, Wagner is not played, because of the association of his music with the Nazis who perpetrated the Holocaust.

It is understandable that humane lovers of Wagner's music, Jewish or otherwise, should have sought to minimize the importance of his antisemitic writings and to consider his music as neutral in itself and untouched by these ideas. On this issue, however, Adolf Hitler is a reliable authority. He considered that Wagner stood alongside Frederick the Great and Martin Luther. He wrote, "Whoever wants to understand National Socialist Germany must know Wagner."[33]

Wagner was initially admired by Nietzsche, who eventually found this variety of antisemitism intolerably vulgar. But that does not mean that Nietzsche was not himself an antisemite. Conor Cruise O'Brien convincingly argues that what Nietzsche had against the Wagnerian type of antisemitism, apart from its vulgarity, was precisely its lingering Christian elements. Nietzsche shared with the Christian inheritance the unchallenged assumption that Jews were bad, but found yet more, now even anti-Christian, reasons for thinking so.

Like Eugen Dühring, Nietzsche thought that those who wished to affirm the Christian tradition "could not turn against Judaism with sufficient force."[34] Dühring had been originally a Social Democrat, attacked by Engels in a famous pamphlet that became a kind of Marxist textbook long after Dühring's own views were otherwise forgotten. Dühring was a failure as an academic, and he attributed his failures to Jewish influence. He became one of the most vicious of all antisemites, attributing all the ills of Germany to Jewish influence and depicting the Jews as a "counterrace" who could neither be converted nor assimilated because of the evil basic to their nature. They must therefore be expelled or even killed.

He claimed to offer a scientific justification of the blood libel, alleging that it was based in ancient human sacrifices offered by the Hebrews and in the desire of contemporary Jews to bind individuals to the community by making them accomplices in crime. He wished to solve the Jewish question by killing and extirpating the Jews.

Nietzsche, for his part, was radically opposed to the Christian ethic, with its emphasis on mercy. This was a reversal of the true Aryan values of "pride, severity, strength, hatred, revenge." Who had been responsible for this transvaluation of values? None other than the Jews.

Paul and Christ, he wrote in *The Antichrist*, were "little superlative Jews . . . One would no more associate with the first Christians than one would with Polish Jews–they both do not smell good." The only New Testament figure who commanded Nietzsche's respect was Pontius Pilate. From Pilate's point of view, as Nietzsche correctly saw, "one Jew more or less, what does it matter?"[35]

O'Brien's conclusion seems just:

> Nietzsche's real complaint against the vulgar anti-semites of his day was that they were not antisemitic enough, that they did not realize that they were themselves carriers of that semitic infection, Christianity. "The Jews," he wrote in *The Antichrist*, "have made mankind so thoroughly false that even to-day the Christian can feel anti-Jewish without realizing that he is himself the *ultimate Jewish consequence*."
>
> Amid the excited vulgar anti-semitism of the late nineteenth century, the reminder that Christianity was a Jewish thing was the most effective argument against Christianity. And to weaken Christianity, especially by this route, was to move towards the abolition of the Christian limit.[36]

By the Christian limit O'Brien means the traditional prohibition of genocide I have often referred to. Once the old Christian hatred of Jews had been radically secularized, and Christian values abandoned precisely because they were Jewish, there was no further moral barrier to genocide. It would not be long before the Nazis would learn Nietzsche's lesson and put it into practice. Nietzsche also wrote of the master race, an idea that especially appealed to the Nazis. It is right to refer to anti-Christian antisemitism, in Nietzsche and in the Nazis, but one should not be misled by the term into supposing that it is not the lineal descendant of its Christian predecessor.

Another of Wagner's admirers was the Englishman Houston Stewart Chamberlain, who married one of Wagner's daughters, Eva, and helped to carry on the Bayreuth tradition. He gave up his British citizenship and wrote in German, about

Wagner, about German authors, and about Christianity. His best known work, entitled in its English translation *The Foundations of the Nineteenth Century*, devoted considerable space to the Jews.

Chamberlain regarded them as a pure race, equal in attainments to the Germans and superior to the Latins. However, if only for this reason, they constituted a substantial threat to the Germans. He argued that King David and the prophets had not been Jewish, and Jesus himself, as a Galilean, must have been an Aryan.

The book became very popular in Wilhelmine Germany; the Kaiser would read it to his children. Later the Nazis and their sympathizers were obliged to read it. Alone among nineteenth-century writers on race, Chamberlain gets a mention in *Mein Kampf*. Generally speaking, Hitler was too anxious to emphasize the originality of his radical antisemitism to acknowledge his own predecessors. In fact, Chamberlain is yet another important link between Christian and Nazi antisemitism.

Perhaps the most famous of all antisemitic slogans, as it subsequently became, was the saying of the Professor of History at the University of Berlin, Heinrich von Treitschke. Consistently with the position of the Enlightenment philosophers, Treitschke argued that if the Jews were to persist in their traditional claim to be a nationality and not just a religion, the legal basis for emancipation would collapse.

At the end of 1879, he began a series of articles on the Jewish question in a journal he edited, the *Preussische Jahrbücher*. The first article began with the sentence, "Even in circles of the most highly educated, among men who would reject with disgust any ideas of ecclesiastical intolerance or national arrogance, there resounds as if from one mouth: *Die Juden sind unser Unglück*."[37] The Jews are our misfortune. Again and again in the years that followed it would be quoted, and it was one of Hitler's favorite phrases. It rings with the self-pity of the oppressor.

FRENCH RACIAL ANTISEMITISM

In 1855, Comte Arthur de Gobineau wrote a four volume work entitled *Essai sur l'inégalité des races humaines*. Gobineau believed in the classic division of the races into the white, the black, and the yellow, and he made the interaction between the races the key to the whole of history. Needless to say, the white or Aryan race was the finest, retaining the greatest potentiality for further development. Its greatest danger lay in degeneration through crossbreeding with the other two.

Gobineau regarded the Latin and the Semitic races as the outcome of such crossbreeding. The Germans were the only remaining representatives of the pure Aryan race. It was up to them to retain their purity, though modern conditions would make this very difficult for them. Gobineau was not intentionally antisemitic, according to his interpreters. His aims lay elsewhere, perhaps in psychological compensation for the misfortunes of the aristocratic class to which he belonged.[38]

However, Gobineau's work was naturally very well received in Germany, and antisemites could certainly use his ideas and did. Gobineau Societies sprang up all over Germany, and the master himself went on regular tours visiting them. Late in life he would spend weeks at Bayreuth as Wagner's guest. Chamberlain, also a member of the Wagnerian circle, was another who took up and developed Gobineau's ideas.

At about the same time that Gobineau was bringing out his work, another French writer and much greater scholar, Ernest Renan, was working along not dissimilar lines. Renan approached things from the standpoint of language, and he made himself an expert on Semitic languages. Nevertheless, he too made the spurious identification between language groups and races, though he did not define the concept of race with precision. In his massive work on the Semitic languages, he wrote, "I am the first to recognize that the Semitic race, as compared to the Indo-European race, essentially represents an inferior store of human nature."[39]

Such ideas did not prevent him from receiving the support of many Jews who admired his expertise, and they supported his claim to the chair of Hebrew at the Collège de France. He wrote in Jewish journals and worked with Jewish scholars. His most influential work, his *Life of Jesus*, reflects similar views about the Semitic race, now completely identified with the Jewish people.

Renan thought that Jews had no interest in the development of human civilization. Their eyes were fixed on the hope of further intervention from God in their own history. He regarded this hope as illusory and a bar to Jewish progress. As Barnett Litvinoff comments, his observation could derive some justification from the Hassidic communities of Eastern Europe and their contemporary descendants.[40] But it would not be long, of course, before the Jews would, as Emil Fackenheim put it, "return into history,"[41] in the form of the Zionist movement. French antisemitism would prove to be one the principal triggers to set off active political Zionism through Theodor Herzl's experiences at the trial and military degradation of Dreyfus.

French antisemitism was mainly Catholic and right wing, even at times counterrevolutionary, though it had a Socialist counterpart, as we have noted already. Antisemitism has always been a component of the nostalgia for prerevolutionary Catholic France that clung to the French Right. The holders of these ideas even came to power for a short time in Vichy France during the Second World War. Antisemitism was less pervasive in France than in Germany, since among Frenchmen there was always a substantial movement, often in the majority, to whom all that the exponents of antisemitism stood for was anathema. Nevertheless, French antisemitism was no less intense than German and sometimes more. Catholic antisemitism gathered strength during the Third Republic, largely in reaction against its anticlerical measures. "The course of French Catholic right-wing politics and journalism in the 1880's was set into the anti-semitic channel into which it was to flow for sixty years."[42]

During that period, its most remarkable exponent was Edouard Drumont, whom O'Brien describes as "the greatest popularizer of anti-semitic ideas and emotions who ever lived (up to the advent of Adolf Hitler)."[43] Drumont was perhaps the supreme example of the modern form of Catholic antisemitism, uniting the old traditional hatred of the Jews as Christ-killers, often expressed in the language of intense and sickening piety, with the new racist doctrines.

The ease with which the new racist antisemitism found a home in the minds of those who stood for the old religious anti-Judaism shows clearly enough that they are not opposites but relatives. If you hate Jews enough, of course, any reason for doing so is welcome, but it was a rare theologically minded Catholic who could reject the new racism while holding on to the old theological rejection of the Jews.

Drumont first brought his ideas before the public in a book called *La France juive*, which he published in 1886. The book was an instant success on the market, proving that what Drumont stood for was not just the outlook of a small lunatic fringe–lunatic though it may well have been. Drumont himself took delight in the numerous approving letters he received from the country clergy, who regarded hostility toward Jews as virtually part of Catholic dogma.

By the end of the year in which it was published, it had already sold 100,000 copies, and in the course of ten years it went through no less than 140 editions. The celebrated writer, Georges Bernanos, was still praising it in the 1930s as a "masterpiece of observation, analysis and erudition." Malcolm Hay remarks that "[i]t was, in fact, a masterpiece of mendacity."[44]

Drumont eagerly promoted the book's circulation outside France, even at his own financial cost. However, since he was quite unscrupulous financially, he probably had other means of recouping his losses on the foreign editions of the book. He sold the Spanish rights for next to nothing, writing, "This is the least I can do for a country like Spain, which originated the tribunal of the Inquisition, a tribunal, patriotic and humane, which the Jews have attacked because it protected Christian honesty against the invading and exploiting Semite." He gave the rights to a Polish publisher for nothing at all, hoping that God would reward him. "Please God that my work may revive in the soul of every Polish patriot hatred for those infamous Jews who have betrayed them."[45] Drumont also had a considerable following in Austria.

What were the ideas set forth in this best-seller of antisemitism? Its principal theme was the by then classic one of the Jewish conspiracy to take over the world, after first destroying Christendom. But as befits a modern work of antisemitism, Jews are now identified as Semites, enemies of the Aryan race. Drumont represents France as already in the clutches of this worldwide conspiracy. Jews were a foreign body, introduced into France at the time of the Revolution, and now more than half controlling it.

This absurd thesis–Jews constituted at that time less than a quarter of one percent of the population of France, most of them poor–was backed up by false statistics, purporting to show that Jews owned more than half of the total French national wealth, all of which they had acquired dishonestly. It gained whatever minimal plausibility it had solely from the prominence of individual Jews, such as the Rothschild family, in the financial world. What made them conspicuous of course was not they were rich, as others also were, but that they were Jewish.

Drumont's sources seem to have been the legacy of traditional German antisemitism, going back even to Eisenmenger in the sixteenth century. Since he did not know German, he must have relied on others to make translations for him, and to direct him to the sources.

He also made use of contemporary materials in German, including the writings of the infamous Austrian professor of Hebrew, August Rohling, whose forgeries had recently been exposed in court when a rabbi deliberately provoked him into bringing a libel action, which Rohling eventually evaded. It was shown that Rohling had no scholarly knowledge whatsoever of the Talmud, on whose alleged contents he had attempted to base his own libels, and was incapable of translating it. Nevertheless, Drumont did not hesitate in 1890 to tell his readers on Rohling's authority that the Jews do not regard Christians as human beings, "since the marriage of Christians, as the Talmud explains, cannot be recognized any more than the copulation of animals."[46]

In 1891, he reminded the parish priests of their traditional belief that ritual murder had been the regular practice of Jews in the Middle Ages, adding that "in every country at the present day where the Jew is his real self *[à l'état de nature]*, such crimes are constantly recurring." The Catholic church, he assured them, had confirmed and ordained belief in these accounts. "To ask a Catholic priest to deny the fact of ritual murder is simply to ask him to admit that the church, by beatifying poor little children whose throats were cut by Jews, has been guilty of the most hateful imposture and made cynical sport of the credulity of nations."[47]

"Drumont united religious, economic and racial sentiments into one single hatred."[48] As one of Drumont's own colleagues said of him, "[He] restated the point of view of the Middle Ages, who hated the Jew because he had crucified the Saviour of the world."[49] He believed that if the Jews could be driven out of France, or otherwise eliminated, peace and prosperity could not fail to follow.

The idea was based on the notion of Aryan racial superiority. The natural goodness of the Aryan French, in the absence of Jews, would put everything right and rescue the poor from oppression. Even a reviewer who was himself an open hater of Jews could not stomach the illogical racism on which Drumont's thesis depended, arguing that if there is really a difference between Jews and others it is the product of history. He regarded the book as dangerous.[50] Most French Jews did not, and failed to take its threat seriously. The threat would be real enough, if anyone took Drumont seriously, and many certainly did.

Drumont approved of anyone who at any historical period had persecuted Jews. He said of the Inquisition, "The Dominicans were ardent patriots such as we are, who did not hesitate to suppress all Jews."[51] He praised the pogroms in Russia, and he suggested that similar methods should be employed to get rid of the Jews of France.[52] Having carefully distinguished on racial grounds between good and bad capitalists, he recommended that the French workers should take violent possession of Jewish property: "On the day when the Catholics, weary of defending a society which has become exclusively Jewish, allow the hungry mob to march on the mansions of the Jewish bankers . . . these beggars of yesterday, now the tyrants of to-day, will be crushed, and their blood will not make a stain any redder than the Kosher meat which they eat.[53]

In a later book, *La fin d'un monde*, he went further and suggested confiscation of the property not only of Jews of German origin, for whom he had a particular hate, but also of those who had lived in France for generations and who were indeed "Frenchmen of the Mosaic persuasion." He proposed to seize all Jewish capital and put it in a National Workers' Bank. He seems to have been particularly skillful at uniting the resentment of the poor with traditional religious and new racial prejudices. The method would be employed by others after him who needed a scapegoat for social ills.

In his *Testament d'un antisémite*, Drumont even alleged that Jews had succeeded in infecting parts of Russia with syphilis.[54] "Drumont's polemic was not merely extravagant; it was obscene, yet he knew what he was doing. He wrote for a public whom he knew would lick their lips over the foulest lie he could tell them about any member of the accursed race."[55] Edmond de Goncourt said of him that Drumont "wrote what everyone was thinking, and he alone had the courage to write."[56]

Perhaps he sank to the lowest depths in his calumny of the Christian convert, Heine. "This exquisite poet, the delicate-minded Parisien, is indeed the brother of the filthy Jew-boy, of the Jew-boys with corkscrew curls from Galicia, who, met together for some ritual murder, look at each other with merry glances while, from the open wound of their victim, issues pure and scarlet the Christian blood destined for their sweet bread of Purim.[57]

As Hay rightly comments, this is the style of Julius Streicher and *Der Stürmer*. Clearly, Drumont wrote for a climate very like that from which the Nazis would later profit. One can wonder what prevented a Holocaust in France. The answer seems to be that, in France but not in Germany, there was a substantial opposition possessing courage and eloquence. When sufficiently provoked, it would stand up and give the lie to such calumnies, as happened in the Dreyfus affair.

Nevertheless, the analogy with Hitler was not devised by Drumont's later critics without solid ground. One of the last surviving members of his own group wrote in 1935, "What Drumont proclaimed, Hitler has achieved."[58] Bernanos, the literary defender of Drumont, wrote in 1938, the year of Kristallnacht, when Jews were already being herded into concentration camps and beaten to death, "I do not believe that M. Hitler and M. Mussolini are demi-gods. But I merely pay homage to the truth when I say that they are men without fear. They would never tolerate in their own country the organization of massacres."[59] Such naïvety can only spring from complicity.

THE DREYFUS AFFAIR

The affair, as the Catholic writer Charles Péguy saw, "was a notable crisis in three histories, in the history of Israel, in the history of France and in the history of

Christianity."[60] In the extraordinary outbreak of antisemitism over the accusation and condemnation of Captain Alfred Dreyfus for giving military secrets to Germany, France came close to the spiritual destruction that actually overcame Germany half a century later, because, as Péguy acknowledged, "she was instinctively antisemitic because of her own Christian past."

That France did not in the end wholly succumb is due to the efforts of a few "heroes,"[61] Péguy among them, who stood up for truth against the massive prejudice of the great majority of their fellow countrymen. As late as the thirties, and perhaps still today, there were Frenchmen who considered it a patriotic duty to continue to believe in the guilt of Dreyfus, even after his innocence had been proved beyond doubt and officially and formally acknowledged by the government of the nation.

It was none other than Drumont who ignited the public movement against Dreyfus. "Had it not been for Drumont, the *affaire* would never have been heard of."[62] The minister for war, Mercier, would probably have taken little notice of the flimsy case against Dreyfus prepared by members of his staff if not for a story that appeared in Drumont's paper, *La libre parole,* under the banner headlines, "Jewish traitor under arrest."

The editor told his readers in an article, "Just as Judas had sold the God of pity and love, so Captain Dreyfus has sold to Germany the plans for mobilisation."[63] Drumont had been tipped off by Colonel Henry, the intelligence officer who was mainly responsible for the intrigue against Dreyfus.

This is not the place to follow the details of the Dreyfus affair, a story often told and readily accessible. What is important for the present inquiry is the dominant role played in the whole affair by antisemitic prejudice, no doubt fomented by Drumont himself. But it was present in abundance to be worked upon, operating powerfully behind the scenes in the attempt to incriminate an innocent man for no other reason than because he was a Jew. It is no less important to see, as the Catholic Péguy so clearly did, the Catholic foundations of this antisemitic frenzy, by now no longer distinct from its new racist taint.

Even when Colonel Henry, the original forger of the famous paper that was the main evidence against Dreyfus, confessed his guilt to the minister for war and committed suicide in prison, *La libre parole* announced that he had been assassinated by the Jews. Dreyfus became a symbol around which all France gathered, on one side or the other, whether *anti-Dreyfusard* or *Dreyfusard.* Eventually, the antisemitic opponents of Dreyfus and what he stood for in the public mind coalesced in the semi-Fascist Action Française.

> Anyone who dared to suggest that [Dreyfus] might be innocent, or that his trial had been illegal, was at once regarded as an enemy of that formidable trinity, *la Patrie, l'Armée et l'Eglise.* "It was not a man who was being degraded for a personal fault," wrote Drumont in *La Libre Parole,* "but a whole race whose shame was being exposed." The Jew had been condemned in the minds of his judges and by the almost unanimous voice of public opinion, even before the evidence, such as it was, had been heard. "I

don't need anyone to tell me," wrote Maurice Barrès [of the notorious Action Française], "why Dreyfus was a traitor . . . or that he was capable of treachery. I know that from his race."[64]

The leader of the French Catholic Party, Albert de Mun, refused to discuss even the possibility that a Jew might be innocent, and he was opposed to the revision of the trial in the light of fresh evidence. One of the handwriting experts at the first trial stated that Dreyfus was guilty, "because all Jews are traitors." A deputy declared in the Chamber that "Dreyfus, whether innocent or guilty, must remain at Devil's Island." In somewhat the same vein, a noble lady expressed her hope that "Dreyfus might be innocent, so that he would suffer more." Drumont, not to be outdone, revived the blood libel once more, and informed his readers that "a great religious sacrifice was being prepared for the feast of Purim."[65]

RUSSIAN ANTISEMITISM

It was in Russia, however, rather than France or even Germany, that antisemitism reached its greatest influence on state policy in the nineteenth and early twentieth century. In the Russian dominions, most Jews were required to live in an area known as the Pale of Settlement, comprising Ukraine, Byelo-Russia, and much of present-day Poland, though a few also lived in the major metropolitan centers. As in Germany, the growth of antisemitism in Russia in the early nineteenth century was a reaction to the earlier spread of Enlightenment views, extending to official thinking and practice.

The first law to be made on the subject of Jews, Alexander I's decree of 1804, had opened centers of learning up to the university level to Jews and provided safeguards for Jewish students. During this period, the policy was to attract Jewish students into the institutions of non-Jewish education, in order to foster the alienation of young people from their traditional religion and culture. Religious Jews therefore opposed the entry of young Jews into these educational institutions, while the maskilim, the advocates of Jewish enlightenment, favored it as a means of breaking down barriers between Jewish and Russian culture.

However, hostility toward Napoleon brought about a nationalistic reaction, in which liberal thinking of all kinds became associated with Napoleon, the enemy. Since Napoleon had shown some friendliness toward Jews, antisemites were able to link Jews with Napoleon. Characteristically for Russia, the reaction was led by the Church. In 1807, only a year after Austerlitz, the Holy Synod passed a measure condemning Napoleon's liberalization of the status of the Jews:

> To the greater shame of the Church he assembled in France Jewish synagogues, ordered to pay honour to the rabbis, and re-established the great Jewish Synedrion, that same godless congregation that once dared to condemn to crucifixion our Lord and Saviour Jesus Christ. [Napoleon] now attempts to unite the Jews scattered by divine wrath over the whole world and to lead them to the overthrow of Christ's Church and

> to (O horrible wickedness overstepping all his impudence) the proclamation of a false Messiah in the person of Napoleon.[66]

For the Holy Synod, as for other antisemites of the day, Napoleon's temerity in improving the lot of the Jews, even for reasons of his own state policy, had made it possible to identify him with the Antichrist, the "false Messiah" of the statement. Antisemitism had begun to take on apocalyptic dimensions.

This revival of ancient hostility did not render the Jews of Russia less loyal to their adopted country. In the campaign of 1812, they rallied to the Russian cause. Some of their religious leaders correctly predicted that if Napoleon were victorious the Jews would be secularized, whereas even though their lot would be worse under the Czar, they would remain religious.[67]

The next Czar, Nicholas I, referred to the Jews as "Zhids . . . leeches . . . the ruin of the Western provinces." But he did remember their loyalty in 1812. In 1828, however, he removed Jewish immunity to military service. This measure made it possible to conscript Jews for twenty-five years of service, under the law even at the age of twelve, and in practice at eight or nine. Young conscripts were submitted to forced conversion, which some avoided only by suicide.[68]

Nicholas' policy aimed at assimilation of the Jews. What he achieved in his army by forcible methods he attempted to bring about more subtly in the educated civilian population by liberalizing measures, correctly understood by the majority of Jews as intended to deprive them of their traditional identity.

Nicholas was succeeded by Alexander II, who adopted a slightly more liberal policy, though one that brought little real change for the Jews. He altered the laws on conscription so that they applied equally to all. No more attempts were made at inducing Jewish conversion and some restrictions on residence were removed. Many Jews now changed their attitude toward state education, and students entered the system in larger numbers. In 1880 the proportion of Jewish students in the state schools was 11.5% of the total and in the universities 6.8%. These proportions had risen from only 1.3% in the schools in 1853, and only a few dozen in the universities, and the numbers continued to increase every year, reaching 35.2% in Odessa and 26.7% in Vilna.[69] Slight as the changes in czarist policy were against a general background of hostility toward Jews, they encouraged hope among educated Jews that liberalization was coming in Russia as it evidently was in Western Europe. But these hopes were not destined to last long.

In 1881 Alexander II was assassinated. O'Brien sees this event as a pivotal moment:

> The assassination of Alexander II is one of the great turning points in world history, and especially in the history of the Jews. It is the moment in which the notion of the inevitable and universal triumph of liberal ideas receives its first great setback. That notion had dominated the thinking and expectations of most educated middle-class people throughout the nineteenth century . . . It drew strength from the overwhelming nature of past successes, the English Revolution, the American Revolution,

the French Revolution. Liberal, secular, universalist ideas were unstoppable; their victory everywhere was only a question of time . . .[70]

The assassination of Alexander, together with the reaction that followed under his successor, Alexander III, was a portent of the twentieth century, still to come. There was nothing inevitable about the march of liberalism. It had to contend with dark forces in the European psyche that had been there much longer than liberal ideas, and were fed by deeper and more powerful passions. Among them was the ancient hostility toward Jews, still blamed for the death of Christ. As O'Brien puts it, "[I]t became horrifyingly apparent that what most united the Russian people—peasant, middle class and Tsar—was a hatred of Jews."[71]

Under Alexander III, antisemitism became an instrument of state policy, spearheaded by the pogroms, murderous riots against Jews, tolerated if not actually instigated by the authorities. The ringleaders were sometimes brought to trial and lightly punished, perhaps as a sop to Western public opinion, but no less frequently the Jews were blamed for the riots, supposedly provoked by their extortions. The trials of the perpetrators often turned into trials of the victims. Everyone knew, too, that if the authorities had really wanted to halt the pogroms they could easily have done so. So the rioters knew that they could get away with violence, extending at times to beating, rape, and murder.

Alexander's adviser in most matters was the Procurator of the Holy Synod, K. P. Pobedonostsev, at different times tutor to both Alexander III and his successor, Nicholas II. The Holy Synod in Russia and other Orthodox countries is the principal governing body of the Church, presided over by the Metropolitan, with other bishops and some leading laymen as its members. The Holy Synod also has a strong influence on the country in general, where the Orthodox Church is also the state church. There was thus nothing anomalous in an ecclesiastical official being the autocratic Czar's principal political adviser.

Pobedonostsev was a highly educated intellectual, author of many academic works and the leading jurist of his time. In his thinking, derived from the French counterrevolutionary, Joseph de Maistre, liberalism was the enemy and the Jews were the carriers of liberalism. Others hoped that the march of liberalism would prove inevitable. People like de Maistre and Pobedonostsev feared that it would, and they pointed to the same evidence.

In Russia, so the argument went, the liberal infection had begun with Catherine the Great and spread under Alexander I. Checked to some extent under Nicholas I, it had broken out again in full force under Alexander II, opening the way to all kinds of revolutionary activity, even costing the Czar himself his life. The time had come to save Holy Russia by putting a stop to liberalism altogether and with it the influence of the Jews.[72]

Pobedonostsev wrote a letter to Fyodor Dostoievsky, the famous writer, in which these ideas are openly expressed:

> What you write about the Yids is extremely just. The Jews have engrossed everything, they have undermined everything, but the spirit of the century supports

> them. They are at the root of the revolutionary socialist movement and of regicide, they own the periodical press, they have in their hands the financial markets, the people as a whole fall into financial slavery to them; they even control the principles of contemporary science and strive to place it outside Christianity.[73]

The destination of the letter ought to remind us of the often overlooked fact that Dostoievsky, so much admired for his literary genius, was one of the foremost exponents of the same nationalist antisemitism. In Russia as in Germany, antisemitism and nationalism went hand in hand. Most of those attached to the Slavophile movement matched love of Holy Russia with a corresponding hatred of Jews.

Unfortunately, there is little evidence that things have changed among Orthodox Christians. Forty years ago, I remember being amazed in my ignorance to hear the political views expressed by the young theologians of the Russian Orthodox emigration in Paris. For them, the root of all evil was the *French* Revolution, not as one would have expected the Communist. While they did not in my hearing express the antisemitic views that went along with such ideas, there is little reason to doubt that they held them. Today, in the Soviet Union, as the collapse of the Communist system brings to the surface ideas that have persisted underground for seventy years, it is clear that intense nationalism, attachment to the Church, and antisemitism still go together and will be hard to separate.

Pobedonostsev is supposed to have uttered a succinct formulation of the policy he urged upon the Czar: one third of the Jews should be converted, one third should emigrate, and one third should die out. There seems to be some uncertainty about whether he actually said this, and some think he did not, for various reasons.[74] But, whether he said it or not, and leaving aside the actual proportions, the remark does sum up the choices state policy intended to offer Jews: unless they had the courage to stand by their faith, and the good fortune to avoid violence, that was in fact what happened to them. A few were converted, many died in pogroms, and a small but significant minority began to make plans for a return to Zion.

Many more looked West, either to the more liberal states of western Europe, or increasingly to the United States, the "*goldeneh medina*," the golden land, where prospects were bright for those who could endure initial poverty and hardship. Bright as they undoubtedly were by contrast, there too the new immigrants would encounter discrimination and occasional violence.

For the first time in European history, antisemitism was now state policy in Russia. It was also a popular policy: all classes in society shared a dislike of Jews. More remarkably, perhaps, as O'Brien points out, Russian state antisemitism did not then arouse international protest, as it did later. "Anyone inclined to meditate on Western rejection of anti-semitism, how deep it goes, and does not go, might give thought to the architecture of the city of Paris. In Paris, there stands a splendid monument to the greatest persecutor of the Jews in modern times, up to the advent of Adolf Hitler. The most exuberantly triumphal of the many notable bridges that span the Seine is the Pont Alexandre III.[75]

Pogroms were especially common in the early 1880s, the years immediately following the assassination of Alexander II and the accession of Alexander III. Their center was the south-western area of Russia, the Ukraine. The pogroms of spring and summer 1881 hit more than one hundred communities.[76]

Initially, the central authorities feared that the pogroms might be a further manifestation of the revolutionary activities that had led to the violent death of the previous czar. They were reassured by an emissary from the Ministry of the Interior, who reported that they could be capitalized for the policy of the state. His superior, Ignatyev, a Slavophile, an opponent of all liberal tendencies and a supporter of Alexander's new policy of autocratic rule, wrote a memorandum to the Czar, in which he argued that the main cause of the riots was the rising economic power of the Jews, who had exploited the main body of the population, arousing them to violent protest.[77] This reasoning seems to have led to the decision to use popular antisemitism as a means of winning the loyalty of the population to its rulers.

Pogroms now also broke out in Poland, apparently stimulated by the perceived direction of official policy, though in this case public figures condemned the violence. In Russia itself, by contrast, writers and intellectuals like Turgenev and Tolstoy remained silent. Further pogroms took place in Russia in 1882 and continued up to 1884.

The czarist regime began to be embarrassed by these excesses, and in May 1882, Ignatyev, who had been associated with them, lost his position. Before his dismissal, however, he had instituted a series of policies known as "Temporary Rules," prohibiting Jews from settling in villages, even in the Pale, from purchasing land outside the towns, and from opening businesses or stores on Sundays or church holidays. These measures were described as "protection of the base population against Jewish exploitation." They had a strongly adverse effect on Jewish livelihood, crowding Jews into the already overcrowded towns and increasing the pressure of competition. They were also taken as a hint by the local population: if antisemitism was so clearly state policy, harassment of Jews in any form was obviously acceptable.[78]

The liberalizing educational policies of the previous czar had brought about the flourishing of a substantial body of Russian Jewish intellectuals. Government service being closed to them, they entered the liberal professions, medicine, law, and journalism. The prominence of Jews in these professions led to a backlash, and the educational institutions began to restrict the entry of Jews. Opponents of Jews claimed that they had introduced a revolutionary spirit into the schools and were thus a bad influence on their Christian fellow students.

Finally, in July 1887, the Ministry of Education itself introduced restrictions on the number of Jews in educational institutions. These were to be limited to 10% in the towns in the Pale of Settlement, 5% in the towns outside it, and 3% in Moscow and St. Petersburg. Many schools were not open to Jews at all. In due course, the same policy was applied to institutions under the jurisdiction of other government departments.

The situation continued until the 1905 revolution, when educational institutions were granted autonomy. Immediately the revolution was put down, the restrictions were again applied, in some cases even to converts from Judaism. However, after the Bolshevik Revolution of 1917, all such restrictions were abolished and only reappeared when Stalin introduced his policy of systematic antisemitism.[79]

In 1894, Alexander III was succeeded by the last Czar, Nicholas II. During his reign, the opposition came to see that the state policy of antisemitism had also the purpose of consolidating the autocratic rule of the czar, and began to oppose it for this reason. Among those who did so were the Slavophile philosopher Vladimir Solovyev, and the writer Maxim Gorki. In reaction, the government now claimed that the whole revolutionary movement was a Jewish plot and again used antisemitic attitudes in the masses to protect its own regime. The Czar was personally antisemitic and encouraged the policy of his government.

The government now actually started to finance anti-Jewish newspapers and attempted to organize pogroms and blood libels. In Kishinev, a local paper spread antisemitism, while local government officials supported a clandestine antisemitic organization. Apparently, in consequence, a particularly brutal pogrom occurred in Kishinev in 1903, in which more than fifty people were killed and over five hundred injured. Hundreds of homes and stores were looted and vandalized. The opposition movement openly blamed the government, while Jews, especially among the young people, began to realize the necessity for self-defense.[80]

During the Russo-Japanese War, which broke out in 1904, the antisemites accused the Jews of sympathizing with the enemy and of spreading revolutionary propaganda in order to weaken Russia. Gangs of hooligans known as the Black Hundreds were formed under the covert auspices of the Union of the Russian People, a prominent antisemitic organization, with the aim of annihilating revolutionaries and Jews. The army and the cossacks took part in their antisemitic riots. Simultaneously, attempts were made to deprive the Jews of the franchise.

When in October 1905, continuing revolutionary pressure forced the czar to sign a proclamation guaranteeing basic freedoms to all citizens, the antisemitic organizations organized patriotic processions bearing aloft the portrait of the czar. The demonstrations soon turned into antisemitic riots. Leaflets inciting the riots turned out to have been printed at police headquarters and financed by a secret fund administered by none other than the Czar. Many hundreds of Jewish lives were lost in the ensuing riots, three hundred in Odessa alone.

In some places Russian intellectuals and workers came to the defense of the Jews, along with their own self-defense organizations, and some even lost their lives. The army and the cossacks suppressed this Russian support for the Jews and in some places themselves took part in the pogroms, even receiving decorations for their good work.

Earlier, the Czar had been forced to agree to the setting up of an advisory council, called the Duma, which limited his own autocratic authority. This body conducted an inquiry into the pogroms, finding that they had been instigated by the authorities. In response, the right wing press and the Orthodox church claimed that many of the deputies in the Duma were Jews, or Poles financed by the Jews. The revolution came to an end in 1907. Stolypin now ruled as a virtual dictator on behalf of the Czar. Anxious to restore Russia's international image, he wished to rein in the anti-Jewish policy of the government, but his proposals were rejected by the Czar.[81]

During the reign of the same czar occurred the famous Beilis blood libel, already briefly mentioned. In 1911, a conference was held of associations of members of the nobility, which issued demands that Russia be rid of the Jews altogether. At the same conference, self-styled experts testified that Jews needed Christian blood for their own religious observances.

Shortly afterward, though it cannot be asserted that it was in direct response, a Jew living in Kiev, Mendel Beilis, was actually accused of kidnapping and killing a Christian boy in order to use his blood for ritual purposes. The libel had in fact been fabricated by the Union of the Russian People, and the police knew who the actual murderers of the boy had been. Nevertheless, in collusion with the Ministry of Justice they brought Beilis to trial and gathered an international collection of "experts" to provide spurious evidence of the accusation. Beilis did not actually receive a court hearing until 1913, having spent the intervening two years in prison. Throughout the trial, the Ministry of Justice brought reports on its progress to the Czar.

In terms that only came into use later, this was widely recognized as a "show trial." Opinion both in Russia and internationally collected around both sides of the case. Beilis was defended by some of the best lawyers in the country, who were able to expose the incompetence and ignorance of the so-called expert witnesses who supported the blood libel in court, while the opposition press brought to light the way in which the Ministry of Justice had staged the whole trial.

An international protest movement took up the cause of Beilis, putting considerable pressure on the Russian authorities. In the end, Beilis was acquitted for lack of evidence, though the jury did not rule on the authenticity of the blood libel itself. The verdict, widely regarded as a defeat for the regime, was popular in liberal and educated circles in Russia itself, although this was not the case in Poland, where the public showed its continuing belief in the blood libel. The most nationalistic party, the National Democrats, organized an economic boycott against the Jews.[82]

When the czarist regime fell in 1917, Jews had reason for relief. A number of assimilated Jews took part in the making of the revolution and the building of the new Soviet state. The most famous names are those of Trotsky and Kaganovich, but there were many others. It seemed to such people that communism would mean the definitive end of antisemitism. It was perhaps less clear to them that their own program also meant the definitive end of Jewish identity.

For a few years, their hopes seemed justified. Lenin himself strongly condemned antisemitism. Soon however, the paranoia of Stalin turned against the Jews, and revived antisemitism with a virulence hardly exceeded in the Middle Ages. Stalin is a perfect example of the process of modern antisemitism. He was brought up as an Orthodox Christian and was even for a while a theological student before he became a Marxist. His conditioned hatred of Jews was not effaced by his Marxist indoctrination but found new justification from aspects of Marxist theory. The strongest element in his makeup was paranoia. In due course, that paranoia focussed on Jews in and out of the party.

Russia was also the source of the most influential antisemitic document ever written, *The Protocols of the Learned Elders of Zion*. During the Second World War, an investigator reckoned that at that time its worldwide circulation was second only to that of the Bible. The *Protocols* purport to tell the story of a secret assembly of international Jewish leaders to discuss their plans for world domination. As has been known in the West since 1920, and in Russia itself from the days of Nicholas II, the document is a forgery. The forgers seem to have been agents of the Russian secret police, working in Paris in the last decade of the nineteenth century.

Its spuriousness was rapidly discovered and recognized even by Nicholas II, personally antisemitic as he was, who wrote in the margin of his copy, "One does not defend a worthy cause by vile means,"[83] and it had little importance as a factor in the history of Russian antisemitism. It was in Nazi Germany, among the international circles of antisemites, and more recently in the Arab world, that the *Protocols* became important. Hitler took it with complete seriousness and made it a principal instrument of Nazi indoctrination and propaganda. In America, Henry Ford, one of the most influential of all antisemites, took it up and financed its distribution, until he too became convinced of its inauthenticity. To this day it is widely circulated in Latin America.

In the Arab world, no one seems to question its truth. Gamal Abdel Nasser personally vouched for its authenticity. King Saud used to distribute copies to whoever would visit his court. I do not know if the practice continues under King Fahd, but there is no doubt that the *Protocols* continue to exert their pernicious influence wherever people wish to think ill of Jews, including the whole Arab world.[84]

The *Protocols* are perhaps the most typical as well as the most influential expression of the theory of Jewish world conspiracy. No traces of such a conspiracy have ever been found by sane investigators, to the extent that they would bother to look. In view of the continuous misfortunes of the Jewish people at the hands of their enemies and detractors, the theory is so improbable that no sensible person would spend time on it.

The origins of the fantasy are not easy to determine. The first signs seem to have appeared in the Middle Ages, when stories circulated of a conspiracy to poison the wells of Christendom. In the eighteenth and nineteenth centuries, paranoid Christians were more worried about Freemasonry, and much of the material that went into such works as the Protocols is really recycled anti-Masonic writing. Soon the idea grew up that Freemasons and Jews could be equated, and allegations began to spread about a Jewish-Masonic conspiracy. In due course, the Jews fitted better as a target for paranoid fantasies, and the Masons were relegated to the background, though not always completely dropped. A quasi-Masonic Bavarian group called the Illuminati, who were actually somewhat anti-Jewish, are still sometimes lumped together with Jews in the paranoid package.

In an earlier chapter, I attempted to account for the standard calumnies against Jews by the mechanism of paranoia. Obviously, paranoia is at work here too. But can we be more specific about how it works? In writing about the Middle Ages, I suggested that paranoid Christians projected on to the Jews unconscious aims of their own. It is certainly not farfetched to point out that the Catholic Church did, and in many respects still does, have the aim of world domination. Under the Kingship of Christ, the Church thought it its own destiny to rule the world under Christ's Vicar, the Pope.

Only reluctantly, and as a result of superior secular power, did the Church abandon this vision in the later Middle Ages. Today, the enormous and growing political influence of the papacy in Eastern Europe makes one wonder if such political aims have been altogether abandoned. At any rate, it is not for Christians to accuse Jews of wishing to rule the world.

ANTISEMITIC PARTIES IN GERMANY AND AUSTRIA

In his article on Anti-Semitic Political Parties and Organizations in the authoritative *Encyclopaedia Judaica*, Jacob Toury states that "[t]he appearance of anti-Jewish parties and organizations . . . constitutes the most important distinguishing mark of modern antisemitism. . ."[85] Certainly these groups, which began to appear in Germany and in the Austro-Hungarian Empire in the period after Germany's success in the Franco-Prussian War, had no precedent. One of the most remarkable features of these parties is the fact that they belonged both to the Right and (to a lesser extent) to the Left of the political spectrum. This is no doubt the reason for the otherwise perplexing capacity of these groups to change their titles and apparent political allegiance, to split up and reunite, according to the needs of the moment. The one consistent factor seems to have been their antisemitism.

Undoubtedly, their antisemitism stemmed from the tradition of Christian anti-Judaism common to the culture in which all of them had been nurtured. The same otherwise inexplicable alliances are recurring today among the enemies of Israel. When the Left and the Right are united against Jews or Jewish causes, Jews have reason for fear.

Conservative groups looked back to the world before the French Revolution, a world dominated by the Church. Anti-Jewishness was unquestionably a part of this world, taken for granted by all but a very few. However, in the prerevolutionary world, anti-Judaism was not yet racial in character. Conservatives embraced the radical new racialist views without hesitation or finding any difficulty in the fact that they were in conflict with an important element in the traditional Christian view of the Jews. Clearly, they felt little remaining force in the older distinction between religion and race.

The Communists identified the Jews with capitalism, as Marx himself had. Since they were not themselves religious, Communists could not object to Jews on theological grounds. As we have seen, however, even the identification of the Jews with capitalism was in fact a modernized form of one of the principal calumnies of the Middle Ages, that identified Jews with the practice of usury. However, the Social Democratic Left in Germany, though also Marxist, managed to escape becoming antisemitic, perhaps mainly because of the strong stand taken by the party leadership.[86]

A new type of political grouping originated in this period, describing itself as Christian-Social. Parties incorporating this expression or its variants in their title were regularly antisemitic. As *Christian*, these parties were against Jews on traditional religious grounds. As *Social*, they were against them as supposedly the chief representatives of the power of financial interests over the little man. They thus combined traditional and modern forms of hostility toward Jews. And they too now considered the Jews as a race with unalterable hereditary characteristics.

Antisemitic parties sometimes openly included the word *antisemitic* in their title. In other cases, they used well understood codes. The terms *Christian* or *German* always meant that the parties in question were antisemitic, as sometimes did the term *Reform*, though the primary meaning of the latter was opposition to liberal advocacy of free trade. The codes were well understood by everybody, and they remained so into the twentieth century. Lucy Dawidowicz cites an example that is not without an element of black humor. The Hungarian dictator of the Second World War period, Admiral Horthy, "joyous[ly] embrace[d] . . . the secretary of the American Y.M.C.A. as the head of 'such an important anti-Semitic organization.' "[87]

Even the term *Socialist* could have an antisemitic meaning in a party title. Among the Sudeten German followers of the antisemitic ideologist von Schoenerer there was a party originally called the *Deutsche Arbeiterpartei*, later renamed the *Deutsche Nazionalsocialistische Arbeiterpartei*, or German National Socialist Workers Party. The antisemitic meaning of the term still held good in the twentieth century. We sometimes forget that the full name of the Nazi party was the *Nazionalsocialistiche Deutsche Arbeiterpartei*, or National Socialist German Workers' Party, an almost identical title. Thus the Nazis embodied at least two of the antisemitic code words in the title of their party, omitting the one they could not use, *Christian*.

Antisemitic parties were not just fringe groups, though they did not attain a political majority at any time. In 1890 five professed antisemites were elected to the Reichstag: in 1893, sixteen antisemitic candidates were elected, of whom half came from Hesse. By this time the German Conservative party had included an antisemitic plank in its platform, and the Agrarian League had entered the arena as another openly antisemitic ultraconservative party. In 1903, eleven antisemites succeeded in being elected and three more gained seats in later by-elections. Just before the First World War, the antisemitic parliamentary groups amalgamated into the *Deutsch-Völkische Partei*, but they did not succeed in maintaining the same degree of electoral support.

However, by this time antisemitism was not confined to the openly antisemitic parties. The liberal groups on the Left, hitherto the bastion of opposition to antisemitism, started to make political deals with the antisemitic parties and began to alienate their Jewish supporters in other ways as well. During the same period, all kinds of clubs and student organizations also formed on an antisemitic basis. Germany's largest white-collar trade union, the *Deutschnazionaler Handlungsgehilfen-verband*, or D.H.V., formed in 1893, adhered to nationalist and antisemitic policies.[88]

Similar developments were taking place in the Austro-Hungarian Empire, though there the antisemites were even more influential than in Germany. In Austria, antisemitism in its Christian-Social form was more closely identified with the Catholic population than in Germany, where Protestant conservatism was the strongest influence in the Christian-Social movement. Even liberals were antisemitic in Austria, since they held pan-German views and were therefore opposed to all minorities. Other minorities were themselves antisemitic, since they identified the Jews with loyalty to the Hapsburgs. In Austria, political antisemitism was pioneered by the clubs and student organizations.[89]

The first important leader in political antisemitism in Austria was Georg von Schoenerer, generally thought to have been an important influence on the young Adolf Hitler. Schoenerer, originally a liberal, gradually went over to the extreme pan-German group. Schoenerer himself had originally been influenced by Dühring, perhaps the most extreme of all nineteenth-century antisemites. Thus, as Dawidowicz points out, a line of descent can be traced from Dühring through Schoenerer to Hitler himself.[90] Schoenerer was accustomed to going around Vienna with his student bodyguard, chanting, "*Was der Jude glaubt ist einerlei, in der Rasse liegt die Schweinerei.*" (What the Jew believes is all one, in his race lies the swinishness.)[91]

In 1888, Schoenerer was sent to prison for assault and his *Deutschnazionaler Verein* began to break up. The Christian-Social movement took its place as the spearhead of political antisemitism, its leading personalities being Karl von Vogelsang and Karl Lueger.

Lueger, originally associated with the Christian Social Union, came to identify himself with a new antisemitic and antiliberal alignment, the United Christians. In the Reichsrat he personally led the Free Union for Economic Reform on a Christian Basis. With the backing of these and other groups he became in due course mayor of Vienna, though the emperor several times prevented him from taking office after being repeatedly elected.

So strong was the antisemitic political influence that in 1902 fifty-one members of the Austrian Diet were antisemites, all of them Christian-Socialists. The Catholic conservatives also courted Lueger, a skilled and charismatic politician. In 1907, after the introduction of a general ballot for the Reichsrat, the representation of the Christian-Socialists rose to sixty-seven. The conservatives then joined with them in a parliamentary alliance, bringing twenty-nine more members into the antisemitic bloc.[92] Lueger is often said to have been an opportunistic politician, playing the antisemitic card only for political gain, while "some of his best friends" remained Jewish. He is famous for his saying, "*Wer Jude ist, das bestimme ich,*" or "I decide who is a Jew."

He may well have used the principle to exclude some personal associates from the force of the antisemitism he advocated politically. The precedent was nevertheless an ominous one. Hitler would use it in the opposite sense, to extend the meaning of the word Jew beyond traditional limits. It is not easy to see how a politician such as Lueger, who did not scruple to use antisemitism for his own political advantage, can be excused from personal antisemitism. No one who cared in the slightest for Jews as human beings would have used such evil forces for his own advantage.

We cannot stress too strongly that these modern forms of antisemitism were no less baseless than their predecessors. It was certainly not in accord with reality to regard converted or assimilated Jews as possessing the same characteristics as their observant and traditional forebears. In Germany as in France, the idea that the Jews monopolized finance was without factual support, in view of the small numbers of Jews in the population and the fact that the majority of them were poor or at most middle-class. Jews were conspicuous to their neighbors because they were Jews, not because they were an enormously powerful influence on society. Paranoia was still at work.

THE MATRIX OF NAZISM

Hitler wanted to claim great originality for his radically antisemitic ideas. In the autobiographical chapters of *Mein Kampf* he plays down the influence of the milieu just described, and when he does refer to such predecessors as Schoenerer and Lueger it is in dismissive terms. Nevertheless, his claim to originality for his antisemitic theories was spurious.

It is impossible to imagine that he could not have been influenced by the ideas that were current in Vienna when he was there. Lucy Dawidowicz brings forward sufficient evidence to support the reasonable assumption that their influence on him was important in the early development of his antisemitic theories.[93] Hitler was original only in the single-minded determination with which he proceeded to put into effect ideas of the removal or extermination of the Jews that others, from Dühring on, had toyed with, without seriously considering how they could be implemented.

In his own writings, Hitler records how he had learned about the Jews in his Vienna period, finally reaching the answer to the question about the nature of German and Austrian Jews that had so much preoccupied him: *the Jew was no German*. Somehow the phrase, which is meant to explain everything, explains nothing. If Hitler had merely been a German racial chauvinist, his insight would have been closer to adequacy. What Hitler came to think about Jews, and perhaps already thought, goes far beyond racism. Later, he said that the Jews were to blame for inventing the conscience. This judgment, in an unintended sense a compliment to Jews, goes deeper. It hints at the ultimate rejection of all morality and decency that the Holocaust came to incarnate.

Whether or not Hitler had learned to articulate his profoundest enmity to the Jewish people at this stage, his theories later received a considerable impetus in their development from his encounters with Alfred Rosenberg. Rosenberg was a Baltic

German familiar with Russian antisemitic theories and activities, as well as with German philosophy. For Hitler and Rosenberg, the Bolshevik revolution was the supreme attempt of Jewry to gain world domination. It was Rosenberg who introduced Hitler to the czarist forgery, the *Protocols of the Learned Elders of Zion*, on which Rosenberg became a sort of expert, writing many articles and pamphlets in commentary on the Protocols. Hitler wrote of the document in *Mein Kampf* that it was "incomparably" done.[94]

Hitler owed something to both the main currents in the Austrian antisemitism of his youth. Ideologically, he was closer to Schoenerer, who represented the romantic, Völkisch, strain in German antisemitism, that idealized a distant, mythical Germanic past, and wished to free the community from all foreign influences. Inasmuch as this type of antisemitism wanted to go back before Christianity to a pre-Christian primitive Germanism, it looks at first sight as though it could have owed nothing to the Christian anti-Judaic tradition.

However, in that case, why was such romantic nationalism antisemitic in particular? Nationalists might well be hostile toward all forms of foreign influence on Germanic culture, but why single out the Jews, who were no particular threat and in many cases actually wished to be assimilated, above all other alien influences? There could be no rational justification for doing so on the basis of his general theory. Schoenerer did not particularly need the Jews as a political scapegoat, and on Hitler's testimony, he had failed to exploit this particular weapon.

The answer is quite clear. Everybody "knew" that the Jews were the enemy of German civilization, because the Germans, like other Europeans, had been taught over the long Christian centuries that the Jews were the enemy of Christian civilization.

Hitler despised the cloudy Teutonic theories of Schoenerer, though he shared them, as lacking political edge. Schoenerer, he thought, had failed to exploit the political potentialities of his own doctrines, or to link them as he should have done with German nationalism.

As for Lueger, Hitler learned from him too, perhaps more than he would acknowledge ideologically, but certainly tactically. He described him as "the best Mayor we ever had,"[95] and given Hitler's views, this must have been primarily a commendation of his antisemitism. He did not like the religious basis of Lueger's antisemitism, however, because he regarded it as unstable: a sprinkling of baptismal water could render a Jew acceptable, and this was anathema to Hitler.

Nevertheless, the obsessive hatred of Jews that reached its ultimate in Hitler cannot be accounted for, even partially, without recognizing that he and Lueger had undergone similar influences. Hitler had "known" from childhood that Jews were bad because he had been brought up in a Catholic milieu. So had Lueger.

He also learned from Lueger, as he had not from Schoenerer, how the antisemitism of others could be politically exploited, doubtless for aims that went well beyond their own. In *Mein Kampf* he did acknowledge learning from Lueger two important lessons: how to appeal to classes that feel threatened and will therefore fight strongly for what they perceive as their interests, and how to use existing instruments such as the church, the Army, or the bureaucracy, for one's own purposes.

Ideologically, however, Hitler criticized Lueger's antisemitism as lacking in rational analysis. "Rational antisemitism . . . ," he wrote in 1919, "must lead to a systematic legal opposition and elimination of the special privileges which the Jews hold, in contrast to the others living amongst us (aliens' legislation). Its final objective must unswervingly be the removal [*Entfernung*] of the Jews altogether." Dawidowicz, from whom the passage is cited, comments, "That paragraph carries, in the post-Auschwitz world, a staggering freight. It prefigures the political realities of the German dictatorship under Hitler, when the Jews were deprived of all rights systematically and 'legally,' and then 'removed altogether,' the ambiguity of the word 'removal' now more apparent than it was in 1919."[96]

What Hitler had done was to put together the strongest elements in all the existing antisemitic ideas, and to conceive of a program of political action capable of mass appeal and implementation.

Whether he had conceived of the Final Solution in any form by the time he wrote *Mein Kampf* is debated among historians. Those "intentionalists" who believe that, at least in germ, the Final Solution was present in his mind even in early days, often cite the sentence from the last chapter of *Mein Kampf* with which Dawidowicz begins her book. "If in the beginning of the War or during the War, twelve or fifteen thousand of these Hebrew corrupters of the people had been held under poison gas, as happened to hundreds of thousands of our very best German workers in the field, the sacrifice of millions at the front would not have been in vain."

Hitler was certainly the ultimate antisemite. Nothing more extreme can be thought, still less done. But it is impossible to imagine these ideas having been created out of nothing, and if they had been, they would never have caught on with others to the extent that made implementation of the Final Solution possible. Without the widespread heritage of anti-Judaism and antisemitism so far described in this book, Hitler would have been taken by everyone for the madman he perhaps was.

The Final Solution required for its execution the obedient or even willing cooperation of hundreds of thousands of Germans and East Europeans. Perhaps only a small minority of these held in full strength the Nazi view of the Jews as a pestilence to be exterminated. But in their cultural environment, antisemitism in a less extreme form had long been something taken for granted, and it weakened the resistance of Germans and others to the radical aims of the Nazis.

If they had found antisemitism morally repugnant and measures taken against Jews horrifying, enough of them would surely have stood up against the actions they were asked to carry out to frustrate their implementation. The fact that some did, even though they were few, demonstrates that there was still a moral choice, even when the Nazis held all material power. Anti-Jewish conditioning, whatever its source, is not absolute in its effects. Conditioning is not determinism.

Even though the full dimensions of what was being done were kept from all but those involved in the actual killings, no one could have failed to have been aware of the disappearance of the Jews, even if they were not involved personally in their rounding up, transportation, and incarceration. In Eastern Europe, among Lithuanians, Ukrainians, and Poles, the Nazis had no difficulty in finding people who hated Jews enough to join the SS in carrying out the Final Solution, as prison guards and as killers. Hitler had chosen his victims well.

Throughout this book, I have constantly emphasized a simple and irrefutable fact. The people of Europe had been taught by the Church that the Jews were bad because they had killed Christ, rejecting the divine revelation he brought. The conviction that Jews were bad was instilled in every Christian child at an early age, long before he or she was capable of appreciating the reasons, such as they were.

Even when in adult life many of these children abandoned the Christian dogma of their upbringing, they were seldom able to rid themselves of a deep conviction that Jews were bad and not to be trusted. Only those with the strongest individual consciences were capable of throwing off such early mental conditioning and those who could were always few. Most often, fresh rationalizations were devised for an ancient conviction. As a result of this millennial conditioning, European people always knew without being told that Jews were bad. They likewise knew that if a scapegoat was needed, Jews were the first candidates who should be thought of.[97]

Hitler's own rationalizations had certainly nothing to do with Christianity, for he despised it in Nietzschean fashion, and he preferred, like Schoenerer, to allude to dark Germanic myths. If ideas explain everything, we must concede that as an anti-Christian antisemite, Hitler owed nothing to Christianity. But they do not.

Hitler's "rational antisemitism" was, like its predecessors, a concoction of the profoundest irrationality, lacking support in evidence or logic. His purpose to exterminate every Jew living on the face of the planet was incapable of serving as means to any goal that could rationally be conceived. Nevertheless, he probably had the capacity to carry it out. Twentieth-century technology and German bureaucratic efficiency would in all likelihood have put a truly final solution within his grasp, had he succeeded in winning the war.

There is some reason to think, however, that this irrationality was in the end self-defeating. The diversion of resources from the war effort to the Final Solution may have been a factor in the defeat of Hitler and his forces by the Allies.[98] The suggestion of some historians, desperately seeking to explain the unexplainable, that after all antisemitism was politically useful to Hitler, fails to explain what it sets out to explain, even lending color to Hitler's own rationalizations.

Irrationality of so dynamic a kind has to be recognized as rationalization of very deep and largely unconscious passions. The genesis of such passions is always to be sought in the experiences of early childhood. They precede all rational processes of inquiry and deduction. Hitler had a Catholic childhood, and indeed (like several of his closest associates) he died still nominally a Catholic, paying his church taxes and technically in good standing, never having been excommunicated. His claim to have been uninfluenced by the Catholic antisemitism of Lueger and others is absurd, for he must have shared it from his childhood on. Where he differed from them was in the intensity of his hate. For him, no sprinkling of baptismal water could transform the Jewish bacillus into a healthy organism.

Christian influence explains the choice of the Jews as the target of hate, but it does not explain the extremity of hatred that filled Hitler and his fellow Nazis. But then, nothing can. Even psychoanalytical explanations of the genesis of hate fail to account for a hatred going beyond all human dimensions. We are left with the mystery of evil.

Christianity had never taught genocide, but neither had it consistently taught that Jews were fellow human beings, entitled to equal rights and consideration with Christians. In its traditional Catholic form, it had no better word to say of the Jews than that they should be preserved in their misery to the end of the world as a witness to their crimes. Having thrown off Christian dogma, Hitler saw no reason to preserve them, and every reason to make them expiate their imaginary crimes, now transformed into racial offenses. But the Church had taught him who the criminals were.

Without the myth, rational investigation of social conditions could never have done that. Actual Jews never resembled the picture in the imagination of the antisemites. They none the less paid the ultimate price for their uncommitted crimes.

11

The Churches in the Twentieth Century

I began with the Holocaust. This book originated in my own attempts to explain to myself how the Holocaust could possibly have happened in a Christian or even post-Christian civilization, and in my dissatisfaction with explanations that seemed to me not to go to the heart of the matter. I concluded that at present we lack the resources to explain hate exceeding all known limits, and (at least for this book) I gave up the attempt to explain it. But something still stared me in the face. The victims were the Jews, and the Jews had been victims before, throughout Christian history, though never to the same degree as in the Holocaust. How could it be that those who had repudiated the Christian tradition still chose the same victims as their Christian predecessors? Out of this question grew the project of attempting to understand the influence of Christian mythology on modern antisemitism.

We are now in a position to see clearly that the Nazi onslaught on the Jews was the ultimate expression of a much older hate, transmitted from generation to generation, and by this time altogether unrestrained by Christian limits. But this hatred of, or at best indifference to, Jews was not confined to the Nazis, though it reached its extremity in them. It was endemic in the Western world. It influenced not only the perpetrators but the spectators as well, and it continues to influence the reaction of the Christianized world to events decades later.

I shall not write about the Holocaust itself. Many writers, some of them distinguished scholars, have told its story eloquently, on the basis of personal recollection or of extremely extensive and detailed research. They have offered their own explanations of the causes of the Holocaust. I have attempted to demonstrate that there is an explanation, a painful one, for the selection of the Jews as its victims. Otherwise, the Holocaust will remain for this book in silence, though it is the real center of its history of hate.

DURING THE HOLOCAUST

What did the Christian world do when the fact of the Holocaust began to be known? At first, not much. Christians did not begin to confront the Holocaust as a theological and ethical challenge to themselves until the sixties. At the time, only a few churchmen allowed themselves to become aware of what was happening to the Jews, and they raised their voice in public protest. The pope, the most influential leader in world Christianity, was not one of these.

In light of the history we have been considering, the only possible conclusion is that the picture of the Jewish people in the minds of Christians outside as well as inside Germany predisposed them to indifference to, or even unconscious connivance with, the Nazi onslaught upon Jews. Christian leaders[1] were not emotionally capable of responding to the knowledge that came into their hands. They were blind to its catastrophic significance. The rank and file were not encouraged to know what the leaders themselves knew, for the same reasons. With few exceptions, the Christian world did not care. Only the emotional shock of the pictures of mounds of corpses and emaciated survivors in the liberated death camps at the end of the war aroused a response from the world. By then it was too late.

During the Nazi years, the churches and their leaders, within and outside Germany, were far more concerned about Hitler's threat to the integrity of the Church itself. They looked on with admiration at the struggle of the Confessing Church in Germany, led by such people as Karl Barth, Dietrich Bonhoeffer, and Martin Niemöller. The Jews remained, as they had so often been, largely invisible to most of the Christian world, including some of its most sensitive and aware members. The threat to the Church was serious, but its leaders generally failed to realize that the Church was only incidentally Hitler's target. Even some who were able to glimpse the mortal threat to the Jews continued to believe that they were under a divine curse, and they interpreted their fate as its fulfillment.[2]

In Germany itself, perhaps only one prominent churchman, Provost Lichtenberg, openly stood up for the Jews, publicly praying for them in his Berlin church and reminding his hearers that a synagogue was a house of God.[3] He paid for his courage with his life. When he was arrested, he asked to be sent to where the Jews were being sent, but he died before he reached the camp to which he was being dispatched.

Dietrich Bonhoeffer, and a very few others, defended church members of Jewish or mixed descent, but even they did not speak up for the Jews themselves, nor it seems did they take account of Hitler's aim of exterminating a whole people. Some believe Bonhoeffer may have regretted this failure in his last days in prison, when he could no longer act on what he came to see. Karl Barth altogether failed to grasp what the real struggle was. Niemöller, on his own testimony, did not think it concerned him when "they came for the Jews." For him also, realization came too late. These were the best and greatest of Germany's Protestant Christians.

Outside Germany, as the reality of the Holocaust going on began to penetrate the consciousness of the most alert, a few churchmen began to sepak out, including the theologians Reinhold Niebuhr and Paul Tillich and the philosopher Jacques Maritain.

In Britain, Archbishop Temple wrote to the prime minister in 1944, when the facts were becoming more widely known, to plead for efforts to save Hungarian Jews. But there are few other records of pressure by Christians on their governments to act decisively to put a stop to the genocide before it was too late for millions more Jews. Nor did these governments themselves, well informed about the death camps from a relatively early date, think it appropriate to do anything about them.

Jewish requests to bomb the railway lines leading to the death camps, or even the camps themselves, fell on deaf ears. Some historians have found the defense that the bombings could not have been successfully carried out convincing. Such defenses might have been more convincing if they had been accompanied at the time by more obvious regret. It is difficult not to conclude that if the fate of the Jews was considered important at all, the allied governments reckoned that victory in the war at large was the best help they could offer them. Besides, as Britain's foreign minister, Eden, argued, they would not have known what to do with great numbers of Jewish refugees. By the time that help became available, six million Jews had perished, along with perhaps five million gypsies, Slavs, Communists, homosexuals, and others, including Germans who had dared to offer resistance to Nazi tyranny.

Not only did the Allied governments fail to do anything whatsoever to stop the extermination of the Jews, they did not even inform the Jews of Europe by radio of the danger they were in, known to the Allies but not yet to the Jews themselves. In a television interview with Bill Moyers, shown on the PBS network in 1991, the Nobel prizewinning writer Elie Wiesel, himself a Holocaust survivor, spoke of his anger at the Allies. He felt an anger at them that he could not feel for the Germans, who had put themselves outside the normal range of humanity. Referring to such people as Roosevelt and Churchill, he said:

> But these were human beings, even great human beings. They knew what we didn't know. We were taken just two weeks before D-Day, and we didn't know that Auschwitz existed. How is that possible? Everybody knew, except the victims. Nobody cared enough to tell us: Don't go. If Roosevelt had gone on the radio and simply said: Jews of Hungary, don't go because Auschwitz is there. . . . If Churchill had done the same. . . . We listened to the BBC, we listened to the radio. I don't understand it. They were good people.

Wiesel did not claim that the Holocaust could have been altogether averted by this kind of warning. But the Jews of Europe had been deceived by the Nazis. In most cases, they had no idea what they were going to. They had been told of resettlement camps, of labor camps. Even the gate of Auschwitz bore the legend *Arbeit macht frei* (work makes free). The deportees had to be safely locked up before they could be allowed to guess what awaited them. The care the Nazis took with deception shows inconvenient for them knowledge would have been. Why was that knowledge withheld from those who most needed it?

There is evidence that the pope was well informed,[4] but at no point did there come from him the unequivocal public condemnation of the measures being taken against the Jews that might have been expected from one carrying his unique moral authority and political influence. On the other hand, during the Holocaust, many

Catholic leaders showed sympathy with or even actively aided the measures being taken against Jews in their own countries, to the point of helping the escape of SS men at the end of the war.

The pope himself determined to say nothing publicly but to use diplomatic efforts behind the scenes, "with reserve and prudence," to help primarily baptized former Jews. He seems to have considered the fate of the Jews themselves outside his public responsibility. Astonishingly, from our present point of view, he attempted to exercise "impartiality" between the Axis powers and the Allies, while reminding all sides of "moral standards." These reminders did not include public protest at the treatment of the Jews. The explanations that have been offered by his apologists do little to excuse what must now appear as a massive moral failure.[5]

AFTER THE HOLOCAUST

The Christian theological response to the Holocaust seems to date effectively not from the event itself but from the postwar work of the Jewish historian Jules Isaac. By his writings and by his personal intervention with Pope John XXIII, he (more than any other individual) succeeded in waking up some influential Christians to the long history of Christian anti-Judaic hostility that lay behind what had taken place in Europe.

John XXIII was in a position to do something about it, and he grasped the opportunity. He made relations between the Church and the Jewish people a principal part of the agenda for the Ecumenical Council he called in the sixties, which has come to be known as Vatican II. He entrusted his friend Cardinal Bea and his Secretariat for Christian Unity with the task of researching the problem and formulating a new statement that might be adopted by the council and become part of the defined faith of the Catholic church. The statement that finally resulted, known as *Nostra aetate*, is now recognized as a turning point in the painful history of Christian-Jewish relations. Nothing of equal authority or decisiveness has come from the Protestant churches corporately, though some remarkable statements have come from individual church bodies in Europe.

The 1960s may well have been the high point of corporate Christian sensitivity to "the Jewish question" in its transformed post-Holocaust form. After that, the churches moved away from concern for the Jewish people in other directions. Historical scholars continued to explore critically the anti-Jewish distortions engendered by the nonhistorical aspects of the Christian myth, as this book has attempted to show. Meanwhile a few courageous theologians attempted to consider the implications of these discoveries, as well as of the Holocaust itself, for Christian faith. We must examine their ideas in more detail later in the chapter. These theologians display not only spiritual sensitivity but also theological boldness and originality that should have placed them in a position of leadership in the Christian thought of our time, if the churches had been more receptive to their work.

While individual theologians, touched by the Holocaust or by their contacts with

Jewish friends, were attempting to purify Christian theology of its millennial anti-Judaism, church bodies, such as the World Council of Churches, the National Council of Churches in the USA, and the synods and equivalent bodies of member churches, were increasingly turning away from the Jewish people toward the new outlook of liberation theology. Whatever its merits in urging Christians to care for the poor and disadvantaged, this theology sets Jesus against his fellow Jews and the Church against Israel.

As a result, the Palestinian cause has enjoyed a popularity among Protestant church politicians in the seventies, eighties, and nineties unmatched at any time by that of the Jewish people. It is impossible to refrain from asking whether this astonishing development can be accounted for otherwise than as the outcome of the continuing influence of the mythology considered in this book.

This Christian anti-Zionism is a perversion of moral and political reality. Injustice to Palestinians assumes vast proportions by contrast with injustice to Jews. No doubt, some of the injustices such church leaders consider the Palestinians to be suffering are real, though not all are. But, whatever they are, and however they arise, injustices to Palestinians cannot justify ignoring in turn the vast historical injustices to the Jewish people that the existence of the state of Israel in part remedies, though it can never undo them.

Nothing can justify the moral obliquity that traduces Israel and the Jewish people by likening their actions to those of racist states, past and present.[6] The churches have been too ready to listen to this kind of hate filled propaganda, some of it emanating from the Middle East churches themselves. If disaster should again come to the Jewish people in their national home, the churches will bear a heavy moral responsibility.

In the nineties, supporters of Israel are in a very small minority among the generally liberal thinkers of the mainline Protestant churches. Evangelical Protestants, now a much more lively and powerful factor in the Christian world than the old mainline churches, are deeply divided on Israel, according to their views on the prophetic scenario for the second coming of Christ. More traditional evangelicals continue to uphold the old anti-Judaism, not infrequently lapsing into racial antisemitism. They consider it a prime duty to work for the conversion of every Jew. Christ will not return before the conversion of the Jewish people has been accomplished.

Another influential wing, prominent among Pentecostals and other charismatics, believes that the conversion of the Jewish people to Christ will not come from human endeavor but will be accomplished by Christ himself on his return to earth. In the meantime, the task of Christian believers is to "comfort" Israel, God's chosen people, in accordance with Isaiah 40:1. Organized missions to Jews are therefore inappropriate, although individual conversions will always be welcomed and not discouraged.

Such Evangelicals are warm and committed supporters of Israel, often embarrassing liberal Jews by their enthusiastic support of positions usually associated with the Israeli Right wing. Although many Jews are understandably suspicious of a group whose support is conditioned upon the expectation that at the end of days Jews will disappear by becoming Christians, it would be foolish to ignore the warmth and commitment of these Christian supporters of Zionism, who are prepared to work hard for their convictions and will not compromise. From a Jewish point of view, it could be said that their hearts are better than their heads.

Thus, in the Christian world the outlook for the Jews and for their Christian supporters in the 1990s had become in general less good than it was in the 1960s. Except among the Evangelicals, numerous but with little influence outside their own circles, those who would speak for the Jewish people and especially for Israel in clear, strong, and theologically grounded terms were very few in number.

The immense swing to liberalism in the mainline Protestant churches over the last few decades turned the leadership (perhaps more than the rank and file) against the Jews. In the Catholic church, the policy of Pope John Paul II has been hard to interpret and apparently equivocal. On the one hand, he has uttered condemnations of antisemitism and made gestures unparalleled by any of his predecessors, with the exception of John XXIII. On the other hand, apparently in line with the Vatican's historic and well documented opposition to the setting up of the Jewish state in Palestine, he has so far continued to withhold diplomatic recognition from Israel, while meeting on seemingly cordial terms with foes of the Jewish people such as Yasser Arafat and Kurt Waldheim.

His policy of allying the Catholic church in Eastern Europe with nationalism against the collapsing Communist empire carries dangers that older Catholic attitudes toward Jews, always prominent among the nationalists, will resurface in a form too virulent for even his authority to control. There is evidence that many Eastern European Catholics feel free to take his public condemnations of antisemitism with less seriousness than ostensibly they merit. We shall now consider all these developments in greater detail.

THE SILENCE OF PIUS XII

During the Holocaust, the leader of the largest and most powerful Christian church, the holder of an office claiming to be the moral and spiritual guide of all mankind, said nothing publicly in condemnation of the assault on the Jews. A debate has been going on over the question ever since 1963, when a young German playwright of Protestant background, Rolf Hochhuth, wrote a remarkable play called in English *The Deputy*,[7] dramatizing the moral issues confronting the pope and his diplomatic representatives during the Holocaust. The play calls the late pope to account before the moral conscience of its audiences. Its presentation led to an international controversy in which the highest levels of the Vatican took part.[8]

Did Pius XII fail to discharge his responsibility as the "Vicar of Christ"[9] and the spiritual leader of the largest and most powerful body in Christendom? His defenders argue that he did all that could have been done, by using the Vatican diplomatic corps to make secret representations to the Axis authorities. They also claim that in the later stages of the war he was instrumental in saving Italian Jews from deportation, though this claim has been questioned by some historians.

The questions raised by the criticism of Pius XII fall into two parts. The issues become clearer if they are distinguished. First, there is Hochhuth's own dramatic question: was not the public silence of the pope in itself an immense moral scandal, regardless of the effect of anything he may have done in secret? Second, and less dramatic, we can ask whether the diplomacy he did use was as well directed and as effective as it could have been.

The two questions are interrelated, however. If diplomacy was actually effective, perhaps the success of diplomatic efforts in saving Jews justified public silence. If the Vatican's diplomatic efforts turn out to have been half-hearted and ineffectual, the first question is reopened with new force. If that was the case, the use of secret diplomacy did not clear the pope of his responsibility to live up to his claims as the moral leader of mankind. He ought to have uttered a public condemnation of the worst moral evil ever to have been perpetrated, while it was actually going on, in largely Catholic countries.

We shall consider the questions in turn. As the title of Hochhuth's play suggests, the question of the pope's public silence turns primarily upon the claims he and all Catholics make for his office. Should not "the Vicar of Christ" have condemned attempts to exterminate the Jewish people at least as publicly and unequivocally as the popes have condemned other actions the Church regards as evil, such as euthanasia, birth control, and abortion?

In reality, the pope's authority does not effectively influence all mankind. Primarily his influence is over those who owe allegiance to him as the head of their church. Granted that, he could at least have spoken to his own Catholic fold, reminding them that to take part in Nazi measures against the Jews was a mortal sin. He could have threatened excommunication against those who did so, invoking the spiritual sanctions that could decisively have influenced the members of his flock.

Not all who took an active part in measures against the Jews were lapsed or lukewarm Catholics. When the Vatican representative, Mgr Giuseppe Burzio, chargé d'affaires at Bratislava, did intervene on behalf of the Jews with the Slovakian prime minister, Vojtech Tuka, the latter bragged of his devout Catholicism. Tuka stated that he attended mass every day, that he had a clear conscience in what he was doing to rid Slovakia of Jews, whom he described as "criminals," and that he had the consent of his confessor for what he was doing.[10] The leader of the Slovak government that cooperated with the Nazis, Mgr Tiso, was likewise a Catholic, and a prelate.

Irving Greenberg, in a remarkable essay that should be read in full,[11] tells how in 1942 the Nitra Rebbe went to Archbishop Kametko of Nietra to plead with him for the intervention of the Catholic church in Slovakia against the deportation of the Jewish population–the rebbe did not yet know about the death camps and was concerned about the threat of hunger and disease. The archbishop, who was personally close to Tiso–the latter had been his secretary for many years–replied, "It is not just a matter of deportation. You will not die there of hunger and disease.

They will slaughter all of you there, old and young alike, women and children, at once–it is the punishment you deserve for the death of our Lord and Redeemer, Jesus Christ–you have only one solution. Come over to our religion and I will work to annul this decree."[12]

The attitude the words reflect can cause us no surprise, after following this history of hate. It is certain that it was still widely shared in the Catholic hierarchy during the time that the Holocaust was actually going on.

There is no reason to suppose that Pius shared it himself. If he did not, we still have to ask why he did not condemn it in resounding terms in his own followers, clerical and lay, while it was still possible to make a difference. Many believe that the moral argument simply settles the question. The pope should have spoken and he did not, and by failing to do so he decisively weakened the credibility of his office.

Worse, by not speaking out, Pius XII involved the Church in contributory moral responsibility for actions it failed to condemn. Perhaps the low spiritual state of Christendom toward the end of the century has something to do with its moral failure during the Holocaust. Because the pope did not speak, the church was then and is now less credible as the Church of Jesus Christ, or as one of the principal moral agencies in a pluralistic world. So powerful is this moral criticism that it can only be effectively answered by demonstrating that if Pius had spoken, the fate of the Jews would have been worse than it was.[13] To this, there is a simple answer. How could it have been worse?

Another related argument is sometimes put forward in defense of the pope. If he had spoken out publicly, he might have compromised diplomatic efforts being made behind the scenes. This argument involves the factual questions concerning the adequacy and effectiveness of the diplomatic efforts actually made. If secret diplomacy was working, and would continue to work, there might have been a case for protecting it by public silence. If it was not, that argument loses its force.

More likely, it was the other way around. If the Nazis could not have been deterred by a public utterance, they were even less likely to be deterred by private representations, which could be safely ignored without public criticism. And if the Jews could have been saved neither by secret diplomacy nor public protest, the spiritual issue remained paramount.

Where would the Church of Jesus Christ stand, with his own people, or with their exterminators? The world, including the Nazis themselves, was left to guess. So important is this spiritual issue that many would argue that effectiveness should not even be taken into account in considering whether the pope ought to have spoken.

Why did Pius XII choose public silence and private diplomacy? The answers that have usually been given turn on analyses of his own personality. Eugenio Pacelli, who became Pius XII, was a member of an aristocratic Roman family and came to the papacy from a career in the Roman Catholic diplomatic corps. He was secretary of state under the previous pope, Pius XI. He had been Papal Nuncio, or ambassador, to Germany before going back to the Vatican. His personal dislike and fear of communism was intense, and like many others he saw Hitler as a prime bulwark against atheistic communism.

For most of the war, he seems to have expected Germany to win, perhaps even hoping that it would, so that it could continue to stem the communist tide. He was concerned about postwar relations between the Church and the German authorities and in particular about the Concordat or treaty he himself had negotiated between the Vatican and Germany. He seems to have been personally timid, disliking confrontation. These factors must have predisposed him to prefer working through the devious paths of diplomacy and the veiled generalities of the traditional Vatican language.

With the release to scholars of many Vatican documents from the period, it is now possible to evaluate the success of the diplomacy that was undertaken; it was quite limited, both in its aims and in its results. John F. Morley, himself a Catholic priest, sums up his carefully researched account of the diplomacy, based on documents in the Vatican archives, in the following measured terms:

> It must be concluded that Vatican diplomacy failed the Jews during the Holocaust by not doing all that it was possible for it to do on their behalf. It also failed itself because in neglecting the needs of the Jews, and pursuing a goal of reserve rather than humanitarian concern, it betrayed the ideals it had set for itself. The nuncios, the secretary of state, and, most of all, the Pope share the responsibility for this dual failure.[14]

Can we now estimate how effective a public protest might have been? When the Church did protest against the use of euthanasia by Germany on mentally ill and other patients in the late thirties, the protest proved effective. The Nazis stopped using euthanasia. Similar protests were made when the Nazis insisted on the Aryan spouses of Jews divorcing their mates. The Catholic bishops of Germany protested, not, however, on behalf of the Jews, as they were careful to state,[15] but in the name of the indissolubility of Christian marriage and the impermissibility of divorce.

However, euthanasia was by no means so central to Nazi policy as the war against the Jews. While the Nazis had many other aims in their program, antisemitism was of its essence. They could not have relinquished it without ceasing to be themselves.

Nevertheless, it does not follow that they could not have been influenced in the decision to adopt a "*final* solution of the Jewish problem." Other, less extreme options existed for the Nazis and were for a while actually adopted, such as the expulsion of Jews from Germany and the other territories under their control. Though some historians argue rather convincingly that the Final Solution was in some form in Hitler's mind from the first, he did not institute it as an explicit policy until it became clear that the world would not take in expelled Jews.

The 1937 Evian conference on refugees had sent Hitler a clear signal that the other nations would not take in Jews in large numbers. By 1939, Britain had determined to go back on the Balfour Declaration and the League of Nations Mandate for Palestine in favor of appeasing the Arabs. Palestine was no longer to be an effective refuge for the persecuted. Nevertheless, even when the war had actually commenced, Eichmann and others still worked with the Irgun in Eastern Europe to evacuate Jews to Palestine, illegally from the British point of view.[16] There was little world enthusiasm for saving Jews by this means–even on the part of the Jewish leadership itself in Eastern Europe and Israel, or so it has been argued.

If the pope had even come out strongly in favor of world efforts to take in Jewish refugees, he would have given a lead to the world outside Germany that could not have been ignored, even by Britain. He might at least have influenced the Nazis to continue their attempts to make Germany and Europe *judenrein*[17] by less appalling means than those ultimately embraced.

With the vigorous leadership of the pope, an evacuation of Jews from Germany and Austria might have been accomplished comparable to the emigration of Soviet Jews to Israel in the nineties. Hitler might even have been deterred from attacking the Jews of Eastern Europe. Millions of Jewish lives might have been saved, even though at considerable cost to themselves and the nations that took them in. These are speculations about might-have-beens, but the fact that they are possible without absurdity shows that the argument that a public protest must inevitably have been ineffective is not decisive.

Even the Nazi leaders were not totally immune to the power and influence of the Catholic church. At least church reaction was something they did take into account in forming policy. This is especially true of Himmler, who had what has been described by one of his closest associates as a love-hate relationship with the Church of his upbringing; he consciously structured the SS on the model of the Jesuit order.[18] Hitler and Goebbels also apparently continued to pay church taxes as Catholics[19] and were never excommunicated. Technically, they remained Catholics in good standing.

What was true of these determined opponents of all forms of Christianity was certainly even more true of large numbers of lesser Nazis, of army officers and of bureaucrats, who had not broken so decisively with the Church.[20] Catholic conditioning in childhood is very powerful, and the explicit threat of eternal damnation is not taken lightly even by one whose adult ties to the Church have become loose. There can be little doubt that the pope had a vast potential influence on the Germans who carried out the Holocaust, an influence he did not choose to exercise.

Asked by the Berlin correspondent of the Vatican newspaper, *L'Osservatore Romano*, if he would not protest against the extermination of the Jews, Pius replied, "Dear friend, do not forget that millions of Catholics serve in the German armies. Shall I bring them into conflicts of conscience?"[21] The conflicts in question would have been, one presumes, between their duty to God and their duty to the Nazi state. Perhaps, too, he had in mind the casuistic argument that if he did not formally condemn actions against the Jews, Germans who took part could be said to have sinned in ignorance, thus incurring a lesser spiritual penalty.

This is false compassion, apart from its implications for Pius' view of the moral priorities between saving Jews and the mental comfort of his own flock. Moreover, the argument is hardly convincing. Even given the anti-Jewish conditioning we have been describing, no one with a Catholic education could have been wholly in ignorance of the fact that actually killing defenseless Jews, or even taking part in measures leading to that end, was a mortal sin, whatever their duty to the state, and whether or not the pope chose to say so. But this does not remove the pope's responsibility to warn and condemn.

On his own premises, the pope must have imperilled the eternal salvation of German and East European Catholics far more by his silence than he could have done by speaking, since he failed to direct them away from actions objectively evil beyond measure. Without the moral support of his outspoken condemnation, hundreds of thousands of Catholics gave in and took part in the most evil act of all history, unrebuked by their spiritual leader.

THE RESCUERS

In the event, Hitler was able to rely on the ingrained antisemitism of Catholic Europe to turn a blind eye on, or even to cooperate with, what was being done to the Jews. Nowhere was there a massive moral protest or refusal to cooperate. There were, as we have noted, a few individuals who protested. Many more actually helped Jews in secret, at the risk of their lives, but it cannot be shown that those who did so were predominantly influenced by Christian motives. Clearly, they shared a Christian culture. In Poland in particular, almost all of them must have been at least nominally Catholics. But they were not conspicuous for their adherence to the Church and its doctrines. Studies of rescuers, several thousand of whom are commemorated as Righteous Gentiles at Yad Vashem in Jerusalem, do not show a uniform pattern of religious allegiance. If anything, those who risked their lives for Jews seem to have been independent spirits, resistant to all forms of indoctrination.[22]

The only case known to me in which a whole community acted together to save Jews is a remarkable one and worth pausing on to analyze it a little. This is the story of Le Chambon, in south-eastern France, a Protestant village of about five thousand inhabitants. Under the leadership of their pastor, André Trocmé, these villagers and farmers saved thousands of Jews over a period of several years, during the German occupation of France, almost every family taking in someone.

The villagers of Le Chambon were Protestants of the Huguenot tradition. Their faith was broadly Calvinist, and like other Huguenots they remembered the history of their own persecution in past centuries at the hands of a Catholic state. As the villagers speak in the beautiful film *Weapons of the Spirit*, made by Pierre Sauvage, himself one of the Jewish children they saved, we can see that they inherited from their Calvinist faith a respect for the Old Testament and for the "people of the book" whom they still regarded as God's chosen people. Their Christian faith took a practical form. The commandment to love the neighbor meant something only if carried out in action.

Theologians may remember the Calvinist idea of the third use of the Law, to guide the actions of the justified person, an idea in fact very close to the Jewish understanding of the role of the Torah. For these Calvinist Christians, simple and untheological as they were, the commandments of God were something to be kept and done. Christian faith in the forgiveness of sins did not remove from them the necessity of action on behalf of other human beings. And so they did act, as if it were the most natural thing in the world, and did not think of themselves as heros.

Le Chambon was unique because here alone a whole community participated in the saving of Jews. But it was not the only case where people of courage corporately stood up to the Nazis and refused to surrender Jews to extermination. The most famous case is that of Denmark, and here an explanation is less easy to come by. The leadership of the king must have been an important factor. When the Germans overran Denmark and demanded the cooperation of the Danish authorities in rounding up Danish Jews, the king threatened to put on the yellow star himself and wear it publicly if any such measures were introduced in Denmark. The Nazis backed off. And in a remarkable story of rescue, all but four hundred of Denmark's Jews were secretly evacuated to Sweden, a neutral country, where they were comparatively safe from the Germans. The operation involved large numbers of Danes.

In Denmark, Jews were widely accepted as a natural part of the community. They were not felt to be an alien presence, as they were in so much of Europe. It is not easy to find a religious explanation. The Danish state church is Lutheran, though it is also the church of Kierkegaard. It shared with the German Lutherans the heritage of Martin Luther's own writings on the Jews. But we may wonder if there is not something in the independent spirit of the Danish people that puts them in the category from which, according to Nechama Tec, rescuers characteristically came.

The king's unique gesture of solidarity with his Jewish subjects, a gesture that did not in the end have to be carried out, showed what might have been possible had the Christian world felt the same solidarity with the Jewish people as the Danish king did. If just the pope had donned the yellow star, how many Jews might have been saved? If the Christian world as a whole had rallied in support of Jews in a similar manner, in all probability there would have been no Holocaust.

Much less well known is the resistance of the Bulgarians to the deportation of Jews. Here again royal leadership played an important role. Early on, King Boris let it be known that he was opposed to anti-Jewish measures. He also stood right up to Ribbentrop face-to-face and refused to cooperate in the deportations of Jews, though later he was forced to submit. Eventually he died in unexplained circumstances.

The Orthodox church also intervened. When Jews were required to wear the badge, Metropolitan Stephan of Sofia delivered a sermon in which he declared that God had determined the fate of the Jews and that they must not be persecuted by men. While the influence of Christian mythology can still be seen in his words, they were compassionate and they had their effect. The metropolitan personally intervened against the measures requiring Jews to wear the star, with the result that the minister of justice demanded the abolition of the measure. The metropolitan himself hid the chief rabbi of Sofia in his home. The Church also allowed many so-called mercy baptisms, involving an agreement that such conversions could be renounced when the war came to an end. Later, large public demonstrations attempted to prevent the deportation of Jews. In the end, the Bulgarians saved all "their own" Jews. The 11,353 Jews from Bulgaria who were taken to the extermination camps and killed came only from the annexed territories in Macedonia and Thrace.[23]

THE POSTWAR CATHOLIC RESPONSE

When in 1960 Pope John XXIII charged the team under Augustin Bea with preparing a statement on relations with the Jews for the Vatican Council, the original intention was that it should form part of the Dogmatic Constitution on Ecumenism, *De Oecumenismo*. This would have been a revolutionary step, redefining the split between Jews and Christians as an internal one within the one people of God. However, the idea did not prove persuasive to the many bishops from Africa and Asia, who thought it singled out what was primarily a European problem for unique attention. They insisted that the Church's relations with other non-Christian religions should also be given attention.

It has been argued that taking the document out of the draft on ecumenism and placing it in a new statement on the Church's relations with non-Christian religions was ultimately to its advantage.[24] The document as a whole attempted to show that non-Christians could in some sense be saved within their own faith. This was a new position for a church that had always held that *extra ecclesiam nulla salus* (there is no salvation outside the Church).

Positively, therefore, the document could at least suggest that Jews could be saved as Jews and did not require conversion to Christianity. Negatively, however, the change meant that the unique relationship of the Jewish and Christian peoples was blurred by assimilation to the more general relationship between the Church and the rest of the human race. The wording of the document attempted to overcome this drawback by stressing in powerful words the Church's inherent relationship to the Jewish people.

This was one very important change that took place as draft succeeded draft in the council discussions. A second change, less positive in its implications, came about at the instigation of those who wanted to stick closely to the anti-Jewish passages in the Gospels. The final draft attempted to deal with this difficulty by a series of balancing statements, in which the negative statement in the Gospels was first conceded and then given less force by a much more positive affirmation. This is how the crucial passage on the responsibility of the Jews for the death of Christ was handled: "Even though the Jewish authorities and those who followed their lead pressed for the death of Christ (cf John 19:6), neither all Jews indiscriminately at that time, nor all Jews today, can be charged with the crimes committed during his passion."[25]

A third kind of change seems to have come about through Arab pressure, both inside the council itself from Arab bishops and outside it from diplomatic representations made to the Vatican by Arab envoys. Earlier drafts had specifically rejected the traditional term, deicide, as used of the Jews, and had used the strong term, *condemn*, of all forms of antisemitism. The Arab lobbyists had argued that to ban the word deicide would tend to legitimate the Zionist state, with adverse political consequences for the Catholic church in the Middle East; the bishops from the area had suggested that there might be fears for the safety of Arab Christians if this happened.

In the final draft, deicide was simply not mentioned. However, the content of the statement itself would certainly tend to rule out any use of the word by Catholic theologians and teachers. At the same time, condemnation of antisemitism, sought by many bishops, was toned down to "deploring,"[26] a somewhat weaker and less technical expression no longer implying that antisemitism was to be regarded as heresy.

Above all, the document never mentions the need for Christian repentance, nor does it ask forgiveness from the Jews, though elsewhere the documents of the council do ask forgiveness for the Church from Protestants, Eastern Orthodox, and Muslims. This is perhaps the greatest weakness of the statement. Perhaps it would not have passed the council if it had. But the absence of mention of repentance has allowed many Catholic apologists to speak of the achievement of the council on the question of the Jews in triumphalist terms, as a sign of great progress, rather than as the first beginning of reparation of an infinite deficit.

Nostra aetate did not say everything that Jews and their friends might have hoped, or indeed that its original drafters hoped, but this does not take away its historic importance. *Nostra aetate* did make it clear, for the first time at that level of authority, that Catholics must not blame the Jewish people corporately for the death of Christ, while insisting on Christianity's debt to its Jewish forebear.

The importance of the document lies even more in its authority than in its details. By virtue of being a statement of an Ecumenical Council, *Nostra aetate* becomes part of Catholic dogma, binding on subsequent popes as well as on priests and laity. Thus, accusing the Jewish people as a whole of the death of Christ has become dogmatically impermissible for Catholics, though many clergy and others, especially at the local level, do not seem to realize that this is now the case. Unfortunately, we can still find Catholic teachers in North America as well as in Eastern Europe who feel free to regard the Jews as Christ-killers. Nor did the Council confront the historical evidence that makes it most likely that even the Jewish authorities did not "press for the death of Christ."

More widely, *Nostra aetate* has been regarded as a landmark by theologians from various churches who want to purge Christianity of its ancient anti-Judaism and more recent tendencies to antisemitism. Such theologians, Catholic and Protestant, stress both the authoritative nature of the document and the way in which it implies that Jews can be saved as Jews and need not be converted to explicit faith in Jesus Christ. Such maximalist interpretations would legitimate the new theologies of a double covenant with both Jews and Christians, or similar variants, and would provide a grounding for those who wish to discontinue missionary work among Jews. The official *Guidelines*[27] for teaching the decisions of the council likewise interpret it in a very positive sense.

THE CATHOLIC CHURCH AND THE JEWS IN THE 1990s

It should not be impossible today, even without dealing with substantial theological issues, for the Church to repudiate every one of the calumnies that have been leveled against the Jews for centuries. The Spanish Inquisition, in itself a terrible assault on the right and duty of human beings freely to choose to worship their God, was intimately connected with the beginnings of the modern transformation of religious anti-Judaism into racist antisemitism. I am not aware that its activities have ever been formally repudiated by the Church and declared contrary to a true Christian faith. If the Church had nothing else to repent of, the monstrous evil of the Inquisition would still require a formal statement of repentance from the highest authority in the Church.

The blood libel has already been officially repudiated a number of times,[28] but exceptions were still sometimes made and the authenticity of a few cases defended. Thus, the libel remains effectively in force, so long as the Church can delude itself that there are some cases of ritual murder, however few. The libel could be repudiated again, formally and without exceptions, and the related charges of host desecration annulled at the same time. Perhaps nobody now believes that the Jews poisoned the wells to cause the plague, but it might still be appropriate for the Church to formally repent for the attitude of mind that caused such charges to be made and believed.

Under the papacy of John Paul II, doctrinal reforms are no longer on the agenda, and traditional piety is being reinstated where it had been eroded by the tide of modernity unleashed by the council. Papal policy toward the Jewish people is hard to read, since it is manifested in contradictory happenings and pronouncements. On the one hand, there are condemnations of antisemitism, expressions of goodwill, and friendly meetings with Jewish leaders,[29] and on the other, continuing refusal to recognize Israel, and unmistakable gestures of moral support to enemies of Israel and the Jewish people, the Arafats and the Waldheims.

However, in the summer of 1989, events occurred that could hardly fail to lead to an unfavorable interpretation of John Paul's own thinking concerning the Jews. In August 1989, the pope himself, over the protests of the Jewish Anti-Defamation League, repeated an earlier statement at a Pentecost sermon, in which he restated the traditional supersessionist view that the Jewish people had broken their covenant with God and that Christ had therefore come to make a new covenant with the world.

At the same time, the long smoldering affair of the Auschwitz convent broke out once more. The convent, housing a small community of Carmelite contemplative nuns, had been set up several years previously in the building just outside the main Auschwitz camp, in which the gas Zyklon B had been stored. They had erected an imposing cross on the site. The purpose of the nuns was to pray and do penance for the souls of the dead at Auschwitz, including the Jewish dead, whose salvation is of course especially in peril in their eyes, since they died outside the communion of the Church.

The convent affair is worth considering in some detail, even if it turns out to have been finally settled by the subsequent negotiations, because it revealed so much about Catholic attitudes toward the Jewish people, nearly half a century after the Holocaust. Nor was it at all certain that even in 1992 we had heard the last of the affair, given the reluctance of Polish Catholicism to yield to the rest of the world on the issue.

Jews found the establishment of the convent profoundly offensive, since it takes away the unique dignity of their suffering by appropriating it for a Christian cause. As a Reuter dispatch from New York put it, Jews see the establishment of the convent as "a Catholic hijack of a Jewish symbol" of disaster and mourning.[30] The nuns had obstinately rejected pleas from Christians and Jews alike to leave the sanctity of the site of Auschwitz untouched.[31]

At the end of August 1989, the Polish church, through the Archbishop of Cracow, Cardinal Franciszek Macharski, repudiated an agreement previously made, after prolonged negotiations and many setbacks, by the Catholic church with Jewish representatives. Macharski, like his predecessor in the same diocese, the present pope, had been among the Poles best disposed to the Jewish people. According to the agreement, signed among other responsible churchmen by four cardinals, under the chairmanship of the Cardinal of Lyons, Albert DeCourtray, the church would remove the convent by February 1989 and resettle the nuns in an interfaith center to be constructed some distance away. The agreement had not been carried out. Meanwhile, Macharski, himself one of the signers of the original agreement, in announcing its repudiation, blamed "the aggressive demands of Jews" for a worsening of relationships.[32]

Cardinal Jozef Glemp, the Primate of Poland, then stepped into the dispute, in an address to pilgrims at a Polish national shrine at Czestochowa. He referred to the agreement to move the convent as a scandal, and he used insulting language to Jews, accusing them of "anti-Polonism," or hostility toward Poles as such. Antisemitism, he said, would disappear in Poland if the Jews gave up their anti-Polonism.

"Dear Jews," he is reported to have said, "do not talk to us from the position of a people elevated above all others, and do not make conditions that cannot be fulfilled." Presumably the conditions that could not be fulfilled were those stipulated in the agreement already signed by the Church. He also referred to supposed Jewish control of the mass media of the world, adding a few further remarks, reported only on radio, of a more traditionally antisemitic kind.[33]

In interviews with Italian reporters a few days later he called for the renegotiation of the original agreement, saying that Macharski had been incompetent and did not speak for Poles as a whole.[34] He also spoke to a reporter from the French paper, *France-Soir*, saying, "This is a very grave matter on the religious level, a very intricate problem. But since the demonstration by the American Jews, the convent has become a political pretext . . . One has to link these events with what is happening in Palestine. This is dangerous, this may cause antisemitism while there is none in Poland (*sic*)."

The Cardinal's words were refuted in the Polish presidential election campaign the following year, when candidates were smeared with antisemitic associations. Even Lech Walesa was pushed into affirming that he was himself of pure Polish descent, in contrast to an opponent. Later, as president of Poland, he formally apologized to the Jews for Polish antisemitism in a speech before the Knesset.

Claude Lanzmann, the maker of the remarkable film about the Holocaust, *Shoah*, made some extremely insightful comments about the attitudes underlying the cardinal's remarks in an interview with the *Jerusalem Post*, from which the above quotation is also taken. He said:

> What is the meaning of this answer? It is obvious. The reasoning is that, "2000 years ago, Jews killed Christ. Their essence is to be deicidal, they are killers. For 40 years, since the Holocaust, these killers have succeeded in passing themselves off as the victims. Now, look at what is happening in Israel; they are killers of children, of teenagers. They are again unveiling their eternal essence as killers. The Holocaust was a mask, in a way. All we thought for 40 years was wrong."[35]

To those who, like Lanzmann, are familiar with the language of antisemitism, Glemp's words therefore had a smell that was unmistakable, that of age-old Catholic antisemitism, including its characteristic paranoia. Clearly, Glemp at least had learned nothing from the Holocaust. The issue undoubtedly brought out latent anti-Jewish attitudes in official as well as popular Catholicism in Poland.

Earlier, in July 1989, when a number of Jewish protesters, led by Rabbi Avraham Weiss, had attempted to demonstrate peaceably and prayerfully on the site against the failure to carry out the agreement, they were met by physical violence and viciously antisemitic words from the workers on the site, doused with paint and urine, beaten up, and ejected. They could get little protection from the Polish police.[36] Glemp even went so far as to imply, in his comments in September, that if they had not been thrown out they would have murdered the nuns. Many Jews saw in his extravagant words an echo of the medieval blood libel.

It is difficult not to suppose that these events were in fact connected with the political triumph of the pope's strategy for his own country. Polish Catholicism is intensely nationalistic, and the identification between church and nation is strong on both sides. The Catholic church, through Solidarity, the union group, had in the summer of 1989 effectively defeated communism in Poland and put its own nominees in power. The new prime minister, Tadeusz Mazowiecki, was a devout Catholic intellectual, though with a much better personal record in his dealings with

Jews than Cardinal Glemp. Polish Catholics were riding high in August 1989, and this must have seemed to some to be the right moment to deal with a fancied humiliation by Jews, whose worldwide influence had supposedly compelled the Poles to back down on the issue of the convent.

The affair of the Auschwitz convent also brought to light strong differences of opinion in the Catholic church on its relationship with the Jewish people. Many Catholic leaders, in Europe and the United States, clearly wished to deal with the Jewish people in the new spirit of Vatican II and perhaps to move even beyond that point. In the United States, the *National Catholic Reporter* carried a highly critical article on Glemp and the Polish church, and an editorial called for the postponement of Glemp's projected visit to the United States.[37] The French Cardinals, DeCourtray and Lustiger, who had cosigned the original agreement to move the convent, were clearly shocked by the Polish turnaround. DeCourtray, rather implausibly and ineffectually, tried to defend Glemp, saying, "He is not an antisemite."

Polish Catholicism seemed mired in the antisemitism of centuries. The attitude of the nuns themselves on the controversy, which had been gradually coming to light, is very significant in this regard. Its importance was probably underestimated by the press, partly from lack of information and partly because those who reported the controversy failed to appreciate the intense respect and reverence in which Carmelite contemplative nuns are normally held by the Catholic clergy, including (or perhaps especially) its senior members.

The attitudes of the nuns may therefore be a significant factor in events. It may not be the case that they were simply pawns in a larger controversy, as they have so far been considered to be. The remarks of Sister Maria to Heather Johnston, cited in Note thirty-one, already gave away much of the real attitudes of the nuns. Somewhat later, an interview given by the mother superior herself, Sister Teresa, was published in a Polish American periodical.[38]

Sister Teresa's remarks are extremely revealing of the underlying issues in the controversy. "Why do the Jews want special treatment in Auschwitz only for themselves?" she asks. "Do they still consider themselves the chosen people?" She accuses the Jews of "creating such a disturbance for us." She denies that there was ever any Polish antisemitism before World War II and according to her, "the Jews were an insignificant minority group in Poland with a majority of privileges." She also accuses Israel of antisemitism for maltreating the Arabs. "Greater anti-Semites are hard to find," she adds, meaning the Israelis themselves.

She also makes much of the presence of Jews in Poland's Communist government in the Stalinist period. However, she fails to get her facts right. Some of those she names were born Jewish, but they never practiced their faith. Others were only Jewish by Hitler's definition. Sister Teresa also never mentions the fact that the tiny remaining Jewish population of Poland suffered terribly under Stalin. During the Gomulka regime, numerous Jews were dismissed from all kinds of government posts.

Sister Teresa emerges from the interview as an unreconstructed antisemite of the old type, with a considerable element of the new anti-Zionism added to the mixture. She concludes the interview by saying, "You can tell the Americans that we are not moving an inch," and adds, "let the Jews understand that the prayers of the Carmelite nuns are also offered for the souls of those victims who were also of the Jewish persuasion."

The pope, himself a product of Polish Catholicism but with a much better personal record in this matter than his compatriots, for a lengthy period remained silent on the dispute, in apparent neutrality, officially declining to intervene in what was described as a local matter of the Polish church.

After some delay, however, in the middle of September 1989, the Vatican issued a statement signed by Cardinal Willebrands, the official entrusted with the guidance of the Church's relations with the Jewish people. It did call for the agreement to be carried out, and it offered financial help to the Polish church from the Holy See for the construction of the ecumenical center in which the nuns were to be rehoused. By 1991, there were reports that construction was actively proceeding. Late in 1991, the foundation stone of a new convent was actually laid, though it is said to be only two hundred meters away from the original site. However, the nuns themselves were likely to continue to offer resistance to any attempt to move them, and it remained to be seen if their prestige would still prove decisive.

Glemp, for his part, continued for a few days after the Vatican intervention to protest that this was not the right way to resolve the problem, saying to reporters that this appeared to be "a forced resolution, and I don't think that would be a very positive way."[39] Eventually, however, he seemed to yield to world pressure and reluctantly backed down. In a letter to Sir Sigmund Sternberg, chairman of the International Council of Christians and Jews, he continued to complain of "shrill voices," but promised to reinstate the agreement. "It is essential," he said, "not only to move the convent outside the perimeter of the site, but also to set up the new cultural centre. This will help us to continue the dialogue that is so dear to us."[40] All the time, however, a Catholic chapel had been in existence at the Sobibor camp, in which only Jews died. No one had even proposed moving it.[41]

Certainly there are nuances, and not every Polish Catholic views Jews in exactly the same way. In particular, relations between Glemp himself and John Paul are said to be cool. The Solidarity paper condemned the words of Glemp, speaking of the infliction of a real and not "paper" pain, hurting the feelings of the children and relatives of the victims of the Holocaust. Behind the utterances of the two cardinals, however, lie centuries of Polish antisemitism, a historical reality no unbiased person could possibly contest.

The memory of Jewish suffering at Auschwitz must be blotted out or transformed into the glorification of Christian martyrs because there is Polish guilt inextricably bound up with the extermination of Jews. There were Polish martyrs, not many, and there were Polish victims of the Nazi camps, numerous, but far fewer than the Jewish victims. But there was also massive Polish complicity in the extermination of the Jews, extending to betrayals of Jewish partisans who had escaped from the ghettos of Poland into the forests to fight the common foe. It was not by accident that the principal extermination camps were set up in Poland and elsewhere in Eastern Europe. No trouble with the surrounding population need be expected there.

Without the continuous Catholic teaching that the Jews killed Christ, a teaching that was continued in the school curriculum of Socialist Poland,[42] Poland could not have become so solidly antisemitic. The Catholic church has its own share of responsibility for the events that happened in Poland, and since it has not repented, the Jews must be blamed.

Eventually, in 1991, the Polish bishops did issue a pastoral letter formally condemning antisemitism as a sin and "contrary to the spirit of the Gospel," and expressing regret for "all the incidents of antisemitism which were committed by anyone at any time on Polish soil . . . and for all injustices and harm done to Jews." But the impact of the statement, perhaps in any case not likely to be strong in view of the centuries of antisemitic tradition it sought to combat, was weakened by attempts at "balance." It made reference to the "injustices and injuries committed by the post-war Communist authorities in which people of Jewish origin also took part." The bishops also criticized Jews for spreading the "harmful" notion that Polish antisemitism is somehow worse than antisemitism elsewhere.[43] The statement is certainly a welcome beginning, but it does not appear to be an impressive call to unconditional repentance for a great and long-standing evil. Finally, Glemp too apologized for his words, acknowledging in the terms of the pastoral letter that antisemitism was a sin against the gospel.

Earlier in the course of the controversy, the pope had issued another of his regular statements condemning all forms of antisemitism. But the statement, like most Vatican pronouncements, did not refer to anything specific, and as usual it did not touch theology, only ethics. The pope's own apparent reiteration of the traditional supersessionist doctrine, earlier in the same week as the repudiation of the agreement on the convent at Auschwitz, also touched a nerve.

It came close on the heels of a vigorous statement by a very different Christian body, the World Evangelical Fellowship, repudiating as altogether incompatible with biblical faith the concept of a double covenant, whose popularity in the mainstream churches its authors probably exaggerated. The statement likewise rejected the notion championed by another evangelical group, the International Christian Embassy in Jerusalem, and its supporters, that the role of the Church at this point in history is to "comfort" the Jewish people. The W.E.F. insisted that Jews need the salvation brought by Christ as much as anyone else, and that it would be unloving for Christians to discontinue their mission to them.[44] Thus two major forces in contemporary Christianity, Catholic and Protestant, were again in agreement that the anti-Jewish theology of supersession is of the essence of Christianity and is no accretion to be removed.

When Archbishop Williamson, of the conservative schism from the Catholic church led by Archbishop LeFebvre, earlier in 1989 reaffirmed all the old Catholic anti-Jewish ideas, using even more antisemitic language than Glemp, he was on solid traditional ground. LeFebvre and his group represent the ideas of the Catholic Right in France, the *intégristes* who opposed reform before, during, and after Vatican

II. Though LeFebvre and his own followers have gone into schism and now characterize the papal church as apostate and even "Satanic," there are many still in communion with the Pope who share most of their attitudes. Politically, the integrists had had disquieting links with Nazism.

Though, like LeFebvre, whose views are similar, Williamson had been excommunicated by the pope as a member of a schismatic body, he was in this respect only following the logic of the pope's own views. The pope may wish to be friendly with Jewish leaders, and his personal record during the Holocaust is excellent, but he cannot purge antisemitism without attacking its mythical and doctrinal roots. There is no sign that he has personally glimpsed the necessity of doing so or even that he could do so if he did. The infallible Church has no mechanism for repenting of its own theological sins.

THE WORLD COUNCIL OF CHURCHES

The World Council of Churches represents the churches of the Eastern Orthodox and Protestant world. It meets every few years in Assemblies at which comprehensive statements of theology and church policy are voted on by the representatives of the member churches and issued to the public. Many of these statements are commentaries on international affairs, including the Middle East.

Between Assemblies, the World Council's affairs are handled by periodic meetings of its Central Committee and by the office of the General Secretary, located in Geneva, Switzerland. Also affiliated with the World Council are comparable national bodies, such as the National Council of Churches in the USA and the Canadian Council of Churches. One such body, with considerable influence on the way the World Council views the Jewish people, is the Middle East Council of Churches, primarily Arab in composition. The World Council also sponsors continuing enterprises such as the Commission of the Churches on International Affairs (CCIA), the Project to Combat Racism, and the Consultation on the Churches and the Jewish People. These bodies, each with their own staff, report to the Central Committee and the Assembly.

The World Council of Churches was founded in 1948 at its first General Assembly in Amsterdam. It brought together in a single organization two earlier ecumenical bodies, known respectively as Life and Work and Faith and Order, which had operated during the previous decades. These ecumenical bodies maintained an office in Geneva during the war years, headed by Willem A. Visser t'Hooft, who became the first General Secretary of the World Council when it was formed. A remarkable leader, Visser t'Hooft had close connections during the war period with the resistance movement to Hitler among the Christians of Germany.

He and his associates who took the lead in the early days of the World Council were identified in various degrees with the "neo-orthodox" or "biblical" theology of which Karl Barth was the greatest representative. Such a theology, since it takes the Christian Bible as a whole with full seriousness, is potentially more favorable to

Jews than are the liberal theologies that consider the Old Testament morally superseded. However, the structure of Barth's own highly christological dogmatics, reflecting many of the themes of the church fathers, left little room for a continuing covenant with the Jewish people.

Then and later, many of the leaders of the World Council, like Visser t'Hooft himself, came from the ranks of the World Student Christian Federation. Having looser ties to the churches, the Federation was often able to pioneer theologically in areas where the World Council could only follow more slowly.

This has worked both for good and for ill. In the forties and fifties, the Federation did remarkable work for Christian unity. Later, when it embraced liberation theology with both hands, the Federation became identified with hostility toward Israel and provided the World Council with leadership that gave greater influence to such ideas. Unlike the World Council, the Federation does not recognize Israel's right to exist but is on record as being in favor of the secular, democratic state of Palestine advocated by the PLO.

The First Assembly at Amsterdam in 1948, reflecting the theological ideas of the period, produced a document that strongly condemned antisemitism, while at the same time it reiterated traditional Christian ideas about the Jewish people. It spoke of the Jewish heritage of the Church, which it was "in honor bound to render . . . back in the light of the Cross. We have therefore to proclaim to the Jews 'The Messiah for whom you wait has come. The promise has been fulfilled by the coming of Jesus Christ.' "

The document went on to recommend that the churches consider missions to the Jews as a normal part of their parish work. The State of Israel, just established, was mentioned only as a factor complicating antisemitism.[45] Evidently it had not yet occurred to the authors of the document that Israel might have theological significance for Christians, if only by refuting some cherished myths about the destined fate of the Jews.

The World Council has, perhaps naturally, tended to reflect changing fashions in theology, and in the period since its origins it has moved far from the ideas of its founders toward an alignment with the Third World and the "liberation theologies" so much in favor there. Simultaneously, the World Council has become much less favorable to the Jewish people, since the liberation theology that has more recently dominated its thinking is strongly anti-Zionist.

Liberation theology is a fusion of some Marxist themes with Christian theology, including the traditional gospel picture of Jesus. It speaks consistently of "the preferential option for the poor" as the proper goal of Christian action, while at the same time it accepts and even emphasizes the mythological picture of Jesus as a religious revolutionary, opposed by the Jewish establishment and martyred by their hostility.

In view of the dominance of liberation theology among the church leaders and ecumenical civil servants who made policy for the World Council over the last two decades or so, it is perhaps not surprising that the influence of the Middle East Council of Churches upon the World Council's attitude toward the Middle East should have been strong. The Middle East Council of Churches reflects the views of a Christian minority in the Middle East, caught between the Arab nationalism of the Islamic majority, and the presence of the State of Israel, in which many of them reside.

To establish their Arab credentials, such Middle Eastern Christians often feel impelled to be even more nationalistic and anti-Zionist than their Muslim neighbors. The residents of the Christian quarter in the Old City of Jerusalem tolerate the increasing number of Muslim residents in their quarter with little difficulty but make a huge fuss if Jews move in, as if their presence were sacrilegious.[46]

The Eastern Orthodox churches pulled the World Council in the same direction. The bishops and theologians from the Soviet Union and Eastern Europe then permitted to take part in international meetings represented churches that took the official line of their governments. It was traditional for the Orthodox churches to obey the state uncritically: this had been their way since Byzantine times. Though in the early stages of Communist rule, Russian Orthodox Christians suffered terribly, eventually they were able to adjust to Communist rule, or at least to find officials ready to do so. However, those who did cooperate eventually lost the respect of many of their flock, and will no doubt gradually be replaced.

During the period in question, anti-Zionism was being fomented worldwide by Moscow. The alliance between the Soviet Union, which had once supported the State of Israel in the United Nations, and the Arab world produced such deadly fruit as the infamous "Zionism is racism" resolution of the United Nations General Assembly, only repealed at the end of 1991, and the automatic majority for any resolution condemning Israel, no matter how farfetched and remote from factual reality. This was the government line that the Eastern European Orthodox churches would be ready to follow in the World Council of Churches. These various influences had their effect. During the eighties and much of the nineties, the World Council of Churches, when it discussed Middle Eastern questions, resembled nothing so much as the United Nations at prayer.[47]

Israel and the Middle Eastern conflict form the subject of a number of statements by World Council bodies. The Commission of the Churches on International Affairs, under the leadership of Ninan Koshy, in 1975 issued a report on *Human Rights in the West Bank*, which claimed that the Israelis had no interest in any peace plan and were flying in the face of international law and public opinion by occupying and settling the West Bank. These are familiar themes of Arab propagandists and their Western supporters, but they do not necessarily correspond with the facts.

In the same year, the CCIA published a report of a visit to Iraq by Koshy and his colleague Stanley Mitton, which praised the Ba'ath party and favorably assessed Iraqi policy toward the Kurds.[48] I have no information on how the authors view their 1975 assessment in the light of the Gulf War of 1991 and subsequent events.

The CCIA adopted a statement on the Lebanon situation in 1981, calling for "the termination of Israeli attacks and interventions against Lebanon and Palestinians in South Lebanon which Israel claims is necessary for its security and a help to

Lebanon; because the security of both Israel and Lebanon depends upon Israeli recognition of Palestinian self-determination and the establishment of a just peace with the Palestinians and Arab countries in general."

The same statement also concluded that "Lebanon should not be sacrificed in the process of enabling the Palestinian people to attain their legitimate rights." Students of Middle Eastern affairs will recognize in the language of the statement several of the code words of Arab propaganda, such as "just peace," "legitimate rights of the Palestinians," and "self-determination for the Palestinians," aimed at Western concerns for human rights, but carrying a different meaning to Arab ears.

The Project to Combat Racism is clearly interested primarily in South Africa and refuses to consider the problems of Jews in Arab lands or in the Soviet Union. Evidently it does not regard racism directed against Jews as a matter of Christian concern. On the other hand, it did hold a meeting in 1980 that spent some time discussing the Palestinian problem. It gave the floor to Riah el-Asal, a Palestinian Anglican priest, who told the meeting that "Zionism is also a form of racism," and said that the church should not be silent on "the blacks in the Middle East," by which he meant the Palestinians.

The World Council itself has almost never shown any concern for Soviet Jewry. On one occasion in 1972, however, the General Secretary, Eugene Carson Blake, wrote to Metropolitan Nikodim asking for clarification of a Soviet policy taxing Jewish intellectuals who wished to emigrate to Israel.

The Consultation on the Church and the Jewish People has had a difficult history. It is the only World Council body specifically concerned with dialogue with Jews and has brought together Christian theologians and churchmen genuinely concerned for righting ancient wrongs and correcting theological distortions. However, it has consistently been ahead of the churches, and its statements have from time to time been considerably toned down before being accepted by the authoritative bodies of the WCC.

It is hard to avoid the impression that its staff members, whose openness to Jews and Judaism has been admirable, have become correspondingly unpopular with their World Council colleagues. They appear to have been viewed somewhat as colonial administrators who committed the unforgivable sin of going native. The rather frequent turnover of staff members for the Consultation perhaps reflects this nervousness on the part of the churches.

Turning now to the more authoritative groups in the World Council, which more closely reflect the views of the member churches, we find a long series of statements on the Middle East critical of Israel and sympathetic to the PLO and its aspirations. In 1974, the Central Committee by implication condemned Israel's annexation of Jerusalem, stating that its future could only determined in the context of a total settlement of the conflict, and that a solution must take into account the rights and needs of the "indigenous" people of the Holy City. (Evidently, like many ill-informed people, the Committee was under the impression that the indigenous people of Jerusalem were Arab. In fact, the Old City alone has had a Jewish majority since at least the last quarter of the nineteenth century.)

In 1980, the Central Committee took a much stronger line, opposing "the Israeli unilateral action of annexing East Jerusalem and uniting the City as its 'eternal capital' under its exclusive sovereignty. The decision is contrary to all pertinent UN resolutions. It most dangerously undermines all efforts towards the just solution of the Middle East problems and thus jeopardizes regional and world peace."

The Committee went on to say that "just as the future status of Jerusalem has been considered part of the destiny of the Jewish people, so it cannot be considered in isolation from the destiny of the Palestinian people . . ." A Dutch delegate called for an amendment affirming Israel's right to exist, but the matter was dropped when the drafters stated that their text did not touch that right.

At the Fifth Assembly in Nairobi in 1975, the meeting received a warm and lengthy message from Yasser Arafat, who evidently regarded the Assembly as at least a potential ally. He had some reason to do so, in view of the World Council's persistent support of all kinds of liberation movements and the expressions of understanding for the PLO and its cause periodically emanating from it.

In September 1970, Blake, the General Secretary, had sent a message to the Central Committee of the PLO condemning the hijacking of civilian aircraft and the taking of hostages but expressing understanding for the frustration of the Palestinian Arabs and their "desire to focus world attention on [their] situation." He went on to say, "We recognize that you have been unjustly excluded from various governmental and non-governmental forums which have made decisions profoundly affecting your future. Until now, the world community has not been able to satisfy your demands for justice and self-determination."

When in 1975 the United Nations General Assembly promulgated its notorious "Zionism is racism" resolution, the new General Secretary, Philip Potter, issued a public statement on November 11, expressing the WCC's deep concern and pointing out that "Zionism has historically been a movement concerned with the liberation of the Jewish people from oppression, including racial oppression." Equating Zionism with racism would not help to solve the Middle East conflict. He therefore asked the UN secretary general to "reconsider and rescind this resolution." However, he was not supported by the Nairobi Assembly, which apart from receiving Arafat's message had given the PLO permission to have a bookstand for the distribution of free literature.

Two member churches, the German Evangelical Church and the United Presbyterian Church in the U.S., wished the Assembly to take a public stand in conformity with Potter's letter. The proposal ran into opposition in the Business Committee, which controlled the agenda; apparently Potter's letter had been opposed by churches in the Arab countries and the Communist bloc. Seeing that their motion would fail, the two churches withdrew it. Thus the Assembly failed to condemn the UN resolution; on the other hand, it criticized the Israeli position on Jerusalem and the occupied territories.

The Assembly repeated earlier World Council statements that "the rights of the Palestinian people to self-determination" must be implemented, while Israel should withdraw from the territories occupied in 1967. However, in conformity with the

Security Council resolutions on the issue, the right of all states to live in peace within secure and recognized boundaries was also affirmed. In calling for the cessation of "all military activity, both regular and irregular, including terrorism," the Assembly did not condemn the PLO as terrorist, as some Western churches wished, because other churches did not regard the PLO as terrorist but as a liberation movement.

The World Council had remarkably little to say on the Camp David agreements, apparently because of sharp internal disagreement on their wisdom. Meeting in January 1979, the Central Committee, instead of welcoming the accords, spoke of the continuing dangers of the unresolved conflict in the region and "the lack of progress towards peace and negotiations involving all parties concerned including the Palestinians."

During the Lebanon war, the Israeli intervention was sharply condemned by the Central Committee at its Geneva meeting in July 1982. The Committee called for the immediate lifting of the siege of West Beirut, which it termed "horrible and scandalous," and affirmed its view that the restoration of Lebanese territorial integrity was fundamental to peace in the region.

The statement then turned to the Palestinian question. The Committee called on the United Nations and all governments to treat "with utmost urgency the resolution of the Palestinian question on the basis of the Palestinians' right to self-determination, including the right of establishing a sovereign Palestinian state." Koshy, the Director of the CCIA, declared that "Israel cannot continue to ignore the Palestinian question or use it as a pretext to justify armed aggression against third parties including sovereign states."

The Sixth Assembly, which met in Vancouver in 1983, continued the same themes, calling for the "implementation of the right of the Palestinians to self-determination, including the right of establishing a sovereign Palestinian state." This time, however, a new theme was introduced: Christians in the West should recognize "that their guilt over the fate of the Jews in their countries may have influenced their views of the conflict in the Middle East and has often led to uncritical support of the policies of the state of Israel, thereby ignoring the plight of the Palestinian people and their rights."[49]

Readers of this book will probably be puzzled at this reference to Western Christian guilt, of which there has been little sign, certainly among those who spoke for the member churches of the World Council. Objectively, of course, the guilt is not small, and perhaps *should* have influenced views of the Middle East conflict, though there is not much sign that it actually did. For moral perversity, this World Council statement ranks with the notorious "Zionism is racism" resolution of the United Nations.

During the same Vancouver Assembly, a small but symbolic incident occurred that also shed some light on the attitude of the member churches toward the Jewish people. Most of the worship services of the Assembly took place in a large tent near the Vancouver School of Theology, on the campus of the University of British Columbia, where the Assembly was held. The faculty of the school has an unusually fine record in the field of Jewish-Christian dialogue, and its recent graduates have all been trained in the historical criticism of Christian anti-Judaism, so that it will not be passed on through their ministry in the churches to their future parishioners.

The lectern used had been borrowed from the Epiphany Chapel of the School. It bears a carving of a tree with the Hebrew words *Etz Chaim*, tree of life. During the Assembly it could be seen that the lectern had been rather clumsily covered up by a weaving that normally hangs from a wall of the chapel, so that the Hebrew words were no longer visible to the worshipers. It is understood that this was done at the instigation of the Eastern Orthodox delegation, who refused to worship in the presence of the Hebrew inscription.

The Melbourne Assembly in 1991 again called for the establishment of a Palestinian state. In the same year, several American churches reiterated the call, including the Episcopal church, to which a number of members of the Bush administration, including the President himself, belonged, the Evangelical Lutheran Church, and the United Methodist Church. The National Council of Churches in the U.S.A. has been if anything more vociferous in support of the Palestinians than the World Council.

In themselves, there is nothing out of the ordinary in all these statements. They are the standard stuff of far Left political rhetoric, or of Arabs and their Western supporters. Even the language and terminology is extremely familiar to anyone who follows the political controversies. What is surprising is the consistent identification of church bodies, on this issue at least, with left-wing political positions of a fairly extreme kind, without any sign of balancing arguments that might indicate that the authors of these statements judge current events in the light of theological rather than political criteria. Perhaps however we should not feel surprise, in view of this history of hate, at the total failure of these churches and their leaders to have any empathy with Jews and their causes and their extreme readiness to sympathize with their sworn enemies.

NEW THEOLOGIES

A more hopeful development has been the appearance since the sixties of works by Christian authors seeking to undo the *damnosa haereditas*, the baleful legacy, of anti-Judaism and antisemitism in Christian thought. Among historians of Christian thought, a new critical principle has emerged in the study of the Christian past. Applying it has brought to light a degree of hostility toward Jews down the ages, in theologians, canonized saints, and ordinary Christians, that was hitherto unsuspected, perhaps because it had been taken for granted and regarded as normal. Without the labors of these historians, the present book could not have been written. Soon, it will be impossible to write the history of Christianity without acknowledging the major part anti-Judaism has played in it.

Among theologians, a few, belonging to various churches, have attempted to confront the implications for theology of these discoveries. Some put the Holocaust in a central position in their thinking, others do not, pointing rather to a millennial history that requires amendment in any case. All struggle with the need to rethink theology in the light of a newly recognized "Jewish-Christian reality," as Paul van Buren calls it in the series title of his four volume work of systematic theology. "The continuing validity of the covenant between God and the Jewish people"[50] is the reality Christian theology must now address.

The thinking of these theologians is being radically changed by the new recognition that the covenant with the Jewish people has never been annulled, as the Gentile church had believed since the close of the New Testament period. It remains fully in force. Hence Christian theology must be rewritten in the light of this reality, which can no longer be evaded.

As we have seen, traditional Christian theology was based on the conviction that the Church has superseded Israel as the people of God, and it is in fact now the true as well as the new Israel. A great part of the theology of the formative period of Christian thought, the period of the church fathers, was structured around this opposition between Christianity and Judaism, between the old and the new. So, still, is much liturgy and many traditional hymns.

The change that is now required, if these theologians are right, is extremely farreaching. It involves abandonment by Christian thought of one of its fundamental assumptions and thus a radical change in its structure. Theologians must now conceive a hitherto unthought of relationship between the Gentile Christian community and the Jewish people. To accomplish this, they must drive a critical wedge into the Christian Scriptures themselves, to separate what is acceptable from what can no longer be maintained in good conscience, in view of the fact that anti-Judaism is by no means absent from even these sacred writings.

Nothing like this has ever been attempted in the history of Christian thought. Even liberal theology, which abandoned much of the supernatural element in Christianity, including the divinity of Christ and his supernatural redemption of mankind on the cross, never questioned the assumption that Christianity is superior to Judaism and intended to supersede it.

Most of these theologians are not liberals in that sense. Some of them are Catholics, and of those who are not most come from the neo-orthodox or "biblical theology" movement in modern Protestant theology. They believe in a biblically attested revelation and in a gospel of divine grace. Most of them therefore hold on to precisely the themes that liberal theology rejected as incompatible with modernity, often including the traditional Christology that regards Christ as divine as well as human. Thus, they claim that their position is not radical but "orthodox," or even, as does Roy Eckardt, " 'conservative,' from the perspective of the enduring covenant between the only God and his people."[51]

On the other hand, they are clearly not fundamentalists, as their willingness to criticize even the New Testament shows. They belong to an important section of modern Christian thought that attempts to unite critical methods of historical inquiry with the affirmation of the substance of traditional faith. This, as well as their openness to the Jewish people, makes their thought extremely creative.

Earlier in this chapter, I suggested that such attributes qualify these thinkers to be regarded as on the leading edge of contemporary Christian thought. With regret, it must be acknowledged that the educated Christian public, especially among the church leadership, does not seem to think so. So far, they remain marginal to the present state of Christian thought, respected more by Jews perhaps than by Christians. In due course, I shall find it necessary to criticize them myself for not going far enough, but first I owe them acknowledgement of the great distance they have traveled along a lonely road, and of the spiritual aspiration to truth, as well as compassion, impelling them along that road.

The task they have taken on is truly difficult. Liberalism by contrast had an easy road. Once the supernatural elements of revelation and redemption have been removed from the structure of Christian thought, there is nothing difficult in remodeling it ad libitum to meet any of the supposed demands of modernity.

These theologians are under very different constraints. They retain most of the elements of traditional orthodoxy while radically criticizing at least one that has always been regarded as no less fundamental. Most exponents of any orthodoxy tend to regard it as an indivisible whole that cannot be tampered with without bringing the whole structure down.

On the other hand, the position of the dialogue theologians has a strength not possessed by those of other orthodox writers. In support of their views, they can point to the testimony of the whole Bible all Christians regard as authoritative and to the actions of the "only God" of which it speaks. They do not find it necessary to diminish the authority of the Old Testament as a vehicle of divine revelation, or to suppose that God has changed his mind about the covenant.

For all of them, the issue of the covenant is central. If the covenant with the Jewish people remains in full force, what is the covenant on which the Church has always relied? Traditionally, Christians have always spoken of two covenants, an old and a new, the second superseding the first. They have claimed that their new covenant is the one promised by the prophets for messianic days, brought by Jesus the Messiah to replace the broken covenant with Israel. Now this traditional position has become untenable. The work of the dialogue theologians attempts in various ways to come to terms with this revolutionary discovery.

Much of their work has taken the form of historical investigation of the role anti-Judaism has played in the development of Christian thought and institutions. The pioneer seems to have been James Parkes, an Anglican scholar of liberal bent, whose interest in the question was sparked off by experiencing European antisemitism when he worked for International Student Services in the period after World War I. Beginning in the thirties, Parkes wrote a long series of historical works dealing with Christian anti-Judaism, with antisemitism, and with the Middle East conflict. He does not seem to have written extensively about the theological implications of his discoveries, though perhaps some of these may be inferred from his writings on other questions.

During World War II, he wrote two popular books under the pseudonym of John Hadham. These offered a simplified account for wartime of what seemed to him essentials of Christianity. Among other traditional elements not emphasized was the doctrine of the Trinity. The God of Hadham's *Good God* seemed to be the one God worshiped by Jews. Later, in his own name, he wrote against the theology of Barth, which he found dangerous in its implications. He saw it, I think, as a kind of crypto-fundamentalism and understood clearly that its exclusively Christological foundation and structure left no real room for Jewish faith or the Jewish people.

Otherwise, writers in this field reflected the new thinking started by Jules Isaac with *The Teaching of Contempt* and *Jesus and Israel*, together with the work done in the period leading up to Vatican II, which bore fruit in *Nostra aetate.* One of the first and most influential writers was Father Edward Flannery, who wrote *The Anguish of the Jews*, which first came out in 1964 (with the imprimatur of Cardinal Spellman!)[52] and has recently been reissued in updated form. His work was also historical, and as his subtitle, *Twenty-three centuries of anti-Semitism*, indicates, he attached great importance to the pagan antisemitism of antiquity, seeing Christian anti-Judaism as continuous with it. In spite of certain unduly defensive aspects, his work remains an astonishing achievement, especially for its time.

Perhaps the next book to have a wide influence was Rosemary R. Ruether's *Faith and Fratricide.* Appearing in 1974, her work gave to the public the fruits of her extensive historical research on the explicitly anti-Judaic works of the church fathers, the so-called *adversus Judaeos* literature. Although she set this part of her book in a wider context, from the New Testament to essentially the medieval period, while offering some reflections on how theology might be changed to remove its anti-Judaic aspects, the strength of the book lay in its research on the church fathers, documenting perhaps for the first time how anti-Judaic Christian theology had been in its formative period.

The book attracted wide attention especially by the compelling and succinct questions it asked. Her formula, "anti-Judaism is the left hand of Christology," for the first time raised serious alarms that anti-Judaism could not be removed from theology without far more drastic changes than anyone had so far supposed, and drew corresponding criticism from those who did not like these implications. Her questions echo through the literature of the subject to the present.

Ruether was also a contributor to a remarkable symposium held in 1974 at the Anglican Cathedral of St. John the Divine in New York City.[53] Her article summarizes her book, to which it is a very clear and succinct introduction. The symposium brought together most of the leading figures, Jewish and Christian, then involved in theological reflection on the Holocaust. Some of the essays, especially Irving Greenberg's, already cited, are remarkably powerful. Unfortunately, the symposium was marred by the inclusion of an anti-Zionist utterance by Gabriel Habib, of the Middle East Council of Churches. Nevertheless, this is a book that should not be forgotten: in its genre, it has yet to be surpassed.

The Canadian theologian Gregory Baum, also a Catholic, like Flannery and Ruether, and himself a consultant at the Vatican Council, has adopted different positions on the topic over the years, as he himself acknowledges. In the late fifties, he attempted to give what he characterized as "a partial response to Jules Isaac" in

The Jews and the Gospel.[54] At that stage, he thought it his duty to defend the New Testament against charges of anti-Judaism and falsification of history.

In his important introduction to Ruether's book, Baum acknowledges that this position cannot honestly be maintained in the glare of the fires of Auschwitz. A radical critique of Christian theology from its beginnings is demanded. He praises Ruether for beginning the task.

Later Baum changed again. His earlier interest in historical criticism, then supported by psychoanalytic insights, was already being replaced by an interest in sociology, which became his new critical principle. At the same time, like Ruether herself, he came to embrace feminist and other semi-Marxist positions, and in his recent articles has emerged as a fairly severe critic of the State of Israel and its policies and to some extent as a supporter of the Palestinian cause.

Ruether has gone even further in the same direction. After the publication of *Faith and Fratricide*, apart from the expected lectures and articles arising from a controversial book, she had not much to say about Christians and Jews, writing and lecturing in the area of feminism and more broadly of liberation theology.

In her most recent book, written with her husband, Hermann Ruether, she gave her earlier admirers a most uncomfortable time by adopting the Palestinian propaganda case lock, stock, and barrel. She writes with some animus against authors like van Buren whose dialogue with Jews had led them to identify with Jewish visions of the rebirth of the state of Israel as a manifestation of the divine rule over history. Like a number of Jewish supporters of the same cause, she seems to have exploited her reputation as an opponent of antisemitism to give credibility to an anti-Zionist position that in anyone else would unhesitatingly be characterized as anti-Jewish.

It is difficult to reconcile two such different books, though the signs of the second are in fact already present in the first. Although *Faith and Fratricide* is dedicated to her Jewish uncle, David Sandow, it already contains sharp criticisms of Zionism. Nevertheless, it would not be hard to use the critical principles of the earlier book against the later one, especially its tendency, in line with the traditional theology of supersession, to spiritualize the meaning of the term Israel so that it loses this-worldly political reality. It now seems that Ruether is not at all comfortable with traditional Jews and only has use for those who are so far on the Left that many other Jews would tend to call them "self-hating."

Was she ever comfortable with religious Jews? Was her critique of Christian anti-Judaism simply part of an intellectual critique of traditional Christianity on a left-wing basis, or did it spring from real compassion for Jews? If the latter, why has she changed? These are questions admirers of her earlier work hope she will satisfactorily answer in due course. At the time of writing, she has not.

Another Canadian writer, Alan T. Davies, wrote a seminal book called *Anti-Semitism and the Christian Mind*,[55] published in 1969, in which he considered the attitudes toward Jews and Judaism of modern theologians writing in the post-Holocaust period. I count the reading of this book as a milestone in the development of my own thinking, for as someone who then specialized in the study of modern theology, I was shocked at the revelation of its inherent anti-Jewishness, at least in so many of its leading exponents. It became clear to me that a type of theology I had viewed with admiration until then was radically flawed and must be completely rethought.

Like Ruether, a symposium on whose work he later edited, Davies does not offer an extended account of how theology must be rethought to eliminate its anti-Jewish tendency. The same is true of Franklin Littell of Temple University, whose passionately written work *The Crucifixion of the Jews* has also enjoyed a wide influence. Littell has worked a great deal through personal influence and through organizations devoted to Jewish-Christian dialogue.

For such adventures into the unknown we must look rather to Roy Eckardt and his wife, Alice Eckardt, who in a series of works first drew attention to the distortions in Christian theology engendered by its anti-Judaism and then made a series of radical suggestions toward righting them. The Eckardts treat the original covenant with the Jewish people as fundamental, seeing Christians, the "younger brothers," as honorary members of that original covenant, with fewer obligations and perhaps a slightly lower status. In their latest work, the Eckardts deny the physical resurrection of Jesus, affirming that he still sleeps, like other Jews, awaiting the general resurrection at the last day.

An even larger project has been undertaken by Paul van Buren, in the series already referred to. He intends to produce a four volume systematic theology of the "Jewish-Christian reality," of which three volumes have appeared at the time of writing. The first, *Pointing the Way*, is a short introduction, and only in the second volume does he adopt the formal style of systematic theology, with interrelated theses and expositions, in the manner of his teacher, Karl Barth. The third volume, dealing with Christology, has recently come out. The final volume is to deal with Redemption, the eschatological portion of his thought.

Nothing like this has ever been attempted before. Unfortunately, perhaps this remarkable enterprise has come too late, when there is no longer an audience for systematic theology and when the fuller discovery of Jesus the Jew has rendered obsolete the historical foundations of van Buren's Christology. Perhaps, however, a critique of his achievement should await the publication of his fourth volume.

Some of the dialogue theologians follow Franz Rosenzweig in speaking of a double covenant. Others think rather of a single covenant into which the Gentiles have been admitted on special terms, as honorary members, as it were. Yet others prefer to speak of two separate covenants, each with their own terms. On all these views, the original covenant with Israel is the foundation, and the new covenant with the Gentiles is established upon its basis and wholly dependent on it.

If the original covenant remains in force, a remarkable consequence follows, of which little has so far been said. The growth of the theology of supersession was accompanied by a battle for the Bible, in which the Church took over the Jewish Scriptures as its own and installed them in its Bible as the Old Testament. If the covenant had been transferred to a new people, so necessarily had the Scriptures that authenticated it.

Upon acknowledging that the original covenant remains in force, the Church should logically return the Scriptures of the covenant with Israel to the people of Israel. The "Old Testament" will thus regain its original Jewish status. For Christians as well as Jews, the Hebrew Bible will have to cease to be merely Old Testament in relation to New, and once again become the book of covenant and Torah. The consequences of this theological revolution have still to be properly explored, but they may turn out to be further reaching than anyone has yet supposed.

We learned in earlier chapters that the belief in Jesus as the Messiah awaited by the Jewish people was originally justified by a radical rereading of the Hebrew Scriptures that in due course transformed them into the Christian Old Testament. Reversing this rereading and returning the Scriptures to their original guardians would presumably entail giving up the new reading of the texts that were used in justification of the infant church's messianic claim for Jesus. As we saw, the earliest form of Christian theology, which still retained its influence many centuries later, was a series of "Testimonies," biblical texts thought to substantiate these claims. Once the Old Testament resumes its role in Christian eyes as the Jewish Scriptures, so that Christians must now read it in much the same way as Jews do, they will in effect have given up the biblical basis for the claim that Jesus was the Jewish Messiah.

The Jews can no longer be accused of rejecting Christ; it is no longer even necessary to find reasons for exonerating them from blame for doing so, in the manner of Vatican II. New grounds will have to be discovered for maintaining a central Christian belief. Christology will presumably have to be rewritten in purely Gentile terms. But renouncing the belief that Jesus was the Jewish Messiah because of its lack of biblical support would deprive Christianity of a vital link with Jewish symbols and with the history of revelation, the very thing these theologians do not wish to abandon.

A second consequence of acknowledging the validity of the original covenant seems likely to be a reevaluation of Gentile rejection of the Torah. In a number of important essays, the New Testament scholar Lloyd Gaston has drawn attention to what he calls "legicide," a "killing" of the Torah by Christians, a symbolic reality unlike deicide, the supposed crime on which his coined word is based. Can this legicide still be justified in the light of the new Jewish-Christian reality? The recognition of Jesus, the Jew, may have to be accompanied by new critique of Paul, the founder of Gentile Christianity. More must be said about this in a final chapter.

If the original covenant remains valid, what can be the basis of the new, or Christian, covenant? It can no longer be biblical, once it is admitted that the Scriptures of the existing covenant belong to the Jewish people and that they retain the right to interpret them in their own traditional way. The Christian interpretation of the Hebrew Scriptures is either made relative, or annulled in favor of the Jewish one. We are left with the shadowy postulates of modern theology, the "Easter faith" of the early Church, as the basis for Christianity, or even more radically with Paul's vision of the risen Christ as the only starting point of Gentile Christianity.

Again, however, this pushes Christianity into a neo-Marcionite position that is the last thing these theologians want. Thus, an unforeseen effect of doing belated justice to Jews may be to make Christianity less Jewish instead of more so. Jews may perhaps welcome this, as the means to avoid a form of confusion that has often embarrassed them, but this can hardly have been the aim of the dialogue theologians themselves.

Given these possible consequences, it is not difficult to see why the new theologies of a double covenant, or their variants, arouse alarm and opposition in some conservative Evangelicals, and not only in them. If the original covenant is still in force, Christ did not die for all men, and the basis for conducting missions to Jews is totally undercut. Once you concede that missions to Jews are unnecessary, perhaps Buddhists will follow, or even secular humanists. Evangelicals are bound to see this as a slippery slope leading to the destruction of all that is most dear to them.

Liberal Christians have tended to ignore this new theology of Jewish-Christian dialogue, having an agenda in which the Jewish people do not figure prominently. The popularity among liberal Christians of issues such as feminism, abortion, gay rights, and the third world has tended to make them less receptive to Jewish concerns. Most religious Jews are less sympathetic to the liberal agenda. On the other hand, traditional Judaism often comes under criticism from liberals for patriarchy and for lack of openness to gays and lesbians and their rights, while its nuanced views on abortion are often confused with those of the Christian Right.

Meanwhile, conservative elements in the Christian world–Catholic, Orthodox, or Protestant–lack the means to come to terms with the new "Jewish-Christian reality." They can understand the need for better treatment of Jews on a personal and social level, and for cooperation on ethical and social issues. But the possibility that radical theological change might be required is beyond their capacity to imagine. Most of them continue to argue that missions to Jews are as obligatory as they ever were. Among conservatives, the theology of supersession still holds sway. The impact even of the Holocaust has not been sufficient to weaken its traditional power.

12

Antisemitisms Old and New

We have learned in the last few chapters how the ancient Christian myth became secularized in the new societies emerging from the crisis of the Enlightenment and the French Revolution. Jews were looked down on and hated as before, but new, no longer explicitly religious reasons were now given. Even in the still more secular societies of the late twentieth century, the Christian myth about the Jews continued to exercise its influence, above and below ground, perpetuating old forms of antisemitism and engendering new ones. There are few in our culture who have altogether escaped it and approach Jews without previous assumptions, simply as people.

Few of the varieties of antisemitism prevalent in the late twentieth century are altogether new. Except for the root of them all, the traditional religious hostility toward Jews of the Christian world, now two millennia old, most modern forms of antisemitism go back to the nineteenth century. Even religious conservatives, whose dislike of Jews was grounded in the old theological and other calumnies, had little difficulty in adding racism to their armory, once others developed the theory. In addition to racial theories, the nineteenth century discovered both left-wing and liberal reasons for disliking Jews. These are very much still with us in the closing years of the twentieth century.

From the mid-nineteenth century onward, the main sectors of opinion in the non-Jewish world each had its own particular theory of why Jews were bad. Whether it was the reactionary Right, hankering after the *ancien régime*, the Marxist Left, looking for a classless utopia in which Jews would have no place, or the liberal center, believing that society could be reformed along ethical lines, all disliked Jews and believed themselves to perceive a Jewish problem.

In the post-Holocaust era, important sections of the non-Jewish world for the first time attempted to acknowledge and undo antisemitism. However, they have not yet succeeded in eliminating it. They have hardly begun to do so. Many people of good will hoped that antisemitism would by now be a thing of the past. If the shock of the Holocaust did not bring it to an end, what would? Unfortunately, with the lesson of the Holocaust unlearned, antisemitism is not dead, even in North America. On the contrary, it is assuming new forms, while the older forms, once thought to be relegated to an insignificant lunatic fringe, are surfacing once more, and even finding public toleration as legitimate expressions of opinion, to be protected by civil rights.

At the same time, two new mutant varieties of antisemitism have appeared: the denial of the historical reality of the Holocaust, and anti-Zionism. Each claims not to be antisemitic at all, though their hateful character cannot be concealed. Both make use of falsification of history to deny the Jewish people and especially the Jewish state their legitimacy in the community of nations.

THE SURVIVAL OF TRADITIONAL ANTISEMITISM

The traditional forms of antisemitism, religiously or racially based and frequently both, are certainly not extinct. After a period of apparent dormancy, they have come to life again, and there are signs that they are even growing in strength. The exponents of religious antisemitism have never admitted their own contributory responsibility for the Holocaust, and many continue to harbor the fantasy that the Jews were being punished justly for their rejection of Christ.

Not a few conservative and neo-orthodox theologians continue to believe that the Jewish people rejected Jesus because of their obstinate adherence to the Torah, which (according to the myth) he had challenged in principle in God's own name.[1] They hold firmly to the theology of supersession, believing that God in turn has rejected the Jews (and the Torah) because they rejected their Messiah. This is the oldest form of the myth still current. It need involve no racial hatred of Jews, but it is mythological, not historical, and it leads to false perception and debasement of Jews and Jewish faith in Christian minds.

Among the more paranoid antisemites of the older type, some of the medieval libels are still believed. In the postwar period in Poland, the last pogrom took place on the pretext of a blood libel. Clearly, Polish Catholics had not yet learned to criticize this libel. Who is to say that it has yet been universally abandoned?

Perhaps the most persistent of all the libels is the identification of Jews with usury. It now usually takes the form of fantasies about Jewish financial control of the economies of the countries where they live. Jews are widely believed to control the banks, the film industry, and the media, and to use this control for their own narrow ends, including the promotion of the state of Israel. Cardinal Glemp obviously retains this image of Jews. So it seems do some politicians in Eastern Europe who hope that this supposedly massive influence can now be used in favor of their countries.

Paranoid fantasies about the Talmud are still circulated by antisemites. Recently a most unpleasant videotape issued by an Evangelical group in the Unites States came into my hands, containing scurrilous libels against the Talmud, alleging that it condoned the sexual abuse of children. The same videotape was viciously anti-

Zionist, actually featuring anti-Zionism in its title. It was further evidence of the inseparability of the old and the new forms of antisemitism.

Among the most extreme conservative antisemites of today, the new racist antisemitism is unmistakably still fused with the old religious hostility, as it was in the late nineteenth and early twentieth centuries. The addition of racism to the old stock of anti-Jewish ideas was evidently too valuable to be let go, even after the Holocaust.

Less is heard now of the racial slurs of the past, though they do reappear in pictorial form in some of the antisemitic cartoons in national newspapers in North America, strongly reminiscent of the scurrilous productions of Julius Streicher's *Der Stürmer*. One cartoonist regularly depicted the then prime minister of Israel, Yitzhak Shamir, as a stereotypical European Jew speaking English with a heavy Yiddish accent.

However, racist antisemitism appears to be more prevalent in Europe than in North America. In France, Le Pen's National Front, said to command four million votes, though best known for its attacks on Arab immigrants, is unquestionably antisemitic in the old racial sense, giving Jews as well as Arabs cause to fear for their safety.

The persistence of the ancient myth is no doubt the explanation of the well documented antisemitism of many Christian biblical scholars. The most famous example from the Nazi period is the theologian Gerhard Kittel, son of the editor of a widely used edition of the Hebrew Bible and himself editor of a highly influential theological dictionary of the New Testament, a work that perpetuated many Christian misunderstandings of Judaism. Kittel was an outspoken supporter of the Nazis. He was eminent enough to draw a measured and dignified reply from Martin Buber.[2]

In recent years, a number of the scholars working on the Dead Sea Scrolls have given evidence of comparably antisemitic attitudes. In 1991, wide publicity was given to the extremely antisemitic remarks of John Strugnell, a British scholar working at Harvard and then the director of the Scrolls project, made in an interview with an Israeli newspaper.[3] He was not alone. Other members of the team refused to set foot in Israel after 1967, and some even refused to acknowledge its existence.

There is no reason to doubt the objective intentions of the vast majority of Christian biblical scholars. However, many of them still seem to think that the primary significance of the Hebrew Bible lies in the prophecies of Christ and the Church it has traditionally been thought to contain. Their theological interpretations of the Old Testament often assimilate it to the New. They treat its ideas selectively, stressing only those elements in its religious thought that they think were brought to fruition in the New Testament, thus largely removing its Jewish character.

I certainly do not agree with those traditional Jews who regard all critical study of the Bible as inherently antisemitic. The history of biblical scholarship has demonstrated that truth obliges us to undertake the historical criticism of even the Scriptures and that criticism is not inherently destructive of faith in a divine revelation attested by the Bible. Certainly such a book as this could not have been attempted without it. Nevertheless, criticism is not always sufficiently self-critical.

One of its most necessary and difficult tasks is to take account of the bias introduced by the critic's own standpoint as a modern person. We can now see rather clearly the ways in which the nineteenth-century critics did not succeed in eliminating their own cultural prejudices, and no doubt our successors will be able to see our own failings more clearly than we can ourselves.

The historical theories associated with Wellhausen and his followers, still widely influential in biblical scholarship, have drawn just criticism because of the assumptions they made about the evolution of religious ideas. These assumptions really were anti-Jewish. They led to a partisan picture of ancient Judaism, according to which it reached its peak in the eighth century with the first literary prophets, supposedly the inventors of ethical monotheism, followed by a degeneration during the exilic period to a priestly and legalistic religion that in its decadence was denounced by Jesus. Moses became a dim and largely legendary figure of little historical importance.

On the basis of this historical theory, they constructed a history of the way the Bible was written and the order in which the various documents of which it was composed were set down in writing. There now seems good reason to believe that this theory was wrong. But the analysis of texts leading to the documentary hypothesis about the origins of the Pentateuch is based on good evidence and sound reasoning. The data cannot be ignored but will have to be reinterpreted in the light of a sounder historical theory. The Israeli scholar Yehezkel Kaufmann[4] made an important beginning, though not all his theories command assent among scholars attempting similar reconstructions.

The influence of archaeology on recent biblical scholarship has also been somewhat questionable. Anti-Jewish assumptions seem to get smuggled in to the interpretation of archaeological evidence without objective justification. This happens when (as is frequently the case) scholars overemphasize the similarities of ancient Israelite religion with its Canaanite surroundings, while failing to stress the all-important differences. In such cases, it is hard not to conclude that such scholars are blind to the distinctive contribution of ancient Judaism to religion and to Western culture. Some archaeologists deny the historicity of the Exodus because they underrate the value of the literary evidence of the Bible by contrast with that of archaeological artifacts, which apparently do not record the event. Would they be so likely to do this if they had not a certain bias against the story on which Jewish faith is based?

In Canada, recent court cases have brought to light the ingrained antisemitism of some Christians, including school teachers, some of whom do not scruple to teach their own hate-filled opinions to the innocent young people in their care. A couple of these cases have received a great deal of publicity, but there is reason to think that they are only the tip of a larger iceberg. Not long ago, at a symposium on the Holocaust for high school students, I told the audience that the Jews did not kill Christ. There was quite an angry response from a group of students of Evangelical

Christian persuasion. One of the teachers, who had been bringing his students to these meetings annually, was heard to say that I should attend his Western civilization course, where I would learn that the Jews did kill Christ. If such opinions are taught in state schools by teachers apparently well enough disposed to the Jewish people to want their students to know about the Holocaust, what can be the teaching of those who are less well disposed?

Opinion is divided on whether legislation against the teaching of hatred and falsehood is the way to deal with it, but that it exists cannot be doubted. In addition to the propagation of antisemitism in the classroom, the Canadian Jewish Congress reported a doubling of such crudely antisemitic incidents as graffiti and vandalism of synagogues in the last years. In the United States, reports of such extreme groups as the Aryan Nations suggest that they are not simply a lunatic fringe that can be ignored, but a real danger. Support is lent to these fears when it is possible for a former, and clearly not very repentant, Nazi and leader of the Ku Klux Klan to run first for the Senate and then for state governor and in each case to stand quite a good chance of winning. In the Louisiana gubernatorial election in 1991, he took most of the white vote. He is said to think he has an important political future ahead of him. We can believe him.

Every now and then, in North America or in Europe, some Christian cleric comes out with the kind of antisemitic utterance that many people had hoped would never be heard again. In the late eighties, a Baptist clergyman attracted a great deal of attention to himself by asserting that God does not hear the prayers of Jews because they are not offered through Jesus Christ. In November 1991, a Dutch clergyman was still able to say that the Holocaust was a punishment for the rejection of Jesus Christ by the Jewish people. These instances could be paralleled at length.

In the former Soviet Union and Eastern Europe, as well as the former East Germany, with the collapse of Communist rule and the rise of nationalism and ethnicity, sinister forces are reemerging from underground. They had been there all along but lacked means of expression under Communist rule, when they were rightly recognized as Fascist. Unfortunately, they also had a religious basis. Movements such as Pamyat in Russia, and the Arrow Cross in wartime Hungary, and the Iron Guard in Rumania united nationalism and highly conservative religion with the old antisemitism of the Catholic and Eastern Orthodox worlds. Untouched by modernity, and kept in deep freeze for forty years, or even seventy in Russia, these movements or their successors were again capitalizing on popular hostility to Communist rule and vying for popular allegiance.

Soon we shall be hearing once more of "Jewish Bolshevism." Indeed, in post-Communist Poland, one of the most common slurs against Jews is that they were prominent in past Communist governments. In these quarters, nothing has been learned from the Holocaust. In Eastern Europe, nationalism has always gone hand in hand with antisemitism. We do not yet know how the new democratic regimes will handle this threat to human decency in their midst.

In the West, the all-out barbarity of uninhibited antisemitism has been confined to groups so far on the fringe of normal society that it has been easy to discount them. The Aryan Nations in the United States and Canada and the various neo-Nazi groups in Britain and Western Europe are small and appear to have little effect outside the paranoid world of their own membership. However, the same was true of Hitler in the 1920s. Economic collapse, always a possibility, could give them the audience they crave and make them a genuine threat to the existence of Jews in the liberal West. Against such hate, liberalism, Christian or secular, has no defense.

LEFT-WING ANTISEMITISM

The origins of the anti-Jewish views of the Left go back to Marx himself, as we learned in a previous chapter. Lenin tried to fight antisemitism, though he certainly held the Enlightenment view that Jews must reform themselves if they wished to be accepted. He had numerous former Jews among his party colleagues, of whom the best known were Trotsky and Kaganovich. Stalin revived antisemitism in its full horror. He purged the party of its prominent Jewish members and instituted systematic persecution of Jews in the Soviet Union. Clearly, Stalin's mentality embraced both the old theological hatreds, acquired in his days in the Church and as a theological student, and the new Marxist reasons for regarding Jews as enemies of the people.

Under Stalin, attempts to salvage Jewish culture were stigmatized as "cosmopolitanism," a punishable political error. After initial support of Israel in the United Nations during the debates about partition and independence, apparently intended mainly as an anti-British move, Stalinist foreign policy turned to anti-Zionism after the 1967 war. Moscow became the world center of the anti-Zionist movement, coordinating Communist and Arab propaganda against Israel. The Stalinist policy of making alliances with the Arab world against Israel led to the infamous United Nations resolution condemning Zionism as racism. The world wide Left, formerly somewhat sympathetic to Israel, from that point turned solidly against it, and does not yet seem to have reviewed its position, even in the light of the demise first of Stalinism and then of Soviet communism itself.

Among those on the Left, the Marxian view that Jews are to be identified with capitalism and imperialism is still strongly held. Marx's own words are seldom known in detail, and perhaps if they were his patent identification with older Christian attitudes might after Auschwitz give some of his later followers pause. The general theory remains uncriticized, however. When socialism triumphs, the destiny of Judaism is to disappear, along with all religion, but not before it has first been reformed by conformity to the ideas of liberal Christianity.

In spite of Marx's criticism of Bruno Bauer, the Left still seems to hold to Bauer's central idea that Judaism must first be liberalized before it disappears along with Christianity. Thus, anti-Zionist Jews, even if observant, are still to be preferred to other Jews, though the ideal Jew is the one who has totally assimilated and shares all the ideas of the Left. However, his or her Jewishness becomes useful when it is necessary to argue that attacks on Israel are not antisemitic in origin. Then the assimilated left-wing Jew will for once acknowledge and even flaunt his or her Jewishness, otherwise something to be forgotten and relegated to silence as a relic of the past.

Since the Left has not abandoned its preference for the totalitarian dictatorships of the Arab world over Israeli democracy, left-wing Jews must continue to be opponents of Israel and supporters of its enemies if they wish to remain in good standing on the Left. We shall shortly examine the phenomenon of anti-Zionist Jews from several angles.

MUTANT ANTISEMITISMS

At the same time as the resurgence of traditional racist and religious antisemitism, the old stock of Judaeophobia has mutated into new forms, adapting itself with remarkable flexibility to changing historical circumstances. If we confine our attention to the justifications offered for hating Jews, we may fail to see the continuity of these new forms of antisemitism with their predecessors. In all cases, however, we can be quite sure that their exponents learned to hate Jews in childhood before as adults they devised these new reasons for doing so. The root of their attitudes remains the old conviction that Jews are bad, engendered above all by the Christian myth and transmitted down the ages from generation to generation, more through the family than through the marketplace of ideas.

The adherents of these new mutations of antisemitism usually find it convenient to deny that they are antisemites at all. If antisemitism only means attacking Jews as a race, perhaps they are not, and a new term is needed. I just used one, Judaeophobia: Alan Dershowitz suggests Judaeopathy.[5] Racism is very widely discredited in the late twentieth century and few like to admit to being racists. However, it is less disreputable to admit to being opposed to Jewish influence on political and cultural affairs, however Jews are now identified. The two most prominent of the new mutant forms of antisemitism are Holocaust denial and anti-Zionism.

DENIAL OF THE HOLOCAUST

The most surprising of the mutants is the historical denial of the Holocaust. It is surprising because of its bizarre improbability, though perhaps it is not really more improbable than the libels so widely believed in the Middle Ages and to some extent even now. The Holocaust is one of the best documented events in human history, supported on the one hand by numerous eyewitness testimonies of survivors and liberators, and on the other by German records, written and photographic. Some of these German files, hitherto inaccessible to historians, have recently been released by the former Soviet Union, whose soldiers had captured them at the end of the Second World War. The historical authenticity of the Holocaust itself is beyond question, whatever debate may still be needed in the establishment of its details. No reputable scholar would for a moment dream of calling it in question.

Holocaust denial is more bizarre than the assertion that the earth is flat, with which it is sometimes compared. After all, the evidence of our senses might lead us think the earth *is* flat. The concept that it is round and moving in space at a high speed in an orbit around the sun is (as the scientists put it) counterintuitive. The only thing counterintuitive about the Holocaust is that the imagination of decent people cannot take in its enormity. But that is not why it is being denied.

The motivation for denial of the reality of the Holocaust is unmistakably antisemitic hate. Most of its exponents have at least some sympathy with Nazism, while some of the most prominent of them are outright neo-Nazis. Nevertheless, Holocaust denial frequently presents itself to the world as historical scholarship, "revisionism," claiming scholarly objectivity.

Those who want to deny the Holocaust allege either that it did not take place at all, that Hitler never ordered it, that there were no gas chambers or crematoria in the death camps, or that the deaths of Jews occurred on a much smaller scale than they really did, being due to poor living conditions, and not to a deliberate policy of extermination. The account the rest of the world believes was made up in order to legitimate the Zionist state. Sometimes there is a less-explicit subtext–if the Holocaust didn't happen, it ought to have; Hitler didn't finish the job.

Revisionism has become a minor "scholarly" industry: the hundreds of articles and books being published are evidently finding a credulous public among antisemites. Among the latter, it appears, are some Arab leaders who see the usefulness of this kind of historical falsification for their own political cause.

Holocaust denial is not a danger to the well informed and historically educated. It is a danger to the young, not yet historically educated, and to the uneducated among their elders. Among such groups, a general skepticism flourishes, fostered by much more sophisticated intellectuals, who hold that any intellectual position is politically motivated. Any statement can be discounted with the reply, "That's just your opinion." Then it is easy for Holocaust denial to be set alongside historical truth as if they were rival opinions, the one no more credible than the other. Or perhaps people will conclude that the truth lies somewhere in between. This is one reason why some people doubt the wisdom of dealing with Holocaust denial by court cases. In Canada, the neo-Nazi Ernst Zundel was permitted through his counsel, Douglas Christie, to call so-called expert witnesses who solemnly trotted out in court the absurdities of Holocaust denial, which were duly reported in the media, and thus given credibility among the uninformed.

Hitler learned that the bigger the lie the more readily it will be believed. There are signs that this lie is gaining ground among those who do not know how to counteract it. It is thus of first importance that the true history be taught in schools as well as universities, incorporated in the regular curriculum. Rightly or wrongly, it is sometimes argued that the reason for teaching African history is that it belongs to the history of the black community in America and is therefore a specifically black concern. In fact, there are other good reasons for teaching it. However, it is not a *Jewish* concern that the Holocaust be taught. The story of the Holocaust should not be taught just to please Jews. It must be taught because it is a major event in all

Western history, without knowledge of which we cannot evaluate our common culture. The history of the Holocaust cannot be confined to Jewish studies. An event of this magnitude must be studied by all. Only knowledge can effectively counteract evil intentioned lying about our past.

ANTI-ZIONISM

The other mutant, anti-Zionism, also frequently depends on historical falsification. In fact, I am inclined to believe that historical falsification has now become the principal weapon of antisemitism. In the case of anti-Zionism, the history of the Middle East conflict is being rewritten to make it appear that in all the five wars between the Arab powers and Israel, even in 1948 and 1967, Israel was always the aggressor and always more militarily powerful than its Arab enemies. Arabs are able by this means to rationalize the "disaster" (as they themselves see it) of military defeat by a weaker adversary, who should have been content to live in second-class status under Islamic rule. Anti-Zionists in the West, whose motives are different, are glad to take up the theme.

Israel is also said to have deliberately expelled all the Arab refugees of 1947–1948, many of whom in fact fled out of panic or even at the instigation of the Arab powers. Much is made of the researches of Israeli revisionist historians, which do tend to show that *some* of the refugees were deliberately expelled, especially from military areas, but fail to overthrow the contemporary evidence from both Arab and British sources confirming that the majority left of their own accord, hoping to return after the annihilation of the infant state.

On the other hand, not only outright anti-Zionists, but even American politicians, take no notice of the carefully considered opinions of international lawyers of the greatest eminence, such as Eugene Rostow and Julius Stone, who find that Israel's occupation of Judaea and Samaria is fully lawful pending a negotiated peace, and even that Israel has a better legal title to the territories, let alone to Jerusalem, than any other claimant.

Those who denounce Zionism as a form of Western colonialism allege that Jews are simply Western people of Jewish faith, without continuity with the ancient people of Israel. They are members of a religion, not a nation, it is asserted, perhaps not even descendants of the ancient Israelites. While anti-Zionists readily accord national identity to Palestinians, whose consciousness of distinct identity at the most generous estimate began just before World War I, they refuse it to Jews, who have been a people for at least three thousand years. Here too we can discern the continuing influence of the Napoleonic bargain.

What is important for our inquiry is the readiness of a good deal of liberal opinion, as well as much of the media, to accept the propagandist rewriting of history as truth. If such people have to decide whom to believe, as between Jews and their enemies, it seems that they will still choose not to believe Jews.

Holocaust denial and anti-Zionism overlap, though they are not identical. Some

Arab propagandists use Holocaust denial in the cause of anti-Zionism, while Holocaust deniers allege that the motive for the fabrication of the Holocaust story is the legitimation of Israel.

The identification of anti-Zionism as a mutant form of antisemitism is complicated by routine denials of anti-Zionists that they are antisemitic. Some of them are actually Jews themselves, though in many cases Jews who only identify themselves as such when it is necessary to criticize the state of Israel.

Nevertheless, the overwhelming consensus of the Jewish people regards Israel as a necessary and even central expression of its life. Most Jews see Israel as an essential means of self-protection should antisemitism again become violent in other societies. The overwhelming response of the worldwide Jewish community to the recent emigration of Soviet Jews to Israel is testimony to this consensus, if any were needed. No one can systematically deny the legitimacy of the State of Israel and still care for Jews. Anti-Zionists often defend themselves by arguing (correctly) that not all criticism of the state of Israel is necessarily antisemitic, while using this principle to excuse utterances that in relation to any other state would at once be recognized as passing beyond the bounds of friendly or even legitimate criticism of acts and policies. While it is incontestable that not all criticism of Israel is antisemitic, in the non-Jewish world most of it is. Persons of good will who wish to criticize Israel will be careful to criticize specific policies and actions, without joining with those who call the legitimacy of the state as such into question, and they will be careful not to apply to Israel criteria that would not be used of other states in the region, or of their own. Anti-Zionists do not subject themselves to such restraints.

Among Jews, Zionism had its opponents from the first, though they have grown less numerous over the years. Jewish opposition to Zionism has taken several forms. Some very traditional Jews believe that the return to Zion, though constantly prayed for, can only be accomplished by the Messiah. The State of Israel, a modern secular state, is not the community governed by the Torah that the Messiah is expected to establish. Its establishment was brought about for the most part by secular and unbelieving Jews, most of whom wished to break with the religious traditions of their people and set up a secular socialist state. Those who hold such traditional beliefs regard the State of Israel as something still to be hoped for, not a present reality.

Such views would naturally lead to non-Zionism, but not inevitably to anti-Zionism. However, a small minority within this religious non-Zionist group is so deeply opposed to the secular preemption of the work of the Messiah that they become actively anti-Zionist, in a few cases to the extent of supporting Yasser Arafat and even Saddam Hussein.

While this chapter was being written, the *Jerusalem Post* and the *Jerusalem Report* reported that the "foreign minister" of Neturei Karta, a small but extreme non-Zionist group in Israel, wished to join the Palestinian delegation to the Madrid Peace Conference in order to "safeguard the rights of the Palestinians." There was some ambiguity in the term *Palestinians*. He may have meant by the term those Jews who are descendants of Jewish residents of Palestine before the Zionist immigrations. Neturei Karta's praise of Arafat and his proposed "secular democratic state of Palestine" suggests that these very religious Jews feel politically, at least, closer to the Palestinians than to their fellow Israelis.

As with other anti-Zionists, however, it is not unfair to suspect that the rabbi in question dislikes the State of Israel more than he likes Palestinians. Neturei Karta even sent representatives to the antipeace conference held in Iran by radical Islamic groups the week before the Madrid conference opened. Most Jews regard such attitudes as bizarre, but it is interesting to discover how far Jewish anti-Zionism can take its exponents. Among secular Jews, such attitudes are less surprising.

Successfully assimilated Jews have also strongly opposed Zionism. During the discussions in the British War Cabinet during the period leading up to the Balfour Declaration, the most vehement opponent of the proposal to issue a declaration in support of Zionist goals was the secretary of state for India, Edwin Montagu, himself a Jew, though much more strongly identified as an Englishman. Montagu argued that Judaism was a religion, not a nationality, and to say otherwise was to suggest that he himself was not an Englishman.[6] Other prominent representatives of Anglo-Jewry joined him in this opposition, including the famous rabbinical scholar Claude Montefiore.

Such Jews, whose families had lived in Britain for generations, had become well accepted in English society, and they feared that the establishment of a Jewish state in Palestine would be a breach of the Napoleonic bargain, leading to loss of their acceptance and social privileges. They might be accused of dual loyalty, or even eventually banished to Palestine, where they had no inclination to live.

Today, in the United States, where Jews nowadays enjoy a degree of acceptance perhaps hitherto unknown in any non-Jewish society, similar attitudes lurk beneath the surface. Many American Jews are much more strongly identified as Americans than as Jews. They have made it in American society, and they do not wish to do or say anything that could disturb their peaceful coexistence with their Gentile neighbors. In particular, they are exceptionally sensitive to the possible and antisemitic charge of double loyalty. They must never be thought of as owing greater allegiance to Israel than to the United States.

The reaction of the American Jewish community to the Pollard affair, when an American Jew was accused of spying for Israel, was very symptomatic of these attitudes. Most Jewish leaders did their utmost to distance themselves from Pollard as quickly and thoroughly as possible, even when it appeared to more detached observers that his sentence, and that of his wife, was clearly, even scandalously, unjust and excessive.

Many Jews would therefore tend either to keep silent when Israel is under criticism or to join with American criticisms. In social and political matters, they tend to share the liberal views of many of their fellow-Americans. Since liberal opinion in the later decades of the twentieth century has been generally hostile toward Israel, this makes it easy for such Jews either to join with or fail to criticize anti-Zionists. Unfortunately, members of this group are also to be found among the appointed leaders of major Jewish organizations in the United States, consulted by the administration on policy toward Israel and other Middle Eastern powers.

However, this group does not tend to be vociferous in its criticisms of Israel. A third Jewish group does. Members of this group are anti-Zionist on principle but for almost exactly opposite reasons to those of the religious opponents of Zionism. This group has its historical antecedents in the Jewish Left in prerevolutionary Russia. Despairing of all Jewish attempts to deal with antisemitism head-on, many Jews turned to an alliance with the secular Left, including the Communists, hoping that the abolition of the Christian state, together with all forms of religion, would bring a final end to antisemitism. They were ready to pay the price: total submergence of historical Jewish identity in a classless, religionless utopia.

Many Jews were active in the Communist party in the early phases of the Russian Revolution, before Stalin brought traditional antisemitism back to the Soviet Union and turned on many of his former colleagues. Because they saw abandonment of Jewish identity as the most effective solution to antisemitism, they were bitterly opposed to Zionism, the opposite solution. Zionism stood for the reaffirmation of the historical identity of the Jewish people and the building of a Jewish state in the historical land of Israel.

Some of the bitterest opponents of Zionism today are assimilated left-wing Jews such as Noam Chomsky, who view Israel in Marxist terms simply as an outpost of Western and especially American imperialism. Are such assimilated "non-Jewish Jews"[7] antisemites? Of course they cannot be racist antisemites. But since many of them are bitterly opposed to the maintenance of the historical identity of the Jewish people in their own country, with the means to defend itself, they can legitimately be regarded as exponents of a new mutation of antisemitism.

Can Jews be antisemites in any sense? Of course. We have seen how from time to time the worst and most dangerous opponents of Jews have been converts to Christianity, who did not hesitate to spread false information about their former religion to their new friends, providing the basis for persecution. Sometimes it seems that membership of the secular Left functions like a new religion for assimilated Jews, replacing their old faith, but not the tenacity with which they hold it.

Jews can also learn to hate their own religion and history by internalizing the antisemitism of the majority culture. Denying their own past, they attempt to merge into the environment as inconspicuously as possible, changing their religion, their names, and their way of life. If they cannot by these means obliterate their Jewish identity, they will attempt to clear themselves of the stigma of a Jewish past by joining the critics of other Jews. Often such "self-hating Jews" are among the most vociferous anti-Zionists and the foremost friends of Israel's enemies. Such Jews should no doubt be regarded with compassion as victims of antisemitism, though the behavior of other Jews shows that a different choice is possible.

When all this has been granted, I have no doubt that anti-Zionism is not only a form of antisemitism but at present *its typical form*. It is the most seductive and plausible of the varieties of antisemitism prevalent today, and it is the most easily rationalized as something other than what it is. Nevertheless, when Middle East history is falsified, when Israel is judged by standards that the critics certainly would not apply to their own country, let alone to other countries in the region where Israel is situated, while atrocious acts by Israel's enemies are passed over and excused, antisemitism is certainly at work, whether in Jews or Gentiles.

MEDIA REPORTING OF THE MIDDLE EAST CONFLICT

I do not know whether the extremely widespread bias in media reporting of the Middle East conflict is to be attributed to outright anti-Zionism among journalists, or the more diffuse prejudice about Jews to be considered under the heading of liberal antisemitism. I suspect the latter. In fact, many of the reporters most guilty of distortion are Jews themselves.

Some have argued that its real cause is a new policy among journalists not to attempt to get at the truth, as they formerly did, but to be neutral in any conflict. Probably, therefore, as I have found myself, most journalists under criticism from well informed people for the nature of their reporting of the Middle East conflict would say that it is their duty to be evenhanded, not to support one side more than another. Their critics, they say, want them to support Israel, and if they did, they would be under no less pressure from Arab critics and their supporters. And then, like all good anti-Zionists, they usually go on to point out that not all criticism of Israel is antisemitically motivated.

Whatever the reason, the bias is a reality, both in the United States and Canada, and certainly in Europe. This reality becomes obvious to anyone who consistently follows media reporting both in the North American electronic and in the print media, while also having access to other sources of information. Without such alternative sources, it is extremely difficult to obtain accurate information on the history of the conflict, on its real issues, or even on day-to-day events.

This is not simply a general impression. It has been systematically documented by media monitoring groups such as CAMERA (Committee for Accuracy in Middle East Reporting in America). Reading their reports shows that the situation is even worse than might be gathered from a general impression. The bias and distortion take various forms, selective reporting, the use of headlines not supported by the story underneath, the repetition of old pictures to give the impression that incidents of beating of captured stone throwers are repeated more often than they are, the slanting of captions to present Israel and Israelis in an aggressive posture, killing without provocation. In television reporting, the brevity of the reports inevitably distorts a complex and historically tangled situation by compressing it into slogan form.

Often, however, the slogans are key words of Arab propaganda. The perception of the viewer is automatically biased by terms such as "the West Bank"–Jordan's name for the territories in Western Palestine it seized in 1948, previously known as Judaea and Samaria; "the occupied territories seized by Israel in 1967"–for the disputed territories that came under Israeli administration as a result of victory in a defensive war, when Jordan attacked Israel in 1967; "Arab East Jerusalem" for an indeterminate area, including the Old City, which has had a Jewish majority for over a century, together with almost wholly Jewish suburbs developed since 1967, as well as areas outside the Old City that are nowadays predominantly inhabited by Arabs; "self-declared security zone"–referring to the obvious fact that Israel itself designated an area of South Lebanon essential to its own security; such a term would not be used of comparable actions by Arab countries. Some of these terms are less inaccurate than others. All of them indicate a wish on the part of the media not to associate themselves with an Israeli point of view on any matter where Arabs have put forward a different one.

Yitzhak Shamir, when prime minister of Israel, was constantly stigmatized as a "hard-liner" because he believed in his people's historic claim to Judaea and Samaria and did not give away his country's bargaining positions in advance of negotiations. He was often contrasted unfavorably with his "moderate" opponent, Shimon Peres, believed, rightly or wrongly, to be ready for substantial territorial compromise. Shamir's "right-wing" orientation was constantly emphasized, even though he presided over a social and economic system considerably to the Left of that of the United States or even perhaps of Canada. Generally speaking, the left-wing parties in Israel, including small fringe ones, get much more favourable media coverage than governments that have received the support of the Israeli people in democratic elections. Similarly tendentious information is conveyed in the historical snippets that usually accompany wire service reports from the area.

More damaging, however, is the way the intifada has been reported. The stone-throwing teenagers were romanticized, while the Israeli soldiers, who are not much older, were demonized. The threat to life and limb they faced from stones and molotov cocktails was minimized. Every occasion when the soldiers defended themselves with small arms fire was magnified out of proportion and sometimes treated as an unprovoked attack upon defenseless civilians. Sometimes the stone-throwing incidents were deliberately staged for the TV cameras.

I do not believe that the Israeli soldiers were always free of blame. Reports by Israeli journalists of brutal beatings during interrogations cannot be disregarded as mere fabrications. Clearly, troops trained for modern warfare are not well adapted for the gentler and subtler measures required by riot control, when casualties among their adversaries are to be avoided instead of sought. No one should minimize the natural revulsion the Palestinians must feel at being under occupation, with only limited civil rights, for so long, with no clear solution in sight, even though truth also requires us to admit that much of the blame must go to the uncompromising attitude of their own leaders. Honest reporting, as displayed in Simcha Jacobovici's movie, *Deadly Currents*, will not minimize the hardships and distress of the Palestinians. But it will not depict Israeli youths in uniform, or their elders in the civil administration, as brutal Nazis, as so often happens.

The media also often fail to tell us that when such abuses become known, they are dealt with by the process of law and those found guilty punished. Even if not every case is prosecuted, the law provides for it, and it does happen regularly. This is something without counterpart in the Arab world. In 1990–1992, substantially more Arabs died in the territories at the hands of fellow Arabs, on the pretext that they were collaborating with the Israeli occupation, than as casualties from Israeli riot control.

Lack of space in an already lengthy book precludes further examination of the details of media bias. An excellent introduction to the subject is to be found in a videotape reporting the Boston Conference of CAMERA in 1989. Surveys are presented of the way in which several major newspapers, including the New York Times and the Boston Globe, and TV networks, have reported Middle East News, together with some remarkable addresses. Most notable among these were those of the civil rights advocate and lawyer Alan Dershowitz and of the historian David Wyman, who is not Jewish, unlike most of the other participants in the conference.

The most interesting question for the present inquiry is why this bias exists. I assume that those who have documented it have proved that it does, since their reports are confirmed by my own observation and knowledge. As we have seen, it is found among both Jewish and non-Jewish journalists: there are very few exceptions to the rule that Israel will receive a bad press. I believe that it is the result of a generally liberal outlook among journalists, in itself far from reprehensible, which predisposes them (among other effects) to sympathize with the underdog, regardless of the circumstances. Israel, once the underdog, is now perceived as the "overdog" in the Middle East. Moreover, antisemitic prejudice cannot easily accept a strong Israel, using military means for national goals, as other states do. Israel should be more Christian and turn the other cheek when attacked. No comparable demands are made by the community at large upon African or Arab states, or even upon the warring factions in Yugoslavia.

Israel received a great deal of journalistic sympathy until after the end of the Six-Day War and was perhaps even falsely romanticized by the media, much as the Palestinians are today. The remarkable victory in that war was favorably reported at the time, and the whole world, with the exception of the Arabs and their supporters, shared some of the emotion of Israelis and Jews at the recovery of Jerusalem and the Western Wall. Even the Yom Kippur War was more fairly reported, although Israel was less well treated on that occasion by the rest of the nations of the world, especially the Europeans, who did their best to prevent Israel from being supplied with arms, while the Arabs could continue to rely on Soviet help.

The turning point came with the Lebanon War, where for the first time Israel exercised the choice to attack an adversary in its perceived national interest. All previous wars (with the possible exception of the Sinai campaign of 1956, in which Israel was involved by its then allies Britain and France) had been unavoidable defensive conflicts. Much was made by Menachem Begin at the time of the right of Israel to behave like a normal state in using war as a means to achieve national goals. In this case, the aim was to ensure the protection of northern Israel from terrorist incursions, and more broadly, to eliminate the military threat of one of its principal adversaries, the PLO. The threat was real enough, as the invading forces discovered when they captured vast stocks of arms.

However, the effective turning point was the decision to push on and enter Beirut, with the aim of smashing all resistance and setting up a Christian government in Lebanon that would sign a peace treaty and in effect enter into an alliance with Israel. The public relations debacle was completed by the Christian massacres of Muslims, Lebanese, and Palestinians in the camps of Sabra and Chatilla, motivated by revenge for the killing of their leader Bashir Gemayel by their Muslim enemies. Israel was and is widely blamed for the massacres, especially on the Left, and accused of perpetrating them itself. Arabs and their supporters especially conceal the fact that the atrocities were the work of a Lebanese group practicing the Arab custom of revenge killing. It may be said, however, as the Kahan Commission did, that Sharon could perhaps have prevented the massacre if he had been determined to do so.

From then on, Israel was under suspicion by liberal journalists. Never mind that Sharon may have exceeded his mandate, that most Israelis disliked what was done and were immensely relieved when in 1985 the national unity government under Peres extricated them from the Lebanese quagmire, with the exception of the security zone in the south. In the journalistic mind, Israel became associated with militaristic power, and with the brutality of its Christian allies in Lebanon, for which it was not responsible, though they ought to have been restrained. A classic example is the brilliant but misleading best-selling book *From Beirut to Jerusalem*, by the Pulitzer prize winning journalist Thomas Friedman, who continues to write on the Middle East for the New York Times, more recently with somewhat greater fairness.

The damage done to Israel's media image by the Lebanon war was greatly accentuated by the intifada. The intifada may have been the first war fought primarily through the media. (Perhaps the Gulf War was the second, though the destruction was no less a reality for that.) So skillfully did the Palestinians use the Western media to damage Israel's reputation that one could wonder if the whole concept of the intifada was a brilliant and calculated invention of propagandists who understood the American mind much better than anyone in authority in Israel. Perhaps not. More probably it developed spontaneously, proved a gift to television reporting, and then was used for all it was worth.

Given the nature of the intifada and of television reporting, there is no way that Israel could have failed to look bad. But no attempt was made by the world media to counteract this built-in advantage to the stone-throwing youths by more honest and objective reporting. As a result, North American opinion, including Jewish opinion, swung substantially away from Israel, permitting the Bush administration, not a friend to Israel, to use means of pressure on Israel to fall in with American interests that would not have been possible to previous administrations. What made all this feasible was a climate of opinion now to be considered more specifically.

LIBERAL ANTISEMITISM

Although there can be fierce argument about the new forms of antisemitism, they are relatively easy to identify. The majority culture is pervaded, however, by another, subtler form of antisemitism, whose existence is often denied, especially by Jews. This form of antisemitism is not explicitly ideological. It consists of a prejudice disposing those who harbor it to think somewhat badly of Jews without necessarily finding specific religious, racial, or political justification for doing so. It also disposes people to give undeserved credence to the arguments of more overt antisemites. The pervasive liberal mentality of our time is the background radiation left by the distant big bang of the Christian myth about the Christ-killing Jews.

Liberal antisemitism is often unconscious and indignantly denied when attention is drawn to it. With very few exceptions, everyone brought up in a Christian (or sometimes a post-Christian) home shares some degree of anti-Jewish prejudice, subtly conditioning their reactions to Jews even when the adult conscience repudiates such prejudice.[8] Those who are alert to its existence, because they have confronted it in themselves, can recognize that it is far more widespread than many Jews suppose.

Liberal antisemitism is not always explicitly Christian, but it depends upon the traditional Christian interpretation of the Sermon on the Mount, generally cited by liberals as the finest statement of the ethics they subscribe to. As we saw, this interpretation sets Jesus against his own people and tradition, and it sets the perfectionism of his ideal against the practical realities of political and national life, judging the latter by the former. Politically, this leads liberals toward pacifism, the ethic of loving the enemy and turning the other cheek being applied to relationships between states, which do not seem to have been in Jesus' mind at all. Among liberals, religious and otherwise, it is taken for granted that the Old Testament teaches revenge and hatred and that it is an outmoded book to be discarded except for its historical interest and literary beauty. As a guide to personal and corporate life, it is no longer taken seriously in the liberal world.

Even those who are no longer attached to Christianity frequently retain the impression that the Old Testament teaches an outmoded and barbaric morality, ethically superseded by the teaching of Jesus. Jews are supposed to be vengeful, and incapable of forgiving those who have injured them. They are supposed to be very interested in money and outstandingly skillful at amassing it. Such attitudes have a much wider influence than it is comfortable to admit.

Liberals, however, would be shocked and horrified to be told they were antisemitic. Such an admission would be incompatible with the liberal self-image as someone exceptionally righteous and ethically motivated. Indeed, it sometimes seems that in such circles to call someone an antisemite is a worse offense than being one.

Enlightenment views of Jews remain widespread in liberal circles. Under the influence of such ideas, Jews are not attacked on religious grounds, though there is still an echo of Christian moral superiority, but rather for insisting on their national identity instead of merging with the majority culture as simply one religious group among others. Today, anti-Zionism is the most vigorous descendant of the old Enlightenment view, expressed so clearly by Clermont-Tonnerre during the French revolution: Everything for Jews as individuals, nothing for them as a nation.

Clearly, liberals still share the Enlightenment opinion that Jews are only acceptable in modern society if they reform themselves according to liberal ideals, abandoning their sense of themselves as a nation or people, and contenting themselves with being "Frenchmen of the Mosaic persuasion." The Napoleonic bargain is likewise still embraced by many Jews anxious about their reception as fellow citizens in modern society.

Liberals are inclined to be pacifists, or at least to regard resort to arms by nation states as almost never justifiable. On the other hand, they are less shocked by the terrorist activities of groups they regard as politically deprived of their rights. American liberals especially tend to believe that if you adopt a forgiving and tolerant attitude to your enemies, they will be won over to friendship. In the Middle East, such expectations are apt to prove delusory.

Semi-Christian liberals are readily influenced by the diffuse antisemitism of Christian culture as a whole to dislike Israel for two reasons. Modern Israel is easily identified with the Jewish establishment that liberal Christianity believes Jesus opposed, and it is resolved to defend itself by force of arms, including reprisals where necessary against its attackers, whereas Jesus taught the forgiveness of enemies. Worst of all, Israel is believed to possess nuclear weapons and is presumably prepared to use them in a sufficiently extreme situation. The wide popularity of books purporting to reveal Israel's nuclear secrets is instructive, especially in view of the fact that belief in the existence of an Israeli nuclear option has evidently contributed to peace in the Middle East by deterring further Arab attacks on Israel. For nuclear pacifists, including some well respected scientists, Mordechai Vanunu, who betrayed his country's purported nuclear secrets to the press, is a hero.

For the liberal pacifist mind, it would be much more ethical for Israelis to become the victims of Arab genocidal hate, a phenomenon in any case difficult for the liberal mind to take in. In this context, we should not be surprised that Israel briefly regained in liberal circles the popularity it lost by winning in 1967 by suffering the Scud attacks of Iraq in 1991 without retaliation, in order to please America.

The liberal attitude is in these respects a clear descendant of the ancient notion that the Jews should be preserved, but in misery. More generally, liberalism denies national identity to Jews, like the ideas of the Enlightenment from which historically it is descended. It calls for their toleration as individuals with human rights, while according little or no legitimacy to Jewish consciousness of being a nation or people. Thus liberalism has an inherent tendency to anti-Zionism, reinforced by the new image of Israel as militarily strong and perhaps at times ruthless in the means it adopts to survive in a hostile and highly dangerous environment.

ANTISEMITISM IN THE BLACK COMMUNITY IN THE U.S.

Antisemitism in the black community in the United States is a phenomenon whose existence can no longer be denied or ignored. The first signs of it emerged as early as the Second World War, but the majority of blacks were then friendly to Jews. I do not know whether black antisemitism should be classified as liberal, left wing or traditional Christian antisemitism. From here, it looks rather like a mixture of all three. Its growth is disturbing, and also disappointing, in view of the massive participation of young American Jews in the black struggle for civil rights in the sixties and following years.

Antisemitic slurs have come from the lips of well respected and presumably responsible politicians. Jesse Jackson, as well as indulging in slurs of his own, refused to condemn the outright antisemitism of Louis Farrakhan of the Islamic Nation. Black intellectuals in their eagerness to establish the legitimacy of Afro-American contributions to world culture do not hesitate to defame Jews. As for Farrakhan, one does not know whether to attribute his outspoken antisemitism to a Christian upbringing or to newly embraced Islam. Evidently, Islam allows him to abandon traditional Christian restraint in the expression of sentiments widely shared beneath the surface.

In the summer of 1991, racial hostility broke out in the Crown Heights district of Brooklyn, New York, a traditionally Jewish district now increasingly inhabited by disadvantaged blacks. A car in the Lubavitcher Rebbe's motorcade, driven by a Hasidic youth, mounted the curb and accidentally killed a black child. The grieving black community was encouraged by unwise leaders to regard the accident as an intentional and politically motivated killing. This in turn led to the revenge killing of an Australian Hasid.

Doubtless, the social factors in the incident were important and need to be analyzed, but nothing can excuse the deliberate fostering and manipulation of antisemitism in the black community by leaders, including Christian clergymen, who ought to know very well what they are doing. In their poverty and frustration, the blacks have begun to look for scapegoats. They are choosing the one that is traditional in a Christian society. Here, too, it is not difficult to discern the enduring influence of the Christian myth.

The presence of antisemitic ideas among black intellectuals has been courageously documented and criticized by one of their own number, Professor Henry Louis Gates, Jr., in an important article in the *New York Times* for 20 July 1992.[9] Hardly less disturbing, because of its influence on the wider culture, especially among youth, is the emergence of antisemitic allusions in the songs of rap artists such as Ice Cube and the group Public Enemy. As reported in the press, including the *Jerusalem Report* and the bulletin of the Simon Wiesenthal Center, *Response*, Public Enemy's record *Welcome to the Terrordome* alluded to the old myth that the Jews crucified Christ, while expressing negative attitudes toward the agelong Jewish claim to be the chosen people. Ice Cube, who later denied that his words were antisemitic, apparently complained in his album *Death Certificate* of white Jews exercising authority over blacks. However, if these singers really do not wish to be antisemitic, the remedy is in their own hands.

Rap stars enjoy enormous popularity in the white youth culture. They are also respected by liberals because of their affirmation of black identity. In fact, they are "politically correct," much more so than Jews. A number of people, including all the campus chaplains, protested to the radio station of the University of British Columbia, when it aired the Public Enemy album, but without result. Thus, there is the likelihood that this new form of antisemitism, which is also very old, will gain considerable currency among young white people also.

THE INFLUENCE OF CHRISTIAN LIBERALISM ON JEWISH INTELLECTUALS

In the closing pages of this chapter, I want to turn to an even more delicate subject, even harder to pin down with specific citations and examples. Several times it has been necessary to point out that Jews are sometimes conduits for attitudes others can recognize as antisemitic. Even the explanations given above do not sufficiently account for all aspects of the phenomenon.

Some of those most prone toward hostility to important elements of traditional Jewish culture and values are themselves Jewish secular intellectuals, in Israel as well as in the diaspora. Very often they feel themselves to be upholding Jewish values just when in fact they are advocating modern liberal ones against those traditional in Jewish culture. Much of the Israeli peace movement is justified ideologically by arguments typically presented as Jewish, but to a detached eye much more obviously liberal Christian.

Some of the Israeli Left seem to carry the Christian precept to love their enemies as themselves to lengths hardly envisaged even by Christians. Politically, these Israelis love their enemies *more* than themselves. In what other country could politicians in opposition lobby their country's strongest ally to apply sanctions against it to influence it to make concessions to its enemies?

How is this possible? One important reason is that modern secularity was not a Jewish development. It originated within the Christian culture, for reasons unique to Christian history. A Jewish secularity might have developed autonomously and even smoothly, without a total rupture with the religious past, but in historical fact it did not. The potentiality was there in the mainstream Jewish tradition, but the circumstances under which Jews lived in the Christian world prevented its development until modernity was in full tide. By then it was too late for an indigenous Jewish version to develop. Jewish secularity is now a branch of the Christian version.

The Jewish movement of enlightenment, or haskalah, appears to have been modeled on the already existing movement in the Christian world. Even Baruch Spinoza, often regarded by Jewish philosophers as the founder of modernity, was under strong Christian influence from his background in the conversos of the Spanish domains, from whose ranks his family came. They had only recently returned to Judaism. Spinoza's excommunication by the Amsterdam community had the result that his ideas had little influence on his fellow Jews until modernity had largely become established in the majority culture.

Jewish philosophers sought comparable reforms to those which their Christian counterparts called for in their own tradition. Jews were attempting to join in a new and dynamic movement that held out the promise of overcoming antisemitism by lessening the influence of the church on society, while giving Jews a place in society appropriate to their talents. The discovery of the individual by the Enlightenment held out the promise that Jews could enter society simply as individuals, not qua Jews.

Such a pivotal figure as Moses Mendelssohn had clearly absorbed many ideas from philosophers of Christian background. He was acceptable to Enlightenment philosophers like Lessing just because he had reformed himself according to the program the Enlightenment set forth for Jews if they were to become acceptable. Would he have defined his own program of Jewish enlightenment in exactly the same way if there had not been such a powerful Christian model before him? And would not his descendants perhaps have remained Jewish if Jewish enlightenment had in fact been a spontaneous Jewish development?

Modernity, it seems, was already established in its main outlines before Jews sought to enter it. Although it was a rebellion against existing forms of Christianity, modernity was really an internal rebellion, perhaps a palace coup, within Christian culture. It broke with much that was traditionally Christian, but it also retained many Christian assumptions. We have already seen that it did not free itself from traditional Christian hostility toward Jews, though it often found new reasons to justify it, sometimes borrowed from pagan antiquity.

Its views on religion, though often negative, were still derived in part from traditional Christian polemics against Judaism. The distinctions between ritual observance and ethics, between priestly and prophetic forms of religion, so dear to modern liberal religion, seem to have their ancestry in the thought of Paul. (As we saw, one recent Jewish writer on Paul, Alan Segal, actually believes that Paul invented the otherwise modern distinction between ritual and ethical commandments.)

Liberals, like many Protestant Christians, saw Jews in the image of the hated Catholics, and began confusedly to think of "Jewish priestcraft." The inclination to pacifism, so characteristic of American liberalism, certainly originated in a particular reading of the sayings of Jesus that first made its appearance during the Radical Reformation of the sixteenth century. No comparable Jewish source for such attitudes comes to mind. Many Jewish teachers in the pre-Zionist period advocated not returning evil, much in the manner of Jesus' teaching. But this was in part the result of political powerlessness, and in any case referred primarily to individual, not political actions. The passivity and resignation to the divine will with which Zionists often charge their diaspora ancestors should not be confused with the political pacifism that so often involves taking the side of the enemies of one's own country.

Perhaps the case should be made at greater length on a future occasion, but I believe that many Jewish intellectuals, in Israel as well as in North America, have been far more Christianized than they suspect. They fail to realize that modernity is not neutral between Jewish and Christian cultures. Still less is it in practice more favorable to Judaism, as many delude themselves into thinking. While hostile toward both religions, modernity retains in secularized form much of the ancient Christian hostility toward Judaism, though often embraced by secular Jews as a defense against memories of an Orthodox upbringing found oppressive at the time. But the gift is poisoned.

Coming to terms with modernity is an essential task for all religions. For Jews especially, the method cannot be simple acceptance. It can indeed be argued that some of the central themes of modernity, that have proved their value and must be defended against all kinds of religious reactionaries, are congenial to Judaism in ways that they are not to Christianity. The inherent goodness of human beings in spite of their proclivity to evil, the capacity of human reason to understand the world both scientifically and historically, the moral responsibility of individuals for their own actions, and the freedom that alone makes individual responsibility possible, these are values to be defended by all. They can easily be grounded in a Jewish philosophy without submitting to identification with an oppressive majority culture. Jewish intellectuals have less need than most, therefore, to bow down to the idols of modernity. Nevertheless, they ought to be on their guard over what they borrow from developments not native to their own tradition. Modernity's hostility toward religion can be turned with particular vehemence against Judaism.

Identification with the oppressor is a well understood psychological defense against the pain and shame of ill-treatment by one stronger than oneself, too strong for retaliation to be possible. The victim frequently internalizes the hate and becomes a self-hater. The phenomenon has often been identified among contemporary Jews, and mention of it does not need further justification. Psychologists speak of the Stockholm syndrome, originally a case of captives absorbing the ideology of their captors. Jewish self-hatred is a similar phenomenon.

I do not think it has yet been recognized how pervasive it is, and how potentially dangerous when unrecognized. Lack of confidence in one's own religious, philosophical, and cultural tradition can likewise lead to identification with outside critics. If the whole world thinks we are wrong, surely there must be something the matter with us, Jews have sometimes reasoned. And this reasoning can be used by the sophisticated as well as the simple to argue for surrender where steadfastness would be appropriate. Internalized antisemitism can lead to attacks on religious and philosophical traditions too valuable to be discarded in the name of a modernity more Christian than Jewish.

If this is what the phenomenon of Jewish self-hate really is – and it is hard to account for otherwise – it calls for compassion as well as criticism. Nevertheless, in any form, Jewish self-hate is without objective justification. It is highly dangerous to Jews, not only politically but spiritually. Self-hate colludes with the antisemites. It could lead to the collapse of a spiritual tradition that directly and indirectly has given more to the world than any other, or at best to its confinement to a narrow fundamentalism.

Internalized antisemitism could also lead to failure to defend the hardly won

Jewish state against ideological as well as military attacks, and therefore to moral weakness threatening its long-term survival. It is plain to me that internalized antisemitism, comprehensible and forgivable as it may be, is not necessary. Jews are in fact free to make other and wiser choices, and many are doing so. Perhaps, if Jews can learn to recognize the sources of such attitudes in the Christian myth they may find them less tempting to themselves.

13

Ending Antisemitism?

For most of the nearly two thousand years we have been considering, Christianity has been the major cultural influence upon non-Jewish society. Secularization began during the Enlightenment, but it would be a mistake to suppose that its influence quickly became universal. Among the educated classes, who until relatively recently remained a small minority, the influence of Enlightenment philosophy and in due course of scientific and even historical thinking grew. But even among them it was by no means the only intellectual influence or always the dominant one.

The Bible remained an important part of everyone's education, even among those less influenced by the norms of Christian behavior. It has often been pointed out that one reason why the Balfour Declaration was possible was because of the familiarity with the Bible of such men as Balfour himself and David Lloyd George, the British Prime Minister of the day. Thus, the influence of Christianity could also sometimes mitigate its own tendency to make people suspicious of and hostile toward Jews. Among the educated classes, this biblical influence remained strong even in the interwar period.

After the Second World War, education became both more democratic and more secular. Far more people received a high school education, but that education said far less about the Bible than had the former education of the elite. Against the background of our own different type of education, many of us who taught first year religious studies classes in the last decades were astonished at the biblical ignorance of the students coming from the public education system. Students who had never heard of Adam, let alone more obscure figures in biblical history, were not uncommon.

Thus, the influence of the Christian myth on the general public at the present time is much less direct than in the preceding period. While a substantial minority, especially in the United States, still adheres to various Christian churches, and fundamentalism is displaying new vigor, the main influences upon the public mind are secular. This is equally true of those influences that are hostile toward Jews. Outside the explicitly Christian groups, the forms of antisemitism encountered are largely the secularized varieties that first made their appearance in the nineteenth century or later.

These secularized varieties of antisemitism have thus acquired a life of their own. Separated from the Christian stock from which they originated, they also lack the restraints once imposed on them. The most extreme case was of course the antisemitism of the Nazis, which raged unchecked by any of the traditional Christian limits. Familiarity with the Old Testament and especially respect for it as the word of God also tend to mitigate New Testament anti-Judaism. Such influences are largely absent today, and they cannot be appealed to in defense of Jews. We do not yet know whether exposing the Christian roots of antisemitism will have any effect on those who embrace its secularized forms.

The damage done by the mythology about Jews Christianity has spread in our culture is beyond calculation. Can this damage now be undone? Certainly the past cannot be undone. Nothing will bring the six million victims of the Holocaust back to life on this earth, to say nothing of their predecessors down the ages, victims of persecution and pogrom. We cannot hope by any form of rational argument to reach those who are committed to hate. Arguing with them only gives them a further opportunity to develop their own rationalizations. We can only address those who are open to truth and flexible enough to change attitudes that have become habitual.

When we consider the forms of antisemitism examined in the previous chapter, it appears that some of them are held by people who consider themselves motivated by rational argument and who should therefore be capable of amending their opinions in the light of newly recognized facts. Marxism claims to be scientific socialism, not religious dogma, and therefore it should be subject to empirical testing. This is part of what Marxism means by praxis. Liberals claim to be motivated by reason above all, and see their liberalism as consonant with a scientific attitude to the world.

Nevertheless, we cannot be optimistic about the effectiveness among such groups of a direct appeal to reason through confrontation with historical fact. In fact, since antisemitism altogether lacks rational basis, it is safe to say that no one is an antisemite as a result of any rational process. Since antisemitism did not originate by a rational process, we cannot expect a rational process to undo it. Worse still, because of the confidence of Marxists and liberals that they are solely influenced by rational processes, they will deny altogether and on principle the influence of unconscious motivations such as suppressed hate.

In the academic world, outside the natural sciences, the most common form of analysis is sociological or political, not psychological. Such thinkers deny the influence upon themselves or others of unconscious inner motivation, and recognize only that of the social or political situation. Thus, the denial of many liberals that they are antisemitic, because their ideology does not allow for it, is hard to breach, even though their antisemitism may be obvious to anyone sensitive to its symptoms.

On the Left, Marxist and semi-Marxist, ideological self-criticism seems overdue in view of the breakdown of Soviet communism. Marxism appears to have been refuted by events as an explanation of history or an economic theory, and it is being abandoned wholesale in the former Soviet Union and the rest of Eastern Europe. Will this lead to renunciation of the antisemitism that Marx's own writing fostered and Stalin put into practice both domestically and internationally? So far, there is not much sign that this is happening, though some of the governments of the new Eastern European democracies are reconsidering their communist predecessors' shunning of Israel.

On the other hand, just when Marxism is breaking down in the political arena, a Marxist type of thinking, explicit or implicit, seems more influential than ever among Western intellectuals. Not without reason, Raymond Aron called Marxism the opium of the intellectuals. Even when the thinking of the intellectual world is not explicitly Marxist, it treats political and economic forces as the sole explanation of reality. Even the current "politically correct" ideology in the universities seems to do this. Where Jews are concerned, it runs into contradictions. Antisemitism is clearly incorrect. On the other hand, it is "correct" to support the Palestinians. So it must be denied that anti-Zionism has anything to do with antisemitism. I doubt therefore whether the discoveries about Christian history we have been considering can be expected to have a strong or rapid effect on the secular world. Who can be reached?

CASTING OFF INTERNALIZED ANTISEMITISM

Perhaps the first to be considered are the victims themselves. It may be that their potential role in bringing antisemitism to an end is larger than they or others suspect and may even be the most important of all. Of course, the responsibility to do so is not theirs. But the refusal of many Jews to continue to be victims by colluding further with antisemitism, either by submitting to it or by internalizing it, is already having an effect, and as more Jews join with determination in the same refusal, it will have more. Jewish self-affirmation, including pride in the Jewish religious and cultural heritage, can be an effective counter to diffuse prejudice, though it may not touch the insanity of hate.

When Jews stand up for themselves with confidence in their own heritage and the conviction that it still has a great deal to give to the rest of the world, they act with dignity, and they do not attract so easily the antisemitism of others. Behaving like a victim can attract oppressors, while refusing to do so gives them less to latch on to. Self-respect wins the respect of others, not always, but often enough to make a difference.

The most important task for Jews themselves, however, is to bring to light, and fully relinquish, all forms of internalized antisemitism. Jewish self-hatred is more dangerous than antisemitism itself, because it weakens those who are potentially strong enough to withstand it. The most dangerous enemies of the Jewish people at the present time are the self-haters and those who feel the need to stand well with the majority culture, making psychological and political concessions in order to do so.

I am convinced that the bullying tactics applied by the Bush administration to Israel in the negotiations leading up to and following the Madrid peace conference of October 1991 could not have had the degree of success they did without the ambivalence of the American Jewish leadership, the majority of whom (according to polls published at the time) did not support the policy of the Israeli government on Middle East peace.

If indeed the Jewish lobby was normally as powerful as President Bush claimed at the time, invoking a stereotype that itself bordered on antisemitism, its power had been greatly diminished by lack of conviction in its politically active supporters. On the other hand, there is good reason to doubt that the opinions of these leaders coincided with that of their own constituency, who (as other polls have suggested) may well have been much more in harmony with the policies of Israel than the leadership was.

THE NON-JEWISH WORLD

However, there are developments in the non-Jewish world that give cause for hope. There are individuals whose consciences are sensitive to evil and whose affinity with truth compels them to criticize even traditions they personally hold dear. These can be addressed, even by a history as critical as this. They can be challenged to do more than has yet been done to undo the damage of centuries. The weapon of truth can be leveled against the demons of hate. Some who have not yet learned of this shameful history can hear it and respond.

We might think that the way to undo the harm would be to begin with what is happening now. We should perhaps direct our moral and intellectual forces first against the contemporary forms of antisemitism, hoping for immediate restraint of at least the newest forms of anti-Jewish hate. We might persuade secularized Christians not to perpetuate prejudices that depend on myths that they have consciously repudiated. Anti-Zionists might perhaps be persuaded that they really are antisemites after all, in spite of their denials, and might feel compelled to change.

I doubt it. Perhaps it would be more fruitful to go straight to the roots of the tree of antisemitism. Again, since its principal root is uncaused hate, which cannot be touched by any appeal to reason and truth, our success will certainly be limited. But at the level of justification for antisemitism, a critical process has actually begun.

CRITICIZING CHRISTIAN HISTORY

Historians have begun to trace the history of the myth, its origin and development, as we have learned in earlier chapters. Theologians have tried to explore the consequences of the abandonment of anti-Judaic mythology. A number of them have given up the allegation that the covenant God made with the Jewish people has been annulled in favor of a covenant with the Gentile church, and they have attempted to devise new theologies giving validity to Judaism alongside Christianity.

It may be fruitful for historians who study antisemitism to enter into dialogue with these thinkers and ask them (in view of the history we have traced here) if they have gone far enough in their movement of return. They wish to go back to a time in the development of Christianity when it was not yet anti-Jewish. How far back is that? What would Christianity look like if *all* of its anti-Jewish elements were removed? We must return to these questions shortly and discover if they can be answered.

If the Church as a whole could learn to abandon its anti-Judaism, it might become a wholesome influence on secular society, in view of the millions who still adhere to the Christian tradition all over the world. Purged of anti-Judaic hostility and ceasing to teach the untruths of tradition, the Church could become the most effective ally of the Jewish people in its own struggle to repel the forces of hatred. Repentant Christians could enter into dialogue on the issue with liberals and Marxists. They might after all be able to persuade them that they need have no interest in perpetuating the effects of a myth in which they do not in any case believe.

THEOLOGY AND ACTION

It is therefore finally time in this inquiry for us to enter into debate with the theologians. Theology attempts to understand and express the meaning of faith by means of words and concepts. In our day, it has become almost a dirty word, for Christians as well as secularized people, synonymous with boring intellectualism without the vitality of the Spirit. Many suspect that theology has become obsolete as a means of articulating and communicating religious faith.

Except for theologians themselves, therefore, theology no longer carries the emotional charge that strongly influences action. Nevertheless, it remains the foundation of all church teaching. Teaching at the level that influences the broad mass of church people can only be changed if the myth is first changed. This is in the first place the task of theologians, though it will take more than theology to give a purified myth the psychic power it will need to inspire a community to spiritual heights.

Antisemitism will not be brought to an end without changes in our whole culture, but perhaps the beginning will be made with theology. If it is true that elements of the Christian myth are at the root of modern antisemitism, the tree cannot be cut down unless the axe is first laid to its root. The tools of theology must be employed in the demolition and perhaps eventual reconstruction of the Christian myth.

Antisemitism has been based on lies. The first lie was that the Jewish people opposed the teaching and the claims of Jesus and brought about his death. During the centuries that the Church has been able to ignore the Jewishness of Jesus, that lie has taken on a dangerous life in the Christian mind, and it has spawned other lies.

The Christian world has grown to be profoundly anti-Jewish, and for much of its history outright antisemitic, though never officially so. Because of the part the Jews play in the Christian myth, many of the themes of Christian teaching and preaching could not be announced without speaking ill of the Jews. The very contrast of old and new, so important to the Church that it is enshrined in the names of the two sections of its Bible, is inevitably to the disadvantage of the Jews. But the Church could never have been anti-Jewish, however, let alone antisemitic, if it had remembered who Jesus was. Historic Christianity has betrayed and forsaken Jesus himself, in exact proportion to its own anti-Jewishness.

In the years of the Holocaust, the Church was brought to the test on its attitude to the people of Jesus and found wanting. As Emil Fackenheim has pointed out, if Jesus of Nazareth had been alive during the Holocaust, it is almost certain that he would have ended his days in an extermination camp, either as a *Muselmann*, spiritually destroyed,[1] or (as I believe, far more probably) in the gas chamber, saying the Shema Israel with his last gasp along with his fellow Jews.[2] If Jesus had been there, where would the Church have been? Would it have been with its Lord?

Where was the Church? With a few shining exceptions, it was not with Jesus' people, and therefore it was not with Jesus. Since that time, the spiritual decline of the Church that betrayed Jesus has become slowly more plain to see. The Church presents the strange spectacle of a still powerful and flourishing institution that has lost its own center, and it is drawing its energy from forces not native to itself. Failure to come to terms with the lesson of the Holocaust is at the root of that loss.

THE AUSCHWITZ COMMANDMENT

In itself, the cataclysmic event of the Holocaust may perhaps have been totally devoid of meaning. However, many Jews have come to believe that a voice nevertheless spoke to them from Auschwitz. Emil Fackenheim wrote of a 614th commandment, of "a commanding voice from Auschwitz":

> What does the voice from Auschwitz command?
>
> Jews are forbidden to hand Hitler posthumous victories. They are commanded to survive as Jews, lest the Jewish people perish. They are commanded to remember the victims of Auschwitz lest their memory perish. They are forbidden to despair of man and his world, and to escape into either cynicism or otherworldliness, lest they cooperate in delivering the world over to the forces of Auschwitz. Finally, they are forbidden to despair of the God of Israel, lest Judaism perish.[3]

Jewish survival becomes a categorical imperative for Jews after Auschwitz. That means first of all surviving physically, and then it means surviving as Jews, instead of submitting to death as a people through assimilation to the surrounding culture.

Did that voice say nothing to the Church? Many believe that the same voice spoke in no less explicit tones to the Christian world: You shall not ever again hate or bear false witness against your Jewish neighbor. After Auschwitz, it is clear beyond argument that antisemitism and even anti-Judaism are forbidden to the Church. More, it is now no less clear that these attitudes, whether personal or theological, always had been forbidden, although the Church had allowed itself to indulge in them for almost all its history.

No Christian could easily call in question the necessity of responding to such a voice, once heard. What would it take to respond? How deep does the taint of antisemitism and anti-Judaism go? Many, including the pope, clearly believe that after Vatican II the only further response needed is a change of personal attitudes toward individuals, the avoidance of insulting language in sermons and theological statements, and improved relationships in the community.

Others see that anti-Judaism is not just an ethical matter, but *structural*. It affects the Christian myth itself. It goes to the very heart of Christianity. Thus it raises a truly appalling question: Does Christianity derive much of its vital energy from its anti-Judaism?

Some theologians would agree that it does, but not for the same reason. They will argue, and tradition is on their side, that there is such a thing as "essential anti-Judaism," a conflict between the Church and Judaism that has nothing to do with antisemitism. It is needed for the Church's existence as a separate body in the world.[4] As we saw earlier, some of the most influential theologians of our time are continuing to maintain that Christianity exists because Jews have gone astray. Yet the history we have retraced in this volume shows clearly enough that no distinct line can be drawn between anti-Judaism in theology and its social consequences in hatred of actual Jews. The one has always led to the other, and it always will.

Others show by their actions, if they do not argue explicitly, that they think the Church has better things to do than working on its anti-Judaism. There are many other things on the agenda for today that clearly seem more important to Church leaders and to laity alike. There are problems such as abortion, homosexuality, the position of women in the church, the ordination of women and of homosexuals, the Church's role in the third world, and so forth, which loom much larger than the almost forgotten question of the Church and the Jews. But the word addressed to the Jews from the ashes of Auschwitz, and the word addressed to Christians, are not optional suggestions for a future agenda, for they are matters of life and death.

If the Jewish people were to award posthumous victories to Hitler, it would not survive, and Hitler would have accomplished his final solution after all. But if the Church continues on its ancient path of anti-Judaism, it will not survive spiritually. It will have no right to its claim to be the Church of God, for its God chose the Jewish people to be his own, and its Christ was a faithful Jew. The anti-Jewish church may live on, but it will be an institutional shell, preoccupied with power. And perhaps it will have lost the connection with the Spirit that might enable it to answer all those other questions wisely.

The history of the Church since the discovery of the extermination camps, and especially in the last few years, gives little confidence that the word from Auschwitz has yet been heard. The signs of spiritual decline are too many to be ignored. The mainstream churches are rapidly losing theological conviction. Cut off from their original center, they are succumbing to the forces of fundamentalism, on the Right, and on the Left to a liberalism that cuts the remaining ties with the Jewish origins of the Church, and with the Jewish ethics that Christianity once largely observed. Is it not probable that the reason is that the Church has not accomplished the repentance that its God required?

THEOLOGICAL REPENTANCE

Some of the most sensitive of contemporary theologians argue that the Church can only recover its waning vitality by undertaking theological repentance for its teaching about the Jews. All forms of repentance begin with facing truth about the past. In that case, the first task of Christian theologians who have become aware of the need for repentance is to confront the history of Christian anti-Judaism and antisemitism. As we have seen in the course of this inquiry, some are doing so. But they are few at present, and they do not have the ear of their churches, preoccupied as the latter are with other matters.

Nevertheless, if present-day scholarship is at last uncovering the truth about the hostility toward Jews that has distorted Christianity from very early times, that truth can no longer be ignored. Facts such as these cannot be pushed aside as irrelevant without adverse effects on the spiritual condition of the Church.

Acknowledgment of truth ought to lead to corrective action. Whatever in Christian mythology and teaching has spread a false image of the Jews must now be corrected. The old image of the Jews as Christ-killers who rejected and betrayed Jesus must be eliminated from all Christian teaching and replaced with a truthful one. But history also needs to influence theology. How far is it necessary to go in theological reform to achieve a Christianity purified from all antisemitism and the anti-Judaism that is its root?

Whatever the ultimate theological consequences, at least it is certain that the Church needs to repent right now of its indifference to the people of Jesus, not only during the Holocaust, but in the years after it up to the present day, for the indifference has continued until now, in spite of all that we have learned about the Holocaust.

In its present infatuation with liberation theology in all its forms, large sections of the Church have begun to share with the secular Left the idolatry of the Palestinians that mesmerizes it. As we have seen, liberation theology distorts the truth about Jesus' relation to his own people, and is no less hostile toward that people than traditional Christian theology has always been. Without that distortion and that hostility, it probably could not exist as a theology, as opposed to a political program, which may not need theological justification.

Now Israel is being forsaken by the Church as the Jews of Europe were in the thirties, before the Final Solution began to be fully implemented. It is not alarmist to point to the continuing intent of Israel's Islamic and Arab neighbors to eliminate "the Zionist entity" from the map of the Middle East. Without the support of the Christian and post-Christian world, Israel's long-term survival is still far from assured. However, the Christian and post-Christian world is deluding itself if it supposes that Islamic hostility stops with Israel. The more fundamentalist forms of Islam that appeal to the masses in the Islamic countries see the whole West as spiritually decadent and ripe for conquest by Islam in accordance with its original mission. Islam has no Christian squeamishness about the means it employs. While the West worries about supposed injustice to the Palestinians, the regions further East are working toward the Islamic bomb, in which they may well have the assistance of some Islamic republics formerly part of the Soviet Union.

Blind to this greater danger, the Church is proving that today as in past centuries it can only live with the Jewish people when they are in misery; then, there may be efforts, halfhearted ones, to preserve it from destruction. The Vatican has repealed some, though not all, of the worst elements in its traditional anti-Jewish theology. On the other hand, it has never recognized or entered into diplomatic relations with the State of Israel. It continued to flirt with Arafat and lend its moral support to Waldheim while taking steps to initiate diplomatic relations with the former Soviet Union, once the archenemy. Could the Vatican ever recognize that Jerusalem is Jewish, not Christian?

What can we conclude from the actions of the Vatican, if diplomatic relationships with "godless atheistic Communism" are politically possible while the same relations with the Jewish state remain impossible? The World Council of Churches has again and again put its prestige behind the Arab cause, showing minimal understanding for Israel and the historical and theological justification for its presence in the Middle East. Feelings of guilt for the Holocaust,[5] never very profound, are wearing off as the Holocaust recedes into the past and older attitudes reassert themselves. Guilt, it is now apparent, failed to lead to effectual repentance.

Ancient distrust and hatred of the Jewish people now manifest themselves once again, though in disguised form, in hostility toward Israel and failure to recognize the legitimacy of Jewish struggle for existence in their own land. Or else the legitimacy of that struggle is formally recognized but hedged about with so many qualifications that it is nullified. The Church cannot accept an Israel that will defend itself with arms and refuse to relapse into misery.

For Christians at least, the legitimacy of Israel is guaranteed in the Scriptures that the Church calls her own and designates as the Old Testament of the Christian Bible. This legitimation can no longer be evaded by the traditional Christian method of spiritualizing this-worldly realities of which the Bible speaks, in order to refer to Israel as a purely spiritual domain. Either the Church recognizes the divine authority of the biblical legitimation of Israel, or it renounces the authority of its own Scriptures.

There are other signs showing that this is actually what the Church is doing. The dominant liberal ideology of the mainstream Protestant churches increasingly treats the ethics of the Torah as outmoded. Marcionism, the rejection of the Old Testament, is again the favorite heresy of enlightened liberal Christians. It is quite consistent that the divine gift of the land to Israel is treated as an ancient myth without authority for our time, or so spiritualized that it refers to no reality in this world. But if that is an ancient myth, so no less is the Church's claim that the prophecies were fulfilled in Jesus and that the gift of the covenant is really given to the Church.

REMOVING ANTI-JUDAIC ACCRETIONS

Repenting of indifference, even real hostility, to the State of Israel will be difficult enough for the Church of today, and perhaps it cannot be achieved until other and even greater road blocks have been cleared away. A far larger, immensely more difficult task would be the abandonment and formal repudiation of every one of those elements in Christian thought and Christian society that have harmed the Jews. Are those elements simply historical accretions, ethical false steps, impurities that have filtered into an originally pure faith, once devoid of hostility toward Jews and Judaism?

Many take it for granted that this is the case. A number of Evangelicals have told me that a "real Christian" can never be anti-Jewish. But many saints have been, and it is not clear how real is "real." If the anti-Jewish elements in Christian mythology are only historical accretions, they can be removed without damage to the integrity of Christian faith.

Certainly, that would be the next step. Some scholars and theologians who stand by the traditional shape of Christian teaching are endeavoring to take it. They are now going right through Christian history, attempting to weed out anti-Jewish accretions in order to purify their faith. Our own traversal of the ground has shown how deep those accretions, if such they are, go, and how far they have permeated Christian teaching and Christian society. In the end, it will be seen whether they are only accretions.

RETURNING THE JEWISH BIBLE TO THE JEWISH PEOPLE

Where does accretion stop and substance begin? What happens when the pressure of truth and the drive to repentance begin to call in question part of the substance of faith? Every theologian who has attempted to discern the pattern of repentance agrees that as a minimum the theology of supersession must be eradicated from Christian teaching. Christians must instead affirm that God's covenant with the Jewish people is still fully in force. Even this would be extraordinarily difficult for the Catholic Church in particular, as the pope's remarks about the old and new covenants in his 1989 Pentecost addresses imply. Is it necessary to go even further?

It is now historically clear that anti-Judaism did not begin only in the second century, when the theology of supersession first became explicit. Anti-Judaic hostility is unmistakably present in the later parts of the New Testament itself. The sacred Scriptures of the Christian Church are contaminated with the poison of anti-Jewish untruth. Ever since it has been a recognizable religion at all, Christianity has been anti-Jewish.

We saw in earlier chapters that the theology of supersession entailed the take over by the Church of the Jewish Scriptures and a reinterpretation of their meaning so substantial that it is not an exaggeration to call the Old Testament a different book with the same text. Clearly, if the Old Covenant has been superseded, its book belongs to the people of the New Covenant. On the other hand, if Christians must now acknowledge the continuing validity of the covenant with the Jewish people, they must likewise acknowledge the right of the people of the Old Covenant to their own Scriptures and to their own interpretation of them. As we saw, Chrysostom thought such an acknowledgment would simply invalidate Christianity. He may have been right. This is the risk these theologians run in their attempt to right historical injustice.

If the changes these theologians call for are to be accomplished, Scripture itself will now have to be viewed very differently. If it is the vehicle of divine revelation, that revelation was given to the Jewish people. The New Testament itself can no longer be given absolute status, either as a vehicle of undisputed truth – in the light of this history, the proverbial phrase "gospel truth" takes on a new and ironical meaning – or as equally authoritative in all parts. It can no longer provide the authoritative principle of interpretation of the Jewish Scriptures. The new theologies effectively entail the return of the Old Testament to the Jewish people and the dismantling of much of the New as authoritative Scripture.[6]

RETHINKING THE CHRISTOLOGICAL INTERPRETATION OF THE OLD TESTAMENT

The basis for regarding Jesus as the Messiah of the Jewish people is the Old Testament, not the original Hebrew Scriptures. Returning it to its original guardians will necessarily entail giving up the christological or typological interpretation of the Hebrew Scriptures, whereby they are seen as a prophetic witness to Christ. The messianic status of Jesus will thus be undercut from its roots. Thus, either the link between Jesus and the Jewish people would be cut, and his person and role interpreted through purely Gentile categories, or (in line with recent historical scholarship) he will have to be recognized as fully Jewish and unrelated to later Christian developments. Could Christianity survive such changes in any recognizable form?

Here is a crisis that perhaps no other religion has ever faced, a contradiction within faith itself. Christian consciences, awakened by the Holocaust, can no longer tolerate anti-Judaism, still less antisemitism. Conscience demands truth. Yet every believer has to acknowledge the authority of Scripture. Sacred Scriptures say one thing, the awakened conscience and historical truth another. How can the dilemma be resolved?

There is naturally no complete agreement on the way in which it should be done. As we saw in a previous chapter, the issue of the covenant is central. If the covenant with the Jewish people remains in force, what is the covenant on which the Church relies? Can Paul's own wrestling with this issue, especially in the later chapters of Romans, guide the contemporary church? Most of the dialogue theologians seem to pin their hopes on this possibility, although our earlier examination of the historical role of Paul makes this seem far from certain.

PAUL AND JESUS

Will reversing the ancient theology of supersession be enough? The theologians have still to take account of the discovery that Jesus was a fully observant Jew. No one to my knowledge has yet proposed that in faithfulness to Jesus himself the covenant with the Gentiles ought always to have been understood to include the observance of the Torah, or (what would amount to the same thing) the revival of Jewish Christianity. All these theologians base their own thought upon Paul's conviction that God meant to deal with the Gentiles (and perhaps the Jews also) in a new way, without Torah. Their theologies are extremely Pauline in structure even when they are not in detail. They treat as beyond question Paul's decision to bring the gospel to the Gentiles without Torah.

Can Paul provide the vital link between historic Christianity and Jesus the Jew, ensuring that at last Christian theology will not be anti-Jewish and therefore in contradiction with Jesus himself? Our earlier examination of Christian origins may lead to the conclusion that the decision to risk everything on Paul is more questionable than has been supposed. Going back behind the anti-Jewish passages in the later strata of the New Testament to Paul is not enough in itself. The theologians must at the same time demonstrate that nothing in the teaching of Paul was openly or latently anti-Jewish. If they cannot show this conclusively, they have not yet found a sure New Testament basis for a Christian theology altogether purged of anti-Judaism.

The traditional interpretation of Paul and Jesus depicts both as highly critical of the Torah. Jesus is supposed to have died for his criticism of Jewish legalism, while Paul's decision to bring a Torah-free gospel to the Gentile world has been thought to be continuous with Jesus' own teaching. Paul was supposed to have set the Gentiles free from the Torah because it was a form of slavery to commandments, for Jew or Gentile.

The traditional reading of the New Testament firmly linked Paul with Jesus. This is a coherent view, suggesting a consistent development from Jesus through Paul to the early Gentile church. But it is anti-Jewish. Not only does it assume that both Paul and Jesus were profoundly anti-Jewish, but it involves a gross distortion of the way Jews themselves understand the Torah and experience living within it.

It is not enough, therefore, to go behind the anti-Jewish portions of the New Testament and return to Paul, unless he can be understood in quite a new way.

Thus, these theologians also depend for the success of their enterprise on some form or other of the newer interpretations of Paul, briefly examined in Chapter 4. Of those studied, it appears to me that only that of Gaston and similar thinkers looks like being adequate for the purpose, and it is in fact followed by Paul van Buren in his own reinterpretation of systematic theology for the age of the Jewish-Christian reality.

There is a difficulty, however, with which even Gaston has not so far dealt. On these assumptions, Paul does not explain to his readers why the gospel for the Gentiles should be Torah-free, as he clearly did in the traditional interpretation. The natural implication of a theory such as Gaston attributes to Paul would be for the Gentiles to enter the original covenant themselves and to experience the Torah as blessing and life, along with Jews.

This conclusion would certainly have been the natural one for the midrashic writers on whose opinion of Torah outside the covenant Paul is thought to depend; this was a period when Jews were still active in proselytizing. The same alternative could hardly have failed to occur to Paul himself, though it seldom occurs to his modern interpreters as a realistic possibility. It was also the obvious one for many other Jews who believed that Jesus was the Messiah, but opposed Paul's abandonment of the Torah.

If Paul still regarded the Torah as a source of blessing and life for Jews, why should he not have wished to extend the same divine gifts to Gentiles? The question ought to puzzle Christians, if they are not anti-Jewish, and all the more so if we have now to assume that Paul was also not anti-Jewish. But Paul does not answer it expressly in any of his letters, if the new interpretation is correct.

As I argued in Chapter 4, the underlying answer appears to be that Paul thought that God had an even greater blessing to offer, to Jews as well as Gentiles, the blessings of the new age, the overcoming of death and the pouring out of the divine spirit on all flesh. Paul's theology can only be rendered intelligible if we understand that it is eschatological through and through. He had an absolute conviction that the last days had come, and that the return of Christ in glory and the end of history would be accomplished shortly, in the lifetime of those then living.

This conviction was for him at least based on his resurrection vision of Christ, in which he became convinced that Christ had risen from the dead and commissioned him, Paul, as Apostle to the Gentiles. The foundation of what Paul calls "my gospel" is not the tradition of the Jerusalem church, which included some of those who had known and followed Jesus in his lifetime, but his own vision.

Even on this interpretation, Paul's view may seem less compelling once Christians stop thinking of observing the Torah as intrinsically bad, as they have for twenty centuries. Once they start thinking of observing Torah as good, among other weighty reasons because Jesus himself did so, they will perhaps begin to think that more explanation is required. Even if Paul thought he had something better than the Torah to offer the Gentiles, why does he disagree so vehemently with other Christian Jews who believe that the Gentiles should first join the Jewish people and receive the promises of the new age along with them? Since the promises were, after all, made to Jews in the first place, that might be the more natural position to take.

If Paul's Torah-free gospel for the Gentiles depended on his expectation that the new age had already been inaugurated and would very shortly be consummated, today it comes up against such formidable difficulties that it has to be said that it is now no longer viable. In its original eschatological context, such a theology was perhaps not anti-Jewish. Separated from that context, as it soon was, it rapidly became anti-Jewish and remains so today.

Can it now be restored to its original eschatological context, divorcing it from the ecclesiastical evolution it led to? After twenty centuries, there are still no reliable signs of the dawning of the new age, unless the State of Israel is one. Only by radically spiritualizing its original historical meaning has the Church managed to hang on to the ghost of Paul's eschatological expectation. It is no longer possible to take such an expectation as the basis of important theological decisions, affecting the foundations of the Church's faith, as well as the way its Jewish brothers and sisters are to be regarded and treated.

Thus, in the light of our earlier inquiry, the New Testament foundations of the new dialogue theology appear much weaker than at first glance. Whatever validity the gospel of Torah-free Christianity had for Paul himself does not seem easily transferrable to the end of the twentieth century, after Auschwitz and after the historical and theological discoveries of our own time.

We now turn to a yet more formidable difficulty in the way of the new theology of the covenant (or covenants). On the most favorable interpretation of Paul, there is still a massive gap between Jesus and Paul. Not only did Jesus make no criticism of the Torah, seeking only obedience from the heart, he had no interest whatever in a Gentile mission. There is even evidence that he actually discouraged it.[7]

The new interpretation of Paul reopens a long suspected discontinuity between Paul and Jesus. The last generation of New Testament critics thought the gap identified by earlier critics had been closed. If they could suppose that Jesus died for his own criticisms of the Torah, they could see Paul as maintaining the essential thrust of Jesus' own life and teaching. Though they thought that there was little we can know about Jesus in detail, it seemed clear to them that Jesus had died as a rebel against established Judaism.[8]

Today, it is no longer open to us to suppose that Jesus died for his opposition to the Torah. Nor is there the slightest evidence that in his preaching of the kingdom of God he looked forward to a time when the Torah would be abolished and Jew and Gentile alike would live without it.

In relation to Jesus, Paul turns out to be an innovator, and a very drastic one. What justified his innovations? It is clear that in his own thinking the real justification for Paul's actions lay in his vision of the risen Jesus. As Sanders points out, not infrequently in Paul's writings the effective reason for a decision is not mentioned, but remains in the background of his thought, taken for granted by him if not by his readers. Paul presumably "knew" that the gospel for the Gentiles had to be Torah-free, because it was part of what he learned in his vision of the risen Christ.

At any rate, he did not get the idea from the Jerusalem church, most of whose members took a very different view.

If Paul knew that from a vision, can we? Visions are incommunicable, self-authenticating for the visionary himself, but of doubtful authority for others. In a theological context, if they are to have validity and authority, they need more objective support.[9] While we can guess at the eschatological background of Paul's ideas, it is not specific enough to provide a justification for what shows signs of once more becoming a highly controversial decision. Worse, its eschatological foundation has been refuted by history. Jesus did not return in the lifetime of Paul and his converts. Twenty centuries have gone by and that shortly-to-be-expected return has still not occurred. And the theory lacks a basis in Jesus' own life and teaching as we now understand them.

The question of Torah for the Gentiles is accordingly once more an open one, as it has not been since the first century. Future dialogue theologians must address it head on. They will no longer be able to take for granted the abandonment of Torah as the basis of a new covenant with the Gentiles.

Paul cannot easily replace Jesus as the foundation of a *Christian* faith. To put it another way, there cannot be a Christ without Jesus. Paul could speak of Christ, while ignoring the historical Jesus, because he took him for granted. He believed in the risen Christ at the right hand of God, who had sent the Spirit as a token of a final salvation very soon to be made manifest. Contemporary Christians cannot ignore the historical Jesus. What we are coming to know about Jesus does not fit what Paul said about him.

If contemporary Christianity attempts to found theology on Paul alone, ignoring the discontinuity with Jesus, it is in danger of corroding the foundations of faith with dishonesty. As their more conservative opponents clearly see, the theologians could unwittingly create a new religion, a Paulinism without Jesus, which has no common basis with traditional Christianity. Such a religion might continue to bear the name of Christianity, but it would be cut off from its roots. And perhaps it would not succeed in its own lofty aim, of finally purging Christian theology of the corruption of anti-Judaism.

EARLIEST CHRISTIANITY

The dialogue theologians do not depend exclusively on Paul, though his importance for them cannot be exaggerated. They also depend on their reconstruction of the preaching of the original disciples to their fellow Jews. Should the search for a form of Christianity altogether free from anti-Judaic taint perhaps go back behind even Paul, to this "early witness?"

What in fact was the "early witness"? As I pointed out in the fourth chapter, the earliest form of the Christian message must actually have been thoroughly Jewish. It could not have included (as the theologians seem to suppose) a proclamation of

Jesus as a divine Savior, or even as a new means of forgiveness, supplanting those contained in the Torah.

So far as we can reconstruct it, its content was the proclamation of Jesus as a messiah altogether unknown to Jewish tradition, buttressed by interpretations of scriptural texts that were so radically novel that they proved to be unacceptable to the Jewish people. The early witness, like the teaching of Jesus, was not an embryonic form of Christianity, but a form of Judaism, soon to become sectarian.

If Jesus really was the Messiah, in spite of not resembling in any way the figure of prophecy, the people as a whole must be blinded by an unbelief so deep that it amounted to apostasy from the covenant. It must follow that believers in Jesus constituted the faithful remnant of apostate Israel. It would be no great step to regard that remnant simply as Israel. The second-century theology of supersession was not explicitly present in the "early witness," but its seeds were. On Gentile soil, those seeds would grow and proliferate, assuming radically anti-Jewish forms.

Is there an alternative to reliance on the early witness? Theologians can no longer have confidence that a purely Pauline Christianity speaks for God, who made a covenant with Israel, or for Jesus, who lived and taught within that same covenant. Turning to the early witness, we find that it too contained the seeds of the theology of supersession.

We have thought of Christian repentance, or *teshuvah*, return, piercing through and abandoning layer after layer of antisemitic and anti-Jewish development in Christianity. At the end of that painful road back, it discovers that the beginning was not Christian at all, but Jewish. Nevertheless, even this sectarian Judaism contained latent elements of anti-Jewishness. To be sure of avoiding anti-Judaism, theology has to go behind even the beginning of Christianity as an identifiable religion. It must go at least to the early claim that Jesus was the promised Messiah. We now begin to guess that it may have to go back further still.

CAN THE CHURCH STILL CLAIM THAT JESUS WAS THE MESSIAH?

Along the road of repentance, Christian thought now meets once more, with even greater urgency, Rosemary Ruether's famous question of 1974: Can the Church say Jesus is Messiah, without at the same time saying Jews be damned? Her question has been ignored by most theologians, or treated as unworthy of serious consideration, but it will not go away.

My own answer to it is no. The Church cannot say that Jesus is Messiah in a sense that has nothing in common with the Jewish understanding of the term, without also accusing Jews of blindness to what is fundamental to their faith. Whether the consequence of this blindness is held to be damnation eternal or temporal depends on the times. At present, since heaven and hell are less vivid to most contemporary Christians than to their predecessors, it is historically that the

Jews have to be damned. Even Ruether herself seems now prepared to damn Jews in their return to history in their own state.

A Christianity continuing to claim that Jesus is or was the Messiah in any sense cannot avoid being opposed to the Jewish people and the Jewish faith, and all the more today when the state of Israel has been reborn. What would a Christianity that abandoned that claim be? Could it still be called Christian at all?

THEOLOGY AND HISTORY

I have assumed that history has something to do with faith and therefore with theology. It is a commonplace among Christian theologians that Christianity is a historical religion. It does not deal with heavenly abstractions or timeless truths, but with actual historical happenings, past, present, and future, interpreting them in the light of faith in the God who revealed himself to Israel. Its traditional creed nails the Christian religion to history with the words, "suffered under Pontius Pilate." If so, it must meet the test of history.

History cannot deliver faith, but it provides the basis for it. For a historical religion, in the tradition of the Bible, faith must mean at least that in certain historical events, God was at work. In that case, there must be reasonable ground for thinking that the historical events happened and in more or less the way faith claims, or the claim is void. History as a discipline can never give us certainty, but if faith is bound up with it, we are entitled to ask for a reasonable degree of probability, the kind of probability on which we would base any other important decision in our affairs.

Christian theologians have been aware of these difficulties for a long time. Modern theology actually began with the encounter with critical history. In fact, our present inquiry has highlighted some of the basic problems of modern Christian theology, bringing them into sharper focus. This encounter with critical history began in the German universities of the nineteenth century, and it has since spread over the theological world. Protestant thought was affected first, but since the middle of the twentieth century Catholic theologians have begun to deal with the same problems, as biblical scholarship has spread into the Catholic world.

New Testament scholars now have at their disposal a great deal of accurate knowledge about first century Judaism, and they can and do read the Gospels in the light of it. The influx of this knowledge has opened up new possibilities of understanding Jesus, because he can be fitted into the newly revealed Jewish world, as he cannot into early Christianity. A new alternative now faces New Testament criticism, which I have defined as *consistent Judaism or consistent skepticism.* Either we know that Jesus was a Jew in heart and soul, or we know nothing about him worth knowing.

The alternatives are not of equal weight. They are not equally well evidenced, so that the choice between them could be a matter of personal preference or theological style. The evidence for Jesus the Jew is good evidence, and it will prevail, except where old prejudices and habits of thought are too strong. There will always be differences of opinion about details, differing interpretations of particular sayings and incidents. But all of them will now have to be understood within the framework of first-century Judaism.

Once again, as they did in the nineteenth century, the theologians will have to take the evidence for the historical Jesus into consideration when building their theology. Faced with the same problem at a much earlier stage in its development, many nineteenth-century theologians of the liberal school and great numbers of Christians along with them had concluded that Jesus must now be looked on primarily as an ethical teacher, and that the task of the Christian was to follow him in building the kingdom of God on earth.

This liberal theology had profound weaknesses, which have tended to discredit its own practice of taking the historical Jesus fully into account. It was highly assimilated to the post-Enlightenment secular culture that surrounded it, as well as to the nationalism of the new European states. It had no sense of radical evil and therefore could not respond to the great crisis of the thirties and forties, when the Church had to encounter Hitler. It no longer had the spiritual power of the original Christian faith, and it could not energize people to stand up to the almost absolute evil appearing in human history. Liberal theology did not even begin to recognize the Jewishness of Jesus.

But the revived Reformation theology that succeeded it also proved to have weaknesses. Some of its leaders, like Karl Barth and Dietrich Bonhoeffer, did stand up to the Nazi onslaught on the Church with great courage, and Bonhoeffer defended Jews within the Church, but even they failed to grasp the theological significance of the fact that Hitler's real conflict was not with the German church but with the Jewish people. The theologians did not know how to teach Christians to stand up for the Jews when they were in mortal peril. If some nevertheless did so, it was not because of the guidance of their leading theologians.

At the theoretical level, this neo-orthodox theology opened up a new gap between theology and history that could not fail to lead either to instability or to dogmatism. Theology would be vulnerable to fresh discoveries, as proved to be the case, or it would tend to bias historical inquiry by dictating its results in advance, as also in fact happened.

The most important advances in New Testament scholarship since that time have come from taking the Jewish matrix of Christian origins more seriously and understanding it more exactly. The consequent rediscovery of the Jewish Jesus throws the neo-Reformation theology into confusion. Either it must admit frankly that it is not interested in the results of historical criticism, even when they have a high degree of probability, and thus implicitly give up the claim that Christianity is a historical religion, or it must radically alter the content of theology to conform it to the discoveries of the historians.

Abandoning the links with history would lead to a new kind of abstract spirituality having little in common with the Christian past. Alternatively (with a twist toward what may be called neo-liberalism) theology could remodel Jesus to suit its own needs, as various forms of liberation theology are doing at the present time. Thus, we now have new versions of the myth: the feminist Jesus, the black Jesus, and the revolutionary Jesus. In such a theology, Christianity is indeed said to be based on Jesus, but the Jesus it is based on never existed.

Must the path of Christian repentance, following the second alternative, lead further back still, further than anyone has dared to go yet, behind Paul, and even behind the early witness? Could it lead all the way to Jesus the Jew? What would it be like to go in this more Jewish direction?

THE ALTERNATIVES FOR CHRISTIANS

The simultaneous discovery of the anti-Jewishness of Christianity and the Jewishness of Jesus has created a crisis for Christian faith, still realized by only a few, yet rendered maximally urgent by the Holocaust and the events of the rest of the twentieth century. The divine-human figure at the center of the Christian myth turns out to have been a Jew with nothing distinctive in common with Christianity. When we consider the implications of this discovery for orthodox Christianity, Catholic and Protestant, they are nothing less than startling.

If Jesus was indeed God incarnate, it follows that in becoming a believing and observant Jew God must have validated Judaism for all time against its religious rivals, including Christianity. This is not a contradiction the Christian mind can tolerate. Alternatively, Christians may have to realize that the doctrine of the Incarnation itself was developed at a time when anti-Judaism was the central organizing principle of Christian theology. Perhaps the doctrine of the Incarnation cannot be separated from the complex of anti-Judaic ideas around which Christian theology was originally structured. The abandonment of anti-Judaism in theology may be impossible without relinquishing the central doctrine of divine incarnation.

The spread of the myth led step by easy step to the antisemitism that culminated in the Holocaust. True, when the myth first took shape it was not antisemitic, in the modern sense, for racial ideas were altogether absent. But the myth was anti-Jewish from the first, and over the centuries it became more so in the popular mind.

The anti-Judaic myth continued to evolve, and in due course it became the basis for modern racial antisemitism and its post-Holocaust successors. None of the steps was a long one, and each seemed to follow more or less logically from its predecessor. This long incremental development culminated in the loss of two-thirds of European Jewry in the Holocaust and continuing international hostility toward the Jewish people in their reborn national state. Christians can no longer evade the suspicion that the course of this development was not accidental, but that it was the natural unfolding of something latent from the first. At least the possibility must be squarely faced.

The resulting crisis of faith allows the Church few viable alternatives. The first option is to use what the psychoanalysts call the mechanism of denial, to turn away from the discoveries of critical history because they are too painful to be taken in and responded to. This is the path of fundamentalism, being taken by increasing numbers all over the world today. Fundamentalism manages to hold on to traditional Christianity by denying all historical discoveries that conflict with its own version of tradition, while welcoming with open arms any that seem to support it. In particular, fundamentalism cannot come to terms with the Jewishness of Jesus, and (without an honorable inconsistency) it can only continue to affirm the anti-Jewish elements in the New Testament.

Yet fundamentalism cannot be ignored, because it is not only a defensive reaction against historical findings that do not fit a myth. It also contains a legitimate protest against the moral and cultural decadence of a world that has lost contact with its spiritual roots.

Unfortunately, fundamentalism cannot provide the remedy for the evils it correctly discerns, because of its own fundamental dishonesty and refusal to come to terms with historical truth. Christian fundamentalists are committed to viewing Judaism through a distortion of the true nature of Jewish faith, since they also read Paul in traditional ways. Even those fundamentalists who are most friendly to Israel and the Jewish people look forward to their ultimate extinction by conversion to Christ.

If the choice is made to confront the disturbing results of historical research, there are really only two alternatives left for the Christian world. The first and for many today the much easier alternative is to abandon the traditional concern for the historical basis of the faith, cutting the links between Christianity and its Jewish parent and treating Christianity as one possible myth among many others. In the late twentieth century, this neo-Marcionite theology is far more prevalent in the mainstream churches than is generally realized.

In the second century, the Church struggled with the claim of Marcion that Christianity was an altogether new religion without basis in Judaism. Its God was wholly other than the God of the Jews, and its Christ had not been predicted in its Scriptures. The Church defeated Marcionism at the cost of further radicalizing its existing anti-Judaism. The Jewish Scriptures were retained but transformed into an Old Testament read as one long indictment of the Jews.

Modern liberal Christians are not Marcionite in any exact sense. They do, however, share Marcion's view that the God of the Old Testament is a different and inferior God, and that Judaism is an inferior religion. In practice, they have already jettisoned the Old Testament. But they cannot do this, as we can now see, without also parting with Jesus himself, since his own life was rooted in the Torah. Moreover, they cannot even maintain anything like the traditional Christology, for it too was rooted in the Jewish Bible, albeit in a very novel reading of it.

The neo-Marcionite solution, dropping the Christian connection with Judaism and the Old Testament, accords with the religious pluralism forced on all of us by the global village. It allows Christianity to ally itself with the other world religions instead of with the Jewish people and its biblical faith. It fits the fascination with non-Western forms of spirituality that influenced so many of us in the sixties—and it was no fad, for we were being introduced to genuine spiritual riches, even if few of us knew how to make use of them for ourselves.

In this ecumenical or generic spirituality, Christianity is one optional element in a program of human growth. It is historically transcended in favor of a wholly modern pan-human spirituality, abandoning the concreteness of the biblical faith. It is no accident that those who adhere to this program generally have less sympathy for Judaism than for any other religion in the mythical mixture, for Judaism is rooted in history and cannot be subsumed in timeless myth. Of this alternative such a thinker as Joseph Campbell is a popular and distinguished representative.

The alternative would be to return to the God of the biblical revelation, whom Jesus knew and worshipped. By moving in this authentically theological direction it becomes once more possible (as it is not for liberalism) to recognize radical evil and the ultimate triumph of God over it.

Such a theology would now involve a rethinking of Christianity from its roots. It would be necessary to rethink theology, not only in the light of historical discoveries, but also and even more in the light of the biblical faith in the one God, who revealed himself through the events of Israel's history, who gave the Torah through Moses, who spoke by the prophets, who has not abandoned his covenant with his original people, and who continues despite all appearances to rule his world and will finally manifest himself as its true and only King. For such a faith, Jewish and perhaps also Christian, God remains Lord of history, in spite of all its confusion, and in spite of the apparent prevailing of evil.

This is the God in whom Jesus believed and whom he found to be near. I would be the last to minimize the difficulties of such a faith, especially after Auschwitz.[10] Nevertheless, there is no existing alternative that can seriously be called theological, in the sense of remaining rooted in the biblical tradition. Along no other path can Christians begin to meet the agonizing problems of an anti-Jewish Christianity once more encountering the Jewish Jesus.

Today, the task for Christian theologians is to rethink from the foundations up the relationship of Christianity to Jesus, and to Judaism, the religion of Jesus. This course is the most risky, for Christianity may not survive it. But if it succeeds at all, whatever does survive will have sound spiritual roots, sounder by far than those from which other alternatives stem, because it will be based on honesty and on truth, and on openness to the God who revealed himself in the history of Israel, whom Jesus called Father.

In short, contemporary Christians appear to be faced by a choice between mythology and history. For two thousand years, Christianity has been based on a myth that presented Jesus as an opponent of the way of Torah by which his people lived and as the innocent victim of their hostility and blood lust. The myth has inspired large sections of the human race, and it would be grotesquely unfair to suggest that all the consequences have been negative.

The mythic Christ has served as a potent image of divine compassion, assuring people who saw themselves as sinners of divine mercy and forgiveness, and teaching them to extend the same mercy and forgiveness to others. The recollections of the actual Jesus preserved through the myth have offered Christians a powerful model to foster the development of their own innate spirituality. Through the myth, faith in the one God and knowledge of the Hebrew Scriptures have been spread throughout the world.

Tragically, these spiritual benefits for so many millions could not be achieved without the propagation at the same time of the anti-Jewish mythology whose development we have attempted to understand. Now sensitive Christians are confronted with the realization that these elements in their myth are historically indefensible and ethically unacceptable. Could there be a Christianity that jettisoned the myth while retaining its spiritual energy and transforming power?

Put in the simplest terms, it appears to me that Christians must now choose between a faith based on the traditional myth, even in a purified form, and one based on the rediscovered historical Jesus. They cannot have both. They must choose between the Gentile religion of Paul and Jesus the Jew.

Going back just one step behind Paul would presumably mean attempting to revive Jewish Christianity in some form. It would mean establishing once more a sect (however large) of observant Jews believing in Jesus as the Messiah. Today, that sounds uncomfortably like "Jews for Jesus," an evangelical or fundamentalist Christian group that addresses a mission to Jews with the claim that it is unnecessary for them to dispense with Jewish customs in order to believe that Jesus is the Messiah and to be saved by him. Apart from the total inadmissibility of missions to the Jews after the Holocaust, it is clear that such an outlook is incompatible with Jewish faith and observance and could never be acceptable to genuine Jews.

Such Jewish converts to Christianity might retain "Jewish customs," but they would no longer be living by covenant and Torah. For the "messianic Jews," Jesus is not just the Messiah but the divine Savior of fundamentalist belief. If critical history is right, Jesus would have been the first to protest against such a distortion of his message to his fellow-Jews. This is not Jewish Christianity, and in all probability it cannot be revived today. Too much has happened since its day, and we have learned, or ought to have learned, too much from history.

There is nothing in the life and teaching of Jesus, as he now appears to the best Christian scholarship, to give any basis for a Torah-free mission to the Gentile world. Clearly, Jesus himself had little or no interest in any mission to the Gentiles, but if he had, it is certain that he would have shared the view of the Pharisees that Gentiles could and should become Jewish proselytes. Paul's Torah-free Judaism for Gentiles (a real oxymoron) was a discovery, or invention, of dazzling brilliance and huge historical consequence, but it had nothing to do with the real Jesus.

Any form of Christian faith or thought that takes Paul as its starting point is committed to the myth at the expense of history, and thus is without solid defense against the anti-Judaic tendencies of the myth. But the return to history is also at the expense of myth and its imaginative power to inspire and transform. Could a new myth grow up around the rediscovered Jewish Jesus? It seems unlikely. Myths cannot be created artificially, in spite of the attempts of some intellectuals to create new ones or recreate some that have died a natural death.

Even to consider this possibility is to evade the real challenge of history. No Gentile religion whatsoever can be plausibly based on the historical Jesus. The only religion that could legitimately be based on Jesus is some form of Judaism.

Thus, as we probe further in the light of the Holocaust and of historical discovery into the dilemma of contemporary Christianity, we find the issues becoming sharper still. The choice between mythology and history is also a choice between any form of traditional Christianity and the religion of Jesus himself, Judaism. Once *all* the anti-Jewish elements have been removed from Christianity, what is left turns out to be Judaism.

JESUS OR CHRISTIANITY?

Here, finally, we have come to the heart of the contemporary crisis of Christendom. *Christianity without Jesus is unimaginable. Christianity with Jesus may be impossible.*

According to the universal tradition of Christianity, Jesus is the ultimate authority for Christians. We now find that the only kind of religion for which Jesus himself can plausibly be taken as an authority is the Torah-observant Judaism of the early first century. This is the unequivocal outcome of the research that now reveals Jesus as an observant Jew, in no conflict with the Torah or its guardians. Christianity as the world has always known it, Catholic or Protestant, orthodox, neo-orthodox or liberal, has turned out to be devoid of foundation in Jesus himself.

Is Christianity then fatally flawed and without historical basis? Is its chronic anti-Jewishness, often and easily sliding over into antisemitic hatred, a defect so grave as to vitiate its spiritual contribution to human beings? The question is not easily answered. Most Christians, aware only of what is good and spiritual in their religion, and unaware of what Christianity has done to Jews, will repudiate the suggestion with indignation, wondering how it could even be raised. Many Jews, the victims or the descendants of the victims of such hatred, will be more disposed to doubt the validity of the Christian claim to have benefitted mankind. In the end, only God can strike the balance.

The spiritual crisis, however, cannot be separated from the theological one, and together they must be confronted by contemporary Christians. I believe that the double crisis for Christianity, precipitated by its failure in the time of the Holocaust to stand up for the Jewish people, together with the discovery by modern scholarship of the Jewishness of Jesus himself, now demands an honest response. If Christianity is not already fatally flawed by its own antisemitism and by its concomitant desertion of Jesus, not to face the crisis would now create a fatal flaw. But the crisis is deep; it goes to the very roots of Christianity. Not just its anti-Jewishness but its non-Jewishness are now in question.

Christianity now appears to the critically alerted eye as an amalgam and not a pure substance. Its Jewish origins have been adulterated at a very early stage with much that it is not only non-Jewish but inherently antithetical to the Jewish spirit, so purely embodied in Jesus himself. Is it possible that Christian humanism, the passion for truth, justice, and human brotherhood in which Christians rightly rejoice, and its compassion for sinners, belong to the Jewish element transmitted through Jesus himself, whereas the power seeking, the cruelty, the support of and connivance at injustice and oppression, and above all the antisemitic and racial hatred that can, even today, successfully invoke the Christian name, represent pagan pollution of that original pure stream?

If that turned out to be so, the way forward for Christianity could only be to purge itself of its pagan elements, the adulteration of the pure metal of Jesus' Jewish legacy, and to identify itself more radically than ever before with its own origins. The contemporary struggle for the soul of Christianity turns into an agonizing wrestling with the question that must now be raised: can there be any conclusion of the movement of repentance, or return, short of actual return of the Church to the Jewish people?

If we go back even further than the beginnings of Christianity as a religion, back to Jesus himself, we are brought to nothing else but Judaism. If Christians are not antisemites, perhaps they are – or should be – Jews. If Christians wish to be faithful to Jesus, they must be where he is, not where the enemies of his people, and therefore his enemies, are.

Many will find such a prospect terrifying. They have heard so many bad things about Judaism that to join Jesus in adhering to its ways seems like a betrayal in itself. The fear and reluctance evoked by the prospect of being Jewish in order to remain faithful to Jesus is the measure of the antisemitism in every Christian mind.

Historical criticism, such as we have been practicing in this inquiry, is also a spiritual task, a task of discrimination between the real and the unreal, between the true God and idols. By removing corruptions and impurities from faith, it opens up freer channels between man and the divine reality. In fact, it is one modern form of the ancient struggle against paganism and idolatry, so destructive to human beings and their spiritual identity. When Christians strip away the layers of their historic anti-Jewishness, they break at the same time with form after form of idolatry.

If they are willing to respond to it, the repentance to which the voice from Auschwitz calls Christians with a categorical and divine imperative will indeed sweep away much that has been precious to them. It will not and cannot sweep away their God or the assurance of his compassion and forgiveness for sinners.

These certainties have always been regarded as the center of the gospel, and they were the heart of Jesus' own teaching. As we can now see, that teaching was fully Jewish. Theological repentance will not sweep away what was once called "the essence of Christianity." Almost everything normally associated with Christianity may have to go, but the spiritual essence remains, with its purity enhanced. Christianity's essence is and always was Jewish.

Christians have now to make a revolutionary discovery. What they found spiritually attractive in Jesus and won their hearts, his teaching of compassion and forgiveness, his courage in standing up to his critics, his single-mindedness to the point of death, all this is Jewish. They thought they were being attracted to anti-Jewishness, when all the time it was Jesus' Jewishness that attracted them. If they love Jesus, how can they not love his own people and his own faith? Can they then allow Jesus himself to teach them the way into Jewish faith and life?

The logic of Christian repentance in the time after Auschwitz, once fully faced, leads the Church to nothing less than a grand *return* to its origins, to "the rock from whence it was hewn." Christians cannot be sure of dealing with the Church's poisoned heritage of antisemitism and the anti-Judaism that was its precursor without returning all the way to Jesus himself. This is the final conclusion of our inquiry into the history of Christian anti-Judaism.

Short of Jesus the Jew, we cannot be certain that there is any theological stopping point in the movement of return that would not once more set the development rolling that culminated in the horrors of the Middle Ages and the twentieth century. But there can be no return to Jesus without a return to Judaism, to the people with whom God made his covenant, for that is where the real Jesus is to be found.

COULD THE SYNAGOGUE RECEIVE THE CHURCH?

If we could imagine the Church, like the prodigal son, now setting forth on the long journey back to the Father's house, repenting of the sin of antisemitism, and leaving the husks of fundamentalism and liberation theology, we can be sure that it would receive the Father's welcome. But if it were to knock on the door of the synagogue and ask for admittance, what would it find within?

Perhaps there would be a welcome, though we cannot be certain of it in advance. But even so, the returning Church would find a house hardly less disordered than its own. Contemporary Judaism too has been disrupted by the crises of modernity, and the immense trauma of the Holocaust has only made those stresses more intense. While Jewish life displays a spiritual vitality absent in the last decades from its Christian counterpart, I do not believe that Judaism in any of its branches has yet found an adequate response to modernity, let alone to the cataclysmic events of the Holocaust and the rebirth of the state of Israel, though each may have some contribution to offer to a synthesis that has not yet appeared. It may take decades or conceivably centuries for a new synthesis to emerge in response to a crisis no less great than that which led to the emergence of rabbinic Judaism in the period after the loss of the Temple and of Jerusalem. Unfortunately, though the need is not less, we do not see today leaders of the creativity, daring and innovativeness of the Rabbis of the first and second centuries. Perhaps future generations may be able to identify them among our contemporaries where we cannot.

Judaism has its own equivalents of fundamentalism and liberation theology, desperate attempts at isolation from modernity, and also wholesale surrender to it. Is it ready, with the best will in the world, to receive a repentant church and to give it a home within the covenant? Jews are seldom enthusiastic about even individual converts. Not infrequently, they regard them as crazy. How could the Jewish people cope with a mass return of the Gentile church?

Is contemporary Judaism ready to repossess Jesus and install him where he belongs, among its own spiritual teachers? Jesus is the only bridge across which the repentant church could ever walk back to its original home. But he cannot be a bridge until Jews fully acknowledge him as their own. This is not so easy for Jews as Christians may suppose. Many Jewish thinkers, however, do now believe that the time has come to repossess Jesus for his own people. Such thinkers see him, as we have endeavored to show him in this book, as unequivocally Jewish.

Traditionally, however, Jews have accepted Jesus somewhat at Christian valuation, and therefore as a deluded teacher and false messiah, responsible for hideous atrocities carried out upon themselves. Some eminent Jewish scholars continue to hold Jesus responsible for Christianity. Jews cannot repossess Jesus until they are able to detach him in their own minds from responsibility for all that Christians have said about them and done to them in his name. Many Jews find the new picture of Jesus as disconcerting as Christians do, but for very different reasons. Only gradually can they be expected to absorb the results of historical scholarship and accept Jesus as the brother he always was.

If Jesus was a brother to Jews, and never meant to be anything else, is it possible that he would actually have something to say in the contemporary debate amongst his fellow Jews, even after twenty centuries of Christian hostility in his name? It is not easy to imagine Jesus being at home in any of the clashing movements into which contemporary Judaism is divided, all of them reactions to the crisis of modernity.

It is impossible to suppose that he would be in favor of abandoning traditional observance, for he knew its spiritual value from within, because he himself lived it. It is equally difficult to suppose that he would support fundamentalist insistence on the minor details of observance while "neglecting the weightier matters of the Torah,"[11] because he denounced it in his lifetime. Jesus would certainly stand today for the *halachah* but equally certainly for a compassionate and flexible interpretation of it.

We should beware, however, of enlisting his symbolic support for any modern program. Jesus was not a modern man, and perhaps has no immediate answers for such specifically modern problems. He was however one of the most spiritual of human beings of whom we know anything, and spirituality is timeless.

Modernity in its inception and subsequent developments was a revolution against all religious constraints, including religiously sanctioned ethics; it was a refusal to allow the forces of human vitality and creativity to be bound down and restrained by religious law. In its most exacerbated form, modernity had to see itself as a rebellion against Judaism, for the Torah was the law of God. Nazism was not only a revolt against modernity, a romantic retreat to an unreal past. It was also a part of modernity itself. On Kristallnacht, the Nazis broke open the ark in the synagogues, seized the Torah scrolls, tore them up, and trampled them into the mud.

As a rebellion alone, modernity has proved spiritually empty, and its disastrous consequences are becoming more evident every day in the Western world. The liberation of the human intellect in science and technology has brought many material benefits. We can never go back on the discovery of the individual and of moral maturity that the Enlightenment brought, which is the foundation of democracy as well as of individual spiritual health: we will always remain both free and responsible in all our actions, whether we accept the fact or not. But for Judaism, these ideas are not such novelties as they were for the Christian world.

How have we moderns used that freedom of choice? The signs are that we have by no means learned to use it. The modern revolution has brought about the liberation of the ego, but it has not yet liberated the true Self (what was traditionally called the soul) from the ego. That is a far greater task, and it still lies before us as modern people.

Religion was not free from blame in the modern revolt. Whether Jewish or Christian, it did indeed function oppressively, producing guilt and rage, which were often directed unjustly at God, instead of the human corruptions to which religion is subject. Our growing disillusionment with modernity cannot lead us back to a form of religion untouched by that rebellion against its oppressiveness, or even rendered more oppressive still in reaction against the evils of modernity, as in Iran. There must be a third choice, a path for modern man to the spirit.

We have looked at Jesus' deep anger at professed guardians of the Torah who cleaned the outside of the cup while leaving the inside filthy, the whitewashed graves who looked outwardly pure but were inwardly full of all kinds of pollution. His anger was so intense that it is an embarrassment to Christians who have to think of him as perfect. They could only live comfortably with it by interpreting it as a divine attack on Judaism as such. Instead of seeing what its true target was, obsessive and compulsive religiosity, devoid of love and compassion, wherever it may be found, they conveniently chose to misinterpret it as a fundamental criticism of Judaism.

We have seen that this interpretation is false. Jesus did indeed clash with some other Jews and they with him. But he never clashed with the Jewish way. Like the prophets who were his model and inspiration, and like the grand tradition of Jewish spirituality in all times, Jesus set forth a clear path between the alternatives of obsessiveness and laxity. It is the path of love.

Love by its nature is always free or it would not be love. Love cannot be commanded and in fact it is not. In the Shema, which Jesus quoted when invited to summarize the Torah, the commandment is not simply to love God, for this is natural and inevitable, as it is natural and inevitable to love one's parents, but to love him in a particular way, with the whole heart, the whole soul, and the whole strength of a human being. It is to love without division of loyalty, for God himself is one.

In the form it eventually assumed in the Jewish prayer book, the recitation of the Shema goes on to speak of various symbolic actions that Jews have traditionally taken literally, actions not important in themselves, for they are not themselves love, but as reminders, reminders which in one form or another human beings find necessary. The whole structure of the Torah can thus be seen as the way in which a people is constantly reminded to love God, who has chosen Israel simply because he loved this insignificant and rebellious people and for no other reason.

Jesus was fully at home in the Torah because he lived out of the love at the heart of his own being. Love taught him that God has compassion for the sinners and does not wait for them to return before reaching out to them. But love also taught him that it is not enough for the sinner to repent in a moment of revulsion from his past. He needs fully to return to the way of life, the Torah of God. But in turn love taught him that observance, however necessary, is only the framework and the reminder: love itself is the essence. Such a teaching is timeless. It is vital for Christians to remember that Jesus shared it with the sages of his own people.

Unfortunately, however, the Jesus the Gospels record was silent on a matter of at least equal importance, either because the gospel writers were not interested in his teaching on it, because he had nothing to say on the subject, or because he looked forward to its realization only in the kingdom of God whose nearness he proclaimed. I mean the corporate, even political aspect of what Martin Buber terms "realization," the actualization of divine love and justice in the historical life of a community. During the centuries when Jews were absent from history, without political power, such an ideal was inherently unrealizable, and was postponed altogether to a messianic age hoped for always but never apparent. No doubt its complete realization also belongs to the messianic age.

The return of the Jewish people into history, away from Christian tutelage, opens up possibilities that cry out for realization, not only for its own sake, but for that of the nations. Yet Christianized, Diaspora thinking continues to influence even those who claim to have cast it off most. Whether among the pietists or the secularists, the Christian divorce between piety and politics prevails, even in Israel. If the covenant is still in force, it obliges a whole people, no less than in biblical times, to live by the love and justice enshrined in the Torah. This means laws and political relationships, not just individual observance. Neither the religious nor the secularists in Israel appear to have grasped the immense challenge to creative thinking and action inherent in Israel's calling to be the people of God, not as a religious abstraction but as concrete historical reality.

These thoughts run through Buber's remarkable and apparently now less known series of addresses on Judaism.[12] His thought moves in long sweeps, and almost defies brief quotation. One address, however, ends with these pregnant words:

> Bergson speaks of an "active mysticism." Where is this to be found, if not here? Nowhere else is man's essential doing so closely bound up with the mystery of being. And for this very reason the answer to the silent question asked by the modern world is found herein. Will the world perceive it? But will Jewry itself perceive that its very existence depends upon the revival of its religious existence? The Jewish state may assure the survival of a nation of Jews, even one with a culture of its own; Judaism will live only if it brings to life again the primal Jewish relationship between God, the world, and mankind.[13]

FINAL THOUGHTS

Many will say that to speak of a grand return of the Church to Jesus the Jew and to his own Jewish people, from whence it came, is visionary, and can have little to do with the here and now, the practical task facing the Church. Visionary it is, and it suggests something even more visionary.

Perhaps if the grand return were ever to be accomplished, it would be the ultimate fulfillment of a hope of which the leaders of the early church all dreamed in different ways, the prophetic hope of the bringing in of the Gentiles in the last days to worship the God of Israel. Christianity would never have existed if the leaders of the early Church had not shared this hope. Paul thought it would be accomplished in one way, James in another. Perhaps they were both wrong. Their hope has not yet begun to be realized. Perhaps the first glimpses of its possibility are now coming into view.

The painful story of Christian antisemitism shows that that hope has so far been frustrated. The Church has not proved to be a way in to the covenant for the Gentile world. Rather, it has kept the Gentiles away from the covenant. It has, to be sure, made known the one God to millions who might never otherwise have heard of him. It has spread the knowledge of Jewish ethics all over the world. It has provided a vehicle for the expression of the innate spirituality of many righteous among the nations.

It has also carried anti-Judaism to regions that might otherwise never have heard of Jews, and it has polluted the purity of biblical faith with much that is pagan and destructive to the human spirit. Nevertheless, if a repentant church were ever to return to its origins and rejoin the Jewish people *en masse*, that would be a bringing in of the Gentiles beyond anything Paul in his day was able to conceive.

I am no prophet, and I should step no further into mysteries that perhaps belong to messianic times. Certainly I cannot guess how far away those days are. If God is God, he will beyond doubt one day assert his kingship over this world of confusion and loss of spirit. Human beings can only attempt to be ready.

The double crisis, created by the Holocaust and by historical discovery, sets before Christians the most revolutionary choice that has faced them since the Church first split off from Judaism. I fully expect that the reaction of most will be to ignore the pressing need for choice and go on as before. In the foreseeable future, it is not likely that the Church as a whole will make any such grand return to its origins. What conclusions individuals will draw is for them to decide in their own hearts.

Much of the scholarship on which this book is based is new, and it will take time to be more widely absorbed. Its newness does not mean that it can be discounted. I do not believe that these issues, once raised, as modern historical experience and modern scholarship raise them, will ever go away until they are resolved. I did not invent them: I have only drawn attention to them. My hope is that others will also see them and respond to them in time to prevent a second catastrophic outcome for the Jewish people, a catastrophe that this time could involve the whole world.

Appendix: The Three Accounts of Peter's Acclamation of Jesus as the Messiah

Mark 8:27–33	*Matthew 16:13–23*	*Luke 9:18–22*
Jesus and his disciples set out for the villages of Caesarea Philippi, and on the way he asked his disciples, "Who do people say I am?"	When he came to the territory of Caesarea Philippi, Jesus asked his disciples, "Who do people say the son of man is?"	One day, when he had been praying by himself in the company of his disciples, he asked them, "Who do the people say I am?"
They answered, "Some say John the Baptist, others Elijah, others one of the prophets."	They answered, "Some say John the Baptist, others Elijah, others Jeremiah, or one of the prophets."	They answered, "Some say John the Baptist, others Elijah, others that one of the prophets of old has come back to life."
"And you," he asked, "who do you say I am?" Peter replied: "You are the Messiah."	"And you," he asked, "who do you say I am?" Simon Peter answered: "You are the Messiah, the Son of the living God."	"And you," he said, "who do you say I am?" Peter answered, "God's Messiah."

	Then Jesus said: "Simon son of Jonah, you are favoured indeed! You did not learn that from any human being; it was revealed to you by my heavenly Father. And I say to you: you are Peter, the Rock; and on this rock I will build my church, and the powers of death shall never conquer it. I will give you the keys of the kingdom of Heaven; what you forbid on earth shall be forbidden in heaven, and what you allow on earth shall be allowed in heaven."	
Then he gave them strict orders not to tell anyone about him;	He then gave his disciples strict orders not to tell anyone that he was the Messiah.	Then he gave them strict orders not to tell this to anyone.
and he began to teach them that the son of man had to endure great suffering, and to be rejected by the elders, chief priests, and scribes; to be put to death, and to rise again three days afterwards. He spoke about it plainly.	From that time Jesus began to make it clear to his disciples that he had to go to Jerusalem, and endure great suffering at the hands of the elders, chief priests, and scribes; to be put to death, and to be raised again on the third day.	And he said: "The son of man has to endure great sufferings, and to be rejected by the elders, chief priests, and scribes, to be put to death, and to be raised again on the third day."
At this Peter took hold of him and began to rebuke him. But Jesus, turning and looking at his disciples, rebuked Peter. "Out of my sight, Satan!" he said. "You think as men think, not as God thinks."	At this Peter took hold of him and began to rebuke him: "Heaven forbid!" he said. "No, Lord, this shall never happen to you." Then Jesus turned and said to Peter, "Out of my sight, Satan; you are a stumbling block to me. You think as men think, not as God thinks."	

Notes

INTRODUCTION

1. The word *antisemitism,* coined in nineteenth-century Germany (German, *Antisemitismus*) was originally a disguised way of expressing the writer's real meaning. Hatred was cloaked in pseudoscientific language by the reference to "Semitism," a concept corresponding to nothing in the real world. Antisemites are hostile to *Jews,* not to "Semitism." Over the years, different interpretations of the word have led to different spellings in English, of which the most widely used is probably "anti-Semitism." The pioneering author James Parkes always believed that it should be spelled "antisemitism" in English, without a hyphen, as in German. (The German initial capital is imply the result of the practice of capitalizing all nouns in written German.) He thought that the word should be used to designate the hating attitude of antisemities, and should not be dignified with a capital, while further currency should not be given to the phony concept of Semitism by separating it from the rest of the word by means of a hyphen, and giving it a capital letter. Some careful writers follow him in this spelling. I believe it would be the best solution, if sufficient agreement could be obtained. See also p. 325.
2. YHWH is a conventional transliteration of the four Hebrew consonants of the name of God, not to be pronounced by Jews, and usually represented in the English versions by "the LORD," corresponding to the Hebrew Adonai, which is actually read where these consonants are found in the text. (In Hebrew Bibles, the vowels of Adonai are placed under the four letters of the original divine name. When a late medieval Christian writer, ignorant of this practice, encountered such texts, he thought the divine name was Jehovah, which is approximately how the resulting word, as it seemed to him to be, would have sounded. Of course, the biblical writers never called God Jehovah.) Though in early times it must have been pronounced more freely, and forms of it seem to enter into personal names, by Jesus' time it was pronounced only once a year on the Day of Atonement, within the Most Holy place. The custom now growing up among Christian writers of spelling out a vocalized form of the consonantal name (which is by no means certainly correct) is offensive to observant Jews and should be avoided.
3. The term *deicide* has been used for much of Christian history as a description of the Jews. Literally, it means God-killing. Of course, God cannot be killed. However, since it was

believed that the Jews killed Christ and that Christ was God incarnate, it was thought suitable to magnify the supposed crime by the use of this term. Few would now defend it.

4. The table is reproduced in Chapter 6, pp. 204ff.
5. I am here quoting Rosemary Ruether. In her important book *Faith and Fratricide*, (San Francisco: Seabury Press, 1974), she uses the phrase to characterize the Christian view of the behavior of the Jewish people throughout their history, of which the killing of Christ was thought to be the paradigm. In Chapter 6, I will consider her findings at length.
6. The phrase is Heinrich Heine's. He himself, born Jewish, had purchased the ticket, but later came to reproach himself for doing so.
7. Many of the early Zionists were of course Marxists themselves. But this was before the Left allied itself with the Palestinians and found it convenient to denigrate Israel as a manifestation of imperialism and colonialism.

CHAPTER 1

1. This feature of the Christian myth has at least one partial parallel, and it is a highly significant one. In the story of the origins of Islam, the Prophet is said to have hoped to win many converts among the Jews of his own area, because his message fulfilled and completed, or so he thought, what they themselves already believed. He was disappointed, and met with almost total rejection and even active hostility from the Jews of the locality. Muhammad was led to order the massacre of hundreds of Jews at Medina. This story is primarily responsible for the very unfavorable reputation of Jews among Muslims, which often descends into actual antisemitism. Islam, like Christianity, is a theology of supersession. Because all that is true in former revelations is contained in the revelation to Muhammad, Judaism must be regarded as totally superseded and without further validity. (For the theological implications of the term *superseded*, see Chapter 5 in particular.)
2. See Joseph Campbell, *The Hero with a Thousand Faces*, 2d ed. (Princeton, NJ: Princeton University Press, 1968).
3. From the Apostles' Creed, probably the most widely used Christian statement of faith.
4. Among these were a Pakistani film that represented Rushdie as Jewish, presumably the worst insult its makers could think of.
5. So Rushdie informed his readers in an important article in the periodical *Granta* (reprinted in a first American edition under the title of *In Good Faith* [New York: Viking Penguin, 1990]). More recently, he announced his conversion to Islam and apologized to Muslims for any pain he had caused them by what he wrote, though without withdrawing any of it. So far, there is no indication that these actions have eliminated the threat to his life.
6. See E. P. Sanders, *Paul and Palestinian Judaism* (London: SCM Press, 1977), pp. 33–59, and *Jesus and Judaism* (Philadelphia: Fortress Press, 1985), pp. 24ff; Geza Vermes, "Jewish Studies and New Testament Interpretation," *Jesus and the World of Judaism* (Philadelphia: Fortress Press, 1984), pp. 62–66.
7. See David Flusser, *Jesus*, trans. Roland Walls (New York: Herder and Herder, 1969); Hyam Maccoby, *Revolution in Judaea* (London: Orbach and Chambers, 1973); Geza Vermes, *Jesus the Jew: A historian's reading of the gospels* (London: Collins, 1973; Philadel-

phia: Fortress Press, 1983); *Jesus and the World of Judaism* (Philadelphia: Fortress Press, 1984); E. P. Sanders, *Jesus and Judaism* (Philadelphia: Fortress Press, 1985); James H. Charlesworth, *Jesus within Judaism: New light from exciting archaeological discoveries* (New York: Doubleday, The Anchor Bible Reference Library, 1988).

All these writers have an exact and extensive knowledge of first century Judaism. Not all of them are equally consistent in starting from Judaism and interpreting the gospel record from that perspective. Sanders and Charlesworth still retain some of the habits of the guild of New Testament scholars to which they belong. Sanders still starts with Christianity and attempts to account for its origins in the work of Jesus. Thus, he ends up with much of the skepticism of his predecessors, while attempting to fill the gap with what can only be called speculation, inadequately supported by evidence. Although Vermes' illuminating comparison of Jesus with other Galilean Hasidim may not be the whole story, it does unequivocally set Jesus where he belongs, in his Jewish context, and as a result is able to show that far more of the gospel record than has recently been supposed has a foundation in real history.

8. Charlesworth, *Jesus within Judaism*, Preface, p. xi.
9. Sanders, *Jesus and Judaism*, p. 2.
10. Vermes, *Jesus and the World of Judaism*, p. 1.
11. It is legitimate to infer this from the fact that Yemenite Jews, who had been separated from the mainstream of Judaism for many centuries, turned out to be wearing the earlocks when they were brought to Israel in 1948. The practice of cutting the rest of the hair close in order to emphasize the earlocks is however obviously modern and is not followed by the Yemenites. The New Testament is silent on the point, which was doubtlessly taken for granted at the time.
12. Jane Schaberg, *The Illegitimacy of Jesus* (San Francisco: Harper and Row, 1987).
13. Most scholars who study religions have now adopted the neutral convention of referring to dates formerly called A.D. as C.E. (common era) and those formerly called B.C. as B.C.E. (before the common era). It is important to realize that the convention of referring to dates as A.D. and B.C. discriminates against Jews.
14. Hubert Cunliffe Jones with Benjamin Drewery, eds., *A History of Christian Doctrine* (Edinburgh: T. and T. Clark, 1978).
15. C.H. Dodd, *The Founder of Christianity* (London: Collins, 1971; New York: Macmillan, 1970).
16. The dates suggested in the text are somewhat later than those most commonly favored by New Testament scholars. The reason for my preference for a later dating is the new evidence, to be discussed in Chapter 4, suggesting that the breach between Christianity and Judaism both began later and was more gradual than used to be supposed. Since the later Gospels reflect this breach, they must have been written after it began to occur.
17. Christology is the branch of theology devoted to the doctrine of the person of Christ, his relationship to God and to human beings. More broadly, it means the views held by Christian groups on these matters.
18. Randel Helms, *Gospel Fictions* (Buffalo, NY: Prometheus Books, 1990), is a useful and easily read account of a literary critic's approach to the study of the Gospels. On pp. 26f he gives a list of most of these linking phrases.
19. Albert Schweitzer, *The Quest of the Historical Jesus* 3d ed. (London: Black, 1954).
20. Henry J. Cadbury, *The Peril of Modernizing Jesus* (London: SPCK, 1962).
21. In *The Quest of the Historical Jesus*, Schweitzer devoted a whole chapter to the subject of eschatology and skepticism, entitled in the English translation, "Thoroughgoing

scepticism and thoroughgoing eschatology." I prefer "consistent" as a translation of Schweitzer's German, *consequente.* The upshot of the chapter is that although the two methods had sometimes worked hand in hand, in the end a choice would have to be made between them. Schweitzer believed Jesus could only be understood by means of what he called eschatology. The condensed expression in the text summarizes the way in which Schweitzer's views were subsequently referred to by New Testament interpreters.

22. Simon bar Kosiba, who became known as Bar Kochva (son of the Star), led a revolt against the Romans in the fourth decade of the second century. Rabbi Akiva, the greatest sage of the time, and other rabbis, recognized him as the Messiah, and placed great hopes in his campaign to free the land from Roman rule. However, it failed, and Bar Kochva lost his life.
23. Cf. Sanders' careful examination of this and other views in the Introduction to his *Jesus and Judaism.*
24. See, for example, Robert Alter and Frank Kermode, eds., *The Literary Guide to the Bible* (Cambridge, MA: The Belknap Press of Harvard University Press, 1987); Helms, *Gospel Fictions.*
25. Helms, *Gospel Fictions,* gives the grounds for this view on the basis of a good deal of literary evidence.
26. See Chapter 2, pp. 80f.
27. For an interesting and revealing example of the effects of this methodology when carried to an extreme, see James Breech, *The Silence of Jesus: the authentic voice of the historical man* (Toronto: Doubleday, 1983). While the concept of the silence of Jesus is attractive, much of the silence Breech attributes to him is the result of the negative application of the "criterion of dissimilarity" to pare down the list of sayings accepted as authentic to a bare minimum.
28. Much of the information in this section may be familiar to Christian readers, but it will be new to Jewish and to most secular ones.
29. See Chapter 4 for an account of the way in which belief in Jesus' resurrection grew up.
30. In fact, some Jews had already made this kind of Greek reinterpretation of their own faith. We find it in Philo and other Hellenistic Jews, and it may well have been the foundation for the reinterpretation carried out by Christians. But the Christian version went much further, breaking up a unity Philo had preserved between Jewish history and Jewish practice, and its allegorical meaning.
31. Unfortunately, the vast majority of scholarly work on Jewish Christianity is not easily accessible to the general reader. One article that is appeared in a symposium edited by Arnold Toynbee, *The Crucible of Christianity* (London: Thames and Hudson, 1969), a large and beautifully illustrated "coffee table" book. The article, by Jean Daniélou, is entitled, "That the Scriptures might be fulfilled."

    However, Daniélou's definition of Jewish Christianity is so broad that the usefulness of the article is much lessened. Nevertheless, it contains much of the greatest interest. Daniélou develops his views at greater length in *The Theology of Jewish Christianity* (Philadelphia: Westminster Press, 1965, 1967). Other sources are given in the bibliographical references in Helmut Koester, *Introduction to the New Testament; Vol. 2, History and Literature of Early Christianity* (Philadelphia: Fortress Press, 1982), pp. 198 ff.
32. On Jewish-Christian gospels see Koester, *Introduction to the New Testament,* pp. 198ff.
33. Gnosticism is discussed in the next section.
34. On Gnosticism, see, for example, Hans Jonas, *The Gnostic Religion: the Message of the Alien*

God and the Beginnings of Christianity (Boston: Beacon Press, 1958), and Elaine Pagels, *The Gnostic Gospels* (New York: Random House, 1969).

35. These writers, who are all heavily influenced by esoteric Islam, belong to a group they themselves call the "traditional" school. Their work has been popularized in North America by Huston Smith and Jacob Needleman. See Huston Smith, *Forgotten Truth: the primordial tradition* (New York: Harper and Row, 1976); Seyyed Hossein Nasr, *Knowledge and the Sacred: the Gifford Lectures, 1981* (New York: Crossroad, 1981); Fritjof Schuon, *The Transcendent Unity of Religions*, with a valuable introduction by Huston Smith (Wheaton, IL: Theosophical Publishing House, 1984). The original edition of this book, published in 1957, was the first writing of this school to gain widespread attention. See also Schuon, *Esoterism as Principle and as Way* (United Kingdom: Perennial Books, 1981), and *Survey of Metaphysics and Esoterism* (Bloomington, IN: World Wisdom Books, 1986).
36. For a brilliant intuitive reconstruction of ancient Egyptian esoteric teaching, see Isha Schwaller de Lubicz, *Her-Bak: the Living Face of Ancient Egypt*, trans. Charles Edgar Sprague (London: Hodder and Stoughton, 1954; New York: Inner Traditions International, 1978), and *Her-Bak: Egyptian Initiate*, trans. Ronald Fraser (London: Hodder and Stoughton, 1967; New York: Inner Traditions, 1978).
37. See James M. Robinson, ed., *The Nag Hammadi Library in English* (San Francisco: Harper and Row, 1977).
38. Monophysites hold to the slogan of Cyril, "One Nature of the Incarnate Word, and that divine." The Orthodox interpret this to mean that they deny that Jesus was really human.

CHAPTER 2

1. When I made this point in a lecture, a Jewish listener reminded me of the prominence of guilt in much contemporary Jewish life. It is clear that this is not the authentic tradition, and it is not easy to see how it got into modern Jewish culture.
2. While the actual expression, the "oral Torah," seems to have originated somewhat after Jesus' time, there is no reason to doubt that the idea itself was widely accepted, especially among the considerable section of the population that was favorable to the Pharisees and their ideas.

   If those biblical scholars are right who believe that the final text of the written Torah is the outcome of a lengthy process of oral tradition and the combination of variant traditions into a single one, it may well be that the traditions incorporated in the oral Torah are also of great antiquity. At least symbolically, the rabbinic claim may be true that the oral Torah was given at Sinai. At least, it no longer seems possible to regard rabbinic Judaism as a revolutionary transformation of the Judaism Jesus knew.
3. It seems likely that the Torah was originally read in a three year cycle instead of an annual one, as later.
4. At Herod's summer home and fortress on Masada, overlooking the Dead Sea, a mikvah has been found fully conforming to the rabbinic regulations found in later texts. Others have been found in many places, including the Galilee, from approximately the same period. At Nazareth, near the Catholic church of the Annunciation, an early dwelling is shown as the Virgin Mary's house. It too contains a mikvah, of which the pious pilgrim must suppose she made use. Those who show the discovery to pilgrims and visitors have perhaps not considered the implications of this.

5. One of Pilate's own inscriptions, which has been found, describes him as PRAEFECTUS.
6. See Hyam Maccoby, *The Myth-Maker: Paul and the Invention of Christianity* (London: Weidenfeld and Nicholson, 1985), Chapter 5, and *Revolution in Judaea* (London: Orbach and Chambers, 1973). Maccoby believes that Jesus belonged to a Zealot wing of the Pharisaic movement.
7. It is interesting that Jesus is represented as taking the side of the Pharisees against the Sadducees on the issue of the bodily resurrection. See Mark 12:18–27; Matthew 22:23–33.
8. Geza Vermes presents his views persuasively in his *Jesus the Jew* (London: SCM Press, 1983). However, it is fair to say that his contentions have recently come under severe criticism from Jacob Neusner and his school, who argue that the documentary evidence does not permit us to conclude that there ever was a distinct group of Galilean charismatics.
9. Matthew 7:29; Mark 1:22.
10. Matthew 10:6; 15:24.
11. Doubt has been cast by scholars on the authenticity of such phrases, since they may be summary versions by the tradition or the gospel writers of teaching given on various occasions in various words. Whether or not they were later summaries, they do seem to be a fair representation of how Jesus understood his own work.
12. The Hebrew and Aramaic word *malkut*, usually translated kingdom, actually means kingship or sovereignty, reflecting the Jewish way of thinking of God as the king of the universe, *melech ha-olam.* (This way of addressing God is still familiar to every Jew, since it is part of so many of the "blessings" that are the fundamental units of Jewish prayer.) Kingdom in the sense of domain is actually rendered by a different Hebrew word from the same root.
13. Cf. 1 Samuel 8 and the following chapter.
14. Since the concept appears to be central for Jewish tradition, it is not likely to have been a novelty introduced by second-century Rabbis. On the other hand, we do know that the later Rabbis were very cautious about all forms of messianism, in view of the unprecedented disasters messianic movements had brought upon the people in the revolts against the Romans. They had every reason to hold them responsible for the destruction of the Temple and the removal of the divine presence from the midst of the people. The Rabbis themselves believed that the Messiah was more likely to be brought by patient keeping of the Torah than by revolutionary movements designed to force God's hand. This was probably also the view of those who earlier in the century did not join with the Zealots in their own revolutionary plans. For these reasons, it is only probable, not certain, that the concept existed in Jesus' time.
15. Jesus is recorded as having spoken of an easy yoke and light burden of his own, and many Christian interpreters have seen here a contrast with a supposedly difficult yoke and heavy burden of the commandments of the Torah. As we are now in a position to see, this is not a Jewish concept, which may lead us to be suspicious of the saying. If the utterance is authentic, however, it may have been spoken in the name of God, and the meaning may be that the Torah is an easy yoke when accepted from the heart.
16. It is not easy to give references for an outlook so pervasive in Judaism. I may mention, however, Lawrence Fine, "Kabbalistic Texts," in *Back to the Sources: Reading the Classic Jewish Texts*, ed. Barry W. Holtz (New York: Summit Books, 1984), the reference that

actually set me thinking along these lines; Chapter 4, "Nearness and Distance–the Omnipresent and Heaven," in Ephraim E. Urbach, *The Sages: the World and Wisdom of the Rabbis of the Talmud* (Cambridge and London: Harvard University Press, 1987); Emil Fackenheim, *What is Judaism? An interpretation for the present age* (New York: Summit Books, 1987), pp. 282ff.

17. From R. Jose ben Halafta, cited by Urbach, *The Sages*, p. 68.
18. Jeremiah 23:23.
19. There has been much debate about which of these translations is the right one. It is at least suggestive that all of them could equally well be renderings of the same Hebrew or Aramaic word. The Hebrew/Aramaic root can be transliterated as KRB. In Hebrew, *karov* means near, or among, or within. (B is often softened to V in pronunciation, especially at the end of words.) Presumably when Jesus thought or spoke about God's kingship *nearing* his contemporaries, he used a form of the verb from the same root. See now Ben F. Meyer's presidential address to the Canadian Society of Biblical Studies, 1989, "How Jesus charged language with meaning: a study in rhetoric," *Studies in Religion/Sciences religieuses,* 19: 3 (1990): 273–285.
20. Theologians often interpret this passage as implying that Christian believers share by adoption in the Sonship which Christ possesses by birth, as it were, as the divine Son. However, it is more likely that Paul, addressing Gentile believers, thinks of them as coming by adoption to share the privilege of being children of God that Jews had by birth into the covenant people.
21. See Vermes, *Jesus the Jew*, pp. 192–213.
22. Isaiah 65:1.
23. Mark 2:17; Luke 15:7.
24. Mark 6:56 and parallels.
25. Matthew 23:5; 6:16:18.
26. Matthew 5:21 etc.
27. The portions of the sermon with which we are concerned are to be found in Matthew 5:17–48. It would be a good idea for the reader to have the passage handy while reading the next pages.
28. Deuteronomy 18:15.
29. Matthew 5:17.
30. Luke 16:17.
31. See Chapter 1, pp. 28f.
32. See, e.g., Eugene Fisher, *Faith without Prejudice* (New York: Paulist Press, 1977), p. 66, citing David Daube, *The New Testament and Rabbinic Judaism*, p. 58.
33. Leviticus 19:2.
34. Cf. Geza Vermes, *Jesus and the World of Judaism* (Philadelphia: Fortress Press, 1984), pp. 70f.
35. Mark 10:1–12.
36. However, while this was the strict legal position, in practice injured women were encouraged by the Rabbis to initiate proceedings that would end in divorce, even though it remained the husband's responsibility to make the necessary legal declaration setting the wife free.
37. W. Gunther Plaut, *The Torah: a Modern Commentary* (New York: Union of American Hebrew Congregations, 1981), pp. 571ff.
38. Matthew 5:43.

39. Some recent writers have suggested that Jesus may have intended a reference to attitudes found among the Qumran sect. In the Manual of Discipline, new members of the community swear an oath to love the sons of light and hate the sons of darkness. If so, Jesus may have been opposed to the Essenes, rather than to the Pharisees, as the gospel tradition implies. Cf. Yigael Yadin, "The Temple Scroll–the longest Dead Sea Scroll," in *Understanding the Dead Sea Scrolls: a Reader from the Biblical Archaeology Review*, Hershel Shanks (New York: Random House, 1992), p. 105.
40. Cf. Eugene Kaellis, *Towards a Jewish America* (Lewiston and Queenston: The Edwin Mellen Press, 1987), pp. 91ff.
41. In his important book, *Jesus and Judaism* (London: SCM Press; Philadelphia: Fortress Press, 1985), E. P. Sanders argues at length that Jesus very likely exempted his repentant followers from such normal requirements of repentance, including restitution and a Temple sacrifice, considering it sufficient to follow him. If so, they would have remained technically sinners when they became his disciples. There is, of course, no direct evidence to support this view; it is actually a speculative suggestion to account for the opposition aroused by Jesus' association with sinners. The evidence suggests, on the contrary, that Jesus took the normal requirements for granted. The cause of Jesus' offense must, I believe, be sought elsewhere.
42. These parables belong with those of the lost sheep and the lost coin, all found in Luke's Gospel.
43. Luke 15:11–32.
44. Pesikta Rabbati 44, 184b-185a, as cited by Bernard J. Bamberger in *The Torah: A modern commentary*, ed. W. Gunther Plaut (New York: Union of American Hebrew Congregations, 1981), p. 869.
45. Luke 18:9–14.
46. Abraham Isaac Kook, *Abraham Isaac Kook: The Lights of Penitence, the Moral Principles, Lights of Holiness, Essays, Letters and Poems*, ed. and trans. Ben Zion Bokser (New York: Paulist Press, The Classics of Western Spirituality, 1978), p. 96. Rav Kook is here quoting Berakoth 34b. Maimonides comments on the Berakoth passage in *Mishneh Torah, Hilkoth Teshuvah*, 7:4, cited by Arthur Hertzberg in *Judaism: The Key Spiritual Writings of the Jewish Tradition* (New York: Simon and Schuster, 1991), p. 192 and n. 59.
47. Mordechai Hacohen, *Al HaTorah*, 5:503, cited Plaut, *The Torah*, p. 1402. The saying as quoted here seems to be a version of a saying of Rabbi Nachman, also quoted by Elie Wiesel in two different versions in his books on the Hasidim, *Souls on Fire* and *Somewhere a Master*.
48. Vermes, *Jesus the Jew*, pp. 28f; *Jesus and the World of Judaism*, p. 46.
49. Mark 7:20.
50. Michael Grant, *Jesus: An historian's review of the gospels* (New York: Scribner's, 1977), p. 77.
51. Fackenheim, *What is Judaism?* pp. 133ff.
52. Matthew 5:28.
53. Matthew 23:27. The reference to scrupulousness about contracting impurity from the dead is at most implicit in the saying as we have it, but it has a great deal more point if the allusion was actually intended.
54. Mark 7:15ff. However, Mark's interpretation (verse 20), that Jesus intended to abolish the dietary laws, is certainly incorrect. Jewish parallels can be found for even this saying.
55. Matthew 23:23.
56. Shabbat 31a.
57. Mark 12:28–34. Cf. Matthew 7:12, where Jesus actually repeats Hillel's summary in a

positive form. Though Matthew makes the exchange much less cordial than it is in Mark, he identifies Jesus' interlocutor as a Pharisee.

58. Mark 2:27. Cf. R. Simeon ben Menasiah's saying, "The Sabbath was given to you and not you to the Sabbath," from the Mekhilta, cited Vermes, *Jesus the Jew*, p. 180 and n. 71.
59. Luke 7:36–50.
60. Vermes, *Jesus the Jew*, pp. 207–9 and notes ad loc. Those who are familiar with the regulations concerning the relations between the sexes in Jewish Orthodoxy today, and even more those of the ultra-Orthodox groups, will readily recognize the modern form of the same tradition. Compare also the Pharisaic criticism quoted above of the Pharisee who bruises his head trying to avoid looking at a woman. Jesus' informal behavior with women was probably the most outrageous thing about him, from the point of view of his critics.
61. See Chapter 3, pp. 105ff.
62. Matthew 8:22; Luke 9:59f. Comparison of the two versions suggests that following Jesus was the same as joining in the proclamation of the kingdom of God.
63. Sanders, *Jesus and Judaism*, p. 255.
64. Vermes, *Jesus and the World of Judaism*, p. 167, note 57.
65. Luke 14:26f; cf. Matthew 10:37ff.
66. As Eugene Kaellis pointed out to me, on Jewish principles we do not have to assume that Jesus was always consistent. He could have had lapses, or he could have given different advice to different individuals, according to his perception of their spiritual needs at the moment.
67. Vermes, *Jesus the Jew*, pp. 99–102. Celibacy was attributed to Moses in particular, but also to other, lesser prophets.
68. Matthew 19:29. The reward may have included the comradeship of others in the present.

CHAPTER 3

1. Julius Wellhausen, *Einleitung in die drei ersten Evangelien* (1905), p. 113, cited by Geza Vermes, *Jesus and the World of Judaism* (Philadelphia: Fortress Press, 1984), p. 147, n. 17.
2. Cf. Vermes, *Jesus and the World of Judaism*, p. 13.
3. Recent Catholic pronouncements have sought to exculpate the Jewish people corporately from the guilt of Christ's death by stressing that, according to the New Testament, it was not the people as a whole that sought his death, but only their leaders. We shall see in Chapter 5 that this is not in fact the unanimous view of the New Testament writers. Certainly, the popular myth made no such fine distinctions. In this chapter, I expect to show that even the leadership did not directly seek his death.
4. See Chapter 5.
5. For a fuller account of the development of messianic expectation in early Judaism, see, e.g., Emil Schürer, *The History of the Jewish People in the Age of Jesus Christ*, vol. 2, ed. and rev. Geza Vermes, Fergus Millar, and Matthew Black (Edinburgh: T. and T. Clark, 1979), pp. 488–554. Summarized in Geza Vermes, *Jesus the Jew* (London: SCM Press, 1983), pp. 130–140.
6. 2 Corinthians 3:14. The interpretation in the text is the traditional one; for a very different explanation of the verse and its context, see Lloyd Gaston, *Paul and the Torah* (Vancouver: University of British Columbia Press, 1987), pp. 151–168.

7. The story in the Gospels of Jesus' temptations in the wilderness, told briefly by Mark and in a more expanded and legendary form in the Q tradition reproduced by Matthew and Luke, may well have a basis in history. The accounts seem to suggest the rejection of a temptation to make use of spiritual power even for good purposes. Jesus may have thought of the role of the Messiah, especially if he had no clear conviction of being called to it, as a way of power.
8. It will be easier to follow this section if the reader looks up the passages in the New Testament and keeps marks in the three synoptic gospels at the place. For additional convenience, I have included the text of all three versions in an Appendix. They are set out in parallel columns, so that the reader can easily see similarities and differences between the three versions.
9. Cf. Randel Helms, *Gospel Fictions* (Buffalo, NY: Prometheus, 1988), pp. 39f.
10. The passage is stylistically coherent, but its content is somewhat less so, depending on how some of the key words are to be translated. If we follow modern translations, as I have in the text, in translating the Greek *psyche* as life instead of soul, we have a Jewish doctrine of the supreme value of life mixed in with a Christian one about the renunciation of earthly life to gain spiritual life. What did Jesus really mean?
11. Mark 8:34ff and parallels.
12. Vermes, *Jesus the Jew*, p. 147. The fixity of Christian tradition is no doubt the reason why the point is missed by the vast majority of Christian commentators. For Vermes, it is evidently so obvious that he lays no special stress upon it.
13. Rock, in Aramaic *Kepha* (cf. Paul's Greek *Kephas* in his letters), is the origin of the name Peter, *Petros* in Greek, from *petra*, rock. Since, if the analysis in the text is correct, this was not the occasion on which Shimon bar Yonah received the name he was to be known by, this was almost certainly also not the reason. Could it be suggested that we have here an example of Jesus' usually underrated sense of humor? If there is one characteristic of Peter that stands out from the various New Testament references to him, it is instability.
14. Matthew's insertions exhibit some puzzling features. Their purpose must in any case be to remove the ambiguities still left by Mark's more subtle handling of the difficulties of the tradition. Where did he get the new material from? It contains features unparalleled elsewhere in the Gospels. Only here is Peter called by his full original name in its Aramaic form, Simon bar-Jonah.

    In fact, this is not the only Aramaic touch in the passage. Hints of Aramaic are unusually common here. On the other hand, scholars have had difficulty in suggesting an Aramaic word of which church (*ecclesia*) would be an appropriate translation.
15. While the Roman claims could not have been at issue for Matthew at this period, it is possible that some earlier claims of Antioch were. In approximately the period that Matthew was writing his Gospel, the bishop Ignatius was exerting a wide spiritual influence over the churches of the region, from his base in Antioch. In fact, he was acting like a sort of archbishop, and may have been the first to do so.

    Perhaps one of Matthew's subordinate purposes (or that of the tradition he reproduced) in introducing this passage was to legitimize this role by linking it to the preeminence of Peter, the traditional founder of the see of Antioch. However, this is speculative, and we do not need to speculate about Matthew's principal purpose in inserting this material, whether he composed it himself or drew it from the traditions of the church of Antioch. It was to make it crystal clear to his readers that Jesus had regarded himself as the Messiah, the son of God, just as Matthew's church did.

16. The vehemence of Jesus' rebuke remains puzzling, even on this explanation. Did Peter's words perhaps revive for Jesus a temptation once rejected? When he calls Peter Satan, is the voice once heard during his temptations in the wilderness echoing once more in his mind? Now an even more decisive rejection is necessary, when the temptation comes from his own closest friends.
17. See pp. 105ff. Cf. also Charles P. Anderson, "The trial of Jesus as Jewish-Christian polarization," in *Anti-Judaism in Early Christianity*, vol. 1, Paul and the Gospels, ed. Peter Richardson (Waterloo, ON: Canadian Corporation for Studies in Religion, 1986), pp. 114ff.
18. The explanation of the inconsistency may lie, as Helmut Koester suggested, in the origins of the book as a gnostic or esoteric document, later edited from the point of view of a writer who believed in the Gentile church's proclamation of Jesus' death and resurrection as the source of the world's salvation. On this view, there are really two quite inconsistent views of Jesus' person and role in the same Gospel, and the writer has not altogether succeeded in harmonizing them.
19. Vermes, *Jesus the Jew*, pp. 169–177, *Jesus and the World of Judaism*, pp. 89–99.
20. The definite article preceding "man," which is there in the Greek but left untranslated in the English versions, must represent the Hebrew definite article, or its Aramaic equivalent, which goes with the second noun in such compound genitive expressions, known as the construct state. In biblical Hebrew, the equivalent expression, *ben adam*, most common in Ezekiel, does not have the definite article; thus the usage must be an Aramaic one, and the reference cannot be to the biblical passages in Hebrew.
21. Vermes, *Jesus and the World of Judaism*, p. 98.
22. Matthew 21:1–11; Mark 11:1–11; Luke 19:35–40; John 12:12–19.
23. Cf., e.g., Helms, *Gospel Fictions*, pp. 102ff.
24. Mark 11:15–19 and parallels.
25. John 2:21.
26. John 2:19.
27. Mark 14:53–15:15; Matthew 26:57–27-26.
28. Luke 23:66–71. See the comments of Gaston in Richardson, op. cit.
29. John 18:19–19:16.
30. See, among other criticisms, Vermes, *Jesus the Jew*, pp. 36f; Anderson, art. cit., pp. 107–126.
31. In Mark's version, Jesus is represented as saying that he will be seen on the right hand of "Power," another expression that avoids the direct use of the divine name. It is paradoxical that he is said to have blasphemed in the very context in which he is shown as avoiding doing so.
32. Vermes, *Jesus the Jew*, p. 36.
33. See Chapter 5, p. 162.
34. See Chapter 5 for a more detailed examination of the way in which the gospel writers transform the tradition they have received into something substantially more anti-Jewish when they describe how Jesus met his end.
35. Josephus, *Antiquities of the Jews*, 17:85–89. Luke (13:1) mentions a bloodbath of Galilean pilgrims, but the incident that led to Pilate's final recall seems to have been a massacre of Samaritans. Pilate was also notorious for his violations of Jewish religious sensibilities.
36. Matthew 27:25.
37. Vermes, *Jesus the Jew*, p. 144; *Jesus and the World of Judaism*, pp. viii–ix, 12.

38. John 11:49f; 18:14.
39. Cited by Vermes, *Jesus and the World of Judaism*, pp. viii–ix, from Josephus, *Jewish War* 6:300–305. The case is that of Jesus, son of Ananias, who was arrested in 62 C.E. for prophecies of doom for the Temple and the people. He was beaten but suffered his punishment with resignation, and he went on prophesying. Some of the leaders began to wonder if he was inspired by God. However, in order to neutralize a possible disturbance, they handed him over to the Roman governor, and he was flayed to the bone. Eventually, the Procurator decided he was mad and released him.
40. However, if this was indeed the reasoning of the priestly leadership, it apparently would not have been condoned by the later Rabbis of the Talmudic period, who regarded each human life as of infinite value that could not be quantified. Perhaps, therefore, their predecessors, the Pharisees of Jesus' own time, would also have objected to this sacrifice of an individual for the benefit of larger numbers.

CHAPTER 4

1. Matthew 15:24.
2. Cf. Randel Helms, *Gospel Fictions* (Buffalo, NY: Prometheus, 1988), p. 53.
3. Cf. C. H. Dodd, *The Apostolic Preaching and its Developments* (London: Hodder and Stoughton, 1936), etc.
4. First Corinthians 15:3. Several scholars have argued that the term translated "received" is a technical term implying a controlled tradition, and directly translating a Hebrew term (*lekabbel*) having the same meaning.
5. First Corinthians 15:4ff. The Greek word used by Paul, translated in the older versions as, "he was seen of," is generally regarded as a technical expression used in the language of the time to mean visions. It is fair to say that some scholars disagree with the common opinion, and believe that Paul distinguishes between resurrection appearances and religious visions.
6. Pinchas Lapide, *The Resurrection of Jesus: A Jewish Perspective*, trans. Wilhelm C. Linss (London: SPCK, 1984), p. 39. However, Lapide himself, an Orthodox Jew, accepts the historicity of the resurrection of Jesus!
7. Readers unfamiliar with the scholarly study of the New Testament need to know that Mark's authentic text ends at 16:8, in the middle of a sentence. The remainder of the chapter as we have it in the English versions was added by a later writer.
8. Geza Vermes, *Jesus the Jew* (London: SCM Press, 1983), p. 41.
9. In the last chapter of Luke's Gospel, he gives an account of a resurrection appearance of Jesus to some disciples who had formerly hoped he was the Messiah and now felt compelled to renounce their expectation on account of his death. In this late account, the Church's new reading of Scripture, to take account of a suffering Messiah, is put into the mouth of the risen Jesus. This may well reflect a tradition that it was not in the lifetime of Jesus but in the early days of the Church that the new interpretation was first devised.
10. For the reasoning here attributed to the early leaders, cf. Donald Juel, *Messianic Exegesis* (Philadelphia: Fortress Press, 1988), pp. 13, 25f.
11. See pp. 138ff.
12. Isaiah 7:14, cited in Matthew 1:23.
13. Toward the end of 1991, press reports spoke of the discovery in a previously unpublished Dead Sea Scroll of allusions to a slain Messiah. It is of course too soon to evaluate their significance and whether they have any bearing on the Christian concept.

14. Cf. Juel, *Messianic Exegesis*, pp. 99ff. Helms, *Gospel Fictions*, pp. 125ff.
15. However, there is one case in which we know that the texts from Isaiah were interpreted messianically, and it seems to have been the exception that proves the rule. Targum Jonathan does read the text messianically, but in order to do so it removes all reference to the sufferings of the servant now thought of as the Messiah, and reassigns the suffering to his opponents!
16. Cf. Juel, *Messianic Exegesis*, pp. 121ff.
17. This reproach is found in the criticisms of Christianity by Origen's opponent, Celsus, in the late second century.
18. Marcion, a Gnostic of the second century, argued that the Jewish Bible was the revelation of a different God, and should not be retained as Scripture by the Church. See the next chapter for a fuller discussion of the controversy.
19. The concept of the Church as the new or true Israel does not seem to be expressed in so many words until the second century, in the writings of Justin Martyr. Before that, we hear instead of the new covenant or of the remnant. This development probably already involves a breach of the Church with the Jewish people. The concept is certainly latent in the sectarian language of first-century Christianity.
20. Second Corinthians 3:14ff. In the text, I have given the traditional interpretation of the passage. However, it has many exegetical complications, and other meanings are possible. See Lloyd Gaston, *Paul and the Torah* (Vancouver, BC: University of British Columbia Press, 1987), pp. 161 ff.
21. Geza Vermes, "Circumcision and Exodus iv. 24–26–Prelude to the theology of Baptism," *Scripture and Tradition in Judaism* (Leiden: E. J. Brill, 1961), pp. 178–192.
22. I do not think it is necessary to invoke these explanations in order to account for the development that took place. In a sense there was preparation in the lifetime of Jesus, in the tenacious belief of some of the disciples, notably Peter, that Jesus was the Messiah, in spite of his own denials. No doubt, as Donald Juel emphasizes, the fact that Jesus had actually been crucified under the title of "King of the Jews" strongly reinforced the same convictions. The other factor that should not be underestimated is the energy imparted to the disciples by their conviction that Jesus had been raised from the dead, giving them psychological certainty that Jesus' life and death belonged to a divine plan, and that the messianic age was here and now unrolling.

    In view of these two factors, I do not see anything in these developments, remarkable and rapid as they certainly were, which requires further explanation, especially explanations that raise new and probably insuperable difficulties of their own.
23. Genesis 1:2; the Hebrew words in the text are traditionally translated "without form and void."
24. First Thessalonians 2:15.
25. John 8:44.
26. Hyam Maccoby, *The Myth-Maker* (London: Weidenfeld and Nicholson, 1985).
27. The Ethics of the Fathers, the most widely read text in the Talmud, uses the phrase as a theme and chapter heading. In fact, Paul does appear to show his own knowledge of and even agreement with this belief in Romans 11:26 (as Alan F. Segal points out in his *Paul the Convert* [New Haven, CT: Yale University Press, 1990], p. 280), thus showing that it existed in the first century in Pharisaic circles. Cf., however, Romans 9:6, which appears to assert the opposite.
28. See Maccoby, *The Myth-maker*, Chapter 7, "Alleged Rabbinical style in Paul's writings."

However, in *Paul the Convert,* Segal credits Paul with expertise in rabbinical exegesis and dialectics.

29. In assessing the value of this argument, it is important to remember that the second century assumed that all the letters traditionally attributed to Paul were his, including Colossians (and Hebrews). Colossians is probably the most "Gnostic" letter in the Pauline corpus.
30. Philippians 3:5f. I translate "Hebrew" as "Hebrew-speaking," following the margin of the New English Bible; usually the contrast between Hebrew and Hellenist refers to speech in the New Testament. It would be redundant for Paul to claim to be a Hebrew in the context, but meaningful to claim a knowledge of Hebrew, since he was also a Greek-speaking diaspora Jew.
31. Second Corinthians 3:7ff. Cf. E. P. Sanders, *Paul, the Law and the Jewish People* (Philadelphia: Fortress Press, 1985), pp. 139ff.
32. Contemporary scholars base their views of Paul's ideas on the letters regarded as certainly authentic, Romans, 1 and 2 Corinthians, Galatians, Philippians, 1 Thessalonians, and Philemon. They use the remaining letters attributed to him by the New Testament only with caution, as they do the much later Book of Acts, which disagrees in important respects with Paul's own testimony.
33. See pp. 138f for a discussion of what these requirements were. The *halachah,* which literally means walking, is the actual legal system which governs the actions of Jews who live by covenant and Torah. It is the official and current interpretation of the way in which the Torah is to be observed.
34. Alan Segal thinks that Paul was essentially the first to make the modern distinction between the ethical and ritual commandments of the Torah, regarding the first as obligatory and the second as dispensed for Gentile converts, and perhaps for all believers in Christ, even those of Jewish origin.
35. The principle of unity in the Christian community was clearly of first importance to Paul. In churches containing both Jewish and Gentile converts, problems of eating together and intermarriage bulked large; if the community was to remain united, someone had to make concessions. In Galatians, he clearly and emphatically regards it as the duty of the Jews to make the concessions. But elsewhere, in Corinthians and Romans, he suggests that others should respect Jewish scruples about meat that may have been offered to idols, and himself offers to become a vegetarian for this purpose (1 Corinthians 8:13; cf. Segal, *Paul the Convert,* p.237). He never concedes that for the sake of unity it would be appropriate for the Gentile converts to observe the dietary laws as a whole.
36. In the so-called Pseudo-Clementine Homilies and Recognitions, variously dated from the early in the second to the late third centuries, Paul seems to appear in the guise of Simon Magus.
37. Lawrence H. Schiffman, *Who Was a Jew? Rabbinic and Halakhic Perspectives on the Jewish-Christian Schism* (Hoboken, NJ: Ktav, 1985).
38. Though not all the traditions recorded in the Mishnah can be precisely dated, it is often possible to trace rulings and debates back to the period of the second Temple, the period of Jesus and Paul. As Schiffman shows, the regulations governing Jewish identity, and the requirements for becoming a Jew if one had not been born Jewish, can usually be assigned a date in the Second Temple period. These regulations were not created by the tannaim themselves. They simply transmitted them, with certain refinements, to later generations.

39. Schiffman, *Who Was a Jew?*, pp. 9ff.
40. Matthew 23:15.
41. Schiffman, *Who Was a Jew?*, pp. 19ff.
42. See especially Galatians 5:2ff. However, the whole letter deals with this theme.
43. Paul says he did not baptize converts himself, except in rare instances. He did not wish to give anyone the impression he was baptizing in his own name. See 1 Corinthians 1:14ff.
44. Romans 13:10.
45. Second Corinthians 11:24. Cf. E. P. Sanders, *Paul, the Law and the Jewish People*, p.192; Gaston, *Paul and the Torah*, p.135.
46. Galatians 2:19. Cf. Gaston, *Paul and the Torah*, pp. 71, 76–79.
47. Galatians 2:18.
48. It is not easy to discover from Paul's writings in what sense he believes Jesus to be the Messiah. On the one hand, so axiomatic is it that Jesus is the Messiah that the Greek equivalent of the word, *Christos*, very often functions as a proper name, and no longer as a title, in Paul's letters. On the other, he never refers to Jesus as the King Messiah of Jewish expectation. Most probably, he regarded Jesus as the Messiah because he now believed that God had raised him from the dead and exalted him to his own right hand, and would soon send him to judge the world, and thus inaugurate the full messianic age of prophetic expectation.
49. Segal believes that the phrase refers to the ritual commandments.
50. Cf. Joel 3:1–5. The passage is quoted in full in Acts 2. Evidently the text was of particular importance to the Christian movement.
51. Galatians 6:16.
52. See Gaston, Chapter 7, "Paul and Jerusalem."
53. In 1 Corinthians 12:13, Paul comes very close to saying in so many words that Jews were also baptized: "for in one Spirit we were all baptized into one body, Jews as well as Greeks, slaves as well as free, and we were all made to drink of one Spirit." In Galatians 3:27–29 he strongly implies that both Jewish and Gentile converts were baptized, arguing from this that there is no difference between them. It is remotely possible to interpret both passages as meaning that the baptism of the Gentile converts brought them into unity with the existing Jewish people, but this does not seem to be the natural interpretation.

    It is generally thought today that Paul was not the author of the letter to the Ephesians. However, its author is also regarded as one of the most reliable interpreters of Paul's own thought. He speaks resoundingly of "One Lord, one faith, one baptism, one God and Father of us all." (Ephesians 4:6.) In the context, this must imply that he knew of a single baptism administered equally to Jews and Gentile converts.
54. Acts 1:5, 2:38ff., 18:25–19:7.
55. See Romans 6:3–4 (cf. Colossians 2:12); 1 Corinthians 12:13.
56. Acts 21:21.
57. Cf., e.g., Gaston, *Paul and the Torah*, pp. 79, 123. Rosenzweig's own views on the relations of Jews and Christians are to be found in Franz Rosenzweig, *The Star of Redemption*, trans. Wm. W. Hallo (New York: Holt, Rinehart and Winston, 1971).
58. Galatians 2:2.
59. Galatians 2:1–10.

60. Cf. Gaston, *Paul and the Torah*, p. 68 and n.11. His interpretation of the passage is not the same as mine, however, since he does not think food was the issue, as I do. See also Segal, *Paul the Convert*, pp. 230f.
61. On Paul's apostasy for the sake of the gospel, see Gaston, *Paul and the Torah*, pp. 76–79.
62. Acts 10:9ff. See Helms' analysis of the way in which the passage was built up by Luke from Old Testament texts, *Gospel Fictions*, pp. 20f.
63. For the above reconstruction of the events, cf. Maccoby, *The Myth-maker*, pp. 145–8. His version does not differ from mine on the issues of Jewish law involved, but does on the role of the emissaries of James in relation to Paul, where he takes a more traditional view, less firmly rooted in the text.
64. Galatians 2:14. The English versions do not always make it clear that the Greek word is actually "Judaize." "Living like a Gentile," the action attributed to Peter, is set in opposition to Judaizing, and therefore we can infer that it meant "Gentilizing," following Gentile practices, not abandoning the Jewish faith. Just as Peter, while remaining a Jew, is living like a Gentile, he expects the Gentiles, while remaining such, to live like Jews, according to Paul's argument. As we have seen, even apostasy did not cut the tie with the Jewish people. Repentance would wipe it out. It seems that whatever Peter actually did, he repented of it.
65. The highly theological paragraphs that end Chapter 2 of Galatians, following on the account of the dispute with Peter, are no longer thought to continue Paul's reported words to Peter but represent his own theological commentary on the incident. For a remarkable new interpretation of these paragraphs, see Gaston, *Paul and the Torah*, pp. 65ff.
66. In later writings, 1 Corinthians and Romans, Paul seems to think that in a community where his principles are solidly established, it is not necessary for Gentiles to claim their full freedom from Torah, and they may make voluntary concessions for the sake of unity. The point for Paul is that salvation is based on faith in Christ, not observance of the dietary laws. In Galatians, he addresses a situation where the principle itself appears to him to be at stake.
67. Galatians 2:4.
68. Sanders, *Paul, the Law and the Jewish People*, pp. 18, 20.

CHAPTER 5

1. Second Peter 3:16.
2. Cf. Alan F. Segal, "Judaism, Christianity and Gnosticism," in *Anti-Judaism in Early Christianity*, vol. 2, *Separation and Polemic*, ed. Stephen G. Wilson (Waterloo, ON: Canadian Corporation for Studies in Religion, Wilfrid Laurier University Press, 1986).
3. First Thessalonians 2:14–16.
4. John C. Hurd, "Paul Ahead of his Time," in *Anti-Judaism in Early Christianity*, ed. Peter Richardson with David Granskou, vol. 1, *Paul and the Gospels* (Waterloo, ON: Canadian Corporation for Studies in Religion, Wilfrid Laurier University Press, 1986). Cf. also Stephen G. Wilson, *Separation and Polemic*, p. 164.
5. The present form of the Blessing in question differs considerably from the ancient text, now referring to slanderers, not heretics.
6. Lawrence H. Schiffman, *Who was a Jew?* (Hoboken, NJ: Ktav, 1985), pp. 76ff.

7. The phrase was coined by the great twentieth-century Jewish philosopher Franz Rosenzweig.
8. Segal, "Judaism, Christianity and Gnosticism," p. 141.
9. It is interesting that Jewish tradition confirms the chronology of the Fourth Gospel for the date of Jesus' death.
10. Schiffman, *Who was a Jew?*, pp. 69ff.
11. It was formerly the view of most critics that a powerful factor in the divinization of Jesus, who was already being addressed and spoken of as Kyrios, Lord, was the Church's application to him of Septuagint texts containing the word Kyrios, but referring to God. These are the texts where most of the English versions have LORD, corresponding to Adonai, which is read where the Tetragrammaton is written. Kyrios had the same function in later editions of the Septuagint. In view of the discovery of fragments of Bibles of the period containing the Tetragrammaton in Hebrew letters in these places, this theory has become dubious. Other factors must have been at work.
12. Schiffman, *Who was a Jew?*, pp. 62ff.
13. Ibid., pp. 55f, 77f.
14. Ibid., p.77.
15. Randel Helms, *Gospel Fictions* (Buffalo, NY: Prometheus, 1988), pp. 28, 102, 134, etc.
16. Charles P. Anderson, "The Trial of Jesus as Jewish-Christian Polarization," in Richardson with Granskou, *Paul and the Gospels*, p. 125.
17. Cf. Anderson, "Trial," p. 119.
18. This fact puts in question the well-intended assertion of the Second Vatican Council that according to the New Testament it was not the Jewish people as a whole that pressed for the death of Christ. Matthew wishes to persuade us otherwise.
19. Erwin Buck, "Anti-Judaic Sentiments in the Passion Narrative according to Matthew," in Richardson with Granskou, *Paul and the Gospels*, pp. 166ff.
20. Matthew 26:63. Cf. Helms, *Gospel Fictions*, p. 120.
21. Matthew 26:39; Buck, "Sentiments," p. 169.
22. Matthew 27:1; Buck, p. 170.
23. Matthew 27:3–10; cf. Buck.
24. Matthew 27:17 and 21. Buck.
25. Matthew 27:22 and 25; Buck.
26. Matthew 27:24; cf. Deuteronomy 21:7f.
27. Matthew 27:43; Buck, p. 170.
28. Cf. Buck, and Benno Przybylski, "The Setting of Matthean Anti-Judaism," in Richardson with Granskou, *Paul and the Gospels*.
29. Cf. Buck, p. 178.
30. While recent discoveries from the Dead Sea Scrolls tend to contradict the view of earlier scholars that the Messiah is never referred to as the Son of God in Jewish messianic texts, even where he may be spoken of in this way there is no thought that he is therefore divine. Rather, like the king in the Psalms, he is adopted as God's son when he is anointed king. The New Testament likewise refers to Jesus as God's adopted son. See Donald Juel, *Messianic Exegesis* (Philadelphia: Fortress Press, 1988), pp. 61, 77–81.
31. Jesus' reported confession that he is "the Son of God" is without legal significance, since it establishes no halachic offense; cf. Lloyd Gaston, "Anti-Judaism and the Passion Narrative in Luke and Acts," in Richardson with Granskou, *Paul and the Gospels*, p. 146.
32. Gaston, "Passion Narrative," p. 145.

33. Ibid.
34. Luke 23:25–56. Cf. Gaston, "Passion Narrative," p. 149.
35. Gaston, "Passion Narrative," p. 147.
36. Ibid., p. 148.
37. Ibid., pp. 150f.
38. S. G. Wilson, "The Jews and the Death of Jesus in Acts," in Richardson with Granskou, *Paul and the Gospels*, p. 157.
39. Acts 22:3. Gaston, among others, doubts if Paul and Gamliel ever met.
40. John 19:7. Clearly, the author of this text shares with the earlier writers the assumption that Jesus, in claiming to be the Messiah, had claimed divinity for himself, a view inconceivable for Jews but natural for Christians.
41. David Granskou, "Anti-Judaism in the Passion Accounts of the Fourth Gospel," in Richardson with Granskou, *Paul and the Gospels*, p. 202.
42. Ibid., pp. 208f.
43. Charles P. Anderson, "Hebrews among the letters of Paul," *Studies in Religion/Sciences religieuses,* 5 (1975): 258–266, and "Who wrote the Epistle from Laodicea?" *Journal of Biblical Lite*rature, 85 (1966): 436–40.
44. Jeremiah 31:31–34.
45. Martin B. Shukster and Peter Richardson, "Temple and *Beit Ha-midrash* in the Epistle of Barnabas," in Wilson, *Separation and Polemic*, pp. 17–31.
46. Ibid., p.23.
47. The translation in the text, following Shukster and Richardson, is based on the Latin version of Barnabas. This reading well fits the authors' interpretation of the Letter (and cf. *Barnabas* 13:1) but it is by no means the only possible text; cf. Robert A. Kraft, *The Apostolic Fathers, A New Translation and Commentary*, vol. 3, *Barnabas and the Didache* (New York: Nelson, 1965), p. 90. We cannot say with certainty whether the early exponents of the double covenant theory referred to by Barnabas were Jews or Christians.
48. Alan F. Segal, *Two Powers in Heaven: Early Rabbinic Reports about Christianity and Gnosticism* (Leiden: Brill, 1977), and "Judaism, Christianity and Gnosticism," in Wilson, *Separation and Polemic*, pp. 133–161.
49. See Chapter 4, p. 148.
50. Marcel Simon, *Verus Israel: A study of the relations between Christians and Jews in the Roman Empire*, trans. H. McKeating (New York: Oxford University Press, Littman Library, 1986), p. 408.
51. I take this phrase from the dialogue theologian Paul van Buren, who considers it should replace the tendentious term New Testament.
52. For the summary, see Harold Remus, "Justin Martyr's Argument with Judaism," in Wilson, *Separation and Polemic*, p. 67.
53. Ibid., pp. 76ff.
54. Stephen G. Wilson, "Melito and the Jews," in Wilson, *Separation and Polemic*, pp. 97f.
55. Ibid., p. 88.
56. Melito, *Peri Pascha,* lines 711–716, as cited by Wilson from S. G. Hall, *Melito of Sardis "On Pascha" and Fragments* (Oxford: Clarendon, 1972).
57. See Chapter 11, p. 364.
58. We should not forget that the Gnostic writers themselves liked Paul and thought him on their side. Those modern scholars who have seen affinities between Paul's theology and Gnosticism have some ancient authority to support them.
59. Some have seen in this aspect of Marcion's theology a common feature with the

revolutionary modern theology of (especially the early) Karl Barth, who has been accused of a kind of Marcionism on the ground in part of his characterization of God as wholly other. I think this was always a misreading of Barth, but it is certainly so of his mature work, which is right in line with the anti-Judaism of Christian orthodoxy in the second and succeeding centuries in asserting systematically that all God's dealings with the world, in revelation or redemption, come through Christ.

60. See David P. Efroymson, "Tertullian's Anti-Judaism and its Role in his Theology," Ph.D. thesis, Temple University (Ann Arbor, MI: University Microfilms, 1977), and his "The Patristic Connection," in Alan T. Davies, ed. *Antisemitism and the Foundations of Christianity* (New York: Paulist Press, 1979); also Stephen G. Wilson, "Marcion and the Jews," in Wilson, *Separation and Polemic*, pp. 45–58.
61. Efroymson, "Tertullian's Anti-Judaism," p. 228.
62. Efroymson, "Tertullian's Anti-Judaism" and "The Patristic Connection," pass.
63. See Rosemary Ruether, *Faith and Fratricide* (San Francisco: Seabury Press, 1974), especially Chapter 3.
64. Cf. Lloyd Gaston, "Retrospect," in Wilson, *Separation and Polemic*, p. 164.
65. Ruether, *Faith and Fratricide*, p. 124.
66. Efroymson, "Tertullian's Anti-Judaism," pp. 13f.
67. Ibid., Chapter 4.
68. Tertullian, *Against Praxeas*, 31, as cited by Efroymson, "Tertullian's Anti-Judaism," pp. 116f.
69. Efroymson.
70. Tertullian, *Against Marcion*, 4:25:3, as cited by Efroymson, p. 119.
71. Efroymson.
72. Ibid., pp. 120–121.
73. Ibid., p. 123.
74. Ibid., p. 122–125.
75. Ibid., p. 146.
76. Ibid., p. 158.
77. Ibid., p. 159.
78. Tertullian, *Adversus Judaeos*, 6:1–2, as cited by Efroymson, "Tertullian's Anti-Judaism," p. 164.
79. Efroymson, p. 180.
80. Ibid., p. 191f.
81. The Arians were an important group in the early Church who considered that Christ though divine existed on a lower level of divinity than the Father. He was like the Father, not one with him in his divinity.
82. Pelagius, after whom Pelagianism is named, was a British monk (his name may mean Morgan) who taught that God's moral commands imply the capacity to obey: ought means can. He thus denied the Augustinian doctrine of original sin, then being formulated. His views were not unnaturally characterized as Jewish, since Jews also do not believe in original sin. But the term had become highly opprobrious.
83. Efroymson, "Tertullian's Anti-Judaism," p. 226, emphasis added.

CHAPTER 6

1. J. M. Hussey, *The Byzantine World* (New York: Harper Torchbooks, 1961), p. 12.
2. Text in English in J. Stevenson, ed., *A New Eusebius* (London: SPCK, 1957), pp. 300ff.

3. James Parkes, *The Conflict of the Church and the Synagogue* (New York: Hermon Press, 1974), p. 185.
4. Ibid., p. 199. As we shall see, it is not completely accurate to say that things got steadily worse for the Jews. There were occasional improvements, but they did not last. The overall trend of events was as Parkes described it.
5. Text in translation in Jacob R. Marcus, *The Jew in the Medieval World: A Source Book: 315–1791* (New York: Atheneum, 1975), p. 4. The last sentence, dealing with converts to Judaism, is given in the original Latin in Edward A. Synan, *The Popes and the Jews in the Middle Ages* (New York: Macmillan, 1965), p. 169.
6. *Codex Theodosianus*, 16, 9, 1. Cf. Parkes, *Conflict*, p. 179.
7. Parkes, p.178.
8. Ibid., pp. 179f. Text in English in Marcus, *The Jew in the Medieval World*, p. 5.
9. *Cod. Theod.*, 16,8,7; 16,8,6. Text in English in Marcus, p. 4f.
10. S. Safrai, *From Roman Anarchy until the Abolition of the Patriarchate*, in *A History of the Jewish People*, ed. H. H. Ben Sasson (Cambridge: Harvard University Press, 1976), p. 353.
11. See Marcus, *The Jew in the Medieval World*, sec. 2, "Julian and the Jews," pp. 8–12.
12. Safrai, *Roman Anarchy*, pp. 353f.
13. Parkes, *Conflict*, p. 180. Cf. Julian, *Epistle* 51. Decree of Valens in *Codex Theodosianus*, 12, 1, 99.
14. Parkes, p.181.
15. *Cod. Theod.* 16, 7, 3; Parkes, p. 181.
16. *Cod. Theod.* 3, 1, 5; Parkes.
17. Safrai, *Roman Anarchy*, p. 354.
18. Parkes, *Conflict*, p. 181.
19. *Cod. Theod.* 16, 8, 26, April 9, 423. Safrai, *Roman Anarchy*, p. 355.
20. Parkes, *Conflict*, p. 185.
21. *Cod. Theod.* 3, 7, 2; 9, 7, 5. Parkes, p. 182.
22. The original Theodosian law is lost, but it is reproduced in *Codex Justiniani* 1, 9, 7. Parkes.
23. Parkes.
24. *Cod.Theod.* 7, 8, 2; 13, 5, 18; 16, 8, 8. Parkes, p. 189.
25. *Cod. Theod.* 16, 8, 9. Translation from Parkes.
26. Parkes, p. 200.
27. *Cod. Theod.* 16, 8, 16; Parkes, p. 201.
28. *Cod. Theod.* 16, 8, 24, Parkes.
29. Parkes.
30. *Cod. Theod.* 16, 8, 23, Parkes, p. 202.
31. *Cod. Theod.* 16, 9, 3, Parkes.
32. We shall hear a good deal more of Chrysostom later in this chapter.
33. *Cod. Theod.* 16, 8, 10, 11 and 15. Parkes, *Conflict*, p. 231.
34. *Cod. Theod.* 9, 45, 2; cf. 16, 8, 23; Parkes, p. 232.
35. *Cod. Theod.* 16, 8, 13; 12, 1, 165; Parkes.
36. Parkes.
37. Ibid., p. 205.
38. *Cod. Theod.* 16, 8, 28; English in Parkes.
39. *Cod.Theod.* 16, 8, 18; Parkes, 234.
40. Cf. Parkes, p. 234.
41. Parkes, p. 235; Safrai, *Roman Anarchy*, p. 355.

42. *Cod. Theod.* 16, 8, 29; Parkes, p. 235; Safrai, p. 355.
43. *Cod.Theod.* 16, 8, 21; Parkes, p. 236. The language of this ruling is very reminiscent of the similarly balanced phrasing of the later Western Constitution on the Jews, known by its first words as *Sicut Judaeis non*. See n. 103.
44. Cf. Parkes, p. 238.
45. Parkes, pp. 238f.
46. See pp. 195.
47. Safrai, *Roman Anarchy*, p. 359.
48. Cf. Henry Chadwick, *The Pelican History of the Church*, vol. 1, *The Early Church* (Harmondsworth, Middlesex: Penguin Books, 1967), p. 209.
49. On Aquila himself, see p. 208.
50. Safrai, *Roman Anarchy*.
51. "His law is not 'antisemitic.' It is 'grandmotherly.' " Parkes, *Conflict*, p. 253.
52. Edward H. Flannery, *The Anguish of the Jews* (New York: Macmillan, 1965), p. 67. Flannery's account of the period after Justinian is the clearest I have been able to find, and I have mostly followed it closely in the text.
53. Marcus, *The Jew in the Medieval World*, sec. 21, Doc. 1 and 2, Ambrose to the Emperor Theodosius, and Ambrose to his sister (excerpted). Cf. Parkes, *Conflict*, pp. 166ff.
54. Cf. Robin Lane Fox, *Pagans and Christians in the Mediterranean world from the second century AD to the conversion of Constantine* (London: Penguin Books, 1988), pp. 664ff.
55. For the English of the canons referred to in the text, see Marcus, *The Jew in the Medieval World*, pp. 101f. Yaffa Eliach in her *Hasidic Tales of the Holocaust* (New York: Oxford University Press, 1982), pp. 198ff, tells the story of Nazis seeking the prayers of Jews during an air raid near the end of the war.
56. Raul Hilberg, *The Destruction of the European Jews* (New York: Harper and Row, Colophon Books, 1979), pp. 5ff.
57. Our guide in this section will be Rosemary Ruether, whose study of the negation of the Jewish people in the church fathers is the core of her influential book *Faith and Fratricide* (San Francisco: Seabury Press, 1974).
58. Ruether, p. 118.
59. Ibid.
60. E.g., Stuart E. Rosenberg, *The Christian Problem: A Jewish View* (New York: Hippocrene Books; Toronto: Deneau, 1986), p. 68.
61. Modern versions frequently render the Hebrew correctly, e.g., New English Bible, "A young woman is with child, and will bear a son, and will call him Immanuel." This translation also clearly brings out the contemporary, rather than eschatological, reference of the prophecy.
62. In fact, the prophetic criticism of the Jewish people in no way implies that their behavior was worse than that of others. The prophets displayed unique moral sensitivity, especially about social evils, sensitivity which they themselves attributed to God. Cf. Abraham J. Heschel, *The Prophets* (New York: The Jewish Publication Society of America, 1962), p. 9 and pass.
63. Ruether, *Faith and Fratricide*, p. 131.
64. Ibid., p. 125.
65. Eusebius, *Demonstration of the Gospel*, 1, 6, 17, cited by Ruether, p. 125.
66. John Chrysostom, *Orations against the Jews*, 6, 2, ascribing the statement incorrectly to Ezekiel (16:31, 23:3). Cited by Ruether, p. 125.

67. *Letter of Barnabas*, 4, 8.
68. Ruether, *Faith and Fratricide*, pp. 125f.
69. Ephrem the Syrian as cited by Ruether, p. 128.
70. Ruether, pp.127f.
71. John Chrysostom, *Orations against the Jews*, 5:6, basing himself on a reading of Deuteronomy 28:56 and Lamentations 4:10, taken altogether out of context.
72. Chrysostom, *Orations against the Jews*, 6, 2.
73. Ruether, *Faith and Fratricide*, p. 129.
74. Augustine, *Against the Jews*, 7 (10), cited by Ruether, p. 130.
75. Ruether, pp. 130f.
76. Cf. Archbishop Carli's introduction to D. Judant, *Judaisme et Christianisme, Dossier patristique* (Paris: Editions du Cedre, 1969), cited by David P. Efroymson, "Tertullian's Anti-Judaism and its Role in his Theology," Ph.D. thesis, Temple University (Ann Arbor: University Microfilms, 1977), p. 229: "an authentic datum of tradition," an "untouchable form of Catholic doctrine."
77. Genesis 25:23. Ruether, *Faith and Fratricide*, p. 133.
78. Cf. Justin, cited by Ruether, p. 148.
79. Ruether, p. 146f. Ruether gives as a correct translation: May their loins quiver. Cf. the authoritative new translation of the Jewish Publication Society, Third Section, *The Writings,* which has: May their loins collapse continually.
80. Cyprian, *Testimonies*, 20, cited by Ruether, *Faith and Fratricide*, p. 135.
81. Ruether, p. 137.
82. Ibid., p. 13, emphasis in original.
83. Ibid., pp. 137f. The description of the Church as the true Israel appears as early as Justin, *Dialogue with Trypho*, 123.
84. Ruether, p. 139.
85. Ibid., pp. 140f.
86. Ibid., p. 142.
87. Ibid., p.149. Cf. Joshua Trachtenberg, *The Devil and the Jews* (Philadelphia: The Jewish Publication Society of America, 1983), p. 32, and see his whole chapter on "The Antichrist."
88. Ruether, p. 149.
89. Ibid., p. 150.
90. Ibid., p. 151.
91. Eusebius as summarized by Ruether, p. 151.
92. Ruether, p. 151f.
93. Ibid., p. 153f.
94. The test usually cited was Leviticus 18:5. Cf. also Deuteronomy 8:1, 3.
95. Ruether, *Faith and Fraticide*, p. 155.
96. Ibid., p. 156.
97. Ibid., p. 160.
98. NEB. Cf. the same Psalm passage, 40:6–7, as more correctly translated by the same English version: If thou hadst desired sacrifice and offering, thou wouldst have given me ears to hear.

    The new Jewish Publication Society translation has: You gave me to understand that/You do not desire sacrifice and meal offering. The translators note that the meaning of the Hebrew is not clear. However, the unclarity lies in the syntax rather than in the word mistranslated "body," which certainly means "ears."

99. Ruether, *Faith and Fratricide*, p. 160.
100. Cf. for example the famous icon painted by Rublev, one of the most beautiful and famous of all icons, which depicts this scene, and also represents the table at which Abraham entertains the angels as the eucharistic table, furnished with bread and wine.
101. Ruether, *Faith and Fratricide*, p. 161.
102. Ibid., p. 164.
103. John Chrysostom, *Against the Jews*, 1:6. Harold Remus, "Justin Martyr's Argument with Judaism," in *Anti-Judaism in Early Christianity, vol. 2, Separation and Polemic*, ed. Stephen G. Wilson (Waterloo, ON: Canadian Corporation for Studies in Religion, Wilfrid Laurier University Press, 1986), p. 80, cited from R. L. Wilken, " The Jews and Christian Apologetics after Theodosius I *Cunctos Populos*," *Harvard Theological Review* 73 (1980): 451–471.
104. Cf. Malcolm Hay, *The Roots of Christian Anti-Semitism* (New York: Freedom Library Press, 1981), pp. 35f, 68f.
105. Gregory, Letters, VIII, 25, translated by Edward A. Synan in *The Popes and the Jews in the Middle Ages* (New York: Macmillan, 1965), p.46. The first words in Latin of the sentence translated in the text are *Sicut Judaeis non* . . . Marcus, *The Jew in the Medieval World*, pp. 112f, has a translation of Gregory's letter to Fantinus, the papal administrator, or *Defensor*, of Palermo.
106. Synan, *The Popes and the Jews in the Middle Ages*, p. 46.
107. Cf. Max L. Margolis and Alexander Marx, *A History of the Jewish People* (New York: Atheneum, a Temple Book, 1980), p. 298.
108. Text in Latin and English in Synan, *The Popes and the Jews in the Middle Ages*, app. 6, pp. 229ff.
109. Cf. H. H. Ben Sasson, in ed. Sasson, *A History of the Jewish People*, pp. 407ff.

CHAPTER 7

1. Edward H. Flannery, *The Anguish of the Jews* (New York: Macmillan, 1964), pp. 89f.
2. An eyewitness account by a Vancouver resident, Willie Cooper, was published in the *Jewish Western Bulletin*, 20, July 20 1989.
3. Peter Abelard, *A Dialogue of a Philosopher with a Jew, and a Christian*, ed. and trans. Pierre J. Payer (Toronto: Pontifical Institute of Mediaeval Studies, 1979), pp. 32f.
4. For the Jewish understanding of *kiddush haShem*, or hallowing of the divine name by voluntary martyrdom, see H. H. Ben Sasson, ed., *A History of the Jewish People* (Cambridge, MA: Harvard University Press, 1976), pp. 414–418, and Jacob Katz, *Exclusivity and Tolerance* (New York: Behrman House, 1961), pp. 82–92.
5. Cited by Malcolm Hay, *The Roots of Christian Anti-Semitism* (New York: Freedom Library Press, 1981), p. 27.
6. Ibid., pp. 41f. Hay writes at length about St. Bernard, comparing his reactions to the attempted murder of Christians with those where Jews were the victims. He shows from Bernard's own writings that he took the lives of Christians with much greater seriousness than those of Jews. Hay's noble scorn for ecclesiastical whitewashing of Bernard does him honor.
7. Letter of Bernard to the Archbishop of Mainz in Bernard of Clairvaux, *The Letters of Bernard of Clairvaux*, ed. and trans. Bruno Scott James (Chicago: Henry Regnery, 1953). Cf. Hay, *Roots*, p. 49.

8. Hay, *Roots*, p. 43.
9. Cf. Deuteronomy 15:3.
10. Ben Sasson, *History*, p. 473. The foregoing account is based on the full and careful treatment of the matter by Ben Sasson, pp. 469–475 and 389–392.
11. Ibid., p. 472.
12. Cited by Ben Sasson, *History*, p. 479.
13. Ibid.
14. Ibid., pp. 478f.
15. Cf. Augustine's reply to Faustus the Manichean, which sets forth the argument in detail. Like Cain, Jews bear a mark that serves both as a sign of guilt and as a means of protection against the extremity of vengeance. Circumcision was frequently taken to be this mark. This may be the source of the medieval view that the Jews are to be preserved, but in misery, as a witness to their crimes. Augustine also preserves the older view that a Jew converted to Christianity is no longer a Jew. A translation is reproduced in Frank E. Talmage, ed., *Disputation and Dialogue, Readings in the Jewish-Christian Encounter* (New York: Ktav and ADL, 1975), pp. 28–32.
16. Ben Sasson, *History*, p. 480.
17. Jacob R. Marcus, *The Jew in the Medieval World* (New York: Atheneum, 1975), pp. 131–135, reproduces a lengthy extract from William of Newburgh's chronicle. See also Ben Sasson, *History*, p. 473. There is a careful study of the whole incident, as well as of the social and financial situation of the Jews in medieval England in R. B. Dobson, *The Jews of Mediaeval York and the Massacre of 1190*, Borthwick Papers, no. 45 (York: University of York, Borthwick Institute of Historical Research, St. Anthony's Press, 1974). See especially pp. 26–37.
18. Hay, *Roots*, p. 46.
19. Ben Sasson, *History*, p. 473.
20. Marcus, *The Jew in the Medieval World*, pp. 121–126, reproduces the story at length from the contemporary chronicler Thomas of Monmouth, who seems to have been exceptionally credulous even by medieval standards.
21. Marcus, *The Jew in the Medieval World*, pp. 127–130.
22. Ben Sasson, *History*, p. 482; Flannery, *Anguish*, pp. 98f.
23. Cited by Flannery, *Anguish*, p. 99.
24. The blood libel eventually spread to the Middle East. In 1840 it was alleged that sixteen Jews murdered a Catholic priest and his servant and used their blood in the baking of the unleavened bread of Passover. In 1986 the Syrian Minister of Defense, Mustafa Talas, published an updated version of the nineteenth century pamphlet in which the allegations had been contained under the title of *Fatir Sahyun* (The Matzah of Zion), and the book was widely distributed in Syria. ADL Bulletin, June 1989.
25. Simon Wiesenthal Center *Response*, 10:2 (September 1989).
26. Flannery, *Anguish*, p. 100.
27. Ibid.
28. Joshua Trachtenberg, *The Devil and the Jews* (Philadelphia: The Jewish Publication Society of America, 1961 [original edition, 1943]).
29. Marcus gives an English translation of the relevant canons, *The Jew in the Medieval World*, pp. 137–141.
30. Abba Eban, *My People*, new ed. (New York: Behrman House and Random House, 1968; paperback edition, 1984), p. 180.
31. Ibid.

32. Marcus, *The Jew in the Medieval World*, pp. 145–150; Ben Sasson, *History*, p. 485.
33. Ben Sasson, *History*, p. 486.
34. Marcus, *The Jew in the Medieval World*, pp. 145–148.
35. Cf. Ben Zion Bokser, "Talmudic forgeries: a case study in anti-Jewish propaganda," *Contemporary Jewish Record* (July–August 1939), 6–22. I owe this reference to my former student Mark Weintraub, B.A., M.A., Ll.B.
36. Barbara W. Tuchman, *A Distant Mirror: The Calamitous 14th Century* (New York: Ballantine, 1978), pp. 109, 113.
37. Ibid.
38. Ibid., p. 113.
39. Ibid.
40. Ibid., p. 115.
41. Ibid., pp. 115f.
42. Ibid.
43. Eban, *My People*, p. 183.
44. Ben Sasson, *History*, pp. 578f.
45. Ibid. pp. 579f.
46. There have been many advances in the psychoanalytic tradition since Freud. The references in the text to Freud's views should not be taken to indicate that I myself hold to them in detail. I have made use of them in the analysis in the text simply because they are well known and easily followed. In the areas discussed the most controversial points are probably those which deal with the nature of the instinctual drives. Although modification may be needed, I still believe that the Freudian picture of the structure of the mind is broadly correct.
47. Theodor Reik, *Myth and Guilt: The Crime and Punishment of Mankind* (New York: Grosset and Dunlap, 1970), pp. 20–26.
48. Cf. Erik H. Erikson, *Young Man Luther: A Study in Psychoanalysis and History* (London: Faber and Faber, 1959).
49. Reik, *Myth and Guilt*, pp. 175f.

CHAPTER 8

1. The Reformed tradition is the one mostly influenced by Calvinism. In the English-speaking world, the Presbyterian and Congregationalist churches belong to the Reformed tradition. Calvin himself held a more traditional theology, and it was only after his time that these developments took place.
2. See now José Faur, *In the Shadow of History: Jews and Conversos at the Dawn of Modernity* (Albany, NY: State University of New York Press, 1992), for the beliefs, ideas, and historical influence of the conversos. Some of the information in the book is summarized, and placed in a striking new context, in his article "Correlations: The German and the Iberian Experience," *Midstream* 38:5 (June-July 1992): 20–22.
3. Eban, *My People*, new ed. (New York: Behrman House and Random House, 1968; paperback edition, 1984), pp. 187–194.
4. Cf. H. H. Ben Sasson, ed., *A History of the Jewish People* (Cambridge, MA: Harvard University Press, 1976), p. 588.
5. Jacob R. Marcus, *The Jew in the Medieval World* (New York: Atheneum, 1975), pp. 173–178.
6. Eban, *My People*, p. 191.

7. Ibid., p. 196.
8. On this, see *The Enlightened: the writings of Luis de Carvajal el Mozo*, ed., trans., and with an introduction by Seymour B. Liebman (Coral Gables, FL: University of Miami Press, 1967).
9. *Notes on the Correct Way to Present the Jews and Judaism in Preaching and Catechesis*, June 1985, IV, 22. Geoffrey Wigoder, *Jewish-Christian relations since the Second World War* (Manchester and New York: University of Manchester Press, 1988), p. 15.
10. Note 15.
11. Translation from Marcus, *The Jew in the Medieval World*, pp. 166f. The explanations in brackets, however, are mine and replace the ones in his text.
12. Heiko A. Oberman demonstrates conclusively the continuity of Luther's theology from his earliest writings on the Jews in the second decade of the century up to the end, in his extremely important little book, *The Roots of Antisemitism in the Age of Renaissance and Reformation*, trans. James I. Porter (Philadelphia: Fortress Press, 1984). This section of the chapter is based on his book, for the most part.
13. Erik H. Erikson, *Young Man Luther: a Study in Psychoanalysis and History* (London: Faber and Faber, 1959).
14. In German, Lutherans refer to their church as the Evangelical Church, meaning the church of the gospel. This term has quite a different meaning from the same word used of a considerably different group in the English-speaking world, much disapproved of by Lutherans.
15. Marcus, *The Jew in the Medieval World*, pp. 167–169.
16. Oberman, *Roots of Antisemitism*, pp.10, 35, etc.
17. Cf. Ben Sasson, *History*, p. 646.
18. Originally, however, Christianity had itself been divided into many sects, and all these had lived within the Roman Empire alongside other religions. When it abandoned the Torah, Gentile Christianity also lost a religiously based social legislation. It did not substitute its own but took over the existing system of Roman law. Thus, the roots of a more secular understanding of the state lay deep in Christian history and could offer resources for dealing with the breakup of the unitary society of Christendom. It seems likely to me that the reason secularity, and even modern science, developed only in the Christian world has something to do with this original distinction between religion and communal life, originating in the minority status of Christianity within the Roman world. This distinction plays no part in religions such as traditional Judaism, and Islam, or for that matter Hinduism. Once the medieval unity broke up, the possibility of the secular state naturally re-asserted itself. As is frequently said today, the Constantinian era in Christian history had an end as well as a beginning, and clearly the Reformation was the beginning of its end. See also Chapter 1.
19. Cf. Oberman, *Roots of Antisemitism*, Epilogue, pp. 138ff.
20. Cf. Oberman, Chapter 4.
21. See Chapter 9.

CHAPTER 9

1. See the discussion of Jewish rites of conversion in Chapter 4. These were developed in the Second Temple period, after the return from exile. Evidently no need had been previously felt for anything of the kind, though conversion in some sense had certainly

been known; witness the story of Ruth the Moabite woman, the ancestor of King David.

2. Of course the word *religion* already existed and is found in classical Latin. But it does not have the precise meaning we now associate with it. Rather, it refers to the religious attitude, instead of to what we call religion, or a religion. Later, the term was used for particular groups, such as those we call religious orders. Only gradually did the word take on its modern connotation.
3. At first sight, the Roman Empire looks like an exception to this generalization. However, although the Roman Empire could find room for a wide variety of religions, it could do so while maintaining its unity by means of the ecumenical equivalence of the gods; worship of the Emperor, which was acceptable to all within the ecumenical understanding, furnished the "glue," as it has been termed, which held the whole together.

   The Jewish people were the exception that proved the rule. The God they worshiped could not be assimilated to Olympian Zeus or Jupiter Capitolinus on the principle of ecumenical equivalence. The Jews fought hard and at great sacrifice to maintain a distinction that was vital to them. In the end, the Romans conceded the point, for the most part, by regarding Judaism as a national religion of a unique kind. This made Jewish proselytism problematic, and whenever it was vigorous, there was the possibility of countermeasures. Eventually, Jews everywhere were granted Roman citizenship, without having to renounce their religion and its restrictions on interreligious assimilation.

   Christianity, on the other hand, was not a national religion and equaled Judaism in its refusal to join the ecumenical consensus. That is why the Christians were persecuted as "atheists." They would not worship the ecumenically accepted gods, and like Jews, they refused to worship the emperor. Nevertheless, they accepted the validity of Roman law in the social sphere, having abandoned the social legislation of the Torah when they split with Judaism. Even when Christianity became the state religion, the concept of a separate civil law remained in force. That, I believe, is the reason Christianity alone among the great world religions could develop a concept of secularity.

   Students of Eastern religions may also wonder whether the coexistence in India of Hinduism, certainly a traditional religion in the sense referred to in the text, with Buddhism and Jainism, may not also be an exception to this generalization. I think the answer is that Jainism and Buddhism were not regarded, as Islam would later be, as different religions, but as sects within Hinduism, which did not disrupt the unity of society. Once Islam was introduced into the subcontinent, communal strife began, and is still a serious problem in the modernizing societies of India and Pakistan.
4. Cf. Quran 5:82; 5:51; 2:61; 3:12.
5. The PLO weekly magazine, *El-Istiqlal*, serialized in its issues of December 13 and 20, 1989, a five-thousand-word article systematically denying the historical reality of the Holocaust. The magazine, published in Cyprus, serves as the PLO's official organ in the Israeli-administered territories of the West Bank and Gaza. This is the first time the PLO had chosen this form of enmity to Jews. More traditionally, they have said the Holocaust was not the fault of the Arab world and that they should not have to pay for it. The reference is taken from the Simon Wiesenthal Center's *Response*, 2:2 (May 1990). The center sent a letter to Secretary of State James Baker, requesting that the U.S. officially protest in the context of its dialogue with the PLO.

6. It has been argued by the Israeli scholar Yirmiyahu Yovel that modernity and secularism owe more to Spinoza than to any other thinker, and Spinoza was of course a Jew. Yovel himself argues, however, that it was his Marrano heritage far more than his actual Jewishness that influenced Spinoza's thinking, and that he sought a foundation for secularity that should be neither Jewish nor Christian. The thesis is controversial and subject to further critical examination by other historians of thought. Even if Yovel is right, it appears that the foundations of Spinoza's thought lie precisely in the *Christianized* Judaism of the Marranos.
7. See, for example, Paul Hazard, *The European Mind [1680–1715]* (Cleveland and New York: Meridian, 1963).
8. *Nathan the Wise* came out in 1779. A conveniently accessible translation of the allegory of the rings can be found in Frank E. Manuel, ed., *The Enlightenment* (Englewood Cliffs, NJ: Prentice Hall, 1965), pp. 63–68.
9. Cited in H. H. Ben Sasson, ed., *A History of the Jewish People* (Cambridge, MA: Harvard University Press, 1976), p. 742.
10. Ibid.
11. Arthur Hertzberg, *The French Enlightenment and the Jews* (New York: Columbia University Press, 1968), pp. 300ff.
12. It is not without interest that Marx, so often referred to as a Jew but in fact a post-Christian antisemite, was heavily exposed to Voltaire in his youth.
13. Hertzberg, *French Enlightenment*, p. 313.
14. Cited in Ben Sasson, *History*, p. 745.
15. Cited by Ettinger, "The Modern Period," in Ben Sasson, *History*, p. 745.
16. Hertzberg, *French Enlightenment*, p. 276.
17. On Fichte, see Alan Davies, *Infected Christianity: A study of modern racism* (Kingston, ON: McGill-Queen's University Press, 1988), pp. 30–33.
18. As cited by Ettinger, "Modern Period," p. 745.
19. For a vivid personal account of these events, see the relevant chapters in Yitshaq Ben-Ami, *Years of Wrath, Days of Glory: Memoirs from the Irgun* (New York: Robert Speller and Sons, 1982).
20. Cited in Ben Sasson, *History*, p. 746.
21. Cited from Ettinger, p. 747.
22. Hertzberg, *French Enlightenment*, pp. 264ff, and the preceding pages.
23. Ibid., p. 1.
24. Ettinger, pp. 746f, 760.
25. Abba Eban, *My People*, new ed. (New York: Behrman House and Random House, 1968; paperback edition 1984), p. 259.
26. Ibid.
27. Ettinger, pp. 761f. Eban, pp. 258–261.
28. Eban, p. 261.
29. Cited from Ettinger, p. 762.
30. Cited from Eban, p. 263. See the context in Eban for a fuller account.
31. Eban, pp. 263–266.

CHAPTER 10

1. On Bauer, Marx, and the twentieth century New Left, see (from a slightly different point of view) the excellent analysis of Shlomo Avineri, "Radical theology, the New

Left, and Israel," in *Auschwitz: Beginning of a New Era?*, ed. Eva Fleischner (New York: Ktav, 1977, pp. 241–254; also Milton Himmelfarb, "Response to Shlomo Avineri," in Fleischner, *Auschwitz*, pp.267–272.

2. Since he was born of a Jewish mother, if she had not yet converted to Christianity by the time he was born Marx would be considered a Jew halachically. However, his own baptism and membership in a Christian church would in any case have constituted him an apostate, a condition from which he could have returned by repentance, without reconversion. But in Orthodox Jewish eyes, he was only in this minimal sense Jewish. As a Jewish apostate, his descent made him potentially, not actually, Jewish.
3. Isaiah Berlin, *Karl Marx: His Life and Environment* (New York: OUP Galaxy Books, 1963), pp. 26ff.
4. E.g., Erich Fromm, foreword to T. B. Bottomore, ed. and trans., *Karl Marx; Early Writings* (New York: McGraw-Hill, 1963), pp. iv–v.
5. Dennis Prager and Joseph Telushkin, *Why the Jews?* (New York: Simon and Schuster, Touchstone Books, 1985), p. 138.
6. Sidney Hook, *From Hegel to Marx: Studies in the Intellectual Development of Karl Marx* (London: Victor Gollancz, 1936), p. 278n.
7. Cited by Prager and Telushkin, *Why the Jews?*, p. 139.
8. Ibid.
9. Prager and Telushkin call them "non-Jewish Jews," following Isaac Deutscher, who uses the term in a positive sense about himself and people like him. They devote a chapter to them. From medieval converts to Christianity to current Jewish apologists for the Arab enemies of Israel, converts from Judaism have been among the most dangerous enemies of the Jewish people.
10. English translations are to be found in Bottomore, *Karl Marx; Early Writings*, pp. 1–40.
11. Berlin, *Karl Marx: His Life and Environment*, p. 99.
12. *Bruno Bauer on the Jewish Question*, Bottomore, p. 10.
13. *Bauer on the Capacity of the present-day Jews and Christians to become free*, Bottomore, p. 32.
14. *The Jewish Question*, Bottomore, p. 21.
15. Other translators have "haggling," which may convey the idea better.
16. *Capacity*, Bottomore, p. 34.
17. Ibid.
18. Ibid., p. 36.
19. Ibid., p. 37.
20. Ibid.
21. Ibid., p. 39.
22. Ibid., p. 40.
23. Even Hitler admired his writings on the Jewish problem.
24. Prager and Telushkin, *Why the Jews?*, citing Jacob Katz, *From Prejudice to Destruction, 1700–1933*, p. 121.
25. Prager and Telushkin, citing George Lichtheim, "Socialism and the Jews," in his *Collected Essays* (New York: Viking Press, 1973), p. 424.
26. Ibid.
27. Ibid.
28. Cf. Leon Poliakov, "Theory of Race," in *Anti-Semitism* (Jerusalem: Keter, Israel Pocket Library, 1974), p. 179.
29. Cited by Poliakov, "Theory of Race," p. 181.
30. Cited by Ettinger, p. 804.

31. We should notice that Wagner shows himself to be an adherent of the new racialism by identifying Mendelssohn as a Jewish musician, when in fact he was a Christian, in spite of his Jewish descent. Much of his music is clearly in a Christian tradition.
32. For a fuller account, see Barnet Litvinoff, *The Burning Bush: Antisemitism and World History* (London: Fontana/Collins, 1989), pp. 179–185.
33. Cited by Lucy S. Dawidowicz, *The War against the Jews, 1933–1945* (New York: Holt, Rinehart and Winston, 1975), p. 7.
34. Eugen Dühring, *Der Judenfrage* (1865), cited by Conor Cruise O'Brien, *The Siege: The Saga of Israel and Zionism* (New York: Simon and Schuster, 1986), p. 57.
35. Dühring, *Der Judenfrage*, citations from O'Brien, *The Siege*.
36. Ibid., p. 58.
37. Cited by Dawidowicz, *War against the Jews*, p. 36.
38. Cf. Alan T. Davies, "The rise of racism in the nineteenth century: symptom of modernity," in *Modernity and Religion*, ed. William Nicholls (Waterloo, ON: SR Supplements no. 19, Wilfrid Laurier University Press, 1987), p. 48.
39. *Histoire générale et système comparé des langues sémitiques* (Paris, 1855), p. 4. Cited by Litvinoff, *Burning Bush*, p. 188.
40. Ibid.
41. Cf. Emil L. Fackenheim, *The Jewish Return into History: Reflections in the Age of Auschwitz and a New Jerusalem* (New York: Schocken Books, 1978).
42. O'Brien, *The Siege*, p. 62.
43. Ibid. For the best account of Drumont known to me, see Malcolm Hay, *The Roots of Christian Anti-Semitism* (New York: Freedom Library Press, 1981), Chapter 7.
44. Hay, *Roots of Christian Anti-Semitism*, p. 183.
45. Cited by Hay, p. 182.
46. Ibid., p.185.
47. Ibid., citation, p. 185. Since of course the blood libel is a lie, one can hardly dissent from Drumont's view that it is the most hateful imposture in human history.
48. Ibid., p. 179.
49. Jean Drault, cited by Hay, p. 178.
50. Ferdinand Brunetière, in *Revue des deux mondes*, cited by Hay, p. 180. Brunetière began his review of *La France juive* with the words "I have little use for Jews; in fact I have no use for them at all." Cited p. 198.
51. Cited by Hay, p. 178.
52. Ibid.
53. Ibid., citation, p. 181.
54. Ibid., p. 191. Compare the contemporary calumny of some antisemites in the former Soviet Union, who accuse Jews of deliberating infecting the population with AIDS.
55. Ibid.
56. Ibid., citation, p. 186.
57. Ibid.
58. Jean Drault, cited by Hay, p. 192.
59. Cited by Hay, p. 193.
60. *Notre jeunesse*, p. 64, cited by Hay, p. 211.
61. Péguy's word for the resisters: "We were heroes. This must be said, in all simplicity, for I am sure that no one else will say it for us." Cited by Hay, p. 212.
62. Hay, p. 194.
63. Ibid.

64. Ibid., p. 196.
65. Ibid., pp. 196, 198f.
66. Cited in O'Brien, *The Siege*, p. 32, from Salo W. Baron, *The Russian Jew under Tsars and Soviets* (New York: Macmillan, 1965).
67. O'Brien, p.33.
68. Ibid.
69. Cf. the article "Numerus Clausus" in *Anti-Semitism*, p. 157.
70. O'Brien, *The Siege*, pp. 34ff.
71. Ibid., p. 34.
72. Based on O'Brien, p. 37.
73. Cited by O'Brien, p. 38, from Byrne, *Pobedonostsev*.
74. Cf. O'Brien, p. 38.
75. O'Brien, p. 40.
76. Ettinger, p. 881.
77. Ibid.
78. Ibid., p. 883.
79. "Numerus Clausus," pp. 158ff.
80. Ettinger, pp. 886ff.
81. Ibid., p. 887.
82. For details see Ibid., pp. 887f. A concise and detailed account is also to be found in the *Encyclopaedia Judaica*.
83. As cited by Leon Poliakov, "Protocols of the Elders of Zion," in *Anti-Semitism*, p. 136.
84. On the *Protocols*, see Norman Cohn, *Warrant for Genocide* (London: Eyre and Spottiswoode, 1967), the standard work, and much more briefly, the *Encyclopaedia Judaica* article.
85. Jacob Toury, "Anti-Semitic Political Parties and Organizations," in *Anti-Semitism*, p. 139.
86. Cf. Dawidowicz, *War against the Jews*, p. 42.
87. Dawidowicz, p.34.
88. Toury, "Anti-Semitic Political Parties," pp. 142f.
89. Ibid., pp. 143f.
90. Dawidowicz, *War against the Jews*, p. 39.
91. Cited by O'Brien, *The Siege*, p. 59.
92. Toury, "Anti-Semitic Political Parties," pp. 144f.
93. In the first chapter of Davidowicz, *War against the Jews*.
94. Ibid., p. 16.
95. Cited from Hitler's *Table Talk* by O'Brien, *The Siege*, p. 61.
96. Dawidowicz, *War against the Jews*, p. 17, citing a letter from Hitler to his military superior in the Press and Propaganda Office, who had asked for enlightenment on the Jewish question.
97. Whether Hitler chose the Jews because he needed a scapegoat for his political aims or scapegoated the Jews because his political aims were to eliminate them is debated. Both views can be supported from his recorded utterances. On the one hand, he said that if the Jews had not existed it would have been necessary to invent them, while on the other hand he acknowledged that the theory of race lacked scientific foundation but was politically useful for his primary aim.
98. As Dawidowicz and others have pointed out, hatred of Jews also overcame rational policy during the war itself. Resources were diverted to the Final Solution that were badly needed for the war effort, perhaps contributing to Germany's defeat by the Allies.

Or perhaps we should agree with Dawidowicz that Hitler's real war was the one against the Jews, and in that war he was not defeated.

CHAPTER 11

1. In fairness it has to be said that the same was true of not a few Jewish leaders, especially in America. Cf., e.g., most recently Alan M. Dershowitz, *Chutzpah* (New York: Little, Brown, 1991), pp. 279–282.
2. Cf., for example, Richard Rubenstein, *After Auschwitz* (Indianapolis: Bobbs Merrill, 1966), pp. 47–58, on his interview with Dr. Heinrich Grüber, Dean of the Evangelical (Protestant) Church in East and West Berlin.
3. Some less prominent pastors did rescue and protect Jews, but the enterprise required secrecy.
4. It is known that the Vrba-Wetzler report on Auschwitz did reach Pius, and actually elicited his intervention with Admiral Horthy on behalf of the Jews. But this was still behind the scenes. In any event, the pope had good information even before the escape of Rudolf Vrba and Alfred Wetzler from Auschwitz and the circulation of their report, which gave the first detailed and accurate account of the measures of extermination being taken in the death camps.
5. See, e.g., the various contributions to Eric Bentley, ed., *The Storm over the Deputy* (New York: Grove Press, 1964).
6. Most offensive to many were the words of the Anglican Archbishop Tutu on his visit to Israel, when he blamed the Jews for not forgiving their enemies and insisted that the cause of the Palestinians was fully comparable with that of black South Africans. Meanwhile, and in his presence, Palestinian posters in Arabic, which he could not read, were saying, "Today the Saturday people, tomorrow the Sunday people."
7. Rolf Hochhuth, *The Deputy* (New York: Grove Press, 1964).
8. The most important of the reactions are conveniently collected together in Bentley, *Storm*.
9. The title of Hochhuth's *The Deputy*–in German *Der Stellvertreter*– plays on the pope's title as the *Vicar* of Christ in a way that cannot be rendered in English. *Vicar* means deputy or representative substitute, as *Stellvertreter* does in German. But the play could hardly be called *The Vicar* in English.
10. John F. Morley, *Vatican Diplomacy and the Jews during the Holocaust 1939–1943* (New York: Ktav, 1980), p. 94.
11. Irving Greenberg, "Cloud of Smoke, Pillar of Fire: Judaism, Christianity and Modernity after the Holocaust," in *Auschwitz, Beginning of a New Era? Reflections on the Holocaust*, ed. Eva Fleischner (New York: Ktav, 1977), p. 11f and note.
12. Michael Dov Weissmandl, from whose book in Hebrew the report is taken by Greenberg, also describes a conversation of his own with the "papal nuncio" in 1944. According to his account, the nuncio told him, "There is no innocent blood of Jewish children in the world. All Jewish blood is guilty. You have to die. This is the punishment that has been awaiting you because of that sin [sc., the killing of Christ]. "

    In fact there was no papal nuncio in Slovakia, though Rudof Vrba also describes a meeting with the "papal nuncio," after his escape from Auschwitz, during which he gave him full details of what was going on there, and the "nuncio" wept. (Rudolf Vrba and A. Bestic, *44070: The conspiracy of the twentieth century*, new expanded ed. [Bellingham,

WA: Star & Cross, 1989], pp. 256f.)

It seems much more probable, as the historian J. S. Conway implies in his appendix to Vrba's book, that the "nuncio" Vrba met with was in fact the chargé d'affaires, Mgr Burzio, whose intervention on behalf of the Jews has been described above. Probably, therefore, Weissmandl either did not understand Catholic titles or did not correctly remember who had said these things. Was it really Archbishop Kametko?

13. This was the claim of Cardinal G. B. Montini, later Pope Paul VI, in his response to the showing of *The Deputy*. Or did Montini mean "harm" to the Catholic church rather than to the Jews? See Bentley, *Storm*, pp. 66ff.
14. Morley, *Vatican Diplomacy*, p. 209. Morley's book extends to 1943, the latest date whose documents were open to scholars when he did his research. If the strong statement condemning the pope, the final paragraph of his book, is compared with what he said in its opening pages, it may be fair to conclude that Morley did not expect to find the pope responsible for Vatican inadequacy, and did not welcome his own conclusions. If anything, this gives them additional weight.
15. Guenter Lewy cites the letter of Archbishop Bertram, writing to the Minister of the Interior on November 11, 1942, in which the writer takes care to point out that the Catholic protest was not due "to lack of love for the German nationality, lack of feeling of national dignity, and also not to underestimation of the harmful Jewish influence upon German culture and national interests." Lewy, "Pius XII, the Jews and the German Catholic Church," in Bentley, *Storm*, p. 205.
16. See the vivid account from the Irgun point of view in Yitshaq Ben-Ami, *Years of Wrath, Days of Glory: Memories from the Irgun* (New York: Robert Speller and Sons, 1982).
17. Literally, clean of Jews. The expression "ethnic cleansing," used in the former Yugoslavia in 1992, had a similar meaning.
18. Walter Schellenburg, *The Labyrinth: Memoirs of Walter Schellenburg* (New York: Harper, 1956), cited by Hochhuth, *The Deputy*, pp. 309ff.
19. In Germany, everyone normally paid part of their taxes to the support of the church to which they belonged, unless they specifically contracted out.
20. Guenter Lewy states that 22.7 percent even of the SS remained Catholic, in spite of all attempts to detach them from religion. "Pius XII," p. 208.
21. Cited by Lewy, "Pius XII," p. 216.
22. See the work of Nechama Tec on rescuers: *When Light pierced the Darkness: Christian rescue of Jews in Nazi-occupied Europe* (New York: Oxford University Press, 1986), and *In the Lion's Den, the life of Oswald Rufeisen* (New York: Oxford University Press, 1990).
23. For a fuller account see, e.g., Nora Levin, *The Holocaust: the destruction of European Jewry, 1933–1945* (New York: Thomas Crowell, 1968), pp. 548–560; also Martin Gilbert, *The Holocaust: A history of the Jews of Europe during the Second World War* (New York: Henry Holt, 1985), pp. 547f.
24. Thomas F. Stransky, C.S.P., "The declaration on non-Christian religions," in *Vatican II: An inter-faith appraisal*, ed. John H. Miller, C.S.C. (Notre Dame: Notre Dame Press, 1966), p. 339.
25. Austin Flannery, O.P., ed., *Vatican Council II, The Conciliar and post-conciliar documents* (Boston: St. Paul Editions, 1980), pp. 738ff. This sentence, carelessly reported in the press, offended many Jews by its suggestion that they were to be absolved for a crime they had not committed. The saying went around that the council had absolved Arthur Goldberg, then the United States ambassador to the United Nations, for killing Christ.
26. Ibid., p. 741.

27. Ibid., pp. 743ff. The *Notes* issued in 1985 carry on and extend the positive interpretation of *Nostra aetate.* Both are reproduced in an appendix to Geoffrey Wigoder, *Jewish-Christian Relations since the Second World War* (Manchester: Manchester University Press, 1988).
28. The Vatican took symbolic action in conformity with Vatican II by terminating the cult of Simon of Trent, another of the fictitious child martyrs whose cult kept antisemitism flourishing in the Church.
29. See Pope John Paul II, *On Jews and Judaism, 1979–1986*, ed. Eugene J. Fisher and Leon Klenicki (Washington, DC: United States Catholic Conference, Inc., 1987).
30. *The Globe and Mail*, 30 August 1989.
31. The former president of the Canadian Council of Churches, Heather Johnston, visited Auschwitz in the summer of 1989 and actually spoke to some of the nuns as a woman and a fellow Christian. She had a lengthy conversation with Sister Maria, who was "bright and articulate." Johnston said in an interview:

> When I asked Sister Maria about reports indicating that the convent might be moved to allay understandable Jewish sensitivities, she firmly replied: "We have never ever promised to move. We have never received any official documentation."
>
> I was saddened. At first I thought that it was a case of the hierarchy of men not including women in this or any other conversation indicating a possible move. But then I had reason to believe that nowhere was such a move even being discussed. Sister Maria was not at all open to where I came from. I asked her, "Surely, the essence of our common Christian faith is love. Couldn't the convent, out of concern and love for the Jewish people, move?"
>
> Adamantly, Sister Maria replied: "I don't see why we should."
>
> "I could not touch her heart," sighed Heather Johnston.
>
> She tried another tactic. "What if the Pope were to use his good offices to ask the convent to move?" I asked Sister Maria. To which she replied, incredulously: "Our Pope? He will never ask us to move! He's from here!"

The above quotation is taken from an interview with *The B'nai Berith Covenant*, September 1989, p. 7.

32. *Time* magazine, 21 August 1989, carried an account of the repudiation of the agreement by Macharski, which seemed to be an accurate report of the facts and of the background to them. Catholic leaders in the United States, according to the *New York Times*, 3 September 1989, also called for the honoring of the agreement, or for the nuns voluntarily to go the second mile and move out.
33. *Globe and Mail.*
34. The *New York Times*, 3 September 1989.
35. "Antisemitism without Jews," an interview by Michel Zlotowski, Paris correspondent, with Claude Lanzmann, *Jerusalem Post*, 15 September 1989.
36. A full account of the demonstrations by the Jewish group, and of the events on the spot, written by one of its leaders, Glenn Richter, was published in *The Jewish Western Bulletin* on 17 August 1989, and doubtless in other Jewish periodicals across the continent.
37. "Glemp stumbles on rock-hewn Jewish history," by Peter Hebblethwaite, and Editorial, "Postpone Glemp's visit," *National Catholic Reporter*, 15 September 1989.
38. The interview was reported by Alan Dershowitz, a Harvard law professor and civil

rights activist, in *The Jerusalem Post*, citing an article in a Polish-American weekly, *The Post Eagle*. The article reproduces an interview given by Sister Teresa to a Colonel Francis A. Winiarz, a retired U.S. Air Force psychologist active in Polish American affairs. See "A pious anti-Semite," *Jerusalem Post*, International Edition, 2 December 1989, p. 8B.

39. *Time*, Canadian edition, 2 October 1989, p. 21.
40. Ibid.
41. Letter in *Jerusalem Post*, International Edition, 24 February 1990.
42. Personal communication from Erwin Nest, Executive Director of the Canadian Jewish Congress, Pacific Region, who was himself a student in the postwar Polish school system.
43. Quotations are taken from an article by Alfred Lipson, *Midstream*, 37:5 (June–July 1991) 30–32. The article, besides containing the fullest account of the letter available to me, is an illuminating and authoritative account of the current situation in Polish Catholicism as it affects Jews.
44. Statement by the World Evangelical Fellowship, meeting at Willowbank, Bermuda, April 26–29, 1989. I owe the text of this statement to Dr. James I. Packer, one of its authors.
45. Cited by Wigoder, *Jewish-Christian Relations*, p. 5.
46. The incident in which a group of religious Jews succeeded in purchasing through an intermediary a building in the Christian quarter of Jerusalem known as St. John's Hospice, and began to move in, was highly symptomatic. Many Israelis and other Jews considered the move provocative but failed to notice the intense antisemitism of the Christian reaction, especially among the Greek Orthodox.
47. I am reminded of the brilliant play on words by the theologian Paul van Buren in a speech at Jerusalem in 1984 at which I was present, when he referred to the United Nations as "the United Goyim."
48. Cited by J. A. Emerson Vermaat, "The World Council of Churches, Israel and the P.L.O.," *Midstream* (November 1984) 3–9. Vermaat is a Dutch journalist who has closely followed the affairs of the World Council and its constituent bodies. His article contains a convenient summary of World Council statements on the subject. Subsequent citations from the same article.
49. "Gathered for Life: Official Report," VI Assembly, World Council of Churches, Vancouver, Canada, 24 July–10 August 1983 (Geneva: World Council of Churches, 1983).
50. Paul M. van Buren, *A Christian Theology of the People Israel: A theology of the Jewish-Christian Reality, p. 2* (New York: The Seabury Press, 1983), p. xv.
51. A. Roy Eckardt, *Elder and Younger Brothers: The encounter of Jews and Christians* (New York: Schocken Books, 1973), pp. xix f.
52. Edward H. Flannery, *The Anguish of the Jews: Twenty-three centuries of antisemitism* (New York: Macmillan, 1964).
53. Rosemary R. Ruether, "Antisemitism and Christian theology," in Fleischner, *Auschwitz*, pp.79–92.
54. Gregory Baum, *The Jews and the Gospel* (New York: Newman Press, 1961), reissued in revised form as *Is the New Testament Anti-Semitic?* (New York: Paulist Press, 1965).
55. Alan T. Davies, *Anti-Semitism and the Christian Mind* (New York: Seabury, 1969). Cf. also his introduction to Alan T. Davies, ed., *Antisemitism and the Foundations of Christianity* (New York: Paulist Press, 1979), a symposium on Rosemary R. Ruether's *Faith and Fratricide* (San Francisco: Seabury Press, 1974), and the responses it drew.

CHAPTER 12

1. Cf. Wolfhart Pannenberg (perhaps the leading Protestant theologian of the day), "Protestant Theology and the Jews Today," in *Jesus, God and Man*, trans. L. Wilkins and D. Priebe (Philadelphia: Westminster Press, 1968), pp. 254-255:

    > With this message [sc., the message of the resurrection of the one who was rejected in the name of the law] the foundation of Jewish religion collapsed. The point must be held fast today even in the discussion with Judaism. One may not be taken in by benevolent statements of liberal Jews about Jesus as a prophet or allow that the conspiracy for Jesus's death was merely a failure of the Jewish authorities. There may be some truth in such explanations. But the conflict with the law in the background of Jesus's collision with the authorities must remain apparent in all its sharpness: either Jesus had been a blasphemer or the law of the Jews–and with it Judaism itself as a religion–is done away with.

    Cf. p. 260. "In the light of Jesus's resurrection not only the circle of his Jewish judges but in principle every Jew who lives under the authority of and is bound to the law thereby is shown to be a blasphemer."
2. See F. E. Talmage, *Disputation and Dialogue: Readings in the Jewish-Christian Encounter* (New York: Ktav and ADL, 1975), pp. 51ff.
3. The interview with Strugnell is now available in English translation in Herschel Shanks, ed., *Understanding the Dead Sea Scrolls: A Reader from the Biblical Archaeology Review* (New York: Random House, 1992), pp. 259–263. See also editor's own article on the controversy, pp. 262–274.
4. See Yehezkel Kaufmann, *The Religion of Israel, from its beginnings to the Babylonian Exile*, ed. and trans. Moshe Greenberg (Chicago: University of Chicago Press, 1960).
5. Alan M. Dershowitz, *Chutzpah* (New York: Little, Brown, 1991), p. 121.
6. On Montagu see David Fromkin, *A Peace to End all Peace: the fall of the Ottoman Empire and the creation of the modern Middle East* (New York: Avon Books, 1990), pp. 294f.
7. The expression was coined by Isaac Deutscher, to refer to deracinated Jews such as himself. He saw the future of Jewish culture as belonging to such non-Jewish Jews. The phrase has been taken up by others but used in a less positive sense.
8. I was glad to note that David Wyman, the distinguished historian, also drew attention to this in his address to the Boston CAMERA conference, recorded on the videotape already mentioned.
9. The *New York Times* article is discussed in its historical context by Marvin Weitz in *Midstream* (October 1992) 11–13.

CHAPTER 13

1. In the jargon of the concentration camps, the word *Muselmann* (i.e., Muslim) came to be used for a person whose physical and mental debilitation was so complete that they had lost the will to live. Essentially, the *Muselmänner* were walking corpses. Probably the word originated from the common view of Muslims as people who resign themselves to fate.
2. Emil L. Fackenheim, *To Mend the World: Foundations of Future Jewish Thought* (New York: Schocken Books, 1982), pp. 280f, 286–288.

3. Emil L. Fackenheim, *God's Presence in History: Jewish affirmations and philosophical reflections* (New York: Harper Torchbooks, 1970), p. 84.
4. Cf. even Edward H. Flannery, *The Anguish of the Jews* (New York: Macmillan, 1964), p.60: "A distinction–difficult to draw–must be recognized between the ambiguous phenomenon of 'Christian antisemitism' and 'anti-Judaism' which legitimately and essentially constitutes a part of Christian teaching and apologetics."

   William Le Saint, in *Judaism and the Christian Seminary Curriculum*, ed. J. Bruce Long (Chicago: Loyola University Press, 1966), pp. 90–92: "Theological, or essential, anti-Judaism is found in all the Fathers of the Church. The early Christians said that Jesus of Nazareth was the Messiah; this the Jews denied. Accordingly, the Fathers of the Church thought of the Jews as essentially anti-Christian, and of themselves not so much as anti-Semitic as anti-anti-Christian. . . . Essential, or axiomatic, antisemitism always has been and, in my view, always will be a part of the Christian tradition." Cf. Richard Longenecker, in Long, *Seminary*, p. 102, "I would propose that Christianity is inherently anti-Judaic but . . . that does not make it anti-Semitic per se." These citations are taken from David P. Efroymson in "Tertullian's Anti-Judaism and its Role in His Theology" Ph.D. Thesis, Temple University (Ann Arbor, MI: University Microfilms, 1977), p. 229, n. 12. He comments, "The evidence from Tertullian tends to make one less enthusiastic about such a view. One is tempted to ask how, concretely, such an essential or inherent anti-Judaism would differ from Tertullian's."
5. Cf. the preposterous claim of the Vancouver Assembly of the World Council of Churches that guilt for the Holocaust had caused the churches to give insufficient weight to the Palestinian cause.
6. There are a few signs that these issues are being faced. Among historical scholars Lloyd Gaston, and among theologians Paul van Buren, are now careful to speak of the Hebrew Scriptures as the Bible, and the New Testament books as "apostolic writings."
7. Sayings of Jesus, such as Matthew 10:5, discouraging a Gentile mission, are not likely to have been preserved by the Gentile church unless they were authentic, and too important to be ignored. Jesus' attitude toward Gentiles was not positive. Vermes, perhaps provocatively, characterizes it as xenophobic.
8. Cf. the citation from Wolfhart Pannenberg, "Protestant Theology and the Jews Today," in *Jesus, God and Man*, trans. L. Wilkins and D. Priebe (Philadelphia: Westminister Press, 1968), in n. 1 to Chapter 12.
9. Catholic theology has always maintained that visions and locutions, such as (in its view) may genuinely have been accorded to mystics and saints, cannot be relied to establish any doctrine. Here too the famous rabbinic story, commenting on the phrase "It is not in heaven," in which even a divine revelation does not determine the question the rabbis themselves must decide, could serve as a warning to Christians.
10. Cf. Irving Greenberg, "Cloud of Smoke, Pillar of Fire: Judaism, Christianity and Modernity after the Holocaust," in *Auschwitz: Beginning of a New Era?*, ed. Eva Fleischner (New York: Ktav, 1977). This is still the best statement I know on the difficulty and necessity of faith after Auschwitz.
11. Matthew 23:23.
12. Martin Buber, *On Judaism*, ed. Nahum N. Glatzer (New York: Schocken Books, 1967).
13. Ibid., "The Silent Question," p. 213.

Bibliography

Abelard, Peter. *A Dialogue of a Philosopher with a Jew, and a Christian.* Edited and translated by Pierre J. Payer. Toronto: Pontifical Institute of Medieval Studies,1979.

Alter, Robert, and Frank Kermode, eds. *The Literary Guide to the Bible.* Cambridge, MA: The Belknap Press of Harvard University Press,1987.

Baum, Gregory. *The Jews and the Gospel.* New York: Newman Press, 1961.

________. *Is the New Testament Anti-Semitic?* rev. ed. of *The Jews and the Gospel.* New York: Paulist Press, 1965.

Ben Sasson, H. H., ed. *A History of the Jewish People.* Cambridge, MA: Harvard University Press, 1976.

Ben-Ami, Yitshaq. *Years of Wrath, Days of Glory: Memoirs from the Irgun.* New York: Robert Speller, 1982.

Bentley, Eric, ed. *The Storm over the Deputy.* New York: Grove Press, 1964.

Berlin, Isaiah. *Karl Marx: His life and environment.* New York: Oxford University Press, Galaxy Books, 1963.

Bernard of Clairvaux. *The Letters of Bernard of Clairvaux.* Edited and translated by Bruno Scott James. Chicago: Henry Regnery, 1953.

Bonhoeffer, Dietrich. *Widerstand und Ergebung: Briefe und Aufzeichnungen aus der Haft.* Edited by Eberhard Bethge. Munich: Chr. Kaiser Verlag, 1951. ET *Letters and Papers from Prison.* London: SCM Press.

Bottomore, T. B., ed. and trans., *Karl Marx: Early Writings.* New York: McGraw-Hill, 1963.

Breech, James. *The Silence of Jesus: The authentic voice of the historical man.* Toronto: Doubleday, 1983.

Brennan, Gerald. *South from Granada.* Harmondsworth, Middlesex: Penguin Books, 1963.

Buber, Martin, *On Judaism.* Edited by Nahum N. Glatzer. New York: Schocken Books, 1967.

Campbell, Joseph. *The Hero with a Thousand Faces.* 2d ed. Princeton, NJ: Princeton University Press, 1968.

Chadwick, Henry. *The Early Church: The Pelican History of the Church.* Volume 1. Harmondsworth, Middlesex: Penguin Books, 1967.

Charlesworth, James H. *Jesus within Judaism: New light from exciting archaeological discoveries.* New York: Doubleday, Anchor Bible Reference Library, 1988.

Cohn, Norman. *Warrant for Genocide.* London: Eyre and Spottiswoode, 1967.

Cunliffe Jones, Hubert, with Benjamin Drewery, eds. *A History of Christian Doctrine.* Edinburgh: T. and T. Clark, 1978.

D'Entreves, A. P. *Aquinas, Selected Political Writings.* Oxford: Oxford University Press, 1952.

Danièlou, Jean. *The Theology of Jewish Christianity.* Philadelphia: Westminster Press, 1965.

Dawidowicz, Lucy S. *The War against the Jews, 1933–1945.* New York: Holt, Rinehart and Winston, 1975.

Davies, Alan T. *Anti-Semitism and the Christian Mind.* New York: Seabury Press, 1969.

Davies, Alan T., ed. *Antisemitism and the Foundations of Christianity.* New York: Paulist Press, 1979.

Davies, Alan T. *Infected Christianity: A study of modern racism.* Kingston, ON: McGill-Queen's University Press, 1988.

de Carvajal el Mozo, Luis. *The Enlightened: The writings of Luis de Carvajal el Mozo.* Edited and translated by Seymour B. Liebman. Coral Gables, FL: University of Miami Press, 1987.

Dershowitz, Alan M. *Chutzpah.* New York: Little, Brown, 1991.

Dobson, R. B. *The Jews of Mediaeval York and the Massacre of 1190.* Borthwick Papers No. 45. York: University of York, St. Anthony's Press, 1974.

Dodd, C.H. *The Apostolic Preaching and its Developments.* London, Hodder and Stoughton, 1950.

_______ *The Founder of Christianity.* London: Collins, 1971.

Eban, Abba. *My People.* new ed. New York: Behrman House and Random House, 1984.

Eckardt, A. Roy. *Elder and Younger Brothers: The encounter of Jews and Christians.* New York: Schocken Books, 1973.

Efroymson, David P. "Tertullian's Anti-Judaism and its Role in his Theology." Ph.D. thesis, Temple University. Ann Arbor, MI: University Microfilms, 1977.

Eliach, Yaffa. *Hasidic Tales of the Holocaust.* New York: Oxford University Press, 1982.

Erikson, Erik H. *Young Man Luther.* London: Faber and Faber, 1959.

Fackenheim, Emil L. *God's Presence in History: Jewish affirmations and philosophical reflections.* New York: Harper Torchbooks, 1970.

_______ *The Jewish Return into History: Reflections in the age of Auschwitz and a new Jerusalem.* New York: Schocken Books, 1978.

_______ *To Mend the World: Foundations of future Jewish thought.* New York: Schocken Books, 1982.

_______ *What is Judaism? An interpretation for the present age.* New York: Summit Books, 1987.

Fisher, Eugene. *Faith without Prejudice.* New York: Paulist Press, 1977.

Flannery, Edward H. *The Anguish of the Jews: Twenty-three centuries of antisemitism.* New York: Macmillan, 1964.

Flannery, Austin, O.P., ed. *Vatican Council II: The Conciliar and Post-Conciliar Documents.* Boston: St. Paul Editions, 1980.

Fleischner, Eva, ed. *Auschwitz: Beginning of a New Era?* New York: Ktav, 1977.

Flusser, David. *Jesus.* Translated by Roland Walls. New York: Herder and Herder, 1969.

Fox, Robin Lane. *Pagans and Christians in the Mediterranean World: From the second century AD to the conversion of Constantine.* London: Penguin Books, 1988.

Fromkin, David. *A Peace to end all Peace: The fall of the Ottoman Empire and the creation of the modern Middle East.* New York: Avon Books, 1990.

Gaston, Lloyd. *Paul and the Torah.* Vancouver, BC: University of British Columbia Press, 1987.

Gilbert, Martin. *The Holocaust: A history of the Jews of Europe during the Second World War.* New York: Henry Holt, 1985.

Grant, Michael. *Jesus: An historian's review of the gospels.* New York: Charles Scribner's Sons, 1977.

Hay, Malcolm. *The Roots of Christian Anti-Semitism.* New York: Freedom Library Press, 1981.

Hazard, Paul. *The European Mind (1680–1715).* Cleveland and New York: Meridian, 1963.

Helms, Randel. *Gospel Fictions.* Buffalo, NY: Prometheus, 1988.

Hengel, Martin. *Between Jesus and Paul.* London: SCM Press, 1983.

Hertzberg, Arthur. *The French Enlightenment and the Jews.* New York: Columbia University Press, 1968.

Heschel, Abraham J. *The Prophets.* New York: The Jewish Publication Society of America, 1962.

Hilberg, Raul. *The Destruction of the European Jews.* New York: Holmes and Meier, 1985.

Hochhuth, Rolf. *The Deputy.* New York: Grove Press, 1964.

Holtz, Barry W., ed. *Back to the Sources: Reading the classic Jewish texts.* New York: Summit Books, 1984.

Hook, Sidney. *From Hegel to Marx: Studies in the intellectual development of Karl Marx.* London: Victor Gollancz, 1936.

Hussey, J. M. *The Byzantine World.* New York: Harper Torchbooks, 1961.

John Paul II. *On Jews and Judaism, 1979–1986.* Edited by Eugene J. Fisher and Leon Klenicki. Washington, DC: United States Catholic Conference, Inc., 1987.

Jonas, Hans. *The Gnostic Religion: The message of an alien God and the beginnings of Christianity.* Boston: Beacon Press, 1958.

Juel, Donald *Messianic Exegesis.* Philadelphia: Fortress Press, 1988.

Kaesemann, Ernst. *Essays on New Testament Themes*. Studies in Biblical Theology 41. London: SCM Press, 1964.
Katz, Jacob. *Exclusivity and Tolerance*. New York: Behrman House, 1961.
Kaufmann, Yehezkel. *The Religion of Israel: From its beginnings to the Babylonian Exile*. Edited and translated by Moshe Greenberg. Chicago: University of Chicago Press, 1960.
Koester, Helmut. *Introduction to the New Testament. Vol. 2, History and Literature of Early Christianity*. Philadelphia: Fortress Press, 1982.
Kook, Abraham Isaac. *Abraham Isaac Kook: The Lights of Penitence, The Moral Principles, Lights of Holiness, Essays, Letters and Poems*. Edited and translated by Ben Zion Bokser. New York: Paulist Press, Classics of Western Spirituality, 1978.
Kraft, Robert A. *The Apostolic Fathers: A new translation and commentary. Vol. 3, Barnabas and the Didache*. New York: Nelson, 1965.
Lapide, Pinchas. *The Resurrection of Jesus: A Jewish perspective*. Translated by William C. Linns. London: SPCK, 1984.
Levin, Nora. *The Holocaust: The destruction of European Jewry, 1933–1945*. New York: Thomas Crowell, 1968.
Litvinoff, Barnett. *The Burning Bush: Antisemitism and world history*. London: Fontana/Collins, 1989.
Maccoby, Hyam. *Revolution in Judaea*. London: Orbach and Chambers, 1973.
_______ *The Myth-Maker: Paul and the invention of Christianity*. London: Weidenfeld and Nicholson, 1985.
Manuel, Frank E., ed. *The Enlightenment*. Englewood Cliffs, NJ: Prentice Hall, 1965.
Marcus, Jacob R. *The Jew in the Medieval World: A Source Book: 315–1791*. New York: Atheneum, 1975.
Margolis, Max L., and Alexander Marx. *A History of the Jewish People*. New York: Atheneum, 1980.
Morley, John F. *Vatican Diplomacy and the Jews during the Holocaust 1939–1943*. New York: Ktav, 1980.
Nasr, Seyyed Hossein. *Knowledge and the Sacred. The Gifford Lectures, 1981*. New York: Crossroad, 1981.
Nicholls, William, ed., *Modernity and Religion*. Waterloo, ON: SR Supplements no. 19, Wilfrid Laurier University Press, 1987.
O'Brien, Conor Cruise. *The Siege: The saga of Israel and Zionism*. New York: Simon and Schuster, 1986.
Oberman, Heiko A. *The Roots of Antisemitism in the Age of Renaissance and Reformation*. Translated by James I. Porter. Philadelphia: Fortress Press, 1984.
Pagels, Elaine. *The Gnostic Gospels*. New York: Random House, 1969.
Pannenberg, Wolfhart. *Jesus, God and Man*. Translated by L. Wilkins and D. Priebe. Philadelphia: Westminster Press, 1968.
Parkes, James. *The Conflict of the Church and the Synagogue: A study of the origins of antisemitism*. New York: Hermon Press, 1974.
Poliakov, Leon. "Theory of Race." In *Anti-Semitism*. Jerusalem: Keter, Israel Pocket Library, 1974.
Prager, Dennis, and Joseph Telushkin. *Why the Jews?* New York: Simon and Schuster, Touchstone Books, 1985.
Reik, Theodor. *Myth and Guilt: The Crime and Punishment of Mankind*. New York: Grosset and Dunlap, 1970.
Richardson, Peter, ed., with David Granskou. *Anti-Judaism in Early Christiantity. Vol. 1, Paul and the Gospels*. Waterloo, ON: Canadian Corporation for Studies in Religion, 1986.
Robinson, James M., ed. *The Nag Hammadi Library in English*. San Francisco: Harper and Row, 1977.
Rosenberg, Stuart E. *The Christian Problem: A Jewish View*. New York: Hippocrene Books, 1986.
Rosenzweig, Franz. *The Star of Redemption*. Translated by Wm. W. Hallo. Notre Dame, IN: Notre Dame Press, 1985.
Rubenstein, Richard. *After Auschwitz*. Indianapolis: Bobbs Merrill, 1966.
Safrai, S. *The Era of the Mishnah and Talmud (70–640)*. In H. H. Ben Sasson, ed. *A History of the Jewish People*. Cambridge, MA: Harvard University Press, 1976.
_______ *From Roman Anarchy until the Abolition of the Patriarchate*. In H. H. Ben Sasson, ed. *A History of the Jewish People*. Cambridge, MA: Harvard University Press, 1976.
Sanders, E. P. *Paul and Palestinian Judaism*. London: SCM Press, 1977.
_______ *Paul, the Law and the Jewish People*. Philadelphia: Fortress Press, 1985.
_______ *Jesus and Judaism*. London: SCM Press; Philadelphia: Fortress Press, 1985.
Schaberg, Jane. *The Illegitimacy of Jesus*. San Francisco: Harper and Row, 1987.

Schiffman, Lawrence H. *Who was a Jew? Rabbinic and Halachic Perspectives on the Jewish-Christian Schism.* Hoboken: NJ: Ktav, 1985.

Schuerer, Emil. *The History of the Jewish People in the Age of Jesus Christ. Vol. 2. Edited and revised by Geza Vermes, Fergus Millar, and Matthew Black. Edinburgh: T. and T. Clark, 1979.*

Schuon, Fritjof. *Esoterism as Principle and as Way.* United Kingdom: Perennial Books, 1981.

_______ *The Transcendent Unity of Religions.* Introduction by Huston Smith. Wheaton, IL: Theosophical Publishing House, 1984.

_______ *Survey of Metaphysics and Esoterism.* Bloomington, IN: World Wisdom Books, 1986.

Schwaller de Lubicz, Isha. *Her-Bak: Egyptian Initiate.* Translated by Ronald Fraser. New York: Inner Traditions International, 1978.

_______ *Her-Bak: the Living Face of Ancient Egypt.* Translated by Charles Edgar Sprague. New York: Inner Traditions International, 1978.

Schweitzer, Albert. *The Quest of the Historical Jesus.* 3d ed. London: Black, 1954.

Segal, Alan F. *Two Powers in Heaven: Early rabbinic reports about Christianity and Gnosticism.* Leiden: Brill, 1977.

_______ *Paul the Convert: The apostolate and apostasy of Saul the Pharisee.* New Haven, CT, and London: Yale University Press, 1990.

Simon, Marcel. *Verus Israel: A study of the relations between Christians and Jews in the Roman Empire.* Translated by H. McKeating. New York: Oxford University Press, Littman Library 1986.

Smith, Huston. *Forgotten Truth: The primordial tradition.* New York: Harper and Row, 1976.

Stevenson J., ed. *A New Eusebius.* London: SPCK, 1957.

Stransky, Thomas F., C.S.P. *Vatican II: An inter-faith appraisal.* Notre Dame: Notre Dame Press, 1966.

Synan, Edward A. *The Popes and the Jews in the Middle Ages.* New York: Macmillan, 1965.

Talmage, Frank E. *Disputation and Dialogue: Readings in the Jewish-Christian Encounter.* New York: Ktav and ADL, 1975.

Tec, Nechama. *When Light Pierced the Darkness: Christian rescue of Jews in Nazi-occupied Europe.* New York: Oxford University Press, 1986.

Toury, Jacob. "Anti-Semitic political parties and organizations." In *Anti-Semitism.* Jerusalem: Keter, Israel Pocket Books, 1974.

Toynbee, Arnold, ed. *The Crucible of Christianity.* London: Thames and Hudson, 1969.

Trachtenberg, Joshua. *The Devil and the Jews.* Philadelphia: The Jewish Publication Society of America, 1983.

Tuchman, Barbara W. *A Distant Mirror: The Calamitous 14th Century.* New York: Ballantine, 1978.

Urbach, Ephraim. *The Sages: The world and wisdom of the Rabbis of the Talmud.* Cambridge, MA: Harvard University Press, 1987.

van Buren, Paul M. *A Christian Theology of the People Israel. P. 2, A theology of the Jewish-Christian reality.* New York: Seabury Press, 1983.

Vermes, Geza. *Scripture and Tradition in Judaism.* Leiden: E. J. Brill, 1961.

_______ *Jesus the Jew: A historian's reading of the gospels.* London: SCM Press, 1983.

_______ *Jesus and the World of Judaism.* Philadelphia: Fortress Press, 1984.

_______ *The Dead Sea Scrolls in English.* 3d ed. London: Penguin Books, 1988.

Vrba, Rudolf, and A. Bestic. *44070, The conspiracy of the twentieth century.* Bellingham, WA: Star & Cross, 1989.

Wigoder, Geoffrey. *Jewish-Christian Relations since the Second World War.* Manchester: Manchester University Press, 1988.

Wilson, Stephen G., ed. *Anti-Judaism in Early Christianity.* Vol. 2, *Separation and Polemic.* Waterloo, ON: Canadian Corporation for Studies in Religion, 1986.

Index

About the Author

William Nicholls is Professor Emeritus of Religious Studies, University of British Columbia, Vancouver, Canada. He was born in England and educated at Cambridge University. His first book, *Ecumenism and Catholicity,* was awarded the Norrisian Prize in Divinity at Cambridge. After serving in the Anglican ministry in England and Scotland, he founded the Department of Religious Studies at the University of British Columbia in 1961 and was its head until 1983. From 1984 to 1985 he was Visiting Professor of Religious Studies at the Hebrew University of Jerusalem. His publications include *Systematic and Philosophical Theology.* He has been involved in Holocaust education since 1975.